The Indo-Europeans

The Indo-Europeans

Archaeology, Language, Race, and the Search for the Origins of the West

JEAN-PAUL DEMOULE

Translated by
RHODA CRONIN-ALLANIC

OXFORD
UNIVERSITY PRESS

Oxford University Press is a department of the University of Oxford. It furthers the University's objective of excellence in research, scholarship, and education by publishing worldwide. Oxford is a registered trade mark of Oxford University Press in the UK and certain other countries.

Published in the United States of America by Oxford University Press 198 Madison Avenue, New York, NY 10016, United States of America.

© Oxford University Press 2023

Originally published in French as: Mais où sont passés les Indo-Européens? Le mythe d'origine de l'Occident © Editions du Seuil, 2014, Collection La Librairie du XXIe siècle, sous la direction de Maurice Olender.

All rights reserved. No part of this publication may be reproduced, stored in a retrieval system, or transmitted, in any form or by any means, without the prior permission in writing of Oxford University Press, or as expressly permitted by law, by license, or under terms agreed with the appropriate reproduction rights organization. Inquiries concerning reproduction outside the scope of the above should be sent to the Rights Department, Oxford University Press, at the address above.

You must not circulate this work in any other form and you must impose this same condition on any acquirer.

Library of Congress Cataloging-in-Publication Data
Names: Demoule, Jean-Paul, author. | Cronin-Allanic, Rhoda, translator.
Title: The Indo-Europeans : archaeology, language, race, and the search for the origins of the West / Jean-Paul Demoule ; [translated by] Rhoda Cronin-Allanic.
Other titles: Mais où sont passés les Indo-Européens? English
Description: New York : Oxford University Press, [2023] | Includes bibliographical references and index.
Identifiers: LCCN 2022054572 (print) | LCCN 2022054573 (ebook) | ISBN 9780197683286 (paperback) | ISBN 9780197506479 (hardback) | ISBN 9780197506493 (epub) | ISBN 9780197506486
Subjects: LCSH: Indo-Europeans—Ethnic identity. | Indo-Europeans—Historiography. | Ethnology—Political aspects. | Civilization, Western. | Indo-European languages—History. | Archaeology and history.
Classification: LCC GN539 .D4613 2023 (print) | LCC GN539 (ebook) | DDC 305.809—dc23/eng/20230112
LC record available at https://lccn.loc.gov/2022054572
LC ebook record available at https://lccn.loc.gov/2022054573

To the memory of Maurice Olender and of Phil Kohl

Epigraph

"The reader might be led to believe that the discipline of linguistics is still in its infancy, and he is gripped by the same skepticism that Saint Augustin expressed, almost fifteen centuries ago, when he declared, in reference to similar works, that the explanation of words depends on one's imagination, just like the interpretation of dreams"

Michel Bréal (1866)

"In truth, when we become aware of the extraordinary fruitfulness of the comparative approach in the area of Indo-European studies . . .; and when we recognize the elusive nature of the realities to which the substantives which qualify the adjective "Indo-European" refer, we tell ourselves that the researcher, when he attempts to explore the relationships between the human spirit and the cultures, fabricates myths himself. In this instance, Freud perhaps offers us a foothold and the inestimable gift of lucidity: speaking of the theory of drives, a theory that he invented and that forms the basis of his scientific work, he remarks on several occasions that it is "in a manner of speaking, our mythology"

Charles Malamoud (1991)

Contents

Preface	xv
The official Indo-European hypothesis: The twelve canonical theses	xviii

I OVERTURE

From the Renaissance to the French Revolution

1. The search for a long-anticipated discovery	3
The Indo-European "Golden Legend"	3
Uncertain inventors	5
The search for an anticipated discovery	7
A recurring discovery?	8
Why was Leibniz unable to publish in German?	10
Schizophrenic Europeans	11
The slow secularization of the world	13
India, an alternative myth	15

II FIRST MOVEMENT (1814–1903)

All is resolved!

2. The invention of comparative grammar	19
The search for origins	19
On the superiority of (Indo-) European languages	21
Comparative grammar, a German science?	23
Colonialism as an understanding of history	25
August Schleicher and the botany of languages	27
The young Turks of comparative grammar	29
Other possible models so soon?	30
3. From India to Germania, the return of the wheeled cradle	33
The Indian cradle	33
An ephemeral Earthly Paradise	36
The return of the homeland	38
Those who refused to repatriate the homeland	41
From texts to objects	42
Imagined communities	43
The rise of archaeological excavations	45

viii CONTENTS

More primitive	47
Bathing, kissing, and chastity	50
Linguistics of absence	53
The return to Germania	54
Pan-Germanism and anti-Semitism	56
Occultist beliefs	58
The ambiguities of official linguistics	61

4. The invention of "scientific racism"	63
God and the polygenists	64
The art of measuring skulls	66
From divine right to nation	68
The terrors of the "Count" de Gobineau	70
A science of man?	71
Who are the French?	74
On the origins of the Aryans	77
Are the Prussians German?	79
The three positions of French anthropologists on the Indo-European question	81
Moderation among German anthropologists	84
Does "race" exist?	87
The Count and the Aryan	88
Sex, fantasies, and racisms	90
The first symptoms of political racism	93
The mismeasure of man	94

III SECOND MOVEMENT (1903–1945)

Crimes and errors

5. From comparative grammar to linguistics: A language of leaders?	99
The ambiguities of Ferdinand de Saussure	99
Antoine Meillet, chief and master	102
A language of chiefs	103
Do you speak a "language of civilization"?	106
An instinct for conquest and a love of wide open spaces	108
Linguistic sentiment?	111
Meillet versus Schuchardt	112
The triumph of structural linguistics	114
And what if there never had been an Original People?	116

6. From Aryan Pan-Germanism to Nazism	119
The methods of archaeology	119
Kossinna's law	121
The Kossinnian Indo-German narrative	123
"A pre-eminently national discipline"	124

CONTENTS ix

Erasing the memory of Kossinna	127
Nazism, one of the possible horizons for the Aryans	129
The Atlantis of the Far North	131
Sects and secret societies	133
Hitler himself was not a believer	136
The rallying of archaeologists	137
SS against SA and the pillaging of conquered lands	140
International cowardice and complicity	143

7. A circling cradle	146
"Culture circles" of the European Neolithic	146
Uncertain European chronologies	149
Childish, not Childeish!	151
Regarding the superiority of declensions	152
Skulls and words	155
The dominance of the Nordic theory	157
Eminently respectable universities	159
Weaknesses in the Nordic hypothesis	162
A die-hard Asiatic cradle	164
Excavations in Central Asia	166
A return to (Eastern) Europe	169
The Pontic Steppes endure	171
Marxism and archaeology	174
Marr, Stalin, and linguistics	175

8. Excesses and crimes of racial theories	179
Ordinary racism and institutional racism	179
The anthropological dead-end	181
Genetics to the rescue	183
Eugenics and scientific charlatanism	184
The dreams of German geneticists	186
From skulls to crimes	187
And what of France?	190
Those who collaborated	194

IV THIRD MOVEMENT
(1945–THIRD MILLENNIUM)
All is re-resolved!

9. The return of the Aryan, pagan, extreme right (1945–present)	199
A truly "New" Right?	199
The "magician" prodromes	200
A view from the (extreme) right	202
From Gobineau to Konrad Lorenz	204
A re-armed extreme right	205

x CONTENTS

The limits of "entryism"	208
Contemporary "Aryan" ideology	210
A racial "*Que sais-je?*"	213
The "racist" International	218
Close collaborations	220

10. From racial anthropology to biological anthropology — 223
    The twilight of the "races" — 223
    Medals and survivals — 225
    From skulls to red blood cells — 227
    A truly new synthesis? — 229
    We have rediscovered the Indo-Europeans! — 230
    Racism by means of psychology and IQ — 236

11. What archaeology tells us today — 238
    The first Europeans — 239
    The Neolithic revolution — 242
    Sedentary hunter-gatherers — 243
    The rise of chiefdoms — 245
    What happened on the steppes? — 248
    From the Copper Age to the Bronze Age — 249
    New power networks — 252
    From proto-history to history — 254
    The search for the Indo-Europeans — 255

12. Archaeology: What if the Indo-Europeans had always been there? — 257
    A nebulous autochthony — 257
    Paleolithic continuity? — 259

13. Did the Indo-Europeans really come from Turkey? — 262
    Ex oriente lux — 263
    A new hypothesis? — 264
    The language of the original Homeland — 267
    From Indo-European to Indo-Hittite? — 267
    Part of the family tree of all the world's languages? — 269
    Concerning the difficulties of classification — 271
    The linguistic impacts of agriculture? — 273
    The return of Troubetzkoy — 275
    A nonverifiable model — 278
    How can we rid ourselves of the initial brief? — 281
    An incomplete critical approach — 283

14. Did the Indo-Europeans really come from the Black Sea Steppes? — 286
    A (very) old hypothesis — 286
    From Vilnius to Los Angeles — 288
    Initial cautiousness — 290

CONTENTS xi

The return of the steppes	292
Feminism and invaders	294
A new demonstration?	296
A unified and coherent theory?	301
The horse, of course . . .	303
. . . And the chariot, naturally!	309
Warrior invasions or a vicious circle?	311
And what of genetics?	314

15. From prehistory to history: The rediscovered routes taken by the
Indo-Europeans? — 318

How do we prove a migration?	318
The coming of the Greeks	320
An Early Bronze Age arrival	322
Tiles, gray ware, and princely tombs	325
The arrival of the "Aryans" in India?	327
The world of the steppes and national issues	331
Invisible migrations and *Kulturkugel*	334
The mysteries of the Tocharians	337
Our ancestors, the Celts	339
Romans and Italics	343
Hittites and Anatolians	345
Their ancestors, the *Germani*	347
Slavs or *Germani*?	348

16. Georges Dumézil, a French hero — 351

A sense of the epic	351
The three functions	352
The original texts	355
The "Dumézil affair"	357
Occupation and occultism	360
One College, two Academies, and a New Right	364
Trifunctionality and Indo-Europeanness	368
By excess and by default	370
Heritages and heredities	373
The unavoidable detour into archaeology	375
Other mythologists?	376
Dumézil and the myths	379

17. Linguistic reconstructions and models in the twenty-first century — 381

Discovering original sounds?	381
What exactly are we reconstructing?	385
Of roots and words	387
Thinking in trees	389
The tree of all the world's languages	390

xii CONTENTS

An apple, a hat, and a car	393
Measuring the speed of language evolution	395
From the tree to the network	396

18. Words and things of the Indo-Europeans — 399

The dead-ends of linguistic paleontology	399
Demonstration by absence	402
From words to meaning	404
Regarding Indo-Europeanness	405
A primordial poetry?	407
From words to things and creating the "impression of reality"	409
Indo-European or universal?	411
How to always be right	413

V FINALE AND SECOND OVERTURE

19. Models, countermodels, ideologies, and errors of logic:
   Are there any alternatives? — 419

How languages change	420
Invisible conquerors and secular empires	421
Cultures and ethnic groups	423
Archaeological culture as Nation State?	424
Lessons from the barbarians	427
Languages and material cultures	429
Languages without frontiers	430
The inadequacy of trees	432
"No language is totally pure"	434
Mixes and interferences	435
Substrates, adstrates, and superstrates	438
Pidgins and creoles	439
Sprachbund and the Balkan laboratory	442
"Areal" linguistics	445
The tools of sociolinguistics	446

Epilogue — 449

An alternative vision: The twelve Indo-European antitheses	451

Appendices — 455

1	Simplified chronological table of the main archaeological cultures and civilizations in Eurasia (from 300,000 BCE to the present)	456
2	Dates of emergence of the major Indo-European languages	458
3	August Schleicher's tree of the Indo-European languages	460
4	The development of the Indo-European languages according to Gamkrelidze and Ivanov (1985)	460

5	A Map of some of the solutions of the Indo-European homeland problem *proposed since 1960*	461
6	Map of the main archaeological cultures defined in the 1930s	461
7	The Indo-European migrations, after Gustav Kossinna	462
8	The early historical distribution of the main Indo-European–speaking peoples	462
9	The neolithization of Europe	463
10	The spread of Indo-European languages, after Colin Renfrew	463
11	The spread of Indo-European people, after Marija Gimbutas's theories	464
12	Map of the Chalcolithic cultures in the fifth millennium BCE	465
13	Map of the Chalcolithic cultures in the fourth millennium BCE	465
14	Map of the Chalcolithic cultures in the third millennium BCE	466
15	Map of the Chalcolithic cultures in the second millennium BCE	466
16	Comparative trees of human genes and language families	467
17	The Indian linguistic area, after Colin Masica	468
18	Relationships between the Indo-European languages, after Paul Heggarty	468
19	Relationships between the Indo-European languages, after Alfred Kroeber	469

Bibliography	471
Index of personal names	533
Index of placenames	543
Index rerum	549
Index of languages	557
Index of names of peoples	561

Preface

Europe is haunted by a ghost: the ghost of the Indo-Europeans. Having departed from a specific point in Eurasia several millennia ago, this conquering and enterprising people are thought to have gradually taken control of virtually all of Europe, as well as India, Iran, Pakistan, Afghanistan, and neighboring regions, imposing their order, language, and culture wherever they settled. Out of their language all known Indo-European languages would gradually emerge like the branches of a tree. Likewise, their original way of thinking would have structured the mythologies, epics, and institutions of the speakers of these languages before the Christianization of Europe partly, but only partly, wiped them out. Driven by the same spirit, these European peoples set out to conquer the rest of the planet some five centuries ago, thereby spreading Indo-European languages and imposing their way of life and thinking throughout the world.

Today, as Europeans seek reasons to live together, beyond "free and fair" competition and opaque regulations, are they perhaps secretly reunited by a community spirit whose origins lie in the mists of time? And behind this "European miracle," so often celebrated but already in decline, is there perhaps an "Indo-European miracle"? At the same time we are aware that, under the guise of the "Aryans," these "Indo-Europeans" provided a pretext for the worst ideologies of the 20th century: But was this not simply an accidental subversion which has already been healed and which has no descendants today?

Through the convergence of linguistics, history, archaeology, mythology, and biological anthropology, in recent years our knowledge of this subject has grown steadily. Prudently put to one side after the Second World War, the Indo-European question became increasingly mediatized in the 1970s and even more so in the 1990s by the self-proclaimed "New Synthesis," which gave us the single family tree of all the world's languages and all the world's genes. DNA analysis of paleogenetics, as well as developments in quantitative linguistics and its sophisticated mathematical models, added a touch of modernism and technology to this well-worn subject. At the same time, the number of archaeological excavations, especially those carried out ahead of major infrastructural developments, has continued to grow and to add to our understanding of ancient European societies. Indeed second- and third-hand publications on the Indo-European question abound as if the issue has already been resolved and all that is needed is to present the well-established results to the wider public.

xvi PREFACE

It is therefore an opportune time to undertake a critical overview of this three hundred-year-old problem and retrace the systematic and dogged construction of an alternative origin myth to the Bible; in the latter instance, Europeans (Christians or of Christian tradition) were beholden, in a pathetic schizophrenia, to their worst enemies within and favorite scapegoats, the Jews. In the same way, Europeans invented a "continent" for themselves by arbitrarily excluding the easternmost part of Eurasia and even a so-called white or Caucasian "race," which would prove just as difficult to delimit convincingly. This critical overview is necessarily accompanied by an assessment of the contribution of the various sciences involved in the debate today, including their methods and techniques, but also all of the questions that remain unresolved. This overview is also an intellectual history of the West and of the fields of knowledge that it has regarded as central for reconstructing, or imagining, its origins.

The subject of this book was suggested to me many years ago by Maurice Olender, to whom I am indebted for his tenacity and patience (and also for rereading the original French text) and with whom I shared the same interests and the same questions regarding this issue. It was on the occasion of the "Dumézil" colloquium that he organized on February 7–8, 1981, at the Centre Thomas-More, in Arbresle near Lyon; it followed the publication of my first article entitled "Les Indo-Européens ont-ils existé?" in *L'Histoire* in 1980. Since then, I have continued my inquiries, regularly publishing articles and presenting conferences papers while at the same time working on the current book.

Over the long term, this work has benefitted from discussions, some of which have been quite heated, with a number of colleagues including Gabriel Bergounioux, Patrice Brun, Serge Cleuziou, Anick Coudart, Michel Danino, Pierre Encrevé, Henri-Paul Francfort, Gérard Fussman, Marija Gimbutas, Blagoje Govedarica, Éric de Grolier, Augustin Holl, Jean-Marie Hombert, Ivan Ivanov, Jean-François Jarrige, Kristian Kristiansen, Bernard Laks, Sander van der Leeuw, Jan Lichardus, Marion Lichardus-Itten, János Makkay, Charles Malamoud, James Mallory, Laurence Manolakakis, Nikolaï Merpert, Marcel Otte, Colin Renfrew, Alain Schnapp, Natalya Shishlina, Bohumil Soudský, Dmitri Telegin, Henrieta Todorova, Gilles Touchais, Zoï Tsirtsoni, and Christophe Vielle.

I have also benefitted from briefer, occasional, but always fruitful exchanges on the same subject with, among others, Alexandra Yurevna Aikhenvald, Morten Allentoft, David Anthony, Raimo Anttila, Esther Banffy, Louis-Jean Boë, Céline Bon, Catherine Breniquet, Joachim Burger, Georges Charachidzé, Gilles Col, Bernard Comrie, Eugen Comşa, Valentin Danilenko, Pierre Darlu, Fabrice Demeter, Alexandre Demoule, Jean Deshayes, Julien D'Huy, Ann Dodd-Opritesco, Paul Dolukhanov, Daniel Dubuisson, Georges Dumézil,

Manfred Eggert, François Émion, Alexandre François, Roslyn Frank, Romain Garnier, Eva-Maria Geigl, Russel D. Gray, Alain Guénoche, Jean Guilaine, Xavier Gutherz, Wolfgang Haak, Harald Hauptmann, Eric Hazan, Paul Heggarty, Javier de Hos, Volker Heyd, Guillaume Jacques, Guy Jucquois, Elke Kaiser, Alain Kihm, Philip Kohl, Guus Kroonen, Charles de Lamberterie, André Langaney, Jean Lassègue, Olivier Lemercier, Jean-Loïc Le Quellec, Marsha Levine, Jean-François Lyotard, Vladimir Makarenkov, Angela Marcantonio, Arek Marcziniak, Emilia Masson, Laurent Métoz, Pierre Moret, Rafael Moreira, Ali Moussa, Salikoko Mufwene, Robert Nikolaï, Thomas Pellard, Asya Pereltsvaig, Daniel Petit, Georges-Jean Pinault, Kostantin Pozdniakov, Nicolas Ragonneau, Yuri Rassamakin, David Reich, Petre Roman, Merritt Ruhlen, Laurent Sagart, Jean-Michel Salanskis, Louis de Saussure, Win Scutt, Bernard Sergent, Patrick Seriot, Victor Shnirelman, Guy Stroumsa, Pierre-François Souyri, Mark Thomas, Marc Van der Linden, Bernard Victorri, Tandy Warnow, Nicolas Witkowski, and Marek Zvelebil.

It goes without saying that none of these researchers is responsible for the ideas presented in this work and, indeed, that a large number of them hold quite opposite views.

As a guide to the reader, at the end of this Preface I have provided a list of the twelve canonical theses of classic Indo-European theory, which can be usefully compared to the twelve alternative propositions that I present in this work.

The transcription of words from other alphabets in the Latin alphabet is always problematic. I have attempted to use standard English transliterations (based on Czech in the case of Cyrillic) throughout, but it should be noted that the name of the same Slavic author, for example, might be spelled differently depending on whether he published in English, French, or Cyrillic. There remains a degree of relative "fuzziness" in this regard. On occasion, I have simplified or omitted a certain number of diacritical signs used in various languages: I apologize in advance to non-specialist readers. An asterisk (*) before a word indicates a reconstructed Indo-European root, which is not attested as such in real languages. In order to avoid breaking up the text, I have opted to present references and bibliographic justifications as footnotes, which essentially provide only this type of information; readers may thus choose to ignore them as soon as they encounter them unless they wish to immediately pursue a given issue in more depth. The bibliography on this subject is of course immense, and I have therefore decided to limit myself to those references that are most pertinent. A growing number of older publications are now available on the Internet; given the constant evolution of the situation I have not indicated them here. As regards citations from other languages, the translation of texts in foreign languages, unless indicated otherwise, are my own.

xviii PREFACE

The official Indo-European hypothesis: The twelve canonical theses

Thesis 1. The Indo-European languages, spoken three thousand years ago in at least the major part of western Eurasia and today throughout much of the world, include twelve principal subfamilies (see Appendix 2) and have been organized by linguists into a single family tree springing from a reconstructed shared original language.

Thesis 2. The kinship link between these languages was discovered by English scholar William Jones in 1786, was formalized by German scholar Franz Bopp in the early twentieth century, and has continued to be refined ever since.

Thesis 3. The reconstruction of the original language (*Ursprache* in German) and of the family tree of Indo-European languages (*Stammbaum*) is based on two centuries of linguistic research and on the most up-to-date methods of quantitative linguistics.

Thesis 4. This shared original language was spoken by an original People (*Urvolk* in German).

Thesis 5. This original People lived in an original Homeland (*Urheimat* in German), namely a specific and delimited region of Eurasia, localized thanks to linguistic paleontology and archaeology.

Thesis 6. Linguistic paleontology allows us to reconstruct the natural environment, economy, and culture of the original People using words that are common to all or a great majority of Indo-European languages.

Thesis 7. The diffusion of the Indo-European languages occurred through migrations and conquests from the original Homeland by peoples who can be traced in the archaeological record and who are the direct forebears of peoples described in Classical and Medieval texts (see Appendix 8).

Thesis 8. Biological anthropology, through the study of skeletons and through the analysis of bone chemistry and DNA, allows us to reconstruct the paths of these migrations.

Thesis 9. Comparisons between the different religions and mythologies of ancient Indo-European peoples allow us to reconstruct their original mythology, just as comparisons between various surviving texts allow us to reconstruct their institutions and even their poetry.

Thesis 10a. The convergence of all of these scientific disciplines allows us to localize the original People and their original Homeland in the steppes to the north of the Black Sea in the fifth millennium BCE (see Appendix 11).

Thesis 10b. The convergence of all of these scientific disciplines allows us to localize the original People and their original Homeland in Anatolia (Turkey) in the seventh millennium BCE.

Thesis 10c. The convergence of all of these scientific disciplines allows us to localize the original People and their original Homeland on the shores of the Baltic in the tenth millennium BCE (see Appendix 7).

Thesis 10d. The convergence of all of these scientific disciplines allows us to localize the original People and their original Homeland in various other points of Eurasia (see Appendix 5).

Thesis 11. The misuse of the Indo-European phenomenon by various nationalist ideologies, and particularly by national-socialism and contemporary extreme right groups (sometimes referred to as "New Right"), is nothing more than a marginal phenomenon that has nothing to do with scientific research.

Thesis 12. Today, the question of the development and history of Indo-European languages, and of the peoples who spoke them, can essentially be considered as resolved.

I
OVERTURE
From the Renaissance to the French Revolution

1

The search for a long-anticipated discovery

The history of Indo-European studies reads with all the straightforward clarity of a family saga, with its founding fathers, child prodigies, and even misguided sons. It also forms part of the catalogue of great scientific sagas, on a par with the discovery of penicillin, gravity, and electricity. Of all the discoveries claimed by the social sciences, it is probably one of the few that the "hard" sciences (i.e., sciences concerned with physical matter and nature) are willing to acknowledge. Not only was the recognition of resemblances between the languages that we now term "Indo-European" an achievement in its own right, but the comparative grammar of these languages also became the foundation on which general linguistics was gradually constructed as a scholarly discipline over the course of the nineteenth century: indeed, it is the only social science to have developed, and successfully applied, widely recognized mathematical models, much to the envy and fascination of other social sciences. As early as the mid-nineteenth century, the German grammarian Schleicher made specific reference to Darwin in the construction of his family tree of Indo-European languages. In parallel, biologists taking this biologically inspired tree at face value are today attempting to uncover traces of the Indo-European migrations hidden deep within the human genome.

The Indo-European "Golden Legend"

The saga had its pioneers, those who at the end of the eighteenth century had the intuitive genius to spot relationships between languages, initially by comparing Latin, Greek, and Sanskrit. The best known of these pioneers was Sir William Jones who, in the nineteenth century, inspired three generations of mainly German linguists. The first generation was led by the German Franz Bopp (from 1816), and the Dane Rasmus Rask (from 1818),[1] who defined the principles and tools of comparative grammar and who extended the corpus to include all Indo-European language families (Germanic, Celtic, Slavic, Baltic, Persian, Armenian, Albanian). The second generation was that of August Schleicher, who was the first to construct a family tree of these languages based on the natural sciences model (in 1861, only two years after the publication of Darwin's *Origin*

---

[1] Bopp, 1816, 1833–1852; Rask, 1818 (written in 1814), 1932–1937.

4   OVERTURE

of the Species); he was also the first to write a short fable in the reconstructed "primordial language" (*Ursprache*).[2] And finally, the generation of Leipzig "Neo-Grammarians" who, deeming the methods of their predecessors insufficiently rigorous, defined a corpus of phonetic laws capable of explaining both the evolution and reconstruction of languages, laws "that would not tolerate any exceptions." Out of this century of German scholarship would emerge an etymological dictionary of Indo-European (initiated by Walde) and a comparative grammar of Indo-European languages (by Brugmann and Delbrück), two key tools that still remain indispensable to this day.

While the twentieth century saw linguistics emerge from the strict bounds of comparative grammar to become a general discipline, the three great principles of the previous century (i.e., the comparative method, the family tree-model, and the regularity of phonetic laws) would remain the cornerstones of Indo-European studies. Quite simply, the development of the structuralist method based on the work of Ferdinand de Saussure provided researchers with new tools, particularly in the realm of phonology, the study of the speech sounds of languages. The reconstruction of the "primordial language" progressed further and the discovery of previously unknown Indo-European languages, such as Tocharian in Chinese Turkestan (in the 1910s) and Hittite (in the 1920s), provided perfect confirmation of the method's efficacy. After the Second World War, the study of Indo-European culture spread beyond Leipzig, Berlin, and Paris to become a global field of research. Up until recently, the *Die Sprache* journal could list almost 2,000 published works on this subject per year.

From the 1930s onward, work on ancient texts by Emile Benveniste, in the area of institutions, and by Georges Dumézil, in the area of religion, have greatly added to our understanding of the functioning and mentality of the first Indo-European societies, if not those of the "primordial" Indo-European people itself. Archaeologists meticulously combing the soils of Europe uncovered increasingly precise evidence for the great prehistoric migrations of Indo-European peoples and were able to retrace the phases and chronology of these movements. By the beginning of the twenty-first century, 200 years after its initial emergence, this field of research was sufficiently well-established that numerous books were published with the aim of disseminating its results to the wider public. Biologists, for their part, would also uncover confirmation of their own hypotheses. The aberrant subversion of Indo-European studies in the name of the "Aryan race" by National Socialists, and by their spiritual heirs today, hardly needs mentioning: this misappropriation has unjustly prompted certain individuals of dubious intent to cast aspersions on the field of study as a whole.

---

[2] Schleicher, 1861, 1863a and 1863b, 1868.

THE SEARCH 5

Such is the Golden Legend, more detailed accounts of which can be readily found elsewhere.[3]

Uncertain inventors

There is an air of Archimedes's bathtub and Newton's apple about the Indo-European discovery in so far as a certain number of long-known resemblances suddenly gained new meaning, leading to a general reinterpretation and the creation of a new paradigm. However, there was no Newton or Archimedes of comparative grammar, although various nations haggled discretely over the privilege of claiming the first discoverer as one of their own: such controversy more usually surrounds important technological inventions (e.g., the phonograph, airplane) than great scientific discoveries.

In this, as in other domains, English-speaking hagiographers have long imposed one of their own, Sir William Jones, as the discoverer. Jones was a colonial administrator in India who was introduced to Sanskrit through managerial necessity: he was tasked with the translation of a corpus of legal documents written in the ancient language of the colony. The announcement of the discovery can be dated precisely to February 2, 1786, when Jones gave a lecture in Kolkata on the occasion of the third anniversary of the founding of the Asiatic Society. On page 10 of his discourse he declares that

> The Sanscrit language, whatever be its antiquity, is of a wonderful structure; more perfect than the Greek, more copious than the Latin, and more exquisitely refined than either; yet bearing to both of them a stronger affinity, both in the roots of verbs and in the forms of grammar than could possibly have been produced by accident; so strong indeed, that no philologer could examine them all three without believing them to have sprung from some common source, which, perhaps, no longer exists: there is a similar reason, though not quite so forcible, for supposing that both the Gothick and the Celtick, though blended with a very different idiom, had the same origin with the Sanscrit; and the old Persian might be added to the same family, if this were the place for discussing any question concerning the antiquities of Persia.[4]

This passage is so often quoted that the rest of his discourse tends to be overlooked. In fact, nowhere else in the text does he deal with this linguistic

---

[3] Among other excellent hagiographies, cf. Benfey, 1869; Robins, 1967; Mounin, 1967; Pedersen, 1931; Meillet, 1937; Römer, 1985; Auroux, 2000; Malmberg, 1991; Sergent, 1995.

[4] Jones, 1799; 1807a, pp. 34–35; regarding Jones, cf. also Cannon, 1987, Vielle, 1994.

6 OVERTURE

kinship, and indeed philological reasoning is generally absent in his other works (he died in 1794). The 1786 lecture was entitled "The Hindus" and was presented as a very general exposé of all aspects of ancient Indian civilization—religion, philosophy, literature, architecture—areas in which Jones demonstrated similar zeal for comparative studies. He drew parallels between the Sphynx and the pyramids of Egypt and the colossal Buddhist statues of India. He compared the physical traits of modern Abyssinians with those of Bengali mountain populations which, together with references from Greek and Roman authors, led him to state that "all these indubitable facts may induce no ill-grounded opinion, that *Ethiopia* and *Hindustàn* were peopled or colonized by the same extraordinary race." Hence his final conclusion that "the Hindus . . . had an immemorial affinity with the old Persians, Ethiopians, and Egyptians; the Phenicians, Greeks, and Tuscans; the Scythians or Goths, and Celts; the Chinese, Japanese, and Peruvians; whence, as no reason appears for believing that they were a colony from any one of those nations, or any of those nations from them, we may fairly conclude that they all proceeded from some *central* country, to investigate which will be the object of my future Discourses."[5]

What general impression might the attentive reader get from Sir Jones's text? That an enlightened amateur, like many after him, was suddenly gripped by the scholarly excitement of jumbled comparison; that it was impossible for him to grasp the history of known human civilizations other than through the lens of an "Adamic" or "Babelian" model (he stated in 1792, the year of his death, that "the language of Noah is irredeemably lost"[6]); that as a colonial administrator for an empire on which the sun was destined never to set, he could only perceive the world in terms of universal colonization emanating from a *central* point. Sir Jones was indeed a precursor, but to an even greater extent than is usually realized: as soon as it appears, comparative grammar becomes inextricably associated with an "Adamic," colonialist model which completely overwhelms it.

In the face of their counterparts in the English-speaking world, French inventors always seem to be unjustly condemned to languish in obscurity (Charles Cros preceded Edison, Clément Ader preceded the Wright Brothers). Similarly, Sir Jones was preceded by the unassuming Jesuit, Cœurdoux. In 1767, this missionary from Pondichéry presented the eminent Parisian Hellenist, Abbé Barthélémy, with a grammar and dictionary of Sanskrit along with an essay "*Question posée à Monsieur l'Abbé Barthélémy et aux autres membres de l'Académie des belles lettres et inscriptions.*" The question mentioned in the title was "How is it that a large number of words in the *Sanskritam* language are also found in Latin and Greek, particularly in Latin?" Cœurdoux provided numerous

[5] Jones, 1799, p. 34, 1807a, pp. 45–56; emphasis in original.
[6] Jones, 1807b. See Vielle, 1994.

THE SEARCH 7

examples of shared vocabulary (words for "I" and "four"), morphology (augment of verbs, the dual, the privative "a"), and phonetics. He rejected the explanation of a possible influence from the Greek kingdoms founded in Bactria in the wake of Alexander the Great's conquests. Unfortunately, the Academy, already disinclined at this period to encourage innovation, refused to publish his paper although it was read in session. Anquetil-Duperron, the Iranologist who discovered and translated the sacred texts of the Avesta, was charged with providing a response. He disdainfully dismissed the discovery, firmly attributing the similarities between the languages to the legacy of Alexander the Great. It was, in effect, unthinkable that the history of the world be viewed in any way other than through the lens of Classical Antiquity. It would take until 1808 for the Academy, by then struck by remorse, to publish Cœurdoux's paper following a dissertation by Anquetil-Duperron.[7] However, it came far too late to allow the Jesuit priest to take his rightful place in history. Sir Jones's paper had appeared twenty years earlier, and the German school of philology was already gathering momentum.

The search for an anticipated discovery

Sir Jones had, however, a long line of predecessors. Since the Renaissance, numerous scholars had highlighted the close lexical and morphological resemblances between certain far-flung languages. As early as 1538, the Jesuit Thomas Stephens had compared the structure of Latin to that of Indian, while, shortly after, the Florentine merchant Sassetti noted the resemblances between number names in Sanskrit and Italian. Similarities between Persian and German had been noted in the sixteenth and seventeenth centuries by Bonaventure Vulcanius, Juste Lipse, and Abraham van der Mijl. In 1686, the Swede Andreas Jäger forwarded the hypothesis of a kinship between the languages that would eventually be termed "Indo-European" by Sir Jones exactly 100 years later.[8]

Moreover, philological comparison had never been confined to the study of Indo-European languages. As early as the Middle Ages, Jewish scholars had already commented on the similarities between the Hebrew and Arabic lexica.[9] Later, the Swedish officer Philipp Johann Tabbert von Strahlenberg, when captured by the Russians after the Battle of Poltava in 1709, made the most of his subsequent forced sojourn in Siberia by writing a monograph (published in 1730) on the northern regions of the Russian Empire.[10] He included a "*tabula*

---

[7] Cœurdoux, 1808.

[8] Concerning the pioneers, cf. Arens, 1969; Auroux and Horde, 1992; Bonfante, 1953–1954; Borst, 1957–1963; Devoto, 1962; Diederischen, 1974; Droixhe, 1978, 1984; Drosdowski, 1966; Fellmann, 1975; Hemmerdinger, 1971; Metcalf, 1974; Römer, 1985; Streitberg, 1915.

[9] Dotan, 1987; Van Bekkum, 1983; Valle Rodriguez, 1983.

[10] Strahlenberg, 1730.

8   OVERTURE

polyglotta," a table juxtaposing the translation of a type list of fifty essential words (names of numbers, family relations, parts of the body, environment, etc.) in thirty-two different Northern Eurasian languages. The table groups the languages, depending on their affinities, into five or six classes including Finno-Ugric languages, Turkish languages, etc. Two and a half centuries later, "glottochronology" would still follow this same model.

Should we then, as we are prompted to do by official history, consider all of these scattered intuitions simply as symptoms of three centuries of gestation, all leading up to Sir William Jones's grand entry onto the scene? Are they, to quote the words of one language historian, manifestations of a "call of history"?[11]

A recurring discovery?

Let us take a leap forward in time. During the 1950s and '60s, as we will see in Chapter 14, numerous excavations in the areas around the Black Sea revealed the remains of great civilizations dating to the end of the Neolithic (i.e., Chalcolithic); these civilizations invented, among other things, copper and gold metallurgy. During the fourth millennium BCE, these civilizations appear to have collapsed in the face of an influx of nomadic pastoralists whose existence was also being revealed by new excavations and who, in the southern steppes of the Ukraine, domesticated horses and buried their high-ranking dead under earthen mounds known as *kurgans*. In 1963, these new archaeological discoveries led Lithuanian-American Marija Gimbutas to propose a general overview and to suggest that these nomadic pastoralists were the "proto-Indo-Europeans" that researchers had been seeking for the past 200 years: "The existence of Indo-European homelands advocated by linguists for more than 100 years is no longer an abstraction; results achieved by archaeological research make it possible to visualize the homelands, at a certain time and place, as a historical reality."[12] This hypothesis—which at the time appeared to be revolutionary and which has since become predominant among archaeologists advocating the reality of an original homeland—is based on archaeological arguments, the validity of which we shall examine in more detail at a later stage.

However, thirty years earlier, well before the discovery of this rich archaeological evidence, the French linguist Emile Benveniste was already in a position to claim: "If one studies, in an unbiased fashion, the distribution of languages, terms and objects, the earliest migrations and conflicts between peoples, the succession of religions, and the chronology of material cultures, one is inevitably

---

[11] Droixhe, 1978.
[12] Gimbutas, 1970, p. 155, 1973, 1977; see Chapter 14.

led to search, if not for the cradle, at least for the first center of dispersion of the Indo-European peoples in southeastern Russia."[13] It is true that when he refers to the risks of a biased approach in his 1939 text, he is explicitly targeting the "Nordic" theory of Nazi archaeologists, a theory which, he states a little further on, "has recently found renewed favor in Germany, for obvious reasons."

However, let us once more step back 235 years. In his *Nouveaux essais sur l'entendement humain* (written in 1705 and published in 1765), which is written in the form of a dialogue between himself (under the name Theophilus) and Locke (under the name Philalethes), the German philosopher Leibniz deals with the question of language. He states that most known languages have "common roots," which supposes the existence of a "common origin for all nations" and, therefore, of a "primordial root language." He even proposes a classification of the languages according to the resemblances between them: he illustrates his theory in the form of a family tree, an approach which was well ahead of its time. Describing the cousinly resemblances between Celtic, Greek, and Latin, he concludes that "we can surmise that they arise from the common origin of these people of Scythian descent *who came from the Black Sea*, crossed the Danube and Vistula, from whence some might have moved on to Greece while others would populate Germany and Gaul; this follows the hypothesis that Europeans came from Asia."[14]

In these lines, which closely mirror those of Benveniste and Gimbutas, but which were written eighty years before Sir William Jones's famous lecture, Leibniz does not claim to have made a new discovery. He is merely stating what he considers to be given facts, albeit it with some reservations: he warns against following the example of Flemish scholar Van Gorp, also known as "Goropius Becanus," who in the mid-sixteenth century rose to fame for his fanciful etymologies.[15] However, Leibniz adds that Van Gorp "was not far wrong when he claimed that the Germanic language, which he called Cimbrian, retained as many, if not more, traces of something primordial than even Hebrew."

There is nothing more to add. At the dawn of the Age of Enlightenment, one of the greatest Western philosophers takes two facts for granted: all human languages derive from one primitive language, of which those who will later be known as "Indo-European" form a separate branch, and the original homeland of the speakers of this branch is situated on the shores of the Black Sea. Three centuries later, have we really made much progress?

[13] Benveniste, 1939, p. 16.
[14] Leibniz, 1993 [1765], p. 228 (emphasis added); Olender, 2008, p. 2.
[15] See Olender, 2008, p. 2; Metcalf, 1974.

10 OVERTURE

Why was Leibniz unable to publish in German?

But Leibniz also makes a crucial admission. The true ideological motivation behind his linguistic research goes far beyond the simple furthering of scholarly
knowledge: it concerns the origin, status, and, ultimately, the historical mission
of the German language and hence of the German people itself. While he hides
behind Van Gorp in *Les Nouveaux Essais*, he had suggested a few years earlier
in an essay devoted "to the practice and improvement of the German language"
(unusually published in German) that "the origin and source of the European
character should, for the most part, be sought with us."[16] But the "Theophilus"
("He who loves God") of the *Nouveaux Essais* did not dare pursue a hypothesis
that came close to heresy by identifying German, rather than the language of the
Bible, as the primordial language.[17] However, even though he published the bulk
of his work in French and Latin, the only cultured languages likely to be read by
the European élite at the time, he actively worked to transform German, up to
then fragmented into rural dialects, into a language in its own right. But for this
endeavor to be taken seriously, German, too, had to be vested with its own origin myths.

Nevertheless, neither Leibniz nor Van Gorp was an innovator. The search for
indigenous Germanic origins dates back to at least the twelfth century when a
follower of the "visionary" Hildegard von Bingen demonstrated in Latin "that
Adam and Eve spoke German, because this language, unlike Latin, has not split
into multiple languages," has remained a single entity, and is, therefore, primordial.[18] Such claims would be repeated, even though learned patriots would continue to seek to reconcile the biblical narrative with the mythological traditions
reported by Tacitus in his *Germania*, which presented the Germans as a barbaric
but virtuous people who remained in touch with nature, in contrast to Roman
society which was in decline at the time. Thus, the Germans were descended
from Ashkenaz, the eldest son of Gomer, eldest son of Japheth who, himself, was
the son of Noah; but Ashkenaz is also identified as the nephew of Tacitus's Tuisto,
or as Tuisto himself, the mythical ancestor of all Germans.[19] In any case, the glorification of the Germanic past has, from an early date, relied solely on the testimony of Tacitus, who was guided more by his own ideological agenda than by
any regard for ethnographic accuracy: from the very beginning, therefore, it has
been based on a historical nonsense.[20]

---

[16] Leibniz, 1838, p. 466 (quoted in Gessinger, 1992, p. 395).

[17] See Belaval, 1947; on Leibniz and language, see also Gessinger, 1992; de Mauro and Formigari,
1990; Olender, 2008, pp. 2 and 5; Schulenburg, 1973.

[18] Borst, 1957–1963, vol. II/2, p. 659; Poliakov, 1971/1987, p. 91.

[19] Poliakov, 1971/1987, pp. 85–122; Borst, 1957–1963, vol. II/2 and III/1; Daube, 1940.

[20] Von See, 1970, 1981; Ridé, 1966, 1976.

THE SEARCH   11

It is widely accepted that, with the Reformation, a decisive step was taken toward German cultural autonomy. The Bible was translated into German, which was promoted to the status of a sacred language, and Germanic values were glorified in the face of a decadent Roman Church.[21] Clearly there are several possible readings of this Western religious revolution. The relationship with the divine rids itself of the "magical" practices characteristic of traditional societies: ritual is simplified, images are banished, the clergy is stamped out and the entire community of the faithful now has access to communion under both kinds, the theophagic reality of communion is reduced to simple symbolism, and the sacrament of confession disappears and with it the money-spinning practice of selling "indulgences." For the individual, this new spirituality would eventually turn morality into a matter of personal responsibility. In terms of understanding the world, it rendered the divine principle so abstract that, in the eighteenth century, it would eventually be reduced to a simple affirmation of the rationality of reality (as in the case of Leibniz) under the remote supervision of a Grand Architect or Supreme Being, until it eventually vanishes. In putting the emphasis on an individual's personal relationship with the Divine, and in rejecting the universal ("catholic") pretentions of the Church of Rome, the Reformation allowed the affirmation of community and national identities. In rejecting the existing rites and myths, it also gave European nations the chance to escape the tragic paradox that had haunted them for almost a thousand years: the origin myth through which they perceived the world was, through a strange accident of history, an imported myth!

Schizophrenic Europeans

It is undoubtedly accidental that what was, in fact, only one of many Jewish heresies rapidly found itself in a position to satisfy the aspirations of populations living within an Empire in crisis and for whom the official imperial religion had absolutely no meaning. And yet it was thanks to this empire, which unified a large part of the ancient world, that the new religion was able to spread so quickly, initially in its dissident version and then in its official form. Eventually it surpassed all other religions and its prestige became such that it appealed to several minor barbarian kings who, one after the other, besieged and carved up the Empire and subjugated its citizens. And then, once the map of the New Christian Europe had been redrawn to include a set of new nations at the end of the first millennium AD, Europeans suddenly realized that the only people who had not adopted their

---

[21] Poliakov, 1971/1987, pp. 98–104; Joachimsen, 1951.

12 OVERTURE

religion were the Jews, the very people who had transmitted (and in fact written) the sacred Book which everyone now claimed to follow; these Jews lived among them in de-territorialized communities.

As ethnologists have pointed out, any traditional ethnic group anywhere in the world who can claim to have its own indigenous origin myths calls itself "the Men" or an equivalent and usually refers to its neighbors in less than flattering terms which tend to minimize their humanity (e.g., "The barbarians," "the mutes," "the raw meat eaters," "the Blacks," etc.). Europeans, however, even though they lived within a myriad of states constantly at war with one another, could not really deny the humanity of their neighbors since they worshipped the same God in the same sacred tongue, under the authority of the same Supreme Pontiff; it was even less possible to deny the humanity of the Jews, who lived among them and revered the same Book, a book filled with foreign tales. The Jews would, therefore, come to represent, for a long time, the disturbing strangeness of the "Other," undeniable but different, who is always there. Pogroms, confiscations, and expulsions would be the only response—and an impotent one at that—to this otherness.

In many ways, the Reformation offered European nations the possibility to progressively reappropriate and rewrite their origin myths. But the Reformation was also one of the many manifestations of the intellectual rupture of the Renaissance, with its radically new approach to knowledge, territory, and history. From this new exploratory relationship with the world would emerge a number of facts that would sound the death knell of the biblical myth: the discovery of New Worlds that the Bible never mentions; the rediscovery of pre-Christian Classical Antiquity, whose knowledge appeared to be far superior to that of the waning "Gothic" Middle Ages; the development of an astronomy that was so incompatible with the biblical tradition that it was initially deemed "heretical," etc. As time went by, criticism became sharper, the Inquisition lost ground, and society became secularized. As early as 1654, the Flemish linguist Boxhorn would claim, without fear of consequences, that Hebrew could not be the mother of all tongues.[22] A century later, the learned Court de Gébelin published a genealogical tree of all the world's (known) languages: this tree sprang from an assumed "Primordial Language" and within it Hebrew was neither older nor more venerable than Chinese, Turkish, Peruvian, Sami, or Celtic, the last being seen as the source of all European languages.[23]

---

[22] Auroux and Horde, 1992, p. 543.
[23] Ibid.

The slow secularization of the world

At the time when Leibniz wrote the *Nouveaux Essais*, the prevailing situation was one of compromise: the Babelian myth, which was already significantly weakened, was cobbled together with the indigenous Germanic myth. Other related disciplines also found themselves in a similar situation. Even though the Adamic model was impeding the development of prehistory in the face of the discovery of increasingly concrete evidence, certain concessions were, nonetheless, being made. Discussions on the existence of prehistoric man focused on the possibility of discovering evidence for Antediluvian man, whose remains might have survived the Flood. And this was far from easy: the remains of a skeleton discovered at Öhningen on the shores of Lake Constance, which appeared to point in this direction, would soon after be revealed as the remains of a giant salamander.[24]

The entire eighteenth century would, therefore, be devoted to the painstaking establishment of a world view freed from the shackles of the Christian myth. Although it had imposed a non-European, foreign origin myth, Christianity was at the same time Universalist. Its abandonment as part of the quest for indigenous origins, and also in the face of growing evidence for which it could not provide answers, would allow different relationships with the "Other." For, at the same time that Europeans were searching for their roots in the European continent (or at least attempting to discard their supposed Middle Eastern origins), they were also embarking on the discovery of new worlds. These worlds sometimes confronted them with evolved cultures that were capable of resisting them by force, as in the case of the Ottoman Empire, or capable of rejecting them, as in the case of China and Japan. But, in other instances, such as in Africa and America, the indigenous cultures were conquered and annihilated. Were these other people, who are never mentioned in the Bible, really human? The Age of Enlightenment would also witness the emergence of scientific racism and, thus, the rejection of the "other." Both would evolve together and would justify the development of this origin myth, as will be amply demonstrated as the Indo-European saga unfolds up to the present day.

In his *Systema Naturae*, the naturalist Carl von Linné (Linnaeus), whose classification of animal and plant species still holds sway today and serves as a model for all other sciences, meticulously identifies four varieties of human: *Europaeus albus*, described as "ingenious and inventive"; *Americanus rubesceus*, "swarthy and irascible"; *Asiaticus luridus*, "proud, greedy . . . yellowish, melancholic"; *Afer niger*, "cunning, lazy, neglectful . . . black, phlegmatic." A little later, commenting on the differences between Hottentots and

---

[24] Laming-Emperaire, 1964. See also Schnapp, 1993.

14 OVERTURE

Europeans, he concludes that "it would be difficult to persuade oneself that they share the same origin."[25] Such statements abound throughout the eighteenth century, even among the greatest minds of the day, from Diderot to Hume and from Buffon to Voltaire.

Voltaire would risk body and soul to defend freedom of thought while at the same time affirming that Whites are "superior to these negroes, just as the negroes are superior to monkeys, and as monkeys are to oysters."[26] This is also the same Voltaire who, in his *Dictionnaire philosophique* of 1764, violently refers to the Jews, "our masters and enemies whom we believe and detest" as "the most abominable people on earth."[27] And it is precisely because we no longer wish to "believe" the Jews, that Voltaire, along with others, promotes an alternative original world, the newly "discovered" India. In the quest for a "primordial nation, who taught and misled the rest of the earth," Voltaire is supporting the astronomer Bailly when he states "I have long regarded the ancient dynasty of the Brahmins as this primordial nation."[28] Voltaire also adds linguistic arguments in support of his thesis: Did not the name "Abraham" come from the word "Brahma"?

All of these contradictions would eventually permeate the *Encyclopédie*. On the one hand, the tone of the work is broadly favorable to the idea of "monogenism," and the position of Hebrew as the mother of all other languages is reaffirmed. On the other hand, the entry for "Negroes" is quite damning: "Not only are they distinguished by their color, but they differ from other men by their facial features . . ., appearing to constitute a different species of man. . . . If by chance honest men are encountered among the Negroes of Guinea (most of them are always vicious), they are mostly inclined towards debauchery, revenge, theft and lying." Should we, therefore, deplore—in a pointless expression of regret—that the age of enlightenment triggered the momentous decline of the Judeo-Christian model with its proclaimed Universalism, as the Catholic Church sometimes claims? This would mean overlooking the massacres and enslavement perpetrated in the Church's name and the lack of consistency among its professed followers with respect to the commandments "Thou shalt not kill" and "Love thy neighbor as thyself." Nevertheless, this decline in no way impeded the emergence of a Universalism freed from religion.

[25] Linné, 1758; cited in Poliakov, 1971/1987, pp. 183–184.

[26] Voltaire, *Traité de métaphysique*, in *Œuvres Complètes*, ed. Moland, t. XII, p. 210; cited in Poliakov, 1971/1987, p. 200.

[27] Cited in Poliakov, 1968, t. III p. 105.

[28] *Lettres sur l'origine des sciences et celle des peuples de l'Asie adressées à M. de Voltaire par M. Bailly, et précédées de quelques lettres de M. de Voltaire à l'auteur*, Paris, 1777, p. 3; cited in Poliakov, 1971/1987, p. 211.

THE SEARCH   15

India, an alternative myth

Like Voltaire, the *Encyclopédie* also falls under the spell of India: in the corresponding entry the *Encyclopédie* states that "the sciences were probably more ancient in India than in Egypt." This opinion was also held by Buffon who, in *Des époques de la nature*, evokes an original people who occupied an area somewhere to the east of the Caspian Sea (not far from the location of Leibniz's original people) and whose ultimate descendants were the "Brahmins of India." However, it is in Germany that this myth of an Indian origin would become an alternative to be reckoned with. This theme, already evident in the work of Kant, would be further developed in the 1780s by one of his followers, the Lutheran pastor Herder, who was one of the founders of German Romanticism and whose two main works shortly predated William Jones's *Discourse*. The Indian myth would flourish with Romanticism—and with the advent of comparative grammar.[29] Friedrich Schlegel's essay, *Über die Sprache und Weisheit der Indier*, published in 1808, would become one of its focal points.

Jones's "discovery" is, therefore, no more than a hagiographical reconstruction. By the time his *Discourse* was delivered, theories regarding relationships between the future Indo-European languages were already part of a 300-year-old tradition. The same is true of the long-established school of "fanciful linguistics" into which Jones falls when he attempts to establish a link between the Hindus and the Egyptians, Etruscans, Chinese, Japanese, and Peruvians. This is a tradition within which Spanish is commonly seen as being derived from Basque, French from Celtic or Greek, Chinese from Egyptian, and Amerindian languages from Pre-Greek Pelasgian.[30] Neither a beginning nor an end, Sir Jones is just another symptom: at the time when he is writing, the myth of the mother tongue is already as old as the Bible, the Eurasian alternative has been developing tentatively since the Renaissance, and the magic of India is already well established.

But Jones was writing three years prior to the French Revolution, a defining rupture that would drag all of Europe into nearly thirty years of historic upheaval. At the end of these 300 years of transition, initiated by the Renaissance and Reformation, a new era begins, an era characterized by the desire for democracy, by Romanticism, and by the awakening of national consciousness. The Christian view of the world, with its myths, order, and universality, inexorably disintegrates. The issue of languages will be particularly revelatory of new ways of thinking. It is precisely at the end of these three decades of seismic change that the first comparative grammar of Indo-European languages is born.

---

[29] *Vom Geist der ebräischen Poesie*, I, 1782; *Ideen zur Philosophie der Geschichte der Menschheit*, 1784–1791; regarding Herder, and more generally the Hindu myth in Germany, cf. Gérard, 1963, Willson, 1964, Schwab, 1950, Olender, 2008, pp. 11–12.

[30] Auroux and Horde, 1992, p. 576 note 17.

II
FIRST MOVEMENT (1814–1903)
All is resolved!

In 1903, Antoine Meillet, the most important French Indo-Europeanist linguist of the first third of the twentieth century, wrote that the comparative grammar of Indo-European languages had reached a point "beyond which it could not move." In his mind, he was drawing a line under a century of scholarship, principally undertaken by German researchers for whom the search for the Original Language (*Ursprache*) of an Original People *(Urvolk)* was bound up with the aspiration for German political unity that was essentially defined by its linguistic unity. This century also witnessed the frenzied search for the Original Homeland (*Urheimat*) of the Original People, for which there were many suggestions, all, or almost all, proposed within an overall logic of reappropriation: this homeland was progressively repatriated from the once dreamed-of India, back toward Europe, and eventually to the Baltic since the term for Indo-European in German is *indo-germanisch*. The emerging discipline of physical anthropology, then defined as "the scientific study of human races," also came to the rescue and found in the Indo-European question an ideal field of application and a magnifying glass that highlighted the underlying racial prejudices. Only a handful of linguists attempted to temper the dominant model (*Ursprache—Urvolk—Urheimat*) and suggested, without much success, other possibilities such as the mixing of languages.

2

The invention of comparative grammar

Ultimately, why should we concern ourselves with all of these pioneers from a distant past? The true founders of comparative grammar were not Jones or Leibniz, but the German Franz Bopp and the long-ignored Dane Rasmus Rask. In 1816, Bopp published his historic work *Über das Conjugationssystem der Sanskritsprache in Vergleichung mit jenem der griechischen, lateinischen, persischen und germanischen Sprache* (On the Conjugation System of Sanskrit in Comparison with that of Greek, Latin, Persian and Germanic), which would eventually lead to the publication of his monumental grammar *Griechischen, Lateinischen, Litauischen, Altslawischen, Gotischen und Deutschen* (Comparative Grammar of Indo-European Languages Including Sanskrit, Zend, Armenian, Greek, Latin, Lithuanian, Old Slavonic, Gothic and German) between 1833 and 1849. Rask, for his part, produced *Research on the Origin of the Old Norse or Icelandic Language*, which was edited in 1814 and published in Danish in 1818, but only translated into English in 1993.[1] From this point onward, linguistics, which would long be identified with the comparative grammar of Indo-European languages, became an autonomous entity, definitively freed from the ideological issues and methodological wanderings of its centuries-long gestation. Nevertheless, in the two centuries following Bopp and Rask, we witness the episodic and marginal annexation of the fruitful and true science of linguistics by the delusional science known as "racial anthropology," in the words of Léon Poliakov; just as the true and fruitful knowledge of nuclear physics has at times been hijacked for military applications without calling into question its theoretical foundations.

The search for origins

However, we do not wish to dismiss two centuries of comparative scholarship on the basis that they are tainted by the theories and applications of "scientific racism," as is often called for. Instead, by only considering the uncontested practitioners of comparative grammar, we propose to question what shaped these interpretive models beyond the facts; in short, why create such elaborate

[1] Rask, 1993 [1818].

20 FIRST MOVEMENT (1814-1903)

interpretive models if the facts did not require them, or at least not exclusively? Sometimes these interpretive models are developed explicitly (as is the case with Schleicher's botanical paradigm and his "genealogical tree" of Indo-European languages), but for the most part they are implicit. Often, and this is undoubtedly a characteristic of Indo-European linguistics, linguists, including the most eminent, maintain a double language. On the one hand, they claim to confine themselves to describing the similarities, relationships, and correspondences between languages without seeking to reconstruct an actual language or, even less so, an original People. On the other hand, and we see it in the twentieth century with Antoine Meillet and Émile Benveniste, they sometimes resort to surprising shortcuts, symptoms of ideological presuppositions regarding languages and cultures that do not always match the facts but which are nonetheless emphasized with undoubted skill.

The beginnings of comparative grammar are all the more exemplary because neither Bopp nor Rask propounded ideologies of identity that exalted the ideas of "land" and "race." In this regard, two phrases by Bopp are frequently cited. The first, published in the introduction to his Grammar, states that "the languages dealt with in this work are studied for themselves, that is as objects and not as a means of knowledge."[2] In effect, this statement amounts to a refusal to make languages subordinate to cultural history and is particularly aimed at his mentor Karl Joseph Windischmann and the metaphysical school of the historian Georg Friedrich Creuzer, but also at the entire European linguistic tradition which we have just discussed. This sentence is often compared to the last sentence (the authenticity of which is often questioned) of the Cours de linguistique générale by the founder of structural linguistics Ferdinand de Saussure: "The true and unique object of linguistics is language studied in and for itself."[3] More anecdotal, but just as ideologically charged, another sentence by Bopp expresses his preference for the use of the term "Indo-European" because, he states, "I cannot approve of the expression 'Indo-German' since I cannot see why the Germans should be taken as representatives of all of the peoples of our continent."[4] An unassuming and obstinate scholar, Bopp, who had previously received an education in linguistics in Paris under Sylvestre de Sacy and Antoine-Léonard Chézy, was therefore far removed from the romantic and India-centered enthusiasms of his contemporaries, such as Schlegel for example.

As regards Rask, whom Meillet considered "more modern" than Bopp, his "Research" was admittedly only a response, emitted in the context of a competition, to a question posed by the Danish Academy of Sciences in 1811: "Identify

---

[2] Bopp, 1833-1852 [1866-1874], t. I, p. 8 (in the translation by Michel Bréal).
[3] Saussure et al., 1972 [1985, 2nd ed.], p. 317.
[4] Bopp, 1833-1852 [1866-1874], t. I, p. 21.

the source from which the ancient Scandinavian language is most likely to have derived; establish the character of this language and its relationships . . . to Scandinavian and Germanic." Even though he was awarded the Danish Academy's prize in 1814, to conduct further studies in India, he quickly lost interest in this quest for origins and turned his attention instead to a proposed general grammar of all languages.

More of a "genealogical" linguist, he can be regarded as one of the first "typological" linguists, if not one of the precursors in the field of "Universal Grammars" that would come to characterize the "generative" linguistics of the late twentieth century.

It is somewhat pointless to continue to evoke the errors of a fledgling science. Certainly, it can be noted that Bopp succeeded in integrating languages such as Lithuanian (in 1833), Slavic (in 1835), Albanian (in 1854), Armenian (in 1857), and Celtic (in 1838) within an initial "core" of identified Indo-European languages (Sanskrit, Greek, Latin, Persian, Germanic); in the case of Celtic, he relied on the 1838 work of Adolphe Pictet[5] and, from 1854 onward, he deigned to acknowledge the work of Johann Kaspar Zeuss, an obscure high school teacher. However, by applying the same methodology, he also managed to add Caucasian, Indonesian, and even Melanesian and Polynesian languages to his 1840 table! In doing so, he reconnects with the old tradition of a universal mother tongue, but he also anticipates speculations that have recently reentered the spotlight with renewed vigor.[6]

On the superiority of (Indo-) European languages

On a more fundamental level, from the outset, the constructions of Bopp and Rask contain two basic paradigms which are taken for granted and which partly emerge from previous centuries, but which continue to persist at the heart of Indo-European linguistics today: the first is the paradigm of a mother tongue and the second is the paradigm of language as a biological entity. Noticing the resemblances between languages, Bopp writes in 1820, "I am inclined to regard all of these idioms as gradual modifications of a single and unique primitive language."[7] This primitive language ought to allow us to retrace the very origins of language, when each elementary concept is necessarily linked to a primordial monosyllabic root. Today's school of comparative linguistics refutes this ultimate consequence but not the initial premise.

[5] Pictet, 1837; on Pictet, see Chapter 3, pp. 34–35.
[6] See Chapter 17, pp. 390–392.
[7] Bopp, 1820; cited in Bréal, 1866, p. xliii.

22   FIRST MOVEMENT (1814–1903)

Rask, who makes explicit reference to the zoologist Linnaeus, postulates that languages are natural entities that lend themselves to classification. In his opinion, "language is an object of nature and the knowledge of language resembles natural history. . . . This is not mechanical; on the contrary, it is the highest triumph of the application of philosophy over nature since it allows us to reveal the real system of nature and confirms its truth."[8] It is also in the continuation of the work of Linnaeus and his followers that Rask revisits the classification of human "races" in order to make them coincide with the classification of languages by intertwining, if not merging, both systems. Thus he introduces a succession of levels: Dialect, Language, Branch, Root, Class, and Race. For instance, the regional Bornholm dialect is included within the "Danish language," which in turn forms part of the "Scandinavian branch," part of the "Germanic root," the "Gothic class" and the "Sarmatic race." The latter, also referred to as "Japhetic" and sometimes "Caucasian," corresponds to the speakers of Indo-European languages. It is distinct from the "Scythian race," which encompasses languages that are today considered as Finno-Ugric, Ural-Altaic, and Dravidian, as well as Basque and Celtic (the latter was not yet identified as Indo-European) and which was believed to have spread throughout a large part of Europe "until the chain was broken by a large invasion of people belonging to our race (this race I call 'Japhetic,' for want of a better term)."[9] Thus, from the onset, Rask's system carries with it, without any particular factual evidence apart from the affinities between Indo-European languages, a certain conception of the history of the continent which would remain unchanged for the following two centuries. "Skull-measuring" anthropologists would soon lose no time in using Rask's authority as an endorsement of their own work, beginning with the Swede Anders Retzius, the inventor of the "cephalic index." They would use Rask's work in their quest to identify anthropological evidence for the invasion of dolichocephalic Aryans[10] in an interdisciplinary vicious circle that would become typical of Indo-European studies.

Bopp, for his part, adopted the ternary classification of languages (inflecting, agglutinating, and isolating) proposed by the Schlegel brothers, which he found to be "eminently sensible" and precisely reflecting the "natural realms." There was no doubt that isolating languages (such as Chinese) correspond to the mineral realm, agglutinating languages (such as Turkish) to the plant realm, and inflecting or declined languages (the Indo-European languages) to the animal realm. The works of the time are full of vibrant *paens* to the glory of declensions, and the wonderment of these scholars—who no doubt struggled with their

---

[8]   Cited in Hjelmslev, 1951 [1973], p. 8.

[9]   Rask, 1932–1937, vol. 2, pp. 245–247; cited in Rousseau, 1981; see also Hjelmslev, 1951 [1973]; Bjerrum, 1980.

[10]   See Chapter 4, p. 67.

Greek and Latin declensions at school—is almost palpable in the face of Sanskrit which appeared to "preserve" an even more elaborate system of declensions. The exaltation of European superiority, therefore, even managed to pervade simple grammatical description while the theme of increasing complexity was also linked to that of decadence.

Comparative grammar, a German science?

Is it an accident that Bopp and Rask both sprang out of the Germanic cultural milieu and that, for at least a century, comparative grammar remained an essentially German science, even though the first manuals of Sanskrit were English and the first great center for linguistic studies was Paris, where Bopp himself came to receive his linguistic training? We have already seen that, since Leibniz, the emergence of an alternative original mythology was closely associated with the desire to develop a German language. Both quests are totally entwined with Romanticism and national awakening. In fact, the German language was the only tangible marker of a German identity which, at the time, was splintered between two great empires and a constellation of small principalities; this was particularly true in the wake of the 1814 Vienna Congress. "Men are much more shaped by language than language is shaped by men" wrote the Philosopher Fichte,[11] author of the famous "Addresses to the German Nation" who, in 1807, took a stand against the Napoleonic invasion following the defeat at Jena-Auerstedt. This observation is echoed in the words of Wilhelm von Humboldt: "Between the soul of a people and its language, there is complete identity; it is not possible to imagine one without the other."[12] This "organic" conception of the nation is precisely the opposite of that of the French Revolution, which saw the nation as being founded on a "community of citizens."

German was not managed, as was the case in France, by specialists concerned with establishing a standard from their base in the capital where they published their grammars and dictionaries. On the contrary, it was characterized by a multitude of dialects and a rich popular tradition which some scholars, including the Brothers Grimm, were beginning to record. Even today, two-thirds of Germans understand and speak a dialect; in contrast to France, there is no social stigma attached to speaking the national language with a regional accent. Because French fitted easily into the semantic and linguistic mold of Latin, from which it sprang, there was less of an inclination in France to perceive the complexity of the language within the wider Greco-Latin culture. The change over from a multiplicity

---

[11] Fichte, 1978 [1808], p. 109.
[12] Humboldt, 1974 [1836], p. 179; Id., 2000.

24 FIRST MOVEMENT (1814–1903)

of dialects to a German that became the language of worship, and then of literature, philosophy, and science, after centuries of effort had barely reached its culmination during Bopp's time. Kant and Hegel, who also implemented Leibniz's linguistic program, not only had to develop and define several concepts in the German language, but were also confronted with the possibility of expressing the same concept either by its Latin root, which was generally inherited from the French, or by its German root. This mother language, which was mother to the whole plethora of German dialects in existence at the time (known as "Common" German by linguists), this long-disappeared primordial entity, was at the same time the mirror image and the retrospective guarantee of the hoped for unity, that of a "reunified" Germany.

Thus, the emergence of the Indo-European concept at the heart of Germanness cannot be attributed to an accident, to a cultural tradition with a natural leaning toward perseverance in scholarly research, nor even simply to the quest for mythical or real origins driven by a rising sense of national identity. On a much more fundamental level, the study of the language, regardless of where we look, was for German society a compulsory initial step in the way it portrayed itself and the world.

This can easily be verified by contrasting it with the situation in France. In France, the new foundation myth did not correspond to a real cultural need. France, the eldest daughter of the Catholic Church and as such universal, spoke a daughter language of the language of the Church, Latin. More generally, Catholic countries that spoke Romance languages had little interest in the issue of language, unlike Protestant countries with their national Churches who prayed in their national languages. Thus, in France, a long-unified state whose language was also that of the entire European elite and of its diplomats (even whenever France was defeated), the original references were provided by Greece and Rome, whose cultures had civilized the Gaulish barbarians to the point of erasing their language. Despite many attempts, which were as unfruitful as they were artificial, the "Gaulish ancestors" would never be granted even the slightest role as founders of the nation. Regarding the Germanic Franks, who would ultimately lend their name to the country and the language, they would also be absorbed both culturally and linguistically within the conquered Gallo-Roman population, leaving almost no trace apart from the all-important reference to the "founding" baptism of Clovis, who had felt politically obliged to adopt the religion of his new subjects. References by the aristocrats of the *Ancien Régime* to their supposed Frankish origins are not even worthy of scholarly debate.

Therefore, in his interpretation of the linguistic similarities pointed out by Fr. Cœurdoux, Anquetil-Duperron could not have but seen a Greek influence on India; just as Joseph de Guignes, in 1770, when reminding us that "an infinity of travelers have already noted that in the Indian languages, and even in Sanskrit, the

THE INVENTION OF COMPARATIVE GRAMMAR   25

scholarly language of these peoples, there were many Latin and Greek words,"[13] explained these commonalities in terms of contact and borrowings since the notion of a genealogical connection was still very underdeveloped. Thus, in France the study of language was not a genealogical undertaking but rather an attempt at logical formatting, symbolized by the *Grammaire de Port-Royal*; French, as the universal language of Reason, identified itself with language per se. This was an intellectual tradition that saw language as a pure form, which the German comparative grammar would banish to the backstage before it would reemerge in the works of Saussure and structural linguistics and eventually flourish in the United States under the "generative grammar" of the 1960s.

This is the reason why Bopp was not translated into French until 1866 by Michel Bréal, who was the equally late holder of the first chair of comparative grammar at the Collège de France. 1866 also saw the founding of the famous Société de Linguistique de Paris, which is still in existence. The oft-quoted second article of the Society's statutes proclaims: "The Society does not admit any communication concerning either the origin of language or the creation of a universal language."[14] In the same way, the archaeology of the national territory occupied, until quite recently, a subordinate place reserved for local scholars. Instead, French archaeology was focused on the civilizations of Greece, Rome, and the Orient, and it was in these distant lands that prestigious institutions, charged with amassing illustrative collections and filling the Louvre, were founded.

Colonialism as an understanding of history

The only accidental element at the origin of comparative grammar is the fact that neither Rask nor Bopp was an ideologue and that, in this regard, they were the exception to the rule. For, in Bopp's immediate circle we find Jacob Grimm, the elder of the story-telling brothers, who was the author of the first great German grammar, which began to be published in 1819. In the introduction to *Geschichte der deutschen Sprache* (History of the German Language), first published in 1848, Grimm declared that this was a "totally political"[15] work. The phrase is undoubtedly that of a liberal who was opposed to the authoritarian Prince of Hanover (he chose to quit the University of Göttingen) and who struggled above all for German unity. However, his declaration cannot but evoke the subtitle of the 1912 work by archaeologist Gustaf Kossinna: *Die deutsche Vorgeschichte,*

---

[13] Guignes, 1777, p. 327 (cited in Auroux and Horde, 1992, p. 560).
[14] Auroux, 1989; see Bergounioux, 1984.
[15] Grimm, 1848, p. vii (*"durch und durch politisch"*).

26 FIRST MOVEMENT (1814–1903)

eine hervorragend nationale Wissenschaft (German Prehistory, a Pre-Eminently National Discipline).[16] Kossinna, who died in 1931, would become, in terms of his methods and objectives, the principal inspiration for National-Socialist archaeology.[17] Alongside the Grimm brothers we find the linguist August Friedrich Pott, who established the principles of etymological research and defined the first phonetic rules which would facilitate comparisons.[18] But Pott was also responsible for introducing the work of the French racial theorist Gobineau[19] to Germany through his 1856 book *Die Ungleichheit menschlicher Rassen, hauptsächlich vom sprachwissenschaftlichem* (The Inequality of the Races, Particularly from the Point of View of Philological Science), which shares the same title as Gobineau's 1853 essay. It was through reading Pott that Wagner discovered the work of Gobineau; in fact Gobineau's book was initially poorly received in France but it went on to have a long (and sinister) success in Germany before reappearing later in France, just as Tocqueville had predicted in a bid to console its author.

However, these German specificities did not exhaust the new comparative paradigm, and they explain why it also prospered outside Germany. While the model of a mother language had a particular resonance in Germany, and while the call of mythical India was stronger there than elsewhere, the biological model of language was much more widely adopted at a time when the new (and anti-biblical) idea of biological evolution of species was making itself felt; this notion was fully described for the first time by Charles Darwin in the middle of the nineteenth century. Furthermore, the colonial-diffusionist model, as expressed so clearly by Jones, allowed the spatial and not just temporal process of the expansion of the mother language to be interpreted. At the dawn of the nineteenth century, at the end of three centuries of Great Discoveries, Europe had passed the stage of exploratory curiosity and coastal trading vis-à-vis the rest of the world. Instead, it was entering a historic phase of generalized territorial appropriation which, within the space of a century, would give it direct control over most of the planet. This became Europe's perception of itself, and the colonial model became the only model deemed suitable to explain linguistic affinities between languages. Indeed, through the elaboration of a new origin myth, this model also became the ultimate implicit justification for the violent destruction which Europe visited on other civilizations throughout the world.

---

[16] Kossinna, 1912.
[17] See Chapter 6, pp.121–129.
[18] Pott, 1833–1836, 1856.
[19] See Chapter 4, pp. 70–71.

August Schleicher and the botany of languages

It was only with August Schleicher and the mid-nineteenth-century generation of Indo-European scholars, the second such generation, that the two models of comparative grammar (the biological model and the model of a mother language) would be fully developed and articulated within a general botanical model. A botanist by training, Schleicher would render the comparative paradigm explicit and would go on to explore all of its logical consequences. It was Schleicher who first put pen to paper to draw a family tree (*Stammbaum*) of the Indo-European languages (see Appendix 3, p. 678). He would be also be the first to define the strict laws of phonetic correspondences in the comparison of languages, thereby prefiguring the work of the neogrammarians; he would also pioneer the systematic reconstruction of words of the primordial language (the *Ursprache*), placing an asterisk before each reconstructed form (e.g., *ekwos* is the reconstructed form derived from words designating "horse" in various languages), a practice that continues today. This method even allowed him, in what was certainly more than an idle challenge, to write a short fable in the reconstructed "mother language": "The sheep and the horses."[20] At the same time, Schleicher occupied a prime position in the academic world. Professor at Prague and then at Jena, in 1852, he founded along with Adalbert Kuhn the *Beiträge zur vergleichenden Sprachforschung auf dem Gebiete der arischen, celtischen und slavischen Sprachen*, the journal of reference for Indo-European studies (which is still in existence under the title *Historische Sprachforschung*). He died prematurely in 1868 at the age of forty-seven.

Schleicher's reference to biology is explicit and fully assumed. His principal work, the *Compendium der vergleichenden Grammatik der indogermanischen Sprachen* (A Compendium of the Comparative Grammar of the Indo-European Languages) appeared in 1862, two years after the publication of Darwin's *On the Origin of Species*.[21] It was followed two years later by *Die darwinsche Theorie und die Sprachwissenschaft. Offenes Sendschreiben an Herrn Dr. Ernst Häckel* (Darwinian Theory and the Science of Language. An Open Letter to Dr Ernst Häckel), in which he states,

> Languages are natural organisms which, independent of human will, and in accordance with set laws, are born, grow, mature, grow old and die; thus they too manifest this series of phenomena that we generally refer to under the term of life. The science of language is therefore a natural science.[22]

---

[20] Lehmann and Zgusta, 1979.
[21] On Schleicher and Darwin, see Bergounioux, 2002.
[22] Schleicher, 1868, p. 3.

28 FIRST MOVEMENT (1814–1903)

This naturalistic, biological vision has colored the study of Indo-European languages right up to the present day. The zoologist Ernst Häckel (or Haeckel), Schleicher's discussion partner and friend, introduced Darwin's work to Germany; he became a social Darwinist thinker (founder of the Monist League[23]) and was a member of the Pan-Germanic movements of the late nineteenth century. A prolific zoologist and theoretician of the recapitulation of phylogenesis by ontogenesis, he also classified human "races," with the "Indo-Germanic race" being the most noble and the African being closest to the ape.[24] However, Schleicher specified in his second book that he had not yet read *On the Origin of Species* when he wrote the *Compendium* and that he intended, in the light of Darwin's work, to better explain the theoretical foundations underlying the new linguistics. This detail is not unimportant. In effect, he is reminding the reader that the evolutionist paradigm was being applied throughout the sciences of the mid-nineteenth century and that Darwin's work was but one of its expressions. He is also indicating that this paradigm was already well-established, as we have seen, since the origins of comparative grammar. Schleicher's other explicit reference is Hegel's *The Philosophy of History*. Just as the Hegelian spirit of the world (*Weltgeist*) frees itself from nature by separating itself dialectically, it is also incarnated in the spirit of humanity (*Geist der Menschheit*) to produce language and, more particularly, in the spirit of each people (*Volksgeist*) to produce different languages. And every language develops through three successive phases as defined by Schlegel: the isolating phase, the agglutinating phase, and, finally, the flectional phase. Beyond these there is no possible progress or even preservation, there is only decadence.

As the Swedish historian Ulf Drobin noted, "Schleicher's system is coherent. To retain the system while rejecting the assumptions of the system appears to be less coherent."[25] In fact, up until now, historiographical judgments regarding Schleicher by Indo-Europeanists provide an excellent illustration of the "doublespeak" they employ: they inevitably laud Schleicher's role as a pioneer; they explicitly regret, to various degrees, certain "excesses" (the idea of decadence, the historical reality of reconstructed forms, the fable, and even the family tree); yet, at the same time, his model is implicitly applied in its entirety. In his *Histoire de la linguistique* (A History of Linguistics), written when structuralism was at the height of its triumph (1967), Georges Mounin wrote the following regarding Schleicher's family tree (*Stammbaum*) of languages:

[23] See Chapter 3, p. 57.
[24] Concerning Haeckel, see Pichot, 2000.
[25] Drobin, 1980.

This scheme—which has remained popular in works of general interest—did not survive criticism: less than ten years after Schleicher, the idea of common periods (or common sources, represented by branches placed between the trunk and the terminal twigs), symbolized by rigorously clear-cut bipartitions, seems unacceptable in the light of well-attested facts.[26]

Less than twenty years after this statement, an overview published by two Soviet linguists, Tamaz Gamkrelidze and Vjačeslav Ivanov, which many Indo-European scholars hailed as a landmark publication, included a *Stammbaum* of the Indo-European languages.[27] The production of family trees continued to grow in pace with the popularity of automatic methods of classification.[28] The implicit application of the Schleicherian botanical model, together with the frequent refusal to explicitly accept all of its consequences, constitutes a dilemma to which we must return at a later stage.

The young Turks of comparative grammar

From Schleicher onwards Indo-European studies will follow two principal directions: one remains confined to comparative grammar and simply aims, by applying the same general principles, to augment the volume of data and increase the rigor of its approach; the other, once the reality of the reconstructed language (the *Ursprache*) is accepted, sets out on the quest for the primordial People (the *Urvolk*) who spoke this language, with a subsequent obligation to identify the original Homeland (the *Urheimat*) as well as its material and spiritual civilization.

The third generation of German linguists, that of the Neogrammarians (Brugmann, Osthoff, Delbrück, Ascoli, Verner, Paul, etc.), are often presented as the instigators of a methodological revolution. However, this is no more than one of many such sociological phenomena that litter the history of science, a skillfully publicized clash of generations. Judging their mentor Georg Curtius to be outdated, even though he was the first to introduce the use of comparative grammar in the traditional teaching of Greek and Latin, two young grammarians from Leipzig University, Karl Brugmann and Hermann Osthoff, openly challenged his authority and launched a new journal, the *Morphologischen Untersuchungen auf dem Gebiet der indo-germanischen Sprachen* (Morphological Research in the Field of Indo-European Languages), in 1876. The first issue began with a

---

[26] Mounin, 1967, p. 201.
[27] Gamkrelidze and Ivanov, 1984; see Appendix 4.
[28] See Chapter 17, pp. 393–394.

30   FIRST MOVEMENT (1814-1903)

manifesto, signed by the two authors, in which they called for a more rigorous approach to linguistics, yet all the while setting the old generation against the new. They adopted the nickname *Junggrammatiker* which ironically echoes the "Young-Turks" of the declining Ottoman Empire who were hungry for renewed power.

The most notable methodological success of these Neogrammarians was the definition of a number of phonetic laws that accurately took account of the resemblances and differences between Indo-European languages. On several occasions they reiterated that these laws "do not suffer any exception," and this was precisely, in their view, one of the fundamental bones of contention between them and their elders, whom they deemed to be too lax. By applying these laws, Brugmann and Delbrück were able to produce their monumental work *Grundriss der vergleichenden Grammatik der indogermanischen Sprachen* (Elements of the Comparative Grammar of the Indo-European Languages),[29] now outdated but never surpassed. However, in reality, the Neogrammarians did little more than apply Schleicher's program: comparison, phonetic laws, reconstruction. Likewise, successive generations of twentieth-century linguists would not attempt to distance themselves from their results. Instead, newly discovered languages (Tocharian, Hittite, and Mycenaean Greek) were integrated within the comparison of languages; the techniques of structural phonology were successfully applied to the comparison; tenacious and systematic studies were patiently multiplied. Even now, at the beginning of the twenty-first century, we still find the work of Brugmann and Delbrück recommended in introductory bibliographies, albeit accompanied by a cautionary note. Indeed, the same can also be said for Meillet's work, *Introduction à l'étude comparative des langues indo-européennes* (Introduction to the Comparative Study of Indo-European Languages), which was also published more than a century ago.

Other possible models so soon?

While the Neogrammarians continued to tweak their laws that did not "suffer exception," dissenting voices belonging to the same generation were already being raised within the German philological community. As early as 1870, two of Schleicher's students, Johannes Schmidt and Hugo Schuchardt, who both went on to become professors at the University of Graz in Austria, called into question the infallibility of their mentor's canonical botanical model. Johannes Schmidt, who died at the age of fifty-eight, developed the "wave theory" of language change (*Wellentheorie*).[30] While up until then it had been postulated that

---

[29] Brugmann and Delbrück, 1897–1916.
[30] Schmidt, J., 1872.

THE INVENTION OF COMPARATIVE GRAMMAR   31

each language was a separate homogenous entity that evolved independently of others, just like the branches of a tree, Schmidt proposed a completely different model: that of a handful of pebbles thrown into a pool of water, with each pebble creating concentric waves that spread out from the point of impact before eventually crossing each other. According to Schmidt, the evolution of languages was similar, occurring through contacts and interferences. He did not necessarily question the kinship relationships between Indo-European languages, but he was more interested in the processes that gave rise to linguistic innovations. He states that

> [e]verywhere we look we observe transitions, without abrupt breaks, from one language to another, and it is undeniable that, in general, the further west an Indo-European language occurs, the further it is from its original state, while two bordering languages always share certain characteristics that are specific only to them.[31]

His attempts were generally not taken up by others, and almost a century would pass before the phenomenon of contact and interference became one of the most novel and productive fields in linguistics.[32]

In contrast, Hugo Schuchardt's working life was much longer; he died in 1927 at the age of eighty-five, having spent most of his life teaching in Graz. He carried out truly pioneering work on the Romance languages, Basque, Celtic languages, and Caucasian languages, and he also became interested in Volapük, a project for a universal language that was briefly popular in the nineteenth century. He vigorously challenged the Neogrammarians in an attempt to demonstrate the pointlessness of their beloved "laws."[33] Nevertheless, throughout his life he remained a solitary researcher even though his students admired him and, on the occasion of his eightieth birthday, honored him with the *Hugo Schuchardt-Brevier*, an anthology of his most important articles presented in the form of a breviary.[34]

However, his name is most closely associated with the study of pidgin and creole languages, particularly those of the Pacific and the West Indies, and more generally with the phenomena of language mixing. He shared this interest in linguistic interferences with Schmidt, but he developed it much further, to the extent that he can be considered the founding figure of Creolistics. While engaged in thorough studies on the edges of the Austro-Hungarian Empire, he worked on the linguistic contact zones and on the language mixing phenomena (*Mischsprache*) between Slovenian and German on the one hand, and

---

[31] Ibid., p. 26.
[32] See Chapter 19, pp. 434–446.
[33] Schuchardt, 1885.
[34] Schuchardt, 1922; see also Schuchardt, 2011.

32 FIRST MOVEMENT (1814–1903)

between Slovenian—as well as Serbo-Croatian spoken on the Dalmatic coast—and Italian on the other.[35] Thanks to this, Schuchardt could calmly assert that "With sounder arguments than those used by Max Müller when he stated that 'there is no mixed language' we can affirm that no language is totally pure"—or, in the original German *"Es gibt keine völlig ungemischte Sprache."*[36] From the 1910s onward, these studies prompted Schuchardt to engage in heated exchanges with the French linguist Antoine Meillet who was opposed to the existence of mixed languages. However, here we are encroaching on the next chronological phase. Therefore, we will return to these debates at a later stage[37] and also in the final chapter,[38] just before the final sections that deal with alternative linguistic models to the *Stammbaum*.

As we will see, it is only by freeing itself from the comparative grammar of Indo-European languages that linguistics would mature into an autonomous science in the twentieth century, when, for a while, it would even stand as the most prestigious of the human sciences. Precisely because of this, comparative grammar failed to benefit from novel methodologies, some of which even contradicted its most fundamental assumptions. However, it was in the field of Indo-European studies that the founder of structural linguistics, Ferdinand de Saussure, produced his earliest work in Leipzig in the company of the Neogrammarians.

[35] Schuchardt, 1884.
[36] Ibid., p. 5.
[37] See Chapter 5, pp. 112–114.
[38] See Chapter 19.

3

From India to Germania, the return of the wheeled cradle

Since the challenge facing the Indo-European linguistic community from the outset concerned a cultural and soon-to-be racial community, it was natural that any advances in comparative grammar would be accompanied by intense research into the original Fatherland (or "Cradle" or "Homeland"), the *Urheimat*, and into its primitive culture; this latter might even involve a raciological characterization of the primitive People, the *Urvolk*. However, prior to the last third of the nineteenth century, this research had no foundations in archaeological reality. Arguments that might be used to support an Asian or Indian origin for the Indo-Europeans were, by turns or simultaneously, geographical, historical, botanical, linguistic, or even raciological. From the Himalayas to the Baltic and from the Caucasus to the North Pole, the places of origin proposed were so diverse and contradictory[1] that a significant number of Indo-European linguists, in a wait-and-see approach, decided that it was more prudent to await future archaeological evidence before making a definitive identification of the original homeland from which the primordial language, which they were attempting to reconstruct, emanated. However, in this apparent chaos, there was a single overriding logic: the progressive repatriation of this mythical origin to Europe.

The Indian cradle

Since William Jones's "discovery," and for the first two thirds of the nineteenth century, India and its neighboring regions were seen as the perfect original Homeland by the vast majority of scholars. It was from there that the term "Aryan" became synonymous with "Indo-European."[2] Indeed, the earliest Indian texts mention the noble and pious "Aryans" who were promptly adopted as representatives of the original People, an interpretation that, as we shall see later,

---

[1] Historiographical summaries of these locations are found in Schrader, 1907; Reinach, 1892; Scherer, 1968; Mallory, 1973, 1989; Römer, 1985.

[2] On the history of the term "Aryan" and associated terms, see Siegert, 1941–1942; Koerner, 1982; Olender, 1989, p. 34; Arvidsson, 2006.

34 FIRST MOVEMENT (1814–1903)

lacks foundation.[3] The hypothesis of an Indian origin was explicitly presented in Schlegel's book (1808) and quite quickly the location was narrowed down: the original birthplace was identified as northern India, on the high plateaus of the Pamir and Hindu Kush, located at the western extremity of the Himalayas, a region divided today between Pakistan, Afghanistan, and Tajikistan. This happens to be the region where the great central Asian rivers, the Amu Darya (the Oxus of ancient times) and the Syr Darya, have their source. Numerous works published throughout the nineteenth century reaffirm and vehemently argue that this area was the original Homeland.[4] In 1829, a German scholar, Johan Gottlieb Rhode, even identified the reasons for the Indo-Europeans' departure from this area: a sudden cooling of the climate, which he inferred from an obscure paragraph in the Avesta, the sacred text of the Persian Zoroastran religion which appears to date back to the beginning of the first millennium BCE (the earliest surviving manuscripts date to the thirteenth century AD).[5]

However, it is to a Swiss artillery officer, Adolphe Pictet, that we owe the most detailed description of daily life in this original Homeland.[6] His great work, *Les Origines indo-européennes, ou les Aryas primitifs, essai de paléontologie linguistique* (The Origins of the Indo-Europeans, or the Primitive Aryans, an Essay in Linguistic Paleontology) (1859–1863), is based on a method that he pioneered: namely, linguistic paleontology. According to this theory, words which are still shared among most Indo-European languages must logically refer to the environment, technology, and institutions of the original People before they spread out. His work is made up of five parts which describe in succession the geography, ethnography, natural history, material culture, social life, and, finally, the intellectual, moral, and religious life of these "primitive Aryans," "a race destined by fate to one day dominate the whole world, . . . privileged among all other races by virtue of the beauty of its blood and by the gift of intelligence, [dwelling] within a majestic but severe nature"; a "fertile race [that] strove to create . . . a language that was admirable by virtue of its richness, vigor, harmony and the perfection of its forms."[7] He concludes by enthusiastically extoling the "Aryans" for

> the harmonious balance of their faculties and aptitudes, which is already perceivable to a high degree in the formation of their language and which presided, from the earliest times, over their social organization. A happy nature, where

---

[3] See Chapter 15, pp. 328–331.

[4] Among many others: Rhode, 1820; Pott, 1833–1836; Lassen, 1847; Grimm, 1848; Pictet, 1859–1863; Hehn, 1873; Virchow, 1874; Sayce, 1884; Van den Gheyn, 1889; Müller, F. M., 1888, 1889; Deniker, 1900; etc.

[5] Rhode, 1820.

[6] On Pictet, see Olender, 2008, pp. 93–105.

[7] Pictet, 1859–1863, vol. 1, pp. 1–2.

FROM INDIA TO GERMANIA   35

energy was tempered by gentleness, a lovely imagination and a powerful reason, an active intelligence and a spirit that was open to impressions of beauty, a genuine sentiment of truth and duty, a healthy morality and elevated religious instincts, such are the qualities which together gave them, along with the consciousness of their own value, the love of freedom and the constant desire for progress.[8]

This "majestic but severe nature" in which the "Aryans" frolicked was ancient Bactria in present-day Afghanistan, a mountainous land that to some extent resembled Pictet's native Switzerland. The arguments for this Asian homeland were, up to this point, as evident as they were tenuous. It is because, for some scholars such as Schlegel (but not Jones, as we have seen), Sanskrit appeared to be the mother language that India was immediately identified as the original homeland; this interpretation was, however, soon abandoned. It was also because, as pointed out by the philological compiler Adelung in his 1806 work *Mithridate*, Europe is "geographically just an extension of Asia that its first inhabitants must undoubtedly have come from Asia." Similarly Pott was led to exclaim: "Out of the East came the light! . . . the march of civilization has always tended to follow the light of the sun."[9] Conveniently, linguistic paleontology reinforced this hypothesis. Suggested by Rask in 1818, it was further developed in the context of the Polynesian migrations by the English historian John Crawfurd in 1820, in his search for shared words in the various Polynesian languages in order to define an original Polynesian culture. Linguistic paleontology was first applied in the quest for the Indo-Europeans by the orientalist Julius Klaproth in 1830; he drew attention to the birch, a tree that would henceforth become renowned in linguistic circles. In fact, birch is the only tree name to be attested to both in the Indo-European languages of Europe (*birke* in German, *bereza* in Russian, etc.) and in Sanskrit (*bhurja*): Klaproth concluded that "these people did not find trees that they knew in their new home [Europe], apart from birch, which grew on the southern slopes of the Himalayas." Frédéric Gustave Eichhoff, Kuhn, and finally Pictet, would subsequently definitively systemize linguistic paleontology, focusing in particular on institutions and the economy.[10]

Hence, in 1864, just after the publication of Pictet's work, Alexandre Bertrand, Director of the *Revue archéologique* and future head of the new *Musée des Antiquités Nationales*, would describe the Asiatic origin of the "Aryan civilization" as an "incontrovertible axiom" that was scientifically proven and accepted by "all of the scholarly institutions of Europe": "to attack it is, in a word, to attack

[8] Ibid., vol. 2, p. 755.
[9] Pott, 1833–1836, vol. 1, p. xxi.
[10] Crawfurd, 1820; Klaproth, 1830; Eichhoff, 1836; Kuhn, 1845.

36 FIRST MOVEMENT (1814–1903)

science itself."[11] It was using these same terms that he intervened in a series of discussions on the "origins of the Aryans" held by the newly founded *Société d'anthropologie de Paris* (SAP).[12] A practitioner of archaeology, the "older sister of anthropology," Bertrand expounded what were already considered the two pillars of the archaeological method: stratigraphy, which allows us to distinguish between superimposed and distinct layers left behind by successive civilizations and thus to establish their chronology; and the study of the geographical distribution (known today as *spatial analysis*) of remains which allows us to establish the geographical extent of civilizations.

Since menhirs and dolmens constituted the only readily visible archaeological remains in Europe at this time, albeit concentrated in the west and north of the continent, and since excavations of these sites did not reveal any metal, it followed that they were the traces of this primitive native population who "at an early stage retreated northwards to the edge of the world, and who, constantly fleeing the invading civilization, moved from island to island, from coast to coast, and even across the ocean, ended up, after failed attempts at transformation, dying out or being completely absorbed within the new populations."[13] In this way, Bertrand pasted an "axiomatic" model over an "irrefutable" geographical distribution, which was, however, open to other interpretations. This axiomatic model was a fusion of two other models: on the one hand, the projection, at the scale of prehistoric time, of the colonialization of "barbarian" Europe by Greco-Roman civilization—the only form under which the European elites could envisage the formation of their own civilization and its extension in modern times—and, on the other hand, the original biblical account, whose geographical locus would be shifted from the Near East to India.

An ephemeral Earthly Paradise

In contrast to the weak evidence, this preference for India as the original homeland did not spring out of nowhere. We have seen that, throughout the eighteenth century, the Brahmins gradually replaced the Hebrews in the quest for a primordial civilization, the mother of all other civilizations. For 1,800 years, Western humanity had known that it was born in a specific and real place, the Garden of Eden, or the Earthly Paradise. The Book of Genesis (Gen. II, 8–12) tells us that, shortly after creating Adam, God placed him in the Garden of Eden, a paradise planted with all sorts of edible fruit trees, including the Tree of Life and the fateful

---

[11] Bertrand, 1864, and particularly pp. 369–370; see also his contribution in the same volume of the *Bulletins de la Société d'anthropologie de Paris*, pp. 316–317.

[12] See Chapter 4, pp. 81–84.

[13] Bertrand, 1864, p. 379.

Tree of Knowledge of Good and Evil, and watered by a river that split into four outside the garden to form the Tigris, the Euphrates, and the mysterious Pishon and Gihon. Then, in an attempt to provide Adam with a "suitable companion," God created all of the animals, and, in a last ditch effort, Eve. During the Middle Ages, Eden was naturally situated somewhere in the Near East and most likely in the mountains since it had survived the Flood and God had made it inaccessible. The Crusades and in particular the Age of Great Discoveries pushed the location of Eden further eastward. Luther, in his reforming purge, declared that Eden had been destroyed by the Flood, and Voltaire, faced with the failure of explorations to find its location, stated a little later that "God is a really poor geographer."

However, theologians were unrelenting, and at least thirty works were dedicated to identifying the location of Eden.[14] The most famous of these stubborn theologians was Pierre-Daniel Huet, Bishop of Avranches and protégé of Bossuet, who published his *Traité de la situation du paradis terrestre* (Treatise on the Location of the Earthly Paradise) in 1691. As early as 1670, the philosopher François Bernier placed Eden in Kashmir, and this attraction for the high mountains of Asia would continue into the Age of Enlightenment. Pastor Johann Gottfried Herder, a precursor of romantic orientalism, urged the abandonment of "these corners of Arabia and Judea, these muds of the Nile and Euphrates" in favor of "climbing the heights, the summit of Asia": "History, which dates everything to this beginning, will have another beginning and another outcome."[15] It is true that, at this point, Eden was becoming secularized and the burning issue was the origin of humanity in general, without the necessity to follow sacred texts to the letter.

However, is it accidental that, at the dawn of the nineteenth century, the homeland of the original Europeans and the Earthly Paradise, the biblical origin of all humanity, found themselves in the same location? And that it was the second that provided the template for the first? As we have seen, the original Homeland has three main characteristics: it is located far away in an inaccessible mountainous area; life there was idyllic, characterized by abundance and peace; one day a "Fall" occurred that triggered a departure and dispersal. If we replace God with Climate, then the secular version of the Fall scenario would continue to have a bright future. A little later, just such a climatic catastrophe was invoked by Armand de Quatrefages and several others to explain the original scattering of humanity, which it was believed had formerly been concentrated in the circumpolar regions.[16] More generally, the catastrophe story, and particularly that of a climatic catastrophe, would become one of the lasting and inevitable scenarios

[14] Jouty, 1991.
[15] Cited in Poliakov, 1971/1987, p. 213.
[16] Quatrefages, 1887, p. 133; Reinach, 1892, p. 12.

38 FIRST MOVEMENT (1814–1903)

used to explain the major steps in human history. For a time it even became the dominant scenario used to explain the origins of man; six million years ago, following the formation of the Rift Valley, the desertification of East Africa forced our primate ancestors to be resourceful and bipedal in order to survive. Similarly, another phase of desertification is cited by Gordon Childe to account for the earliest domestication of plants and animals 12,000 years ago.[17] These scenarios, which disregard a certain amount of factual evidence, in reality just reproduce and perpetuate the founding myth of the "Fall."[18]

The return of the homeland

Thus, for several decades, the northern highlands of India would become this strange land of compromise where the retreating biblical myth would gradually yield to the triumphant Indo-European myth. However, as René Gérard ably demonstrated,[19] India was little more than a romantic interlude for European intellectuals, a temporary substitute that was based on far too many misinterpretations. In line with certain reactionary aspects of Romanticism, it was even seen as a kind of regressive maternal image, an original and faraway homeland which stood as the polar opposite of the French Revolution and its call to the people to seize their destiny here and now by obliterating the old order.[20] However, in its quest for new benchmarks, Romanticism participated just as actively in the nurturing of new national sentiments and soon it would be Europe itself which would, almost definitively, become the original Cradle of the Indo-Europeans. In 1848, the year of great national uprisings, most of which were crushed, an elderly Belgian geologist, Jean Julien Omalius d'Halloy, became one of the first to cast doubt on the dogma of an Asian origin. His only predecessor was the German historian Heinrich Schulz who, in his 1826 work *Zur Urgeschichte des deutschen Volksstamms* (Prehistory of the German People),[21] had categorically discounted the idea that "white humanity" could have originated anywhere other than Europe. Little by little, from the midnineteenth century onward, more and more scholars would revise the arguments that up to now favored India simply by inversing them. By the end of the nineteenth century, whether lapped by the waters of the Baltic or of the Black Sea, the original Homeland had become European. However, while India was just a short-lived distraction, the abandonment of the biblical model did not occur

[17] See Chapter 7.
[18] Stoczkowski, 1994.
[19] Gérard, 1963; Schwab, 1950.
[20] Poliakov, 1971/1987, pp. 41 and 232.
[21] Schulz, H., 1826 (cited in Römer, 1985, p. 70); Omalius d'Halloy, 1848.

without misgivings, even though, for the most part, it was not a conscious move. Thus, we sometimes observe the emergence of two other forms of compromise, both of which were marginal and recurrent. The first of these continued to suggest a Near-Eastern location, either in Mesopotamia, where certain influences of Babylonian on the primordial language were noted (Schmidt), or else in the Caucasus, where Noah's Ark was said to have made landfall and from whence the first post-diluvian people were believed to have spread out; the archaic aspect of old Persian and certain toponyms seemed to support this thesis (Heinrich Friedrich Link, Hermann Brunnhofer).[22] The second, which revived the long tradition of a Hebrew mother tongue, cited potential proof of linguistic contacts between the original Indo-Europeans and original Semites.[23] However, as far as we are concerned, the main interest of these ideas lies in the fact that they were trotted out once more, virtually unchanged, at the end of the 1980s,[24] when, after a century in obscurity, they were hailed as new discoveries, the fruits of the most recent research in genetics, linguistics, and archaeology.

The rooting of the original homeland in Europe would therefore involve turning all earlier arguments on their head. If Sanskrit (and Persian) appeared archaic, then the recently studied Lithuanian and Old Slavonic, both Indo-European languages of Europe, appeared to be just as old; moreover it was the languages of emigrants (e.g., Quebec-French and Castilian as spoken by the Jews of Thessalonica) that tended to be most conservative while the autochthonous languages were more likely to innovate.[25] And even if certain migrations appeared to come from the east, did not most of the historical migrations, and the most durable, come from the west (the Sea Peoples, the Celts of southern Europe, the Scythians in Persia, the Goths)? And it was indeed European peoples who continued to display an expansionist drive while their old Asian colonies of Persia and India "having mixed with various less gifted races, completely lost their taste for long distance migrations and conquest by assimilation."[26] Furthermore, when we look at the distribution of Indo-European languages, we see that their widest territory lies in Europe, which, if we follow Schleicher's botanical analogy, must surely mean that this was their original territory.[27]

Ultimately, linguistic paleontology would be enlisted to explain absences, as well as presences, in the primordial Indo-European language: there was, for example, no common root for elephant, tiger, or camel, all of which are species indigenous to Asia (in a departure from his own rules, Pictet had already been

[22] Schmidt, J., 1890; Link, 1821; Brunnhofer, 1885.
[23] Hehn, 1870; Delitzsch, 1873; Hommel, 1879; Reinach, 1892.
[24] See Chapter 10, pp. 229–230. pp. 229–230. and Chapter 17, pp. 390–392.
[25] Omalius d'Halloy, 1865; Hirt, 1892; Reinach, 1892, pp. 26–27.
[26] Lindenschmit, 1880 (in preface); see also Omalius d'Halloy, 1865.
[27] Latham, 1862.

40 FIRST MOVEMENT (1814–1903)

forced to place camels in the original Homeland since these ruminants are well-known natives of Central Asia). Sometimes the struggle was indecisive: since, with the exception of birch (and possibly beech), there are no common roots for the names of trees apart from among European languages, it followed either that, coming from Asia, the future Europeans created these names for the new vegetation that they encountered on the edge of Europe before splitting into various groups or, alternatively, that, coming from Europe, the Indo-Iranians simply lost these words because they no longer had a use for them in an Asian context. A third alternative exists: that there were no trees in the original Homeland. All three of these hypotheses were amply discussed in the literature. As regards the common root for the "sea," it could point to any European or Asian coast, but it might also originally have been used to describe any large body of water, be it fresh or salt.

Within Europe, two regions received particular attention: on the one hand, the southeast, essentially the steppes to the north of the Black Sea (also known as the "Pontic Steppes" from the ancient Greek name for the Black Sea: the *Eúxeinos Póntos* or "favorable Sea"), with some minor variations (the Balkan Peninsula, southern Belarus); and, on the other, the Baltic region. The first and more popular of the two propositions represented a convenient solution as it constituted a veritable bridge between Europe and Asia. In 1892, Salomon Reinach, Director of the *Musée des Antiquités Nationales*, presented it as a "new theory," backed up by "serious arguments" and as "the conclusion to which modern science appears to have led"; Reinach was a staunch despiser of the "oriental mirage," which, thirty years later, would lead him to endorse the Glozel archaeological hoax.[28] This "new theory," which was championed by Émile Benveniste in 1939 and "rediscovered" by Marija Gimbutas in the 1970s through the Soviet archaeology, was none other than that originally forwarded by Leibniz. Proposed by several authors including Robert Gordon Latham, who pointed out the resemblances between Sanskrit and Balto-Slavic and therefore proposed an intermediate point of origin, necessarily placed in Europe for "botanical" reasons,[29] it was systemized in 1883 by German linguist Otto Schrader. His *Sprachvergleichung und Urgeschichte* (Linguistic Comparison and Prehistory)[30] was followed in 1901 by the imposing *Reallexikon der indogermanischen Altertumskunde* (Dictionary of Indo-European Realities).[31]

---

[28] Reinach, 1892, p. 121.

[29] Latham, 1862; Benfey, 1868.

[30] A first edition appeared in 1883, a second augmented edition in 1890, a third augmented edition in 1907.

[31] Schrader, 1901; a second edition, completed by Alfons Nehring after the death of Schrader, appeared between 1917 and 1929: Schrader and Nehring, 1917–1929.

Those who refused to repatriate the homeland

Two countries, for different reasons, resisted this repatriation of the original homeland to Europe: the first was Russia, where the Aryans had been explicitly appropriated to bolster nationalist sentiment.[32] The cultured Russian elites sought to affirm their belonging to Europe, and thereby their "Indo-Europeanness," but also their originality, even though, from a Western perspective, they were often seen as Asian barbarians. At the same time, the Tsarist Empire continued to extend its territory eastward (the Far East) and southward (Central Asia). A compromise was therefore established in the mid-nineteenth century: the original homeland was indeed in Central Asia as the writer Aleksej S. Khomyakov[33] asserted from 1840 onward, and, by seizing these regions, the Slavs were simply freeing their Aryan brothers (Tajiks and Afghans) from the yoke of the Turkish-speaking peoples. Dostoevsky himself claimed to belong to the "Aryan" people. Moreover, the ancient, Persian-speaking Scythians provided a convenient geographical and chronological link with the original People. However, unlike in Western Europe, this Aryan ideology never gave rise to racist rhetoric (regardless of the pervasiveness of anti-Semitism in these regions).

The other European country that resisted the repatriation of the Cradle was the United Kingdom. On the one hand, British intellectuals of the nineteenth century traditionally remained reserved regarding raciological rhetoric and thus regarding the Indo-European question as it was treated at the time, and they also avoided historical migrationist and invasionist explanations. At the same time, as has been pointed out by the historian Marlène Laruelle, British colonialism used the Aryans to justify its imperialism, just as the Russians did. In the same way that the Russians attempted to play the Persian-speaking Tajiks against the Turkish-speaking populations, the British would promote the idea of the "Aryanness" of the Brahmin caste, whose original purity ought to be restored through the intervention of their British Aryan brethren, thereby rescuing them from decadence and political fragmentation arising from their prolonged contact with inferior populations.[34] A significant proportion of the Indian elites would nonetheless remain reticent toward this solution in so far as it posed an obstacle to the unity of India.

---

[32] Laruelle, 1999, 2010; Laruelle and Taguieff, 2005.
[33] Khomyakov et al., 1873; Laruelle, 2010.
[34] Laruelle, 2010; Leopold, 1970; Greenberger, 1969; Parry, 1972; Trautmann, 1997.

42 FIRST MOVEMENT (1814–1903)

From texts to objects

The growth of prehistoric archaeology would lend Indo-European studies, up to then quite academic, a degree of "reality" which would render the *Reallexikon* (Dictionary of Realities) more concrete. This discipline had an undeniably long history. In England, megalithic monuments were being scrutinized as early as the twelfth century AD, while in France, in 1685, Abbot Cocherel undertook an excavation at Houlbec-Cocherel in Normandy, which revealed a collective Neolithic grave containing skeletons and stone axes. Fr. Bernard de Montfaucon describes this discovery, along with others, in his *Monuments de la monarchie française* of 1729–1733, the first overview of French archaeology. From 1727 onward, President de Robien, a councilor in the Parliament of Brittany, carried out several excavations in the Locmariaquer region and produced numerous detailed sketches of his discoveries.[35] At the same time, following a period during which surviving works of art from classical antiquity were fortuitously collected, the first systematic excavations of Pompeii began. However, classical archaeology posed few epistemological problems: ancient texts existed, in both Greek and Latin, which archaeological "rediscoveries" backed up, and thus archaeology was little more than an "auxiliary" discipline which aided in the interpretation of the texts. Furthermore, undeciphered texts, particularly from Egypt and the Near East, would soon be decrypted. Subsequently, the first half of the nineteenth century witnessed the development of systematic tools for collecting objects and revealing monuments in the field; from Bonaparte's expedition to Egypt, which thirty years later would lead to the deciphering of the Rosetta Stone by Champollion, to the foundation of the first Western institutes for archaeology overseas, such as the *École Française d'Athènes*, founded in 1846.

However, the only text available to prehistorians was the Bible and even though animal fossils had been collected throughout the seventeenth and eighteenth centuries, by 1831, Cuvier still believed that man post-dated them because he was created on the sixth day. To suggest that the days of creation corresponded to geological periods constituted a nonliteral interpretation of the Bible and was grounds for excommunication up until at least the end of the nineteenth century. Very ancient human remains were simply interpreted through the lens of the Book of Genesis; these were "antediluvian" people, predating the Flood. However, the 1850s witnessed both the publication of Darwin's *On the Origin of Species* and a multiplication of prehistoric discoveries; the latter ranged from the controversial identification of Neanderthal man, whose remains were found in a small cave outside Düsseldorf in 1896, to the discovery by customs official Jacques Boucher of flint tools on the terraces of the River Somme, the authenticity of which was

---

[35] See Daniel, 1950; Laming-Emperaire, 1964; Schnapp, 1993.

confirmed by several visiting English geologists and paleontologists in 1859. Boucher published the finds between 1847 and 1864 in his *Antiquités celtiques et antédiluviennes* (Celtic and Antediluvian Antiquities).[36] The Neanderthal discoveries and those of the Somme were not without consequences for the Indo-European question; they proved that Europe had very likely been inhabited since the dawn of humanity and that the hypothesis of migrations from the East could be abandoned definitively.

From the beginning of the twentieth century onward, efforts were made to systemize prehistoric discoveries within the framework of a global sequence. Christian Jürgensen Thomsen, founder and director of the National Museum in Copenhagen, Denmark, a country with a long history of careful and systematic collection and protection of archaeological remains, classed the museum's collections into three "ages": the Stone Age, the Bronze Age, and the Iron Age. But even these three ages were still compatible with the mythical ages described by certain ancient writers such as Plato. Megalithic monuments—dolmens and gallery graves constructed of large blocks of stone—which German folk tradition interpreted as Huns's beds, were often attributed by French and English scholars to the Celts, the oldest native people referred to in those inevitable ancient texts, thereby giving rise to "Celtomania."

Imagined communities

"Celtomania," which existed from the mid-eighteenth century to the mid-nineteenth century, consisted of an exaltation of an imaginary Celtic past concocted from snippets of information regarding the Celts provided by Roman and Greek authors mixed with archaeological evidence of dolmens and menhirs, fantastical and romantic representations of the past, and even literary fakes such as the famous Works of Ossian, which inspired generations even though it was actually written in 1760.[37] Salomon Reinach summed up (with a high degree of irony) the Celtomaniac credo: "The Celts are the most ancient people on earth, their language, the mother of all languages, has been preserved, almost intact, in Bas-Breton; they were deep philosophers, whose revelations were transmitted to the Bardic schools of Wales; the dolmens are the altars on which their priests, the Druids, offered up human sacrifices; the stone rows are their astronomical observatories."[38] The close ties that Celtomania formed with Indo-European aspirations, of which it could be seen as a marginal and degraded form used by

---

[36] Boucher de Perthes, 1847.
[37] Laming-Emperaire, 1964 (pp. 106–114); Reinach, 1898; Piggot, 1937; Michell, 1982.
[38] Reinach, 1898, p. 111.

44 FIRST MOVEMENT (1814–1903)

local scholars to promote nativist patriotism, are clear for all to see. However, as this aspiration developed, Celtomania was the first to suffer. The Celts, with their Indo-European language, must have come from Asia along with metalworking—but no metal was found beneath properly excavated dolmens. Thus these monuments must have belonged to the primitive population of Europe that had been colonized and civilized by the Celts.[39] All at once the Celts became trivial, stripped of their megaliths and all of their evocative, fantastical power; they were no longer worthy of anything more than "normal," modest philological and archaeological study. Thus Celtomania virtually disappeared with the end of Romanticism and as a scientific approach was gradually applied to Celtic archaeology, even though it has survived in a marginal way right up to today among various para-religious and para-scientific groups. It was, nonetheless, one of the first independent forms of prehistoric archaeology to emerge.

Celtomania would also survive in the use of the notion of "Celticness" for nationalistic purposes, which would be attempted in France, with little success, by certain political leaders, from Napoleon III to Marshal Pétain, and through the medium of countless school books.[40] This exploitation of Celticness would never kindle much enthusiasm in France, however, since the Gauls had officially been vanquished by their own indiscipline and barbarity and found themselves forcibly civilized to the extent that their descendants spoke the language of their conquerors. Moreover, it was only in periods of defeat, after the war of 1870 or during the period of collaboration with the Nazi regime, for instance, that the idealized figure of Vercingetorix would acquire a significance that was expiatory or even Christic. Unified for centuries, France had no need to resort to archaeology in order to assert the legitimacy of its territory, and France's elites instead turned to Greece, Rome, and the Near East to renew links with the origins of their cultural heritage. The search for archaeological objects attesting to ancient roots within the territory was therefore left in the hands of local notables, curates, doctors, teachers, and their learned societies.

The situation was very different in most other parts of Europe, which were divided among four great "multinational" empires—Austrian, Ottoman, Russian, and, more recently, German—or else fragmented into small principalities such as the Italian or German peoples. The national sentiment and democratic aspirations of Romanticism found in the supposed grandeur of the past a justification for revolting against current oppression and a pretext for the hostile annexation of neighboring territories. Thus "imaginaned communities"[41] gradually took shape, in whose name all too real massacres

---

[39] Bertrand, 1864.
[40] Viallaneix and Ehrard, 1982; Pomian, 1992; Buchsenschutz and Schnapp, 1993; Demoule, 2012a.
[41] Anderson (B.), 1983; Thiesse, 1999.

were perpetuated, from the Balkans to Ireland, right up to the dawn of the twenty-first century. Throughout the nineteenth century, in almost every large city of Europe, "National Museums" were established where archaeological finds that bore witness to a long indigenous history were amassed. In France, however, the Salomon Reinach, founded by Napoleon III, was relegated to Saint-Germain-en-Laye, a residential suburb at the outer limits of Paris. These museums financed archaeological excavations, published journals and books, and protected ancient monuments.

The rise of archaeological excavations

The second half of the nineteenth century was characterized by the institutionalization of archaeology: university chairs, learned societies, and regularly held international congresses defined the rules of the new discipline and diffused its findings. Thomsen's "three-age" system was refined and rendered more accurate by successive contributions from John Lubbock, Gabriel Mortillet, Paul Reinecke, and Joseph Déchelette. The constraints imposed by Genesis and the Greco-Roman texts were overturned, opening up a vast chronological vista on human history.[42] National traditions, but also the potential for discoveries, gave rise to varied focuses of interest. In France, an abundance of cave sites and a penchant for the universal meant that research tended to focus on the earliest periods of prehistory to the detriment of "recent" prehistory (namely, the Neolithic and Metal Ages). In Germany, the northern half of which had been covered by ice and therefore uninhabitable for much of the Paleolithic, researchers were more interested in the megaliths of the Late Neolithic and the tumuli of the Bronze and Iron Ages, which were believed to have been erected by the ancestors of the Germanic people. It was similar in Scandinavia, where archaeologists excavated megaliths and tumuli but also shell middens, *kjøkkenmødding*, left behind by Mesolithic hunter-gatherers along the Danish coastline. In Italy, excavators focused their attention on the Latium area in order to understand the prehistory of Rome, but investigations also targeted the *terramare*, extremely rich Bronze Age sites typical of northeastern Italy. Following a drop in the water level in Lake Zurich in winter 1854, the lake shores of Switzerland began to reveal the buildings, ceramics, and stone and wooden tools of a new civilization, that of the lake villages or *palafittes*; these settlements, composed of pile dwellings, were among the first communities to practice agriculture and animal husbandry, and similar sites also occur in eastern France and southern Germany.

---

[42] Groenen, 1994; Coye, 1997; Gran-Aymerich, 1998; Hurel and Coye, 2011; Trigger, 1989.

46   FIRST MOVEMENT (1814–1903)

But, in terms of public profile, the most significant events of the period were the excavations undertaken by Heinrich Schliemann. This rich German businessman, who as a child (if we are to believe his autobiography) dreamed of the stories of the Trojan War, embarked at the age of forty-six on a career as an amateur archaeologist. Beginning in 1871, he successively rediscovered Troy, Mycenae, and Tiryns; he showed that these towns, which were believed to be mythical, did indeed exist. Despite the use of questionable methods, he was, nonetheless, the first archaeologist to investigate prehistoric *tells* (i.e., hills composed of a complex accumulation of superimposed settlements) and excavate them layer by layer, thus applying a geological approach to classical archaeology; up until then, field work consisted of the ad hoc collection of art objects destined for study by historians and philologists. Schliemann also knew how to surround himself with qualified collaborators such as the architect Wilhelm Dörpfeld, who arrived fresh from the German excavations at Olympia, or the anthropologist Rudolf Virchow, who became one of his firmest supporters. He also had considerable media savvy, publishing "live" daily updates in the *Times* and the *Telegraph*. Through this faculty of "rediscovery," archaeology opened up a new space for the imagination within which the search for Indo-European origins would eventually flourish.

In fact, Schliemann himself believed that the Indo-Europeans once occupied Troy. Certain clay spindle whorls (which he interpreted as ritual objects because "they were much too elegant") retrieved from the deepest levels bore incised swastikas.

The Trojans were, therefore, an Aryan race, as is clear from the evidence of symbols engraved on terracotta discs. The nation which succeeded the Trojans was also long-lived as it occurs in every soil layer between a depth of 10 and 7 m. It was of Aryan origin for it featured numerous Aryan symbols; and I believe that I have demonstrated that several of these also belonged to our ancestors at a time when the Germans, Pelasgians, Hindus, Celts and Greeks all belonged to one nation and spoke a single language.[43]

While most archaeologists pursued their research without any particular interest in the Indo-European question, Indo-Europeanist scholars, who were hitherto confined to the field of linguistics, were now presented not only with a new temporal space but also a huge quantity of tangible objects. Thus, while Pictet only had Homer and Virgil to turn to when reconstructing the primordial society, Schrader was able to situate some of his Indo-Europeans on the shores of Alpine lakes and to physically touch the "reality" of these people. However, these mute

---

[43] Schliemann, *Trojan Antiquities*, report dated April 24, 1872, cited in Schliemann, 1992, p. 76.

objects are obstinate and cannot be put in just any old chronological order; in fact, from now on they have to be considered seriously.

More primitive

It is worth lingering a while on the achievements of Schrader because, like the monumental philological works produced by the Neogrammarians at the end of the nineteenth century, in terms of their level of ambition, the works of Schrader constitute the first and last attempts to integrate all available linguistic, archaeological, mythological, and historical data. This is why his *Linguistic Comparison* and his *Reallexikon* (the latter is an alphabetic presentation of the former, which is itself more demonstrative and methodological) still feature in bibliographies today. Moreover, in terms of a century of Indo-European studies, this synthesis marks the first official appearance of the "steppic theory," which places the original Homeland in southern Russia and Ukraine. More recent works claiming the same ambition in fact reproduce the same approach and the same errors of logic.[44]

This conscientious and systematic scholar, for whom "the expression 'Indo-European' (*indo-germanisch*) designated a purely linguistic notion, a fact that can never be over emphasized,"[45] was never driven by nationalistic ideology. In the name of scientific argument, he fought against locating the *Urheimat* in Germany or Scandinavia, an idea that would soon predominate in Germany. In his dictionary, under the entry for "Racial questions" (and not "Race"), the reader is referred to the heading "Physical makeup (*Körperbeschaffenheit*) of the Indo-Europeans," which is something else entirely. And within this section, which borrows from the work of the anthropologist Virchow, who as we will see later held a moderate position, Schrader refutes the idea of an Indo-European "racial entity": "Nowhere has the objective study of ancient skulls revealed a totally homogenous population. On the contrary, in all periods going back as far as the Stone Age, we see the co-existence of dolichocephaly, mesocephaly and brachicephaly." As regards eye and hair color, "we must take it as a certainty" that they are not linked to skull proportions.[46] To believe in a racial entity would be to preclude the possibility of marriages outside the group; in reality, we cannot exclude the possibility that Indo-Europeans "also purchased

---

[44] See Chapter 18, pp. 399–403.

[45] Schrader and Nehring, 1917–1929, I, p. 540; all of the citations that follow are taken from this second edition of Schrader's dictionary, as are the page numbers in brackets (in Arabic numerals) and the volume numbers (in Roman numerals).

[46] Ibid., vol. I, pp. 632–633.

48   FIRST MOVEMENT (1814–1903)

or kidnapped their women from foreign tribes (and why not from non-Indo-Europeans?)" (I, p. 631).

The fact that Schrader's Indo-Europeans have little in common with those of Pictet cannot simply be put down to the increase in archaeological discoveries; in fact, it is also due to the development of what was a new discipline at the time, ethnology. Of course, at an early stage, the exploration of Black Africa and the discovery of the Americas opened the door to historical reflection, and, from as early as 1724, the Jesuit Lafitau in his *Mœurs des sauvages américains comparées aux mœurs des premiers temps* (Customs of the American Indians Compared with the Customs of Primitive Times) risked proposing almost sacrilegious comparisons between Greco-Roman Antiquity and the "savages." The systematization of ethnographic observations initially made by missionaries and soldiers would, over the course of the nineteenth century, renew the vision of "primitive" societies, which oscillated continually between the idealization of the "good savage" and the denial of their humanity. And because they were "primitive" in the true sense, these societies were presumed to display, in an embryonic stage, features that true civilizations went on to develop. Thus, they did not possess true religions, much less philosophies, but only obscure beliefs in the primordial forces of nature and meteorological phenomena inhabited by a vague principle, "Mana." It is precisely this ethnology that would be developed by Lucien Lévy-Bruhl and subsequently by James Fraser. In fact, it was not until the 1940s that "primitivism" gradually gave way to the structuralist approach. The religious historian Max Müller had attempted to find connections between the Greek pantheon and that of the Vedic hymns of India; thus he equated Uranus with Varuna and the Centaurs with the Gandharvas.[47] Abandoning these linguistically dodgy assimilations and instead basing his assumptions on the absence of shared names for deities in the various languages, Schrader described an Indo-European religion that was entirely orientated toward the adoration of primitive natural forces: the sun and the earth, the moon and water, wind and fire.

The entire life of the "Primitive People" (*Urvolk*) was thus "primitivized." With characteristic meticulousness, Schrader, who had included alphabetical entries for almost everything, from "Abortion" to "Beer," from "Butter" to "Family," "Bell" to "Chastity "and "Pan" to "Polygamy," devoted almost two pages to "rest rooms" (in German *Abort*). Beginning with the statement that "the installation of rest rooms is still unknown in many parts our country (Germany) today," he goes on to suggest that "as long as Indo-Europeans had lived in villages, toilet facilities

[47] On Max Müller, see Olender, 2008, pp. 82–92.

were totally absent and it was only with the establishment of urban centers, and then only among the upper echelons of society, that they made their appearance, perhaps under the civilizing influence of the East (toilets and water conduits are, for example, attested at a very early date in ancient Babylon)." This lack of toilet facilities is confirmed by the absence of a shared vocabulary referring to them, even though such a vocabulary does exist for the body parts concerned, "an unthinkable phenomenon if the designations, today usually veiled, by which we refer to these things had, in one way or another, been habitual practice in ancient times" (I, pp. 4–5). As a kind of consolation, under the heading "Flower," Schrader informs the reader that

> [a]s regards all that refers to fields and gardens, the growing of flowers is the most recent conquest of European humanity. The pragmatism of prehistoric people had prevented them from discovering the attraction of these objects, so cherished by ladies and poets, in the same way that their ears remained deaf to the song of the lark and the nightingale. This only changed when flower scented perfumes from the East reached Europe and when man's relationship with nature, at least in the upper echelons of society, began to become sentimental. (I, p. 151)

In this primitivist vision, archaeology and linguistic paleontology come to support each other mutually, or indeed circularly. Today, we know that most of the proto-historic populations of Europe lived in quadrangular houses built of timber and clay but which only survive in the archaeological record as barely perceptible variations in soil color. It was not until the 1920s in Germany (the 1960s in France) that archaeological techniques had developed to the point where these faint traces could be observed. In contrast, the pits that these populations dug in order to extract and mix clay for building, and which were subsequently used for waste disposal, were easy to spot; they appeared as roughly circular, dark stains and were filled with broken and discarded objects (tools, pottery, animal bone). Archaeologists mistakenly identified these pits as Neolithic houses and coined the term "pit-dwellings" (*Grubenhaus, maisons en fosse*). Schrader believed that he could confirm this interpretation; a certain number of shared Indo-European words for "house," such as *sala* in Sanskrit, *höll* or *halle* in Germanic, or *cella* in Latin, are close to the French verb *cacher* ("to hide"); the Latin *celare* also gave rise to the verb *celer* ("to hide") in old French. The primitive Indo-European house, therefore, must have been buried: "this is why we can attribute pit-dwellings to the primitive Indo-European era" (I, p. 448). The archaeology of the time suggested this mistaken interpretation to Schrader, who then kindly returned the favor.

50   FIRST MOVEMENT (1814–1903)

Bathing, kissing, and chastity

In several entries, Schrader paid a good deal of attention to Indo-European practices involving the body and sexuality, all the while being careful to apologize for the primitiveness of the Indo-Europeans and seeking to reassure the bourgeois reader while remaining, above all, scientific. Thus, under the heading "Bath" he states,

> [w]hile the idea of "washing" existed in the primitive vocabulary, we can nonetheless ask ourselves what use the original people made of it in relation to their own bodies. On the basis of what we know, we cannot claim that there was a particularly developed desire for cleanliness in prehistoric times, and bathing on the occasion of a birth, marriage, death, numerous expiatory obligations, etc. would never have been invested with such importance and solemnity if this had been an everyday practice. (I, p. 71)

On the basis of various historical accounts (Homer, Caesar, Tacitus) and ethnographic evidence (Russian and Baltic), he felt confident enough to state that

> [w]hether a bath was cold or hot, taken in rivers, wooden huts, tents, chambers or pits, all ancient Indo-European peoples shared the idea that there was nothing shocking in a man undressing in front of a woman on such occasions, and vice versa. (I, p. 77)

Regarding "Chastity" (*Keuschheit*), he notes that "in terms of sexual life, prehistoric times were still characterized by an attitude of complete candor or astonishment, and even reverence" (I, p. 582). Of course the existence of pederasty could not be denied, but this undoubtedly came from the East where

> [t]his repugnant lust appears to find a natural cause in physiological tendencies resulting from the high degree of corporeal indolence among Orientals. . . . However, we cannot ignore the fact that modern medicine considers the homosexual impulse to be congenital among a non-negligible number of individuals belonging to all peoples, even though, having originated elsewhere, it has found a broadly favorable ground in Europe. (I, p. 610)

Concerning amorous practices, "the history of the kiss remains to be written" and "it is difficult to resolve the issue of when the love kiss (*Liebeskuss*), the particular kiss performed with the mouth and which relegated all other forms of kiss to the background among civilized peoples, is first attested among Indo-European peoples" (I, pp. 669–670). On the question of marriage (under the entry for "Woman," we find: "See Marriage"), Schrader abruptly begins his entry "Concubine" (*Beischläferin*) as follows: "Polygamy prevailed in primitive Indo-European times" (I, p. 86). Indeed, evidence for it abounds among the Hindus, Persians, Germans, Slavs, and Celts. In the end, the only exceptions are the Greeks and Romans, undoubtedly due to the influence of wives originating from Asia Minor, "who were not inclined to give up their place to another [?]" (II, p. 197; the question mark is Schrader's).

Thus, little by little, Schrader's "method" takes shape, created by the juxtaposition of diverse approaches that utilize the following sources of information:

1. Data provided by linguistic paleontology: the existence of a common root in the various different Indo-European languages guarantees that the referent of this root (animal, plant, tool, action, institution, etc.) existed at the time of the original People and within their original Homeland; its absence implies that it did not exist, or did not yet exist. For example, there were no toilet facilities but there were sheep;

2. Data provided by what we could call "historical paleontology": if all of the peoples who are historically attested, right up to the present, and who speak Indo-European languages, have a certain object, practice, or institution in common, then we can postulate that this was also the case in the original Homeland. Hence, primitive Indo-Europeans had long hair, wore beards, and cheated on their wives with impunity;

3. General historical data: since all peoples who speak an Indo-European language are, by definition, Indo-European, it is permissible to create entries in order to summarize our knowledge concerning each one of them (Macedonians and Thracians, Lycians and Scythians, Armenians, Persians, and Slavs) as well as their non-Indo-European neighbors (Finns), but also to reflect on any objects that might be pertinent for the cultural history of Europe, and this even if they do not belong to the "common vocabulary," whether they be plants (wormwood or the date palm), techniques (the potter's wheel or the chair), practices or institutions (tattooing or wills);

4. Ethnographical data: it is this information that allowed Schrader to offer a much less idyllic picture of the original People than that developed by Pictet. But, in addition to a certain "average" representation of primitive societies (*die sogenannte Naturvölker*, "the peoples we refer to as naturals," I, p. 610), Schrader, for the reasons outlined in the previous point, also draws on European rural ethnography, which provides him with numerous illustrations (building techniques, agricultural tools, etc.), and also on certain popular myths. The vast majority of these borrowings (75%) are from the Slavic and Baltic worlds and, secondarily, the Germanic world, while the rest of Eurasia is more or less ignored;

52 FIRST MOVEMENT (1814–1903)

5 Archaeological data gleaned from iconography, particularly iconography from the Greco-Roman world (Trajan's Column and the Adamklissi monument in Romania, both of which illustrate the "barbarian" adversaries of Rome; the frescoes of Knossos) but also iconography from Egypt and Assyria illustrating aspects of daily life, and, in a few cases, from the "barbarian" world (Scandinavian petroglyphs, the Gundestrup cauldron, Scythian jewelry, etc.);

6 Archaeological data gleaned from excavations, such as those discussed above: Scandinavian and northern German megaliths and tumuli, Swiss lake villages, northern Italian *terramare*, Scythian objects, discoveries at Mycenae and Knossos. From this point of view, Schrader provides, through his dictionary entries, a summary of the state of archaeological knowledge in Europe at the end of the nineteenth century. This work prefigures the weighty *Reallexikon der Vorgeschichte* (Dictionary of Prehistory) which was published in fifteen volumes by the same publisher between 1924 and 1928, under the direction of Max Ebert, professor at the University of Berlin. However, as we saw in the case of the "House," it often happened that archaeology had a circular relationship with linguistic paleontology;

7 Images that were generally accepted by academics at the time of Wilhelm II regarding the customs and functioning of human societies, as well as a number of particular prejudices, such as a very ambivalent attitude toward assumed Eastern influences—which were simultaneously seen as beguiling, corrupting, and civilizing—on the European world.

The almost circular ambiguity of Schrader's enormous undertaking is evident and yet his work is rarely called into question in terms of its scholarship, particularly in light of the state of knowledge at the time, and even less so in terms of any potential nationalist bias. It is a work of linguistic paleontology, summarizing the findings of this philological method, but embedded within an archaeological, historical, and cultural dictionary of Europe and its margins, which in itself is not specifically Indo-European unless we admit that everything that is European is Indo-European. In fact, this was Schrader's belief, as indicated in the subtitle of the *Reallexikon*: "Elements of the cultural history of the peoples of ancient Europe." However, this is circular reasoning since we have no proof that tattoos or dolmens, chairs, or lake villages, were in fact Indo-European; as we shall see later, many present-day Indo-Europeanists do not accept that this was the case even though they support Schrader's general hypothesis. Be that as it may, the association of linguistic paleontology with compelling historical and archaeological data, illustrated by more than 200 plates and illustrations, creates an illusion of "reality" that leads the reader to accept the theory as fact. Indeed, the same applies to all other similar works undertaken up until the present day.

Linguistics of absence

There remains the "hard core" that is linguistic paleontology, a field in which Schrader, who was himself a linguist and who benefitted from the development of comparative grammar, showed more rigor than Pictet, of whom he was often critical. However, as we have seen, Schrader's linguistic approach is essentially the linguistics of absence. On the basis of the virtual absence of common words for trees in the "shared vocabulary," a fact for which three mutually exclusive explanations can be offered,[48] Schrader deduces that there were no trees in the original Homeland: for him, the Indo-Europeans would have invented new names when they arrived at the fringes of the great European forest, having left the original treeless steppes of Russia behind. Similarly, on the basis of the rarity of common words relating to agriculture, specific to the languages of geographical Europe and in contrast with the shared roots for most domestic animals (with the exception of "pig"), Schrader comes to the conclusion that the original Indo-Europeans were essentially nomadic; this is confirmed by the shared terms for "wheel" and "cart." Uncertainty regarding the meaning of a common root for "mountain" suggests that the original Homeland offered particularly monotonous views!

A number of problems arise for which ad hoc solutions are immediately proposed. The bear, which is a forest or mountain dweller, appears in the common vocabulary: if we follow Schrader's reasoning, then we have to envisage bears wandering across the steppes. Fish, which are abundant in the great rivers of Russia and the Ukraine, are absent from the common vocabulary: in this case we have to presume a dietary disinterest, or even a taboo, which subsequently disappeared once the Indo-Europeans arrived in Europe, as evidenced by the large amount of fishing equipment present in the Swiss lake village sites. Only the salmon occurs in the shared vocabulary (with the root *laks*), but it appears that this species only lives in the Baltic; in this case, the word is given to mean "fish" in the general sense. The absence of a common root for salt (**sal*) in the Indo-Iranian languages must be connected to dietary preferences. In fact, Schrader is never far from Ferdinand Justi's[49] caricatural comment on "negative" linguistic paleontology: if there were no words for illnesses in the shared vocabulary, it is simply because the Indo-Europeans were never sick!

All of which shows that, ultimately, reasoning was of little importance: the original Homeland was situated in the Steppes, period. It is easy to see what objections could be made against Schrader's reasoning in support of any other location: clearly, if certain words were lost, then the same could be true of any other

---

[48] See this chapter, p. 40.
[49] Justi, 1862.

54   FIRST MOVEMENT (1814–1903)

words. The link between nomadism and the cart is also an abuse; after all, sedentary farmers also have carts. Schrader's vision, which was more "primitive" than Pictet's, in fact contained just as many preconceptions. He paints a picture of a warrior society because, he claims, "in prehistoric times, war was, in a manner of speaking, the normal state of relations between different tribes, naturally interrupted by periods of rest which had to be guaranteed by the exchange of hostages and oaths" (I, p. 630). However there is no specific linguistic reasoning behind this claim. Just like there is nothing to prove that Indo-European people disliked flowers: in the Near East, Paleolithic people were already laying flowers in graves 40,000 years ago. Schrader's underlying imaginary matrix starts to reveal itself. It is a world of great invasions of Scythians then Huns, Magyars then Tatars, intrepid nomadic pastoralists and horsemen who swept forth from the Steppes (Schrader illustrates his entry for "Cart" with the image of a Tatar example even though these people are undoubtedly non–Indo-European). Hence the prominence of Scythian objects and tumuli, as well as of Russian and Ukrainian ethnographic material, in Schrader's iconography (and here Leibniz raises his head again); it is in these areas that we find the most "steppic" and possibly the most primitive of all modern Indo-European peoples (Schrader borrows nothing from Celtic or Latin peoples, nor from the Slavs living within the German and Austrian Empires). Purely incantatory in nature, these illustrations clearly do not have any demonstrative role.

Schrader's work establishes a new image of the Indo-Europeans as warlike nomadic invaders from the steppes, an image that still survives today with new archaeological arguments but with the same flaws in logic, marred by circular reasoning and amalgamation, and which is popular with the majority of Indo-Europeanist archaeologists and linguists who are only too happy to follow suit.

The return to Germania

Schrader, however, had a struggle on his hands against those of his more radical compatriots who wished to repatriate the original Homeland to Germany and southern Scandinavia. It was inevitable that German Unification, finalized and proclaimed in the Hall of Mirrors at Versailles in 1871, following the capitulation of the French Imperial Army at Sedan in 1870, would also call upon the Indo-Europeans for support. 1871 also saw the publication in Stuttgart of a posthumous study by the philologist and philosopher Lazarus (also known as Ludwig) Geiger, nephew of the reforming rabbi Abraham Geiger; the paper, entitled *Über die Ursitze der Indogermanen* (Regarding the Original Residence of the Indo-Europeans) was part of a larger compilation entitled *Zur Entwicklungsgeschichte der Menschheit* (The Evolution of Humanity). The bitter irony of history is that

Geiger, a conservative Jewish thinker who was interested in the issue of language, thus became the first author to officially situate the original homeland in Germany, a position that the French were quick to consider "chauvinist."[50]

The reasoning behind Geiger's claim remains linguistic and largely tree-based; in particular it relies on the famous "beech argument." The German *Buche* and the Latin *fagus* used to designate this tree may be derived from an original root **bhagos*, which we also find in Greek (*phègos*, but in this case meaning "oak"), Russian (*buzina* or *boz*, but meaning "elder"), and especially in an Indo-Iranian language, Kurdish (*buz*, but meaning "elm"). Since, along with birch, this is the only tree name common to the Indo-Europeans of Europe and Asia, and since beech only grows west of a line drawn between Odessa and Königsberg (present day Kaliningrad), we could safely deduce that the original Homeland lay in Germany. However, at this stage, the reader should be sufficiently familiar with linguistic paleontology to realize that the "beech argument," which became an essential element in all discussions regarding the original Homeland, can in fact be used to demonstrate the exact opposite. Moreover, the commonality of the root among the various languages, with such variation in meaning, is not accepted by many linguists.[51] The reference to Königsberg, which at this time was one of the main cities of Eastern Prussia, is not entirely innocent: this city marks the eastern frontier of the Second Reich.

Henceforth, it would be possible to speak of a correspondence between "Germanic" and "Indo-European"; it is this that the German term "*indogermanisch*" has always unconsciously implied, even though the first attested use of the term was by the Danish-born French geographer, Conrad Malte-Brun, in his *Géographie universelle* (Universal Geography) first published in 1810.[52] Or rather, with the establishment of the Germano-Scandinavian locus, the secret desire embodied in this term finally found its fulfillment.

Thus, in the last quarter of the nineteenth century, Indo-Germanic-ness became a key component of Pan-Germanist ideology, of its assertion of German greatness and its military victories, and of its territorial claims for a unity that was still considered incomplete. Numerous Pan-Germanist scholars would follow in Geiger's wake, but often these should more accurately be described as amateur Indo-Europeanists rather than true academics.[53]

The most famous of these is undoubtedly Karl Penka, a high school teacher in Vienna, whose *Origines Ariacae*, dedicated to Herder, "the father of anthropology and of the anthropological conception of history," painted a vast panorama that Salomon Reinach would describe as a "historical novel."[54] In Penka's vision, at

[50] Geiger, 1871; Reinach, 1892, p. 48.
[51] Passler-Mayrhofer, 1948; Friedrich, 1970; Mallory and Adams, 1997, pp. 184–185.
[52] See Shapiro, 1981.
[53] On the Germanic myth in Germany, see Ridé, 1966.
[54] Penka, 1883; Reinach, 1892, p. 73.

56 FIRST MOVEMENT (1814–1903)

the time of the great glaciations, people would have abandoned northern Europe, apart that is from the most courageous and strong who would go on to forge an exceptional, tall, blond, and blue-eyed, "race," the Indo-Europeans or primitive Aryans. It is they who would build megalithic monuments and amass the substantial coastal shell middens known as *kjøkkenmødding*. They would subsequently head off to conquer the rest of Europe, imposing their language and their culture wherever their conquests took them. Thus the Slavs are Aryanized Mongols and the Greeks Aryanized Semites; the Finns, on the other hand, who are often blue-eyed and blond, are Aryans who lost their language. Penka utilized linguistic paleontology to support the hypothesis of a Nordic Homeland; thus, this was a Homeland in which beech and birch abounded along with animals from the shared vocabulary, such as the eel which lives in Northern Europe or the oyster whose shells form the famous Danish middens. But Penka was also one of the first to systemize the racial argument which we will later examine in greater detail. His work provoked numerous debates and articles in scholarly journals; it was met with enthusiasm by the French racist ideologue Vacher de Lapouge and with reservation by German philologists.

Pan-Germanism and anti-Semitism

The last years of the nineteenth century were marked by economic crisis and by the rise of racist and anti-democratic movements and ideologies. In France, the Dreyfus affair and the prevailing climate of virulent anti-Semitism are telling examples. In Germany and Austria, we witness the rise of Pan-Germanist and anti-Semitic movements. This trend was particularly forceful in Austria where the German-speaking population, the ruling ethnic group, represented only a third of the populations that once belonged to the former multinational empire. In order to maintain coherence, Emperor Franz-Josef was forced to approve a number of reforms: Hungarian autonomy from 1867; the obligatory speaking of German among civil servants, and of Czech in Bohemia, from 1897 onward; the abandonment of censitary suffrage, which benefited German landowners, in favor of universal suffrage (for men); constitutional reforms; etc. Furthermore, following the defeat of Austria by the Prussians at Sadowa, a sudden halt was called to the unification of all German peoples. Instead they would remain divided between two multinational empires ruled over by Wilhelm II and Franz-Josef, respectively. Finally, the Industrial Revolution and the rural exodus led to an influx, particularly in Vienna, of mixed populations from all over the empire, thereby creating a fertile breeding ground for xenophobia and scapegoats. In 1909, Adolf Hitler, who was living an impoverished life in Vienna, where he had just failed the entrance examination to the Academy of Fine Arts, sought to

FROM INDIA TO GERMANIA   57

vent his frustration at his social failure in the city: "The racial conglomeration of the Imperial capital is repugnant to me. . . . The giant city appears to me to be the incarnation of racial ignominy."[55] Furthermore, hundreds of sporting and cultural associations, exalting the German national (*völkisch*) ideal, sprouted up in both Germany and Austria where they were grouped together under the banner of the *Bund der Germanen.* This movement, which was both anti-Slav and anti-Semitic, was headed by Georg von Schönerer who founded the journal *Die unverfälschte deutsche Worte* (Unadulterated German Words). It drew inspiration from the works of nationalist and conservative thinkers such as Paul de Lagarde, Julius Langbehn, and Arthur Moeller van den Bruck; from the ideological racism and anti-Semitism of Vacher de Lapouge, Ludwig Schemann, and Houston Stewart Chamberlain[56]; and also from the "scientific racism" of the social Darwinists. In 1906, Ernst Haeckel, translator of Darwin into German and friend of Schleicher,[57] founded the Monist League, which advocated eugenics, the struggle between races, and racial purity, and whose cause was supported by Ernst Krause, Otto Ammon, Ludwig Wilser, and Ludwig Woltmann.[58]

Wilser and Woltmann were among the most exalted of Germanomaniac scholars along with, for example, Matthäus Much and Count Hans von Wolzogen. Wolzogen was one of the leading lights of the Bayreuth Circle, which promoted the works of Wagner, as well as being a disseminator of the works of Gobineau in Germany and co-author of an anti-Semitic petition addressed to Bismarck. He describes the Germano-Aryan era as follows:

> As the children [of the Gods], these Germanic tribes burst forth into the midst of Semitico-Roman culture and lent it the pure strength of their blood. . . . As soon as they entered history, with the frankness of their blue eyes, their proud heroic stature, their simple patriarchal customs, their free communal associations, their loyal warlike confederations, their representations of the gods and their simple, honest, heroic traditions, they must undoubtedly have appeared from the outset as the true manifestation, without blurring or mixing, of the most noble ancient branch of the white race. Such is the Aryan.[59]

Ludwig Wilser, a doctor and amateur prehistorian, entered into a bitter dispute with Penka regarding which of them first identified the original Homeland

---

[55] Hitler, 1925–1926 [1940], p. 135. See Goodrick-Clarke, 1989, p. 22.
[56] See Chapter 4, p. 57.
[57] See Chapter 2, p. 28.
[58] On Pan-Germanism in general, see Goodrick-Clarke, 1989, pp. 11–23; Mosse, 1964, 1975; Stern, F. R., 1961. On "scientific racism" and the social Darwinists, see Pulzer, 1964; Gasman, 1971; Zmarzlik, 1963; Weindling, 1989. See also Chapter 8.
[59] Wolzogen, 1882, p. 85 (cited in Römer, 1985, p. 66).

58 FIRST MOVEMENT (1814–1903)

as Scandinavia: he claimed his theory was the result of an "epiphany."[60] In any case, he was one of the first to attribute the invention of writing to the Aryan-Germans: he held that all Mediterranean forms of writing were derived from Germanic runes—even though it is a well-known fact that the latter were a very late and limited adaptation of the former. This "discovery" was met with great acclaim, first by the archaeologist Gustaf Kossinna, and then by Nazi ideologists. Matthäus Much, detractor of the "Oriental mirage," went even further: copper metallurgy, the domestication of plants and animals, and geometric decoration were all Scandinavian inventions and, therefore, Aryan.[61] Kossinna would even attempt to claim for himself the authorship of these "discoveries." For his part, Ludwig Woltmann claimed that he could identify clearly Germanic racial types in the portraits of great figures of the Italian Renaissance.[62]

Occultist beliefs

At this point we are at the frontier between scientific charlatanism and mystical ramblings. The Germanomaniac Indo-Europeanists would engage in both with equal fervor. The Ura-Linda Chronicle, a literary hoax produced in Holland in the 1870s, told how, in the third millennium BCE, a Germanic people from Friesland left from the shores of the North Sea to found Athens and bring writing and monotheism to the East. Forgotten for a time, this so-called chronicle found favor once more under the Nazi regime. But the theme of the great original ancestors also coincided with the rise of numerous esoteric movements in the late nineteenth century; this esotericism fed off the continuing decline of Christianity in its literal form, deepening economic and social crises, and also, it has to be said, the development of depth psychology, which offered a much more complex and opaque image of the human psyche. These trends were also expressed in the visual arts, through symbolism; in literary fiction; and in what would soon be dubbed "science fiction." In general, this period saw a proliferation of esoteric publications, places of worship, and sects.

One of the most famous of these movements was "theosophy," founded in New York City, in 1875, by a Russian immigrant, Helena Petrovna Blavatsky, who claimed to have been initiated into the teachings of the secret masters of a "Great White Lodge" somewhere in the Himalayas; these masters were the survivors of the collapse of the continent of Mu (Plato told a similar tale of having received knowledge of the destruction of Atlantis from Egyptian priests, but this

---

[60] Wilser, 1899 (among others); see Römer, 1985, pp. 71, 76–79.
[61] Much, M., 1902.
[62] See Römer, 1985, p. 95.

FROM INDIA TO GERMANIA   59

was in fact no more than a political fable intended for his contemporaries). In reality, Helena Blavatsky unscrupulously plundered the literary fiction of her time, such as, for example, *The Last Days of Pompeii* and *The Coming Race* by the British author Edward Bulwer-Lytton, as well as scholarly works by orientalists such as Louis Jacolliot, who published *Les Fils de Dieu* (God's Sons) in 1873. In *Isis Unveiled* (1877) and *The Secret Doctrine* (1888), she presents a syncretic hodgepodge of Egyptian and Hindu inspiration, fleshed out with cosmic cycles, electro-spiritual forces, reincarnations, and "root races."[63] She claimed that five such races succeeded each other on earth: the "Astral race," the Hyperborans, the Lemurians (who would die out because they succumbed to monstrous cross-breeding), the Atlanteans, and finally the current "Aryan race."

The template for these "esoteric" or "occultist" stories is always the same: somewhere on a mountain summit or in the depths of a cave (or both), mysterious beings, inheritors of the ancient wisdom of a long-dead civilization, continue to control the world through a small group of privileged initiates who are sworn to secrecy. With an accentuated pathology, this template rehashes that of many religious systems. It also takes inspiration from Freemasonry, but the latter, a product of the Century of Enlightenment, was at its origin driven more by the pre-revolutionary ideas of fraternity and mutual support than by fantasies of power. This template was also present in the short-lived Celtomania movement of the early nineteenth century.[64] In the face of the declining credibility of Christianity, these new beliefs hoped to benefit from the growing prestige of the sciences: Darwinian biology, prehistory, and also the discovery of new and invisible forces such as electricity, X-rays and, more recently, radioactivity.

In Germany and Austria, these ideas fell on fertile ground due to a combination of factors: the nationalist identity crisis, which we have already highlighted; the particular cultural vigor that was associated with Romanticism in these countries; and certain late nineteenth-century tendencies toward a "return to nature," a reform of life (*Lebensreform*), which was expressed in a fashion for naturism, vegetarianism, and alternative medicines.[65] This latter trend could take politically liberal forms but could also merge with the reactionary aspirations of the nationalist *völkisch* mystique; this component would later become a key component of Nazi ideology.

The Austrian Guido von List developed a specifically "Aryo-Germanic" adaptation of theosophy. He claimed to be the reincarnated last descendent of the ancient Aryan priesthood, the *Armanenschaft*. This title is derived from the name of one of the three Germanic tribes mentioned by Tacitus, the Irminones.

---

[63] In particular, see Goodrick-Clarke, 1989; Stoczkowski, 1999.
[64] See this chapter, pp. 43–44.
[65] Krabbe, 1974; Cluet and Repussard, 2013.

60   FIRST MOVEMENT (1814–1903)

Applying a "trifunctional" interpretation, List identified the Irminones as priest kings while the other two tribes, the Istaevones and Ingaevones, were warriors and farmers, respectively. He also claimed to have rediscovered the million-year-old secret Aryan language. He rehashes the entire theosophical cosmology, with its Atlanteans and their aircraft, its "past" races, its cyclical floods, its reincarnations, and its drowned Atlantis, which is evidenced by surviving megalithic monuments. He also drew inspiration from the Aryan *Sexualreligion* of theosopher Max Ferdinand Sebaldt von Werth when describing the ancient "Aryan sexual religion," which was replete with bacchanalia but also careful to maintain the purity of the race through eugenics. The sacred wisdom of the Aryans was, he claimed, passed down to us through the Kabbalah, the Templars, and the Rosicrucians.

However, this knowledge and the "purity of the Aryan race" were under threat from a combination of Jews, parliamentarianism, feminism, plutocracy, and modern art, all of which were lumped together within an imagined underground "Great International Party." List enjoyed considerable celebrity within *völkisch* circles, and his plays were performed during major Pan-Germanist festivals. In 1911, his disciples created the Guido von List Society, which included an inner group known as the "High Armanen Order." As Grand Master, List preached a return to a peasant lifestyle and painted a detailed picture of a strictly hierarchized future Aryan state where pure Aryans would be exempt from all hard labor and could devote themselves to study and the noble professions. Racial and matrimonial laws, patriarchy, racial identity papers, birthright, slavery, and domination of society by an elite with sacred authority, which was both absolute and initiatory: in short, List's program already encapsulated the entire Nazi program, the Nuremberg racial laws, and the organization of the SS.[66]

Of course each century is burdened by its own baggage of para-sciences and para-philosophies: it is when official science abandons the idea of a possible origin for the Aryans, and perhaps for humanity as a whole, in India that Helena Blavatsky, a century after Voltaire, decides to locate her "Great White Lodge" of the "unknown Masters" there; it is when academic Celtomania, with its fake Poems of Ossian and its mythical druidic heritage, dies out that the amateur Germanomaniacs, with their fake Ura-Linda Chronicle and their "Armanist" hallucinations, burst onto the scene. But List's Aryan mysticism and his racist program did not simply fade into obscurity. From the beginning of the twentieth century, several secret societies would rapidly pick up this mystical baton and continue to run with it: thus we encounter the Order of the New Templars, founded by the "ariosophist" Adolf Joseph Lanz, one of whose lodges, the *Thule-Gesellschaft* (Thule Society), would play an important role in the foundation of

---

[66]   List, 1908, 1914; on List, Goodrick-Clarke, 1989.

the Nazi Party.[67] One of List's disciples, Ernst Lauterer, known as "Tarnhari," would go on to collaborate with the anti-Semitic *völkisch* writer, Dietrich Eckart, who would become Hitler's mentor and to whom *Mein Kampf* is dedicated; the *Münchener Beobachter*, which would subsequently become the *Völkischer Beobachter*, the journal of the Nazi Party from 1920 onward, published an obituary for List following his death in 1919. It is no surprise then, that a little later, with the publication of Louis Pauwels's *Le Matin des magiciens* (The Morning of the Magicians), we see this "occultist" trend resurface within the ideology of the French New Right movement of the 1960s and 1970s.[68] More than just a malignant offshoot, the "occultist" aspect of Germanomania (or Aryanomania) is also a magnifying glass that lays bare some of the models as well as the ideological and fanciful preoccupations which drove the quest for ancestral origins.

The ambiguities of official linguistics

Professional Indo-Europeanists who worked in academic circles attempted to distance themselves from these amateur ravings. The linguist Hermann Hirt, professor at Leipzig and then at Giessen, argued, against Schrader, for an original Homeland in Scandinavia: for him, the bear and the bee of the common vocabulary excluded a homeland in the Steppes, while the beech, the sea, salt, willow, and birch pointed to the Baltic.

> There lives, even today, the wolf and the bear, there swarm the bees whose honey was used to make the sweet beverage, the *medhu, of the Indo-Europeans, there grew tall trees which, with the aid of fire, could be hollowed out to make boats, there one could adore the Divine in the vast forests that inspired religious terror. However, there was no space to maneuver a horse; the lion and the tiger are lacking in this region. Finally, we must remember the archaic character of the Lithuanian and Slav languages; the peoples who spoke these languages, closer to their land of origin and sheltered from invasions, preserved them better than others.[69]

However, Hirt considered the works of Penka and Wilser in the field of linguistics (a field in which they were "controllable") to be "not only insufficient, but not even worthy of criticism." In fact, "the notion of Indo-Europeans has a linguistic sense, and only a linguistic sense. It should only be used in this context."[70]

---

[67] Ibid.; Römer, 1985, pp. 96, 136; Daim, 1958.
[68] See Chapter 9, p. 201.
[69] Hirt, 1892 (republished in Hirt, 1968, p. 23).
[70] Hirt, 1905–1907, p. 549.

62 FIRST MOVEMENT (1814–1903)

Regarding the idea of a "single" race, he states: "Only linguistics has the right to speak of a 'people' because this is the necessary assumption underlying the reconstructed primitive language; as regards whether or not these people shared homogenous racial characteristics, we are incapable of providing proof and, in any case, it is of little importance to us."[71] Of course Hirt believed that the Indo-Europeans had achieved "all that which is most noble in human civilization" and that their linguistic branch was "the most significant and most energetic at a global scale."[72] But for him, they remained barbarians and most of the traits of their civilization (the plough, bronze-working, and the cart) were essentially borrowings from Egypt and Mesopotamia.

Hirt, who was born a generation after Schrader, represents a turning point. Outside the hallowed halls of academia, he was the first to lend linguistic and scholarly respectability to the Scandinavian Homeland theory. However, as we shall see, his contemporary, the archaeologist Gustaf Kossinna, professor at Berlin, had no such methodological scruples. For most of the generation working in the early twentieth century, the equations "Germans = primitive Indo-Europeans" and "historical Germania = the original Homeland" gradually became, with certain nuances, a fait accompli. At the same time these equations increasingly assumed a racial definition and content. It is in this intellectual atmosphere, where the boundaries between official science and amateur ravings would become increasingly permeable, that the next generation grew up, the generation of national-socialism. Even though Kossinna died in 1931, two years before Hitler seized power, and Hirt in 1936, both were fully "reclaimed" by the Nazi movement. Research into the "racial" identity of the original People was not initially part of the plan. It was gradually, from the second half of the nineteenth century onward, while physical anthropology with its dubious methods took hold in Europe, that debate arose regarding the "Indo-European race." The underlying stakes were high: namely, the justification of inequalities between peoples and between human beings.

[71] Hirt, 1892, p. 465.
[72] Hirt, 1905–1907, pp. 3 and 176.

4

The invention of "scientific racism"

Racism is a modern notion. Of course it is common for human groups to demean other neighboring groups, but the use of "race" as a justification is a characteristic of the West and its "scientific" approach to the world. In Corneille's famous play, when the father of Rodrigue, le Cid, is slapped in the face by the father of Chimène, he proclaims "Go on, and take my life, after this insult—The first that e'er made red with shame the brow of any of my race." At this time, however, the word "race" still meant "family" or "line" in the broad sense of the word. This word—"race"—which appeared in the same form in French, English, and German, came from the Italian *razza*, which itself is an evolution of the Latin word *ratio* (which also gave the word "*raison*" in French); at the beginning of the Middle Ages it also took on the meaning of "species" or "varieties" of animals and fruits.[1] As regards humanity, mankind still formed one single family, descended from a single ancestor, Adam, via Noah, survivor of the Flood, and his three sons Shem, Ham, and Japheth. But as the West spread its colonial reach across the world, Christian universalism would soon discover its limits.[2] On the one hand, it became increasingly difficult to account for the variety of physical appearances encountered in the new territories, and commentators were forced to twist the biblical text to accommodate a fourth son of Noah or to identify the Amerindians as one of the "lost tribes" of Israel. On the other hand, the well-understood interests of the new colonial empires demanded that their spiritual authorities come up with the best justification for the new world order and their need for cheap labor.

Hence, long debates occurred as to whether these new peoples really possessed souls or whether they could simply be domesticated, like animals. "Discovered" in 1492, the Amerindians were not considered to be *veri homines* ("true men") until the issuance of a papal bull to that effect in 1537. In any case, Shem and his descendants bore a mysterious biblical curse which was enough to justify the enslaving of the Blacks; the link between Shem and the Africans was itself the result of a relatively recent Talmudo-casuistic extrapolation. Rare attempts at "soft" colonization, such as the Jesuit missions in Paraguay, were rapidly brought to heel. However, budding scientific stringency, which was spreading its net over

---

[1] Tournier, 1992.
[2] Jouanna, 1976.

64 FIRST MOVEMENT (1814–1903)

the world, meant that there was a duty to understand these discoveries and these peoples. On the one hand, it was essential to classify, as Linnaeus was attempting in his *Systema Naturae*, by distinguishing four varieties of humans with unequal qualities.[3] Before Linnaeus, in 1684, François Bernier had divided humanity into five "races" of men according to appearance and geography: this was the first use of the word "race" in its "modern" sense.[4]

But it was also important to explain such striking variety, especially since, over and above differences in appearance, there seemed to be clear differences in destiny, with one race being destined to prevail over all others. Or perhaps this difference had always been there, which would imply polygenism, with humankind having several independent places of origin; in this case what would become of the Bible? Or, if all humankind descended from a single man (and woman), this difference would have to be chronological. The "monogenistic" Adamic model would eventually accommodate two variants: either the "White race" emerged through a gradual progress of civilization from the savage level of the Blacks or from earlier apes (this was the belief of Lord Monboddo[5]); or, alternatively, in a more orthodox view, the "White race" existed from the beginning and had been created by God, but, in certain hostile environments, was liable to "degenerate" into "inferior races." This opinion was held by many, including the naturalist Buffon who, in order to verify the hypothesis, proposed that a number of Black people from Senegal be transported to Denmark to see if, over the course of generations, they would recover their original beautiful White skin.

God and the polygenists

The continued weakening of the biblical model allowed more and more space for polygenist theories to flourish. Following the philosopher David Hume, in 1799, the English surgeon Charles White in his *Account of the Regular Gradation in Man* affirmed the reality of polygenism and launched an attack on Buffon both for his theory on the influence of environment on "race" and for his definition of species based on internal interfertility; after all, is it not possible to create hybrids by cross-breeding different species? These two points would be at the heart of all nineteenth-century debates on the subject. As regards the superiority of the "White race," it was easy for White (whose name says it all) to state that "Where shall we find, unless in the European, that nobly arched head, containing such a brain . . .? Where that variety of features, and fullness of expression . . .? In

---

[3] See Chapter 1, p. 13.
[4] Bernier, 1684; Poliakov, 1971/1987, pp. 164–165 (and more generally, part II, chapters I–II).
[5] Greene, 1961.

THE INVENTION OF "SCIENTIFIC RACISM" 65

what other quarter of the globe shall we find the blush that overspreads the soft features of the beautiful women of Europe, that emblem of modesty, of delicate feelings, and of sense? . . . Where, except on the bosom of the European woman, two such plump and snowy white hemispheres, tipt with vermillion."[6]

With impeccable historical logic, from the early nineteenth century until its demise under the influence of Darwin's theory of evolution, polygenism found its greatest theoreticians in the slave-holding United States. The real issue at stake was clearly understood by scholars at the time. The first was the Swiss naturalist Louis Agassiz, a disciple of Cuvier, who, in 1840, took up a post at Harvard University where he founded the zoological museum. Originally a strict creationist, Agassiz's interest in polygenism developed after his arrival in the United States and following the trauma he suffered on encountering Black slaves: he expressed his distress in a series of devastating and pathetic letters addressed to his mother.[7]

But polygenism required a foundation of solid arguments and this was the task that Philadelphia-based Samuel Morton set himself: his approach involved collecting and measuring skulls, and, by the time of his death in 1854, his collection numbered more than a thousand. In his voluminous *Crania Americana*, he claimed to be able to demonstrate that, on average, Whites had a larger skull that the other "races" and, therefore, in his opinion, possessed greater intelligence. More recently, the paleontologist Stephen Jay Gould has shown in detail how Morton obtained these results through unconscious manipulation of the figures and statistics.[8] For example, in order to measure the volume of a skull, Morton filled it with mustard seeds which he tamped down to a greater or lesser degree, in all good faith, to get the desired results. The results were much less satisfactory when the mustard seed was replaced by iron granules.

At Morton's side were his friend George Gliddon, American Consul in Cairo, and Josiah Nott, who published tables of the differences between "races" in *Types of Mankind* (1854) and *Indigenous Races of the Earth* (1857); they decried "all those who believe that the Hebrews and the Hottentots, just like the camels and giraffes, emerged from a single and unique stock." Nott traveled throughout the southern United States delivering lectures on "niggerology," while one of the main medical journals in the South hailed Morton on his death as a "benefactor." But Europe also had its polygenists: the French naturalist Bory de Saint-Vincent, for example, author of *L'Homme (homo), essai zoologique sur le genre humain* (Man, a Zoological Essay on the Human Race), member of the 1828 scientific mission to Morea and supporter of the Greek uprising against the Ottoman

---

[6] White, 1799, p. 135. Cited in Stanton, 1960, p. 17.
[7] On American polygenism, see Ibid.; Gould, 1981.
[8] Ibid., chap. II.

66   FIRST MOVEMENT (1814–1903)

Empire; or the extremely racist military pharmacist and Bonapartist Jean-Joseph Virey, whose *Histoire naturelle du genre humain* was translated and published in the United States in 1837, under the title *The Natural History of the Negro Race.*[9]

The art of measuring skulls

Morton, however, was not the first collector and measurer of skulls. From Hamlet to the anamorphosis in Holbein's *The Ambassadors*, the skull long served as an invitation to moral edification and meditation on the vanity of the world before becoming an object of scientific research in the Age of Enlightenment. Johann Friedrich Blumenbach, professor at Göttingen, is generally credited with having founded the discipline of physical anthropology. He amassed the first large collection of skulls for the purpose of classification. As is evident from the title of his frequently translated and republished 1775 work *De generis humani varietate nativa* (On the Natural Varieties of Mankind), Morton was a committed monogenist. It was he who defined and coined the term "Caucasian" to refer to the "White race": "I have taken the name of this variety from Mount Caucasus, both because its neighborhood, and especially its southern slope, produces the most beautiful race of men, I mean the Georgian; and because all physiological reasons converge to this, that in that region, if anywhere, we ought with the greatest of probability to place the autochthones of mankind. . . . Besides, it [the skin of the Georgians] is white in color, which we may fairly assume to have been the primitive color of mankind, since . . . it is very easy for that to degenerate into brown." Even today, the term "Caucasian" is the official term used by North American police forces in their data sheets. A little earlier, in 1770, the Dutch physician Peter Camper invented the notion of "facial angle": from the ape to the European, and passing through the Blacks and the Kalmyks, the angle between the skull's horizontal and the "facial line," which extends from the incisors to the curve of the forehead, becomes increasingly obtuse and is thus a measure of intelligence (it is somewhat inconvenient that this angle is more acute in European adults than in European children[10]).

However, although measuring was the price that had to be paid in the search for a "scientific" definition of "races," it was not a straightforward exercise because of the complex volume of the skull. The Camper index and variations thereof were applied with great zeal and, following the observations of the English monogenist James Cowell Prichard, a distinction was made between "orthognathic" and "prognathic" facial profiles, the former being a straight profile and the latter

---

[9] Blanckaert, 1981.
[10] Camper, 1791; Blanckaert, 1987; Barsanti, 1986.

THE INVENTION OF "SCIENTIFIC RACISM"   67

having a forward projecting, muzzle-like jaw.[11] The most famous of the cranial indices was the "cephalic index," first proposed by the Swedish anatomist Anders Retzius, in 1842. This approach involved measuring the ratio between the length of the skull, from back to front, and its width, as viewed from above: if the width is no more than three-quarters of the length (index of 75% or less), then the head is said to be "long" or "dolichocephalic"; if the width is greater than 80% of the length (index of 80% or more), then the head is "short" or "brachycephalic."[12] In fact, Retzius went beyond this simplistic cephalic index by combining it with other indices which allowed him to distinguish between "dolichoce-phalic orthognathic" (Germans, Celts, Scandinavians) and "dolichocephalic prognathic" populations (Greenlanders, Caribbeans, Africans, Australians) and between "brachycephalic orthognathic" (Slavs, Lapps, Finns, Persians) and "brachycephalic prognathic" populations (Tatars, Mongols, Malaysians, Papuans, and certain Amerindians); he continued this diversification right up until his death in 1860. But the "cephalic index" was the easiest approach to apply and therefore outlived its inventor.

Observing the European populations as he had classified them, Retzius was confronted with two facts. On the one hand, in Scandinavia there was a clear difference between the Lapps and Finns, on one side, and the Swedes, on the other, and the former did not speak Indo-European languages. On the other hand, there was a lack of homogeneity within Indo-European–speaking populations. The Slavs, in particular, stood apart with their round heads. There was, therefore, no homogeneity in Blumenbach's so-called Caucasian race, which was a reworking of Linnaeus' *Homo europaeus* and which Prichard, the creator of "prognathism," had baptized the "Indo-Atlantic race," a clear allu-sion to the bearers of the Indo-European languages. To Retzius's new classi-fication, which in reality only subdivided earlier geographical classifications, the Indo-European model as applied during the first half of the nineteenth century naturally proposed an interpretive scheme, but one based on twinned arguments. Since the Indo-Europeans had come from Central Asia and subse-quently spread throughout Europe, and since the Celts and the Germans, who were attested to in the writings of ancient authors, were two of the components of this wave, it is normal to identify the Indo-Europeans with these "dolichoce-phalic orthognathic" peoples occupying a major part of western Europe (who are furthermore often blond). And it follows, therefore, that the "brachyce-phalic orthognathic" peoples who speak non–Indo-European languages, such as the Lapps, the Finns, and also the Basques, were the survivors of the native populations that occupied Europe prior to the arrival of the "Aryans." In fact,

[11] Prichard, 1813.
[12] Retzius, 1846, 1864; Blanckaert, 1989b.

68   FIRST MOVEMENT (1814–1903)

Retzius's theory explicitly relies on the authority of Rasmus Rask, one of the "inventors" of the Indo-European linguistic concept.[13] As regards the dolichocephalic populations, it was difficult not to notice that in Europe they were generally "endowed with the best faculties of the soul."[14]

But the issue of the internal heterogeneity of Indo-European speakers remained. It is clearly evident that not all Europeans who speak an Indo-European language are tall, blond, and dolichocephalic. Which populations, therefore, are closest to the original "race"? And where did the others come from? The third quarter of the nineteenth century, a period when national movements, crushed in 1848, came to fore in most parts of Europe and when Italian and German unities were forged through warfare, was also the period when anthropological schools became institutionalized and defined their tools and protocols of choice.

From divine right to nation

Until the emergence of the idea of "nation" at the end of the eighteenth century, the people of Europe were subject to two powers. One, a universal, "Catholic" (in the true sense of the word) spiritual power, which one obeyed as a human being, a descendant of Adam. The other, a temporal power, fragmented into a mosaic of territories fashioned by the fortunes of war and marriages between the various reigning families, to which one was a subject. While the legitimacy of a sovereign lay in a "Divine" right, nothing defined the extent of his territory—apart, that is, from the last treaty signed. The subject populations, however, in opting for self-determination, would draw their own new legitimacy from a feeling of shared belonging, the clearest manifestation of which was a shared language which would allow them to understand each other; in Germany, this language was acquired after a hard struggle. Henceforth, boundaries should coincide with languages, thus signaling the end of multinational empires. But if the new science of anthropology allowed the identification of the physical traits specific to the various peoples, then it followed that there existed, beyond a collective spirit, a physical incarnation of the national sentiment. Not only is there a memory of our history, but also of our blood, our "race" (today we talk of a "genetic memory"). The family and its ancestors became a metaphor for the nation: in short, ethnic differences are also racial differences.[15]

---

[13] Blanckaert, 1989a, pp. 182–183; see also Rousseau, 1981. See Chapter 2, pp. 20–21.
[14] Retzius, 1864.
[15] Blanckaert, 1981; Liauzu, 1992; Moussa, 2003; Guiral and Temime, 1977.

THE INVENTION OF "SCIENTIFIC RACISM" 69

The degree to which this new vision of the world took root varied depending on the prevailing political situation. In France, national unity and a national language had been acquired long before through the obliteration of what we might today term "nationalities"; these nationalities were vigorously denied legitimacy by the "single and indivisible" Republic. Furthermore, the aspiration for change did not concern unity or boundaries but rather democracy, a model that France had invented and felt duty-bound to export. In Germany, the opposite was true: the Napoleonic upheaval had a double effect. On the one hand, it gave birth to new sentiments through its temporary overturning of the old regime, but, on the other, it also wounded these same sentiments through its military annexations and, even more so, through its incidental political emancipation of German Jews[16] (Napoleon subsequently reinstated some of the discriminations against French Jews). We have already seen why comparative grammar, in its very origins, had to be a German science and how, from Schlegel to Grimm, it maintained an organic relationship with the development of German nationalism.

However, as an explanatory principle of history, the notion of "race" was met with a degree of approval in France. In 1825, in the introduction to the *Résumé de l'histoire d'Écosse* (An Outline of the History of Scotland) by republican journalist Armand Carrel, the historian Augustin Thierry wrote: "New physiological studies, in accordance with a deeper examination of the great events that have changed the social state of various nations, prove that the physical and moral constitution of peoples depends more on their lineage and on the primitive race to which they belong than to the influence of climate."[17] Consequently, from Sieyès to Guizot, attempts were made, somewhat artificially, to explain the French Revolution—and indeed the entire history of France—in terms of a "racial struggle" between the aristocracy, who were seen as being of Frankish and Germanic origin, and the vanquished "Gaulish" population. As a result, the works of both Herder and Schlegel became immensely popular among French Romantic historians in a France that was dying of boredom under the July Monarchy: Edgar Quinet translated Herder while Michelet translated Grimm. In 1831, Michelet alluded to "the long struggle between the Semitic world and the Indo-Germanic world."[18] Thus, according to Léon Poliakov, "this mixture of spiritualist nationalism and materialist scientism began to take a form that would eventually give rise to racial determinism."[19]

[16] Sterling, 1969.
[17] Cited in Poliakov, 1971/1987, p. 42.
[18] Cited in Ibid., p. 227.
[19] Ibid., p. 231.

70 FIRST MOVEMENT (1814–1903)

The terrors of the "Count" de Gobineau

France also witnessed the publication of the famous *Essai sur l'inégalité des races humaines* (Essay on the Inequality of the Human Races) by "Count" Arthur de Gobineau. The book took the form of an immense, imaginary, historical panorama spanning 1,200 pages (Gobineau never reread what he wrote!), which told the story of the "races" since their creation: the author remained faithful to the biblical account. Horrified by the notion of racial-mixing, he took it upon himself to evaluate the degree of purity of the various ancient populations, with the great "Aryan race" having gradually become mixed with the yellow and black "races." Using some creative linguistics, he made a connection between the (Greek) word "Pygmy" and the word "Finn," via two Sanskrit roots, *Pi* and *Han*, which meant that the Pygmies were dwarf yellow invaders from the North (the present-day Finns being Germanic half-breeds). He recognized that the Blacks displayed undeniable "artistic genius" and that the Jews were "a strong people, a free people, an intelligent people" who once "provided the world with as many doctors as merchants."

Ultimately, the *Essai* served as an introduction to the history of Gobineau's own mythical ancestor—the tall, blond, and ferocious Viking pirate, Ottar Jarl. Alas, Gobineau was not a count but the son of a drab, lower middle-class monarchist from Bordeaux while his mother, horror of horrors, was a beautiful but fickle Creole from the West Indies. Gobineau was neither tall nor blond, but was small, dark, and sickly. It is no surprise that the *Essai* finishes with a series of poignant and mournful prophecies regarding the imminent end of the world.

> The white species has thus disappeared from the face of the Earth. . . . The proportion of Aryan blood, already subdivided so many times, which still exists in our countries, and which alone supports the structure of our society, each day takes a step closer to the extreme limits of its absorption . . ., to finally expire in all forms of mediocrity: mediocrity in physical strength, mediocrity in beauty, mediocrity in intellectual prowess, one can almost speak of annihilation.

And then will come a time when, with "the last breath of our species, the globe, now dead, continues, but without us, to trace its impassive orbs in space."[20]

Notwithstanding its literary quality, the *Essai* is a symptom of a fairly transparent delusional pathology, and Gobineau emerges as the very epitome of what today's commentators would call a "mad scientist." But, in 1853, the boundaries between mythical thought and scientific thought were far less clear-cut. In fact, Gobineau would be cited as an "acceptable" author in the anthropological

---

[20] *Essai*, 1967 re-edition, pp. 870–872. On Gobineau, see Young, 1968.

THE INVENTION OF "SCIENTIFIC RACISM" 71

journals that would soon appear in France and elsewhere, even though he had little influence at the time in his native country, a fact often emphasized in France; for the liberal Tocqueville, Gobineau's insistence on the importance of "blood" is the system of a "horse trader rather than that of a statesman," worthy only of publication in the *Revue des haras* (Stud Farm Review).[21] Nonetheless, Gobineau received a letter from Ernest Renan praising his "vigor" and "originality of spirit" in a France "which believes little in race, precisely because her own is practically erased. . . . The French language, which is nothing but detritus of the fourth or fifth class, is certainly one of the reasons why the French Spirit has not accepted, and lends itself with great difficulty to, the true principles of comparative philology. All of this could only come from a people such as the Germans, who still hold onto their primordial roots and speak a language whose causes lie within itself."[22] Renan, whose courses in the Collège de France were banned for being blasphemous by Napoleon III, devoted much of his work to the opposition between a "Semitic race" and an "Indo-European race," one stuck in the monotheism of its desert birthplace, the other inventive and colorful; however, being a linguist, he constantly wavered in his definitions, sometimes referring to "anthropological races" and sometimes to "linguistic races."[23]

Most of Gobineau's readers were German, and, for a long time, Wagner was one of the most avid. He invited Gobineau to Bayreuth, dedicated his works to him, and, when listening to his own opera, *Siegfried*, he declared: "*Das ist Rassenmusik, das ist für Gobineau!*" (That is racial music, that is for Gobineau!)— at least that is what is recounted by Ludwig Schemann, an anti-Semitic ideologist who, in 1894, founded the Gobineau Society.[24] As we know, Wagner's ideological responsibilities have been the subject of much debate; most recently, his great-grandson Gottfried Wagner denounced the Wagner family's collusion with Nazism, while, in the same year, Eric Eugène denied that Wagner ever approved of Gobineau.[25]

A science of man?

At the end of the 1850s, such was the intellectual climate within which most of the anthropological societies that would go on to codify this new "Science of man" were founded: 1859 saw the founding of the Society of Anthropology of

---

[21] Jardin, 1977, p. 216. See also Moussa, 2003.
[22] Letter to Gobineau dated June 26, 1856, *Œuvres*, t. X, pp. 203–205 (cited in Poliakov, 1987, p. 235).
[23] Olender, 2008, pp. 51–81.
[24] Schemann, 1913–1916, p. 558. See this chapter, p. 93.
[25] Wagner, G., 1998; Eugène, 1998.

72 FIRST MOVEMENT (1814–1903)

Paris (SAP; which took over from the Ethnological Society), and this was quickly followed by similar societies in London (1863), Moscow (1863), Berlin (1869), Vienna (1871), and elsewhere. There were several burning issues of the day: in terms of human origins, it was the debate between monogenists and polygenists; as regards national ideologies, it was the role of "race" in the development of each country; as regards history and politics, the main issues were widespread colonial expansion and its justification; in terms of methodology, the challenges were to divide all humanity into "races," each of which was to be rigorously defined by a series of objective and repeatable measurements, and to define the epistemological status of these "linguistic," "geographical," "historical," and "anthropological" "races." The new discipline developed three fields of observation: the human body, "primitive" civilizations, and archaeological research on the origins of mankind. It was only at the end of the century that these three fields would separate to become three independent sciences. History and philology, however, would only occupy a marginal position, or, more precisely, would become the preserve of the new amateur "anthropologists," mainly doctors and anatomists. The internationally renowned SAP[26] exemplified all of the contradictions of the discipline: the application of a scientific methodology to a nonscientific subject in the name of what were often unstated ideologies.

The founding of the Society by doctor and anatomist Paul Broca was viewed with some suspicion by Napoleon III's cronies, who no doubt confused "anthropology" with "philanthropy." Broca stated as much on the occasion of the banquet celebrating the twentieth anniversary of the Society: "Did this hitherto unknown noun 'anthropology' perhaps disguise a political society?" The first meetings had to be held "under the surveillance of the Commissioner of Police for the Sorbonne Area."[27] Nonetheless, as early as 1864, the Society was recognized as being of "public benefit." Paul Broca was one of the founders of modern anatomy, and our brains contain a "Broca's area": a lesion in this area can cause "Broca's aphasia." He led a double career as a doctor and a scientist; a member of the Academy of Medicine, he also became a senator for the Republican Union toward the end of his life. For twenty years, up until his death in 1880, he maintained an iron grip on the debates, work, and scientific orientation of the Society in which he remained "general secretary" for life, regularly producing programmatic statements on the state and advancements of the discipline.

---

[26] On the Society of Anthropology of Paris, which is still in existence, see, in addition to its *Bulletins* and *Mémoires*, Blanckaert, 1981; Blanckaert et al., 1989; Blanckaert, 1989c; Harvey, 1983, 1984; Williams, 1983; Schiller, 1979. See also Moussa, 2003; Reynaud Paligot, 2006; Liauzu, 1992; Guiral and Temime, 1977.

[27] *Bulletins de la Société d'anthropologie de Paris*, 1879, p. 711.

THE INVENTION OF "SCIENTIFIC RACISM"   73

Broca, himself the son of a surgeon in the Imperial Armies, and more than 80% of the members of the Society had a background in medicine so it was natural that anatomy would be at the center of their interests. As stated in the statutes, the aim of the Society is "the scientific study of the human races" by means of measurement. Broca developed an arsenal of instruments for measuring skulls: the craniograph, craniophore, cranioscope, craniostat, endograph, stereograph, pachymeter, orbistat, goniometer, sphenoidal hook or Turkic hook, optical probe, and tropometer. Each session of the Society was an occasion to present a skull or head sent in by a generous correspondent. On one occasion, the subject was the "head of an individual called Abdallah from the Province of Oran, who was infamous for his numerous ambushes during which he killed about thirty of our men. . . . His head was cut off and preserved by dipping it in a box full of sea salt every night; you can see for yourself the results of this simple procedure."[28] On another occasion, the subject was "the skull of a Chinese man killed during the attack on the forts of Takon as part of the French expedition to Peiu-Ho in 1860. This Chinese man was killed by a sabre blow. . . . It is a good example of the impact that a sabre blow can produce. . . . The origin of the subject makes the conformation of the face interesting as it is perfectly Chinese."[29] On yet another occasion the brain of a Chinese man was received from Saigon "in a tin box filled with alcohol and soldered shut." Alas, on arrival "it was completely rotten and filled the air with a dreadful stench": in future it would be necessary to first dry out the brains and then to pack them more carefully.[30]

There was intense rivalry in terms of ingenuity: Ernest-Théodore Hamy, who followed in the footsteps of Quatrefages, "offered to the Society, a chromatic scale of Negro skins. . . . These are a series of coffee beans, which have been roasted to a greater or lesser degree, and each of which bears a number"[31]; Doctor Gustave Le Bon, racist theoretician and author of "Psychologie des foules"[32] (The Crowd: A Study of the Popular Mind), procured the cranial dimensions of hat makers' clients in order to compare skull sizes between the sexes and social classes (in 1879, he received a prize from the Society for his endeavors). Broca himself issued fifty pages of instructions for the accurate measurement of faraway populations intended for those traveling abroad. He contributed copiously to the Society's collection of skulls, which numbered 630 specimens after only four years and 3,500 on Broca's death. In order to remedy a lack of "Basque skulls" in the collection, he engaged the help of a Spanish colleague and, together,

[28] *Bulletins de la Société d'anthropologie de Paris*, 1862, p. 237.
[29] *Bulletins de la Société d'anthropologie de Paris*, 1879, p. 697.
[30] *Bulletins de la Société d'anthropologie de Paris*, 1879, p. 175.
[31] Ibid., p. 255.
[32] On Le Bon, see Olender, 2009, pp. 29–35.

74 FIRST MOVEMENT (1814–1903)

under the cover of night, they disinterred over fifty specimens in the Spanish Basque cemetery of Zaraus.[33]

The overriding challenge of the anthropological program was clear: to demonstrate the intellectual superiority of the "White race," whose military superiority at the time was blindingly obvious: "a more or less white skin, silky smooth straight hair, an orthognathic face are the most ordinary prerogative of the peoples that are at the pinnacle of the human series. . . . A people with black skin, woolly hair and a prognathic face have never been able to spontaneously rise to the level of civilization."[34] Broca and his colleagues were not racist extremists, but enlightened, anti-slavery republicans; to their minds, this "natural" superiority should never be used to justify the excesses of colonialization. For all that, their "scientific" proof was little more than a series of pathetic setbacks, with each anthropological measurement being ultimately exposed as inconsistent.[35] Brain size and head size were the first measurements to be applied: on average, Germans had larger brains (which could just as easily be attributed to their consumption of beer!), but so, too, did Asians and even European criminals. Relatively long forearms should be indicative of a close relation with the apes, but the lowest value was in fact that of the "Hottentot Venus," who belonged to the South African Bushman people (of Khoisan origin, Sawtche, who was better known as Saartjie Baartman, was taken from Africa in 1810 and brought to England and then to France, where she was exhibited as a fairground "freak." After her death in 1815, Cuvier preserved her remains in formaldehyde and also made a cast of her body, which was exposed in the Musée de l'Homme until 1974; her remains were finally returned to South Africa in 2002, following the enacting of specific legislation). The "occipital hole" of the skull, through which the vertebral column passes, shifted to a more forward position as human beings' upright stance evolved; however, this hole is in fact located closer to the rear of the skull in Whites than in Blacks. Toward the end of the nineteenth century, anthropologists finally threw in the towel. Psychologists, however, lost no time in taking up the cause by developing the notion of IQ.

Who are the French?

For many years, two specific and related controversies came to occupy central stage in the debates, and these were faithfully and avidly reproduced in the *Bulletins* of the SAP: the mixing of "races" and the origin of the

---

[33] *Bulletins de la Société d'anthropologie de Paris*, 1862, pp. 579–580; Dias, 1989.
[34] Broca, 1866, pp. 280 and 295.
[35] Gould, 1981, chap. III.

THE INVENTION OF "SCIENTIFIC RACISM" 75

Indo-Europeans. The first session focused on a paper by Broca on "the Ethnology of France": revisiting the theories of Edwards, the first "French" anthropologist[36] who in part based his work on Julius Caesar, Broca used data compiled on the sizes of army conscripts to confirm that France had two "Gaulish" races: in the north, the "Kimris," who were tall, blond, and dolichocephalic, and, in the south, the "Galls" who were small, dark, and brachycephalic. The natural environment and the Roman and Germanic invasions had little influence on these populations. Ultimately, "cross-breeding . . . had no untoward consequences for the population, since the strength, health, fertility and longevity of the men . . . are, on average, the same in the departments where the races underwent the least mixing and those where they underwent the most." As Broca stated, the "duty" of the anthropologist is to "provide a strong impetus to research that might throw scientific light on our national origins." Therefore, the implications are clear: there is a permanency to "races" (otherwise racial anthropology would have no subject); within the boundaries of its territory, the French population has been autochthonous for a long time; and, even though this population is evidently not homogenous, the heterogeneity is stable and the mixing has been beneficial (which runs counter to Gobineau's theory).

Broca did not have a choice: if the possibility of "racial mixing" was accepted, then a given "race" risked becoming diluted and transformed. Consequently, throughout the inaugural year of 1860, the Society's sessions focused on the nature of the possible crosses between "races" before finally raising the question of the "perfectibility" of "races." Behind the history of the French population, it was really the status of the "race" and the issues surrounding colonialism that were at stake. For certain anthropologists, the "races" were perfectible and colonialism was beneficial; such was the opinion of Jean Louis Armand de Quatrefages de Bréau, a monogenist Protestant and holder of the chair of Anthropology at the *Musée national d'histoire naturelle*, who maintained that wild animals (including one of the museum's she-wolves) could be domesticated. It was also the opinion of the German doctor Franz Pruner-Bey, who was also monogenist and who liked to remind his readers that bountiful nature sometimes allowed savages to live simply: "Let us not demand too much of the Negro; he is content with little."[37]

Conversely, Perrier, chief doctor at *Les Invalides*, was a supporter of Gobineau even though he rejected "his theory on the regenerating role of the Germanic peoples."[38] Georges Pouchet, another doctor, believed "like Perrier, in the inequality of human races, and in the permanence of this inequality. . . . There are

[36] Broca, 1860; Edwards, 1829; regarding Edwards, an Englishman settled in France, see Blanckaert, 1988.
[37] *Bulletins de la Société d'anthropologie de Paris*, I, 1860, p. 492.
[38] Ibid, p. 196.

76 FIRST MOVEMENT (1814–1903)

races who willingly allow themselves to be beaten. This was confirmed for me in Egypt [where], in order to ensure their obedience, I too had to beat people for whose services I was paying."[39] Adolphe Bertillon, the father of the "anti-dreyfusard" inventor of fingerprinting Alphonse Bertillon, even thought that religion was inseparable from "race," in keeping with Renan's theories. All, however, were in agreement regarding the benefits of French colonization, particularly in Algeria; this French colonization was seen to be quite the opposite of English colonization, which was an assault on the conscience and exterminated whole populations, as in Tasmania. Broca attempted a compromise: there are "un-civilizable races" just as there are "untamable animals" (the museum she-wolf only had three legs which rendered her more docile); there are other races that are capable of "civilizing themselves" and "the further apart the mother races, the more defective the cross-breeds will be."

These preoccupations colored Society debates regarding the Indo-Europeans throughout the 1860s and particularly in 1864. The debate had been initiated in 1862, by Belgian polygenist linguist Honoré Chavée who believed that Semitic and Indo-European languages were racially inscribed within the "cerebral organization" of their respective speakers.[40] He was thus on the same wavelength as Ernest Renan, who was present on the occasion of the lecture and who, despite some reservations, approved of Chavée's approach.[41] This was part of a wider debate in which the issue took on an international dimension, conducted most notably between two other scholars, the Hungarian Islamologist Ignaz Goldziher and the German philologist and philosopher Heymann Steinthal.[42]

Broca had no choice but to react since it was language that provided Chavée with the basis for his concept of "race" and it was through the radical alterity of these two linguistic structures that he deduced the polygenism of the two "races." In a lengthy paper, Broca insisted that "type" [i.e. "race"] is infinitely more permanent than language"[43]: we can change our language, and there are numerous historical examples of this, but we cannot change our "race." Anatomical measurements were to remain the basis for all human science, and Broca restricted the meaning of "ethnology" and "ethnography" to the study of a particular "race."

---

[39] Ibid, pp. 433–435.
[40] Chavée, 1862a, 1862b. On Chavée, see Auroux, 1982, p. 8; Hovelacque, 1878.
[41] See this chapter, p. 71.
[42] Olender, 2008, pp. 115–135, 2009, pp. 26–27.
[43] Broca, 1862.

THE INVENTION OF "SCIENTIFIC RACISM" 77

On the origins of the Aryans

Tackling the issue of Indo-European origins and migrations from an anthropo-logical point of view (in Broca's sense of the word) meant adhering to Retzius's model, described above (Retzius became a member of the SAP shortly before his death in 1860); said model involved the colonization of Europe, with its dark-skinned, brachycephalic natives, by tall, blond dolichocephalics from Asia, whose purest representatives were the Germans (in their Scandinavian version) and the "Celts"; a more or less implicit corollary of this model is the assump-tion that the dolichocephalics were "superior." Within the SAP, this model was supported by Franz-Pruner-Bey, a cultivated doctor of German origin who was given the honorary title "Bey" by his grateful patient, the Viceroy of Egypt, Abbas Pacha.[44] However, remaining faithful to the position he took in 1860, Broca—a stocky, dark-skinned brachycephalic—was unable, like his French peers, to ac-cept a model which reduced them, in accordance with his principle of the per-manency of "race," to mere descendants of poorly assimilated slaves and applied to them the colonial model that they themselves applied to others. He eagerly threw aspersions on Retzius's intentions but failed to realize that his arguments could be reversed.

> We must not forget that dolichocephalic and brachycephalic characteris-tics were first studied in Sweden, and then in England, the United States and Germany; and that in each of these countries, particularly in Sweden, the dolichocephalic type clearly predominates and that there is always a natural tendency for people, even those most free of prejudice, to attach a notion of su-periority to the dominant characteristics of their own race.[45]

He also embarked on a hunt for dolichocephalics both among living "indige-nous" populations (hence his nightly raids on the Basque cemetery at Zaraus) and beneath Neolithic dolmens; he sought and translated in the Society's *Bulletins* contributions from foreign researchers who described such discoveries in Great Britain (John Thurnam), Switzerland (W. His), and even in Sweden, where Retzius's own son, together with Baron von Düben, discovered dolichoce-phalic skulls beneath a dolmen thereby "hammering the final nail in the coffin of Retzius's doctrine."[46]

Thus French indigeneity was saved and Aryan invasions had never occurred: "What spread throughout Europe was not a race but a civilization

---

[44] Blanckaert, 1989b; Wrotnowska, 1975.
[45] *Bulletins de la Société d'anthropologie de Paris*, 1861, p. 513.
[46] *Bulletins de la Société d'anthropologie de Paris*, 1868 p. 381; Blanckaert, 1989b.

78 FIRST MOVEMENT (1814–1903)

which, in a manner of speaking, was transmitted from population to population, since good is as contagious as bad"; "And in this way, from neighbor to neighbor, from one migration to another, century after century, people who were still Celtic by language, but less so by blood, spread out in all directions to the edges of Europe."[47] Peoples with blond hair and brown hair, with long heads and round heads, had all been occupying their own corners of Europe since the dawn of time. Certain members of the Society went even further. The aforementioned Belgian geologist Omalius d'Halloy, who had been among the very first to suggest the idea of a European origin for the Indo-Europeans as early as 1848, contributed to the ongoing debate by reiterating his original ideas but without much elaboration.[48] Others, such as the polygenist doctor Eugène Dally, completely rejected linguistics and dubbed the entire approach an "Aryan" fantasy.

Pruner-Bey, who fiercely defended the classic model, attempted to preserve the unity of the Indo-European "race" by giving it a high level of variability.

> Skin color varying from white . . . to yellow and olive. Hair of whitish yellow to jet black. . . . Skull and face harmonious, orthognathic, and decidedly oval or tending towards this shape in its dolichocephalic and brachycephalic extremes. Facial features of more or less harmonious proportions. Skeletal details that, among the human races, are furthest from the proportions . . . of anthropomorphic apes.[49]

But in the face of such laxity, even when "harmonious," can we still talk of "race"? In strict anthropometric terms, there was no evidence whatsoever for a large-scale migration in any part of Europe. Nevertheless, as we have already seen, Pruner-Bey was vigorously supported in his theories by the archaeologist Alexandre Bertrand.[50] It was not simply a clash between two disciplines, but also a confrontation between two types of scientific background, with medical doctors on one side and antiquarians on the other.

But the outcome of the scientific conflict and struggle for influence between Broca and Pruner-Bey was eventually decided in a brutal and highly symbolic manner. In 1870, the Prussian army defeated the French; the Germans had prevailed over the Celts. Bavarian-born Franz Pruner-Bey, Egyptian by title and Parisian by adoption, was forced into exile and his name disappeared from the list of members of the Anthropological Society; when his name is cited, it is with a phonetically unnecessary umlaut added ("Prüner-Bey"), no doubt in a bid to emphasize his Teutonic origins. He retired to Pisa, where he died in 1882, two

---

[47] Broca, 1864, pp. 313–315.
[48] Omalius d'Halloy, 1848, 1864, 1865; see Chapter 3, pp. 38–39.
[49] Pruner-Bey, 1864, p. 122.
[50] See Chapter 3, pp. 35–36.

THE INVENTION OF "SCIENTIFIC RACISM" 79

years after Broca; he received no obituary from the Society. He had, however, savored a brief and bitter revenge.

Are the Prussians German?

The war of 1870, the principal objective of which was the extension of German unity, was the first modern "national" war. However, it was also the start of a serious economic depression that would last twenty-five years and exacerbate national sentiments. Reunified Germany yearned for a national ideology, which it would shortly find in the Wagnerian Epic (the Tetralogy was created in1876) and in the exaltation of "blondness," which up until then was regarded as a sickly complexion.[51] It was from this founding moment onward that German scholars, following in the footsteps of Lazarus Geiger, began to claim that the original European homeland was indeed Germany and that the "Original Race" was therefore the "Germanic race," in whose existence and homogeneity they had unwavering belief. The French, even though they could not reasonably claim the same, would at least do their best to deny their adversaries this honor. From the onset of war, both parties glorified this clash between the two peoples as a clash between "races."

For the monogenist Armand de Quatrefages de Bréau—who incidentally was a tall, blond Protestant—the Prussians, whose king had just crushed France in his quest to unify Germany, could not possibly belong to the "Germanic race" and thus could not be Aryan. In February 1871, while the museum where he worked was under cannon fire from the besieging enemy, he explicitly reiterated Pruner Bey's theses in the *Revue des Deux Mondes*, and, without acknowledging it, he also rehashed Gobineau's strange opinions regarding the Finns. The Prussians, he believed, belonged to the "Finnish race" who, along with the Basques and a handful of others, constituted the native European stock who were eventually colonized by the Aryans. They were, in effect, "a people who pre-dated all history," "semi-barbarians who nurture a jealous hatred for a superior civilization," of which the 1870 war was a contemporary manifestation. They undoubtedly belonged to the "White" root stock, but to an "allophyllic" (i.e., "other") branch which was neither "Aryan" nor "Semite." Of course these "others" were also present in France. Quatrefages identified them in Brittany, but, he writes, "the children of our ancient Armorica have proved themselves in many ways, so we can now accept, without repugnance, a certain ancestral community with them", since we have "aryanized" them. Thus, the "true" Germans are much closer to the French than to the Prussians. This conflict was, in fact, based on a fateful

[51] Bierhahn, 1964; Poliakov, 1971/1987, p. 298.

80   FIRST MOVEMENT (1814–1903)

error: "Thanks to the idea of antagonism between the races, which has been brought to the fore and exploited with Machiavellian dexterity, all of Germany has risen up in the name of Pan-Germanism"; this is why, as Quatrefages prophesizes in the last line, "she will pay cruelly for the mistake she has made in basing her future on an anthropological error."[52]

After a year of inactivity due to the war, and after "order had been restored" following the violent crushing of the Paris Commune, the Anthropological Society reconvened in July 1871. A lecture was presented by Charles Rochet who, thanks to the occupation of Paris, had had the opportunity to observe the Prussians at close quarters and compare them to the Bavarians. He confirms Quatrefage's thesis: the Prussians are definitely Finns. The idea was further discussed during a subsequent meeting and was supported and approved by many members, including Lagneau[53] who would become president the following year. In his inaugural speech, he talks of

[a]n implacable war, wrongly considered as a war between races. Between civilized nations, with such a complex ethnogeny, the diversity of races should not be a motive for mutual destruction. A threat to the future of Europe, ambitious claims lurking under the cover of Panslavism, Pangermanism, or other theories that are more linguistic than ethnological, can lead to wars of conquest; the anthropological sciences, which allow us to identify numerous dissimilar ethnic elements within a single nation, in no way legitimize and indeed completely repudiate these nefarious claims.

In a call for an international scientific community, surpassing partisan hostilities, he reminds his audience

[h]ow, often, certain political principles, by which a nation claims only one of its various ethnic components as original, at the expense of all others, prove to be poorly founded. . . . Moreover, a nation, which like ours, counts among its ancestors Celts, Gauls, Aquitani, Ligurians, Belgae, Burgundians and Franks, brings together physical and intellectual aptitudes that are as great and as diverse as those of any other European nation.[54]

This sentiment was strongly reaffirmed by another Society member, Abel Hovelacque, ordinarily a specialist in human evolution, who two years later insisted on publishing an entire work, *Langues, races, nationalités*,[55] dedicated

[52] Quatrefages, 1871; Poliakov, 1971/1987, pp. 296–297.
[53] Rochet, 1871.
[54] *Bulletins de la Société d'anthropologie de Paris*, 2nd series, 7, 1872, pp. 4–5.
[55] Hovelacque, 1873; see Dias, 1993.

THE INVENTION OF "SCIENTIFIC RACISM" 81

to the same issue. He denounces chauvinistic German science and, implicitly, its poster boy Pruner-Bey, the creator of such fictions as "Mongoloid Basques," "Dolichocephalic Celts," and "other fantastic inventions of German origin, even though they were produced in Paris." This is why "it is just as inadmissible to claim to base the notion of nationality on race as it is to base it on language," since the nation is not a biological inevitability but rather a common desire, "a choice of free association which the republican democracy places at the top of its demands."[56] In fact, Hovelacque, a Radical Party militant, would eventually become President of Paris City Council and Member of Parliament. It was evident that the French nation could not be based on the notion of "race" or on language, neither of which would provide any unity; the linguistic plurality was evident, with the Basques, Bretons, and especially the inhabitants of Alsace-Lorraine, even though their languages were ultimately doomed to be swept aside by the official language of the one undivided Republic. Being one of only two European democracies at the time (Switzerland being the other), it was equally impossible for national unity to be expressed in the person of a monarch. In 1891, Michel Bréal, Professor of linguistics at the Collège de France and translator of the works of Bopp, echoed Hovelvacque's words:

> After ethnography had been used to serve causes that humanity now repudiates, it is now the turn of linguistics to find itself exploited. It would appear that this latter application of science is even more abusive and disagreeable because this time it does not involve skin color or hair type, but a product of the mind.[57]

Such was the position, determined by history, of the vast majority of French intellectuals; the only mavericks were those, like Vacher de Lapouge who, at the end of the century, would seek to question the democratic conception of the nation.

The three positions of French anthropologists on the Indo-European question

Thus, in the second half of the nineteenth century, the Indo-European paradigm, in so far as it postulated an original "racial homogeneity," could have no foundational significance in France. Moreover, the world had witnessed how it had been exploited, in the name of science, by its German inventors. The debate would, however, continue for two decades, particularly within the SAP, which

---

[56] Hovelacque, 1873, pp. 8 and 22.
[57] Bréal, 1891, p. 631; see Dias, 1993, p. 95.

82 FIRST MOVEMENT (1814–1903)

remained perhaps the only forum in France where the Indo-European question could be debated since it brought together anthropologists, ethnologists, and prehistorians (at least until 1904, when the latter founded their own society, the Société Préhistorique Française). For a number of years (1873, 1879, 1887, and 1889) entire successive SAP sessions were devoted to the Indo-European question.

Three conflicting positions emerged within the SAP; all three opposed Retzius's model of dolichocephalic invaders. The first, which became entrenched, was that of Broca, who maintained it right up until his death: blond- and brown-haired people are both indigenous to Europe, Aryan languages are simply a product of linguistic diffusion, the primacy of craniometry and its immutable "races" must not be questioned. The great Aryan migrations from Asia are, therefore, just a myth. And, since nothing has ever changed, we can still find living direct descendants of even the most ancient prehistoric "races," such as the Neanderthals or Cro-Magnons.[58]

The second position was that the Aryans did indeed come from Asia but that they were brown-haired brachycephalics who dominated the blond natives. This was the position supported by Prefect Julien Girard de Rialle, the French-based Hungarian Orientalist Charles de Ujfalvy, and the army veterinarian Charles-Alexandre Piétrement.[59] Piétrement believed that the Aryans "belonged to a brachycephalic type with brown hair, whose purest surviving representatives are the Savoyards and the Galtchas [Tajiks]"; they "Aryanized a group of blond-haired dolichocephalic people, either through force of arms or through the attractiveness of their civilization." This is the reason why Hector, the brother of blond-haired Paris, abductor of Helen, was brown-haired. This point of view was confirmed by the fact that the domestication of the horse could be traced to Central Asia and by the sacred Iranian texts of the Avesta which, when describing a country "where the longest summer's day is equal to the two shortest days of winter, and where the longest winter's night is equal to the two shortest nights of the summer," had to be talking about a region situated at a latitude of 49° north, around Lake Balkhash in Kazakhstan. Of course, nothing really indicated that these late texts were seeking to describe any actual historical reality, and professional philologists, including Bréal, had no problem in dismantling the argument.[60] The abuse of philologico-astronomical interpretations was by no means rare, and certain other publications from the same period even attempted to locate the original Homeland at the North Pole, an original theory that continued

---

[58] *Bulletins de la Société d'anthropologie de Paris*, 3rd series, 2, 1879, pp. 318–319, 330–331; also see Boule, 1921, p. 292.

[59] Piétrement, 1879, and *Bulletins de la Société d'anthropologie de Paris*, 3rd series, 2, 1879, pp. 189–194, 203–212, 260–271.

[60] Schrader, 1907, pp. 108–109; Reinach, 1892, p. 61.

THE INVENTION OF "SCIENTIFIC RACISM" 83

to receive support in some quarters until recently.[61] Ujfalvy, who propounded the same anthropological thesis and who provided lengthy descriptions of the Tajiks, putative inhabitants of the original Homeland, sarcastically described Pösche and Penka as "the scholars from Northern Germany," for whom "the Aryan is tall, blond and dolichocephalic; such was their opinion which they believed to be absolutely sacrosanct. That is to say, that the German is the purest representative of the ancient Aryan race (?) in Europe." Pösche and Penka responded in the same tone, accusing Ujfalvy of adopted jingoism.[62] A little later, the Italian anthropologist, Giuseppe Sergi had few qualms about rehashing this theory of the original brown-skinned Aryans from the Hindu Kush.[63] Incidentally, general accounts of the "human races" published in France at this time more often than not persisted in locating the cradle of humanity, and as a consequence that of both blond and brown-haired Indo-Europeans, in Central Asia and more specifically in Pamir.[64]

The third position voiced within the SAP was that of European repatriation. First forwarded by Omalius in the 1860s, it would be vigorously defended by Clémence Royer in subsequent decades.[65] This controversial scholar, the first translator of Darwin and by extension the first promoter of "social Darwinism" in France, stated in her preface to the *Origine des espèces* that the most courageous "races" had overcome the others since "man, having become the stronger, could impose himself on the mate that pleased him most; and hence woman, who had nothing to do but please and submit, became more and more beautiful, in accordance with man's ideal, man who himself became even stronger, having only to fight, command, and protect." Thus we see the "reckless and blind" error of Christianity and democracy which scorned natural selection: "while all care, all devotions of love and pity are considered to be owed to the deposed and degenerate representatives of the species, there is nothing to encourage the development of the emerging force or to propagate merit, talent and virtue."[66]

There is a degree of coherence when, in the context of the Indo-European question, such robust biological racism is associated with a thesis that is both Euro-centrist and migrationist; this is in contrast to Broca's "entrenched" anti-linguistic autochtonism. In the opinion of Clémence Royer, "a race that is powerful enough to overrun all of Europe and all of western Asia cannot have had its origins in a Pamirian valley; mountain peoples are peoples who have retreated and defend themselves; they are never conquering peoples." Yet "the blond

[61] Warren, 1885; Tilak, 1903. See Chapter 9, p. 216.
[62] Ujfalvy, 1884, 1887a, 1887b, 1896.
[63] Sergi, 1903.
[64] Quatrefages, 1887; Deniker, 1900.
[65] On Clémence Royer: Blanckaert, 1982; Fraisse, 1983; Thuillier, P., 1981; see also Royer, 1870.
[66] Royer, 1862.

84   FIRST MOVEMENT (1814–1903)

European race, as a whole, appears to have always been a race of travelers, a race that is essentially war-like and conquering." "In the end, these high plateaus of Asia can be discounted; once we wanted to believe that these plateaus were the birthplace of everything but all they have ever given rise to are avalanches."

> For a long time it was supposed that Semites, Aryans and Mongols may have shared a common birthplace somewhere on top of a mountain, from whence the three races then dispersed and quickly turned their backs on each other, in accordance with the story of the "tri-color" descendants of Noah's three sons; this is simply the invention of a myth which, unlike its ancient counterparts, does not even have the merit of symbolizing history. It amounts to a retelling and a renewing of the tale of the Earthly Paradise, with less poeticism and even less common sense.[67]

However, it was difficult for Frenchwoman Clémence Royer to accept the Germanic and Scandinavian hypothesis. She therefore settled for an origin on the Black Sea, in the Balkan Peninsula, close to Schrader's steppes. The proximity to Turkey made it possible to reconcile this original Homeland with the Near Eastern origins of the European Neolithic as proposed by prehistorians—Gabriel Mortillet being the first[68]—and botanists alike. The geographical isolation of the region might explain why a distinct "race" emerged there. She even suggested, in an elaborate geological fantasy based on continental drift theory, that an ancient Balkano-Caucasian island had existed and was the birthplace of the "Aryan race"; the other "races," for their part, emerged in a parallel and polygenist fashion in other geographically isolated ancient locations. As time went on, the Germanic hypothesis gathered momentum and even found support in France, where some of its adepts generated controversy; among these was naval officer Lombard, who addressed the SAP in 1899.[69]

Moderation among German anthropologists

It would be a mistake to think that all of German Europe at that time unanimously rejoiced in the exalted vision of a Germanic cradle for the "Aryan race." A prominent detractor was pathologist Rudolf Virchow, who was one of the founding members of the Berlin Anthropological, Ethnological, and Prehistoric Society in 1869, and who had once collaborated with Schliemann. As a liberal

---

[67] In particlar, see *Bulletins de la Société d'anthropologie de Paris*, 3rd series, 2, 1879, pp. 198–203, 240–249, 281–288; ibid., 2nd série, 8, 1873, pp. 905–937.

[68] Mortillet, 1879.

[69] Lombard, 1889; see Déchelette, 1914, vol. 2, pp. 9–10.

THE INVENTION OF "SCIENTIFIC RACISM" 85

and a representative of the progressive party opposed to Bismarck, he held a very moderate view (his prudence had even led him to view Neanderthal man as a congenital idiot).[70] Naturally, German anthropologists had been shocked by Quatrefages aspersions regarding the "Germanity" of the Prussians and initially responded harshly[71] before opting for a conscientious, methodical, and scientific riposte. Under the auspices of the fledgling Berlin Anthropological Society, Virchow, a native of Pomerania (an area only recently Germanized), initiated a large-scale official survey involving all primary school teachers in Germany, Austria, Switzerland, and Belgium. The aim was to record the eye color and hair color of 15 million school children. The survey went on for ten years and confirmed the obvious: Northern Germany was predominantly blond and was, therefore, the heartland of Germanity, whence came the majority of German aristocrats; further south, the indigenous dark-haired stock tended to predominate. As for the German Jewish school children, 11% were blond and a certain number had blue eyes.[72]

But this characterization of modern Germans bore no relation to the original Homeland that Virchow continued to place in Asia. Moreover, he writes: "Who can actually prove that the Aryans were white skinned with blue eyes and a long skull?" Indeed, "anyone who is familiar with Greek literature knows that white skin, blond hair and blue eyes have always been regarded, since the dawn of Antiquity, as extremely rare features that never failed to attract attention" and, therefore, cannot be regarded as defining characteristics of the original "race."[73] In 1889, he came to the conclusion that "the typical Aryan, as postulated in theory, has not yet been discovered."[74] Along with colleagues such as Julius Kollmann, he noted that remains found in megalithic tombs exhibited a total lack of anthropometric homogeneity: not only did brachycephalics and dolichocephalics occur together, but between these two "types" there was a wide range of intermediate "types."[75] Faced with these facts, committed Germanomaniacs like Matthäus Much attempted to identify the dolichocephalics as the masters and the brachycephalics as their slaves,[76] but this argument was more than a little circular! Liberal German anthropologists strove to distance themselves from the rapidly expanding Germanomaniac movement at the end of the nineteenth century, and Kollmann was eager to affirm during one of the Society's meetings

[70] On Virchow: Andree, 1976; Hermann, 1981; Kümmel, 1968; Boas, 1902; Massin, 1996; Trautmann-Waller, 2004.
[71] Virchow, 1872; see Poliakov, 1971/1987, pp. 297–301.
[72] Virchow, 1886.
[73] Virchow, 1874.
[74] Virchow, *Correspondenzblatt der deutschen Gesellschaft für Anthropologie, Ethnologie und Urgeschichte*, 20, 9 (1889), p. 121.
[75] Schrader and Nehring, 1917–1929, I, pp. 630–634.
[76] Much, M., 1902, p. 344.

86 FIRST MOVEMENT (1814-1903)

that "all of the European races are . . . equally talented when it comes to cultural exploits."[77] On one occasion Virchow ventured as far as asking whether there might be "a form of autochtony of Germanic-type peoples of Northern Europe,"[78] but he went no further.

As we have seen, the linguist Hermann Hirt, who believed in the Scandinavian original Homeland, attached no significance to the idea of a homogenous "race," a notion that was "impossible to prove" and "moreover, without importance."[79] At the turn of the nineteenth century, leading German Indo-Europeanist Otto Schrader[80] could, without fearing criticism from colleagues, present an entirely negative account of the contribution of anthropology to the Indo-European issue.

> Anthropology, and in particular craniology, despite its means, is incapable of producing clear definitions of human races, either in Prehistory or in historic periods. On the contrary, whether it is in the present or the past, wherever we turn, we are confronted with transitional and mixed forms.[81]

As regards the root stock, Schrader notes, in an involuntary but ironic echo of Broca, that "this dispute, in which the French have an understandable preference for brachycephalic original Indo-Europeans, and the Germans for dolichocephalics, has become entrenched for reasons that are more often national than scientific."[82] In his book *The Origin of the Aryans,* the English Canon Isaac Taylor (who borrowed heavily from Schrader for his "solution" and opted for a compromise regarding the characteristics of the "original race," which he saw as Asian, brachycephalic blonds) rather humorously summed up the dispute as follows:

> The Germans claim the primitive Aryans as typical Germans who Aryanized the French, while the French claim them as typical Frenchmen who Aryanized the Germans. Both parties maintain that their own ancestors were the pure noble race of Aryan conquerors, and that their hereditary foes belonged to a conquered and enslaved race of aboriginal savages, who received the germs of civilization from their hereditary superiors. Each party accuses the other of subordinating the results of science to Chauvinistic sentiment.[83]

---

[77] Kollmann, 1892, p. 104, 1892; Massin, 1993, p. 213.
[78] Virchow, 1884; cited by Schrader, 1907, pp. 111–112.
[79] Hirt, 1892, p. 465. See Chapter 3, pp. 61–62.
[80] See Chapter 3, pp. 47–54.
[81] Schrader, 1907, p. 116.
[82] Schrader and Nehring, 1917–1929, I, p. 631.
[83] Taylor, 1890, p. 226.

Does "race" exist?

Taylor's pronouncement was somewhat simplistic. On the German side, we have seen how professional anthropologists tended to be moderate in their views while Germanomaniac theses were generally put forward by "amateur" Indo-Europeanists who were following in the footsteps of Penka and Wilser. On the French side, the Indo-European question gradually disappeared from anthropological concerns. Anthropology in France, despite its institutional prosperity (a host of European associations were represented at the fiftieth anniversary of the SAP in 1909), was entering a period of serious epistemological crisis, the causes of which were both external and internal. Despite resistance (particularly in the French Academy of Sciences from which Broca was barred), Darwinism was gradually gaining acceptance. Within the Society, and the most radical free thinkers, such as Mortillet, were its most active propagandists. In 1871, Darwin was finally admitted to the Society, following a proposal by Quatrefages and long-time skeptic, Broca. And so, the idea of a slow, branch-like transformation of all species led to the demise of "classic" polygenist racial anthropology; if all life was in a state of constant evolution, then the notion of "race" was an impossibility and thus the raison d'être of racial anthropology was no more.

In fact, as instruments and measurements improved, "races" tended to disappear. Even Paul Topinard, Broca's spiritual successor, was forced to admit this in 1891: "Race does not exist within the human species, . . . it is the product of our imagination and not of raw, palpable reality. . . . Mankind seems only to display individual variations."[84] German anthropologists, from Johannes Ranke to Erwin Baelz, came to the same conclusion. Felix von Luschan, Professor of Anthropology at Berlin, former student of Broca and representative of the Berlin Ethnographic Museum at the Society's fiftieth anniversary, declared the following in his work *Völker, Rassen, Sprachen*: "All attempts to divide humanity up into artificial groups based on skin color, cranial dimensions or hair type, etc., are totally misguided . . ., similar attempts in the future will increasingly prove to be fruitless wastes of time."[85]

Furthermore, a growing number of studies were revealing the influence of environment on "race." The famous cephalic index could vary as a function of climate and diet, as US-based German anthropologist Franz Boas demonstrated in spectacular fashion: while European immigrants displayed variable cranial proportions, the cephalic indexes of their American-born children tended to become harmonized and approach the national average.[86] Similarly, the heights

[84] Topinard, 1891, pp. 4 and 39.
[85] Luschan, 1922, pp. 1 and 13; see Massin, 1993, pp. 212–213.
[86] Boas, 1911.

88   FIRST MOVEMENT (1814–1903)

of European populations tended to increase as a function of improved hygiene and diet. Consequently, anthropological journals gradually distanced themselves from sweeping raciological ambitions and instead focused on classifying and describing the ever-increasing quantities of anatomical and ethnological data that were being amassed as colonial conquests gathered pace. Of course overviews of the "human races" continued to be published, but they focused mainly on obvious major groups and were of little heuristic interest.[87] And, while the descriptive craniometric tradition remained active in France, centered around the persona of Henri-Victor Vallois, during the first half of the twentieth century and beyond[88] most scientists at least opted to abandon the anthropological fantasies of the preceding century.

The Count and the Aryan

Once the ideology had retreated in the face of moderation and had disappeared from the studies of enlightened and liberal scholars, raciology was reduced to nothing more than an ideological entity left in the hands of political extremists. In Europe, and particularly in France, the 1890s saw the crystallization of an entire extreme right-wing ideological apparatus; this movement had its roots in history, but its rhetoric and actions took new and virulent forms. The Dreyfus affair is its best known manifestation; the case saw Bertillon, the "inventor" of fingerprinting and the son of a founding member of the Anthropological Society (to which he himself belonged) present a doggedly unscientific defense of the fake documents produced by the military authorities. Anti-Semitism, founded on the denunciation of "international plutocracy," was one of the favorite themes of the extreme right in France, which at the time was being rocked by the international economic crisis. Certain theoreticians sought "scientific" justifications for these views. One of the best known was librarian and former magistrate Georges Vacher de Lapouge who, in 1899, published L'Aryen, son rôle social (The Aryan: His Social Role), based on the texts of a series of open lectures that he presented at the University of Montpellier in 1889–1890: a follow-up publication, Le Sémite, son rôle social (The Semite: His Social Role) was planned.

Essentially a product of his time rather than the founder of a school of thought, Count Vacher de Lapouge came from a socialist background and had tried unsuccessfully to have a chair in Anthropology created for him. Instead, under the self-proclaimed title of "anthropo-sociology," he attempted to organize the fin de siècle racist vision of the world into a coherent system: anxiety regarding

[87] Deniker, 1900; Ripley, 1899.
[88] See Chapter 8, pp. 190–193, and Chapter 10, p. 223.

THE INVENTION OF "SCIENTIFIC RACISM"   89

racial mixing and decline, à la Gobineau; inegalitarian "Social Darwinism," à la Clémence Royer (he translated the work of the German Social Darwinist Ernst Haeckel into French); racial prejudices typical of the early years of the SAP; prehistoric fantasies regarding Indo-European origins borrowed from Penka; anti-Semitic clichés and delusions; *Völkerpsychologie*, à la Gustave Le Bon and Alfred Fouillée; eugenics, etc. This heady mix was supported by a plethora of paleontological data and craniometric statistics. He advocated the elimination of undesirables (by means of execution or at least castration, for which he provided a number of chemical recipes). Strongly anti-clerical, he posed as a supporter of "socialism" in the face of "plutocracy" but denounced democracy and the "failure" of the Revolution. Count Vacher de Lapouge was thus typical of the anti-parliamentary "revolutionary right" which was taking shape in the 1890s and which would ultimately lead to the emergence of interwar fascist movements and collaboration.[89] It is no surprise then to find his works cited (discretely) by the French New Right in its attempted ideological refoundation of the 1970s.[90]

Two-thirds of Vacher de Lapouge's book is devoted to an anthropological reconstruction of Indo-European origins. As a Frenchman, the author is faced with the same issues as Broca before him: the multiplicity of European "races," lack of correspondence between languages and "races," and a certain reticence to locate the original Homeland in Germany. He therefore devises a compromise: the *Homo europaeus* "race" (a reference to Linnaeus for whom this term applies to the entire "White race"), also termed the "Aryan race" or "Dolicho-blond race," emerged in the area of the North Sea between Germany, Holland, and Great Britain during the last glacial period, at a time when the sea level was lower. The "Aryan" civilization and languages developed at a later stage in Central Europe through the agglomeration of various populations around the conquering *Europaeus*. Thus, the indigenous dark-haired brachycephalics were part of the Aryan civilization "just as a servant is part of a household" (p. 23).[91]

For Vacher de Lapouge, the concept of an original Aryan people is "modelled on that of the development of peoples as described in the Book of Genesis" (p. 8). Using what was then the most up-to-date philological data, he states:

[There was] no Aryan patriarchal family, or even people, but rather a collection of nomadic peoples, spread out over a vast territory, speaking related languages and undergoing a collective linguistic evolution towards Aryan forms, with each dialect influencing its neighbors. In this dense and complex mass

---

[89] On the "revolutionary right," see Sternhell, 1978, 1983. On Vacher de Lapouge, see Nagel, 1975; Thuillier, G., 1977.

[90] See Chapter 9, p. 215.

[91] The numbers in brackets in each of the quotations refer to the page numbers in Vacher de Lapouge, 1899.

90   FIRST MOVEMENT (1814–1903)

of undefined dialects, a selection process would lead to the disappearance of the weaker dialects and would greatly extend the distribution areas of the strongest. Thus, by suppressing the intermediates, the large linguistic groups took shape, just as French, Spanish and Italian have more recently emerged out of local dialects that had been imposed over vast regions due to accidents of history; these languages are themselves in the process of swallowing up a myriad of other local languages that, like them, sprang from a common Latin source. To this theory, resulting from the old wave doctrine proposed by Schmidt and others, is added a complementary explanation for the increasing simplification of languages. The destruction of grammatical forms is due to the emergence of pidgins in countries where the conquest superimposed peoples that spoke languages too far apart to allow mutual understanding and where families might have parents who spoke different languages. In this way, philologists eventually abandoned the theory of a single Bactrian origin for Aryan peoples, languages and institutions. (p. 9)

Sex, fantasies, and racisms

But this linguistic "modernity" went hand in hand with a simplifying raciology, which we will meet time and time again throughout the twentieth century. The *Europaeus* "race" was thus born in the mists of the North Sea, "in this abundant but austere nature, so uniform, so infinitely sad, where only those endowed with a resilient temperament, a cold and melancholic spirit, a calm but boundless energy, could survive" (p. 151). Little by little, this "race" spread out over the great Northern Plain and eventually reached the forests further south.

It is from the great shady forests of Middle Europe, between the Atlantic and the Black Sea, that the Aryan swarms would emerge and ride forth to conquer the warmth, the light and all that they had been denied during their dull, uniform and severe infancy; and behind these swarms others would come, in their turn, after the enchanting nature, perfumed air, vibrant golden rays, sweeping horizon and the sweet soft life of the Orient and the Mediterranean would have laid the first waves to rest under the perfidious flower-covered earth; because the sun has always attracted the Aryan, has attracted him incessantly, has weakened him, disarmed him and slain him. (pp. 151–152)

This *Europaeus* "race" is therefore blond, blue-eyed, dolichocephalic, and tall in stature; "the whole physiognomy is energetic, and this calm energy is apparent in the gaze"; "from the back, the blond dolichocephalic is readily distinguished from the other races by the elegant form of the neck, torso, and especially the

THE INVENTION OF "SCIENTIFIC RACISM"   91

waist" (p. 26). His brain is "significantly longer and less wide" than that of *Alpinus*, the European "Alpine race." "The male genital apparatus is notable only for its volume," which would be comparable to that of *Afer*, African man, "if the long, voluminous member of the latter was not at the same time flaccid and incompletely erectile" (p. 31). "The large, well-developed *labia*" of the female genital apparatus "attest to a very advanced evolution. This race is furthest from the simian form which lacks large, distinct *labia*." However (and the Count lets his fantasies run wild here), these "voluminous external organs . . ., placed lower down and further back than in the *Alpinus* female" signal an "inferior trait, which we find among the apes" and which render the *Europaeus* woman similar to the "black races" that "naturally practice *more pecudum* copulation."[92] In fact, de Lapouge devotes two whole pages to these "serious" genital issues which "are of very considerable anthropological importance."

From a moral and intellectual point of view (pp. 370–375), the Aryan or *Europaeus* is distinguished by "power of reason and will"; "the nervous system is more powerful, more resistant"; "the intelligence is more adaptable"; "the reason is cold and fair. It calculates everything, calculates well and does so as quickly as required, without excess haste and without indecision"; "the supreme quality of the race, that which characterizes it and sets it above all others, is its will, which is cold, precise, and tenacious and overcomes all obstacles." This "race" is supremely domineering, and in such a natural way that others readily get accustomed to being dominated. As a result, "today we can say that only the peoples of this race are free." This "race" is not just confined to Scandinavia and Northern Germany. We find it in equal proportions in Great Britain and the United States which were, for Vacher de Lapouge, model Aryan states; this went against the grain of the anti-English and anti-American tradition that would go on to characterize the French extreme right. It is probably for this reason that the original Homeland of the "race," now submerged, was located in the North Sea, between the various dolichocephalic countries. However, even in these countries, the "Aryan race" only represents one-quarter of the population, and this proportion drops to 4% in France and 1% in Spain.

This is because the purity of the "Aryan race" is threatened by the dark-haired brachycephalic natives of the southern half of Europe and by the Jews. The former are characterized by "servility, a lack of character and virility" and are found in today's "detritus of intellectuals, critics, decadents, symbolists, cowards, emasculated neuropaths, anarchists, not a man amongst them" (p. 392). "Swarthy, short, stocky, the brachycephalic presently prevails from the Atlantic to the Black Sea"; "he is apathetic and mediocre but keeps on multiplying"; "he is a submissive subject, a passive soldier, and obedient civil servant"; "he never

---

[92] "In the manner of animals," *Translator's note.*

92 FIRST MOVEMENT (1814–1903)

rebels" (p. 481). This is why Vacher de Lapouge makes a point of distancing himself from the anti-Semitism of brachycephalic Drumont, the vehement propagandist of *La Libre Parole*. Because what the brachycephalics were defending was no more than the democratic power of the "inferior classes," which had been won from the dolichocephalics by the Revolution and which they wanted to safeguard against the Jews (p. 464). The opposition was already taking shape between a "vulgar" and popular racism and an "intellectual" racism with pseudo-scientific pretentions; in its own way, this opposition found a voice under the Third Reich and still endures today.

As for the Jews, "they are the same everywhere: arrogant in success, servile in contrary circumstances, wily, sly to the extreme, great amassers of money, remarkably intelligent and yet incapable of creating . . ., afflicted by persecutions . . . that they seem to deserve because of their bad faith, their cupidity and their spirit of domination" (p. 466).

> There is clearly in this two-faced being, something of a woman who deceives and caresses only to corrupt, and something of a haughty domineering priest. While the Jews produce very few violent criminals and a large proportion of thieves, fakers and swindlers, they are more vindictive than gentle, and what they fear most is the policeman and the judge. (p. 470)

"The Jew, following his prodigious aptitudes for speculation and crookery, treats all political affairs as speculations or scams" (p. 476). However, "while *Europaeus* is unquestionably a zoological race, the Jews instead constitute an ethnographic race"; that is to say, there is no "Jewish race," this is a "fake race," which is only defined by its "psychological unity." This is a contradiction that does not halt this positivist "monist": "while this zoological incoherence is reflected in the psychology of the Jews, this very instability is a characteristic of their psychology" (p. 465). This exemplifies the way that anti-Semitism conveniently dispenses with any "scientific" demonstration if it happens to have shaky foundations, just as it did at the end of the nineteenth century.

Yet, despite these racial perils, Vacher de Lapouge, contrary to Gobineau, remains optimistic. The strength of the "Aryan race" is bound to prevail in the long run, provided that a systematic "selectionism" is applied. He cites the example of recent laws passed in several states of the United States which forbade marriage, and even any common law union, for epileptics, "imbeciles," the simple-minded, the mentally ill, tuberculosis sufferers, and alcoholics, and which punished sexual crimes by castration (the author has some reservations regarding this last point, as he makes a distinction between "erotic madness" and rape; the latter "if it did not involve violence" was tolerated and even legal in "ancient societies" and among "non-Christian civilized peoples," p. 505). Therefore, he was able

THE INVENTION OF "SCIENTIFIC RACISM" 93

to triumphantly announce the age of the "coming barbarians," "convinced that in the next century, millions will be massacred for the sake of one or two extra degrees in the cephalic index."[93]

The first symptoms of political racism

In the name of the Indo-European epic, Vacher de Lapouge, "the only great Frenchman" in the words of Willhelm II, placed an already out-of-date physical anthropology at the service of a new political ideology, that of an anti-democratic, racist, extreme right. Following the "normal," if not "enlightened," racism of most of the nineteenth century, which served as a calm justification for colonial conquests, the end of the century witnessed the establishment of a racist political program that was haunted by a dread of decadence and racial interbreeding. Within this climate of hatred of "the other," anti-Semitism grew in strength and was expressed in ways that became increasingly hateful. While Gobineau's work could still pass as the post-Romantic ravings of an isolated pathology, which, in addition, predates any "scientific" racial justification, those who now invoked it would go on to have a very real impact on society.

We encounter ideologists like Otto Ammon, who introduced the theories of racist statistician Francis Galton to Germany, and who, like Vaucher de Lapouge, distinguished between long heads (Bismarck and Moltke) and round heads (socialists and Catholics) within the population and preached racial selection; Houston Chamberlain, Wagner's son-in-law and resident of Bayreuth, author of the *Fondements du xixe siècle*[94]; and Ludwig Schemann, translator and biographer of Gobineau, to whom he dedicated a museum in annexed Strasbourg. In 1894, Schemann also founded a Gobineau Society in the Kaiser's summer residence; its members included Vacher de Lapouge, Paul Bourget, and Albert Sorel. The same Schemann, who considered the Hindus and the Mongols as "semi-animals" and the Africans as a "sub-race," denounced the detrimental impact of Rome and the Jews on the German people; he had the same opinion of Marxism, which he saw as an instrument of the Jews.[95] Furthermore, while Gobineau's "racial pessimism" foresaw the imminent annihilation of the "Aryan race," these new ideologues were determined to resist decline through the application of vigorous measures. While they had, for a time, a degree of influence on the Kaiser— thanks to the support of Count von Eulenburg-Hertefeld—they also embraced the eugenist positions of the "Social Darwinist" movement, which itself was

---

[93] *Revue d'anthropologie*, May 1887, p. 15.
[94] Field, 1981.
[95] Römer, 1985, pp. 32–33; Young, 1968; Weindling, 1989 [1998], pp. 111–113.

94   FIRST MOVEMENT (1814–1903)

promoted by the Monist League. The latter was founded in 1906 by Haeckel, who introduced Darwinism to Germany. And, as we have seen,[96] it attracted leading "Germanomaniacs" such as Ludwig Wilser and Ludwig Woltmann. Schemann and Chamberlain would have a direct influence on National-Socialist ideologues like Alfred Rosenberg and Adolf Hitler.

This political racism, which would mar the entire history of the twentieth century, emerged at the very time when the "scientific" definition of "race" was falling apart under the scrutiny of scientists. There would no longer be "scientific" legitimacy to affirm the superiority of Europeans and, more particularly, that of northwestern Europeans. But colonialism had to maintain a minimum of ideological justification for its domination. In 1908, in the German colony of South West Africa, interracial marriages were forbidden and, where necessary, annulled, and the Germans involved in such unions were ostracized. In the United States, where apartheid was generalized in schools and in all public and private areas, it was hoped, over and above the medical laws that had just been passed, to greatly restrict immigration from Central and Eastern Europe. The development of an alternative "scientific" definition of inequality was now a matter of urgency.

The mismeasure of man

Coincidentally, since the 1860s, a new "science" had developed in parallel: racial psychology, which would go on to form the basis of eugenics. We can even pinpoint its emergence to an article published in 1865, by Sir Francis Galton. Galton was a cousin of Charles Darwin and was eager to apply the latter's discoveries to the management of human beings with a view to improving the species; he developed his ideas further in his 1869 book, *Hereditary Genius*.[97] Galton's theses were simple and explicit: the "human races" are unequal, each has its own characteristics, and well-born individuals are more intelligent than others. In 1883, he invented the term "eugenics" in his *Inquiries into Human Faculty and Its Development*. The aim is to ensure the improvement of the "superior races" and not that of humanity in general, because "There exists a sentiment, for the most part quite unreasonable, against the gradual extinction of an inferior race."[98] As early as 1907 a "eugenics laboratory" was created under the direction of Galton's disciple Karl Pearson, and the following year saw the founding of the Eugenics

[96]   See Chapter 3, p. 28.
[97]   Galton, 1865, 1869, 1883. On Galton and eugenics, see Billig, 1981; Searle, 1976.
[98]   Galton, 1907, p. 200.

Education Society, which brought together all of the leading biologists and geneticists of the day.

In 1911, Karl Pearson was appointed to the new Chair of Eugenics at University College London, where he developed the statistical methods that have now become standards (chi-square, correlation coefficients, standard deviations, etc.); indeed, we often forget the motivations that lay behind these methods and their role in what is termed "biometrics." Pearson's beliefs were radical in terms of racism and heredity. He believed that the Africans belonged to "the lower races of men" and that "they have not yet produced a civilization in the least comparable with the Aryan"; hence "Educate and nurture them as you will, I do not believe that you will succeed in modifying the stock."[99] His convictions were so strong that they did not require any biometric demonstration. His rejection of racial mixing allowed him to justify the genocide of Native Americans and to recommend the expulsion of Africans from White South Africa, thus opening the way for apartheid and, especially, the genocides of the twentieth century. With students like Cyril Burt, Raymond Cattell, Sir Ronald Fisher, and Charles Spearman, the "London School" would soon come to occupy a dominant intellectual and scientific position in the field of psychology throughout the first three decades of the twentieth century.

This school lost no time in adopting the Intellectual Quotient (IQ) test, which was invented in 1912 by the German psychologist Wilhelm Stern who himself built upon the works of Alfred Binet in France; Binet had earlier attempted, in vain, to measure intelligence through craniometry. Originally designed to detect children with learning difficulties, this new tool, whose development coincided with the rediscovery of Mendel's laws of heredity and the emergence of genetics, would contribute to the rise of eugenics, this new ideological movement with scientific pretensions, whose collision with the story of Indo-European origins would forever mark the history of Europe.

[99] Pearson, 1905, p. 21.

III

SECOND MOVEMENT
(1903–1945)

Crimes and errors

The history of the twentieth century is divided into two parts, a before-Auschwitz and an after-Auschwitz. The same can be said of the history of the Indo-European concept. On the one hand, Auschwitz is one of the culminations of the "Aryan" racial logic that emerged during the nineteenth century, reinforced by twentieth-century eugenic doctrines and tragically brought to the fore through the ideology of hate that was born in a Germany ruined by defeat and humiliated by the Treaty of Versailles. Admittedly, most linguists and archeologists continued their research on the Indo-Europeans while keeping their distance from Nazism or actually opposing it. Many, however, held firmly to the image of an Indo-European *Urvolk* that was war-like and conquering. Despite the technical quality and scholarship of much of the work produced, this model or this ideology continued to predominate almost without exception, although there were some attempts to propose more elaborate systems. After Auschwitz, the wayward "Aryan" ideology and any serious attempts at historical synthesis were silenced or forced underground for almost the entire third quarter of the twentieth century, before emerging once again with renewed vigor.

5

From comparative grammar to linguistics

A language of leaders?

In order to pursue its methodological development, linguistics underwent profound changes over the course of the three generations that followed that of the German Neogrammarians. The centers of linguistic innovation moved from Germany to its periphery: Geneva, Paris, Prague, and Copenhagen. Rather than simply observing the evolution of languages, focus was shifted to the description of their functioning at a given moment in time: that is, favoring synchrony over diachrony. But, above all else, comparative grammar ceased to be the very object of linguistics, if not linguistics itself, to become just one of its fields of endeavor. A "general" linguistics was born. These three generations are those of Ferdinand de Saussure, founder of structural linguistics and "structuralism"; followed by that of Antoine Meillet, who in a monumental work attempted to integrate comparative grammar, structural linguistics, and the sociology of language and who reigned over French linguistics until his death in 1936; the last generation was that of the Prague Linguistic Circle, which included Nikolai Sergeyevich Troubetzkoy, and Roman Jakobson, thanks to whom structuralism was borrowed from linguistics and gradually applied to all human sciences.

The ambiguities of Ferdinand de Saussure

It is usually considered that a new form of linguistics, later known as "structural linguistics," came into being through the work of Geneva-born linguist Ferdinand de Saussure who developed it in his *Cours de linguistique générale* (Course in General Linguistics), which he taught in Geneva between 1906 and 1911; this series of lectures was published after de Saussure's death in 1916 by his students based on their lecture notes.[1] On the one hand, linguistics now concerned itself with language in general and was not just restricted to Indo-European languages; on the other hand, language was no longer treated as a collection of independent elements which were seen to evolve in an almost biological manner, but rather

---

[1] Saussure, 1972. On Saussure, see Koerner, 1973; Leroy, 1963. All quotes are from Baskin's 1959 translation.

100   SECOND MOVEMENT (1903–1945)

was considered as a system of differences and oppositions which only makes sense per se at any moment in time. This is the origin of the standard distinction made between the "synchronic" study of a language (i.e., at a given moment in time) and its "diachronic" counterpart (i.e., its evolution over time). Saussure also makes a distinction between "speech," which is how a language is practiced in reality by a speaker, and "language" itself.

Of course this form of linguistics did not simply appear out of nowhere. The way was prepared by growing research on phonetic "laws" and by more general considerations by contemporary linguists such as the Pole Baudouin de Courtenay and the American William Dwight Whitney. But it also owes its development to the generalization of a new machine-based representation. The machine, which up to then had been marginal, permeated all aspects of Western life in the nineteenth century, as both the cause and product of the Industrial Revolution. It provided the scholar with an array of new metaphors and new ways of questioning. The machine is ageless; it is born out of nothing and only exists through the interactions of its various components. It either works or it does not. In place of the idea of isolated elements, each with an individual history, a new notion of the "whole" emerges, a notion which emphasizes synchronicity. This new paradigm emerged within the so-called exact sciences at the end of the nineteenth century with the development of set theory; it then permeated the science of language, which up until then had been marked by biological metaphors, before spreading progressively to all other human sciences.

In theory, structural thought provided the study of Indo-European languages with a novel and powerful tool. It allowed scholars to move beyond a simple genealogical/biological model and rethink the emergence and evolution of languages in an alternative way. Saussure incorporated the social aspect of language and found that the evolution of language was the result, "like any other practice," of "two forces [that] are always working simultaneously and in opposing directions: individualism or provincialism [*esprit de clocher*] on the one hand and intercourse—communication among men—on the other."[2] Language is not an isolated entity but is part of material culture: "This feeling [of divergence between languages] makes primitive people look upon language as a habit or custom, like dress or weapons. The term idiom aptly designates language as reflecting the traits peculiar to a community (Greek *idioma* had already acquired the meaning 'special custom')."[3] It is equally conceivable that languages merge to create a "real, organic mixture or interpenetration of two idioms that results in a change in the system (cf. English after the Norman Conquest)."[4] However, over

[2] Saussure, 1972, p. 281.
[3] Ibid., p. 261.
[4] Ibid., p. 265.

COMPARATIVE GRAMMAR TO LINGUISTICS 101

the following decades, the structuralist method would be applied to the internal descriptions of individual Indo-European languages and even to comparisons between languages, but it had no impact whatsoever on considerations regarding the general relationships between Indo-European languages. The Russian structuralist Nikolai Troubetzkoy was virtually alone among scholars when he took a step in this direction just before his death in 1938.

Like Schliemann, who was attracted to archaeology as a boy after hearing tales of Homer's *Iliad*, Saussure came to linguistics through long childhood conversations with Adolphe Pictet, the first "inventor" of the Aryan homeland and creator of linguistic paleontology[5] who also happened to be a friend of Saussure's grand aunt, Albertine-Adrienne.[6] The Saussure family belonged to the wealthy and cultured Protestant bourgeoisie of Geneva (Ferdinand's great-grandfather, Horace-Bénédict de Saussure, was a philosopher and naturalist who launched a competition for the first ascent of Mont Blanc; in 1787, he accompanied the victors on a subsequent ascent of the mountain). One of Saussure's first works, produced at the age of twenty-one, was a review of the posthumous second edition of Pictet's *Origines indo-européennes*, which appeared in 1878 in the *Journal de Genève*. Saussure's description reveals his emotionally charged fascination with Pictet: "He had an insatiable curiosity, a love for new and distant explorations to the extreme limits of human knowledge. . . . It seems that known facts were simply a platform from which to grasp the unknown, the terms of an equation that must be worked out and, if possible, solved. . . . It was always here, at the frontier between imagination and science, that his thoughts liked to travel."[7]

Saussure studied the comparative grammar of Indo-European languages at Leipzig, then the capital of the discipline. In 1878, he published his famous *Mémoire sur le système primitif des voyelles indo-européennes* (Dissertation on the Primitive System of Indo-European Vowels), which does not depart from a neogrammarian perspective, based on laws, but also considers Indo-European phonetics as a system. The application of a rigorous method of comparison allowed him to suggest that primitive Indo-European languages exhibited particular phenomena—namely, laryngeals—whose existence would later be confirmed by the deciphering of the Hittite language.[8] Most of his research and lecturing career, which began in Paris in 1881 under Michel Bréal and then continued in Geneva, was devoted to the teaching of Indo-European comparatism, particularly in the fields of Germanic, Greek, Latin, and Lithuanian. As we have seen, the famous *Cours de linguistique générale* was a reconstructed work published after

[5] See Chapter 3, pp. 34–35.
[6] De Mauro, 1972, pp. 321–323.
[7] *Journal de Genève* from April 17, 19, and 25. See Olender, 2008, pp. 99–101.
[8] See Chapter 17, p. 382.

102 SECOND MOVEMENT (1903–1945)

his death. While Saussure expresses certain reserves in his lectures regarding linguistic paleontology,[9] his position remains ambiguous and there is no indication that he conceived the relationships between Indo-European languages in any terms other than that of the classic family tree. The second last paragraph of the *Cours* (the last paragraph is probably apocryphal)[10] reveals something of this testamentary ambiguity and his confused feelings toward it: "We now know that Schleicher was wrong in looking upon language as an organic thing with its own law of evolution, but we continue, without suspecting it, to try to make language organic in another sense by assuming that the 'genius' of a race or ethnic group tends constantly to lead language along certain fixed routes."[11]

Antoine Meillet, chief and master

Through his teaching at Paris, Saussure had a determining influence on the next generation of French linguists (the Société de linguistique de Paris was founded in 1866), but it is important to note that this influence was limited to the technical improvement of the comparative method. This was central to the career of Antoine Meillet, Saussure's most prominent French student, who would dominate Indo-European comparative grammar and indeed a major part of the field of linguistics not only in France but also in Europe up until his death in 1936.[12] In the face of a German linguistic tradition in decline, having reached the limits of neogrammarian "phonetic laws" and lacking a leading figure, Paris became the center of scientific influence, largely through the efforts of Meillet. Lecturer at the École pratique des hautes études (appointed in 1902) and at the Collège de France (appointed in 1906), and General Secretary of the Société de linguistique de Paris (where he succeeded Saussure, who in turn had succeeded Bréal), his institutional and intellectual influence on the field of linguistics was comparable to that wielded by Broca in the field of anthropology fifty years earlier.

These dynamic institutions were, however, still quite marginal relative to the official University, whose philological conservatism remained impervious to linguistics and even to comparatism. Meillet published hundreds of literature reviews for the Society's *Bulletin* in an irrevocably incisive style, which, as in the bulk of his work, left no place for doubt.

---

[9] Saussure, 1972, pp. 306–310.
[10] Ibid., pp. 476–477.
[11] Ibid., p. 317.
[12] Two conferences were dedicated to Meillet on the fiftieth anniversary of his death, at Pisa (Quattordio Moreschini, 1987) and at Nanterre (Auroux, 1988), as well as a third at Noirlac in 2000 (Bergounioux and Lamberterie, 2006).

COMPARATIVE GRAMMAR TO LINGUISTICS   103

Over the course of his career he would publish twenty-four works, among them reference works on Latin, Greek, Germanic languages, Slavic, Armenian, Serbo-Croat, and Indo-Iranian languages; he also directed a synthesis of the world's languages. His students, in turn, went on to occupy prominent positions in the areas of general and comparative linguistics in the middle decades of the century; Émile Benveniste, Marcel Cohen, Lucien Tesnière, Pierre Chantraine, Michel Lejeune, and André Martinet dominated the scene in France while Jerzy Kuryłowicz came to prominence in Poland. At the same time, he discouraged the young Georges Dumézil from following a career in linguistics, confining him instead to the study of comparative mythology far from Paris.[13]

Antoine Meillet never spent time searching for the original Homeland of the Indo-Europeans. He never even claimed to be able to reconstruct the original language. The comparative grammar method did not provide a reconstruction of Indo-European as it might once have been spoken: "It is a defined system of correspondences between historically attested languages"[14] and "The aim of the comparative grammar of a group of languages is the study of correspondences that these languages display between one another."[15] Indo-European is thus an abstraction, a rigorous logical construction which, through phonetic and morphological correspondences, links together a certain number of languages. This is of course a "structural" vision in the widest sense. But, for Meillet, language is a "social fact," "language only exists by virtue of *society*." This is one of the lessons that Meillet took directly from Saussure. In fact, Meillet maintained close scientific relations with the entire recently established French school of sociology and in particular with Durkheim, Mauss, and Lévy-Bruhl; Meillet took charge of the linguistic section of their journal, *L'Année sociologique*.

A language of chiefs

So how did Meillet envisage primitive Indo-European society? In his *Introduction à l'étude comparative des langues indo-européennes* he writes,

> Nothing allows us to speak of an "Indo-European race," but there must have been an "Indo-European nation" although we know not where or exactly when. . . . The population for whom Indo-European was the idiom, while they were conscious of their common origins, while they shared common morals

---

[13] See, for example, Dumézil, 1987, p. 59.
[14] Meillet, 1937, p. 47. The italics are Meillet's own and are a device that he rarely uses.
[15] Ibid., p. 13.

104   SECOND MOVEMENT (1903–1945)

and institutions, and while they were capable of coming together and acting as one when the occasion arose, did not form a single political group, did not recognize a single chief for any length of time, and did not display any permanent political unity. The best idea of the political situation in the ancient Indo-European world can be gained from the Greek City states and not from the unity of the Achaemenid Empire. . . . Indo-European speaking populations were led by an aristocracy that had a well-developed political savvy, since it was capable of imposing its language and its social organization, which was both firm and supple, over most of Europe and a large part of Asia, but it only occasionally obeyed the will of a single leader.[16]

Indo-European is thus a "language of leaders and organizers imposed through the prestige of an aristocracy. Clearly very little remains of the informal part of the language."[17]

The existence of a dominant warrior aristocracy is central to Meillet's thinking, and is the subject of numerous passages.

The preoccupation of every Hellenic, Nordic and other leader was to be independent; and it so happens that the Indo-European sentence is made up of words that, because of their flexion, are sufficient in themselves and indicate their own role within the sentence.[18]

Elsewhere,

Over the entire Indo-European range we observe the same pattern: extension to a new domain of the rigorously defined language of a dominant group whose members protect the purity of their language as a title of nobility and who maintain it jealously. The result is that the expansion of Indo-European languages, remarkable in itself, in reality involved the adoption of the same language, Indo-European, by increasingly numerous populations who occupied an increasingly large area.[19]

Likewise,

The wide-spread extension of Indo-European languages is due to the fact that, spoken by a nation with a particular sense of organization and domination,

---

[16] Ibid., pp. 418–419.
[17] Ibid., p. 47.
[18] Meillet, 1928a, p. 164.
[19] Meillet, 1938, p. 48.

they gradually replaced a large number of other languages, just as occurred with Latin in Italy.[20]

And,

> Serving as an organ for aristocrats who were, above all else, concerned to maintain their position as independent leaders, the Indo-European language functioned with words that, themselves, had as much autonomy as possible.... "Vulgar Latin" perpetuates the spoken language of the Indo-European aristocracy; but it developed within a population that was a mixture of people of all origins; these people no longer had anything in common with the leaders, major and minor, of the groups who had spread the ancient Indo-European languages.[21]

But what were these supreme certitudes, which allow us to pass from formal phonetic correspondences to aristocratic warriors, actually based on? The truth is that they are based on virtually nothing. The state of knowledge of the original People and its institutions is that which Schrader presented decades earlier; Schrader's approach was based on linguistic paleontology, which Saussure did not really believe in and which Meillet never mentions. Only the notion of an absence of original political unity could be "justified" linguistically: since the reconstruction never leads to unique forms, it must be assumed that, even at the very beginning, "dialects" already existed in the original Homeland. Meillet identifies these dialects with the origin of the principal Indo-European language groups (Indo-Iranian, Celtic, Germanic, etc.). This is negative evidence. The model of the Greek cities does not really work since, as Meillet (true to the fashionable primitivism of the time) admits "the populations who spoke Indo-European must have had a level of civilization equivalent to the African negroes or the North American Indians."[22] This no doubt explains why Indo-European cities had never been discovered. But, in any case, Meillet had a foolproof argument: "The extension of the language stems from the extension of a type of organization and conceptions, and not of a type of material civilization. The Indo-European leaders who spread this family of languages generally adopted the advantages offered to them by the civilization of those whom they conquered."[23] In other words, there will be no archeological trace of the Indo-European conquests!

---

[20] Ibid., p. 61.
[21] Meillet, 1928b, pp. 272–273.
[22] Meillet, 1937, p. 49.
[23] Meillet, 1938, p. 88.

106   SECOND MOVEMENT (1903–1945)

Meillet's vision is, therefore, completely fanciful, even though it is a direct continuation of nineteenth-century theories. More precisely, it is based only on a chain of assumptions, which themselves are founded on the prevailing wisdom of the time: if there was a linguistic diffusion, then it was because a military conquest took place, and if there was a military conquest, it was because there were leaders; and since the conquests were successful, then it was because these leaders had "great political savvy"; and since there is no material evidence for these conquests, then the leaders must have been content to introduce their language and organization into pre-established civilizations. We should remember that, with Schrader, war was postulated rather than proved (in fact, the shared vocabulary is succinct on this point) and that the notion of "Indo-European nomadism" was founded on nothing more than the rarity of terms relating to agriculture and on the existence of the wheel.

Do you speak a "language of civilization"?

Several other aspects of his thinking complete the world view of the great linguist Meillet, in this dual—almost schizophrenic—language, between the affirmation of an Indo-Europeanity based on purely abstract logical correspondences and an invasionist, war-like vision. In line with his colleagues at the Année sociologique and the prevailing ethnological thinking of the time, influenced by the works of Fraser, Meillet's Indo-Europeans are "primitives"; hence, following in the footsteps of Schrader, he envisages the original religion as lacking identified deities, adoring only "social and natural forces[24]"—an idea that George Dumézil would devote a life's work to refuting. But, as we have seen, the Indo-Europeans also formed a "nation"; after the original separation, more nations would emerge, such as the "Indo-Iranian Nation" and the "Germanic Nation" for instance.

The year 1918 witnessed the end of the Great War, a war that "appears to be the continuation of the long struggle which led to the language of the Indo-European Nation being imposed on a large part of the globe"; the very same year saw the publication of Meillet's *Les Langues dans l'Europe nouvelle* (Languages in the New Europe), in which he paints a linguistic portrait of Europe which is completed in the 1928 edition by the addition of statistical data and a map.[25] Above and beyond being simply descriptive, Meillet's project is political. As a humanist and progressive European intellectual, he is sensitive to the rights of peoples to self-determination and welcomes the end of the great empires. However, he is also worried about the concomitant emergence of new national

[24] Meillet, 1921, pp. 323–334.
[25] Meillet, 1928c. On Meillet's positions, see Caussat, 1988; Perrot, 1988.

languages: "In Europe, the increasing number of new languages of civilization creates an ever-growing unease."[26]

For one thing, this trend hinders communication; Meillet, who was familiar with many foreign languages but who did not speak any, learned that, in the United States, scientists only used English. Furthermore, not all languages deserve the same treatment. For instance, Irish is "a language of peasants" whose status as an official language "will imprison [the Irish people] in a linguistic dungeon"[27]; Basque "is nothing more than a curious survival"; Breton is a "tool that is so crude, of so little use, that no sensible Breton would dream of using it out of preference"; "Lithuanian . . . can hardly be counted as a language of civilization"; the Finno-Ugric languages of Russia are "simple linguistic curiosities." To give the speakers of these languages political autonomy would lead to a situation where they are left behind "in a small local culture, with no view to the outside, no horizons, no future." Even Hungarian "is not an ancient language of civilization. . . . Its literature is not renowned . . .; its structure is complicated and is difficult to learn."[28] As regards the Slavic peoples of Central and Eastern Europe, it would be in their interest to unite within a common state that would allow them to "restore" the original unity of the Slavic language.

For Meillet, an identity must exist between a "language," a "civilization," and a "nation," but only nations that deserve it possess "languages of civilization." The only true civilization is that of the original "Indo-European nation," at least in its Greco-Roman variation: "All [the languages of Europe] were formed under the influence of the same civilization; behind all of them lie the same Greek and Latin models that were imitated everywhere. . . . Despite apparent diversity, European civilization basically has but one language of culture at its root. . . . For almost three thousand years, the whole essence of the civilization was expressed by Indo-European languages."[29] This is why the project of a single artificial language (Esperanto, Ido), constructed on the basis of Indo-European languages, "has the merit of expressing the unity of modern civilization, whose foundations are Greco-Italian. The recently proposed 'Occidental' language demonstrates this unity even better."[30]

All of these converging assertions are not the naïve claims of a scholar ensconced in his ivory tower. They should be taken at face value, but reversed: this is because, for Meillet, there is an inherent superiority in Western civilization and there was inevitably an original national unity. This is the only possible explanation for this prodigious destiny, a primordial unity within which the dream

[26] Ibid., p. 246.
[27] Ibid., p. xi.
[28] Ibid.; citations in Perrot, 1988, and Caussat, 1988.
[29] Meillet, 1929, cited in Caussat, 1988, p. 203.
[30] Meillet, 1928c, p. 279.

108   SECOND MOVEMENT (1903–1945)

of a single recreated language would allow a renewed communion. Such was the power of this ideological vision whose origins lay in the past and which was no doubt shared at the time by many enlightened European intellectuals. This vision found itself superimposed on a phenomenon that was totally unrelated: the existence of phonetic correspondences between a certain number of ancient languages of Eurasia. Although rarely committed to paper, and then only fleetingly in certain passages, this ideological matrix nonetheless continued to inform all Indo-European research in the interwar years; it is this that will serve as the ultimate and obvious interpretation for the works of two of Meillet's most prominent students: the young linguist Émile Benveniste, his official heir, and the young mythologist Georges Dumézil, the unloved pupil.

An instinct for conquest and a love of wide open spaces

Meillet's favorite pupil, Émile Benveniste, who would succeed him at the Collège de France, was born into the Jewish community in Syria. As we see in this cataclysmic description from 1939,[31] in which he expresses his own belief in a steppic homeland, Benveniste takes up the warrior model propounded by his master.

> In their diversity, these invasions . . . never involved vast hordes of warriors. Instead it was a case of small courageous groups, who were highly organized, imposing their order on the ruins of existing structures. . . . They would all preserve, over the course of their particular destiny, the distinctive traits of their original community: . . . an instinct for conquest and a taste for open spaces; a sense of authority and an attachment to worldly goods. In the beginning they appear to be absorbed into the mass of peoples, often more civilized, whom they subjugated. A long silence follows their conquest. But soon, out of the new order that they created, surged a culture initially charged with local elements but which went on to develop in forms that were increasingly novel and audacious. An inventive power marks these creations, to which the language of the masters lent the most complete expression.

The full text deserves a thorough semantic analysis, which would lay bare all of the assumptions contained therein. But the date of publication and the text's ideological closeness to representations of Aryans in pre-Nazi and Nazi Germany are quite chilling. Three years earlier Meillet had contributed, in complete naïvety, to a volume in honor of the elderly German linguist Hermann Hirt, a volume that

---

[31]   Benveniste, 1939; see Chapter 1, pp. 8–9.

COMPARATIVE GRAMMAR TO LINGUISTICS 109

was coordinated by Nazi ideologist Helmut Arntz.[32] In any case, this 1939 article by Benveniste attests to the power of collective representations among Indo-Europeanists at the time, representations that lack any physical foundation—as might be expected, since they were themselves used, in a circular logic, to justify the absence of visible archeological traces for the supposed invasions.

Two years later, in October 1941, that other famous pupil of Meillet, the mythologist Georges Dumézil, used almost identical terms in the opening paragraph of an article in *La Nouvelle Revue Française*; the volume, coordinated by Pierre Drieu La Rochelle,[33] was devoted to methods for "The comparative study of Indo-European religions." Dumézil's text begins,

> Over the course of the 3rd and 2nd millennia before Christ, the most important event in the recent temporal history of mankind occurred: successive waves of conquering troops, who spoke more or less the same language, spread out in all directions from a single region which seems to have been situated somewhere between the Hungarian Plain and the Baltic. What was happening? The disintegration of prehistoric empires? Food supply or climatic difficulties? Innate imperialism, a confused call of destiny, the blossoming into maturity of a privileged human group? We will never know. But the fact remains; over the course of a few centuries, these fierce horsemen rode out centrifugally to overrun all of Northern, Western, Southern and South-Eastern Europe; the former inhabitants disappeared, were assimilated or survived in isolated pockets which slowly melted away.[34]

Then, after three pages that retrace four millennia of roaming by these "Indo-Europeans" ("a purely symbolic compound name, that appeals more to the spirit than to the imagination"), the emergence of historic civilizations, and European colonization of the world, he concludes as follows:

> Europe "speaks Indo-European" and, through its immigrants, imposed its Indo-European language on everyone of significance on three other continents and on half of the fourth. Today, beyond fratricidal wars that may constitute the difficult birth of a stable order, there is only one corner of the earth where a herald of this triumph might emerge. But in all likelihood he will arrive too late.[35]

[32] Arntz, 1936. See Chapter 7, p. 161.
[33] See Chapter 16, pp. 362–363.
[34] Dumézil, 1941a, p. 385; my thanks to Christophe Vielle for bringing this passage to my attention.
[35] Ibid., p. 387.

110   SECOND MOVEMENT (1903–1945)

This article was reused as the preface to Dumézil's book *Jupiter, Mars, Quirinus,* which was also published in 1941. However, a few extra sentences were added to the preface including,

> Of course the question has other aspects. First of all, an ethnic aspect, which has also been studied for a century by the various schools of anthropology using their own methods. It is worth recalling in broad terms the results of this research: the Indo-Europeans belonged to the white race and included representatives of the three principal types of mankind that subsequently settled in Europe, with a striking predominance of the Nordic type.[36]

We will return at a later stage to the ideological assumptions of Georges Dumézil and what lay behind this "innate imperialism," "confused call of destiny," and these "fratricidal wars" that, in the Europe of 1941, "may constitute the difficult birth of a stable order."[37] Respectively progressive republican, former pupil of a rabbinical school, and active ex-sympathizer of Action Française, Meillet, Benveniste, and Dumézil shared a common vision of war-like, centrifugal, Indo-Europeans which underpins all of their work, even though it did not necessarily affect the structuring of their data. Suffice it to say, without anticipating further debate, that in this matter it is important to be able to clearly distinguish between at least three aspects which may operate independently of one another: the personal political opinions of the researcher, the logical models that structure his discoveries, and the ideological representations that underpin his final interpretations.

We also observe how much the original People have changed. They are no longer the "privileged race" described by Pictet, "marked by a happy nature, where energy was tempered by gentleness, a lively imagination and strong reason, an active intelligence and a spirit open to the impressions of beauty."[38] Since the end of the nineteenth century, ethnography, prompted by the work of Schrader, had "primitivized" the Aryans, but, in addition, the spirit of the time was no longer marked by the mercantile optimism of the nascent Industrial Revolution. The world had gone through several economic crises and a world war and had emerged dislocated. A new war was now in progress: violence and evil were an unavoidable part of history, and new political systems were founding their philosophy on this fact. Intellectuals had to take this truth on board and even theorize it. Once again we had become the mirror image of the People at our roots.

---

[36] Dumézil, 1941b, pp. 12–13.
[37] See Chapter 16, pp. 357–360.
[38] See Chapter 3, pp. 34–35.

COMPARATIVE GRAMMAR TO LINGUISTICS   111

Linguistic sentiment?

Within its own logic, the cultural permanence postulated by Meillet required three conditions: continuity of linguistic transmission, homogeneity of the language, and perhaps also a certain form of "heredity." Meillet raised the last issue in the context of phonetic evolutions in certain languages. In Gaul, for example, Latin transformed into French following certain phonetic characteristics belonging to Celtic languages even though Gaulish was no longer in use at the time: "Certain acquired habits could have been transmitted by heredity. This is not the heredity of acquired anatomical characteristics, but rather something completely different, namely the heredity of acquired habits. This heredity is comparable to that observed in certain breeds of dog that are used for specific tasks."[39] Meillet did not develop this "daring" canine hypothesis any further. However, his student Marcel Cohen, one of the founders of the French Communist Party, went further in a book published in 1956, which incidentally opens with a linguistic quote from Joseph Stalin. According to Cohen, Meillet's hypothesis prefigured Lysenko, the agronomist who theorized on the heredity of acquired characteristics in the name of "proletarian biology" (and who was ultimately responsible for the collapse of Soviet agriculture). This notion of heredity could therefore provide a possible explanation for the astonishing continuation of "European civilization" over millennia, an explanation that was more subtle than Chavet's "cerebral organizations,"[40] which were different in Aryans and Semites.[41] This discussion, at the frontier between the psychological and the physiological, was brewing within the social sciences in the 1930s and even permeates Freud's *Moses and Monotheism*. Somewhat later, writing on the subject of Indo-European mythological permanencies, Dumézil refers to "hereditary furrows,"[42] later denying that this was an "organic" interpretation.

The second condition is the homogeneity of language. When speaking of languages, Meillet's implicit model was that of the nineteenth- and twentieth-century nation state, with its uniform official language. He recognizes that languages have dialects and patois but he sees them as a "relatively vague notion."[43] He had quite heated exchanges regarding this matter with Jules Gilliéron, founder of French dialectology. As we shall see, the dialectal reality may render the image of languages much more complex. Moreover, Meillet uses the term "dialect" in a very restrictive way, identifying the "dialects" of original Indo-European as

---

[39] Meillet, 1938, p. 111.
[40] See Chapter 4, p. 76.
[41] Chavée, 1862b.
[42] Dumézil, 1968, p. 570; see also Dumézil, 1987, p. 140; Charachidzé, 1987, p. 13. Dumézil puts the word *sillons* (furrows) in quotation marks.
[43] Meillet, 1928c, p. 16; see Chapter 19, pp. 432–433.

112   SECOND MOVEMENT (1903–1945)

reconstructed "proto-languages" which were supposed to be the sources of the principal Indo-European language families (Proto-Slavic, Proto-Germanic, Proto-Indo-Aryan, etc.).

The last condition required for permanence is linguistic continuity. Language evolves according to "trends" and, so long as there is no brutal replacement of one language by another, speakers "always have the intention of remaining faithful to their traditional language"[44]: this is what Meillet calls "linguistic sentiment." This notion, which is inherently impalpable, particularly in the case of lost languages, explains why there are no "mixed languages" formed through the mixing of two different contemporary languages.

Meillet versus Schuchardt

We have seen how, in the 1880s, German linguist Hugo Schuchardt was the first to describe and theorize mixed languages, in particular pidgins and creoles, the study of which he founded.[45] However, for Broca and those who held fast to the theory of the permanence of the Indo-European language, such a possibility was naturally scandalous since it implies the possibility of interbreeding which, together with transformism, was undermining the very idea of stable "races." If languages could mix "transversely" to form others, the Darwino-Schleicherian genealogical tree of languages would collapse, along with the idea of "nations." Meillet, therefore, spoke out vehemently against the work of Schuchardt. Long before Meillet, the Indo-Europeanist Max Müller, who was also aware of what was at stake, had stated: "*es gibt keine Mischsprache*" ("There are no mixed languages").[46] But, in the meantime, Schuchardt had gathered a significant amount of linguistic data. Through the medium of articles, the heated debate between Schuchardt and Meillet, which began in 1913, continued until the death of the former in 1927,[47] and with a vehemence that the First World War only fueled further since Schuchardt was deeply affected by his country's defeat.

Meillet used particularly authoritative arguments: "Mixed languages are often talked about. The term is inappropriate because it suggests the idea that the situations of the two languages concerned, if not equal, are at least comparable."[48] And "The terms 'crossing of languages' or 'mixed languages' are often used for such cases; but these are simply metaphors; what is essential is the fact, remarkable from a mental point of view, that individuals who have two manners

[44] Meillet, 1938, p. 107.
[45] See Chapter 2, pp. 30–31.
[46] Müller, F. M., 1872, vol. 1, p. 86.
[47] Meillet, 1921, pp. 76–101, 102–109; Schuchardt, 1922, pp. 167–182; Baggioni, 1988.
[48] Meillet, 1938, pp. 107–108.

COMPARATIVE GRAMMAR TO LINGUISTICS   113

of expressing themselves at their disposal, can, without significantly altering one of the languages, add to its system certain structures borrowed from the other"[49]; "regardless of their number and regardless of the scale of these 'borrowings', indigenous elements always persist where people have wanted to speak a given language, and were convinced that they did so. . . . What matters is not to determine the proportion of any one element, but to identify which language the people wanted to speak, and indeed believed that they spoke, and which they transmitted without interruption between the two dates under consideration."[50] As regards creole languages: "Certain linguists will be tempted to refer to mixed languages; the Creole language of Réunion and Martinique is imperfect French, but it is French nonetheless because it is simply an imitation of French that the Negroes created from the French of their masters"[51] (this was a time when the word "Negro" was more commonplace and less pejorative); "dialects that are shapeless mixtures of two different languages, such as the Slavo-Italian or Italo-Slav described by M. Schuchardt, belong to inferior populations; they rarely survive. In cases where they might survive, it is doubtful that we could use them to build a theory; the facts would be much too complicated. We would undoubtedly be faced with indeterminable relationships."[52]

In other words, the facts do not exist, and, if they did, it would be unimportant. All that matters is "linguistic sentiment," the language that the speakers believe they speak. While language is a "social fact" for Meillet, the contributor to the *Année sociologique* has a very archaic understanding of social functioning: society is a "nation," homogenous and whole, in which what people do is what they think they do! However, Meillet was a great linguist, and, in the decade between Schuchardt's death and his own, we see him begin to struggle with some of his beliefs. When Danish linguist Kristian Sanfield published his work on Balkan linguistics, which described remarkable convergences between very different languages,[53] Meillet had reservations but he nonetheless had the work published within the collection that he directed. The following year he concluded an article on Latin and Germanic bilingualism in the French Early Middle Ages with the following statement: "This is a type of investigation which will be of the utmost importance for historical linguistics, and the scope of which has already been indicated by Schuchardt."[54] Indeed, from the beginning, the attention paid to social facts gave rise to a possible contradiction in Meillet's system. In 1911, when discussing the diffusion of languages he stated, "In every case, there is a common

---

[49] Ibid., p. 102.
[50] Meillet, 1921, p. 104.
[51] Ibid., p. 85.
[52] Ibid., p. 106.
[53] Sandfeld, 1930; see Chapter 19, pp. 442–445.
[54] Meillet, 1938, p. 98.

114   SECOND MOVEMENT (1903–1945)

feature: the strength of a political organization and the value of a civilization can constitute ancillary causes: but the root cause which drives this diffusion phenomenon is the particular utility provided by a language that is spoken over a vast area."[55]

The triumph of structural linguistics

On the eve of the Second World War, French linguistics, which still enjoyed a predominant position, had failed to reap the benefits of the new structuralist paradigm and instead continued to view the relationships between the Indo-European languages in terms of Schleicher's model. Moreover, the ideology governing Indo-European origins remained unchanged and widely supported. Meillet was clearly Saussure's heir, but of Saussure the comparatist, the one who had inherited the ultimate key to deciphering the Indo-European reality from Pictet. Meillet had no contact with Saussure the structuralist who, having returned to Geneva in 1911, gradually succumbed to depression and alcoholism[56] and gave up writing but who left behind a largely oral, and soon to be posthumous, legacy through his lectures. Following their publication, Meillet even kept his distance from the *Cours* and all of the direct disciples of the "Geneva Master" whom he felt had strayed too far from concrete linguistics. The accident of individual destinies, the weight of institutions and academic traditions, and the strength of cultural representations would all intertwine to form an effective barrier to innovation.

As a result, it was at the periphery, in Prague and Copenhagen, that the structuralist paradigm gained ground at the end of the 1920s. It was institutionally sanctioned through the foundation of the Prague Linguistic Circle (and its journal *Travaux*) in 1926; through the creation, around the personage of Louis Hjelmslev, of the Copenhagen Linguistic Circle in 1931, whose periodical *Acta linguistica, revue internationale de linguistique structurale* officially gave the new discipline its name; through the first International Congress of Linguists held in the Hague in 1928, which marked the definitive breaking away of general linguistics from comparative grammar; and through the holding of the first International Phonological Meeting in 1930. The main driving force behind the new movement was the Prague Circle and, in particular, Prince Nikolaï Troubetzkoy and Roman Jakobson, who, along with the poet Mayakovsky, sprang from the Russian formalist milieu of the 1920s. These revolutionary origins, which were as much intellectual as political, lent linguistic meetings "the

[55] Meillet, 1921, p. 120.
[56] Mounin, 1972, pp. 48–49.

COMPARATIVE GRAMMAR TO LINGUISTICS   115

working style of a Bolshevik Congress"[57], where hypotheses were succinctly but forcefully presented and discussed; these origins also made the new linguists keenly aware of their pioneering role, of the strategies to be developed, and of their militant duties. The correspondence between Troubetzkoy and Jakobson, published forty years later by the latter and which, in terms of its importance, can be likened to that between Freud and Jung, is full of passion and provides insights into the development of the new methods and the intellectual atmosphere from which they emerged.[58] Incidentally, an anecdotal but violent difference of opinion arose between Troubetzkoy and Dumézil regarding the thorny issue of Caucasian linguistics.[59]

Troubetzkoy's principal and fundamental contribution to linguistics is "phonology": the sounds of a language are not entities that can be studied in a separate and disjointed manner (as was done by the neo-grammarians) but form a system of oppositions that are unique to each language. The long "i" and the short "i" have a distinctive value in English ("sheep" and "ship") which they do not have in French: in French they form a single "phoneme" but in English they form two. Troubetzkoy, who published his first scientific articles at the tender age of fifteen, was interested in ethnology, folklore, and modern history. He established the phonological systems of more than 200 languages and sought to apply the structural method to other aspects of language. At the founding congress held in the Hague in May 1928, when presenting "Proposition 16" concerning the definition of "Language Groups," he introduced, in a short nine-line paragraph, a new notion: *Sprachbund*. He used the term, which makes reference to the notion of "linkage" (*gebunden* is the past tense of the verb *binden* which means "tie" in German) to designate groups of languages that are linked together by a series of resemblances in syntax, morphology, and vocabulary but without systematic or regular phonetic correspondences; it is only if this last condition is met that we can speak of a "family of languages," which, even in this case, does not necessarily imply a common origin.[60] There is often a tendency, especially in English and French, to translate the term *Sprachbund* not as "linguistic alliance" or "linguistic union" (in German, *Bund* is often used to designate an "alliance" or "political federation") but as "linguistic area"; thus we speak of "areal linguistics." It would undoubtedly be better to translate the term as "language network" (even though the word "network" usually corresponds to the German word *Netz*). Troubetzkoy thus greatly enriched the field of interpretations of resemblances between languages, which up until then had been systematically reduced to kinship links implying a common origin. He explicitly takes the example of Balkan languages,

---

[57] Ibid., p. 108.
[58] Troubetzkoy, 1975, 2006; Viel, 1984; Gasparov, 1987; Liberman, 1980; Toman, 1987; Sériot, 1999.
[59] Eribon, 1992, pp. 313–320.
[60] Troubetzkoy, 1930, p. 18; 1939, p. 215.

116   SECOND MOVEMENT (1903–1945)

which we have already mentioned and which were also being studied at the same time by the Danish linguist Sandfeld. Jakobson would also go on to apply this notion, developing it to cover common phonetic traits that languages—even very diverse languages—within the same geographical zones tend to adopt.[61]

And what if there never had been an Original People?

In a nine-page paper presented in Russian at the Prague Linguistic Circle on December 14, 1936 (two years before the Munich Agreement), Troubetzkoy uses these "areal" links to striking effect. Here it is worth quoting two of the most significant passages.

> Certain researchers hypothesize that in the extremely distant past there was a single European language, referred to as Proto-Indo-European, from which all other attested Indo-European languages emerged. But this hypothesis is contradicted by the fact that, no matter how far back in time we go, we always encounter a large number of Indo-European languages. Of course we cannot state that the hypothesis of a single Indo-European language is utterly impossible. But it is in no way indispensable and we can get by perfectly well without it.
>
> The notion of a "language family" in no way implies a common origin for a group of languages in a single proto-language. By "language family" we mean a group of languages that, in addition to sharing common structural characteristics, also exhibit "material coincidences"; it is a group of languages in which a significant number of grammatical and lexical elements display regular phonic correspondences. However, in seeking to explain the regular character of the correspondences, it is not necessary to resort to the hypothesis of a common origin for the languages of the group, since we find the same regularity in large scale borrowings from one unrelated language to another.[62]
>
> We can just as easily envisage an inverse evolution, whereby the ancestors of the Indo-European branches were originally unalike and that it was only over the course of time, through constant contact, through reciprocal influences and borrowings, that the languages came to resemble each other noticeably, while never becoming identical. The history of languages is marked by divergent and convergent evolutions. At times it is even difficult to differentiate between these two types of development. . . . However, up until now, when looking at the "Indo-European problem," we have only considered the possibility of a purely

---

[61] Jakobson, 1938.

[62] Troubetzkoy, 1996 [1936], pp. 211–212. Translated after the French language edition by Patrick Sériot, which at the time of writing is the most complete version in a Western language of the Russian original; a shorter version in German also exists (Troubetzkoy 1939); See Troubetzkoy, 1996, p. 228.

divergent evolution from a single proto-language. This unilateral approach has led all discussion of the problem in an entirely erroneous direction. The true, i.e. purely linguistic, nature of the Indo-European problem has been forgotten. In examining the "Indo-European problem," numerous Indo-Europeanists have introduced, in an absolutely baseless manner, considerations relating to prehistoric archeology, anthropology and ethnology. They have launched themselves into discussions on the dwellings, culture and race of the Indo-European "primitive people," even though this people may never even have existed. For contemporary German linguists (and they are not alone!), the "Indo-European question" is posed more or less in the following terms: "What type of pottery should be associated with the primitive Indo-European people?" However, this question (and most other questions of the same type) cannot be resolved scientifically and is thus futile. The entire discussion is just a vicious circle, in so far as the very existence of the primitive "Indo-European people" cannot be demonstrated; similarly, it is impossible to demonstrate that there is any link between a particular type of material culture and a certain type of language. It is in this way that an imaginary idea, the romantic mirage of the "Primitive People," is formed. By following this mirage, we forget a fundamental scientific truth, that the "Indo-European" notion is an exclusively linguistic notion.

The only scientifically acceptable questions are where and how the Indo-European linguistic structure developed. In answering this question we must confine ourselves to concepts and facts of a purely linguistic nature, which implies that we must identify the particularities of the Indo-European system.[63]

... The "wave theory" previously proposed by Johannes Schmidt can be applied not only to dialects of the same language and to groups of related languages, but also to non-related neighboring languages. Neighboring languages, even those that have no kinship relation, in a way "mutually contaminate" each other, and in the end acquire a series of shared characteristics in their phonic and grammatical structure. All of this can be applied to language families. In the majority of cases, a given language family presents characteristics, some of which resemble those of a neighboring family, and others those of a different neighboring family. In this way, language families form veritable chains.[64]

Troubetzkoy goes on to develop a number of hypotheses. Demonstrating that linguistic "Indo-Europeanity" cannot be based on vocabulary, of which hardly a word is common to all Indo-European languages, nor on morphology, nor on the famous "laws of phonetic correspondence" which are all dogged by exceptions, he attempts to formulate a general definition of this group of languages using

---

[63] Ibid., pp. 213–216.
[64] Ibid., p. 221.

118   SECOND MOVEMENT (1903–1945)

six structural traits; only the combination of these traits will be specific. Then he examines the "areal" relationships between the Indo-European languages and the neighboring linguistic groups (Semitic, Caucasian, and Finno-Ugric languages). Troubetzkoy's iconoclastic endeavor goes no further; in doing so he joins a long line of dissenting linguists, such as Johannes Schmidt, Hugo Schuchardt, Vittore Pisani, and Christianus Cornelius Uhlenbeck, each of whom, in his own way, tentatively explored possible alternative countermodels to the *Stammbaum*. We will return to these models at a later stage.[65]

Troubetzkoy undoubtedly had additional reasons not to like the Indo-Europeans in the form of the original People. He belonged to a "Eurasist" intellectual movement, which saw closer historical and cultural relationships with immediate neighbors in Russia, including the Turkish-speaking and Muslim populations of Central Asia, than with "Romano-Germanic" Europe, which was seen as being more or less decadent.[66] This vision, which emerged, along with an interest in "Aryans," in Russia in the nineteenth century,[67] considers that Russia's historical calling was orientated just as much toward the East as toward Western Europe. Eurasism later fell into obscurity but re-emerged in Russia after the fall of the USSR and the rise of ultranationalist movements.

On March 14, 1938, Adolf Hitler, welcomed by a crowd of 200,000, led his army into Vienna, the city where, as a down-at-heel student, he had failed to be accepted into the Academy of Fine Arts. Troubetzkoy was denounced by Nazi archaeologist Oswald Menghin because of his anti-racist position and expelled from the University. His house was searched, and his archives confiscated. Subjected to rough interrogation at the hands of the Gestapo, Prince Troubetzkoy, the descendant of one of the great aristocratic Russian families, died of heart failure in hospital on June 25, 1938. As he passed away he was still writing the final pages to his famous *Principles of Phonology*. "He died," wrote Roman Jakobson, "suddenly, just like his father did when, in 1905, the Tsar and his bureaucrats moved against him on account of his liberal views."[68]

A year later, it was Prague's turn to be occupied by the Wehrmacht. Jakobson fled to Denmark, then Sweden, and eventually moved to the United States in 1941. The Prague Circle was dispersed, and Jakobson would eventually turn his attention to semantics, literary theory, and other fields. Structuralism spread its influence to ethnology (in New York City, Jakobson met Claude Lévi-Strauss who was also in exile) and then to most disciplines within the Humanities. When peace returned, comparative grammar simply resumed business as usual as if nothing had happened.

---

[65] See Chapter 19.
[66] Sériot, 1999; Laruelle, 1999.
[67] See Chapter 3, p. 41.
[68] Troubetzkoy, 1949, p. xxix, 1996, p. 229.

6

From Aryan Pan-Germanism to Nazism

We left the question of the original Homeland at the close of the nineteenth century, a time when European and more specifically German (because such was the original Homeland of comparative grammar) reappropriation was reaching the end of its historical logic: namely, to locate the point of origin in northwestern Germania, as far away as possible from Asia. Situated on the very margins of Europe, with its back to the sea and ice, this "Homeland" owed its existence to itself, and its inhospitable climate would justify the conquering pride of its "native race." This was also the moment when the three closely intertwined disciplines of ethnology, physical anthropology, and prehistoric archaeology gained their respective autonomy and began to develop their own methodologies, subject matter, and institutions. The great integrating evolutionist family tree, which up until then had provided the narrative for the "natural history of mankind," with its stages, branches, and "races," slowly ceased to be a central reference and concern.

Anthropology witnessed the disintegration of its "races" and had to seek out new raisons d'être in the measurement of intelligence, genetics, and eugenics. Ethnologists could no longer simply resort to classifying societies as "savage" or "primitive" on the basis of the testimonies of missionaries or soldiers; a new generation of ethnologists, including Boas, Haddon, Rivers, Radcliffe-Brown, and Malinowski, were now obliged to go out into the field themselves to observe the actual functioning of these societies, which would become the true object of their research. The metaphor of the machine, which had shaped Saussurean linguistics, began to permeate ethnology; ethnology became "functionalist" with the work of Bronislaw Malinowski, who was studying the societies of the Trobriand Islands at much the same time as Saussure was delivering his *Cours*. The highlighting of the differences between human societies ultimately became more important than the elements that unified them within a single classificatory family tree, all the more so because the Western value system, which up until then was seen as universal, was rendered relative by the vast array of information being collected.

The methods of archaeology

Prehistoric and protohistoric archaeology was also being swamped by a profusion of newly discovered finds and civilizations. It was no longer enough

120   SECOND MOVEMENT (1903–1945)

to simply define "ages" or "eras." The Neolithic lake villages of the Alps and the dolmens on the Atlantic coast had been known for a long time but now new cultures were being identified: the Linear Ceramic Culture (*Bandkeramik* in German) of Central Europe with its decoration of incised volutes, the Corded Ware Culture (*Schnurkeramik*) of northern Europe with is cord-impressed wares, the Fatyanovo Culture of Russia with its coarse vessels and stone axes, and the Tripolye Culture of the Ukraine with its richly painted ceramics (see Appendix 6). In France, prehistorians moved away from the *Société d'anthropologie de Paris* to found their own *Société préhistorique française*, in 1904. On the eve of the First World War, amateur archaeologist Joseph Déchelette, who subsequently gave his life as a volunteer on the battlefield, presented a vast panorama of the new European Prehistory in his *Manuel d'archéologie préhistorique et celtique* (Manual of Prehistoric and Celtic Archaeology).

This new discipline required new methods. At the beginning of the twentieth century, the Swede Oscar Montelius presented the "typological method," according to which each civilization is characterized by significant objects (weapons, tools, personal ornaments, houses, tombs, etc.), referred to as "types," which the prehistorian should be able to define with the same rigor that zoologists and botanists apply to animal or plant species—Montelius explicitly makes this comparison but never defines what a "type" actually is. Using this method he divided the Scandinavian Bronze Age into six successive "periods," which are still in use today, each characterized by a certain number of "types."

The classificatory level above "types" is "cultures" or "civilizations." Up until the end of the nineteenth century, particularly in France, the term "civilization" was used to designate a stage in human evolution: the term "Reindeer Civilization" (also referred to as the "Reindeer Age"), for example, was applied to the end of the Upper Paleolithic, a period in which we find cave paintings and a toolkit rich in reindeer bone and antler. The recognition that civilizations that are clearly contemporary yet different, because they are defined by different "types" could coexist within the vast area of Europe, gave rise to a new use of the term. This arose from the work of German archaeologists, in particular Gustaf Kossinna, who was appointed to the Chair of Prehistory at Berlin University (where he succeeded Virchow) in 1902, and who founded the German Society for Prehistory and its journal, *Mannus*, in 1909.

In Germany, from the mid-nineteenth century onward, there existed a strong academic tradition, beginning with Carl Ritter and taken up by Friedrich Ratzel and Leo Frobenius, of human geography and the study of human societies in their natural context. When applied to ethnology and history, this approach led to the identification of "culture circles" (*Kulturkreise*) that are spread across the surface

ARYAN PAN-GERMANISM TO NAZISM   121

of the globe; each culture circle is defined by specific phenomena (institutions, techniques, languages, etc.) which are themselves susceptible to diffusion and borrowings. This was the approach of the "Historico-Cultural" (*kultur-historisch*) School, which developed at the beginning of the twentieth century under the influence of Fritz Graebner in Cologne and Wilhelm Koppers and the missioner Wilhelm Schmidt, of the *Societas Verbi Divini*, in Vienna.[1] Schmidt, for example, attempted to correlate kinship systems, linguistic structures, and modes of production on a global scale. But, yet again, this involved observing living societies, whose ethnic definition was a given, and grouping them together according to supra-regional and supra-ethnic patterns, thereby characterizing large "cultural" groups.

Kossinna's law

However, in the realm of prehistoric archaeology, the ethnic identity of the societies observed is, by assumption, unknown. The hypothesis forwarded by Kossinna in his 1911 work, *Die Herkunft der Germanen* (The Origin of the Germans), was, therefore, a formidable one and is summed up in one of the most famous phrases in the history of archaeology: "Sharply defined archaeological cultural areas correspond in every era with the areas of particular people or tribes" (*"Scharf umgrenzte archäologische Kulturprovinzen decken sich zu allen Zeiten mit ganz bestimmten Völkern und Völkerstämmen"*).[2] Thus, there is a correspondence between a given archaeological "culture" defined as an assemblage of "types" of characteristic objects, and a given ethnic group. Of course this idea was implicit in earlier research, but, in the absence of archaeological data, such ethnic speculation remained very general and was largely based on philological or anthropological arguments; we can cite as an example the discussions regarding "Aryan migrations" and their relationships with the indigenous Basque or Finnish "substrate." With Kossinna, the dividing up of archaeological data to render it easier to arrange was no longer an exercise in simple classification based on stylistic variations in concrete objects; behind the distribution of a certain number of tools and pottery styles within a single geographical zone there had to lie a "people" or homogenous "ethnic group," with its own institutions, economic system, and language. This hypothesis is far from benign: some fifty years later it was the subject of heated discussion and, as we shall see, as early as the 1930s, the prehistorian Gordon Childe would propose other alternatives. It is also very

[1] Graebner, 1911; Schmidt, W., 1926.
[2] Kossinna, 1911, p. 3. See Klejn, 1974; Römer, 1985; Grünert, 2002; Veit, 1984, 1989, 2000.

122 SECOND MOVEMENT (1903–1945)

simplistic, imposing a very restrictive and narrow interpretation on observed "reality." Ultimately, it is also circular in that it requires that all archaeological material be ordered and then interpreted in terms of a defined "culture," with no other possible alternatives.

But this notion of "culture" is also based on a naturalistic, biological model. Culture is an association of "types" just as the "types" are an association of descriptive traits, defined with reference to the natural sciences. And, just as a "type" of axe gives rise to another, in line with a classic evolutionist model in any chronological system (we also see it applied in the history of art), a culture will naturally give rise to another. Thus the model underpinning this new archaeological methodology for ordering and interpreting data is simply Linnaeus's classificatory arborescent model in its genealogical reinterpretation as proposed by Darwin. It is not surprising that this arborescent model quickly formed close ties with existing family tree models, such as those proposed for "races" and languages. However, the family tree was not the only possible model; the "machine," with its interdependent cogs, would soon become the new operating model for structural linguistics and functionalist ethnology. However, it would take another fifty years for archaeology to abandon the notion of "culture" as a living organism or, more precisely, for an alternative "mechanical" model to be developed by archaeologists, particularly by those who engaged in the New Archaeology which emerged in the English-speaking world in the 1950s and '60s. The only other attempt to develop an alternative model was made by Soviet archaeologists during the Stalinist period, but, as we shall see, it was far from convincing. Ironically, it was at the moment when ethnology abandoned its evolutionist paradigm and renounced the ambitious historical reconstructions so typical of the last third of the nineteenth century (typified by the work of Lewis Morgan, Edward Burnett Tylor, James Atkinson, Hobhouse, McLennan, and Westermarck) in favor of understanding concrete social functioning, at the very moment when ethnology and prehistory parted company, that the latter borrowed an already obsolete tool from the former. Such time lags are not rare in the history of the relationships between sciences.

Nor is it an accident that this cultural model was developed in Germany. Not only was archaeology more professionalized in Germany than elsewhere, but it also played a powerful role in the creation of a national ideology; intellectual and methodological debate was thus very advanced. Furthermore, in contrast to French prehistorians who were more inclined to spend their efforts defining broad, universal chronologies that spanned the ages of humanity, German sciences were marked by an interest in geographical space. This is symptomatic of a nation whose territory, won at the cost of several bloody wars, still remained an issue even though there was no coincidence, either by excess or default, between territory and nationality, between land and blood. From the outset, German

Romantics like Herder, Fichte and his *Addresses to the German Nation*, as well as Schlegel and Hegel, had always envisaged the Nation as a biological entity, both delimited and eternal, and endowed with a "national soul," the *Volksgeist*, which was bound to perpetuate itself indefinitely.

The Kossinnian Indo-German narrative

Trained in German Philology, Kossinna was born in East Prussia, where he grew up within the nationalist climate that accompanied the unification of the German Nation through armed struggle. He was drawn to archaeology because of his desire to retrace the origin of the Germanic peoples and, through them, that of the Indo-Germans; like many others, he took this denomination, which was specific to Germany, literally. His first published work, a lecture delivered in Kassel in 1895, on the occasion of the Anthropological Society's Annual Congress, and dealing with the "the geographic distribution of the Germanic peoples in Germany in prehistory,"[3] set out his scientific program (i.e., building on ancient accounts of the geographical locations of Germanic peoples by the Classical authors) to retrace their history back through time using archaeological evidence. Admittedly, the archaeological evidence was still lacking and even deliberately ignored for the Neolithic period, while he continued to locate the original Indo-European homeland in the region of the Danube.

The rest of his life's work was entirely devoted to the fulfilment of this program: the use of archaeological arguments for preconceived ethnic identifications. These arguments were ever-changing, with the original People being shifted from east to west and identified by turns with the *Linearbandkeramik* culture of Central Europe, the megalith builders of Western Europe, the Paleolithic population of the Périgord, and the Corded Ware culture of Northern Europe (see Appendices 6 and 7). Kossinna was all the more cavalier with archaeological material since he hardly ever conducted excavations himself. He also introduced a new term for his approach—*Siedlungsarchäologie*, or "occupation archaeology"—by which he meant the archaeological identification of the territories occupied by given peoples. The term is historiographically ambiguous because, since *Siedlung* designates both territorial occupation in the widest sense and the occupation of a given settlement "site," *Siedlungsarchäologie* would later be applied to the exhaustive and extensive excavation of individual settlements, a method in which Soviet and Nazi archaeologists, following in the footsteps of SS professor Herbert Jankuhn,[4] would excel.

---

[3] Kossinna, 1896.
[4] See p. 141.

124 SECOND MOVEMENT (1903–1945)

In what was effectively Kossinna's final vision,[5] the Indo-Europeans, descendants of Cro-Magnon man, emerged with the northern European Mesolithic Ellerbeck culture in the early fourth millennium BCE (according to the prevailing chronology of the time). From there, they spread out over all of Europe in fourteen great warrior invasions (the *Züge*). The historical process is evident:

> The Indo-European expansion clearly happened in this way: a vigorous warrior minority subdued a weaker majority, reduced them to slavery and then rigorously kept themselves separate from this enslaved population by applying a caste system; in doing so, they partially smothered the indigenous civilization and replaced it with their own, but, above all, they forced the dominated population to accept the Indo-European language. Otherwise, how could we explain the undeniable domination of the new language of the minority and the preservation over millennia of the purity of the light-skinned Nordic type among the dark-skinned populations of southern Europe?[6]

Regarding this last point, Kossinna could not resist calling on the authority of Vacher de Lapouge.

We also see how little Kossinna's Indo-European vision differed from that presented by Meillet, Benveniste and Dumézil. Incidentally, Déchelette, who had reservations concerning this issue (and the notion of "race"), judged Kossinna's above article as one of only a handful of studies on the Indo-European question in which "the archaeological aspect is discussed with complete competence."[7] We will see later how Gordon Childe, one of the greatest prehistorians of the twentieth century, would share this opinion in his early works. At the time, Kossinna was far from the pariah he would later become in the world of archaeology.

"A pre-eminently national discipline"

Influenced by the theories of raciologist and future Nazi Hans Günther,[8] Kossinna thus identifies the Indo-Europeans with the "Nordic race" defined by the former (i.e., the *Homo europaeus* of Vacher de Lapouge and others). This identification conveniently solved all of the problems: in the absence of evident continuity in the archaeological record from the Mesolithic to the emergence of

---

[5] Kossinna, 1902, 1911, 1912, 1921, 1926. On Kossinna, see Klejn, 1974, 1999; Hachmann, 1970; Eggers, 1959; Römer, 1985; Veit, 1984, 1989; Smolla, 1979–1980 and 1984–1985.

[6] Kossinna, 1902 (republished in 1968, pp. 45–46).

[7] Déchelette, 1914, vol. 2, p. 10, note 2.

[8] See Chapter 8, p. 187.

ARYAN PAN-GERMANISM TO NAZISM   125

the Germanic peoples in historic times, the affirmation of a "racial" continuity supplants its demonstration. Building on the work of Much (to whom he denies the authorship of the "Nordic" homeland only to unduly appropriate it for himself) and others, Kossinna had no hesitation in crediting the (Indo-)Germans with the invention of writing (the attribution of the invention of writing to the Phoenicians is "one of the worst historical lies that we know of[9]"), the domestication of the horse, and the mastering of copper metallurgy.

An armchair archaeologist, Kossinna was first and foremost a professional ideologist. His 1912 work, *Die deutsche Vorgeschichte, eine hervorragend nationale Wissenschaft* (German Prehistory: A Pre-Eminently National Discipline), is explicit. Chapter after chapter, with titles such as "The Superiority of German Taste" and "The Grandeur of Germanic Spiral Ornamentation," he affirms the ancestral cultural superiority of the (Indo-)Germans. He is thus led to the conclusion, two years before the outbreak of the First World War, that "Such a people . . . cannot be looked upon as barbaric, even though the Romans did so, or more accurately, the Romance-speaking successors of the Romans and, with particular partiality, the French . . ., despite their own very real barbarity."[10] He welcomes the declaration of war; then, after the defeat, he endeavors (in vain) to limit the loss of territory in the Baltic area by addressing a memo entitled "Ostmark, the original homeland of the Germans" to the negotiators of the Versailles Treaty. In this way, he became the first to use archaeology as a support for territorial claims. A prolonged and heated debate with Polish archaeologists ensued.[11]

From 1912 onward, he affirmed the "value of pure German blood" because "the blood determines the soul"; at the same time he belittled the Celts, the Dacians, and the Slavs. In the same year, when writing an obituary for his favorite student Erich Blume, who was murdered by his wife, Kossinna denounces the "clearly non-Germanic type" of the latter whom he also describes as "a clearly degenerate hybrid." Since the turn of the century he had been corresponding with Ludwig Schemann, the racist and anti-Semitic disseminator of Gobineau's work in Germany.[12] In 1913, as the outbreak of war grew near, Kossinna's German Society for Prehistory (Deutsche Gesellschaft für Vorgeschichte) became the Society for German Prehistory (Gesellschaft für Deutschen Vorgeschichte). In the same year, Heinrich Class, the leader of the German ultra-nationalist party, the Pan-German League (Alldeutscher Verband), became a member. The following year, in the Society's journal *Mannus*, Karl Felix Wolff attacked the Jewish Indo-Europeanist linguist Sigmund Feist, who had refuted the identification of the Germans with the Indo-Germans; among other things, he describes Feist

[9] Kossinna, 1911, p. 12.
[10] Kossinna, 1912, p. 229.
[11] Schnapp, 1977, pp. 19–20, 1981; Klejn, 1974.
[12] See Chapter 4, pp. 93–94.

126 SECOND MOVEMENT (1903–1945)

as a "product of the raceless civilization (*Rasseloser Zivilisationsmensch*)" and a "stateless citizen of the red and gold International (*Weltbürger der goldenen und roter Internationale*)." Feist resigned from the Society of which he was a founding member.[13]

After the First World War, under the influence of Hans Günther, Kossinna went further and, like Vacher de Lapouge before him, undertook to estimate the proportion of "true" Nordic blood in the German people. Ultimately he was forced to admit that said "race" was only present in 60% of the population and that the proportion of "pure" Nordics was only 6–8%. Fortunately, "within the soul of every German the ideal of the Nordic essence is firmly anchored."[14]

Furthermore,

> It is one of the laws of racial psychology that within a racial branch the dolichocephalics always constitute the enterprising portion of a given population, turned toward adventure and travels, conquering, but also creative, inventive, aspiring toward progress and endowed with an aristocratic ideal, while the brachycephalics form that part that is obstinate, conservative, little inclined to progress, adventure or war-like sorties, politically democrat and thinking only of their own interests.[15]

Kossinna followed a tradition of glorifying the "national spirit" (*Volksgeist*) and national unity which traced its roots back to Romanticism, Grimm, and Schlegel; of course he was living within a climate of intensifying nationalism that would eventually lead to the Second World War. But he lent this cause the support of institutional archaeology, and, at the same time, by sweeping away the earlier warnings of Virchow, Hirt, and Schrader, he strengthened the links between archaeology and raciology. Penka, Poesche, and Much were amateurs, but Kossinna, who relished in belittling Much, was a university professor in the capital of the Reich.

At the same time, Kossinna did not reign over the discipline of prehistory in all of Germany, just over the eastern part. He had extremely heated personal arguments with Karl Schuchardt, Director of the Department of Archaeology of the Berlin Museum and founder of the *Prähistorische Zeitschrift* (Prehistoric Journal); and, even though he held the title of Professor, he was never actually tenured. His work, and in particular the equating of ethnic group with archaeological culture, was immediately criticized by eminent academics such as the classical historian Eduard Meyer, Rector of Berlin University; the prehistorian

---

[13] Wolff, 1914; Feist, 1913; Smolla, 1979–1980, p. 5; on Feist, see Feist-Hirsch, 1970; Römer, 1981. On the subject of "blood," see Olender, 2009, p. 18.

[14] Kossinna, 1926, p. 128.

[15] Kossinna, 1921, p. 68.

ARYAN PAN-GERMANISM TO NAZISM   127

Moritz Hoernes, Professor at the University of Vienna; and the linguist Otto Schrader. The equation "*ein Volk, ein Topf*" ("one people, one pot") was held up to ridicule. After his death in 1931, and the rise to power of Hitler in 1933, his disciple Reinerth strove, by all means at his disposal, to take control of German prehistory. However, he ran into opposition from a large section of the university establishment (including Karl Schuchardt) which, admittedly, had to seek the protection of Himmler and the SS to preserve its position.

Erasing the memory of Kossinna

After the crushing of Nazism, the official historiographers of archaeology "forgot" Kossinna. There is no mention of his work in the book by British archaeologist Glynn Daniels, *A Hundred Years of Archaeology*, which was, for a long time, the principal reference on the subject; it was re-edited several times and revised in 1975 under the title *A Hundred and Fifty Years of Archaeology*. Just like the Vichy government in the official political history of France, Kossinna was tacitly seen as some sort of momentary aberration, his work an inexcusable enslavement of science to an extremist ideology. In West Germany, as in all of the Western Bloc after the Second World War, archaeologists turned away from all explicitly ethnic approaches[16]; in East Germany, archaeologists, officially won over to Marxism, did not have to acknowledge Germany's Kossinnian past. Nonetheless, Kossinna provided bad answers to real questions, questions regarding the formation of ethnic entities and the identification of ethnicity through material culture.

In spite of what anyone might say, and even though the identifying of ethnic groups through material archaeology had previously been attempted by Virchow (in the context of medieval Slavic fortifications), Tischler (in the context of Germanic material in Prussia), and Montelius (in Scandinavia), Kossinna was the first to have so forcefully defined the approach, founded on the equation "archaeological culture = ethnic entity," and to have applied it systematically. In fact, Kossinna's Polish students, such as Kostrzewsky, were content to simply inverse the arguments to declare "Slavic" those territories that their master considered "Germanic." The English-based archaeologist Gordon Childe, who, as we shall see, drew on Marxism in order to understand cultural history, considered the Kossinnian equation to be evident and acknowledged its influence in his first great syntheses written in the 1920s.

More generally, since Kossinna, this equation has underpinned all archaeological research throughout Europe, both East and West; behind a given "archaeological culture," defined as the delimited geographical distribution of a

---

[16] Wolfram, 2000.

128 SECOND MOVEMENT (1903–1945)

certain number of associated "types" of objects, there had to be a homogenous political, religious, socioeconomic, even linguistic community—in other words, an "ethnic group." This ethnic group is envisaged as an objective entity, likely to perpetuate itself for centuries before transforming, through internal mutation or crossbreeding, into a new homogenous, objective entity. The use of vocabulary from the fields of biology and kinships is typical of descriptions of archaeological "cultures." And, evidently, it is on this model that all attempts to identify the original Indo-European people archaeologically have been based right up to the present day, to the extent that certain German archaeologists have recently attempted to rehabilitate Kossinna by showing, quite rightly, that all he did was define, with conviction, a method that most Continental European archaeologists have continued to use ever since.[17]

Yet precisely because it is officially deemed to be simplistic, Kossinna's work should act as a magnifying mirror concerning the relevance of the *ein Volk, ein Topf* equation, since it is not the only possible interpretive model. Even prior to the Nazi defeat, certain German archaeologists, such as Hans Jürgen Eggers and Ernst Wahle, had the courage to subject it to reasoned criticism. The former insisted on the complexity of material culture, which is not a simple reflection of living society but includes objects with various statuses (utilitarian, funerary, symbolic, etc.) and variable life spans; a few years for ceramic objects, several decades for metal objects, and several centuries for religious insignia or symbols of status. In contrast to historians, who treat their written sources critically, archaeologists do not subject their own "documents" to any prior critical assessment; however, "even archaeological remains can lie!"[18]

Ernst Wahle, a former student of Kossinna, published an article in 1941 with the unequivocal title: "The Ethnic Significance of Protohistoric Cultural Provinces: The Limits of Knowledge of Protohistory."[19] The formation of a new culture results from a general rearrangement, which follows accelerated innovation processes, in the face of which the question of genetic filiation with the immediately preceding culture is of very little interest, particularly since archaeology has great difficulty in grasping and describing moments of rapid change. However, these reflections emanating from the German scientific world remained marginal, and it was not until the emergence of the New Archaeology in the United States and Great Britain in the 1960s and '70s that an independent debate would open on archaeological resources and cultural functioning. Once again, the ethnic question would be swept under the carpet.

---

[17] Smolla, 1979–1980 and 1984–1985; Veit, 1984.
[18] Eggers, 1939, 1950, 1959.
[19] Wahle, 1940–1941, 1964; see also Malina and Vašíček, 1990, pp. 105–109; Veit, 1989.

ARYAN PAN-GERMANISM TO NAZISM   129

Archaeology, therefore, paid a heavy price for believing that it could skim over a fundamental debate on Kossinnism, which remains the underlying paradigm for most archaeological "solutions" to the Indo-European problem. The discipline accepted, without question, Kossinna's premises so long as they were not exploited for patently ideological purposes and continued to apply a model of cultural evolution that sprang from biology and the Romantic tradition of the *Volksgeist*, which was central to European nationalisms, a model that was all the more dangerous because it was both implicit and taken for granted. Archaeology was completely helpless when, with the recent re-emergence of nationalist sentiments, it found itself once again summoned to support the most unreasonable ethnic and territorial claims, from the Balkans to the Caucasus and from India to the Middle East: a sweet revenge for Kossinna!

Nazism, one of the possible horizons for the Aryans

It may seem out of place at this point to turn our attention to Nazism, its exploitation of the Indo-European question, and the terrifying consequences that followed as a result. After all, the period has already been the subject of innumerable historical studies; National-Socialism has been described as an aberrant, and thus marginal, subversion of Indo-European studies, and, in the end, we might run the risk of laying false blame on these studies through a bogus trial. Nevertheless, we hope, on the one hand, to show that, like Kossinna who preceded and indeed prefigured it, Nazism was one of the potential final destinations for the Indo-European myth; on the other hand, the behavior of scientific communities in their relations with Nazism as a field where "scientific" theories found concrete application deserves our closer attention. Linguists, archaeologists, anthropologists, and geneticists found in Nazism the official culmination of their work; they received honors and funding, which, in return, meant making concessions to the pervasive climate of terror and to political and racial persecutions. Outside Germany, foreign scientists did not show much solidarity with their threatened colleagues. Indeed, we could go as far as to say that their indifference, cowardice, and even weak intellectual complicity gave tacit license to the repression. Finally, even today, it is pretty clear that certain so-called scientific works in the field of Indo-European studies are directly descended from Nazi ideology.

For the purposes of clarity, this section examines the role of archaeologists (and, by extension, linguists) while other issues, such as the destiny of the concept of "race" in the first half of the twentieth century and the more fateful and bloody role of anthropologists and geneticists, will be looked at later.[20]

---

[20] See Chapter 8.

130　SECOND MOVEMENT (1903–1945)

One of the traits of Nazi ideology is that, in the continuity of the Germanomaniacs of the last quarter of the nineteenth century, it definitively equated "race" and "culture"; up until then, no professional scientist—be they anthropologist, linguist, or archaeologist—had made this claim. As we have seen, the official stated ideology can be summarized as follows: the original "Aryan" People, which coincides with the blond, dolichocephalic "Nordic race," spontaneously emerged in northern Germany and Scandinavia in prehistoric times, and the historical Germanic peoples were their purest descendants; the Aryan invasions spread Indo-European civilization to parts of Eurasia but it became bastardized through contact with indigenous peoples; the Jews, who, like parasites, infiltrated the economic and cultural systems of the West, constituted the greatest threat to the survival of the Aryan "race" and cultures whose "purity" had to be restored by all possible means.

In chapter XI ("People and Race") of *Mein Kampf*, published in 1925–1927,[21] Hitler writes,

> It would be futile to attempt to discuss the question as to what race or races were the original standard-bearers of human culture and were thereby the real founders of all that we understand by the word humanity. It is much simpler to deal with this question in so far as it relates to the present time. Here the answer is simple and clear. Every manifestation of human culture, every product of art, science and technical skill, which we see before our eyes today, is almost exclusively the product of the Aryan creative power.... He is the Prometheus of mankind, from whose shining brow the spark of genius has at all times flashed forth, always kindling anew that fire which, in the form of knowledge, illuminated the dark night by drawing aside the veil of mystery and thus showing man how to rise and become master over all the other beings on the earth.... If we divide mankind into three categories—founders of culture, bearers of culture, and destroyers of culture—the Aryan alone can be considered as representing the first category. (pp. 317–318)

But "the adulteration of the blood and racial deterioration conditioned thereby are the only causes that account for the decline of ancient civilizations" (p. 324). Also, faced with the mortal threat from the "Jewish parasites," "In place of preaching hatred against Aryans from whom we may be separated on almost every other ground but with whom the bond of kindred blood and the main features of a common civilization unite us, we [the National-Socialist movement]

---

[21] The page numbers in brackets in the following citations refer to the official German edition of *Mein Kampf* published in one volume by the NSDAP Press. The translation proposed here is borrowed from James Murphy's translation published in 1939.

ARYAN PAN-GERMANISM TO NAZISM 131

must devote ourselves to arousing general indignation against the maleficent enemy of humanity and the real author of all our sufferings" (pp. 724–725).

The other prominent Nazi ideologist was Alfred Rosenberg, who was responsible for the regime's cultural policies, first as head of the Nazi party's *Kampfbund für deutsche Kultur* (Militant League for German Culture) and then as head of the *Amt Rosenberg* (Rosenberg Service), an official body for cultural policy and surveillance. His major work, *Der Mythus des 20. Jahrhunderts* (The Myth of the Twentieth Century),[22] over one million copies of which were published in1930, is a weighty tome of more than 700 pages which Hitler himself admitted to never having read in its entirety: it retraces the story of Germanic racial genius, which was now under threat from bastardization, Jewish parasitism, Christianity (an Eastern religion), and Marxism. He calls for the creation of a "racial-organic" state within a restored Germany because "Odin, as the eternal mirror of the ancient spiritual force of Nordic mankind, lives today as he did 5000 years ago."[23] He relies heavily on the work of Leibniz, Herder, and Nietzsche, but also on that of Chamberlain, Vacher de Lapouge, and Hermann Wirth.

The Atlantis of the Far North

In fact, Rosenberg's theory on the origin of the Aryans and the "Nordic Race" was borrowed from Wirth. According to Wirth, this warlike and "creative race" originated in a northern Atlantis, now disappeared beneath the waves, from whence they spread out toward North America and the rest of Europe, bringing with them their writing—as evidenced by numerous rock carvings on both continents. Of Dutch origin, but engaged as a volunteer in the German army during the First World War, which earned him the title of "Professor," Wirth taught Dutch at the University of Berlin. 1n 1933, he republished the Ura-Linda Chronicle, that famous literary hoax which we mentioned in an earlier chapter[24] and set up the Hermann Wirth Society as a vehicle for his bold ideas. The society received the support of several academics such as Gustav Neckel, holder of the Chair of Nordic Studies at the University of Berlin and editor of the Medieval Scandinavian poems of the *Edda*, and the linguist Walther Wüst.[25] Wirth was appointed as the first president, under the control of Himmler, of the SS cultural institute, the *Ahnenerbe* (Heritage of the Ancestors). The Nordic Indo-European Atlantis had appeared previously in the work of Vacher de Lapouge,[26] who was

[22] Rosenberg, 1930.
[23] Ibid.; pp. 678–679 of the 1942 edition.
[24] See Chapter 3, pp. 58 and 60.
[25] Wirth, 1928; on Wirth, see Römer, 1985, pp. 77, 95, 136, 142; Kater, 1974, pp. 11–15; Schnapp, 1977, p. 6.
[26] See Chapter 4, p. 89.

132   SECOND MOVEMENT (1903–1945)

building on the ideas of Penka, and in the work of Guido von List. The scenario tells of how severe living conditions in the original Homeland forged the exceptional spirit of the Aryans, a virtual rehash of the biblical story of the Fall. This biblical link was made by another Germanomaniac, Karl Georg Zschaetzsch who, despite situating the Aryan Atlantis in the Azores, discovered in the Bible the story of the Aryan Exodus from their Eden, a story that had subsequently been subverted by the Jews. Phoenician writing naturally originated from runes, Jacob was an Aryan prince, the name of the city of Hebron must be linked to the Celtic Eburones tribe, and that of Zschaetzsch to Zeus! He thus claimed world domination for the Aryans, whose "race" stretched back more than 30,000 years.[27] Hermann Wieland would go on to develop the same idea.[28]

Here we remember how Plato's Atlanteans had been given a makeover by the theosophist Helena Blavatsky, and subsequently by Guido von List, whose Germanomaniac fantasies prompted him to reconstruct the "primitive Aryo-Germanic language" spoken a million years ago by the Armanian priesthood and call for a program of Aryan racial purification.[29] List's work was adopted by Vienna-born Adolf Joseph Lanz, also known as Jorg von Liebenfels, inspirer of Wirth and founder of "Ariosophy."[30] In 1905, this former Cistercian monk, expelled from the order for "sins against the flesh," published his Theozoologie oder die Kunde von den Sodoms-Äfflingen und dem Götter-Elektron (Theozoology, or the Science of the Sodomite Apelings and the Divine Electron), according to which the Bible is really a cryptic teaching intended to warn the Aryans against racial mixing. In fact, the original man-gods copulated with animals (in the Bible, the verbs "to name," "to know," "to cover" actually mean "to copulate"), thereby giving rise to the "human races," among which the "Aryan race" is the least corrupted. As in the works of List, the ancient Aryan religion has been passed down to the present day by a chain of secret initiates, through Christ, the Kabbalah, the Templars, the Rosicrucians, and, finally, List and the Atlantomaniacs Zschaetzsch and Wieland.

In the face of the growing threat from racial mixing and from "inferior races," but also from feminism, socialism, and democracy, only a strict eugenic program could reinstate the ancient super powers of the Aryans: the strict subjugation by their Aryan husbands of women, who, because of their bestial nature, are spontaneously attracted to the "inferior races"; the creation of "eugenist convents" (Zuchtkloster) where females of reproductive age would copulate with pure Aryans; subjugation of the "inferior races," doomed to slavery or extermination through sterilization, castration, or incineration "as a sacrifice to God." As with

[27] Zschaetzsch, 1922; see Römer, 1985, p. 66.
[28] Wieland, 1925.
[29] See Chapter 3, pp. 59–61.
[30] Goodrick-Clarke, 1989; Daim, 1958; Römer, 1985, pp. 96, 136; Lanz-Liebenfels, 1905, 1918.

ARYAN PAN-GERMANISM TO NAZISM 133

the work of List, this prefigures, virtually word for word, the future program of the Nazi Party, with its crematoria and the SS racial reproduction centers of the *Lebensborn* organization.[31]

In 1905, Lanz founded the *Ostara* magazine (named after a Germanic spring goddess), a "Newsletter of the Blond," the "first and only collection of illustrated publications of the Aryan aristocracy." The magazine dealt with the "races," sex, women, the psycho-physiology of blonds compared to the other "races," occultism, etc. According to Lanz, 100,000 magazines were printed, and it is known that Hitler was a loyal reader.[32] In 1918, Lanz published an issue entitled *Die Blonden als Schöpfer der Sprachen, ein Abriß der Ursprachenforschung* (The Blonds as Creators of Languages, an Outline of Research on Primitive Languages), in which he demonstrates that only blond, dolichocephalic Aryans were capable of creating languages, while the "inferior races" of humanity, confined in their isolating and agglutinating languages, were only capable of borrowings. In fact, this was just an extension of the evolutionist theories of Schlegel, Bopp, and Schleicher on the superiority of inflective languages. Lanz also collaborated on one of the journals linked to Ernst Haeckel's Monist League, *Das Freie Wort* (The Free Word). In 1907, Lanz founded the *Ordo Novi Templi* (Order of the New Templars) on the model of the Templars and Teutonic Knights. He acquired a medieval ruin, the Burg Werfenstein, perched above the Danube, which became the order's headquarters and over which flew a flag bearing the Swastika—this symbol was already important to Helena Blavatsky and Guido von List. The order celebrated "racial purity"—members of the order should have an "Aryoheroic" countenance—and its ultimate goal was the rebirth of the Aryan elite through eugenic selection and the extermination of the "inferior races."

Sects and secret societies

The same model was applied by several other German extremist groups and sects founded by the disciples of List and Lanz. The best known were the *Hammer* groups (named after Thor's hammer) founded in 1902 by Theodor Fritsch, agitator and author of an *Anti-Semitic Catechism*. In 1912, these groups were federated within the *Reichshammerbund* (Reich Hammer League), under the directorship of Karl August Hellwig, retired army colonel and member of the List Society; he was assisted in his efforts by a twelve-member Council of Armanians. The League was flanked by a secret society, the *Germanenorden* (Germanic Order), which called for the "religious rebirth of the Aryo-Germans" and the

---

[31] See Chapter 8, p. 190.
[32] Daim, 1958; Goodrick-Clarke, 1989, pp. 127–149 and 269–284.

134   SECOND MOVEMENT (1903–1945)

creation of an "Armanian Empire" free of "parasitic and revolutionary inferior races."[33] Clad in white robes and wearing horned helmets, the members of the Order held secret ceremonies complete with Wagnerian music, "Wotan's spear," "the Grove of the Holy Grail," and swastikas. The Order was responsible for a number of political assassinations under the Weimar Republic, including that of Matthias Erzberger, former minister for finance and signatory of the armistice.[34]

A lodge of the Order was founded by the explorer Rudolf Glauer (self-proclaimed Baron Rudolf von Sebottendorff) in Munich in 1917; the lodge was baptized the Thule Society, and its emblem was a dagger surmounted by a swastika. This is an allusion to Pytheas, an explorer from the Greek colony of Massalia (Marseille) who is known from a handful of fragmentary texts. Pytheas traveled to Britain in the fourth century BCE, where he heard tell of an island called Thule situated further north—a probable reference to the Shetland or Faroe Islands. To Germanomaniacs, however, Thule was the now drowned polar homeland of the original Aryans. Glauer also organized a Thule Combat Group which, in 1919, took part in the bloody counter-revolutionary repression that followed the short-lived Munich Commune led by Jewish journalist Kurt Eisner. The Thule Society was frequented by a number of future Nazi Party ideologists, including Alfred Rosenberg and the anti-Semitic writer Dietrich Eckart, who was a mentor to Hitler before his death in 1923. Glauer also owned the *Münchener Beobachter* (Munich Observer), an anti-Semitic rag which would become the *Völkische Beobachter* (People's Observer), the leading Nazi party newspaper. Over time a plethora of smaller groups sprouted up around the Thule Society and its members; these included the Deutscher Arbeiterverein, founded by Karl Harrer, and the Deutsche Arbeiterpartei (the German Workers' Party), founded in January 1919 by Drexler, Dannehl, and Harrer. In September 1919, Hitler joined the ranks of the latter and, in February 1921, transformed it into the National-Sozialistische Deutsche Arbeiterpartei (NSDAP; National Socialist German Workers' Party), the Nazi Party.[35] The emblem of the Thule Society, the Aryo-Germanic swastika, was adopted as the official emblem of the new party.

Yet another group was the Edda Society (named after the collection of medieval Scandinavian legends of the same name) founded by Rudolf Gorsleben, who preached a racist, occultist religion founded on the magic of runes (Gorsleben saw runes everywhere, in crystals, coats-of-arms, and even in the frameworks of half-timbered houses!) and warned against the threat of cross-racial breeding (a single impure sexual union could, "through impregnation," permanently contaminate the concupiscent Aryan female). In his journal, *German Liberty*, which

[33] Ibid., pp. 177–192.
[34] Ibid., p. 192.
[35] Phelps, 1963; Goodrick-Clarke, 1989, pp. 212–214.

ARYAN PAN-GERMANISM TO NAZISM 135

later became *Aryan Liberty* (*Arische Freiheit*), he collaborated with, among others, leading Nazi ideologist Hans Günther. Lurking among a host of authors on racist and occultist matters, we find Lanz's editor, Herbert Reichstein, who published the official journal of the Ariosophical Society, the *Zeitschrift für Menschenkenntnis und Menschenschicksal* (Journal for the Knowledge of Man and His Destiny), which was devoted to runic magic and Aryan clairvoyance. It also published articles on Hans Hörbiger's "Ice theory," full of glacial catastrophes and submerged "races," and also on the Hollow Earth Theory, imported from the United States—all manner of ravings that fascinated Lanz and several Nazi Party dignitaries.[36]

A number of sects attempted to reconcile paganism and Christianity, taking up the idea of an Aryan Christ whose original significance had been subverted, as claimed earlier by Chamberlain and now by Dinter.[37] In 1933, purely neo-pagan sects attempted to unite under the *Deutsche Glaubensbewegung* (German Faith Movement) founded by Jakob Hauer, former Protestant missionary and Professor of Sanskrit and Indian religion at the University of Tübingen.[38] In several works, such as *Deutsche Gottesschau* (The German Vision of God, 1934) and *Glaubensgeschichte der Indogermanen* (The History of Indo-Germanic Faith, 1937), Hauer invented from scratch an original Indo-European religion and deplored the disappearance of Indo-European belief in reincarnation. The raciologist Hans Günther was an ardent supporter. Despite Rosenberg's ambitions to recreate Germanic, or Indo-Germanic, religion, most of the Nazi leadership did not show much enthusiasm for it; they were anxious to avoid confrontation with the Christian churches and the Vatican, and, in any case, the military situation would soon require all of their attention.

Thus, in this Germany, weakened after the defeat of the First World War and ravaged by economic crisis and inflation, small groups of marginal pseudo-intellectuals communed with tin-pot mystics to glorify a submerged heroic past and dream of an elite that would lead them to revenge and restoration, all the while damning the coalition of degenerate peoples and Jews, the traditional scapegoats of European crises. And yet, the same crisis and humiliation would grant a historical role to these men who in ordinary times would never have been read, let alone published.[39]

---

[36] Goodrick-Clarke, 1989, pp. 245–246, 302; Ley, 1947.

[37] Gentile, 2013, pp. 231–257.

[38] Rapp, 1920; Linse, 1983; Poewe and Hexham, 2005; Conte and Essner, 1995, pp. 13–64 and 119–188.

[39] On the ideological foundations of Nazism, see, among others, Poliakov and Wulf, 1983 [1959]; Arendt, 1951; Faye, J.-P., 1972.

136   SECOND MOVEMENT (1903–1945)

Hitler himself was not a believer

Aryo-Germanic occultism exercised a direct influence on Rosenberg and others. It inspired Himmler, through the intermediary of his personal magus Karl Wiligut, to create his SS rituals.[40] More generally, in the words of Nicholas Goodrich-Clarke, it was like "an early symptom of Nazism," the crystallization of all the fantasies of exclusion and revenge generated by the Industrial Revolution and then the defeat. It proves that the Nazi horror was not an incomprehensible accident, that it had already been banalized for some time in certain minds. But the most tragically derisory aspect of all is that Hitler himself did not believe in it. In *Mein Kampf*, he castigates those whom he refers to as "wandering scholars peddling Germanic folk-lore," who "rant about Teutonic heroes of the dim and distant ages," "who brandish Teutonic tin swords that have been fashioned carefully according to ancient models and wear padded bear-skins, with horns of oxen mounted over their bearded faces, [who] proclaim that all contemporary conflicts must be decided by the weapons of the mind alone. And thus they skedaddle when the first communist cudgel appears"; they, whose activities "tend to turn the attention of the people away from the necessity of fighting together in a common cause against a common enemy, namely the Jew": this is why "the Jew finds it in his own interest to treat these folk-lore comedians with respect and to prefer them to the real men who are fighting to establish a German state."[41] Always the practical-minded demagogue, Hitler preferred the efficiency of his street-fighting cohorts and the very real lynchings they perpetrated. A classically trained academic painter, he had little fascination for the Germanic past. Indeed, he stated to Speer,

> Why do we call the whole world's attention to the fact that we have no past? It isn't enough that the Romans were erecting great buildings when our forefathers were still living in mud huts. . . . All we prove by that is that we were still throwing stone hatchets and crouching around open fires when Greece and Rome had already reached the highest stage of culture. We should really do our best to keep quiet about this past.[42]

It is said that he admitted that he, "like many *Gauleiter*, only ever read a small part" of Rosenberg's *The Myth of the Twentieth Century* "because, in his opinion, it was written in a manner that was too difficult to understand."[43]

---

[40] Mund, 1982; Goodrick-Clarke, 1989, pp. 249–268; Kater, 1974. See this chapter, p. 140.

[41] Hitler, 1925–1926, pp. 395–397.

[42] Translation from *Inside the Third Reich, Memoirs by Albert Speer*, translated from the German by Richard and Clara Winston, 1970, pp. 94–95; see Chapoutot, 2012.

[43] Bollmus, 1970, p. 25.

ARYAN PAN-GERMANISM TO NAZISM 137

Even more sinister is the fact that Hitler, like Vacher de Lapouge, did not even believe that there was such a thing as a "Jewish race." Thus, he confided to Martin Borman, in his last testament dictated as bombs rained down on Berlin, that "Deep down in his being, the Jew is the 'outsider.' The Jewish race is first and foremost a community of spirit. To this must be added a sort of connection of destinies, the consequences of centuries of persecution. . . . And what is determining for the race, which should serve as a sad proof of the superiority of 'spirit' over flesh, is precisely this incapacity to be assimilated."[44] "If this was Hitler's intimate conviction," concludes the German historian Benno Müller-Hill with regard to the anthropologists, doctors, and biologists compromised by their involvement in Nazism,[45] then "these specialists in the human sciences with their biological ideas, were, for him, just accomplices in murder; idiots no doubt, but useful nevertheless."

The rallying of archaeologists

Wirth, Lanz, List, Eckart, and Rosenberg: when Hitler came to power, each German intellectual had the means to verify the "scientific" references on which Nazi doctrine based its claims of Indo-Germanic supremacy. Nazism did not sneak up and take them by surprise. Before the Anschluss of 1938, the Viennese academic August Knoll showed his students, in an exercise in ridicule, the clear links between Nazism and the writings of Lanz and his colleagues in the *Ostara* magazine.[46] But the First World War had tipped almost the entire scientific community into war-mongering mode; the same thing happened in France but without the particular connotations of Pan-Germanism. Some of the greatest Classical historians, such as Wilamowitz-Moellendorff and Eduard Meyer (one of Kossinna's opponents) found themselves at the head of a radical movement justifying the legitimacy of the conflict; after the war, we find them among the ranks of Wolfgang Kapp's German Fatherland Party, which would attempt to stage a coup d'état in 1920. In 1917, almost 1,700 intellectuals signed a petition against the pacifist motion of the German parliament.[47] In the same vein, in 1934, Theodor Wiegand, director of the Deutsches Archäologisches Institut (German Archaeological Institute; DAI) of Berlin, and the geneticist Eugen Fischer (to whom we will return later) took the initiative of calling for Hitler, already Chancellor, to succeed the recently deceased Marshal-President, Paul von Hindenburg.[48]

[44] Cited in Müller-Hill, 1984 [1989], p. 95.
[45] See Chapter 8, p. 189.
[46] Goodrick-Clarke, 1989, p. 272; Daim, 1958.
[47] Schnapp, 1977, p. 18; Böhme, 1976.
[48] Bollmus, 1970, p. 304, note 23.

138   SECOND MOVEMENT (1903–1945)

Hitler seized power on January 30, 1933, with the active support of members of the business community and carried along by a large grassroots movement, but also following elections that were held within a climate of terror. Almost immediately, within the first year of his coming to power, one-seventh of university staff members were expelled for political or "racial" reasons. On May 10, 1933, a public burning of "undesirable" books was organized. On May 16, the archaeologist Hans Reinerth, former disciple of Kossinna, assistant at Tübingen University, and head of archaeology in Rosenberg's cultural organization, delivered a lecture on the "Battle for German Prehistory."

Raciology, and particularly the awareness of the importance and uniqueness of the Nordic race, must be acknowledged as the foundation of the National Socialist vision of the world, and thus as the foundation of all science. . . . If we want to once again become a great, united people, we have to reach back to this era when the Nordic racial core was still pure and untainted, and associated with an aristocratic civilization that shone its light across the whole of Europe. This was the era of Germanic Antiquity, of German Prehistory. Despite the fact that the proof of the cultural greatness of our ancestors has long been established, thanks to excavated finds, the barbarity attributed today to the Germanic tribes is even worse than that attributed to them by the Romans, their enemies. . . . We have been characterized as indebted to the Mediterranean for as long as there have been people on German soil.[49]

Reinerth is particularly virulent toward the Deutsches Archäologisches Institut (directed by Theodor Wiegand) and the Römisch-Germanische Komission (Romano-Germanic Commission in Frankfurt), directed by Gerhard Bersu, of Jewish origin, accusing these institutions of favoring the archaeology of the Mediterranean world with their "international pacifism" and their "policy of surrender, in the national and political sense" in the face of Poland and France. He denounces several named colleagues and concludes by demanding the creation of an Institute for German Prehistory. Eventually, for want of anything better, he transformed the Society for German Prehistory, founded by Kossinna who had died two years previously, into a State League (Reichsbund) for German Prehistory, of which he immediately became head. He also took over Kossinna's chair of prehistory in Berlin in 1935.

Reinerth is typical of this new brand of young opportunistic academics determined to use their political stances to advance their careers at any cost. He secured the dismissal, among others, of Bersu and the renowned professor

[49] Ibid., p. 154; Schnapp, 1977, p. 3; Krall, 2005; Hassmann, 2000; Fetten, 2000; Halle, 2002.

of prehistory at Marburg, Gero von Merhardt. Both had supported Reinerth in his application for the position of assistant at Tübingen. For him, the ideological issues at stake are those of a national and nationalist prehistoric archaeology confronted by the prestige of classic Greco-Roman or Oriental archaeology; it is a case of North against South. But this confrontation also strays into the Aryan problem: Should the Greeks and Romans be regarded as the pinnacle of excellence of the Aryan people, with the Germanic peoples relegated to a modest periphery (as we saw earlier, this was Hitler's opinion)? Or was the purest form of "Aryan-ness" to be found in Germania—as was the opinion of Kossinna and all the Germanomaniacs, including Reinerth and the Rosenberg Service? This debate had begun in the 1890s, when the young Kaiser Wilhelm II declared the following during a national meeting on education: "Above all else, we are lacking a national foundation. Our principles should be German; we should raise young Germans, and not young Greeks or young Romans."[50]

The opposing opinion of classicists is well illustrated by the historian Helmut Berve, professor at Leipzig who, in the preface to a 1942 collective work on "The New Image of Antiquity" (Das neue Bild der Antike), stated that "the racial instinct that has arisen in our people allows us to recognize that each of these two ancient peoples [the Greeks and the Romans] is, in its own way, part of our blood and of our make-up; it links us to them within the circle of their kinship of being."[51] Berve would also become one of the defenders of the theory of a "Dorian invasion" of Greece. The Dorians, who included the Spartans, were believed to represent a purer "Indo-Europeanness" and to be closer to the Germans than the Ionians, who included the decadent Athenians. This theory, based on a literal interpretation of Greek myths, owes its origins to German historian Karl Otfried Müller at the beginning of the nineteenth century.[52]

Respectable academics tried for a while to demonstrate their passive resistance to the attacks from Reinerth and the Rosenberg Service. Thus, Theodor Wiegand and the prehistorian Karl Schuchardt, a long-time academic rival of Kossinna and moderate nationalist, self-published a manifesto against Reinerth.[53] However, they would soon be forced to find themselves some unlikely allies in the form of Heinrich Himmler's SS.

[50] Cited in Smolla, 1979–1980, p. 3; see Chapoutot, 2012.
[51] Berve, 1942, pp. 7–8; cited in Schnapp, 1977, p. 21.
[52] Berve, 1937; Müller, K. O., 1824. See Will, 1956; Schnapp-Gourbeillon, 1979. See Chapter 15, p. 327.
[53] Bollmus, 1970, pp. 158, 303, 306.

140 SECOND MOVEMENT (1903–1945)

SS against SA and the pillaging of conquered lands

Among the Nazi leadership, Himmler was undoubtedly the most avid follower of Germanomaniac occultism. He engaged the services of a clairvoyant, the retired Viennese army officer Karl Maria Wiligut, who claimed to be descended from the 78,000-year-old line of the Wiligoten (Wiligut's ancestral clairvoyant memory allowed him to see back over 228,000 years to the time of the dwarves and giants). He could also "sense" sacred Aryan places, such as the so-called Germanic sanctuary of the Externsteine, near Detmold, which was excavated by the SS, or the site of Raidenstein near Gaggenau, which was never excavated due to the outbreak of the Second World War. The Externsteine are natural rock formations shaped by erosion, where a small aristocratic residence was constructed in the twelfth century[54]; it was never a Germanic site but this has not stopped it becoming a center for neo-pagan ceremonies in recent years.

In 1933, after a three-year stay in a mental asylum in Salzburg where he was treated for paranoia, Wiligut became head of the Prehistoric Department of the SS and a member of Himmler's personal staff: he was also promoted to the status of General. It was he who chose Wewelsburg Castle as a base for the SS, comparable to the Marienburg of the Teutonic Knights; mammoth architectural plans were drawn up which would have transformed the site into a kind of Nazi Vatican. Wiligut was also responsible for designing the infamous SS insignia ring, the Totenkopfring: decorated with a skull, swastika, and Germanic runes, the rings were to be brought back to Wewelsburg on the death of SS members. He also devised various marriage and warrior rituals.[55] Himmler believed that he himself was the reincarnation of Henry the Lion, Duke of Saxony and Bavaria in the twelfth century and adversary of Frederick I Barbarossa—Alfred Rosenberg saw him as the first true German hero.

Faced with the cultural and historical claims of Rosenberg and his Service, Reichsführer Himmler decided to set up his own think tank in 1935: the Ahnenerbe, which would be composed of forty sections covering a wide range of disciplines from botany to prehistory, and from "Indo-European musicology" to "experiments in the occult sciences." Thus, Himmler sponsored the 1938–1939 SS expedition to Tibet, led by the ornithologist Ernst Schäfer (this was the first German expedition to Tibet). Its members notably included anthropologist Bruno Beger, who would go on to make a name for himself in 1944 by criminally collecting "Jewish skulls[56]" at Auschwitz. Beger took meticulous measurements of the Tibetan population and noted the presence of "several individuals with

---

[54] Halle, 2002.
[55] Mund, 1982; Goodrick-Clarke, 1989, pp. 249–268.
[56] See Chapter 8, p. 188.

blue eyes, children with dark blond hair and a few types with marked Europid traits."[57] In fact, in the line of Helena Blavatsky and her emulators, certain occultists, including Himmler, continued to believe in a Himalayan origin for the Indo-Europeans. After the war, the participants in the expedition, all SS members, claimed that the mission was purely scientific and that its funding by the Ahnenerbe was simply opportunistic in the face of hard times. The expedition, which was welcomed back to Berlin by Himmler himself, did indeed bring back numerous botanical and zoological samples, as well as precious Buddhist works, but Beger's own archives are proof that there was an underlying "anthropological" agenda.[58]

As regards archaeology, Himmler initially surrounded himself with dubious Germanomaniacs, such as Wilhelm Teudt, the "discoverer" of the Externsteine site, and Hermann Wirth, the Dutch Atlantomaniac who was appointed as first president of the Ahnenerbe. But his desire for intellectual respectability soon led him to engage the services of genuine academic archaeologists. First, Alexander Langsdorff, a specialist in Celtic art, and Hans Schleif, director of the excavations at Olympia; then the prehistorian Werner Buttler, a student of Merhardt who would go on to become an adviser to the Minister for Education on matters concerning archaeology and heritage; the classical historian Franz Altheim; and, most notably, the proto-historian Herbert Jankuhn.[59] The latter, who enjoyed an illustrious university career at Kiel after the war, was given responsibility for the "excavations" section of the Ahnenerbe and enjoyed the status of SS Sturmbannführer. With the SS, he excavated the Viking site of Hedeby (Haithabu) near Hamburg, which would remain a reference excavation for German archaeology for many years to come. It was here that Jankuhn developed the concept of *Siedlungsarchäologie*, no longer in the Kossinnian sense of "archaeology of occupation" but in the novel sense of an "archaeology of settlement," focused on the study of the internal organization of villages and their social systems—a similar concept was being developed in Soviet archaeology at the same time.

Of course tensions abounded between Germanomaniac amateurs and their academic counterparts. Theodor Weigel, who, despite his academic credentials, was capable of recognizing runes in the half-timbered structures of German rural houses, denounced the incompetence of the clairvoyant Günther Kirchhoff, the visionary "detector" of Aryan sanctuaries and protégé of that other illustrious clairvoyant, Wiligut.[60] Wirth, who was deemed to be too troublesome, was

---

[57] Beger, 1944, p. 47. Regarding this expedition: Sünner, 1999; Engelhardt, 2008; Hale, 2005; Mierau, 2006.

[58] Conte and Essner, 1995, p. 255 and note 68, p. 405.

[59] Bollmus, 1970; Kater, 1974; Schnapp, 1977, 1980, 1981; Krall, 2005; Pringle, 2006; Wiwjorra, 1996; Mees, 2008; Olivier, 2012; Olender, 2009, pp. 125–126.

[60] Goodrick-Clarke, 1989, p. 260; Bollmus, 1970, pp. 198, 214.

142 SECOND MOVEMENT (1903–1945)

replaced as head of the Ahnenerbe by Walther Wüst, professor of Indo-European linguistics and soon to be rector of the University of Munich; it was in this latter role that he acted as one of the principal accusers of two students opposed to the regime, Hans and Sophie Scholl, members of the Weiße Rose (White Rose), who were arrested and beheaded in 1943. In his main textbook, he denounced any possible family link between Indo-European and Finno-Ugric languages, even though Kossinna himself supported this hypothesis. He attacked "accidental parallels that denigrate our beloved German, our Germanic, through an intolerable closeness to the languages and dialects of backward hunter-gatherers."[61] But the most heated tensions arose between the two competing organizations, those of Rosenberg and Himmler, who would sometimes clash personally and violently over who controlled research. Just as German generals preferred the SS to the SA, academics came out in massive support of the Ahnenerbe, whose forms of control were normally more subtle and partially protected them from vulgar and direct attacks by Reinerth and his cronies. This protection came at the price of scientific concessions (the deep coffers of the SS permitted the excavations of the Externsteine and Hedeby) but, more seriously, entailed undeniable ethical compromises.

The competition between the services became particularly cut-throat when it came to pillaging the archaeological treasures of occupied countries. In the USSR, Reinerth, with the help of Joachim Benecke, Werner Hülle, and Modrijan, ransacked the museums of Kharkov and Kiev. Meanwhile, Himmler, who was named Reich Commissioner for the Consolidation of German Nationhood in 1939, pillaged the museums of Rostov, Novocherkassk, Vorochilovsk, and Pyatigorsk, as well as private collections and libraries, with the aid of the Sonderkommando Jankuhn and the Wiking SS Division.[62] In Poland, the SS of Kommando Paulsen, a Berlin pre-historian, rifled through the museum collections and, with the help of archaeologists Kurt Willvonseder, Wilhelm Unverzagt, and Robert Schmidt, resumed the excavation of Biskupin; the SS also conducted excavations in Croatia, Serbia, and Bulgaria. In Greece, Rosenberg's Sonderkomando Griechenland pillaged Jewish collections and undertook excavations under the direction of Reinerth and Richard Harder, with the help of Siegfried Lauffer and Otto Wilhelm von Vacano, thereby circumventing "normal" archaeological institutions. The principal aims of these undertakings were to demonstrate that Neolithic populations were not yet Indo-European and to pinpoint the arrival of the Aryans, a theme that was also close to the heart of Fritz Schachermeyr, Professor of Prehistory at Jena and one of the principal supporters of the regime in the area of archaeology; he developed the theory of

---

[61] Cited in Römer, 1985, p. 61.
[62] Kater, 1974, pp. 156–157.

ARYAN PAN-GERMANISM TO NAZISM   143

the "race wars" and "de-Nordification" (*Entnordung*) which leads to degeneration.[63] Of course these archaeologists did not necessarily commit crimes against humanity themselves, unlike other Nazi scientists who conducted criminal experiments on prisoners, for example. But, as Alain Schnapp reminds us, "international celebrities like Unverzagt and Jankuhn were not afraid to commit acts that, from an intellectual point of view, were veritable scientific crimes. . . . Unfortunately, we can imagine that it was only their position as archaeologists that preserved them from committing bloody crimes."[64]

International cowardice and complicity

The fact that, in the not too distant future, scientists from other countries would have to succumb to similar demands (during the colonial wars led by France and England, for instance) is not a mitigating circumstance. Rather, the only argument in their defense lies in the fact that the Nazi regime was never the target of condemnation from the international scientific community—condemnation that might have sown the seeds of internal resistance. On the contrary, at times we witness what amounts to tacit complicity. Thus, in 1938, after all their German Jewish colleagues had been expelled from its ranks and after a handful of foreign scientists such as Henri Frankfort and Christopher Hawkes had resigned, the Director of the École Française d'Athènes (French School at Athens), along with Hellenists Robert Demangel, Paul Lemerle, and Pierre de La Coste-Messelière, all accepted to be elected to the *Deutsches Archäologisches Institut*. That same year, the prehistorian Raymond Vaufrey organized a visit for a delegation from Reinerth's Reichsbund für deutsche Vorgeschichte to the Institute of Human Paleontology in Paris, of which he was director. This was followed by a second visit, this time organized by Abbé Breuil and Claude Schaeffer, to the *Musée des Antiquités Nationales* in Saint-Germain-en-Laye. As Alain Schnapp points out, "the satisfactory account of this trip published in the *Germanenerbe* (Heritage of the Germans) journal suggests that the French interlocutors did not challenge the racial prejudices of their Nazi guests by making any allusion to Salomon Reinach,"[65] the former (Jewish) director of the museum in Saint-Germain-en-Laye.

This is the same Vaufrey who, in 1933, in one of the principal French prehistory journals L'Anthropologie, welcomed a circular from the German Minister of the Interior, Frick, imposing his ideological recommendations for the teaching

[63] Losemann, 1977; Schnapp, 1980; Chapoutot, 2008, 2012.
[64] Schnapp, 1977, pp. 17–18.
[65] Ibid., p. 22.

144   SECOND MOVEMENT (1903–1945)

of prehistory: "By endeavoring, above the bickering of the political parties, to give the German people a sense of national dignity and of the greatness of their country, the German political establishment provides an example that our own should follow, if not for their own benefit, then for that of our country."[66] Following the reactions caused by this circular, particularly among English scientists, Vaufrey attempted to justify himself in the following edition: "We must reiterate that, by virtue of its particularly naïve exaggeration, Dr Frick's circular does not strike us as a threat to the future of German science."[67]

Fifty years later, in 1986, on the occasion of the five-yearly Congress of the Union international de sciences préhistoriques et protohistorigues (UISPP: International Union for Prehistoric and Protohistoric Sciences) in England, the English scientists decided, within the context of international sanctions against apartheid, to ban the South African delegation from attending because of the racist policies of their country. The director of the Institut de Paléontologie Humaine (Institute for Human Paleontology), Vaufrey's successor and a member of the directing committee of the Union, Henri Lumley, managed to reverse the decision to organize the Congress in Great Britain and instead to move it to Germany, where the South African delegation would be welcome! This country's onerous racial past clearly did not bother the organizers, even though racism was at the heart of the debate.

As we shall see, French anthropology, with Henri-Victor Vallois at the helm, behaved no better in the face of Nazism. It was in England—a country that never had the slightest interest in the myth of Indo-European origins—and in the United States that archaeologists voiced their condemnation of Nazism's subversion of science. Actions included the aforementioned resignations of Christopher Hawkes and Henri Frankfort from the German Archaeological Institute; outcry published in *Nature* in 1934 against Frick's circular, which was seen as a sign "that Germany is ready to abandon all standards of scientific honesty"; and official support for the Romano-Germanic Commission of Frankfurt under attack from Reinerth, published in *Antiquity* in 1936. At the very moment when Hitler was seizing power, prehistorian Gordon Childe began his first lecture of the 1933–1934 academic year with the words: "No one who has read *Mein Kampf*... can fail to appreciate the profound effect which theories of the racial superiority of 'Aryans' have exercised on contemporary Germany. In the name of these theories men are being exiled from public life and shut up in concentration camps, books are being burned and expression of opinions stifled."[68] Further on,

[66] *L'Anthropologie*, 43, 1933, p. 205; cited in Schnapp, 1980, p. 27.
[67] *L'Anthropologie*, 44, 1934, pp. 447–450; cited in Schnapp, 1980, p. 27.
[68] Childe, *Antiquity*, 7, 1933, p. 410; cited in Schnapp, 1980, p. 24.

he affirms that we must consider anyone who speaks of "racial mentality" as a "charlatan."

After the war, apart from Hans Reinerth, who nevertheless found work directing the private Archaeological Museum in Unteruhldingen (a fantasy "lake city" reconstructed on the shores of Lake Constance), none of the archaeologists compromised by Nazism experienced serious career setbacks; on the contrary, most went on to have illustrious university careers.[69] More recently, on the occasion of the publication of a tribute volume in honor of Herbert Jankuhn, Heiko Steuer wrote that all he saw in the master's past political activity was a concern for the "organization of research and funding," which in no way lessened his "scientific independence."[70]

So, was Nazism just a monstrous and aberrant episode in the normal, if not irreproachable, course of Indo-European studies? At the heart of the canonical Indo-European paradigm, from its origins—if not constituting its very origin— is the opposition between Aryans and Semites, what Maurice Olender called this "providential couple" in the subtitle to his book, *Les Langues du Paradis*. In concluding the preface to this book, Jean-Pierre Vernant writes: "In the two mirror mirages, coupled and dissymmetrical, where European scientists of the nineteenth century attempted to discern their own facial features, by projecting themselves therein, how, today, could we fail to see, as in the murky background of a painting, the emerging silhouette of the camps and the columns of smoke rising from the crematoria?"[71]

[69] Olivier, 2012.
[70] Steuer, 1997, p. 565.
[71] Vernant, in Olender, 2008, p. xi.

7

A circling cradle

Up until the end of the nineteenth century, Indo-Europeanists in their search for the original Homeland essentially used arguments from linguistic paleontology while anthropological "data" (skull measurements) could be distorted to fit virtually any theory. The prehistoric remains known at the time—Swiss Lake villages, caves of the Perigord, Italian *terramare*, and the megaliths of the Atlantic façade—threw little light on the issue. Prehistorians such as Gabriel Mortillet and Joseph Déchelette generally shied away from the subject. But the continuous flow of new excavations conducted over the first quarter of the twentieth century led to such an influx of new data to museums that it became difficult to resist the temptation to utilize it. In his day, Schrader, whose attention was turned toward the steppes, could only cite gold treasures from Scythian tombs, dating to around the fifth century BCE, and contemporary rustic Russian log cabins as proofs of his theory. Now, however, scholars had access to vast assemblages of finds, soon to be baptized "cultures," stretching from the Black Sea to the Baltic.

"Culture circles" of the European Neolithic

In the preceding chapter, we saw how European prehistoric and protohistoric archaeology, intellectually dominated by German research, had begun in the early twentieth century to delineate "cultures," each characterized by particular types of associated tools, pottery, houses, and funerary rites. These cultures were themselves often grouped together within broad "culture circles" (*Kulturkreise*), as defined by German and Austrian ethnologists such as Wilhelm Schmidt and Wilhelm Koppers, to encompass human societies throughout the globe. About half a dozen such *Kreise* spanned Neolithic Europe, a period crucial for the definition of the original Homeland since the subsequent Bronze and Iron Ages witnessed the emergence of historically attested peoples (see Appendix 6).

In Scandinavia and northern Germany, the earliest phase of the Neolithic, which saw the introduction of agriculture and animal husbandry, appeared to be associated with dolmens; commonly referred to as "Huns' beds": these were the remains of megalithic burial chambers, originally covered by earthen tumuli, which contained the skeletal remains of a varying number of individuals. The deceased were accompanied by pottery vessels bearing incised decoration and featuring flared necks. This eventually became known as the Funnel Beaker culture but at the time was referred to as the "Megalithic culture" or "Nordic culture." Several periods can be distinguished within the culture.

In Central Europe (the Czech Republic, Slovakia, Hungary, Poland, Germany, and the Paris Basin), the oldest sites are characterized by very homogenous ceramic styles, with hemispherical vessel shapes and incised decoration consisting of curvilinear ribbon motifs often filled with cross-hatching or dots: these are described as Danubian or belonging to the Linear Ceramic culture (*Bandkeramik* in German and *Rubanée* in French). The houses belonging to this culture were long, rectangular, wooden structures with a roof supported by five longitudinal rows of closely spaced timber posts; Buttler, heritage advisor to the National-Socialist minister for education, carried out an exemplary excavation (covering several hectares) of one of these villages at Cologne-Lindenthal in the 1930s. Incidentally, Buttler also produced one of the first detailed syntheses of the German Neolithic[1] before being killed on the front in 1940.

Subsequently, Central, Northern, and Eastern Europe witnessed the spread of a new culture, the Corded Ware Culture (*Schnurkeramik,* also known as the "Battle Axe culture") characterized by vessels bearing impressed cord decoration and by double- or single-edged, perforated stone axe heads. The dead were buried beneath earthen mounds. The characteristic pottery and axes are found from Scandinavia (here the term "Single Grave culture" is also used because collective megalithic tombs disappeared) to the Ukraine and central Russia (here the culture has been referred to as the Fatyanovo culture since the 1880s), but they also occur sporadically in the Balkans and as far as Troy in Turkey.

In Romania, but also in Moldova and Ukraine, we find villages of well-preserved earthen houses arranged in concentric circles, sometimes built on small earthen platforms and featuring richly decorated polychrome pottery bearing spiral and volute motifs: this is referred to as the Cucuteni culture in Romania (where German archaeologist Hubert Schmidt excavated the eponymous site in 1909–1910) and is called the Tripolye culture in the Ukraine (where, in the 1930s, Soviet archaeologist Tatiana Passek excavated several of these extensive villages following the principles of an archaeology of social structures, which we will return to at a later stage). In Greece (at Sesklo, Dimini, and Servia) and in Bulgaria (where the French Consul at Plovdiv and the École Française d'Athènes excavated the first Neolithic tells), excavations revealed pottery with painted, geometric decoration. These painted wares from Eastern Europe are often compared to the Danubian *Bandkeramik,* with which they share the same repertoire of ornament and the same rules of decoration. For this reason archaeologists sometimes group them together within the same culture circle,

---

[1] Buttler, 1938.

148 SECOND MOVEMENT (1903–1945)

while others include all of the painted pottery of Eastern Europe within a single vast culture referred to as the "Vase Painters" which extends as far as Anau in Turkmenistan and Susa in Iran.

From the Carpathians to the Urals and the Caucasus, the pre- and protohistoric cultures of the steppes inhumed their dead beneath large mounds of earth known as *kurgans*. These monuments, which are visible over long distances, have become better known since the Russian state began, from the late eighteenth century onward, to take control of these vast open spaces. For a long time the *kurgans* attracted the attention of tomb robbers and treasure hunters, particularly since burials dating to the Scythian period (i.e., the last centuries BCE) frequently contain gold ornaments. The oldest examples are the least opulent. In general, they contain a coarse pottery vessel bearing rudimentary impressed ornament produced using a pointed tool, and sometimes a few copper objects or stone "battle axes" are present. The deceased, inhumed in timber chambers or in pits of various depths, are usually placed in a fetal position (as in most of the European Neolithic) and are liberally dusted with red ochre; as a result, these tombs are often grouped together under the term "Ochre Grave culture." Retired Russian army officer and archaeologist, Vasily Gorodcov, founder of the Moscow Archaeological Institute, identified three successive periods within the culture: the Pit Grave culture (*Jamnaja kultura*), the Catacomb Grave culture (*Katakumbnaja kultura*), and the Timber Grave culture (*Srubnaja*). Following on from a 1921 work by German prehistorian Max Ebert, Finnish archaeologist Aarne Michaël Tallgren published a substantial overview of this culture in French in the journal *Eurasia Septentrionalis Antiqua*[2] in 1926, for the benefit of Western scholars.

At the other extremity of the continent, a further circle grouped together, more or less by default, the various western and southwestern European manifestations: this is "the Western circle," as defined by Buttler and Childe.[3] Within this circle we find the lake villages of the Alps and Jura, so-called Chasséen pottery bearing incised geometric ornament, the megalithic "*allées couvertes*" of the Paris Basin (also known as the "Seine-Oise-Marne culture"), the funnel-shaped vessels of the Michelsberg culture of southwest Germany, etc. The term "bag-shaped" (*Beutelstil*) is often used to describe these round-bottomed wares, and Childe suggested that they may have imitated original leather vessels. The coarse nature of their fabric suggests that they were made locally by these populations.

---

[2] Ebert, 1921; Tallgren, 1926.
[3] Buttler, 1938; Childe, 1925.

A CIRCLING CRADLE 149

Uncertain European chronologies

Within this context, studies of French prehistory were scarce on the ground, apart from a few second-hand accounts by amateur archaeologists.[4] On the one hand, and this has only been recognized with hindsight, the neolithicization of France was a late and marginal phenomenon that left fewer traces on the ground than elsewhere in Europe, apart from the Atlantic megaliths, which unfortunately have been pillaged throughout history. But, above all else, archaeology in France remained a largely amateur affair due to the lack, as we have amply pointed out earlier, of a national agenda. In fact, in the interwar years and up until the 1950s, all detailed studies of the French Neolithic, including the definition of the various "cultures," were carried out by foreign researchers, such as Bosch Gimpera, Serra Rafols, Childe, Sandars, Daniel, Hawkes, Piggott, Bernabò Brea, and Vogt.[5] Furthermore, excavations tended to concentrate on Paleolithic cave sites that were easy to identify and symmetrically absent in the loess-covered regions of Central and Northern Europe, which had, incidentally, been blanketed with ice in the Paleolithic.

In France, these excavations were not undertaken as part of an attempt to identify the origins of the modern nation; on the contrary, they were carried out to throw light on the "natural" history of mankind in general. In his *Manuel*, textile manufacturer Joseph Déchelette showed his disdain for the "Aryan controversy," "one of these scientific crossroads that, at the present time, easily becomes a crossroad of errors."[6] In the end, the death of Déchelette at the battle of Chemin des Dames in 1914 (he was skeptical and suspicious of German archaeologist Paul Reinecke's identification of sites belonging to the Linear Ceramic culture, an allochthonous culture, in the Paris Basin), and then the 1929 crash, which ruined dilletantes of independent means, brought this amateur scientific activity to a virtual standstill; it nonetheless remained the principal form of archaeology carried out on French soil until the 1960s. In any case, these amateurs were never interested in the archaeological search for Aryan origins—the quest undertaken by French linguists and mythologists, such as Meillet, Benveniste and Dumézil, instead focused on the origins of European civilization as a whole.

A significant number of these cultures and cultural circles defined in the early decades of the twentieth century still retain their taxonomic value as broad stylistic entities today. But the picture has become increasingly complex with each new discovery, and dozens of other "cultures" have since been

---

[4] For example, Goury, 1931–1933; Poisson, 1928–1929, 1939.
[5] Coye, 1997; Gran-Aymerich, 1998; Hurel, 2007; Hurel and Coye, 2011.
[6] Déchelette, 1914, vol. 2, p. 10, note 2.

150   SECOND MOVEMENT (1903–1945)

added.[7] Furthermore, thanks in particular to radiocarbon dating, the chronological space has been considerably expanded since the 1950s. Up until then, the recent periods of European prehistory, from the Bronze Age onward, were dated by reference to contemporary civilizations in Mesopotamia and Egypt, for which calendars and dates were known. Objects imported from these regions and found in association with "indigenous" objects in Europe allowed connections to be made and a European chronology to be interpolated. For earlier periods, however, archaeologists had to rely on estimates. This is why the beginning of the Neolithic in Europe was initially dated to 2600 BCE; today, we know that it in fact began 4,000 years earlier. Originally believed to have lasted only a few centuries, the Neolithic and Chalcolithic periods are now known to have spanned 4,500 years and are divided into six successive broad chronological horizons (see Appendix 1); three chronological horizons and almost 2,000 years now separate the Danubian and "Battle Axe" cultures, which in the 1920s were believed to be more or less contemporary with each other. Therefore, this temporal flattening, which persisted until the 1950s, renders many details of earlier discussions invalid, in particular all comparisons between Near-Eastern civilizations and European material culture since the latter is now known to postdate the former.

Furthermore, two fundamental problems underlie this research: "racial" identification and diffusionism. The first of these issues will be looked at in greater detail in the following chapter. Most archaeologists, including Gordon Childe, did not dissociate the identification of "races" from the definition of "cultures" and paid particular attention to the skulls recovered from each site. Likewise, comparisons between the shapes and decoration of pottery vessels—often found hundreds, if not thousands, of kilometers apart—with a view to retracing migrations gave rise to numerous prehistoric "fictions" which are now regarded as being of little more than anecdotal interest and marginal in the overall history of ideas.

But, as regards the Indo-European question, just as happened before and would happen again, the archaeological "facts" could be fitted, quite naturally, into the various hypotheses proposed by other disciplines, with the same "facts" being used to prop up diametrically opposed conclusions when required. At this point the reader has no doubt guessed that the Corded Ware culture and "Battle Axe" culture would come to play an important role in these discussions: Could these decorated vases and axes (their name alone evokes war and conquest), which are found scattered all the way from Denmark to the Volga, belong to the *Urvolk*? If this is the case, then in what direction did their diffusion occur?

---

[7] See, e.g., Lichardus et al., 1985; see Chapter 11, and Appendices 12 and 15.

A CIRCLING CRADLE   151

Childish, not Childeish!

Vere Gordon Childe is without doubt the most important prehistorian of the first half of the twentieth century, and his scientific journey typifies the archaeology of this period. His progressive ideas drove him to leave his overly conservative homeland of Australia to settle in Great Britain. As he said himself, he moved from classic philology to prehistory, "like Kossinna," in order to discover "the cradle of the Aryans." In 1926, he published his second work on "the origin of the Aryans," in which he took Kossinna's theories very seriously although he himself favored a steppic origin. In the 1930s, under the influence of both functionalist ethnology and Marxism, he attempted a more complex explanation, partly evolutionist and partly anti-migrationist, of the Indo-European phenomenon. Finally, in 1957, shortly before his retirement and subsequent suicide in the area where he grew up, he acknowledged in a lucid and good-humored scientific testament that his particular quest for the origins of the Aryans was pointless.[8]

In 1925, Gordon Childe presented the first coherent synthesis of these archaeological "facts" under the telling title of *The Dawn of European Civilization*,[9] which is also an allusion to *The Dawn of History* by his mentor John Linton Myres. The entire European Neolithic was presented under "the sole unifying theme" of "the irradiation of European barbarism by Oriental civilization, a traditional dogma in Britain my faith in which had been consolidated as much by a reaction against the doctrines of Kossinna and Hubert Schmidt (which were recognized as slogans of Germanic imperialism more easily after the victory of World War I than they are after the disillusionment of World War II)."[10] He came to prehistory from a background in classical archaeology, which he studied at Oxford under Sir Arthur Evans, the excavator of Knossos, and John Myre. This was a discipline "to which bronzes, terracottas and pottery (at least if painted) were respectable while stone and bone tools were banausic."[11] He therefore had to train himself in prehistory and naturally turned to its most developed form, German prehistory. Trawling through the literature, he became familiar with "the German concept of culture, defined but not constituted by distinctive pottery and representing a people" in order to be able to construct "from archaeological remains a preliterate substitute for the conventional politico-military history with cultures, instead of statesmen, as actors, and migrations in place of battles."[12] This, then, would become his first great work, *The Dawn*. German archaeology also taught him the importance of space, geography, and

---

[8] Childe, 1926, 1958. On Childe, see Green, 1981; McNairn, 1980; Trigger, 1980; Veit, 1984.
[9] Childe, 1925; the French translation (1949), that of the fourth edition, is very approximate.
[10] Childe, 1958, p. 70.
[11] Ibid., p. 69.
[12] Ibid., p. 70.

152 SECOND MOVEMENT (1903–1945)

environment, while English archaeology, just like its French counterpart, was essentially interested in the typology of stone tools which formed the basis for the definition of successive "ages," similar to geological periods.

The following year he tackled his primary interest head-on with *The Aryans: A Study of Indo-European Origins*, which followed on from a B. Litt. thesis on "The Indo-Europeans in Greece," of which only a summary has survived. Speaking of his 1926 publication, he admits that, "inspired by J. L. Myres and behind him Schrader and Jevons, I looked with over-credulous eyes for footprints of Steppe horsemen in the marshes of the Pripet." He then goes on to state that "This was childish, not Childeish!"[13] The work nonetheless provides a very clear picture of the state of the "Aryan question" in the 1920s and summarizes not only the theories of linguistic paleontology but also the various hypotheses regarding the original birth place (Asiatic, Central European, Nordic, and steppic). It also summarizes all of the contradictions of the era, between the malleability of the "facts" and the circular pitfall posed by the notion of "culture," between the quest for a point of origin for the "genealogical tree" and a lucid suspicion of ideological abuses. Childe cannot be accused of ideological extremism or of lacking scientific culture. He also has the merit of being explicit. For these reasons it is worth spending a little more time looking at his work.

Regarding the superiority of declensions

In fact, Childe feels absolutely no sympathy for the glorification of the "Aryan race" and the pseudo-scientific foundations that certain scholars such as Vacher de Lapouge in France, Penka and Chamberlain in Germany, Dean Inge in England, and Lothrop Stoddard in the United States had attempted to lend it: "The correlation between cranial contours and intellectual characters, if any, has yet to be discovered."[14] He strongly criticizes the "fantasies of the anthroposociologists," which he deems "worthless," lacking even "a particle of evidence," and above all "positively mischievous."

> The apotheosis of the Nordics has been linked with policies of imperialism and world domination: the word "Aryan" has become the watchword of dangerous factions and especially of the more brutal and blatant forms of anti-Semitism. Indeed the neglect and discredit into which the study of Indo-European philology has fallen in England are very largely attributable to a legitimate reaction

---

[13] Ibid.

[14] Childe, 1926, p. 163. The page numbers in the quotations that follow refer to the same edition.

against the extravagancies of Houston Stewart Chamberlain, and his ilk, and the gravest objection to the word Aryan is its association with pogroms. (p. 164)

In the introduction to his book, Childe summarizes the linguistic Indo-European hypothesis (he prefers the term "Aryan,"[15] which is shorter and less clumsy) stating that

[l]anguage, albeit an abstraction, is yet a more subtle and pervasive criterion of individuality than the culture-group formed by comparing flints and potsherds or the "races" of the skull-measurer. . . . they [the Aryans] must have possessed a certain spiritual unity reflected in and conditioned by their community of speech. To their linguistic heirs they bequeathed, if not skull types and bodily characteristics, at least something of this more subtle and precious, spiritual identity. . . . The Indo-European languages and their presumed parent-speech have been throughout exceptionally delicate and flexible instruments of thought. They were almost unique, for instance, in possessing a substantive verb and at least a rudimentary machinery for building subordinate clauses that might express conceptual relations in a chain of ratiocination. It follows then that the Aryans must have been gifted with exceptional mental endowments, if not in enjoyment of a high material culture. (p. 4)

Childe credits the Aryans with the development of the first abstract science, the first world religions (Zoroastrianism, Buddhism, and even the monotheism established by the reforming pharaoh Amenhotep IV through the "Aryan" kingdom of the Mitanni), but also poetry and literary qualities.

This hymn to the linguistic superiority of inflected languages brings us back more than a century to the era of Schlegel and German romanticism. It was also important in National-Socialist ideology. For example, Bruno Kurt Schultz, professor of anthropology in Berlin and Prague (who would finish out his postwar academic career peacefully at the University of Münster) and director of the "raciology" (*Rassenkunde*) section of the SS, included the following in a textbook written in 1934: "While we in German, as well in related languages, construct a logical link between the subject of a sentence, the clause of the sentence and its object, this is not the case in most other languages, where meaning is given by the simple addition of suffixes or by the respective positions of the words in the sentence."[16]

---

[15] On the history of the term "Aryan" and associated terms, see Siegert, 1941–1942; Koerner, 1982; Olender, 2008, pp. 11–13.

[16] Schultz, 1934, p. 66; cited in Römer, 1985, p. 134.

154 SECOND MOVEMENT (1903–1945)

Two hundred pages later, having examined the various theories regarding the original Homeland, Childe outlines his own vision of history.

> The victorious expansion of the Nordic culture, whatever its origin, is the dominant fact of European prehistory from 2500 to 1000 B.C. The path of the prehistorian who wishes to draw ethnographical conclusions from archaeological data is often beset with pitfalls. . . . No such reservations impede the interpretation of the almost miraculous advance of the Nordic cultures. In their triumphant progress they repeatedly annexed regions previously occupied by higher types of culture. And such supersession of higher by lower is only explicable in racial terms.
>
> Whether the Nordic culture originated on the shores of the Black Sea or of the Baltic its authors grew from an originally poor and insignificant group to the dominant power in the western world. (p. 200)

And more precisely:

> But what was their contribution to the capital of human progress? We may at least say that they were not merely destroyers. They knew how to profit by and improve on the achievements of their victims. From the fields they had wasted choicer blossoms grew. (p. 207)

In this cataclysmic vision of a history that was born in suffering, we find the same horse-borne migrations that would be described by Émile Benveniste and Georges Dumézil a few years later.[17]

Childe concludes his work with this final paragraph:

> How precisely did the Aryans achieve all this? It was not through the superiority of their material culture. We have rejected the idea that a particular genius resided in the conformation of Nordic skulls. We do so with all the more confidence that, by the time the Aryan genius found its true expression in Greece and Rome, the pure Nordic strain had been for the most part absorbed in the Mediterranean substratum: the lasting gift bequeathed by the Aryans to the conquered peoples was neither a higher material culture nor a superior physique, but that which we mentioned in the first chapter—a more excellent language and the mentality it generated. . . . At the same time the fact that the first Aryans were Nordics was not without importance. The physical qualities of that stock did enable them by the bare fact of superior strength to conquer even more advanced peoples and so to impose their language on areas from which

---

[17] See Chapter 5, pp. 108–110.

their bodily type has almost completely vanished. This is the truth underlying the panegyrics of the Germanists: the Nordics' superiority in physique fitted them to be vehicles of a superior language. (pp. 211–212)

The most remarkable aspect of Childe's 1926 ideology is undoubtedly its contradictions regarding the notion of "race." In fact, as we shall see later, "scientific racism" was beginning to lose ground in the English-speaking world at the same time that it was becoming a terrifying instrument of political power in Germany; French scientists, for their part, occupied an ambiguous position somewhere in the middle. Childe, like most of his contemporaries, still believed that skulls could be measured (with the usual time lag between the anthropology of the time, which was abandoning these methods, and the outdated anthropology being applied by scholars hailing from other disciplines); however, he was also aware of the limits of this technique. Nevertheless he believed that archaeological cultures reflected peoples and that these peoples had a "soul": this is the romantic *Volksgeist* that underpins the notion of "culture" as defined by Kossinna. In this respect, political opinions aside, little separated Childe and Kossinna apart from a difference in opinion regarding the degree to which the genius of peoples is embodied in race. Thus Childe contrasts the inventiveness of the Aryans with the conservatism of Neolithic Danubian farmers and dolmen builders who were "wholly absorbed in the cult of the dead" which "monopolised and paralysed all their activities": "The ferment which transmuted the societies of agricultural clans into heroic tribes of the Bronze and Iron Ages, thus opening the way to initiative and individuality, we regards as Aryan. Thus the Aryans do appear everywhere as promoters of true progress and in Europe their expansion marks the moment when the prehistory of our continent begins to diverge from that of Africa or the Pacific" (p. 211).

Skulls and words

Equipped with this frank and explicit ideological toolkit, which was undoubtedly common to all researchers at the time, Childe examines the various theories regarding the original Aryan Homeland. In the 1920s and 1930s, the four principal locations proposed (from east to west, were Central Asia, the Pontic Steppes, Central Europe, and Scandinavia). These are the four locations that emerged one after the other over the course of the nineteenth century, the same four that still (unequally) divide researchers in these early decades of the twenty-first century. Three disciplines supplied the data: anthropology, linguistic paleontology, and archaeology. Anthropology was still being called upon even though it was incapable of providing any new information. The numerous "racial" classifications

156   SECOND MOVEMENT (1903–1945)

of humanity that were in vogue at the time (i.e., those of Deniker, Coon, Keith, Pittard, Ripley, Sergi, Czekanowski, Montandon, Stolyhovo, Günther, Haddon, Fischer, Eickstedt, Elliot Smith, Fleure, etc.[18]) simply repeated ad infinitum the same hard geographical evidence; the ordering of these "races" within a genealogical tree and within a historical narrative gave rise to convoluted speculations, none of which really stood out above the others. Europe was but one particular example of this: everyone agreed to recognize that Europeans tend to be tall and blond toward the north and short and brown-haired toward the south. Therefore, they were invariably divided into three groups: the "Nordics" in the north, the "Mediterraneans" in the south, with transitional "Alpines" in the middle. Beyond this simple scheme lay a labyrinth of variations and exceptions in which nationalist and hair-based prejudices inherited from the nineteenth century stumbled around and collided with each other in the search for Aryan migrations. Linguistic paleontology was in the same boat. Schrader had already said all (or almost all) that could be said, even anticipating potential objections. Childe pointed out that, depending how we look at the shared vocabulary, the original Cradle could be located virtually anywhere in Eurasia. Each of the so-called arguments, deemed to be decisive either by their presence or absence (the beech, the salmon, the willow, the eel, the tortoise, the sea, the salt, the bear, the lion . . .), could be turned around: either the word could have changed meaning to designate a new reality brought about by migrations, or a "reality" that was believed to be absent in an area to be excluded is suddenly discovered, especially when climatic changes are considered (thus, tortoises did indeed exist in Scandinavia, salmon does exist in the Black Sea, there could have been beech trees to the east of Königsberg, etc.). In the 1920s and 1930s, this in no way dissuaded a new generation of linguists, including Belgian Albert Carnoy, Swede Jarl Charpentier, and Englishman Harold Bender,[19] for example, from applying themselves diligently to the question.

Sigmund Feist, born into a Jewish family and one of the most prudent Indo-Europeanists of his day, repeatedly warned of the dangers of the "method."[20] Significantly, Feist was chosen by Max Ebert, Kossinna's erstwhile student and successor to the chair of prehistory in Berlin and editor of a monumental fifteen-volume Dictionary of Prehistory (Reallexikon der Vorgeschichte; 1924–1928), to write the entry for "Indo-Europeans" (Indo-Germanen) and, indeed, also for "Germanic peoples." Feist begins the entry as follows: "The Indo-Germans, or more rarely 'Aryans,' referred to as Indo-Europeans outside Germany, are not a historically attested people, but are only an abstraction based on linguistic

[18] See Chapter 8.
[19] Bender, 1922; Carnoy, 1921; Charpentier, 1926.
[20] Feist, 1913, 1914, 1916, 1927.

A CIRCLING CRADLE   157

facts."[21] Following a review of the Indo-European languages per se, Feist explains that most of the claims based on anthropology and linguistic paleontology for an original People and Homeland, particularly in Scandinavia, "belong to the realm of myth."

Also of significance (and we will come back to this when we look at the issue of "race") is the fact that the entry is followed by a very brief paragraph on the "anthropology of the Indo-Europeans" by racist raciologist Otto Reche, holder of the chair of anthropology at Leipzig.

> Indo-European: a term borrowed from comparative linguistics and most usually used to designate the blond North-European race (*Homo europaeus*, see this term), but which may provoke confusion since in most of these regions, originally settled by the North-Europeans, race and language have not overlapped for some time due to the bastardization (*Bastardierung*) of the Northern European speakers of Indo-European languages.

In this pre-Nazi era, the *Reallexikon* delimited the scope of the debate. But Feist, as we have seen,[22] chose to quit Kossinna's German Prehistory Society even before the First World War; he was at the receiving end of constant anti-Semitic insults from defenders of the Nordic hypothesis, such as Karl Felix Wolff, Rudolf Much (the son of prominent Germanomaniac Matthäus Much), the brilliant Germanist Gustav Neckel, and even Waldemar Barthel and Carl Atzenbeck, authors of a dictionary of prehistory published in 1936.[23]

The dominance of the Nordic theory

Therefore, in the interwar period, just as anthropology and linguistic paleontology were running out of steam, it was archaeology that provided most of the new arguments in support of the various Homelands. In Germany, the Nordic hypothesis, despite the earlier warnings of Schrader and even Hirt a generation before, became the intellectually dominant theory after the First World War. The narrative that gradually came to predominance through successive contributions from Kossinna (who contradicted himself many times) and his disciples read as follows: following the end of the last glaciation, Magdalenian reindeer hunters, the same people who left us the painted caves of the Perigord (and hence the most prestigious culture of the Paleolithic) moved northward to Scandinavia. It

---

[21] Feist, 1927, p. 54.
[22] See Chapter 6, pp. 125–126.
[23] Römer, 1981 and 1985, pp. 67, 81, 97.

158   SECOND MOVEMENT (1903–1945)

was here that the Pre-Indo-European civilization emerged; this was the culture that produced the Danish shell middens, the Maglemose and Ellerbeck cultures, and the "race" that gave rise to them, namely, the tall blonde dolichocephalics whose character was forged by the unforgiving climate. Little by little, this culture became "Indo-Europeanized," invented pottery and agriculture, erected the first dolmens (certain German archaeologists continued to perceive a southern influence in these structures), and set forth to conquer the world (see Appendix 7). Two currents can be distinguished. First, the "Southern Indo-Europeans" embodied by the Linear Ceramic culture (*Rubané*) and the Painted Pottery cultures of the Balkans (whence, according to Kossinna, they went on to found the Minoan civilization of Crete); from them sprang peoples who spoke *satem* languages: Slavs, Balts, Indo-Iranians, etc. The other current was more specifically Nordic and corresponded archaeologically to the Corded Ware and "Battle Axe" cultures and linguistically to the *centum* languages (languages in which the *s* sound of the *satem* languages is pronounced *k* or *kh*: thus, the French number "cent" occurs as *satem* in Sanskrit and *sto* in Slavic languages, but as *centum* [kentoum] in Latin and *hundert* in German). These correspond to the Germanic peoples, the Celts, the Italic peoples, and the Greeks. This binary *satem–centum* division, which is typical of the time, is considered obsolete today.

The Nordic theory was thus one of the essential ideological components of German nationalism and its political incarnation at the time, Nazism. After the war, following on the work of Hans-Jürgen Lutzhöft,[24] this ideology was qualified as "Nordic thought" (*Nordische Gedanke*) or "Nordicism" and was thus transformed into acceptable "normal thought," comparable to any other "normal thought." It is solemnly described in these terms in several entries in the recent *Encyclopédie philosophique universelle* published by the Presses Universitaires de France. The term "Germanomania" would be much more apt when referring to a pathology of thought founded on an accumulation of scientific errors, the instrument of a politics of hatred and extermination. We will come back to this when looking at the question of "race" since the equation "Original People" = blond "Nordic race," and vice versa, is one of the underlying assumptions of the theory.

But, up until 1945, the Nordic theory was far from being seen as a marginal fact. In addition to the respect Déchelette showed for Kossinna just before the First World War,[25] Childe, writing in 1926, was also able to state

> [a]t the present moment the Scandinavian theory is the most attractive, having been expounded with a wealth of detail and a complete mastery of the archaeological data by such profound students as Kossinna, Schliz and Schuchardt. . . .

[24] Lutzhöft, 1971.
[25] Déchelette, 1914, vol. 2, p. 10, note 2. See Chapter 6, p. 124.

A CIRCLING CRADLE   159

[It] is the most comprehensive and consistent synthesis of Indo-European peoples that has ever been offered. It is the only doctrine the extant expositions of which can pretend to combine the results of recent archaeological research with the data of philology. At the same time it is one of the fairest and certainly the most economical account of the development of a peculiarly European civilization yet propounded.[26]

Eminently respectable universities

Most of the influential academics of the day followed on the path laid out by Kossinna (who did no more than lend archaeological weight to a theory that was initially defined by amateur Germanomaniacs and raciologists, but also by linguists like Hirt); these successors included his personal adversary, Carl Schuchardt, director of the Department of Prehistory at Berlin Museum.[27] Of course there were amateur archaeologists among the ranks of followers, and these tended to be particularly prolific, such as medical doctors Alfred Schliz, a specialist in the Linear Ceramic and Corded Ware cultures, and Georg Wilke, who not only believed that megalithism was invented in Scandinavia, but that it had spread from here to the rest of the world, from Brittany to North Africa and as far as India.[28] But we also encounter chair holders in prehistory, such as Walther Schulz, a former student of Kossinna, professor at Halle and director of the museum (one of the oldest in Europe) in the same city. Schulz was one of the rare university academics to support Rosenberg and Reinerth, and he subsequently continued his work in the German Democratic Republic (GDR) within the same institutions.[29] We also encounter Professor Alfred Götze, who presented the first thesis in German archaeology at Jena and who was one of the excavators of Troy; Herbert Kühn, again a former student of Kossinna and professor at Cologne, but who lost his job and had to flee the country following accusations from Reinerth that he was a "*francophile*" and in a "non-Aryan marriage"[30]; Martin Jahn, yet another student of Kossinna, professor at Breslau (and at Halle, in the GDR, after the Second World War), a member of the prehistory section of Rosenberg's Combat League and subsequently at odds with Reinerth but still defending Kossinna from methodological attacks by Ernst Wahle[31] in

---

[26] Childe, 1926, pp. 166, 179.
[27] Schuchardt, K., 1919.
[28] Schliz, 1906; Wilke, 1918.
[29] Schulz (W.), 1935, 1938. See Bollmus, 1970, pp. 174, 308, 318, 321.
[30] Kühn, 1932. See Bollmus, 1970, pp. 155, 175, 234, 302.
[31] See Jahn, *Nachrichtenblatt für deutsche Vorzeit*, 1941, p. 73 *sq*; Bollmus, 1970, p. 165, etc.; Hassmann, 2000; Fetten, 2000.

160   SECOND MOVEMENT (1903–1945)

1941; and Professor Hans Seger, who preceded Martin Jahn at Breslau and shared the same political opinions.[32] The list goes on.

While not all German archaeologists were preoccupied by the Indo-German question, most nonetheless favored the theory of a Scandinavian or northern German origin for the Corded Ware culture, which at the time was the principal archaeological issue within the Scandinavian hypothesis. More specifically, as Gordon Childe notes with some irony, following the loss of the Danish province of Schleswig-Holstein in 1918, they shifted "the cradle of the Single Grave and other Battle-Axe cultures, and so of the Indo-Europeans, to the more thoroughly Germanic soil of Saxo-Thuringia."[33] This was the case with Gustav Schwantes, professor at Kiel, and Ernst Sprockhoff, who replaced Bersu after he had been ousted as director of the Romano-Germanic Commission[34]—two academics who were favorable to the regime but who fought against the machinations of Reinerth and Rosenberg—and with numerous contributors to Kossinna's journal, *Mannus* (e.g., Tode, Bicker, Agde, etc.).

Within the wider German cultural area, Moritz Hoernes, professor of prehistory at Vienna, remained reserved, but his successor from 1917 onward, Oswald Menghin, was anything but. Menghin was Minister for Education in Austria, an active Nazi, and the only archaeologist, admittedly Austrian, who was forced into exile—in Argentina—after 1945, where he continued his career.[35] He corrected, where required, the re-editions of the syntheses of his mentor Hoernes, particularly with regard to European prehistoric art, and he published a number of racist textbooks.[36] It was he who denounced the linguist Troubetzkoy to the Gestapo and had him thrown out of Vienna University.[37] In Scandinavia, where in the previous generation the Swede Oscar Montelius, founder of typology, and the Dane Sophus Müller, long-time director of the Museum of Copenhagen, not only had no inclination toward Kossinna's Nordic theories but actually opposed them, Nils Åberg, the most influential Swedish archaeologist of the first half of the twentieth century, now set out to revive them.[38] In Finland, Aarne Michaël Tallgren, appointed first professor of archaeology in Helsinki in 1923, and whose journal *Eurasia Septentrionalis Antiqua* created a scientific bridge between Soviet archaeologists and those of the rest of Europe (we will come back to this again later), believed that the Corded Ware culture, identified with the Northern Indo-Europeans, did indeed result from a movement of population from west to east (thereby completely eliminating the Pontic Steppes as a possible original

[32] Seger, 1936.
[33] Childe, 1925 [1957], p. 218 (sixth edition of *The Dawn*; French translation 1949, p. 201).
[34] See Chapter 6, p. 138.
[35] Kohl and Perez Gollan, 2002.
[36] Hoernes and Menghin, 1925; Menghin, 1934, 1935.
[37] Troubetzkoy, 1996, p. 229.
[38] Aberg, 1918.

A CIRCLING CRADLE 161

Homeland). This was also the opinion, expressed in the same journal, of his compatriot and successor Aarne Äyräpää (known as Europaeus). In Poland, the same was true of Leon Kozłowski, prehistorian, politician, senator, and professor at Lvov.[39]

The intellectual prestige enjoyed by the Nordic hypothesis was not based, therefore, on ideological affinities since neither Childe nor Tallgren (among others) can be accused of Pan-Germanist leanings. Instead it stems from the dominant scientific position of German prehistory at the time. Thanks to their network of scientific institutions, universities, libraries, and museums, and thanks also to their decisive contribution, since the nineteenth century, to the construction of a national cultural heritage, German archaeologists of the first half of the twentieth century were able to exploit means and methods of fundamental importance. They were the first to identify the remains of timber and earthen Neolithic houses (it would take another fifty years to do the same in France!), which in the 1930s would allow Werner Buttler to excavate the major Linear Ceramic village at Cologne-Lindenthal. They carried out large-scale investigations of Alpine lake villages in which Reinerth played an active role. This archaeology, which focused on the extensive excavation of ancient settlements, was systemized by Herbert Jankuhn, who applied the approach on the Viking site of Hedeby. The theoretical tools of the time were also German: these were the notion of "culture" defined by Kossinna and the concept of "type" that was first proposed by Montelius but developed by Gero von Merhardt within the "Marburg school," based in the university of the same name. Many young prehistorians from Central and Eastern Europe came to Germany and Austria to be trained, just as Gordon Childe did. The theses of German prehistorians were, therefore, highly influential.

One of the symbolic culminations of the Germanic hypothesis, and the proof of its standing, was the publication in 1936 of a tribute volume in honor of Hermann Hirt—the first linguist to have formulated the theory—on the occasion of his seventieth birthday. Hirt, blind and ill, and who would die within the year, had however refused to accept the idea of an "Aryan race" and had roundly criticized the Germanomaniacs Penka and Wilser. However, his student and editor of the volume, the racist Germanist Helmuth Arntz, "reclaims" the old man in the introduction to the work. Of course, he acknowledges, Hirt had not touched on the racial aspect of the Indo-European problem, but he was aware of it, and, at the very least, he had prepared the way for others, especially since the rise of "the Third Reich, this state that we have built for ourselves" and which Arntz, along with Hirt, "feels in harmony with."[40] In an article published the following year, Arntz voices his approval of the Reich's anti-Jewish laws, the

[39] Tallgren, 1926 (in particular pp. 143 and 227); Äyräpää, 1936; Kozłowski, 1924.
[40] Arntz, 1936, introduction, p. VII. See Römer, 1985, p. 72.

162 SECOND MOVEMENT (1903–1945)

only measures capable of restoring unity to the culture, "race," and language.[41] The principal Nazi raciologists of the time also contributed to the volume: Otto Reche; Hans Günther and his *Nordische Ring* movement; and Bruno K. Schultz, director of the "raciology" section of the SS. However, there were also a number of foreign contributors including (surprise, surprise!) Émile Benveniste, who presented his views regarding Tocharian. It is also true that the academic world of the time believed that it was possible, within a republic of letters, to separate that which pertained to the realm of science, presumed to be objective and neutral, and that which belonged to the private domain, particularly personal political opinions. It would take the Second World War and its atrocities to force people to admit that ideas could in fact kill.

Despite his membership in the Nazi party, the SA, and the paramilitary *Wehrstahlhelm* group, Arntz managed to secure a retrospective career readjustment after the war because, as a victim of score-settling between the SA and the SS, his career had supposedly been hampered; he later became president of the German Documentation Society, then president of the International Documentation Federation, and, in 1998, he received the Grand German Federal Cross of Merit (*Grosse Bundesverdienstkreuz*), the highest German honor.[42]

Also in 1936, in Vienna, ethnologist Wilhelm Koppers oversaw the publication of another collective volume dedicated to *Die Indogermanen- und Germanenfrage* (The Indo-Germanic and Germanic Question), featuring contributions from Nehring and Childe but with no space given over to raciology or the Nordic hypothesis apart from criticisms thereof.[43]

Weaknesses in the Nordic hypothesis

In reality, the Nordic hypothesis has many weaknesses. In addition to its ideological excesses and crude dolichocephalic anthropological hypothesis, it lacks coherence with regards to the usual rules of linguistic paleontology of the time. In Scandinavia, we find neither the fortified towns (*polis, *teichos) nor the horses of the shared vocabulary. Naturally snow and winter are well-attested and there are no tigers, camels, or lions (absent from said vocabulary). But the bee, the eel, and the tortoise (arguments proposed by Hirt and Kossinna) do not exist in all Indo-European languages and are nonetheless ubiquitous on European soil, just like the birch, while the word for beech (*bhagos) has very different meanings. The so-called word for the sea (*mari) only appears to designate a limited body

[41] Arntz, 1937.
[42] Maas, 2010; Klee, 2005.
[43] Koppers, 1936.

A CIRCLING CRADLE   163

of water, and, furthermore, most Greek terms linked to navigation (*okeanos*, *pelagos*, *thalassa*, *agkuros*, *kubernètès*) are not of Indo-European origin. Likewise, fishing and amber, two elements of the economy that were clearly important in Scandinavian prehistory, do not occur in the shared vocabulary. In particular, the hypothesis was wide open to concrete, archaeological criticism. Doubt can even be cast on the fundamental concept of "archaeological culture" and on the associated assumption that "one people equals one pot," as demonstrated by Eduard Meyer and Moritz Hoernes, and then by Ernst Wahle (one of Kossinna's students) and Hans Jürgen Eggers. The presumed filiation between successive Nordic cultures is particularly problematic: in short, no indisputable continuity can be observed between Maglemosian hunter-gatherers and the megalith-builders with their funnel-shaped beakers, and then between these and the Single Grave culture, between the Corded Ware culture and the "Battle Axe" culture, and finally, between all of these and the radiant Scandinavian Bronze Age. We know that, as a last resort, Kossinna used the "racial" argument to support this hypothesis of continuity. The rise of the Corded Ware culture is crucial to this argument: since it is present in an area stretching from Scandinavia to the Russian and Ukrainian steppes, its point of origin could be located anywhere within this vast territory. Russian archaeologist and historian Mikhail Rostovtzeff dates the very rich tumulus burials of the Maykop culture of the Caucasus to the middle of the third millennium BCE at least, on the basis of imports from the Middle East; this culture is related to the Ochre Grave culture of the steppes, which sometimes features "battle axes" and corded ware. Tallgren, using other arguments, proposes a date some 1,000 years later. By the end of his book on the Aryans, Childe is conscious that the choice of one or other of these dates determines the entire direction of the supposed migration and thus the choice between a Scandinavian or steppic homeland: while Childe himself favored the latter, he admits that the question remains unresolved.[44]

An explicit overturning of the Nordic hypothesis in favor of a steppic origin for the Corded Ware culture, had already been suggested by Sophus Müller in Sweden, followed by John Myres, Childe's mentor at Oxford, and then by Harold Peake.[45] Ernst Wahle, then Polish archaeologist Tadeusz Sulimirski and once again Gordon Childe, would attempt to provide archaeological proof for this hypothesis.[46] Sulimirski focused on the typology of cord-decorated wares, whose shapes appeared to be older and more uniform in the east. Furthermore, the distribution of the "Nordic race" did not match that of the Corded Ware culture—a fact that might explain the phonetic oddities of Germanic relative to the other

[44] Rostovtzeff, 1922; Tallgren, 1926; Childe, 1926.
[45] Myres, 1911; Peake, 1922; Peake and Fleure, 1928.
[46] Wahle, 1932; Sulimirski, 1933; Childe, 1936.

164   SECOND MOVEMENT (1903–1945)

Indo-European languages (a phenomenon known as "consonant mutation"). This (astute) idea that the Germans were not "real" Indo-Europeans, but rather some kind of acculturated Finno-Ugric populations with a particular accent, was not new: it dates back to Isaac Taylor, or even to Quatrefages and his "Prussian race." Feist also developed the idea, and we quite often encounter the hypothesis of an allocthonous and mixed origin for the "Nordic race" in the works of non-German anthropologists such as Sergi and Poisson.[47]

Paradoxically, almost a century later, virtually no real progress has been made regarding the genesis of the Corded Ware culture.[48] All of the hypotheses continue to be advanced—varying from a single local origin located somewhere within the territory to multiple points of origin or even the long-standing steppic origin—with no argument being decisive. By contrast, there is a definite lack of arguments in support of an entirely autochthonous origin for the earliest Nordic Neolithic (or Chalcolithic); specifically, it is difficult to argue that the Funnel Beaker culture (or *Trichterbecherkultur*, shortened to TRBK, in German), with its characteristic megaliths, might have evolved from the pre-existing Mesolithic Maglemose and Ertebølle cultures. Instead the discussion has focused on the way in which this first Scandinavian Neolithic might have emerged in conjunction with the Danubian Neolithic (Linear Ceramic culture and derivatives) or its steppic equivalent and on the importance of the indigenous component associated with one or other of these two traditions, or both.

A die-hard Asiatic cradle

Confronted with the Nordic hypothesis, principally championed by the Germans, Indo-Europeanist scholars from other European countries, most of which had been at war with Germany during the First World War, almost exclusively opted for one of the three other "solutions": Central Asia, the Russian steppes, or Central Europe. The Asian hypothesis, which Childe deemed the "most venerable," still had its supporters although they had now abandoned the high plateaus of Pamir for the steppes. Even in Germany, National Socialist philologist Hermann Güntert supported it, to the dismay of his political friends.[49] In 1904, American geologist Raphael Pumpelly, assisted by Hubert Schmidt of the Museum für Völkerkunde in Berlin, had excavated a Neolithic site at Anau in Russian Turkestan which yielded finely painted pottery.[50] In fact, this was a peripheral facies of the Near-Eastern Neolithic which has since been dated to

---

[47] Taylor, 1890; Feist, 1914, 1926, 1932; Sergi, 1903; Poisson, 1934, 1939.
[48] See Chapter 11, p. 250; Appendices 1 and 12.
[49] Güntert, 1934. See Römer, 1985, p. 74.
[50] Pumpelly, 1908.

the sixth millennium BCE. Pumpelly, whose express aim was to search for the "cradle of the Aryans" at this location, rapidly lost heart: Anau was in no way specifically "Aryan," even though the remains of a type of horse, known henceforth as *Equus pumpellii*, were found there. However, the site would nonetheless be used to support the Asian hypothesis. Attempts were even made to group together all Neolithic sites with painted ware, from Egypt to Transylvania, passing through Iran, Anau, Knossos, and Bulgaria, to form a vast "Vase Painter" culture potentially identifiable with the Aryans (in a Kossinnian, contrary version of events, this corresponded to the easternmost reach of the "Southern Indo-Germanic" migrations); in actual fact, these ceramic phenomena were unrelated and spanned several millennia.[51]

Certain similarities had also been noted between European Neolithic wares and those from Turkey whether or not they were attributed to these so-called vase painters. This is why, in 1927, British researcher Adalbert Sayce, one of the first to study the Hittite civilization, would finally opt for a Near Eastern, and more specifically Turkish, origin for the Indo-European languages[52]; prior to this he had defended an origin in the Hindu Kush before changing his mind in favor of a European homeland. He based his opinion on other considerations, most notably of an anthropological nature. Subsequently, this hypothesis would frequently resurface in the context of an association between the origin of Indo-European languages and the emergence of the European Neolithic.

The Asian location also benefited from theories on the origin of mankind that often continued to locate the appearance of early humans in the Hindu Kush; this is a continuation of the early nineteenth-century scholarly tradition of a "mythical India" acting as a temporary stopover for the Garden of Eden. In the 1920s, the discovery in Zhoukoudian, China, of the remains of "Sinanthropus," a local variety of *Homo erectus* dating back half a million years, lent further support to these theories (the oldest form of hominid, Australopithecus, had been discovered in 1925 in South Africa, but researchers were slow to classify this species—which had emerged on the Dark Continent—as "human": its name literally means "southern ape"). The archaeological evidence for the Asian hypothesis was decidedly weak. It was founded on a certain view of the Aryan migrations, namely one modeled on the steppic invaders of the historic period, the Huns and Mongols, who regularly overran Europe. The shared vocabulary includes the horse and the cart and more words connected with animal rearing than with agriculture; furthermore, the horse appears to have played an important role in certain Indo-European religions of the historic period (Rome and India); in addition, the wild horse ("Przewalski's horse") still inhabited the

---

[51] See Childe, 1926, pp. 103–116; Appendix 6.
[52] Sayce, 1927.

166 SECOND MOVEMENT (1903–1945)

Mongolian steppes in the nineteenth century (today it only survives in zoos and reserves), and it plays an important role in local mythologies. Furthermore, certain resemblances had long been noted between Indo-European languages and other linguistic groups (e.g., Finno-Ugric languages, Caucasian languages, and Semitic languages) to the point that, since the beginning of the twentieth century, Holger Pedersen in Denmark and Alfredo Trombetti in Italy had envisaged a common origin for all of these languages and had even attempted to develop a family tree of all the world's languages (we will come back to this point because these theories are once again in vogue). The Asian steppes undoubtedly represent the most convenient contact zone imaginable between these various languages.

Since modern nomads are generally herders, and since the original Indo-Europeans appear to have practiced some degree of agriculture (as confirmed at Anau), several researchers in the 1930s proposed that the original People arose from a fusion between nomadic herders (Finno-Ugrics for the most part) and early agriculturalists (predominantly from the Caucasus or further south), each contributing its own techniques, ideology, and language: this would explain both the linguistic affinities and also some of the incoherencies observed in the reconstructed language. This notion of centripetal "fusion," which is a break from the usual model of centrifugal arborescence, was developed in various fields, including in the area of religions by Viennese ethnologist Wilhelm Koppers[53] and in the area of linguistics by Dutch researcher Christianus Cornelius Uhlenbeck.[54] The previously mentioned collective work,[55] edited in Vienna in 1936 by Wilhelm Koppers, largely reflects this mindset, and its contributors (Wilhelm von Brandenstein, Alfons Nehring—Schrader's successor—Wilhelm Koppers, Gordon Childe, etc.), in direct opposition to the *Festschrift für Hermann Hirt*, opt for a complex, steppic origin, be it Asian or Eurasian, for the Indo-European phenomenon. In France, this idea would be taken up in two works by prehistorian and amateur anthropologist Georges Poisson.[56]

Excavations in Central Asia

The most prominent French orientalist archaeologist of the beginning of the twentieth century was Jacques de Morgan. Having directed the Service des antiquités égyptiennes, he was appointed as head of the delegation from the Ministère de l'Instruction Publique et des Beaux-Arts to Persia in 1897, a position which he held until 1912. Discoverer of the Hammurabi Code and the

[53] Koppers, 1929, 1935, 1936.
[54] Uhlenbeck, 1935, 1937.
[55] Koppers, 1936.
[56] Poisson, 1934, 1939.

A CIRCLING CRADLE   167

Naram-Sin stele, he left behind on his death in 1927 a three-volume synthesis posthumously published under the title *La Préhistoire orientale*.[57] In this book, he retraces the history of Asia, from the origins of mankind to the Iron Age, and writes at length about the Indo-European cradle and migrations. He forwards the idea of a shifting cradle, initially Siberian and then Central Asian, whence the Indo-Europeans, driven out by the cold, spread out toward India, Iran, and Europe in successive waves, bringing with them agriculture, animal husbandry, and metal working. He had virtually no new archaeological proof at his disposal even though he carried out a brief test excavation at the Iranian site of Khargush Tepe, near Astarabad, in 1890. The hypothesis of climatic cooling in the Central Asian homeland dates back to at least 1820, when it was proposed by German Iranianist scholar Johann Gottlieb Rhode.[58] In his turn, Morgan resorts to the *Avesta* for support, and he would not be the last scholar to do so.

Morgan also uses anthropological arguments; he revives the hypotheses advanced in the nineteenth century by certain members of the Société d'Anthropologie de Paris, such as Piétrement and Ujfalvy, who in 1887 called for excavations to be carried out in Central Asia: in Europe, the true Aryans were the brown-haired brachycephalics, also known as the "Alpine race," of Asian origin. Certain anthropologists, such as Sergi[59] in Italy, would develop this theory, which ultimately stripped the blond European dolichocephalics of all original "Aryan-ness." Between the "Nordics" to the north and the "Mediterraneans" to the south, did the anthropological maps not show *Homo alpinus* driven like a great wedge between Central Asia and the tip of the Armorican peninsula?[60] This was a striking racial and historical interpretation of a wider biological phenomenon: the progressive lightening of human pigmentation from south to north in step with the gradual decrease in local sunlight intensity. Thus raciologists were obliged to accept numerous "mixings" in the contact zones between "races."[61]

Morgan vigorously opposed the Pontic Steppes hypothesis developed by Schrader on the grounds that these regions would have been uninhabited and uninhabitable before the late arrival of the brachycephalic Aryans—which forces him to regard as "doubtful" the Ukrainian Paleolithic sites with their spectacular mammoth bone structures dating back to the Pleniglacial period more than 20,000 years ago. Of course, since Morgan's day, nothing has come to light that might support his narrative. In fact, archaeological discoveries have led to a complete revision of the chronological framework on which he attempted to build his theory and which presumed, as in Childe's work, a contemporaneity between

---

[57] Morgan, 1925–1927, vol. 1, pp. 160–200; vol. 3, pp. 380–389.
[58] See Chapter 3, p. 34.
[59] Sergi, 1903. See Chapter 4, p. 83.
[60] Morgan, 1925–1927, vol. 1, pp. 186 and 189.
[61] For example Morgan, 1925–1927, vol. 1, p. 186.

168   SECOND MOVEMENT (1903–1945)

the beginnings of the European Neolithic and the first Near Eastern urban civilizations of the third millennium BCE.

But since it was the brainchild of a prominent archaeologist whose recent excavations had swelled the Louvre collections, this narrative, by then at least half a century old and purely anthropological in its inspiration, was difficult to ignore. Excavations conducted in Central Asia and in Northern Iran in the interwar period aimed, among other things, to identify evidence for the supposed passage of the Indo-Europeans.

The key area appeared to be the Turkmenian steppes to the south of the Aral Sea; the Syr Darya and Amu Darya flow through this area, which opens out to the south, between the Caspian and the Alborz Mountains to the west and the Hindu Kush to the east, toward the Iranian Plateau. This flat-land area lay west of the mountainous region (the high plateaus of Pamir and the Hindu Kush) which had been hailed as the original Homeland throughout the nineteenth century by the likes of Rhode, Pictet, Virchow, and Deniker, all proponents of an Asian cradle. The proposed new location, though less appealing to the imagination, was nonetheless more reasonable: early travelers to this region had noted the presence of *tepes* (*tells* in Arabic), artificial hills formed from the accumulation of successive prehistoric villages. In excavating the example at Anau in the extreme south of Russian Turkmenistan, close to the Iranian border, Pumpelly found himself on the southern periphery of this putative cradle whence the Indo-European hordes may have set out on their conquest of Iran and India. The period between the two world wars saw the excavation of several sites on either side of this frontier. On the Soviet side, excavations such as those carried out by Maruščenko at Akdepe near Ashgabat, were little known before the Second World War. On the Iranian (and Western) side, which was open to foreign archaeologists from 1930 onward, excavations were carried out by a Swedish team under the direction of Ture Arne at Shah Tepe, and by American teams under Frederick Wulsin at Tureng Tepe and Erich Schmidt at Tepe Hissar.[62]

These methodical investigations allowed the material culture of the Neolithic and Bronze Age of this largely unknown region to be identified for the first time. But soon they would also reveal an apparent historical fact: a type of pottery decorated with black geometrical motifs on a red background appeared to replace a more austere type of ware that was uniformly gray in color. Depending on the authors, it was made more or less clear that the former was the work of indigenous farmers while the latter was produced by Indo-European nomads from the steppes. This was the conclusion expressed matter of factly by Schmidt in the context of the end of the "Hissar I" period (characterized by the painted pottery): "There are an insufficient number of skulls at Hissar I and II to determine

[62] Arne, 1945; Schmidt, E., 1933, 1937; Wulsin and Smith, 1932.

A CIRCLING CRADLE   169

with certainty the racial differences between the two peoples but as far as we can tell, clearly elongated skulls appear in layer II while wider skulls appear to have been more prevalent among the people of the painted pottery period."[63]

This racial interpretation was not always unanimously accepted. Otto Reche, a renowned Nazi raciologist (author of the "Indo-European race" entry in Ebert's monumental dictionary of prehistory), was able to affirm from simple observation of photographs that several skulls from Shah Tepe were clearly dolichocephalic and Nordic. The Swede Ture Arne noted (with a degree of malice) in the final publication that, following careful measurement, the skulls in question were in reality "the least dolichocephalic." The authors of archaeological monographs nonetheless felt obliged to include such raciological contributions. The study of the skulls recovered during the excavations of Mohenjo-Daro, which allowed Sir John Marshall to identify the great Indus civilization, were entrusted to anthropologist Arthur Keith, the leading figure of British "scientific racism." In 1931, the latter enthused over the archaeological traces left by the Indo-Europeans: "There was the original homeland of the inventors and pioneers of our modern civilization. From the Iranian uplands, our pioneers descended on the neighboring river lands of India and Arabia, probably using native labour to execute their great schemes."[64]

The question of the gray "Indo-European" wares would gain growing attention, minus the anthropometry, after the Second World War. With the works of Soviet archaeologist Vadim Masson and French archaeologists Roman Ghirshman and Jean Deshayes, the gray wares became the marker of Indo-European migrations across Asia and beyond. In reality, there was no proof that these two categories of ceramics, painted and gray, actually succeeded each other in time. Their shapes are often very similar, and, in certain tombs, at Tepe Hissar for example, both types are even found deposited together.

A return to (Eastern) Europe

Shifting our attention from Asia to Europe, we recall that at this time German archaeology organized the Neolithic of Continental Europe into three cultural circles (*Kulturkreise*: see Appendix 6). Each of the three was used, alternately and contradictorily, to support the hypothesis of a European homeland. The first circle, often qualified as "Nordic" or "Megalithic," encompasses all types of dolmens and related monuments in northwestern Europe (Scandinavia, Germany, and Holland). For most researchers of the time, these manifestations

[63] Schmidt, E., 1933, p. 365.
[64] Keith, *Illustrated London News*, 1931, p. 1000, cited in Cleuziou, 1986, p. 222.

170 SECOND MOVEMENT (1903–1945)

derived, to a greater or lesser degree, from the indigenous hunter-gatherer cultures of the local Mesolithic. In a later phase, and without a clear break in the archaeological record, the Corded Ware (*Schnurkeramik*) culture appeared in this region along with its stone "battle axes," and, in this instance, the culture extended as far as Poland and Ukraine. The second circle corresponds, in its broadest accepted sense, to the Neolithic societies of southeastern and Central Europe; the associated pottery is richly decorated with geometric motifs which are either painted, as in the area from the Balkans to western Ukraine, or incised, as in the Linear Ceramic of Central Europe. The origin of these cultures is still open to debate. Finally, the third circle extends to include Ukraine and southern Russia as far as the Caucasus; it corresponds to the Ochre Grave culture in which the dead, abundantly sprinkled with ochre, were buried in a fetal position within timber-lined shafts or chambers covered by earthen mounds known as *kurgans*.

The problem facing archaeologists searching for the original Homeland was how to order these groupings chronologically and articulate them historically—in other words how to identify the origins, evolutions, migrations, or conquests—and then, potentially, to trace the expansion of the original People. In fact, given the continuing significant uncertainty regarding the records and the absence of accurate physico-chemical dating methods, all of the hypotheses remained possible. Any of the circles could have acted as a point of origin, with the other two either being secondary homelands or independent cultures destined to disappear.

For Kossinna and his followers, the situation was simple[65]: the Scandinavian Mesolithic, which had itself developed from the Magdalenian, characterized by the painted caves of southern France, gave rise to the "Nordic circle" and its dolmens, which can be identified with the original People and the "Nordic race"; this culture extended both eastward (giving rise to the Corded Ware culture and *centum* languages) and southeastward (giving rise to the Linear Ceramic culture, the painted wares of the Balkans, and *satem* languages). The Ochre Graves are either omitted from this picture or are considered as an expression of the Corded Ware culture as attested in the western USSR. As we have seen, this position was predominant even among non-German archaeologists and was, for example, that held by Déchelette, Tallgren, and Childe. Even among the dissenting voices, no one questioned the indigenous nature of Nordic megalithism. The only problematic issue was the direction in which the Corded Ware culture spread; in the 1930s, several archaeologists, including Wahle, Sulimirski, and Childe, proposed that it spread from east to west. In this case, if there was no expansion of the "Nordic circle," it could not be a candidate for the "homeland."

---

[65] See Chapter 6, pp. 157–159.

A CIRCLING CRADLE   171

The Pontic Steppes endure

In the drive to repatriate the Indo-European cradle to Europe, the identification of the Pontic Steppes as the original Homeland, an idea that can be
traced back to Leibniz, was first formulated in detail by German linguist Otto
Schrader. Schrader's meticulous work won over a certain number of historians,
philologists, and anthropologists who, in the first three decades of the twentieth
century, were increasingly non-Germans. In Britain, proponents of Schrader's
theory included John Myres, Professor of Ancient History at Oxford, mentor to
Childe, and the first editor of the journal *Man*; ethnologist and raciologist Alfred
Haddon, one of the founders of field ethnology; historian Harold Peake; and
raciologist and geographer Herbert Fleure.[66] In France, the theory was adopted
by Émile Benveniste in 1939. In the interwar years, the development of archaeological excavation in the region permitted Tallgren, Ebert, and Childe to publish the first archaeological syntheses written in the West. Regardless of whether
or not these investigations agreed with Schrader's hypothesis, it could not be
ignored.

In 1926, Childe presented the steppic hypothesis although admittedly without
total conviction.[67] The finds from the Ochre Graves appeared to support the data
provided by Schraderian linguistic paleontology, as did the natural environment. Indeed, the modest aspect of the tombs themselves seemed to suggest a
nomadic lifestyle. Animal husbandry, including the rearing of horses, was well-
attested by the bone finds, and there was also some evidence for limited agriculture. Clay models provided evidence for wheeled vehicles. Copper was present
in the form of daggers and projectile points, words that are also attested to in
the shared vocabulary. Stone and copper axe heads were reminiscent of types
found in Mesopotamia; the Greek word for axe (*pelekus*) can be compared to
the Assyro-Babylonian word *pilakku* and the Sumerian word *balag*, just as the
Indo-European word for copper, **roudhos*, is reminiscent of the Sumerian word
urud. Similarly, the root of the word for star, **ester*, can be compared to the name
of the Mesopotamian goddess Ishtar, whose ideogram takes the form of a star.
Moreover, the uniform nature of the funerary ritual of the Ochre Grave culture
might reflect shared religious beliefs, perhaps even the adoration of a single main
deity, namely the **Dyeus* of reconstructed Indo-European, and "this cultural
unity would perhaps allow us to infer the currency also of a single language."[68]
Finally, elements common to Indo-European and Finno-Ugric (Finnish, Sami,
etc.) languages, on the one hand, and Mesopotamian, on the other, could

---

[66] Peake, 1922; Peake and Fleure, 1928; Haddon, 1925; Myres, 1911.
[67] Childe, 1926, pp. 183–200.
[68] Ibid., p. 183.

172 SECOND MOVEMENT (1903–1945)

be explained if the original Homeland was indeed located halfway between Mesopotamia and Northern Europe. Furthermore, "The people interred here were generally tall, dolichocephalic, orthognathic and leptorrhine, in a word Nordics. There was, however, at least a small minority of Brachycephals present in the population."[69]

The proof appears tenuous and could undoubtedly be applied to other "cultures" in Europe or elsewhere. Childe is well aware of this fact and very often uses the conditional tense in his account. Important elements in the argument, namely the battle axes and the horse, "cannot, therefore, be regarded as conclusive in view of the mass of evidence collected by the advocates of the Germanist thesis."[70] A crucial point remains the interpretation of the direction of the diffusion of the Corded Ceramic culture, which is found in an area stretching from Scandinavia to Russia (the Fatjanavo culture) and Ukraine, passing through Poland (the Zlota culture); certain vessels are found deposited alongside local pottery in the ochre graves, as in the cemetery of Jakovica. In the 1920s, the dominant opinion favored a movement from west to east; this view was also held by non-German authors such as Tallgren (who in fact attributed a date that was too early to the ochre graves) and Äyräpää in Finland and Leon Kozłowski in Poland.

Max Ebert was alone in developing an original point of view in his 1921 monograph entitled *Südrussland im Altertum* (South Russia in Antiquity). Born in eastern Germany, he became professor of prehistory at Riga, in what was then independent Latvia, as well as at Königsberg, in East Prussia. In the monograph, he concedes that the Corded Ware culture originated in northwestern Europe but also states that its presence in the steppes was only marginal. As regards the "steppic homeland" more generally, he briefly resumes Schrader's arguments to remind the reader that in this hypothesis, which was principally supported by linguists, "each point of the demonstration is contestable from a linguistic point of view."[71] Here he hopes to confine himself to the archaeological evidence, "even though the Indo-European problem is above all a linguistic problem and cannot be resolved using archaeological material alone."[72] In his opinion, the painted pottery of the rich Tripolye culture found in Ukraine stylistically belongs to the Linear Ceramic group. This wider group is itself "in close contact and overlaps" with the Nordic Megalithic culture.

Thus, all of Neolithic Europe, from the Dnieper to the Atlantic, was encompassed by a single cultural complex, that of *Alteuropäisch* (Ancient Europe), within which no clear frontiers existed; it is with this complex that the primitive Indo-Europeans should be identified. Implicitly, tracking back in time,

[69] Ibid.
[70] Ibid., p. 192.
[71] Ebert, 1921, p. 58.
[72] Ibid.

this model leaves open the possibility of an Asian or, more specifically, a Near Eastern origin for the primitive Indo-Europeans since it is generally assumed (and correctly so) that the roots of the European Neolithic lie in this region. This is why Adalbert Sayce placed the primitive Homeland in Anatolia. The material culture of the Ochre Grave group owes nothing to the *Alteuropäisch* culture, nor does it have anything in common with the succeeding Bronze Age cultures, which are identifiable with historic Indo-European peoples; in effect "it vanishes without a trace in the steppes."[73]

Ebert died at the age of fifty in 1929, having taught for only two years at Berlin University. As a consequence, he did not have time to develop his hypotheses further nor to create a research tradition, even though the use of the term *Alteuropäisch* endured to varying degrees in archaeological and linguistic circles to designate the Neolithic substrate of Europe. The identification of primitive Indo-Europeanness with the European Neolithic—admittedly an effective, if only moderately migrationist, solution—would not fully resurface until the 1960s but with no specific reference to its originator, Max Ebert.

Childe himself makes no mention of Ebert in his review of the various theories. He confines himself to citing the hypothesis of British linguist Peter Giles who, in 1922,[74] had proposed, without reference to any particular archaeological culture but for environmental reasons, that the original Homeland was located in Central Europe, in the area between the Carpathians, the Balkans, and the Alps. Childe dismisses the suggestion because the Linear Ceramic culture, which occupied exactly this region in the Neolithic, did not correspond to the specifications laid out by linguistic paleontology. This culture was, he claimed, made up of small, undifferentiated communities of peaceful farmers of Mediterranean origin, in which "the women doubtless made the pots, imitating with feminine conservatism the gourd vessels of their remote ancestors."[75] Without "subscribing to the extravagances of the 'racial psychologists,'" Childe admits that their activities must have lent these Neolithic people "a specific mentality, that of the peasant." It is, therefore, "highly improbable" that this culture's "narrow conservatism, its intense attachment to the soil should ever have developed of itself into that restless love of wandering and acquisitiveness which has not only diffused Aryan languages over half the globe, but also imposed them on so many non-Aryan peoples."[76] This would often be the argument, implicit or otherwise, used against the hypothesis linking the original Homeland and the Neolithicization of Europe.

[73] Ibid., p. 59.
[74] Giles, 1922.
[75] Childe, 1926, p. 140.
[76] Ibid., p. 143.

174   SECOND MOVEMENT (1903–1945)

Marxism and archaeology

At the end of his 1926 work, Childe is clearly in an awkward position. Despite being "elegant," the Germanic theory aroused his ideological reticence. But the steppic theory appeared to lack a strong foundation. Toward the end of his book he seems to have given up trying to decide between these two contradictory hypotheses (e.g., "Whether the Nordic [i.e., Indo-European] culture originated on the shores of the Black Sea or of the Baltic"[77]). The years that followed would at least provide Childe and others with arguments (not always well-founded) in favor of an east-to-west diffusion of the Corded Ware culture. But, in the meantime, as he continued to collect and synthesize archaeological data, he came to realize the extent to which his previous work had been in vain and even "childish." In line with his political sympathies, he also established contact with the burgeoning world of Soviet archaeology. This contact forced him, sometimes reluctantly, to rethink the history of societies.

Up until the October Revolution of 1917, Russian archaeology was largely an amateur affair and its most enlightened practitioners worked under the influence of German archaeology, but also that of Montelius and Déchelette. There existed an Imperial Commission for Archaeology which oversaw research and discoveries under the presidency of Alexej Uvarov. Countess Uvarova personally financed many of the excavations, such as those carried out by Vasily Gorodcov, an army officer who was the first to sketch out a chronology for the ochre graves of the Pontic Steppes. After the revolution, Russian archaeology became professionalized and the Commission was transformed into the State Academy for History and Material Culture (GAIMK), under the direction of Georgian linguist and archaeologist Nicholas Jakovlevitch Marr. The Academy itself subsequently became the central research body known as the Academy of Sciences of the USSR.[78]

During the 1920s, the years of Lenin's New Economic Policy (NEP), the intellectual climate remained liberal and even prolific in the domain of Marxist thought. As regards archaeology, while certain researchers emigrated, such as the economist and classical historian Rostovtzeff, others carried on their research within the same tradition, such as, for example, Vasily Gorodcov, Alexander Spitsyn, and Alexander Miller, former student of Mortillet and professor at Saint Petersburg University. Contacts with the West remained active, thanks chiefly to the Finnish journal *Eurasia Septentrionalis Antiqua*, founded in 1926 by Aarne Tallgren. Apart from his sweeping panorama of the "Pre-Scythian Pontide,"

---

[77] Childe 1926, p. 200.
[78] On Soviet archaeology in the interwar period, see Bulkin et al., 1982; Trigger, 1989 (pp. 207–243); Malina and Vašíček, 1990; Miller, M. O., 1956; Sklenar, 1983; Bloch, 1985; Gellner, 1980; Davis, 1983; Shnirelman, 1995.

A CIRCLING CRADLE 175

Tallgren regularly reported on the progress of Soviet archaeologists whose articles he also published in the journal. He himself insisted on the importance of a material and economic approach to ancient societies and advocated a move away from purely classificatory and typological studies, which he referred to as "formalist," a term also used in the USSR.

Everything would change, however, at the end of the 1920s with the emergence of Stalin's reign of terror. Like all aspects of Soviet society, archaeology was hard hit. Dozens of archaeologists were thrown out of their positions (e.g., Vasily Gorodcov, who was later rehabilitated and decorated), forced into exile (like Alexander Miller), arrested, or simply "disappeared." Tallgren, who was a sympathizer of the revolution in its early days and an opponent of the extreme right in Finland, was one of the first to express his indignation. In 1928, he published an "open letter" to the Soviet academic authorities. In his account of his last trip to the USSR in 1936, published in the journal, he describes the prevailing climate of fear and mentions the "disappearances." In another article dedicated to "The method of prehistoric archaeology," published in the same issue, he denounces interference between politics and science in Germany and in the USSR.[79] Nazi archaeologist Bolko von Richthofen, professor at Königsberg, published a reply in the same journal in 1938, in which he states that raciology was indeed a science and that Tallgren's criticisms could in no way apply to German archaeologists since they, unlike their Soviet counterparts, never cited politicians in their work. The Soviet authorities forbade Tallgren from entering the country again and stripped him of his honorary membership in the GAIMK. He ceased publishing *Eurasia Septentrionalis Antiqua* in 1938 and died in 1945.

Marr, Stalin, and linguistics

Nonetheless, the emergence in the 1920s of a new generation of young archaeologists brought up under Marxism, some of whom were communist militants, also had scientific consequences. The attention now paid to the functioning of societies, and not simply to labeling them according to the form or "type" of their objects, led to larger-scale excavations which aimed to better understand the spatial organization of settlements. The fastidious construction of chronological tables and the search for hypothetical and inevitable migrations gave way to the study of successive socioeconomic transformations—these were issues that quickly attracted the attention of the likes of Tallgren in Finland, Childe in Great Britain, and, a little later, Bosch Gimpera in Spain and Leroi-Gourhan in France. Studies of technology sought to understand the modes of

---

[79] Tallgren, 1936a, 1936b. On Tallgren, see Kivikoski, 1954.

176 SECOND MOVEMENT (1903–1945)

production and the uses of pottery and tools and would soon lead to Semenov's pioneering work using microscopic and experimental analysis to study use-wear traces on lithic tools. Ethnicity itself was no longer seen as the permanence of timeless entities (the *Volksgeist*) but rather as the crystallization, in a given moment of time, of historical and economic processes; Tallgren would incorporate these notions in a work published in Finnish in 1939, "Ethnogenesis, or Reflections on the Birth of Nations."[80] Thus, in 1933, twenty-three-year old Yevgeni Krichevsky would propose a scheme whereby the Indo-European languages emerged progressively from Central Europe and, more specifically, from the Linear Ceramic culture; Childe, although critical, considered the article to be "remarkable."[81]

In the end, this profound shift in perspective died a death in the USSR (Krichevsky himself died in 1942, at the age of thirty-two) because of the paradoxical but symptomatic convergence between the intellectual dogmatism that was part of the Stalinist Ice Age and linguistic theories that had survived from the early nineteenth century: this would be the accomplishment of Nicholas Jakovlevitch Marr, first director of the GAIMK, who died in 1934. On the one hand, according to the evolutionism outlined in 1883 by Engels in *The Origin of the Family, Private Property, and the State*, a notion that was borrowed from American ethnologist Lewis Morgan, humanity was destined to pass through a series of socioeconomic stages. Simple to understand, but still open at a time when archaeological research was in its infancy, the theory would become fossilized under Stalin as a revealed and intangible truth. On the other hand, we recall that the first linguistic classifications, those of the Schlegel brothers taken up by Bopp and many others, distinguished, in an order of growing complexity reminiscent of the "realms of nature," three groups of languages: isolating, agglutinating, and inflective.[82] At the moment when evolutionism was on the rise, Max Müller, a follower of Bopp, had correlated these three classes with three stages of social evolution: the isolating languages were associated with a "familial" organization, the agglutinating languages with a "nomadic" organization, and the Indo-European and Semitic languages with a "state" organization.[83]

Marr, taking inspiration from Engels, revisited this periodization when devising his "stadial theory," in which the isolating languages correspond to the initial stage of "primitive communism," the agglutinating languages to the appearance of division of labor, and the inflective languages to the emergence of class-based societies. Marr also created the group of "Japhetic" languages in which he lumped together the languages of the Caucasus, Hamito-Semitic

---

[80] Tallgren, 1936a, 1939; Kivikoski, 1954, p. 111.
[81] Kriševskij, 1933.
[82] See Chapter 2, p. 22.
[83] Müller, F. M., 1876, p. 69; Römer, 1985, p. 117; Olender, 2008, pp. 82–92.

languages, Basque, and even Burushaki, a well-known but minor isolated language of northern Pakistan. According to Marr, the first human language was founded on four basic roots (*ber, jon, ros, sal*), which can be found in all of the world's languages.[84] Soviet scholars were strongly encouraged to rethink not only the entire field of linguistics but also archaeology in these terms. Thus Vladislav Ravdonikas, leader of the young "Marrist" archaeologists, could state that the Crimea never underwent the slightest population change but rather, over the course of less than two millennia, witnessed an internal linguistic evolution: as society evolved, the local populations saw their Cimmerian language (a "Japhetic" language according to Marr) transform itself into Scythian (a classically Indo-Iranian language), then into Gothic (this time a Germanic language whose Germanity was vehemently denied), and finally into Slav![85] Migration hypotheses were rejected all the more vehemently because archaeology had to tackle another scandal: according to historical sources, the first Russian state, that of Kiev and Novgorod, was founded in the ninth century by a group of Vikings, the Varangians.

Troubetzkoy considered Marr to be utterly mad and, worse still, believed that "Marrism" had "long halted . . . the development of Soviet linguistics," which had become "the laughing stock of the civilized world, and, worse still, which had lost all contact with the truly progressive and revolutionary linguistic movements that had emerged in Europe and America"[86]—an affirmation contained within a scathing, but for a long time unpublished, note in his famous work on the Indo-Europeans.[87] This "madness," taken up by the young Marrists who were characterized, as is often the case in such situations, by a mix of youthful enthusiasm, incomplete scientific education, intolerance, and careerism, would go on to have tragic consequences. Archaeologists who dared to challenge Marr's teachings were at best treated as reactionary idealists and bourgeois nationalists. Linguists did not escape sanction either, and one of the most brilliant, Jevgeny Dmitrievich Polivanov, who was reduced to poverty in 1929 and arrested during the purges of 1937, died in detention in 1938 before being rehabilitated posthumously in 1963. Even though this intellectual stranglehold was relaxed a little during the Second World War (known as the Patriotic Great War in the USSR), the Cold War would once again see the screws being tightened. One of Marr's students, Ivan Ivanovič Meščaninov, would carry Marr's doctrine to even more ludicrous heights; incidentally, he was director of the Marr Institute

[84] Marr, 1923. On Marrism, see Murra et al., 1951; L'Hermitte, 1969; Bulkin et al., 1982; Miller, M. O., 1956; Sériot, 2005.
[85] Ravdonikas, 1932; Bulkin et al., 1982, p. 275.
[86] Troubetzkoy, 1996, pp. 228–229.
[87] See Chapter 5, pp. 116–118.

178   SECOND MOVEMENT (1903–1945)

for Languages and Thought[88] at the same time that agronomist Lyssenko was wreaking havoc on Soviet agriculture in the name of a proletarian biology.

Virtually overnight, in June 1950, Stalin condemned the Marrist doctrine, and Lyssenkism suffered the same fate. In his book *In the First Circle*, Solzhenitsyn describes in novel form the derisory vanity that pushed the dictator to personally venture into a realm so far removed from his daily experience. Stalin's text, which would be diffused and cited ad infinitum, is sprinkled with hard evidence. Contrary to the *new Marrist theory*, language could not be a simple superstructure, the reflection of an economic infrastructure, since more than three decades of socialist revolution had not led to any changes in the Russian language. The dictator and former seminarian states with authority that "language is a medium, an instrument with the help of which people communicate with one another, exchange thoughts and understand each other."[89] But this text should not be dismissed as a collection of naïve, common sense statements, seasoned with the political perversity that regularly drove Stalin to eliminate the elites that had served him for too long, in the USSR as in its satellite states. In fact, it rehabilitates the idea of a unique and homogenous "national language," independent of social and historical conditions and whose only possible evolution is the "improvement of the grammatical structure." In doing so, it reconnects with the tradition of the *Volksgeist*. In 1964, when a degree of free speech began to return within Soviet linguistics, Vinogradov stated that the refutation of Marrism, accompanied by the condemnation of all linguistic sociology, "did not, however, lead to a new lease of life for the discipline since it actually imposed new barriers and new dogmas upon it."[90] Marx and Engels, he reminds the reader, never envisaged language as pure communication but instead considered it as inseparable from ideology.

Paradoxically, Stalin's autodidactic truisms converged with Ravdonikas's baroque evolutionism within the same imperial preoccupation: the perpetuation of national identity over time. And beyond that, they only reinvoke the romantic *Volksgeist* and its fateful Kossinnian avatar—and, to the same extent, the notions of language and nation as defined by Meillet and his school. But, despite the political and intellectual subversion of Marxism by the tragedy of Stalinism, new avenues and new ways of perceiving language and ethnicity were momentarily opened up between Soviet archaeologists, linguists, and ethnologists and, more durably, among those in the West who read their works.

---

[88] Meščaninov, 1949.
[89] Stalin, 1950.
[90] Vinogradov, 1969.

8

Excesses and crimes of racial theories

The extermination of six million human beings in the gas chambers was the extreme culmination of Aryan ideology, although the latter was not its sole cause. To reach this level of horror, as was the case to a lesser degree for so many other "ordinary" massacres, it took the conjunction of exceptional economic, social, political, and moral disasters that followed the collapse of the German Second Reich after less than half a century in existence. But the call for Aryan purity became a façade for the genocide after having gradually prepared the way by rendering it, if not normal, at least imaginable. It allowed a soft acceptance of its intentions to permeate foreign public opinion, and particularly that of foreign scientific elites, so that, in the end, all that was required for its accomplishment was that a blind eye be turned in its direction.

Certainly this blindness was not generalized since, as early as 1933, Gordon Childe denounced the Nazi concentration camps, never imagining that they would later become extermination camps. But condemnation was rare, particularly in France. This silence was due to the continued prevalence, to varying degrees, of racial theories in the ideologies of Western countries in the first half of the twentieth century, despite the fact that the scientific foundations of these theories had started to collapse at the end of the nineteenth century. In addition, research in archaeology and anthropology, which were quite distinct in the nineteenth century, had since become inextricably intertwined in the search for the original Indo-European cradle. There were, nevertheless, subtleties within the various scientific traditions. In Germany, both approaches were merged within the Kossinnian School. In the United States and Great Britain, the interwar period was marked by a progressive decline in "scientific racism," if not in institutional and cultural racism. France, where there was a strong tradition of racial anthropology but where the Aryan question remained marginal, occupied an intermediate position in which the acceptance by certain of its anthropologists of Nazi "racial hygiene" presaged collaboration.

Ordinary racism and institutional racism

Although necessarily intertwined and interdependent, there exist three forms of racism, each a function of the context where it develops and is expressed.

180 SECOND MOVEMENT (1903–1945)

Cultural racism pervades all of a society and informs its vision of the world; *institutional racism* is the political implementation of racism through various forms of apartheid, colonial or homegrown, which are codified to a greater or lesser degree; finally, and of particular interest to us, *scientific racism* aims to lend coherence to the whole (mainly for the benefit of the ruling classes) by establishing rules governing method and validation, this despite all its ideological heaviness and potential contradictions.

These three racisms are also a function of the historical status of the societies that develop them. Up until the 1960s, France and Britain retained extensive colonial empires: in 1918, Germany lost its empire, which had been assembled too late to be extensive; apart from a few external territories which had been purchased or seized by force (Hawaii, Puerto Rico, Alaska, the Philippines for a while, etc.), the United States had constructed a homogenous territory through relatively recent conquests but it was faced with the issue of managing its ethnic minorities (Amerindians, Spanish-speakers), the descendants of African slaves, and continual immigration. For historical reasons, the place of the Jews differs in each of these four nations. Finally, the same nations were impacted on in different ways by the economic crisis: Germany, already morally and economically ruined by the defeat, was of course affected, but so, too, was the United States. Paradoxically, German scientific traditions remained strong, and, in the face of the slow decline of anthropometry, genetics experienced a period of spectacular development.

One must also be aware of certain anachronisms. Up until at least the early 1950s, spontaneous racism openly informed all of these societies—if not all societies in general—to varying degrees. Furthermore, in the nineteenth century, the hypothesis of a polygenetic origin of mankind also offered an escape from the ideological shackles of the Bible and opened up new spaces for reflection. This is why Paul Broca could be seen as a progressive militant republican who juxtaposed his hypothesis of "inferior races" with a desire to improve the unfortunate lot of said races. Likewise, as we shall see, when researchers moved on from measuring skulls to measuring genes, "eugenist" concerns at times took on "progressive" forms, as under the Weimar Republic: the aim was to improve the human species, in the same way that we seek to improve domesticated animal species. These preoccupations can be commendable, the scientific theories incorrect, and the social and political consequences calamitous all at the same time.

In addition, we encounter certain semantic ambiguities, which are sometimes unconscious but never innocent: in this period, when one speaks of "racial hygiene," it can refer either to improving a specific "race" by protecting it from contamination by others or improving the entire "human race" in the sense of a biological species. Furthermore, we know that drawing the line between "good" eugenics (e.g., the prenatal detection and elimination of Down syndrome) and criminal eugenics (infanticide of girls, genocide) demands constant vigilance on the part of universal morality. Finally, up until the 1960s, science had always been viewed in a positive light; it could only contribute favorably to the progress of mankind. This situation changed with the setbacks of the 1970s (economic crisis, pollution, climate change, new pandemics, nuclear accidents), when science began to be perceived as having negative aspects,[1] at least in Western societies.

This ideological climate, markedly different from our own, is not an excuse. On the one hand, minds that rebel against the scientific prejudices of their time have always risen up in the face of a racial vision of the world. On the other, it is precisely because daily racism was so banal that it could lead, with such ease, to the banality of racial crime.

The anthropological dead-end

Up until the 1890s, German scholars, including anthropologists like Virchow and linguists like Schrader, had for the most part a very prudent and moderate view of the racial implications of the Indo-European hypothesis. It was in the last decade of the nineteenth century, at the very moment when, in a context of economic crisis and minority grievances, German nationalism, like so many others, became a reactionary ideology, that the equation between Germans and Indo-Germans became set in stone. The work of philologist and archaeologist Kossinna led to the crystallization of two notions: the general identification of any given archaeological culture with a specific people and the identification of the Mesolithic populations of northern Germany and Scandinavia with the original Indo-European People (*Urvolk*). Coincidentally, Hermann Hirt had conveniently just completed the linguistic demonstration of this link.[2]

The archaeological demonstration, however, posed several problems. While Kossinna believed that the Mesolithic hunter-gatherers of the Ertebølle-Ellerbeck culture had spontaneously given rise to the Neolithic Dolmen culture (later known as the Funnel Beaker culture), the cultural link, seen in the styles of objects, between this latter culture and the Scandinavian Bronze Age that followed it is much less obvious (curiously, today archaeologists are faced with the opposite problem but we will return to this subject later). Therefore, Kossinna, along with all other archaeologists of his day, had to base his hypotheses on the biological continuity of the dolichocephalic "Nordic race," a supposedly well-established fact, in order to support his claims of cultural continuity and with

[1] Blanckaert, 1993. See dossier entitled "La science face au racisme," *Le Genre humain*, 1, autumn 1981.
[2] See Chapter 3, pp. 61–62.

182 SECOND MOVEMENT (1903–1945)

it a Nordic location for the original Homeland. The question of "race" had become central to Indo-Germanic—and thus to Germanic—identity. This was all the more so because the modest nature of the material legacy from this ancient past—a modesty which shocked Hitler himself—offered little support for the archaeological argument.

The anthropometric demonstration also had its weaknesses. At the time when so many popular works offering classifications of the world's "races"[3] were being published, the objectivity of the measurements was being eroded and doubt was creeping in. Among other things, the physical heterogeneity of the German nation was patently obvious. It was difficult, for example, to classify such eminent examples as Adolf Hitler and Joseph Goebbels within the tall, blond "Nordic race." To juggle with the notion of three German "races"—the Nordic, the Dalic, and the Alpine (or their synonyms)—as Broca had done in France with the Kimris and Galls, was a tedious exercise. Kossinna got around the problem by performing a patriotic pirouette, claiming that "in the soul of each German is firmly anchored the ideal of the Nordic essence."[4] But the claim was somewhat weak in terms of the legitimate requirements of a scientific approach. Perhaps "scientific racism" was too important to be left in the hands of archaeologists and anthropometricians alone. In fact, it became clear that the more skull measurements were taken (more than 5,000) the less easy it was to define well-delimited groups (i.e., "races). This did not prevent a number of classic anthropometric studies being undertaken. Thus, in 1939, Harvard professor Carleton Coon published a work on *The Races of Europe* which aimed to update the synthesis published some forty years earlier by William Ripley, to whom the book is dedicated.[5] The "Nordic race" is presented as a depigmented version of the "Mediterranean race." After the war, Coon published another book, this time on *The Origin of Races.*[6]

In the preface to his 1941 work *Jupiter, Mars, Quirinus,*[7] Georges Dumézil claimed that the Indo-Europeans, who "belonged to the white race," "included representatives of the three principal types of people that had settled Europe, with a marked predominance of the Nordic type."[8]

---

[3] See Chapter 4, pp. 87–88.
[4] Kossinna, 1926, p. 128 (cited Chapter 6).
[5] Coon, 1939; Ripley, 1899.
[6] Coon, 1962.
[7] See Chapter 5, p. 110.
[8] Dumézil, 1941b, p. 13.

Genetics to the rescue

In the third quarter of the nineteenth century, a little-known and depressive Moravian monk, Gregor Mendel, carried out repeated experiments on the hybridization of peas in the silence of his experimental garden in the monastery at Brno; the results of these studies were published in German in 1866. He had just discovered the famous three "Mendelian laws" governing heredity, which almost immediately passed into obscurity. Darwin, who was aware of Mendel's work, failed to make the connection with his own theory of evolution. When Mendel died in 1884, his successor as abbot of the monastery, Anselm Rambousek, actually burnt his archives. It would take another thirty-five years for Mendel's laws to be independently rediscovered by Carl Correns in Germany, Erich von Tschermak in Austria, and Hugo De Vries in Holland. Modern genetics, as the "science of heredity," thus came into being and went on to enjoy a period of significant development in several countries. But this new discipline also provided scientific support for two major social and political preoccupations of industrialized nations: concern for public health and, less clearly formulated, a concern to filter, select, or exclude certain populations that made up these states or sought to form part of them.

With the development of the State, health became a collective issue. It was no longer an individual or charitable initiative but became the responsibility of the State; the medical advances made by the likes of Louis Pasteur and Alexander Fleming were reducing the mortality rate spectacularly, and, for the first time, the average height of people was increasing. Health was now a question of everyday, civic discipline, and it was given a suitable Greek name: "hygiene." In the euphoria of these undisputed advances, it is tempting to try to eradicate all forms of illness and, instead of treating identified pathologies, to either eradicate them at their source (i.e., at birth) or at least to implement certain forms of vaccination, be they literal or metaphorical. The control of illness from birth, or better still before birth, was central to what is rather ambiguously known as "eugenics," a concept developed in 1883 by psychologist and statistician Sir Francis Galton.[9] Thus, at the end of the nineteenth century, and often in the absence of any clear debate, the medical profession found itself faced with dizzying new powers. Genetics clearly had a particularly instrumental role to play: it alone could determine whether a serious illness was hereditary or not. Of course, at the end of the day, the radical decisions (sterilization of carriers, or even euthanasia) would be taken by the political powers, but such decisions were rarely taken without prior incitement from the medical powers. Such decisions were not the prerogative of totalitarian regimes: the United States,[10] Canada, Switzerland, and Sweden

---

[9] See Chapter 4, pp. 94–95.
[10] Adams, 1990; Black, 2012; Kühl, 1994; Stern, A., 2005; Kline, 2001.

184 SECOND MOVEMENT (1903–1945)

all practiced forced sterilization in the first half of the twentieth century and up until the 1970s and '80s in some cases—Peru even continued the practice into the 1990s as a means of controlling poverty-stricken Amerindian populations.

But genetics as the science of heredity also lent a new legitimacy to "the scientific study of human races"—the definition of anthropology proposed by Broca. When Franz Boas successfully demonstrated that the famous cephalic index varied as a function of nutrition and that the cephalic index values of immigrant populations could change within the space of a generation or two,[11] anthropometry was abandoned. Wherever cultural racism gave rise to institutional racism, genetics was able to come to the rescue of a moribund anthropology. But while genetics allowed hereditary characteristics to be scientifically identified, it remained to be demonstrated which characteristics were really hereditary and whether stable groups of hereditary characteristics—in other words "races"—actually existed. As would be discovered later, while blue eyes and blond hair are both hereditary characteristics, each is inherited independently of the other. However, despite these significant uncertainties, a certain number of doctors and geneticists, particularly in Germany, would turn into so-called racial theoreticians. By concretely applying the extreme principle of eugenics, they passed, in the name of science, from uncertain science to real crime; very few would subsequently pay the price for their transgressions.

Eugenics and scientific charlatanism

This sinister development was not confined to dictatorships. As we have just mentioned, eugenics was founded in the last quarter of the nineteenth century in England by Sir Francis Galton and Karl Pearson. As part of what was known as the "London school" of racial psychology, their students, Cyril Burt, Raymond Cattell, Sir Ronald Fisher, and Charles Spearman, bolstered by the application of sophisticated statistical tools, proclaimed the inequality of the human "races" during the opening three decades of the twentieth century. In *The Fight for Our National Intelligence* (1937), Cattell, who recommended "the love of excellence" so that "less capable people and races disappear," stated the following with regard to Africans: "Even when the race is, by virtue of its own constitution, naturally good and likeable, an inferior mental capacity results in retardation, rusticity and the dead weight of conservatism."[12] He feared "the twilight of western civilization" and the rise of "sub-humans" who were insidiously attacking the very root of national life.[13] Just as Pearson hoped that the principle of elections could

---

[11] Boas, 1911.
[12] Translated from the French, as cited in Billig, 1981, p. 36.
[13] Translated from the French as cited, in ibid., p. 42.

EXCESSES AND CRIMES 185

be replaced by "an oligarchic class possessing a scientific education," Cattell favored a "benevolent dictatorship" toward individuals with "limited mental capacities." For his part, Cyril Burt noted that "throughout the world, Irish and Jewish emigrants are notoriously faithful to their racial character."[14] And Charles Spearman in *The Abilities of Man: Their Nature and Their Measurements* (1927) states "as regards 'intelligence,' the Germanic stock has on the average a marked advantage over the South European. And this result would seem to have had vitally important practical consequences in shaping the recent very stringent American Laws as to admission of immigrants."[15] In fact, between 1911 and 1930, twenty-four states of the United States enacted laws for the sterilization of socially "inadapted" individuals and thirty others introduced restrictions on mixed marriages, while a federal decree of 1924 restricted the immigration of "racially inferior" people.[16] At the same time, programs of forced sterilization, based on "scientific" eugenics, were also introduced in two Canadian provinces (Alberta and British Colombia), Imperial Japan, Sweden (where the law remained in place from 1934 to 1976), the Swiss canton of Vaud, Australia, Iceland, etc.[17] The apartheid that was officially enforced in the United States until the 1960s, and which was still in force in South Africa several decades later, was based on a supposedly "scientific" racial vision.

However, unlike in Germany, "scientific racism" began to wane in the English-speaking world from the 1930s onward. Even from within the scientific world, racial arguments came under increasing attack from eminent scholars such as Franz Boas in the United States and Julian Huxley in Great Britain. In 1935, the latter, originally a confirmed eugenist and one time president of the British Eugenics Society, published a book co-written with the ethnologist Alfred Haddon entitled *We Europeans: A Survey of "Racial" Problems*, in which the notion of "race" is criticized and rejected.[18] This intellectual and scientific movement would contribute to the formulation of the UNESCO declaration on racism—and Huxley would go on to become the organization's first Secretary General. The reliability of "biometric" research carried out in the name of scientific racism was also questionable; Burt, for example, simply invented some of his own data on twins.[19]

[14] Cited in ibid., p. 34.
[15] Spearman, 1927, p. 379; cited in Billig, 1981, p. 35.
[16] Chase, 1977; Gossett, 1963; Kline, 2001; Kühl, 1994; Finzsch, 1999.
[17] Broberg and Roll-Hansen, 2005.
[18] Huxley, et al., 1935; Barkan, 1992.
[19] Hearnshaw, 1979.

186   SECOND MOVEMENT (1903–1945)

The dreams of German geneticists

German anthropology in the nineteenth century was neither more nor less racist than any other. At the beginning of the twentieth century, Germany was rather less racist than the United States, with its apartheid laws and immigration restrictions (1921 and 1924 laws), the limitations on access to American universities by Jews, the banning of interracial marriages in more than half of the states, and, of course, the Ku Klux Klan, which boasted six million members in the 1920s. In the same way, the new discipline of German genetics was not necessarily destined to be racist, but, just as it was gathering momentum, the ideological context was changing. Like nationalism in general, which had initially been liberating, and Indo-European studies in particular, which up until then had been quite descriptive, the biological sciences as applied to mankind developed within the defensive and reactionary climate of the turn of the century; a climate which, in Germany and elsewhere, marked a large part of existing ideologies and impacted on disciplines with concrete ramifications.

We might wonder what role English eugenists would have played had an authoritarian regime seized power in Great Britain. Happily for them, this question remains theoretical even though a certain number were ideologically sympathetic toward their German colleagues. Their respective journals, *Eugenics Review* and *Archiv für Rassen- und Gesellschaftsbiologie* (Archives for Racial and Social Biology) exchanged courtesies, and the German founder of the Internationale Gesellschaft für Rassenhygiene (International Society for Racial Hygiene), Alfred Ploetz, fervent proponent of the "Nordic race," successfully convinced Sir Francis Galton to become the society's first honorary president.[20] Likewise, Cattel enthusiastically cites the works of Hans Günther as a support for his own anxieties regarding racial degeneration.

In all cases, for German raciologists and eugenists, the rise of Nazism and the enactment of the racist Nuremberg Laws, offered an opportunity to put all of their scientific dreams into practice.[21] Writing in the columns of the *Archiv für Rassen- und Gesellschaftsbiologie*, such renowned researchers as professors Falk-Alfred Ruttke, Ernst Rüdin, Eugen Fischer, Baron Otmar von Verschuer, and Friedrich Lenz enthusiastically supported Nazi anti-Semitic policy and put themselves at its service from the outset. Fischer heralded Hitler's coming to power, stating "We are now building a State of earth and blood, a State founded on the community of the German people united within the *Volkstum*, the Germanic race and soul,"[22] while Otmar von Verschuer recognized in Hitler "the head of the

---

[20] Billig, 1981, p. 44.
[21] Müller-Hill, 1984; Conte and Essner, 1995; Billig, 1981, Weinreich, M., 1946; Massin, 1998, 1999; Kaupen-Haas and Saller, 1999; Römer, 1985; Adams, 1990; Weindling, 1989 [1998]; Olff-Nathan, 1993; Schmuhl, 2005, 2008; Lipphardt, 2008.
[22] Cited in Field, 1977.

EXCESSES AND CRIMES   187

ethno-empire [who] is the first head of state to make data provided by hereditary biology and eugenics a principal factor directing the conduct of the State."

Eugen Fischer's 1904 study on the "Bastards of Rehoboth," individuals of mixed European and African blood from the German colony in what is now Namibia (where the Germans set up some of the first concentration camps in human history to confine the Hereros, shortly after the camps set up by the English in South Africa to contain the defeated Boers), led to the prohibition of all interracial marriages in the colony in 1912. This is undoubtedly one of the first raciological studies claiming to use genetic data (albeit very inadequately).[23] Eugen Fischer, along with phytobiologist Erwin Baur and racial hygienist Fritz Lenz, would subsequently co-author the weighty *Menschliche Erblichkeitslehre und Rassenhygiene* (Human Heredity and Racial Hygiene), first published in 1921 and re-edited many times since.

From skulls to crimes

Among the younger generation of scientists we note the presence of the future Nobel Prize winner and one of the founders of modern ethology, Konrad Lorenz, professor at Königsberg, who, in two articles published in 1940 and 1943, warned against the "genetic decadence" that was threatening "racial purity" and called for "scientifically based racial policy": "The idea of race, which is the foundation of our political regime, has already accomplished much in this regard."[24] In a letter from 1942, he goes as far as stating: "From a purely biological view of race, it is disastrous to see the two foremost Germanic peoples in the world wage war against each other while the non-white races, black, yellow, Jewish and mixed stand by rubbing their hands."[25]

Side by side with the new disciplines of genetics and ethology, traditional craniometry continued to play a special role within the racial context of the Third Reich. The most eminent specialist in craniometry, Hans Günther (nicknamed "Rassengünther"), was obsessed by the "Aryan race." His *Rassenkunde des deutschen Volkes* (Raciology of the German People), published in 1922, was the key reference work in Germany for two decades and its author received multiple honors[26]—he was also lauded by the French Nouvelle Droite (New Right) in the 1970s.[27] In the same spirit, Ludwig Ferdinand Clauss developed a "racial psychology" with its "racial styles," the most splendid of which was the "Nordic

---

[23] Fischer, E., 1913.
[24] Lorenz, 1940, 1943; Billig, 1981, pp. 47–48.
[25] Burkhardt, 1993, 2005, p. 276.
[26] Lutzhöft, 1971; Field, 1977.
[27] See Chapter 9, pp. 206 and 213–216.

188   SECOND MOVEMENT (1903–1945)

soul"; the latter became the title of one of his major works (*Die nordische Seele*), which was regularly republished throughout the 1920s and 1930s. He also defended the theory of an "Aryan Christ."[28] At times, power struggles raged among anthropologists, those associated with the SA (*Sturmabteilung*), such as Friedrich Merkenschlager and Karl Saller, ended up on the losing side here as elsewhere; after the war, this fact allowed Saller to pass himself off as a member of the ideological resistance against Nazism.[29]

However, German biologists' collaboration with Nazism was not limited to providing pseudo-scientific back-up for the regime's propaganda. Some scientists went as far as being complicit in murder. All anthropological institutions were happy to establish "racial certificates" concerning individuals suspected of being Jewish or whose ancestors were Jewish on one side and "Aryan" on the other. In fact, every German was provided with an "Aryan" racial passport (*Ariernachweis*), which outlined the individual's certified genealogy, including his or her parents, four grandparents, and eight great-grandparents.[30] For those whose ancestry was not "pure," the certificates determined whether they could be tolerated or whether they should be sent to extermination camps— in line with the logic of eugenics. Similarly the Third Reich relentlessly organized the elimination or, at the very least, the sterilization of homosexuals, the handicapped, and the mentally ill; in total 400,000 such individuals were sterilized and 70,000 were murdered.[31]

At the University of Strasbourg, an annexed city at the time, the persistence of the craniometric model encouraged the creation of a sinister collection of "Jewish" and "Bolshevik" anatomical casts and skeletons under the direction of three anthropologists associated with the SS *Ahnenerbe*: August Hirt, Hans Fleischhacker, and Bruno Beger (one of the members of the SS expedition to Tibet).[32] They personally selected a hundred of their "study subjects" at Auschwitz and then had them transported to the Natzweiler camp near Strasbourg where they were gassed. However, this was September 1944, and it was no longer possible to install the "collection." The three anthropologists endeavored to erase all traces of their crimes but only managed to destroy a portion of the evidence. Hirt committed suicide in June 1945; Beger continued his anthropologoical research after the war but received a symbolic sentence twenty-five years later; in 1971, Fleischhacker was appointed professor of anthropology at Frankfurt's Goethe University, where Hirt had lectured before obtaining his position in Strasbourg.

---

[28] Clauss, 1934; Conte and Essner, 1995, pp. 76–78. See Chapter 6, p. 135.
[29] Merkenschlager and Saller, 1934; Saller, 1961; Conte and Essner, 1995, pp. 93–111.
[30] Ehrenreich, 2007.
[31] Müller-Hill, 1984 [1989], pp. 15–70.
[32] Conte and Essner, 1995, pp. 231–262; Kaul (F. K.), 1968; Steegmann, 2005; Lang, 2004. See Chapter 6, pp. 140–141

EXCESSES AND CRIMES   189

Finally, we are all familiar with the notorious experiments carried out on deportees by the "Angel of Death" Josef Mengele, assistant of the renowned Otmar von Verschuer. The latter, who continued his brilliant university career after the war, supervised the research carried out by Mengele and by another of his assistants, Karin Magnussen; Magnussen's research involved a program of dissection of the eyes of gypsy children with heterochromia and the study of organs from deportees who had been deliberately contaminated with typhoid at Auschwitz.[33]

After the defeat, Josef Mengele spent five trouble-free years in Germany before being hunted down and forced to flee to Latin America, where he died in 1979. All of his colleagues, doctors and anthropologists, from Eickstedt to Verschuer and Eugen Fischer, were cleared of all accusations and quietly continued their university careers. In their private correspondence, some, such as Verschuer, cynically joked about the *Persilschein*, the "Persil certificates" (an allusion to a famous washing powder whose "whiteness" was its selling point) issued by benevolent "whitening" commissions.[34] In 1949, Baron von Eickstedt revived the raciological journal *Zeitschrift für Rassenkunde* under the new title *Homo. Zeitschrift für die vergleichende Biologie des Menschen* (Homo. Journal of Comparative Human Biology).

In the early 1980s, geneticist and historian Benno Müller-Hill interviewed the last survivors, assistants, and descendants of this generation of scientists.[35] All proclaimed that they had acted in good faith, that they were apolitical, and that they were ignorant of the crimes committed under their watch. They assured the interviewer that some of their best friends were Jews, and they deplored the excessive actions of a few rogue individuals who had, in the past, discredited their science. Some, however, refused permission for the publication of their interviews, despite the accumulation of justifications they contained, leading Benno Müller-Hill to speculate that "it is possible that this mass of ignorance and proclamations of innocence, so easily uttered, appeared appalling to them—whether lies or truth—once put in writing."[36] Ilse Schwidetzky (who was honored by the Société d'Anthropologie de Paris in 1980[37]) virtuously claimed, in a self-justifying history of German anthropology, that her institute, where she acted as assistant to its director Eicksted, had refused to issue "racial certificates." Unfortunately for her, historian Benoît Massin found examples of just such certificates, signed by Schwidetzky herself, within the archives of said institute.[38]

---

[33] Müller-Hill, 1984 [1989], pp. 76–80, 170–175; Schmuhl, 2005, 2008; Olff-Nathan, 1993.
[34] Müller-Hill, 1984 [1989], p. 92.
[35] Ibid.
[36] Ibid., p. 13.
[37] See Chapter 10, pp. 225–226.
[38] Spiegel-Rösing and Schwidetzky, 1982; Massin, 1999, p. 42 and note 105.

190 SECOND MOVEMENT (1903–1945)

Finally, mention must also be made of the SS's *Lebensborn* program, with its reproduction centers set up to produce "racially pure" children through the union of "Aryan" women and members of the SS. Such centers, which also existed in France,[39] were home to about 22,000 children. As part of the wider program, hundreds of thousands of children, officially recognized as "Aryan," were forcibly taken from their parents in occupied territories and entrusted to German families.

And what of France?

While the question of Indo-European origins had little prominence in France, the issue of race, as approached through craniometry, remained central throughout the first half of the twentieth century and even later within the tradition of the Société d'Anthropologie de Paris (Paris Anthropological Society), especially since the vast French colonial empire was prompting questions regarding identity and the management of very diverse populations.[40] So while genetics developed less rapidly than in Germany, craniometry remained a strong tradition, particularly among the followers of Henri-Victor Vallois, and it remained so until the early 1980s.

Of course, as we have seen, in 1891, Paul Topinard, despite being Broca's spiritual heir, was able to claim that "race does not exist,"[41] at the same time that ever-increasing numbers of measurements were dissolving "racial" boundaries. On the eve of the First World War, archaeologist Joseph Déchelette also proclaimed his skepticism regarding "races" and "types."

> Instead of a small number of clearly defined forms, that lend themselves to being grouped within a simple classification, we encounter multiple types encompassing numerous varieties. Furthermore, despite the best efforts of specialists, abundant and often confused theories regarding the origin and distribution of ancient races provide nothing but overly problematic data for our understanding of the primitive history of humankind. In many respects, the general conclusions reached by anthropologists do not agree exactly with the observations of archaeologists. On both sides, so many ingenious but ephemeral doctrines have been built on unsound foundations.[42]

---

[39] On the *Lebensborn program*, see Henry and Hillel, 1975; Lilienthal, 2003; Maroger, 2008; Thiolay, 2012. Also see the documentaries entitled *Lebensborn, les enfants de la honte* by Chantal Lasbats, Capa Presse TV, 1994; and *Les Pouponnières du IIIe Reich* by Romain Icard, 2014.

[40] Reynaud Paligot, 2006, 2007.

[41] Topinard, 1891, p. 4. See Chapter 4, p. 87.

[42] Déchelette, 1914 [1927], vol. 1, p. 482.

EXCESSES AND CRIMES   191

This scientific tradition—imbued with a healthy dose of skepticism, realism, and anti-racism—continued during the interwar years through the work of scholars such as Henri Neuville, Rector Étienne Patte (who was removed from his position by the Vichy government), and Jacques Millot.[43]

But, at the same time and at the other end of the spectrum, raciologists such as René Martial and in particular Georges Montandon were developing racist and anti-Semitic theories that were in line with the prevailing climate. Eugenics was also represented with the work of Dr. Alexis Carrel, who had received the Nobel Prize in 1912 for his research on blood vessels.[44] All three were naturally drawn toward active and even criminal collaboration, as in the case of Montandon.

Between these two minority tendencies there emerged, within the French anthropological and raciological tradition founded by Broca, the school of Henri-Victor Vallois which would come to dominate the field for years to come. Over the course of his career Vallois held many positions including, among others, professor at the Muséum National d'Histoire Naturelle (Museum of Natural History), director of the Musée de l'Homme (Museum of Mankind), director of the Institut de Paléontologie Humaine (Institute of Human Paleontology), director of the anthropology lab of the École Pratique des Hautes Etudes, editor-in-chief of L'Anthropologie, and general secretary of the Société d'Anthropologie de Paris. His articles and reviews in L'Anthropologie set the tone. For instance, the works of Eugen Fischer, Baron Egon von Eickstedt, and Baron Otmar von Verschuer on the subject of "racial hygiene" are greeted with complacency. Furthermore, Vallois was a member of the editorial committee of the Zeitschrift für Rassenkunde, founded by Eickstedt. In 1936, commenting on the final chapter of Eickstedt's Rassenkunde und Rassengeschichte der Menschheit (Raciology and the Racial History of Humanity), Vallois states: "Adopting the notion of the inequality, both anatomical and psychological, between the races, the author concludes by stating that rigorous racial selection is the only way to combat the annihilation of our civilization."[45] Eickstedt's original text included the following statement: "Race, blood and land are more important than parliamentary activity."[46]

And regarding another of Eickstedt's works, dealing with the "Foundations of Racial Psychology," Vallois, who felt that said psychology was "generally little known," expresses his concern as follows:

> Thus, M. von Eickstedt concludes, racial psychology has attained the status of a true science . . . no one, at least in Germany, questions its importance. Will this

[43] Neuville, 1933; Patte, 1938a, 1938b; Lester and Millot, 1939. See Bocquet-Appel, 1989.
[44] Carol, 1995; Schneider, 1990.
[45] Eickstedt, 1934; Vallois, in L'Anthropologie, 1936, p. 429.
[46] Eickstedt, 1934, p. 889: "Rasse, Blut und Boden sind wichtiger als parlamentarische Tageserfolge."

192   SECOND MOVEMENT (1903–1945)

conclusion be shared by all anthropologists? I fear the answer is no. The premature generalizations of certain authors . . . have damaged this science, at least in the minds of many. In order to rehabilitate itself, it will need numerous studies, conducted in a non-partisan manner, and using methods that are deductive rather than inductive.[47]

Commenting in the same year on the results of the work of Austrian anthropologist Rosa Koller, who distinguished between Ashkenazi and Sephardic Jews in Constantinople on the basis of their skulls, he stated: "These cranial configurations could be correlated to the development of certain facial muscles and, thereby, to the characteristic facial expressions of a large number of European Israelites."[48]

On the death of the Aryan race theorist Georges Vacher de Lapouge,[49] Vallois wrote a brief obituary in *L'Anthropologie*.

> Observant and hardworking in spirit, M. Vacher de Lapouge certainly deserved more than the oblivion to which he has been consigned. The excesses of the theories he developed, the over categorical manner in which he presented his "laws" . . . probably explain the void that was created around his research. However, this research contained certain accurate facts and it would be unfair to forget it. . . . It is curious, when we re-read his works, to find therein, already expressed in their entirety, and with all of their practical consequences, the theories on racism that would much later become so widespread in Germany.[50]

He does not elaborate on what these "accurate facts" might be.

In a report on the Demographic Congress held in Paris in 1938, and which brought together German and English eugenists in particular, Vallois sanctimoniously declares: "Certain important lectures were delivered on the problems of racial purity, the superior races and inferior races, eugenics and racial hygiene . . . no conclusion emerges from these presentations, but a fair exchange of views, free of ulterior motives, is always useful between people studying the same problems."[51] 1938, the year that Hitler entered Vienna and annexed part of Bohemia, also witnessed a confrontation on racial issues between the German delegation, led by Fischer, and those from the English-speaking world and Scandinavia at the Internal Congress of Anthropological and Ethnological

---

[47] Eickstedt, 1936; Vallois, review in *L'Anthropologie*, 46, 1936, pp. 427–429.
[48] Vallois, in *L'Anthropologie*, 46, 1936, p. 455; cited in Schnapp, 1980, p. 26.
[49] See Chapter 4, pp. 88–93.
[50] Vallois, 1936, p. 481.
[51] Vallois, 1938, p. 161; cited in Bocquet-Appel, 1989, p. 29.

EXCESSES AND CRIMES   193

Sciences held in Copenhagen; the scientific and political stakes were very clear, but Vallois abstained from the debates.

Under the German occupation of France, Paul Rivet, the left-wing founder of the Musée de l'Homme, was removed from his post as professor at the museum by the Minister for Education, archaeologist and historian Jérôme Carcopino, who incidentally was the author of the law excluding Jews from the teaching professions and also of the so-called 1941 Law or "Carcopino Law" governing archaeology. Vallois and Millot were rival candidates for the post left vacant by Rivet's expulsion. Millot was supported by the museum professors while the Académie des Sciences, which was also consulted regarding the appointment, remained divided. In 1937, the president of the Academy, veterinarian Emmanuel Leclainche, had waxed ironical on the subject of "races": "It is understood that, for scholars, human races no longer exist. But, unfortunately or fortunately, the earth is home to more than just scholars. The ignorant masses still believe that Whites, Blacks and Yellows exist and that they can be easily recognized."[52]

Minister Carcopino, largely on the advice of Abbé Breuil, chose Vallois for the post[53]: the episode was omitted from the obituary notice for Vallois published in 1982 in *L'Anthropologie*, just as it was not mentioned in the special edition of *Bulletins et Mémoires de la Société d'anthropologie de Paris* dedicated to Vallois in the same year. In 1960, Vallois published a favorable review of an anthropological manual written by Otmar von Verschuer, former superior of Mengele,[54] in which its author deplored the fact that "certain biologists," in the name of genetics, question the notion of "race"; in other words, "all of the work carried out for more than a century by hundreds of anthropologists."[55] This was the same Otmar von Verschuer who, in 1942, and in full knowledge of the facts, stated in the *Völkischer Beobachter* that "the unique racial threat represented by the Jews, found a definitive resolution in National Socialist policy."[56]

Vallois's volume on the "Human Races," first published in the *Que sais-je?* series in 1944, was regularly reprinted up until his death in 1981.[57] In the work, he identifies four broad racial groups (including that of "the primitive races"; i.e., the Australians and Veddas) which he in turn divides into twenty-seven "races." The "white races" group notably encompasses the Nordic, East European, Dinaric, Alpine, Mediterranean, Southeastern, Indo-Afghan, Anatolian, Ainu, and Touranian "races."

[52] Leclainche, 1937, p. 1279; cited in Bocquet-Appel, 1989, p. 31.
[53] Ibid.
[54] See this chapter, pp. 186–190.
[55] Verschuer, 1959; Review by Vallois, in *L'Anthropologie*, 1960, pp. 343–344.
[56] Müller-Hill, 1984 [1989], p. 48. Translated into English in 1988.
[57] Vallois, 1944.

194 SECOND MOVEMENT (1903–1945)

Those who collaborated

Vichy policies, which borrowed the term "Aryan" to legally identify "non-Jews," have been studied in detail elsewhere[58] and are somewhat outside the scope of the present study. Nevertheless, it is worth looking briefly at the issue of collaboration within French anthropology, which, although not widespread, was very real. In 1935, medical doctor and Nobel Prize winner, Alexis Carrel, published *L'Homme, cet inconnu* (Man, the Unknown). In the chapter "The Remaking of Man," he makes the following recommendation:

> The conditioning of petty criminals with the whip, or some more scientific procedure, followed by a short stay in hospital, would probably suffice to insure order. Those who have murdered, robbed while armed with automatic pistol or machine gun, kidnapped children, despoiled the poor of their savings, misled the public in important matters, should be humanely and economically disposed of in small euthanasic institutions supplied with proper gases. A similar treatment could be advantageously applied to the insane, guilty of criminal acts.

The preface of the 1936 German edition even states that

> [i]n Germany, the government has taken vigorous measures against the rise of minorities, the insane and criminals. The ideal situation would be to eliminate each individual of this type once they have demonstrated that they are dangerous.[59]

In fact, between 40,000 and 50,000 handicapped and mentally ill individuals died of hunger and cold in French hospitals under the Vichy regime.[60] Alexis Carrel, who in the meantime had signed up to Jacques Doriot's Parti Populaire Français (French Popular Party), was appointed by Pétain as head of the newly established Fondation Française pour l'Etude des Problèmes Humains, which was tasked with "the study of all aspects of the most appropriate measures to preserve, improve and develop the French population in all its activities." The Foundation was dissolved on the liberation of France and Alexis Carrel died following an illness the same year. Cited as a reference in the 1990s by the leadership of the Front National (National Front), his biography and works were rediscovered and the medical faculty at Lyon, which bore his name, was rebaptized (after René Laennec) as were several French Streets. Nonetheless, the Foundation continued

---

[58] Among others, Paxton et al., 1999; Rousso, 1990; Burrin, 1997. See also *Le Genre humain*, 28, November 1994 (*Juger sous Vichy*), and 30–31, summer-autumn 1996 (*Le Droit antisémite de Vichy*).
[59] Bonnafé and Tort, 1996.
[60] Lafont, 1993; Bueltzingsloewen, 2007.

to live on under the guise of the Institut National d'Etudes Démographiques (INED), some of whose directors were subsequently linked to the far right.[61]

René Martial made a name for himself before the war with his 1934 book *La Race française* (The French Race), which received an award from the Académie Française, and with his works on the dangers of racial mixing and immigration.[62] Confronted with the same dilemma as his French anthropological predecessors, he was forced to admit that the "French race" was composed of harmonious racial mixes but that it nonetheless had to protect itself from any mixing with African and Asian "races." The "biochemical index of blood" should allow only immigrants with type O blood to be admitted and should exclude the Jews, who were believed to belong to the B blood group. He was one of the few anthropologists to pay homage to Vacher de Lapouge and his "Aryan" on his death in 1936; he hailed de Lapouge as a "prophet" whose "works were, and still are, consigned to oblivion because they offend all those who preach a *laissez-faire* approach to human racial mixing." Referring again to this in 1942, he states: "The simple use of the word 'race' was already shocking. Jewish-dominated thinking furiously resisted all racial discussion."[63]

Indeed, under the Vichy regime, René Martial was appointed professor of "anthropology of races" at the faculty of medicine in Paris and, in 1942, became the co-director of the new Institut d'Anthroposociologie, set up by the Commissariat général aux questions juives (General Commission for Jewish Questions) and placed under the aegis of the Institut Pasteur and the Académie de Médecine; it was presided over by Claude Vacher de Lapouge, Georges's son who thus exacted a kind of posthumous revenge. In 1943, Martial published Notre race et ses aïeux (Our Race and Its Forefathers), a contribution on the "Jewish question," at the request of the Fondation Française pour l'Etude des Problèmes Humains. He retired before the end of the war and, in 1955, published *Les Races humaines*.[64]

Both a partner and rival of Martial, Georges Montandon, a French citizen of Swiss origin, would go even further in terms of collaboration.[65] Appointed professor of ethnology at the École d'Anthropologie de Paris in 1933, he published *L'Ethnie française* two years later. A friend of the writer Céline, during the war he became director of the newly established Institut d'Etudes des Questions Juives of the Commissariat Général aux Questions Juives directed by Xavier Vallat. As head of the institute he published the *Ethnie française* journal, commissioned the translation of Otmar von Verschuer's book, was closely involved in the design of the 1941–1942 exhibition "*Le Juif et la France*," and, like René Martial, published

[61] Liauzu, 1999.
[62] Schneider, 1990, 1994; Taguieff, et al., 1999; Liauzu, 1999; Larbiou, 2005.
[63] Martial, 1942.
[64] Martial, 1955; Larbiou, 2005; Taguieff et al., 1999.
[65] Taguieff et al., 1999.

196 SECOND MOVEMENT (1903–1945)

a number of racist and anti-Semitic works such as *Comment reconnaître le Juif* (How to Recognize the Jew). He also issued racial certificates (some of which were handsomely paid for) from his office and at the Drancy internment camp; he thus had power of life and death over Jews who had been arrested by the French police.[66] He was seriously wounded by the Resistance during the Liberation of Paris in 1944, but there is a degree of uncertainty regarding the actual circumstances of his death. In the 1960s, he was still being cited in certain anthropological textbooks[67] and would be one of the "scientific" authorities quoted by the Nouvelle Droite in the 1970s.[68]

For Western nations the horror of the genocides committed in the name of science and scientists was so traumatic that, after 1945, the question of "races" had to be totally re-examined; in particular, this re-examination would lead to several UNESCO publications, including Claude Lévi-Strauss' *Race et Histoire*, which was published in 1952. Nevertheless, there was never any in-depth criticism of physical anthropology from anthropologists themselves. The handful of examples provided in this chapter, and to which we will return later,[69] reveal this fact all too clearly. Even in France, anthropologists contented themselves with a name change: "physical" anthropology was simply rebaptized as "biological" anthropology. By the end of the 1960s, barely a generation later, racist "Aryan" ideologies once again began to emerge out of the shadows.

[66] Wieviorka and Laffitte, 2012.
[67] Olivier, G., 1965, pp. 129–132.
[68] See Chapter 9, pp. 310–323.
[69] See Chapter 10, pp. 223–227.

IV

THIRD MOVEMENT
(1945–THIRD MILLENNIUM)

All is re-resolved!

After a quarter century of relative silence, Aryan ideologies as well as voluminous historical syntheses on the subject of the original Homeland of the original People witnessed a new surge in popularity in the 1970s. These ideologies descended directly from National Socialism, and, as if nothing had happened, their publication was heralded in the media with all the hype that nowadays accompanies easy-to-understand scientific discoveries and concepts. Reputable scholars presented century-old theories as new archaeological and conceptual discoveries. Geneticists, linguists, and statisticians developed hyper-sophisticated tools but without changing the underlying interpretive models. Nevertheless, high-quality scholarly works abound in the fields of linguistics, mythology, archaeology, and genetics that do not need to be ultimately interpreted in terms of an original People speaking an original language within an original Homeland. In fact, progress in other fields of linguistics—and indeed of history and archaeology—opens the way for models that are infinitely more complex, fruitful, and interesting.

9

The return of the Aryan, pagan, extreme right (1945–present)

The collapse of Nazism did not mean the collapse of extreme right ideologies. Dictatorships with close ties to fascism continued to exist in Spain and Portugal with the assent, and even support, of Western powers within the new geopolitical context of the Cold War. Numerous Nazi dignitaries escaped judgment, with some taking refuge in South America and Syria. On the South American continent and elsewhere (Greece, Korea, South Vietnam, Iran, Indonesia, South Africa, etc.), the United States and its allies fostered dictatorships that they regarded as a lesser evil in the face of the perceived threat of communist subversion. In the Eastern Bloc countries, anti-Semitism and various forms of cultural racism (against the Roma, for example) continued to prosper more or less openly.

A truly "New" Right?

However, within the democracies of Western Europe, movements more or less explicitly connected to this discredited extreme right would long remain marginal, even though in France the war in Algeria gave them, for a time, a greater degree of visibility. Of course certain small publishing houses produced confidential journals and republished older works and recordings of military or Nazi chants. But after the horrors of the Second World War, followed by the triumphant impetus of the reconstruction and the Trente Glorieuses and buoyed up by the baby boom and spectacular technological successes (the conquest of space, medical innovations, nuclear power, etc.), little room was left for this extreme ideology. The lessons of the Treaty of Versailles had been learned and the idea of once again humiliating a defeated Germany was no longer acceptable.

However, from the 1970s onward, as the memory of Nazism and wartime collaboration began to fade, the optimism of Western societies faltered. The energy and economic crises, new illnesses, increasing anxiety regarding ecology, the slow collapse of communist regimes and the hopes that this raised in the West were all causes for doubt. There was room once again for ideologies of exclusion and scapegoats at a time when immigration from the former colonies, which up

200 THIRD MOVEMENT (1945–THIRD MILLENNIUM)

until then had fueled the economy, began to contribute to rising levels of unemployment. These ideas re-emerged from obscurity with the Front National (FN) in France, the National Front in Great Britain, and the Nationaldemokratische Partei Deutschlands (NPD) in Germany, but they also took new and sometimes covert forms. In France, the movement known as "Nouvelle Droite" would become one of the most mediatized, most developed, and best known examples, even though, strictly speaking it was not a fully formed doctrine but rather an evolving nebulous body made up of individuals, movements, publications, and doctrines and within which we encounter the classic themes of prewar right-wing extremism: hatred of equality, democracy, Judeo-Christianity, American imperialism, the neoliberal plutocracy, and racial mixing; the exaltation of an imperial, aristocratic, elitist, and even "pagan" Europe; and advocacy of racial inequality and, of course, of an "Indo-European heritage." All of this was wrapped up in the traditional "neither left nor right" rhetoric of the extreme right.

In this regard, the Nouvelle Droite is thus not so very "new," even though it and other similar currents in other countries differ from the populist and nationalist extreme right-wing political movements mentioned above, which have flourished in Europe since the 1980s. To be more precise, we can distinguish two broad tendencies within the wider European extreme right movements: one, predominant up until now, is based on traditional Christian conservatism, or even fundamentalism, which is also nationalist and racist and at times has maintained uneasy or even porous relationships with mainstream conservative political parties; the other, less prominent, is more specifically "pagan" and intellectually is in a direct line of descent from Nazism—it is this strand that interests us here.

The "magician" prodromes

We can, at least in France, identify one of its first symptoms with the publication in 1960 of the best-seller by Louis Pauwels and Jacques Bergier, *Le matin des magiciens* (Translated in 1963 as The Dawn of Magic and in 1964 as The Morning of the Magicians), which in turn led to the establishment of the ephemeral magazine *Planète*. This book is largely a compilation by the scholarly para-scientist Jacques Bergier of sensationalist themes that would subsequently proliferate: parapsychology, UFOs, apparently mysterious archaeological discoveries (the Palenque "cosmonaut," the Nazca lines, the ancient batteries in Bagdad Museum), etc.[1] But about one-quarter of the book, which makes uneasy reading, argues that Hitler and his followers, in the pure tradition of "Armanic" and Aryo-Germanic delusions,[2] were "great mediumistic initiates" in contact

---

[1] Pauwels and Bergier, 1960. On this para-scientific trend, see Stoczkowski, 1999.
[2] See Chapter 6, pp. 133–135.

ARYAN, PAGAN, AND EXTREME RIGHT   201

with "the absolute elsewhere," whose "true goal is to create, to undertake divine work, the goal of biological mutation," "the emergence of a humanity made up of heroes, demi-gods and man-gods."[3] The obscure Thule Society, one of the initial components of the Nazi Party, but which disappeared in 1925, becomes "an instrument capable of changing the very nature of reality," " a secret society of initiates in contact with the invisible," the "magical center" of Nazism.[4] The Second World War was ultimately just "a great spiritual conflict."

In an appendix to his remarkable intellectual analysis of *The Occult Roots of Nazism* (curiously enough translated into French by a publishing house affiliated to the Nouvelle Droite[5]), English historian Nicholas Goodrick-Clarke had little trouble highlighting (as if it was necessary) the historical errors and approximations upon which the rare "concrete" elements of Pauwels's "demonstration" were based; in addition to an imaginary "Vril Lodge," Pauwels attributed a central role to the ephemeral Thule Society and to two of its supposed members, Dietrich Eckardt (*sic*) and Karl Haushofer. In reality, the latter was simply a specialist in geopolitics at the University of Berlin who had only very distant links with Hitler and who was never a member of the Thule Society. As regards Eckart, a true inspiration to Hitler, he, too, was never a member of the Thule Society although he did attend society events; in the book, however, he is presented not as an exalted anti-Semitic ideologist, but rather as "a unique character, a poet, playwright, journalist, Bohemian." Not surprisingly we will encounter Pauwels again a little later on.

From 1968 onward, the entire intellectual wing of the Nouvelle Droite was mobilized around two journals, *Nouvelle École* and *Éléments* (to which the journal *Krisis* was added in 1988) and an explicit think-tank, the GRECE or Groupement de recherche et d'études pour la civilisation européenne (Research and Study Group for European Civilization).[6] Those at the head of these journals and associated groups, and in particular Alain de Benoist and Dominique Venner (the latter was a former paratrooper in Algeria and a member of the Organisation Armée Secrète [OAS]), were directly linked to extreme, often violent and anti-Semitic, right-wing organizations such as Jeune Nation (Young Nation) and Europe-Action, or the Fédération des étudiants nationalistes (FEN; the Federation of Nationalist Students). In the 1960s and 1970s, a certain number, such as François d'Orcival, Alain de Benoist, Jean-Claude Valla, Jean Mabire, Patrice de Plunkett, and Michel Marmin, were employed as journalists

---

[3] Pauwels and Bergier, 1960, p. 353.
[4] Ibid., p. 433.
[5] Goodrick-Clarke, 1989.
[6] On the Nouvelle Droite, see Algazy, 1989; *Art Press*, 1997; Billig, 1981; Biscarat, 2000; Brunn, 1979; Camus, 2006; Camus and Monzat, 1992; Desbuissons, 1984; Duranton-Crabol, 1988; François, 2008; Germinario, 2002; Monzat, 1992; Olender, 2009, pp. 95–137; Schnapp and Svenbro, 1980; Taguieff, 1994.

202   THIRD MOVEMENT (1945–THIRD MILLENNIUM)

by the magazines *Valeurs actuelles* and *Spectacle du monde*, which were part of the publishing house owned by Raymond Bourgine; it was here that they first began to diffuse their ideas (and still do in some cases).[7]

Influenced by the 1968 cultural movement, they developed the idea that, in order to one day take political power, it was first necessary to seize "metapolitical" power—in other words intellectual and cultural power. This idea was explicitly borrowed by de Benoist from Italian Marxist revolutionary Antonio Gramsci. After all, was this not what happened in May 1968, when the cultural and social demands that had been formulated over time by the baby boom generation suddenly exploded outwardly onto the political stage? Another example, which was not spotted by *Nouvelle École*, was the inevitable collapse of the USSR which could have been predicted two decades beforehand. At the time, every young Russian's dream was to listen to rock and roll, wear nylon shirts and stockings, and write with ballpoint pens, none of which was available in their country. The regime had ultimately failed to create its own culture despite the Red Army Choirs, traditional folk groups, and Bolshoi Ballet. The Soviet Union first lost the cultural battle before finally losing the economic, technological, and political battles. The first issues of *Nouvelle École* thus developed the "metapolitical" program for this eventual seizing of cultural power of which the extreme right dreamed.

A view from the (extreme) right

Consequently, by 1969, the GRECE's confidential internal bulletin made the following recommendation: "It is important to be careful regarding the vocabulary used. In particular, it is necessary to abandon outdated phraseology; new habits must be created."[8] This program was henceforth put into practice with an undeniable tactical expediency and led to real ideological success. *Nouvelle École* soon displayed all of the characteristics of a high-quality intellectual journal (with financial means that are still opaque). Its scientific patronage committee reads like a scholarly who's-who of far-right personalities, some with direct links to Nazism, and well-known intellectuals of a more neutral leaning, some perhaps even naïve. Amid innocuous themes, the entire, renewed creed of the traditional extreme right is systematically presented but using new arguments. A new rhetoric is added which decries the fact that so little attention is paid to the theories and theoreticians presented, theoreticians who are supposedly systematically ignored or even ostracized. The desire for respectability is also evident in the

---

[7] Duranton-Crabol, 1988, pp. 34–35.
[8] Cited in Brunn, 1979, p. 380.

repeated use of the titles "Doctor" or "Professor" for contributing authors, and regular references are made to Alain de Benoist's library of 30,000 books, with supporting photographs (in an 2012 interview on *France Culture* radio, this collection had become "the largest private library in France, containing more than 150,000 or perhaps even 200,000 works").

The "theoretical" capital of the Nouvelle Droite was synthesized in Alain de Benoist's main work, *Vue de droite* (1977), which he himself described in the introduction as an "anthology," if not an "encyclopedia," since a portion of the work had already been published in the form of articles in various journals.

The first section of the book, presented under the title of "Heritage," opens with a back-lit photograph of Stonehenge's monumental orthostats, imbued with Wagnerian drama. A large part of the book is devoted to the "Monde des Indo-Européens" (the Indo-European World), in which we learn that the thesis of their "Nordic or Germanic" origins is founded on their physical characteristics: "blond hair, blue or light-colored eyes, tall stature, narrow hips, fine lips, strong chin, dolichocephaly," which are "specific to the Nordic and Phalic subraces that emerged from a Cro-magnonoid substrate in a territory encompassing the shores of the North Sea and the Baltic and their hinterlands."[9] In short, this is Kossinna's theory, who incidentally is not cited, although a dozen other German authors are. The steppic theory is also mentioned, but these people of the *kurgans* might only have been "a simple pastoral extension of an Indo-European culture which first developed in Northern Europe." For the "world view" (*"vue du monde"* in French, from the German *"Weltanschauung"*—which is normally translated as "ideology" in standard French) of these Indo-Europeans, de Benoist frequently turns to Georges Dumézil.

As regards the "race" of the Indo-Europeans, a "dynamic, evolutive, statistic" notion, de Benoist invokes the authority of the racist and anti-Semitic anthropologist Georges Montandon, a regular participant in the "racial visits" organized under the Occupation, whose diagnostics could mean certain death (he himself was executed by the Resistance during the Liberation[10]), as well as that of neofascist writer Giorgio Locchi, member of the Nouvelle Droite, who believed that in ancient times "each racial groups had a corresponding specific language."[11] Alain de Benoist also threw into the mix some of the old esoteric themes favored by the extreme right from the Nazi period to the present day. Atlantis, the homeland of the original Indo-Europeans, was of course situated in the North Sea, on the Island of Heligoland, the thesis originally propounded by Alfred Rosenberg in his *Der Mythis des Zwanzigsten Jahrhunderts* (The Myth of the Twentieth

[9] Benoist, 1978, p. 33.
[10] See Chapter 8, pp. 195–196.
[11] Benoist, 1978, p. 37.

204   THIRD MOVEMENT (1945–THIRD MILLENNIUM)

Century)[12] and by Hermann Wirth, the first president of the SS Ahnenerbe; this theory was also taken up after the war by ex-Nazi pastor Jürgen Spanuth on whose authority de Benoist relied and whose works were regularly re-edited by the Nouvelle Droite.[13] Likewise, the Vikings and Templars, and perhaps even the Trojans, had conquered South America and were the true founders of the prestigious pre-Colombian civilizations which the natives would never have been capable of creating themselves—a thesis originally proposed by Jacques de Mahieu, a former combatant with the SS Charlemagne division who took refuge in Argentina after the war and who is another favorite of extreme-right publishing houses.[14] A little further on we encounter works on "lost" civilizations and knowledge, the paranormal, gnosis (with reference to collaborationist author Raymond Abellio), and even UFOs, with reference to Louis Pauwels and Jacques Bergier. The authors of *Le matin des magiciens* and *L'homme éternel* (The Eternal Man) are favorably cited, as are René Guénon and Georges Gurdjieff (the latter was a "mentor" to Pauwels)—two gurus of the interwar years and compulsory references in occultist circles—and the works of Arthur Koestler on parapsychology.

From Gobineau to Konrad Lorenz

As the book unfolds, Alain de Benoist gradually reveals his references and his own vision of the world. Having evoked Nietzsche and the *Wille zur Macht* (will to power), the support provided by the work of ethologist and Nobel Prize winner Konrad Lorenz allows him to propose a biological basis for this will: "The spirit of competition, the appetite for risk, the sense of honor, entrepreneurship and even industrial dynamism, are, like war, by-products of an aggressive impulse in the smallest structures of the organism. To attack this impulse would be to divest the species of its appetite for struggle, its desire to live. To condemn it to death."[15] Konrad Lorenz, a member of the Nazi Party, had at the time, as we have seen,[16] endorsed Nazi racial policy, a fact which provoked major controversy when he was awarded the Nobel Prize for Medicine in 1972. While his scientific work clearly went beyond this aspect, Lorenz was a darling of the Nouvelle Droite, and, in 1975, Alain de Benoist traveled to his home to interview him for his *Nouvelle École* magazine.

---

[12] See Chapter 6, p. 131.
[13] Regarding the Atlantis myth, the reference work is Vidal-Naquet, 2005.
[14] On these "theories," see Adam, 1988.
[15] Benoist, 1978, p. 150.
[16] Billig, 1981, pp. 47–48. See Chapter 8, p. 187.

ARYAN, PAGAN, AND EXTREME RIGHT   205

Two other important scientific endorsements concerning "racial" matters are those of socio-biologist Edgar Wilson and, of course, the theories on heredity and intellectual inequality developed by Hans Eysenck and Arthur Jensen.[17] They allow de Benoist to elaborate his theories on the intellectual inequality of the "races"; he also draws on the works of psychologist Cyril Burt, famously found guilty of falsifying his results on the heredity of intelligence in twins.

In the rest of the work, Alain de Benoist discusses the authors he particularly detests (Marx, Freud, Jesus, and their respective disciples) and those he appreciates: racist ideologists Arthur de Gobineau and Alexis Carrel, socialist revolutionary Georges Sorel, reactionary writers Alfred Fabre-Luce and Jean Cau, Italian fascist esoterist intellectual Julius Evola (who provided the preface for an Italian edition of the infamous anti-Semitic hoax *The Protocols of the Elders of Zion*[18]), and academician Roger Caillois, specialist in the realm of the sacred and feasting. Their books, and the works devoted to them, are the subject of sustained yet biased commentaries; the same applies to his treatment of the works of Richard Wagner and the "conservative revolution" of Weimar Germany. Numerous pages are devoted to the French regionalist movements in Occitanie, Flanders, and Brittany, with special attention paid to those linked to the extreme right, particularly during the Second World War. Toward the end, a long chapter serenely discusses the "Hitler enigma" with abundant indulgent citations from the Führer himself and from certain historians and witnesses—and all without the slightest allusion to the genocide. Similarly, the chapter on "Eternal Japan" stresses the sense of honor of the Japanese elites and the atrocities committed by the Allies.

A re-armed extreme right

In summary, this "anthology" presents itself as a manual listing the themes to be used by the militants of an intellectually revamped and modernized, even rearmed, extreme right; one that is in a direct line of descent from the extreme right movements of the prewar era.

A closer reading of the issues of *Nouvelle École* and *Éléments* both reinforces and refines this impression. For example, in each issue, the section headed "*Éphémérides*" singles out important historical dates and rarely misses an occasion to evoke the atrocities committed by the Allied forces during the Second World War. The iconography employed highlights the work of artists affiliated with the Nazi regime, such as the sculptor Arno Breker, the painter

---

[17] See Chapter 10, p. 205.
[18] Olender, 2009, pp. 74–80.

206 THIRD MOVEMENT (1945–THIRD MILLENNIUM)

Wilhelm Petersen, and the illustrator and lithographer Georg Sluyterman van Langeweyde.[19] One of the illustrations used in *Vue de droite* is particularly telling in this regard: from the pen of Georg Sluyterman van Langeweyde, it represents a proud medieval knight armed with a lance and originally graced the cover of the August 1940 edition of *Germanien*, the journal of the SS Ahnenerbe's "cultural" institute; Alain de Benoist is happy to simply invert the image from left to right and—a tiny detail—replace the swastika on the knight's shield with a two-headed eagle. Other illustrations are lifted directly from *Germanien* to embellish the pages of *Nouvelle École* and the official magazine of the GRECE.

German Nazi archaeologists and raciologists are given pride of place, invariably qualified as "professors," whether as contributors or as the subjects of texts extolling their work, from Hans Günther to Hans Reinerth, via Hermann Wirth, first president of the Ahnenerbe and committed Germanomaniac,[20] or Herbert Jankuhn, the Ahnenerbe's head of archaeology.[21] They are honored with obituaries. Esoteric references, founded on falsehoods, abound in these journals produced by the Nouvelle Droite; hence we encounter references to Atlantis, the Vikings of South America, the fake "Germanic" *Ura-Linda* chronicle, and the continent of Mu, propounded by a certain Louis-Claude Vincent, amateur anthropologist, engineer, and inventor of "bioelectronics." The former French Waffen-SS member Marc Augier, known under the pseudonym Saint-Loup, who was condemned to death in absentia after the war and then pardoned, occupies center stage among the figures of reference; he never denied his past, right up until his death in 1990.

The Nouvelle Droite also maintained close political and intellectual ties with the Club de l'Horloge (the Clock Club), a right-wing think tank founded in 1974 by Viscount Henry de Lesquen du Plessis Casso that sought to build lasting bridges between the mainstream right and the FN. Some of its founding members, such as Bruno Mégret, Yvan Blot, Jean-Claude Bardet, and Jean-Yves Le Gallou, who came from classic right-wing parties but who were also close to or members of GRECE, would go on to enlist with the FN and subsequently Mégret's dissident party. Since 2006, Henry de Lesquen has directed the right-wing radio station Radio Courtoisie. Thus, since the 1970s, an extensive and influential network of associations, clubs, and magazines has been built up with the aim of propagating the ideas of this revamped extreme right: today their reach extends to include the internet and a television station, TV Libertés. The collections of Copernic Editions ("*L'Or du Rhin*," "*Nation armée*," "*Cartouches*," etc.), founded in 1976 by the GRECE, are used to diffuse the works of Hans

[19] Monzat, 1997.
[20] See Chapter 6, pp. 131–132.
[21] See his obituary by Alain de Benoist, in *Nouvelle École*, 46, 1990, pp. 141–142; see Olender, 2009, pp. 125–126.

ARYAN, PAGAN, AND EXTREME RIGHT   207

Eysenck, Oswald Spengler, Julius Evola, and members of the GRECE (Alain de Benoist's *Vue de droite* was re-edited several times between1977 and 1979).

Toward the end of the 1970s, this strategy became very successful indeed. In 1978, *Vue de droite* was awarded the Grand Prix for essay writing by the Académie française, whose Permanent Secretary, Jean Mistler, a former Vichy dignitary, was an admirer of the *Nouvelle École* journal. De Benoist even claims that it was Mistler's idea to send a copy of the 1972 special edition of *Nouvelle École*, dedicated to Dumézil, to all Academicians that ultimately ensured the latter's election to the Académie in 1978.[22] In 1977, biologist Yves Christen, a founding member of the GRECE, even became editor-in-chief of the important popular scientific magazine *La Recherche*; Éditions du Seuil, who were responsible for the magazine, had to remove him when they belatedly became aware of the nature of his views on biological inequality.

In 1978, Michel Poniatowski, Minister of the Interior and number two in Valéry Giscard d'Estaing's government, published a book entitled *L'avenir n'est écrit nulle part* (Nowhere Is the Future Written) which so closely mirrors the theses of the Nouvelle Droite that it could only have been written by one, or more, of its members (incidentally, Alain de Benoist gave it a rave review in *Le Figaro Magazine*). The minister, who vigorously promoted the book in the media, exalted "the genetic heritage" of the Indo-Europeans, "active men, who were as hard on themselves as on others . . ., attached to everything that creates deep roots—family, role, city, culture, race"—whose "spirit of invention, of creation, led them, through a long progressive journey over 4500 years, from the shores of the Baltic to the Moon." And he deplored how the "Indo-European fact was sidestepped and, worse, ignored and is not included in any university faculty program." Indeed, "the history of the West" must be understood in terms of "the same inexhaustible energy, the same readiness for war and thirst for conquest that characterized the Indo-European peoples." For, "it is the Indo-European race that drives the scientific, technical and cultural impetus and that leaves its mark on the development of our societies."[23] In the chapter "Heredity, Milieu and Intelligence," he denounces the "egalitarian error" and uses Hans Eysenck's work on IQ to demonstrate the "inheritability of intelligence," which largely takes precedence over the social and cultural milieu.[24] Konrad Lorenz is also invoked in order to warn against media "over-information" and the "purported intelligentsia."

Other right-wing works that appeared during the same era reflect the strong influence of the Nouvelle Droite. An example is *Le Terreau de la liberté* (1978)

---

[22] See Chapter 16, pp. 364–367.
[23] Poniatowski, 1978, pp. 145–158.
[24] Ibid., pp. 225–248.

208 THIRD MOVEMENT (1945–THIRD MILLENNIUM)

(Freedom's Breeding Ground) by mayor of Nice and government minister Jacques Médecin (he twinned his city with Cape Town at the height of South African apartheid and was later condemned and imprisoned for financial misconduct), who had incidentally presided over the Congress "for the defense of culture" organized in his city by the GRECE. Another is *Renaissance de l'Occident?* (Rebirth of the West?) written by the anonymous Maiastra group that gravitated around Olivier Giscard d'Estaing; or the works of researchers at the Institut national d'études démographiques (INED; National Institute for Demographic Studies) revolving around Jacques Dupâquier[25]; or the publications of the aforementioned Club de l'Horloge; and many others.[26]

But their greatest media success would be the large-scale infiltration by senior Nouvelle Droite members (Alain de Benoist, Jean-Claude Valla, Patrice de Plunkett, Yves Christen, Michel Marmin, Jean Varenne, and Guillaume Faye, as well as several others writing under pseudonyms)[27] of the editing committee of *Figaro Magazine*, a weekly supplement to *Le Figaro* created in 1978 by Louis Pauwels. The magazine was an immediate popular success, soon reaching a circulation of one million, and it disseminated the ideological themes of the Nouvelle Droite to a wider public. Apparently, the readers of *Figaro Magazine* were neither scared off nor even surprised by expressions (often penned by de Benoist) such as "the worship of energy," "the appetite for conquest," "Prometheism," "tragic instinct," "aristocratism," etc., if indeed they even noticed them. Both the classic, conservative Gaullist right, removed from power after Jacques Chirac's resignation from his position as Prime Minister, and the Giscardian right, which was heading for defeat in 1981 in spite of its early reforming measures (voting age lowered to 18, legalization of abortion, etc.), were in ideological disarray. In this context, the Nouvelle Droite offered a body of cultural references that many saw as a breath of fresh air.

The limits of "entryism"

However, this intellectual and political expansion came to a halt in the summer of 1979, when a certain number of intellectuals and journalists finally decided that it was time to act and expose the ideological genealogy of the Nouvelle Droite.[28] A press campaign, initiated by *Le Monde* through an article written by journalist Thierry Pfister, and later joined by *Le Nouvel Observateur* and *Le Matin de Paris*, revealed the strategy of the Nouvelle Droite and highlighted some of its

---

[25] Liauzu, 1999.
[26] Duranton-Crabol, 1988, p. 189.
[27] Ibid., p. 192.
[28] Brunn, 1979; Duranton-Crabol, 1988, pp. 172–203.

ARYAN, PAGAN, AND EXTREME RIGHT   209

"Nazi references," which were confirmed by several in-depth analyses.[29] In 1974, part of this argumentation had already appeared in an anonymous pamphlet published by the so-called Groupement d'action et de recherche pour l'avenir de l'homme (GARAH; Action and Research Group for the Future of Mankind), an obscure traditionalist, Christian group who were appalled by the "pagan" and eugenist references of the Nouvelle Droite; the authors were Michel de Guibert and Georges Souchon, the latter briefly a member of the GRECE.[30] This 1979 press campaign, which generated hundreds of articles and several radio and television programs, forced the Nouvelle Droite to reveal itself and to reply either in a soft-spoken manner, as Alain de Benoist did when he appeared on the *Apostrophes* television program or during his regular contributions on *France Culture*'s Panorama radio program, or more insultingly, as in de Benoist's article (written under the pseudonym David Barney) published in *Éléments* under the title "*Le stade pipi-caca de la pensée*" (The Pee-Pee Poo-Poo Stage of Thought) in which he attacked historian Madeleine Rebérioux, archaeologist Alain Schnapp, and myself.[31]

At the end of 1980, bowing to public pressure and especially to pressure from the traditional, conservative readership of *Le Figaro*, led by Jean d'Ormesson, as well as from the owner of the newspaper Robert Hersant, Louis Pauwels was forced to remove many of his colleagues with links to the Nouvelle Droite from the editing committee of *Figaro Magazine*; shortly afterward, he and Patrice de Plunkett converted to Catholicism. Moreover, with the coming to power of the left in May 1981, the traditional right turned toward new ideological themes, such as economic ultraliberalism, as preached by Ronald Reagan and Margaret Thatcher, in a clear break with Gaullist statism, thus distancing itself from the theories of the Nouvelle Droite. Symmetrically, certain members of the Nouvelle Droite expressed their support of Soviet (or at least Russian) imperialism in opposition to American imperialism in the name of immemorial European values; in this regard they were following in the tradition of national-bolshevism, one of the unexpected elements of the German "conservative revolution" of the 1920s. Likewise, the GRECE looked favorably on the legalization of abortion in the name of eugenism, and certain of its members had a more nuanced attitude toward foreign immigration, citing an ambiguous "right to be different" or even "third-worldism."

The rise of the FN also posed a problem for the members of the Nouvelle Droite. Some, such as Alain de Benoist, favored a continuation of the "metapolitical" struggle outside of standard politics and found the FN party a little too vulgar

---

[29] Schnapp and Svenbro, 1980; Seidel, 1981; Taguieff, 1981, 1984; Olender, 2009, pp. 95–137.
[30] Guibert and Souchon, 1974; Duranton-Crabol, 1988, p. 171.
[31] Barney, 1982.

210 THIRD MOVEMENT (1945–THIRD MILLENNIUM)

with respect to their assumed aristocratism; but others, prolonging the entryist strategy, joined the FN. Among the latter we encounter Pierre Vial, Jean Haudry, and Jean Varenne, who became members of its "scientific council" and its "training institute"; Yvan Blot and Jean-Yves Le Gallou, members of the Club de l'Horloge, entered its political bureau; and Jean Mabire took over responsibility for the FN Jeunesse (National Front Youth) in Upper Normandy. It was only natural that these personalities would follow Bruno Mégret when he split from the FN and formed the Mouvement National Républicain in 1998: in fact, Mégret represented a minority, "pagan" trend within the FN, contrary to the traditional Christian conservative majority trend represented by its leader Jean-Marie Le Pen.

The 1990s were therefore marked by a string of expulsions, scissions, and resignations within the Nouvelle Droite, as is usual in political groups of this type. The "metapolitical" strategy was called into question: Was there not a risk of losing all visibility by choosing to advance behind a mask? This is indeed the drawback of any entryist approach, as was made evident—at the other extreme of the political spectrum—by Trotskyism. Certain historians specializing in the Nouvelle Droite thus speak of "reflux," while others, or the same, point out (fluctuating) doctrinal differences between individual members or currents within this nebulous ideological entity. It is a fact that any historical understanding of a phenomenon can, in the long run, trigger empathy, which can then turn into sympathy—especially since it is difficult to dedicate oneself to the long-term study of an object that one does not like. Consequently, certain intellectuals fell into the trap of engaging in dialog with the Nouvelle Droite and even contributed to its journals, as if the opinions expressed therein were normal and acceptable. In 1993, as a reaction to this, Yves Bonnefoy, Lucy Vines, and Maurice Olender, with the support of philosopher Roger-Pol Droit, published an "Appeal for a Vigilant Europe Against the Extreme Right" in the newspaper *Le Monde*.[32]

Contemporary "Aryan" ideology

In reality, the key elements of the Nouvelle Droite's ideology belong to a political school of thought whose boundaries are somewhat blurred and whose origins in Europe can be traced back to the end of the nineteenth century; Nazism, which itself was multifaceted, was but one of its more monstrous historical

---

[32] Text of the Appeal, names of the first forty signatories and bibliography in Olender, 2009, pp. 244–248; Droit, 1993; Bonnefoy, 2013. Also see the special dossier of the *Art Press* magazine, no. 223, 1997.

manifestations. For the sake of simplicity, let us refer to this as the "Aryan" trend. The Nouvelle Droite, in the strict sense, with its official journals, represents its most intellectual and polished version, but movements that are more radical in their expression, if not in their actions, are closely linked to it and range from clearly identified associations and clubs, which are socially and politically well-integrated, to marginal groups which are, to a greater or lesser degree, informal and violent. Such groups are also found on the so-called "Euro-pagan" music scene and not surprisingly on the internet. The "Indo-Europeans" or "Aryans," sometimes reduced to the "Celts" or "Germans," play a central role in these constructs.

The FN and its current foreign equivalents differ from this "Aryan" trend in a number of ways: their "national populism" assumes a more popular and demagogical stance far removed from aristocratic "Aryan" ideologies, and they are determined to come to power, or at least have a share in it, via democratic means, as has already been the case in Austria, Italy, and Hungary—to the point of accounting for between 15% and 25% of votes in several European countries, including France, in the 2010s. This national-populism is rigidly nationalist and borderline racist, at least in some of its oral expressions, and it is vehemently opposed to foreign immigration, which is held up as a scapegoat. It is traditionalist as regards morality (at least officially) and is often linked to a more conservative, if not fundamentalist, Christianism. From an economic point of view, it was ultraliberal for a long time, as in the case of South American dictatorships (advocating, for instance, the suppression of income tax), before becoming more statist, as in France for example; in this regard it harks back to National Socialism in its original form.

In contrast, within the "Aryan" extreme right, five key ideas can be identified which together shape its credo, regardless of the variations specific to the individual subgroups:

1. From a historical point of view, Europeans are the direct descendants of the prehistoric Indo-Europeans, an exceptional ethnic group which forged itself several thousand years ago on the shores of the Baltic. Their religion and their society were pagan, warlike, aristocratic, and stratified. Thus, in the words of ideologist Guillaume Faye, we must today follow this "pagan conception of society—both libertarian and sovereign, convivial and regalian, animated as much by the principle of pleasure as by the will to power."[33] This includes the resurgence of pagan rituals (real or imaginary), such as those associated with the winter and summer solstices.[34]

[33] Faye, G., 1983, p. 25.
[34] Benoist, 1981.

212 THIRD MOVEMENT (1945–THIRD MILLENNIUM)

This paganism can also be accompanied by esoteric and occultist beliefs (including belief in reinvented Templars) and by regular references to Hinduism, which, it is believed, managed to preserve the ancient hierarchical polytheism of the Indo-Europeans.

2. In order to counter the egalitarian ideology and the notion of human rights that have emerged from Judeo-Christianism, it is necessary to affirm the right to difference, or, in other words, the *right to identity* (i.e., the specificity of cultures, if not races). From this point of view, communitarianism is acceptable as long as the races are distinct, even irreducible, each with its specificity, without it being always necessary to introduce a hierarchy between them. However, social Darwinism remains present, often in the background, while racial mixing is explicitly rejected. Racist, anti-Semitic rhetoric, sometimes closely linked to negationism, is nevertheless present in certain important and official wings of the Nouvelle Droite.

3. To counter the uniformizing, Jacobin national State, it is necessary to build a European ethnic empire, without strong internal borders, but where each ethnic group, within its own territory, has its own identity and enjoys a high degree of autonomy: the Paris Commune, with its program of decentralization and self-management, as well as certain utopian socialists of the nineteenth century, are sometimes paradoxically cited as references. It was in the name of this imperial program that writers such as Drieu La Rochelle and Brasillach embraced Nazism only to be disappointed by its strictly Germano-centric, nationalist application.

4 To counter uniformizing Anglo-Saxon political and cultural imperialism and its ultraliberal economic ideology, it is necessary to develop an economy based on solidarity within the framework of an "organic" society, which might even be socialist, in reference to revolutionary socialists such as Georges Sorel (who was claimed in turn by Mussolini, the conservative pro-Nazi Carl Schmitt, and the founders of the Baas party), if not to national-socialism. This economy might be ecological in nature—a clear continuity of the *Lebensreform* of late nineteenth-century Germany.

5 As regards morals, the Aryan ideology permits abortion in the name of eugenics, just as it does euthanasia and suicide; the suicide of Henry de Montherlant at the age of seventy-seven, after he had been blinded in an accident, is a reference, as is the suicide of Pierre Drieu La Rochelle during the Liberation, or more recently that of Dominique Venner in Notre-Dame de Paris in 2013, and, of course, we must not forget the *seppuku* of Japanese writer Yukio Mishima in 1970. A certain emphasis is placed on male camaraderie (referred to as *Kamaradenschaft* on certain sites), to the extent that male homosexuality is largely tolerated, with the endorsement of German Nazi writer Hans Blüher, Robert Brasillach, Maurice Bardèche, Gabriel

Matzneff, Pierre Gripari (member of the GRECE), Alain Daniélou, Michel Caignet (former member of the neo-Nazi group Fédération d'action nationale et européenne, director of the *Gaie France* magazine, who was also convicted for pedophilia), or German neo-Nazi Michaël Kühnen, a close friend of the latter and author of *Nationalsozialismus und Homosexualität* (1986). Consequently the presence of some of these violent movements in the 2012–2014 demonstrations against same-sex marriage in France was somewhat paradoxical and led to a certain amount of internal confusion.

These five central themes, the importance of which may be easily gleaned from Nouvelle Droite publications right up to the present, prompt a number of reflections. On the one hand, a degree of apparent ideological haziness might suggest, to someone deprived of even a minimum of historical culture, that some of these ideas are novel and perhaps even not far removed from those of some of today's left, such as an interest in regionalist movements, Arab nationalism (sometimes out of anti-Semitism[35]), or even ecology—despite the fact that the return to nature and naturism have been a constant of the German extreme right since the end of the nineteenth century (which, of course, in no way discredits left-wing political ecology, whose agenda is entirely different).[36] Because they diverge from those of the FN on certain issues (e.g., hostility toward strict nationalism, affirmation of the right to difference and their view on abortion, euthanasia, and male homosexuality), we might be led to believe that some of these "Aryan" theses are not extreme right ideas at all. In reality, their secular affiliation is evident through certain elements of Nazism (in its "aristocratic" variation, embodied by the SS) and the postwar extremist movements such as Europe Action. Only the rhetoric and certain literary and scientific references are novel.

A racial *"Que sais-je?"*

Publications, even recent ones, by the Nouvelle Droite on the subject of the Indo-Europeans are revealing. From linguist Jean Haudry's 1981 book in the *"Que sais-je?"* series (re-edited in 2010) to the 1997 special issue of *Nouvelle École* (almost exclusively written by Jean Haudry and Alain de Benoist), including several more recent and more repetitive works, they recycle almost in their entirety the theories of Kossinna and of his Nazi disciples regarding an original Homeland situated in the Baltic or even in a fantastical drowned Atlantis.[37] But in particular,

---

[35] See Olender, 2009, pp. 221–222.
[36] Pouchain, 1999.
[37] Haudry, 1981; *Nouvelle École*, no. 49, 1997.

214   THIRD MOVEMENT (1945–THIRD MILLENNIUM)

from *Vu de droite* to the aforementioned "*Que sais-je?*," the idea of a tall, blond, blue-eyed "Aryan race" is reaffirmed with explicit references to Hans Günther, official raciologist of the Nazi regime and oft celebrated in *Nouvelle École*. These theses also currently feature on a certain number of internet sites, such as that of the Terre et Peuple movement (Land and People; a transparent reference to Nazi exaltation of *Blut und Boden*—Blood and Soil), which was founded and managed by retired university academics Pierre Vial and Jean Haudry. It goes without saying that this "blondness," which as we recall was first proposed by Vacher de Lapouge,[38] is purely fictional as was ably demonstrated by Bernard Sergent[39]: certain heroes were described as brown-haired, such as the Germanic Sigurdr (i.e., Siegfried himself!); the Greek word translated as "blond" is *xanthos*, which also means "tawny" or "red-haired"; and the color red is often associated with warriors in Indo-European mythologies.

In his "*Que sais-je?*" on the Indo-Europeans, which is a follow-on to a first volume almost entirely devoted to Indo-European linguistics,[40] Jean Haudry describes an ideal proto Indo-European society, which for the most part belongs to the realm of fantasy as becomes more and more obvious as the book progresses.[41] This primitive society was supposedly based on anachronistic "national ties" (p. 66). Aristocratic in nature, this society stood against "class struggle" (p. 52) and the "hidden enemy within" (p. 24). Hence, "the Indo-Europeans rejected, in their forms of government, any kind of majority rule, be it democratic or plutocratic" (p. 57). Their moral code would have differed little from the program of the original FN since it supposedly promulgated "measures intended to favor fertility, dissuade celibacy, and repress abortion and homosexuality" (p. 106). The Indo-European religion was "pagan," "tolerant," "free of fanaticism," and ignored "dogma" (p. 71). It was also "esoteric," and certain individuals, with the gift of "supranormal powers," "produced the various phenomena catalogued and studied by parapsychologists" (p. 29). This latter observation is not anodyne because, as we have seen, this constant fascination of the extreme right with esotericism and occultism can be traced in a direct line from Nazism to the Nouvelle Droite.

Ideological references to National Socialism occur literally in the choice of expressions. In Haudry's book, "soil and blood" (p. 49) evokes the Nazi *Blut und Boden*, likewise "living space" (p. 101) and "their taste for open spaces,

---

[38] See Chapter 4, pp. 89–93.

[39] Sergent, 1995, pp. 434–441.

[40] Haudry, 1979; critical review by Jean-Louis Perpillou in *Bulletin de la Société de linguistique de Paris*, t. LXXVI, fasc. 2, 1981, pp. 113–114.

[41] Sergent, 1982; Taguieff, 1984; Biscarat, 2000; Olender, *Le Nouvel Observateur*, February 20, 1982, and the response from Jean Haudry, *Le Nouvel Observateur*, March 20, 1982; Olender, 1983, 2009, pp. 111–115; Demoule, 1982, *L'Histoire*, no. 43, p. 116. The citations that follow are taken from Haudry, 1981, with the corresponding page numbers being indicated in brackets.

ARYAN, PAGAN, AND EXTREME RIGHT   215

their desire for domination" (pp. 122 and 50) echo the concept of *Lebensraum*. Even "the twilight of the gods" gets a mention (p. 88). References become even more explicit toward the end of the book when the author considers the issue of the Indo-European "physical type." He states that the ancient texts "all agree in identifying the Nordic race, if not with the entire population, at least with its upper echelon" (p. 122). This approach is not new: it dates back to Vacher de Lapouge and his *L'Aryen, son rôle social* (The Aryan, His Social Role)[42] in which he provides a series of appended citations from ancient texts describing heroes as tall and blond. Kossinna also used these sources. But, as Haudry notes, this blondness generally only concerns the "upper social stratum," since "the racial unity of the Indo-European aristocracy must have been reinforced through endogamy; its physical type was perceived as a mark of superiority" (p. 124).

In fact, "if the Nordic type was considered as the physical ideal, it was because it corresponded to that of the upper stratum of the population" (p. 123), with the exception, precisely, of the Germanic people—at least as described by Tacitus—who were all of "Nordic type" regardless of their place in society. It follows therefore that the only racially pure Indo-Europeans were the Germanic peoples. What makes it even more explicit, are the names invoked by Haudry as authorities in "modern anthropology": by this he means the works of Nazi raciologist Hans Günther, *Rassenkunde des deutschen Volkes* (Ethnology of the German People, 1933) and *Die nordische Rasse bei den Indogermanen Asiens. Zugleich ein Beitrag zur Frage nach der Urheimat und Rassenherkunft des Indogermanen* (The Nordic Race Among the Indo-Germans of Asia. With a Contribution on the Question of the Original Homeland and the Racial Origins of the Indo-Germans, 1934).[43] He adds to this the recent re-edition of a posthumous work by German nationalist Rudolph Much (d. 1936), son of Matthäus Much, amateur Germanomaniac and inspirer of Kossinna (incidentally, Haudry confuses father and son); this re-edition was courtesy of Herbert Jankuhn, former head of archaeological excavations under the SS ("de-Nazified" at the time and serving as professor at Göttingen University, where he was dean) and of Germanist Wolfgang Lange.[44]

These anthropological "certainties" allow Haudry to identify the original Indo-European cradle. It is no longer in Scandinavia, as suggested by Kossinna, but is now to be found in the Arctic, a hypothesis first mooted by Vacher de Lapouge and Rosenberg. The chapter (pp. 119–121) dedicated to it is entitled "Ultima Thulé." This apparent reference to the Greek traveler Pytheas, who gave this name to an unknown northern island of which he had heard, is in fact a transparent allusion to the Thule Society, one of the secret societies that

---

[42] See Chapter 4, p. 89.
[43] Haudry, 1981, pp. 122–123, notes 36 and 40; Günther, 1933, 1934.
[44] Haudry, 1981, p. 122, note 40; Much et al., 1967.

216   THIRD MOVEMENT (1945–THIRD MILLENNIUM)

contributed to the foundation of the Nazi Party and whose historical role was greatly exaggerated by Pauwels and Bergier. It is also a reference to the Thule Combat League, which was active in the bloody reprisals that followed the 1919 Munich Soviet Republic. In support of his thesis, Jean Haudry invokes obscure passages taken from Celtic legends of medieval Ireland and from the Avesta, the sacred text of the Zoroastrian religion, dated to the first millennium BCE. He also mentions an allusive manuscript text by late French prehistorian Franck Bourdier, as well as the work of an Indian scholar of the early twentieth century, Bâl Gangâdhar Tilak, which had been conveniently translated shortly beforehand by a publishing house linked to the extreme right and which also situated the original cradle at the North Pole.[45] Finally, he reminds the reader that the Indo-European root *sekʷ, which can mean "to track" or "to follow" and also "to see" and "to recount," was indeed one of the "vestiges of the language of a hunting people."[46] Clearly, the evidence is a bit thin. Nevertheless, the Polar origin hypothesis was subsequently reiterated in the special edition of *Nouvelle École* dedicated to the "Indo-Europeans,"[47] an issue entirely written by Alain de Benoist and Jean Haudry. In the same vein, a certain Carl-Heinz Boettcher developed a barely modernized version of the Kossinnian theories in the *Études indo-européennes* journal edited by the Institut d'Études Indo-Européennes founded by Jean Haudry at the University of Lyon III.[48] According to this version, the original People are identified in the Ertebølle-Ellerbeck culture of Mesolithic Scandinavia.

We might be surprised that the respectable Presses Universitaires de France (PUF), presided over at the time by the late Michel Prigent, could have published a work with such blatant ideological references as part of such a prestigious collection. In fact, it was not until 1998, after several re-editions, that the book was removed from the PUF catalogue; it continued to be available for purchase until 2003. An extreme-right publishing company subsequently re-edited the two "*Que sais-je?*" volumes together as one "updated" volume.[49]

The above-mentioned Institut d'Études Indo-Européennes was founded by Jean Haudry in 1981, with the enthusiastic support of Jacques Goudet, then president of the university, but was shut down in 1998.[50] Its staff included several members of the GRECE, such as Indianist Jean Varenne and Germanist Jean-Paul Allard (who became director of the Institute in 1987). At the same time, Lyon III's teaching staff included historian Pierre Vial (specialist in Templar

---

[45] Tilak, 1903; Haudry, 1981, pp. 119–121.
[46] Ibid., p. 121.
[47] Haudry, 1997.
[48] Boettcher, 1996.
[49] Haudry, 2010.
[50] Olender, 2009, pp. 120–123; Rousso, 2004, p. 59, note 24; Biscarat, 2000.

history, sometimes seen through an esoteric lens), law expert Bruno Gollnisch (for a time second-in-command of the FN), sociologist Jacques Marlaud (formerly based in South Africa), Breton nationalist Georges Pinault (veteran of the colonial wars and virtually lacking any university qualifications), and Africanist Bernard Lugan (apartheid propagandist), all of whom had close ties to the extreme right and more specifically to the GRECE. The procedures behind their appointment to this university were sometimes controversial. In the 2000s, these individuals retired and were not replaced. This group of lecturers was directly engaged in negationist research and became involved in a number of controversies. Jean-Paul Allard, Jean-Claude Rivière, and Pierre Zind in particular, as members of the jury, were implicated in the infamous controversy surrounding the thesis presented by Henri Roques at Nantes University in June 1985; the Ministry for Education subsequently revoked his PhD degree. Other controversial works include an article by economist Bernard Notin, also a lecturer at the university, and the 1990 master's degree thesis by bookseller and negationist editor Jean Plantin, granted by other Lyon III academic staff and which was also the subject of an appeal.[51]

These retirements, while they meant the end of any academic recognition, did not lead to the group's disappearance. Pierre Vial and Jean Haudry are active within the aforementioned Terre et Peuple group. The Indo-Europeans occupy a central place on the group's internet site and on others. Likewise, the Association des Amis des Études Celtiques, which has its headquarters in the Sorbonne, is still controlled by Jean Haudry and some of his ideological sympathizers and regularly organizes "seminars" with the same orientation.

An increasing proportion of extreme-right ideologies are now diffused via the internet. There we find dozens of so-called identitarian reference sites, such as the much-visited "François Desouche" site, managed by FN militant Pierre Sautarel and hosted in Sweden, or the web TV channel TV Libertés, created in 2014. Here, too, we encounter the Indo-Europeans, on top of all the usual extreme-right themes, such as exaltation of the "race," islamophobia, condemnation of "Judeo-capitalism," etc. This internet diffusion represents a cultural rejuvenation of these themes which goes hand in hand with another scene, that of so-called Europagan music and Neopaganism in general.[52] However, in a manner of speaking, we can distinguish between a "right-wing" paganism and a "left-wing" paganism. The latter is part of the wider New Age trend and is often associated with feminist, pacifist, and ecological movements, mostly originating in the English-speaking world, like the so-called Wicca movement which preaches an invented primitive mother goddess cult; interestingly, Indo-Europeanist Marija

[51] Rousso, 2004.
[52] François, 2006, 2007, 2008.

218 THIRD MOVEMENT (1945–THIRD MILLENNIUM)

Gimbutas participated in the movement toward the end of her life and has since become one of its figures of reference.[53] "Right-wing" paganism, or perhaps more accurately extreme right-wing paganism, vaunts the diametrically opposite values of brute force within a warrior mythology, which is equally invented, with gatherings and "ceremonies" linked, for example, to the solstices and so-called pagan music concerts. This form of Neopaganism was theorized under a more intellectual form by the Nouvelle Droite and particularly by Pierre Vial and Alain de Benoist.

The "racist" International

The re-emergence of extreme-right ideologies, hitherto disqualified by the defeat of Nazism, was clearly not confined to France, even though it is our main focus of interest. From the late 1960s onward, the United States and Europe witnessed the weaving together of networks which English historian Michael Billig has termed the "Racist International."[54] These networks have a common basis, one founded on non-egalitarian, eugenist, or even racist theories,[55] and on references to a mythical Indo-European past. In the postwar years, British anthropologist Roger Pearson founded the Northern League for North European Friendship, which brought together former Nazis, like raciologist Hans Günther (who at the time was writing under a pseudonym); former SS member Arthur Ehrhardt; Franz Altheim, one time collaborator of Himmler within the Ahnenerbe (after the war he held a professorship at Halle in East Germany and then in West Berlin); and various neo-Nazis and neo-fascists such as Colin Jordan, Alastair Harper, and John Tyndall in Great Britain. In 1960, Pearson established the *Mankind Quarterly* journal, the mouthpiece of "scientific racism," in collaboration with Robert Gayre and, most notably, with Nazi geneticist Ottmar von Verschuer, Mengele's former superior.[56] French anthropologist Henri-Victor Vallois was a member of the journal's honorary committee. Pearson also created a publishing and distribution house, the Institute for the Study of Man, whose neutral title belies the fact that it was largely financed by the Pioneer Fund, an organization which supports racialist and racist publications. Furthermore, Pearson was a member of the World Anti-Communist League and had links to other similar organizations, such as the Moon sect.

In 1973, Pearson, through the intermediary of the Institute for the Study of Man, founded the *Journal of Indo-European Studies*, which would rapidly become

---

[53] See Chapter 14, pp. 294–296.
[54] Billig, 1981.
[55] See Chapter 10.
[56] See Chapter 8, pp. 189 and 193.

a leading reference in the field. The editorial committee was comprised of four members: Roger Pearson himself, archaeologist Marija Gimbutas, Finnish linguist Raimo Anttila, and Belgian Indo-Europeanist Edgar Polomé. Incidentally, Polomé, Pearson and Gimbutas were also part of the patronage committee of *Nouvelle École*. Assuredly, the scientific standing of these three scholars is indisputable, as is that of most of the editorial advisory board of the *Journal of Indo-European Studies*, which initially numbered thirty-six members. However, in their midst we once again encounter Franz Altheim, Himmler's collaborator, who was also on the patronage committee of *Nouvelle École*; indeed several other members, such as Mircea Eliade, Scott Littleton, and Rüdiger Schmitt, belonged to both committees, and it is not always possible to ascertain if these scientists were fully aware of the nature of the journal.

To this day, the *Journal of Indo-European Studies* purports to be a purely scientific publication. This measured neutrality can be read as an example of "metapolitical" editorial action on the part of Pearson, even though in a bibliographical review Edgar Polomé, himself quite conservative, commended the quality of *Nouvelle École*, "the fascinating French journal devoted to original, even if controversial, ideas" on the occasion of the aforementioned 1997 issue dedicated to the Indo-Europeans (in their Kossinnian version).[57] In two pages of praise, Polomé (a French-speaking Belgian) clearly saw no link between the original Nordic or even "circumpolar" cradle proposed by de Benoist and Haudry and the theories of Kossinna and Rosenberg. Indeed, he concludes: "This volume stands out as an excellent *status questionnis* of the IE problem that no serious scholar in the field can afford to bypass." A few pages further on, Polomé also provides a very brief but equally eulogizing account of Alain de Benoist's book *Famille et Société* (1996), which he describes as "fascinating," a "brilliant overview," "amply documented, well written and easily readable."[58]

It is also worth mentioning within the same American context *The Occidental Quarterly* journal and *The Occidental Observer* website, edited by the Charles Martel Society, whose name speaks for itself. The topics covered for the most part focus on threats to the "white race." The editor of *The Occidental Quarterly*, Kevin McDonald, professor of psychology at the University of California, Long Beach, discusses the "eugenist and ethnocentrist strategy" which the Jews supposedly put in place to take control over "the white majorities of Europe and America" and ponders on the existence of a "Jewish race." One of its contributors (who also include Alain de Benoist) is John Day, the author of a voluminous work, *Indo-European Origins: The Anthropological Evidence* (2001), naturally published by the Institute of the Study of Man (in fact it is the second monograph published

---

[57] Polomé, "Book Chronicles," *Journal of Indo-European Studies*, 25, 1–2, pp. 234–235.
[58] Ibid., 25, 1–2, pp. 266–267. Critical review of this book in Le Bras, 1997.

220 THIRD MOVEMENT (1945–THIRD MILLENNIUM)

by this organization, shortly after its tribute to Marija Gimbutas) and which claims to answer the question of Indo-European origins through physical anthropology. Even enriched by a dose of DNA analysis, this anthropology remains biased because it is based on the supposed "Nordic physical type" of the old Indo-European elite attested in ancient texts and, as such, stands in a direct line of descent from the works of Gobineau, Vacher de Lapouge, and Kossinna. The author vigorously dismisses Colin Renfrew's Anatolian hypothesis and instead, without daring to fully admit it, moves toward Kossinna's Nordic hypothesis and his historico-political conclusions: since the Indo-European were an elite, they were in a minority and thus were partly absorbed within the mass of the conquered peoples. This was notably the case of the Roman patricians, all traces of whom were lost at the beginning of the Roman Empire. On this subject, John Day concludes one of his articles as follows: "If we, Westerners, wish to avoid a similar fate, we have a lot to learn from the history of the Indo-Europeans." Deploring the intellectual terrorism visited on the French Nouvelle Droite and "democratic Germany" (the quotation marks are Day's), he cites Nazi anthropologist Ilse Schwidetzky when discussing the decline of peoples.[59]

Close collaborations

Thus, thanks to the Northern League, the "Racist International" benefits from an active network of magazines like *Mankind Quarterly*, *Nouvelle École* and, in Germany, *Neue Anthropologie*, a mouthpiece for the Gesellschaft für biologische Anthropologie, Eugenik und Verhaltensforschung (Society for Biological Anthropology, Eugenics and Behavioral Science), coordinated in particular by neo-Nazis Hans Georg Amsel and Jürgen Rieger, a disciple of Hans Günther. The links between France and Germany are particularly strong. One of the French members of the Nouvelle Droite, Pierre Krebs, lives in Germany and co-ordinates the Thule Seminar (another clear reference to the Thule Society), which defines itself as a *Forschungs- und Lehrgemeinschaft für die indoeuropäische Kultur* (i.e., an "association for research and teaching on Indo-European culture"). Within this association, Krebs successively founded the magazines *Elemente* (from 1986 to 1996), *Metapo* (in reference to the "metapolitical" strategy) from 1999 to 2001, and then *Mars Ultor* (Mars the Avenger, after the Roman god). The internet sites linked to the association use graphic images and iconography that explicitly evoke Nazism, including the "black sun" which graced the floor of the great hall at Wewelsburg, the general headquarters of the SS. The proud motto *Wissen eint! Wille siegt!* (Knowledge unites! Will conquers!) also appears.

---

[59] Day, 2001, 2002; Schwidetzky, 1954.

Among these magazines' French collaborators we encounter, not surprisingly, those involved in *Nouvelle École*, such as Jean Haudry, Pierre Vial, and Guillaume Faye. In the early 1990s, Alain de Benoist was also involved; at the same time he was directing an extreme-right publishing house in Germany, Grabert, which was known for its anti-Semitic and negationist publications, some of which have been condemned under German law.

In Italy, the Nuova Destra was founded, in 1977, by members of various neo-fascist youth groups.[60] Like its French older sibling and model, it publishes a magazine called *Elementi* and proclaims itself to be anti-capitalist, anti-democratic, biologizing, anti-egalitarian, and admiring of Julius Evola. Within this movement we encounter the names of Claudio Mutti, former neo-fascist member of parliament, translator of several negationist works and of the anti-Semitic hoax *The Protocols of the Elders of Zion*; Mario Tarchi, and his magazines *Diorama letterario* and *Transgressioni*; and Alessandro Campi and his magazine *Futur Presente*, which closely resembles *Nouvelle École*.

Likewise, we cannot omit Belgium (both Flanders and Wallonia), which also has links with the French Nouvelle Droite, and its neo-pagan magazine *Antaïos*; Switzerland, with its *Cercle Thulé* (Thule Circle); and Austria, Greece, Spain (or Catalonia, where a homonym of the GRECE exits), etc.[61] The extreme-right internet site "Metapedia," in an explicit reference to "Wikipedia" which it blatantly plagiarizes in terms of its page layout and model, publishes articles in almost twenty European languages. In 2013, entries in Hungarian, which are the most numerous of all, numbered almost 150 000, in contrast to a few thousand entries in most other languages. The predominant themes are the Second World War, fascist movements, anti-Semitism, and negationism.

All of these contemporary movements share a desire to prolong the political and intellectual heritage that German Nazism and Italian Fascism pushed to its ultimate concrete expression. The imaginary perpetuation of a reconstructed "Indo-European" heritage, which is in reality very far removed from anything we know of prehistoric European societies, coupled with cheesy Neopaganism, could remain marginal and anecdotal. However, the marginal groups that gave birth to Nazism began in exactly the same way; in their infancy they did not even enjoy the same intellectual audience as that attracted by the Nouvelle Droite in France. On the one hand, in today's Europe, the clearly populist extreme right has the support of between 5% and 30% of voters, and, on the other, the fringes of the traditional conservative right have been contaminated by extreme right-wing rhetoric.

[60] Ferraresi, 1984; François, 2008.
[61] On contemporary European extreme-right movements: Duranton-Crabol, 1991; Milza, 2002; François, 2008.

222 THIRD MOVEMENT (1945–THIRD MILLENNIUM)

The 2014 publication of the French edition of the present work attracted immediate and vehement criticism from the extreme right. Early on, one of its magazines, *Éléments*, asked me to agree to an interview with their leader Alain de Benoist, a request that I turned down because to accept it would have been to recognize him as a respectable scientific commentator and not an extremist ideologist. As a consequence, a series of very violent, and almost insulting, articles appeared in various extreme-right magazines, including *Éléments*, *Nouvelle École*, *La Nouvelle Revue d'Histoire*, *Valeurs Actuelles*, *Le Figaro Histoire*, *Réfléchir et Agir*, and even in a new magazine dedicated to Indo-European linguistics, *Wekwos*, which also has certain links to the extreme right. Identical attacks also occurred on extreme right-wing radio and TV channels and on social networks—the latter were even more violent because they were expressed anonymously. In the end, I even had to request a mediation from the online encyclopedia Wikipedia because of this behavior. In 2018, *Nouvelle École* devoted an entire issue to the "*Paléogénétique des Indo-Européens*" (Paleogenetics of the Indo-Europeans), which, apart from the usual attacks on my book, examined the results of genetic analyses published in 2015 in support of a migration from the steppes.[62] Since this migration does not correspond to the extreme right's usual thesis, which, in the wake of Nazism, advocates a Baltic or even Polar origin for the original People, Alain de Benoist in his editorial introduction wonders if we should not "go back even further to identify the conditions that gave rise to the PIE" and whether the Yamnaya culture might not originate from "a branch that could have developed from the PIE further north." We might add that the cover of the magazine features a young blond girl belonging to the Kalash ethnic group, a polytheist society living in the mountains of northwestern Pakistan and which continues to resist Islamization. Apart from the fact that blond hair is rare in the region, this fascination for the Kalash, who are "clearly descendants of the Indo-European peoples who colonized the Indian sub-continent," finds echoes in the Third Reich expeditions to Tibet in 1938–1939, where anthropologist Bruno Beger took a particular interest in blond-haired, blue-eyed types in his quest for the primitive Indo-European cradle.

While such reactions were foreseeable, I was nonetheless taken aback by their scale and by the use of certain language which I consider unacceptable. I was thus described as a "negationist" on the pretext that I had denied the existence of the original People. In French, this term is generally reserved for those who deny the reality of the Holocaust. While the process of twisting the meaning of words is typical of extreme right-wing rhetoric, it is nonetheless obscene when it concerns the very real assassination of six million human beings.

---

[62] See Chapter 10, pp. 232–236.

10

From racial anthropology
to biological anthropology

The first half of the twentieth century witnessed the gradual abandonment of craniometry at a rate that varied in different countries and scientific traditions and, at the same time, the emergence of genetics. The second half of the same century saw the continuation of this trend. However, physical anthropology, as the study of skeletons, did not disappear entirely as a scientific discipline but rather found other modes of existence, particularly through the application of novel modern techniques. For its part, genetics appeared to have largely triumphed, although behind the public scientific debate there also lay academic power struggles. The genetic study of living populations seemed capable of doing away with the need to study ancient skeletons, even though the latter constitute the actual physical evidence of past populations; among other things the financial cost was significantly less, and, in principle, there was no longer any need to carry out long and complicated archaeological excavations. However, despite the growing sophistication of DNA studies, the explanatory models used essentially remained those of the nineteenth century, when craniometry reigned supreme. And just as Alfredo Trombetti a century ago retraced the dispersal of humans and their languages from a single central point in the Himalayas, geneticists and linguists set about constructing a Great Tree of all the world's genes and languages in which was embedded the tree of Indo-European languages that were dispersed via the migrations of the primordial People.

The twilight of the "races"

Outwardly, physical anthropology resisted the traumas of the Second World War and the consequences of its subversion by the racial politics of the Third Reich and its dependencies, including Vichy France. Henri-Victor Vallois[1] suffered no career setbacks after the Liberation. He continued to wield enormous influence over French anthropology right up until his death in 1981. His students, such as Denise Ferembach and Raymond Riquet, continued faithfully in his footsteps.

---

[1] See Chapter 8, pp. 191–193.

224 THIRD MOVEMENT (1945-THIRD MILLENNIUM)

The latter, professor of anthropology at Bordeaux University from 1977, tirelessly identified the prehistoric "races" and reviewed some 700 skulls dating to the French Neolithic and Eneolithic.[2] Perfectly representative of French anthropology at the time, he distinguished "paleolithic and mesolithic type races," both indigenous, within which we encounter "tall types" with the "Cro-magnoid type in the strict sense," the "Brünn (Brno) type," and the "Borreby type," which is "not attested in France." Among the "short types" he identified the "Proto-Alpine type" ("defined by its brachycephaly, which was much less accentuated than among current Alpines"), the "Séquanian mesocephalic type" ("*type mésocéphale séquanien*"), and the "Aquitanian dolichocephalic type" ("*type dolichocéphale aquitain*"). Furthermore, he identified the "Neolithic invaders," who could also be divided into "tall" and "short" types. Among the former, we encounter the "Corded Ware race" (defined by Coon, and which corresponds to Schliz's Hinkelstein type, Reche's Type II, Scheidt's East German dolichocephalic form, and Ulrich's Type I). As Riquet notes, "this race corresponds to tall individuals who are markedly dolichocephalic. . . . The origin of this type is not known but perhaps might be found in the area of the steppes to the north of the Black Sea, if it is indeed the case that the Corded Ware culture emerged in these regions as is generally assumed. However, we could just as well consider this race to be indigenous. Along with the Brünn race, it forms one of the essential components of the current Nordic race."[3]

Riquet also recognizes "Coon's megalithic type"; the "Danubian type," which "undoubtedly corresponds to the earliest wave of Neolithic invaders" and which "displays a clearly Mediterranean character," just like the "Baumes-Chaudes race," which is "without doubt a megalithic race." Finally, we must mention the "Early Bronze Age invaders" with the "Dinarics, or more precisely the Dinaroids" (but within which we have undoubtedly "confused the craniologically similar Armenoid type, the true Dinaric type of Balkan origin and the Lorraine type of Central European origin") and the "Insular Iberian race."

Finally, while "the Nordic race in its current form barely existed before the first Iron Age . . ., that which we encounter in the Eneolithic is more often than not the Proto-Nordic: Cro-magnoid and Corded Ware. The relationship that we propose remains in any case open to discussion."[4]

In a tradition that can be traced back to Broca, and which was born out of mistrust on the one hand and probable disinterest on the other, Raymond Riquet never uses the terms "Indo-European" or "Aryan." Nevertheless, the issue remains present in the background in the guise of the "Corded Ware race" that

[2] Riquet, 1951.
[3] Ibid., pp. 205-206.
[4] Ibid., p. 210.

RACIAL TO BIOLOGICAL ANTHROPOLOGY   225

may have originated from the Black Sea region, unless of course it was indigenous and Nordic, which leaves a certain degree of flexibility. We also see how the notions of "race," "type," "culture," and "ceramic tradition" are intertwined and ill-defined and furthermore, without going into the detail of Riquet's work, the extent to which the boundaries between these "races" appear to be blurred and fluctuating, illustrating the observation, already fifty years old at the time, that groups become increasingly ill-defined as a function of the number of anthropomorphic measurements taken; indeed, it was this observation that led Déchelette and others to profoundly question the pertinence of the discipline.

Medals and survivals

We have already seen[5] how German anthropologists, including those most compromised, continued to enjoy peaceful academic careers after the Second World War and how their discipline was never brought into question.[6] In 1956, Eugen Fischer, the "scientific" brains behind the Nuremberg racial laws, enjoyed pride of place at the international congress celebrating the centenary of the discovery of Neanderthal man. It was not until the 1980s that a new generation of scientists, mainly German- and English-speaking, took over the dossier and carried out the necessary critical historical reviews.[7]

These intellectual affinities would culminate in the awarding of the 1980 Paul Broca Prize to German anthropologist Ilse Schwidetzky, under the aegis of the Société d'Anthropologie de Paris and the Centre national de la recherche scientifique (CNRS; French National Centre for Scientific Research), on the occasion of the centenary of Broca's death.[8] Despite her assertions to the contrary, Ilse Schwidetzky, who succeeded Baron Egon von Eickstedt at the helm of the Mainz Institute of Anthropology, was linked to Nazism.[9] Her receipt of the prize provoked a public scandal within the CNRS and a crisis within the Société d'Anthropologie de Paris. In the Society's annual report, Denise Ferembach expressed her regret regarding these "deplorable incidents," which "thankfully, did not greatly impact upon the running of the conference."[10] Nevertheless, the following year (the year of Vallois's death), the Society was forced to organize a special session on "ethical problems in physical anthropology" during which

---

[5] See Chapter 8, p. 189.
[6] See also Kaupen-Haas and Saller, 1999.
[7] Müller-Hill, 1984; Conte and Essner, 1995; Billig, 1981; Weinreich, M., 1946; Massin, 1998, 1999; Kaupen-Haas and Saller, 1999; Römer, 1985; Adams, 1990; Weindling, 1989 [1998]; Olff-Nathan, 1993; Schmuhl, 2005, 2008; Lipphardt, 2008.
[8] Bocquet-Appel, 1996, p. 116.
[9] See Chapter 8, p. 189.
[10] Ferembach, 1980, p. 351.

226 THIRD MOVEMENT (1945–THIRD MILLENNIUM)

were examined, in turn, "the responsibility of the anthropologist; the emotive context surrounding the notion of race—the concept of which cannot be abandoned; the exploitation of scientific works for ideological ends—through the subversion of their true meaning, leading to unjustified attacks on anthropology." Also discussed was "the way in which anthropologists ought to react in the face of attacks made on the discipline."[11]

However, over the course of the 1980s, physical anthropology in France ceased to exist in its traditional form as its proponents passed away one by one. Nevertheless, even if it persisted longer in France than elsewhere, craniometry has not entirely disappeared. It remains an issue in Japan, the country that undoubtedly provides the greatest level of funding for its national archaeology. In certain museums, for example, interactive screens have been installed where, by entering one's physical characteristics, one can determine whether one is "Jomon" (i.e., belonging to the physical "type" supposed to be that of the first Japanese population) or "Yayoi" (i.e., belonging to the population believed to have arrived from the continent in the past few centuries BCE). Such an approach is perhaps understandable in a country where volcanic soils result in poor preservation of skeletal material and thus greatly limit available data; furthermore Japanese anthropology has not been compromised by involvement in crimes against humanity.

In 1973, Indian anthropologist Kumar published, in the first edition of the new *Journal of Indo-European Studies*, an article on "The Ethnic Components of the Builders of the Indus Valley Civilization and the Advent of the Aryans" in which he describes, in line with his colleague Dutta, how the skeletons associated with this civilization constitute "a composite homogeneous group, characterized by certain variants attributable to Proto-Nordic, Proto-Mediterranean, or Mediterranean, Alpine-Armenoid and Veddoid/Proto-Australoid elements." However, he remains reserved as regards the identification of "Aryan types" who supposedly brought down the Indus civilization, even though Indian and English anthropologists in the interwar years believed that they could distinguish them from the indigenous population by virtue of their "high cranial vault, their long face and prominent nose."[12]

Craniometry also persisted at the University of Geneva under Marc-Rodolphe Sauter. In the 1980s, one of his students, Roland Menk, published several studies reinforced by multivariable statistical analysis with the classic aim of identifying "Cro-Magnoids" and "Mediterraneans" within Europe and, in particular, relative to the supposed migrations of Kurgan peoples.[13] Nevertheless, taken at face

[11] Ferembach, 1981, p. 474.
[12] Kumar, 1973; Dutta, 1972.
[13] Menk, 1980, 1981.

RACIAL TO BIOLOGICAL ANTHROPOLOGY   227

value, his results fail to demonstrate any migration of people from the steppes toward Central and Western Europe, which certain scholars might interpret as supporting the hypothesis that the original Indo-Europeans constituted a small, anthropologically invisible, military elite, with all the risks that such an argument based on absence of evidence entails.[14]

Nevertheless, ideological abuses persisted, such as those—already mentioned—committed by a certain John Day, who has clear links with the American extreme right[15] and whose work, *The Indo-Europeans Origins: The Anthropological Evidence*,[16] surprisingly appears as a reference, without any commentary, in several serious anthropological text books.

However, the debate surrounding physical anthropology is not straightforward. Of course, as was already pointed out by Topinard a century ago, "races" in the commonly understood sense, or in the sense evoked by Vallois and Riquet, do not exist. It is impossible to delimit stable "groups" or "types" since an infinite range of intermediaries exist between one "group" and another; this is because dietary differences influence stature and even skull shape, and physical characteristics are partly inherited independently of one another. Nonetheless, humans had a tendency to resemble each other over large regions, if only because of localized traditional marriage arrangements, before recent migratory movements gradually blurred the picture; clearly the environment, temperature, the degree of exposure to sunshine, and natural selection also played an important role.[17] It is a fact that populations of the world react differently to certain foods (e.g., dairy products in Asia) and to certain medicines. Resemblances and differences attest to a long biological history which it will undoubtedly be possible to reconstruct bit by bit. While craniometry, despite a century of attempts, has never proved to be a useful tool at a large scale, very localized studies can, even today, serve to highlight continuities or ruptures in the physical "types" of a given population—with, of course, the usual precautions—and identify genetic relationships.

From skulls to red blood cells

Astonishingly, in France there has never been a critical review of physical anthropology, at least not from within the discipline itself, apart from a few historiographical comments.[18] The discipline simply underwent a name change,

[14] Sergent 1995, pp. 254, 285; Menk, 1980; Schwidetzky, 1980; Xirotiris, 1980.
[15] See Chapter 9, pp. 219–220.
[16] Day, 2001, 2002.
[17] See dossier in *Current Anthropology*, 53, supplement 5: "The Biological Anthropology of Living Human Populations: World Histories, National Styles, and International Networks" (April 2012).
[18] Bocquet-Appel, 1989, 1996.

228 THIRD MOVEMENT (1945–THIRD MILLENNIUM)

switching from "physical anthropology" to "biological anthropology," and moved its focus to other fields such as paleodemography, blood markers, DNA, paleopathology, and "archeothanatology" (i.e., the close study of the process of decomposition of bodies after burial which allows certain inhumation practices to be identified). On the basis of the numbers of dead belonging to a given civilization (and on condition that the burials leave visible traces) and thanks to sophisticated mathematical models, paleodemography can retrace the sizes and evolutions of populations.[19] Human paleontology has also developed with the growing number of field campaigns in Africa over recent decades which have led to the discovery of numerous fossils stretching back eight million years. This reorientation toward more ancient forms of humans has also contributed to the abandonment of raciological classifications of modern humans.

In other countries, however, the term "physical anthropology" continues to be used. In the United States, for example, university anthropology departments are still associated with three disciplines: namely, "physical anthropology," "social anthropology," and "prehistory." Symmetrically, the term "social anthropology," imported from the United States most notably by Claude Lévi-Strauss, and even the term "anthropology" itself, tends to be replaced by the term "ethnology" by French ethnologists.

The study of blood markers began to be developed worldwide in the 1920s, including in France, where it remained on the margins of official anthropology for some time.[20] This research finally received official recognition through the appointment of Jacques Ruffié to a chair of physical anthropology in 1972; in reality, the department focused on genetics and the geographical distribution of blood markers, which would become known as *hemotypology*.[21] The research undertaken sought to characterize certain populations, from the Basques to the Papuans, and one of the central problems encountered was the representativeness of samples with regard to the populations being studied. With the advent of DNA analyses in the 1990s, new methods of characterization were developed, particularly for revealing evidence of ancient migratory movements. Blood markers and DNA analyses also offered a significant advantage in terms of academic resources (or lack thereof): in principle, there was no longer any need for costly overseas archaeological campaigns to collect human material since the same results could be obtained from simple genetic sampling performed on living modern populations.

[19] Bocquet-Appel, 2008; Dutour et al., 2005a, 2005b.
[20] Schneider, 1995.
[21] Bernard and Ruffié, 1966.

RACIAL TO BIOLOGICAL ANTHROPOLOGY 229

A truly new synthesis?

Such was the origin of the success of the New Synthesis in the 1990s. On the basis of a few hundred analyses from around the world, Italian geneticist and statistician Luigi Luca Cavalli-Sforza and his American team were in a position to propose a tree of the world's human genes.[22] In real terms, these few hundred human beings were grouped into "populations" (e.g., "Indians," "Sards," "Bantus," "Europeans," "Filipinos," etc.), and an arborescent classification was proposed to express the relationships of varying degrees of closeness between these different groups. Clearly these proximities could be expressed using other models, and the representativeness of the sample, even if it were extended to several thousands, is insufficient to account for the entire history of humanity. In fact, the explicit premise is that this classificatory tree is a genealogical tree, the tree of all *Homo sapiens* who emerged in Africa through the evolution of local *H. erectus* some 100,000 years ago and who all potentially descend from a hypothetical "African Eve."[23]

Even more audaciously, the team placed its tree of all the world's genes side by side with the tree of all the world's languages constructed by American linguists Joseph Greenberg and Merritt Ruhlen at roughly the same time; the latter was based on the approximately 6,000 known languages, which were assumed to descend from an original shared proto-language, namely that of the "African Eve." It would seem that the two trees strictly coincided. Thus the so-called New Synthesis was born (see Appendix 16): having emerged 100,000 years ago in North East Africa, *H. sapiens* transported their genes and their languages throughout the entire world before dividing up to form successive human groups, each with its own language, which in turn evolved and divided to produce the 6,000 languages currently spoken by seven billion modern human beings. The Indo-European language family is just one part of this whole.

We can understand why this conclusion, illustrated by a plethora of evocative drawings, has succeeded in grabbing and maintaining media attention from the 1990s right up to the present. In fact, for a scientific study to be newsworthy, it must fulfil three conditions: (1) the research should be easy to understand, (2) it should use sophisticated techniques and/or equipment (in this case lexicography and genetics), and (3) it should retrace a great myth (in this case the Tower of Babel and the Earthly Paradise).

However, this coincidence between the language tree and the genetic tree that constitutes the "New Synthesis" can be challenged from a number of angles.[24]

[22] Cavalli-Sforza et al., 1986, 1988, 1994; Cavalli-Sforza, 1997.
[23] Pellegrini, 1995.
[24] Sims-Williams, 1998.

230 THIRD MOVEMENT (1945–THIRD MILLENNIUM)

The term itself was not "new" because sociobiologists had already employed it barely fifteen years earlier to baptize, with comparable modesty and a sense of self-promotion, their own burgeoning discipline, with which the Great Tree clearly had no connection. Essentially the model does little more than rework—by shifting from skulls to genes—the old model produced by Trombetti at the start of the twentieth century, although the Himalayas have now been replaced by the savannahs of East Africa. As regards methodology, the arborescent model is but one way to organize resemblances which could be just as well expressed using more complex networks. We will return to the strictly linguistic criticisms of the Greenberg-Ruhlen model at a later stage.[25] When we look at the details, the much-vaunted coincidences between the two trees are not so clear-cut. Thus, the populations of northern India, who speak an Indo-European language belonging to the Indo-Iranian group, are much closer genetically to their southern Indian compatriots, who themselves speak quite distinct "Dravidian" languages, than they are to European speakers of Indo-European languages. Likewise, Ethiopians are genetically very close to sub-Saharan Africans, even though they speak a far-removed language, classified within the "Afro-Asiatic" group, which also includes Berber and Semitic languages.

In fact, the proximities, or, inversely, the boundaries, between genes and between languages simply express something quite banal: namely, geographical proximities and frontiers, which themselves depend on geopolitics. In the end, these two trees either illustrate something that is self-evident (i.e., we all descend from the first African *H. sapiens*—although, since 2010, we know that in Eurasia *H. sapiens* interbred with local descendants of *H. erectus*, which include Neanderthals)—or, on the contrary, they are unverifiable since neither the "mother language" nor the first hypothetical "proto-languages" are currently identifiable. Furthermore, the details of the first prehistoric migrations remain unclear, and the workings of the "molecular clock," which would date the speed of genetic mutations, are also unknown. The general hypothesis of the Great Tree is, therefore, either banal or unverifiable (or "unfalsifiable" in epistemological terms).

We have rediscovered the Indo-Europeans!

Moving from a global to a continental scale, the same geneticists have also attempted to retrace the movements of ancient populations on the basis of the distribution of living populations. In fact, prior to the publication of the Great Tree, Cavalli-Sforza, along with archaeologist Albert Ammerman, had modeled

---

[25] See Chapter 13, pp. 269–271, and Chapter 17, pp. 390–392.

the "wave of advance" and the demographic progression of the Neolithic farmers who colonized Europe from the Near East. In this instance, his team mapped the distribution and frequency of a certain number of genetic markers among modern Europeans. These distribution patterns were interpreted as the traces of prehistoric migrations. In particular, Cavalli-Sforza claimed to have found genetic traces of the migration of Neolithic farmers from the Near East and then traces of population movements from the Black Sea steppes in the direction of Western Europe—in other words, traces of the supposed Indo-European migrations.[26] These results have been questioned on a number of grounds. The distribution of present-day genes on the European continent tells us nothing about the date at which a given prehistoric migration might have occurred. It is only natural that Europe, located at the western extremity of Eurasia, would have witnessed east–west diffusions—indeed, the reverse would be surprising! But the genetic proximities may be just as easily linked to geographical proximity as to phenomena of linguistic diffusion.[27]

However, technical progress in the domain of DNA analyses has, in recent years, allowed researchers to work not only on samples from modern humans but also on ancient DNA. The most spectacular results were achieved in 2010, when it was discovered, thanks to sequencing of Neanderthal genes, that 2–4% of the genetic makeup of modern Europeans and Asians is composed of Neanderthal genes and thus that, at an early date, there was a degree of interbreeding between modern humans and Neanderthals. Furthermore, the same year witnessed the identification of a new human species, the Denisovans, who were Asian contemporaries of the Neanderthals of Europe and of the first African Sapiens. Other DNA analyses revealed that the first Neolithic farmers were quite distinct from the indigenous hunter-gatherers of Europe and that the latter played a modest demographic role in the establishment of this new mode of production.[28] The hunter-gatherers had not been eliminated but, instead, were absorbed as various population movements occurred over the course of the Neolithic and Chalcolithic. Furthermore, movements interpreted as originating from Eastern Europe were much less numerous than movements interpreted as originating in southwest Europe.[29]

In June 2009, a press statement and video conference released by the CNRS announced "We have re-discovered the Indo-Europeans." In reality, the research carried out by a Franco-Russian team was based on the genetic analysis of twenty-six skeletons from the Krasnoyarsk region of Siberia and dating from between the middle of the second millennium BCE and the middle of the first

---

[26] Menozzi et al., 1978; Cavalli-Sforza et al., 1994.
[27] Rosser et al., 2000.
[28] For example, Brunel et al., 2020; Bentley et al., 2002; Price and Borić, 2013.
[29] Brandt et al., 2013.

232 THIRD MOVEMENT (1945–THIRD MILLENNIUM)

millennium CE.[30] When they were alive, most of the subjects had fair hair and light-colored eyes. In a somewhat hasty extrapolation, the researchers deduced from this that these twenty-six individuals must have originated from the steppes to the north of the Black Sea and that this validated Marija Gimbutas's hypothesis of a steppic origin for the supposed original Indo-European people.[31] However, according to this steppic hypothesis, to which we will return at a later stage, the original dispersion occurred in the fifth and fourth millennia BCE. The individuals analyzed in the Franco-Russian study could therefore originate from a great variety of regions, including the Near East—a competing hypothesis to that of the steppes. In addition, in terms of markers, the genetic resemblances between these individuals and modern humans point toward an origin in Central Europe rather than one in the steppes to the north of the Black Sea.

But, six years later, in 2015, two further articles appeared in the prestigious journal *Nature*. The title of one loudly proclaimed: "Massive Migration from the Steppe Was a Source for Indo-European Languages in Europe."[32] The first article, which emanated from the Max-Planck Institute in Jena (these Institutes grew out of the Kaiser-Wilhelm Institutes of the interwar years but had totally different perspectives), was this time based on sixty-nine individuals scattered between the Volga and the Atlantic and spanning about ten millennia, but with the greatest concentration lying between the ninth millennium BCE (i.e., the Mesolithic) and the second millennium BCE (i.e., the end of the Bronze Age). The authors also considered twenty-five additional individuals who had been analyzed at an earlier stage. The core of the article, justifying the title, focused on genetic resemblances between nine individuals belonging to the Pit Grave culture (*Jamnaja Kultura* in Russian and referred to as *Yamnaya* by the authors) in Russia and four other individuals from the Corded Ware site at Esperstedt in Germany. The first nine individuals were all from the Samara region in the Middle Volga basin within the forest-steppe zone and date from the end of the fourth millennium BCE: thus several thousands of kilometers separate them from the German Corded Ware sites, which date to the first half of the third millennium BCE. The material culture of the Corded Ware culture, and in particular its pottery, is clearly different from that of the Pit Grave culture. We will examine the archaeological problems posed by these differences in greater detail later.[33]

Generalizing the results, the article reduces the entire genetic heritage of European populations of the past five millennia into three components: a founding component originating from indigenous Mesolithic hunter-gatherers, a component originating from the farming colonists who migrated from the Near

---

[30] Keyser et al., 2009.
[31] See Chapter 14.
[32] Haak et al., 2015, Allentoft et al., 2015.
[33] See Chapter 14.

East from the seventh millennium BCE onward, and a component originating from migrations from the steppes from the end of the fourth millennium onward—these are the migrations mentioned just above. The Mesolithic component is virtually invisible in the settlements of the first Western European farmers of the sixth and fifth millennia, but it subsequently reappears undoubtedly because the direct descendants of the hunter-gatherers gradually intermarried with the farmers. The arrival of the migrants from the steppes essentially concerns northwestern Europe in the third and second millennia BCE.

These three components are found intact, without notable additions, in the modern populations of Europe: the Mesolithic foundation is persistent, accounting on average for 10–20% of the genetic heritage of the continent; the "steppic" component declines steadily from north (c. 50%) to south (less than 15%); the Near Eastern component, in contrast, declines steadily from south (80–90%) to north (10–20%).[34] Of particular interest is the fact that, among modern European populations, there is absolutely no genetic difference between those who speak Indo-European languages and those who do not; namely, the Estonians and Hungarians, who speak languages belonging to the Finno-Ugric group, and the Basques, who constitute a separate linguistic group. There is, therefore, no correlation between languages and genes within modern populations. It can be counterargued, using circular reasoning, that over the course of five millennia, all of these populations have had ample time to intermingle. Nonetheless, the fact remains that in the only instance where a correlation can be scientifically observed, the result is negative.

The second study, published in the same issue of *Nature*,[35] and this time led by a team in Copenhagen, was based on 100 individuals. Even though it differs from the preceding article on certain technical points, duly mentioned in the article, and though it also incorporates individuals from further east, the results are generally comparable. The study also draws attention to the fact that the gene for the persistence of lactase production, the enzyme that allows adults to continue to digest milk and which is absent today in numerous Asian and African populations, is a little more frequent than average in the Neolithic of the steppes and among the Corded Ware population, but that an increase in carriers of the gene really only occurs in the Bronze Age (i.e., in the second millennium BCE). The authors also note a tendency over time toward fair hair and light-colored eyes in Northern Europe, characteristics that were already present during the local Mesolithic, while the populations of the steppes essentially have dark hair and eyes.

[34] Haak et al., 2015, figure 3.
[35] Allentoft et al., 2015.

234   THIRD MOVEMENT (1945–THIRD MILLENNIUM)

These articles consider the DNA analyses of 100 Neolithic skeletons from various parts of Europe, principally Germany, Russia, Hungary, and Spain, spanning the period from the Upper Paleolithic to the Iron Age. A certain number individuals from Northern Germany, belonging to the Corded Ware culture of the third millennium BCE, appear to be very close genetically to individuals belonging to the Russian Pit Grave culture (*Jamnaja kultura*) of the late fourth millennium BCE, a fact that leads to the conclusion that the former culture resulted from a "massive migration" of the latter toward northwestern Europe—duly illustrated with arrows on maps. Without going into details (which will be the subject of a forthcoming book), this interpretation poses several problems. For example, Corded Ware pottery has little in common with Pit Grave pottery; steppic populations generally had dark hair and eyes, while the populations of Northern Germany tended to have fair hair and light-colored eyes; the populations of the Remedello culture of Northern Italy (including the famous Ötzi), whose rituals are interpreted as being typically "Indo-European," are not genetically "steppic."

In the years that followed, many additional analyses were published (and continue to be so) in a markedly competitive academic atmosphere, and it would seem prudent to wait a little longer before drawing any conclusions. But, on the one hand, preliminary syntheses have already been published,[36] and, on the other, it is interesting to make an initial assessment regarding the Indo-European question. In fact, the initial picture painted in 2015 was particularly complicated, and the current provisional situation raises several questions:

1. Can these analyses be considered representative?
2. Were the suggested migratory movements massive, even violent, or were they gradual or even slow?
3. Is there a coincidence between biology and culture, or, in other words, are the cultural groups defined by archaeologists homogenous from a genetic point of view?

As regards the first question, at present (2020), more than 2,500 ancient genomes have been published for Europe and the Near East, principally spanning the period between 6000 and 1000 BCE.[37] However, all of the regions, periods, and Neolithic cultures are far from being treated in a representative manner. For example, a component from the Caucasus was added to the "steppic" component after the first publications had appeared. Likewise, the first analyses did not detect a "steppic" presence in the Iberian Peninsula, a fact that was subsequently

---

[36]   Reich 2018; Heyer 2020; Orlando, 2021.
[37]   Olalde and Posth, 2020.

RACIAL TO BIOLOGICAL ANTHROPOLOGY   235

refuted in a new series of analyses.[38] In summary, even though the arrival of steppic populations in northwestern Europe appears to be demonstrated, we are still far from having a complete and detailed picture of the situation. Moreover, ancient DNA is much less well preserved in hot countries, which means that while Central Asia has produced significant data, India has produced virtually none.[39]

The second question concerns the manner in which these populations arrived. In fact, it is spontaneously assumed, and in a somewhat circular manner, that this "massive migration" toward northwestern Europe was warrior-led since it appears that there was a greater proportion of "steppic" men than women involved (even though this interpretation remains controversial[40]); sometimes archaeological arguments are also forwarded, and these will be examined at a later stage.[41] But this is not the only possible interpretation. We could just as easily envisage a very gradual penetration, with regular inputs of genes over several generations, or even a reproductive advantage for the new arrivals over the course of several centuries, as has been observed in other parts of the world.[42] Since the case of each region of Europe needs to be examined in detail, it is, yet again, too early to come to definitive conclusions.

Finally, the last question, concerning the powerful assumption that there is a coincidence between biology and culture, brings us right back to nineteenth-century craniometry. In fact, a 2018 study has shown that an important cultural phenomenon, the Bell Beaker culture, which in the third millennium BCE was discontinuously spread over an area stretching from the Iberian Peninsula to Denmark and Hungary, lacked any genetic homogeneity: while a "steppic" component is present in Central Europe, even as far as Great Britain, it is virtually absent in southwestern Europe, even though material manifestations (e.g., pottery, daggers, funerary practices, etc.) are identical.[43] Furthermore, this "steppic" component diminishes significantly from north to south in Europe, while in historic periods the Indo-European languages were present almost everywhere on the Continent. Finally, this "steppic" genetic component is virtually invisible during the second millennium BCE in Anatolia, where Hittite was spoken,[44] and in Greece, where Mycenaean Greek was spoken.[45] And the further we move back in time, the less genetic homogeneity is observed. Thus the Basques are not genetically distinct from their neighbors, no more so than the Turks later on, while

[38] Olalde et al., 2018, 2019.
[39] Narasimhan, 2019.
[40] Goldberg et al., 2017.
[41] See Chapter 14, pp. 314–317.
[42] Verdu et al., 2013.
[43] Olalde et al. 2018.
[44] Barros Damgaard, 2018b.
[45] Lazaridis et al., 2017.

236   THIRD MOVEMENT (1945–THIRD MILLENNIUM)

the Indo-Iranian speaking Scythians who occupied the steppes in the first millennium BCE were, in contrast, genetically very heterogeneous.

While paleogenetics will undoubtedly continue to enrich our knowledge in the years to come, a certain number of archaeologists have expressed concerns regarding the application of models that are overly simple or even simplistic.[46]

Recent developments in the field of bone chemistry, and particularly in strontium isotope analysis, have provided other interesting results. The quantity of strontium fixed in teeth remains stable and definitive. However, strontium absorbed in the rest of the skeleton evolves as a function of diet. If there is a difference between the two in the case of a given individual, it implies that he or she did not die in the same place where he or she was born. In this way, strontium analysis can reveal movement of people. It is a relatively new and promising method even though, for now, we still do not have enough data to draw detailed conclusions regarding ancient migrations. Hopefully other comparable techniques will be developed over the coming decades.

Racism by means of psychology and IQ

Throughout the nineteenth century and the first half of the twentieth, the true issue underlying research and debate—behind the outward mask of science— was the justification of racism and inequality between humans. The goal was to distinguish the "Indo-Europeans" or their equivalent from the rest of humanity and to demonstrate their specificity or even supremacy. In recent decades, these attempts have not lost any of their original momentum. At the end of the nineteenth century, alongside raciology, new theories of intellectual inequality were being developed by the likes of Sir Francis Galton and Karl Pearson. The work of this "London School" continued into the early twentieth century with Cyril Burt, Raymond Cattell, Sir Ronald Fisher, and Charles Spearman. While there was a clear stepping back from "scientific racism" within biological anthropology, these psychologists continued to develop their theories of inequality.

The movement survived the Second World War through the work of researchers like German-born Hans Jürgen Eysenck, professor of psychology at University College London until 1983[47]; Arthur Jensen, professor of psychology at the University of California, Berkeley; or Nobel Prize in physics winner (for the invention of the transistor) William Shockley. Leading proponents of IQ and enjoying a significant scientific reputation, they argued that Whites are more

---

[46] Frieman and Hofman, 2019; Furholt, 2019a, 2019b, 2021; Hansen, 2019; Hofmann, 2019; Van der Linden, 2016.

[47] Eysenck, 1973. On Eysenck and Jensen, see Billig, 1981.

intelligent than Blacks, that differences in intelligence exist between the social classes (which would explain the lower success rate among the poor), and that criminality is genetically inherited. Eysenck and Jensen were politically engaged, very far right leaning, and their works were widely used as "scientific" references to justify racism in the writings of the French Nouvelle Droite, including in the book published by former minister Michel Poniatowski.[48]

In 1994, the baton was taken up by psychologist Richard Herrnstein and political scientist Charles Murray, whose book *The Bell Curve: Intelligence and Class Structure in American Life*, became a best-seller in the United States. The title of the book refers to the "bell curve" or "Gauss curve" of human intelligence as measured by IQ, and its thesis, based on an impressive body of statistics, is simple: Whites are more intelligent than Blacks and it is therefore a waste of public money to fund social programs for the latter.[49] As we have seen, some 125 years earlier, Clémence Royer, who tracked the Indo-Europeans across Eurasia, was already in a position to assert that "While all care, all devotions of love and pity are considered to be owed to the deposed and degenerate representatives of the species, there is nothing to encourage the development of the emerging force or to propagate merit, talent and virtue."[50] It seems that "scientific racism" is by no means ready to disappear into obscurity.

Thus, the biological anthropology of recent decades presents us with a mixed picture. It appears to have split into a number of highly varied disciplines and methods. It is probable that the continuously evolving techniques of biological analysis will provide increasingly significant results in the future. However, it is essential that they are not just used to prop up historical models that are not only obsolete, but also simplistic and sometimes even politically biased.

[48] See Chapter 9, p. 207.
[49] Herrnstein and Murray, 1994. *Contra*, see Fischer, C., et al., 1996; Fassin, 1997.
[50] See Chapter 4, pp. 83–84.

11
What archaeology tells us today

With respect to the issues of the first half of the twentieth century, early twenty-first-century archaeology has undergone considerable transformation in terms of the volumes of documentation available, diversification of methods and techniques, and the development of explicative models. After the Second World War, all Eastern Bloc countries witnessed a surge in archaeological research because individual states were keen to demonstrate their interest in culture but were also hungry for evidence of national identity. In the tradition of Soviet archaeology of the 1920s, excavations tended to be extensive, with a view to reconstructing all aspects of past social life. But, at the same time, despite the compulsory deferent footnotes to the fathers of Marxism-Leninism, cultural issues remained marked by the Kossinnian paradigm since most of the older generation of scientists had been trained in Germany and Austria, countries whose archaeology was seen to set an example. For some time, France lagged behind because archaeology (just like the Indo-European question) within its territory played only a marginal role in the exaltation of national sentiment.[1] It was only in the 1970s that this delay started to be rectified, when rescue excavations—and subsequently preventive excavations—became more systematic, better funded, and conducted by professional archaeologists; the influence of Central European archaeology, particularly German, Czech, and Polish archaeology, was significant in this regeneration.[2]

An interest in the environment (fauna, flora, soil, and climate evolution, etc.), statistical processing of large amounts of data thanks to developments in computer technology, and research on the origins of objects (identification of raw materials) and their circulation, on their manufacturing techniques (technology), and on their use (microscopic study of use-wear traces) have provided completely new insights into ancient ways of life and have also allowed researchers to reflect on issues in different ways. The emphasis has shifted away from tracing migrations and establishing the genealogies of peoples to studying the economy, techniques, and relationships of societies with their environments. American archaeologists group these manifestations together under the term "New Archaeology." Through a logical and normal generational swing,

---

[1] Cleuziou et al., 1991; Demoule, 1999b.
[2] Demoule, 2012b.

WHAT ARCHAEOLOGY TELLS US TODAY   239

these preoccupations, which were predominant in the 1960s and 1970s, were succeeded in the 1980s and 1990s by a renewed interest in cultural and ideological phenomena; a change of emphasis that archaeologists in the English-speaking world, with a certain sense of scientific marketing, baptized "post-processual archaeology" in reference to the "post-modernism" that dominated human sciences at the time. Since 2000, however, there has been a return to environmental preoccupations linked to rising ecological concerns.

Throughout the third quarter of the twentieth century, archaeologists displayed little interest in the Indo-European question. In Germany, the subject was off limits; in the Eastern Block, archaeologists were officially focused on social and economic history, just as they were (albeit with a different slant) in the English-speaking world. Interest in the issue re-emerged in the 1970s through the work of Marija Gimbutas on the Neolithic of the steppes and her spectacular yet easy to understand theories of successive waves of "Kurgan" invaders. The revived, rehabilitated quest for the original Homeland also became the subject of academic challenges. Soon, Colin Renfrew would propose, with equal or even greater media success, the hypothesis of a Near-Eastern origin for the Indo-Europeans. However, Renfrew in turn would be overtaken in the media by the promoters of the genealogical tree of all the world's languages and all the world's genes. Since the Iron Curtain had dissipated in the meantime, the search for the original Homeland partly abandoned the arena of ideology for that of the media market.

Let us now look at the current state of knowledge and evidence in terms of the overall development of European societies since the appearance of modern humans (see Appendices, 1, 9, 12–15).

The first Europeans

Without going all the way back to the Flood, we recall that Europe has been populated by humans for the past one and a half to two million years, when the first descendants of African *Homo habilis* and *H. ergaster* arrived. These early humans took so many diverse forms and their remains are so rare that it is difficult to construct an accurate family tree: *H. georgicus* from Dmanissi in Georgia, *H. antecessor* from Atapuerca in Spain, and, more generally, *H. erectus* and *H. heidelbergensis*. About 300,000 years ago, human evolution in Europe and western Asia led to the emergence of *H. neanderthalensis* whose cranial capacity and physical appearance, as well as their aptitude for articulated language, were very close to those of modern humans, *H. sapiens sapiens*, also known as "anatomically modern humans." The latter are believed to have emerged about 100,000 years ago through the local evolution of *H. erectus* in northeast Africa.

240   THIRD MOVEMENT (1945–THIRD MILLENNIUM)

Once they had appeared, they set out over a period of tens of thousands of years to conquer all inhabited regions and those that were previously uninhabited (the Americas, Australia, Oceania), eliminating the local descendants, when they existed, of *H. erectus*, Neanderthals included. This is the so-called *African Eve scenario* which forms the basis, from a linguistic point of view, for a single family tree of all the genes and all the languages of the world.[3] Since 2010, this vision has been nuanced by the discovery of a small percentage of Neanderthal genes in European and Asian populations, providing evidence of hybridization, not to mention the existence of *H. floresiensis*, a dwarf form of *H. erectus* or *H. habilis*, on the Indonesian island of Flores as recently as 15,000 years ago.

These modern humans first set foot in Europe about 40,000 years ago from the Near East, passing through the Balkans, apparently spreading from east to west (but also from west to east toward Asia), while the last Neanderthals died out about 27,000 years ago on the Iberian Peninsula. Named after a cave in the Haute Garonne in France, their first culture is termed the Aurignacian and lies within the Upper Paleolithic, the period that characterizes European prehistory following the arrival of *H. sapiens*. The Aurignacian saw the appearance of the first forms of "art": cave paintings such as those at Chauvet in Ardèche, mobiliary art such as the ivory figurines from the Swabian Jura (examples from the caves of Hohlenstein-Stadel and Hohlefels), and, of course, the art of music attested to by flutes fashioned from bird bone (examples from Hohlefels cave and Isturitz in the Basque Country). As regards Indo-European languages, clearly the most economical theory would be that the Aurignacians spoke the ancestor of Indo-European languages, a theory with a long history and which continues to attract support.

The arrival of modern humans in Europe occurred during the last glaciation, known as the *Würm glaciation*, which lasted between about 115,000 and 10,000 before the present era. During this last glacial period, glaciers covered the entire north of Eurasia with a thick ice sheet extending as far south as Belgium and also covering mountainous regions, such as the Alpine arc, further south. In southern regions free of ice cover, where the natural environment resembled modern-day Norway, small dispersed hunter-gatherer groups lived a nomadic existence. For their meat diet they depended largely on hunting large mammals—horses, bison, aurochs, mammoths, and reindeer—which roamed across these spaces in herds. On the basis of the forms of the tools made by these groups, we can identify different cultures such as the Magdalenian of Western Europe, which left us the painted caves of the Périgord and Pyrenees and which represents the final phase of the Upper Paleolithic in these regions.

---

[3] See Chapter 10, pp. 229–230, and Chapter 17, pp. 390–392.

WHAT ARCHAEOLOGY TELLS US TODAY 241

But soon the climate became progressively warmer, in successive oscillations, ultimately reaching temperatures close to those of today. The melting of the thick ice sheet led to a slow rise in sea levels, which up until then were about 100 meters lower than current levels; in fact, they only reached their current levels at about 2000 BCE. Europe at the time was covered by a dense temperate forest, composed mainly of oaks and lime trees. Animal species adapted to the cold, such as reindeer and mammoth, retreated northward while other species, such as the horse, that were more adaptive but preferred the open prairies, became concentrated in steppic zones and particularly in a long band stretching from the area to the north of the Black Sea and the Caspian Sea, through the Carpathians, as far as Chinese Turkestan. Since then we have been living in an interglacial period, destined to last at least another 5,000 years (unless, of course, we modify the climate significantly in the meantime). We possess a relatively coherent picture of Europe over the last 12,000 years, and it is useful, at this stage, to look at some of the main developments, independently of the Indo-European question. While many of the cultures identified by archaeologists in the 1930s[4] remain valid, the picture has become much more detailed thanks to the growing number of excavations undertaken since then. At the same time, the development of radiocarbon dating since the 1950s has considerably extended the durations of the various periods. In Childe's day, for example, the Neolithic was estimated to have lasted no more than a few centuries but we now know that it spanned four millennia.

Some of the hunter-gatherers recolonized northern areas freed from the ice, thereby retaining in part their ancient environment. Others adapted to the new conditions of the temporal forests and turned to hunting red deer, roe deer, aurochs, and wild boar. This period, which witnessed the continuation of a hunter-gatherer way of life within what was now a temperate environment, is known as the Mesolithic.[5] The European Mesolithic is characterized by the disappearance of figurative art; instead, with the exception of Scandinavia and eastern Spain, we find rare abstract motifs painted or incised on pebbles or rock faces. The period is also characterized by a drastic reduction in the size of certain flint tools, described as "microlithic."

Generally, the Mesolithic of a large part of Europe is divided into three principal successive periods, namely the Azilian, the Sauveterrian, and the Tardenoisian. The latter is characterized by very small stone tools, and, in particular, transverse arrowheads featuring a broad cutting edge. The Tardenoisians lived in small bands of a couple dozen individuals who moved about within vast territories; their population density was very low. In coastal regions, certain groups specialized in exploiting aquatic resources including shellfish, fish, and

---

[4] See Chapter 7.
[5] Ghesquière and Marchand, 2010; Bailey and Spikins, 2008.

242   THIRD MOVEMENT (1945–THIRD MILLENNIUM)

marine mammals, which allowed them to settle in these areas for longer periods of time. Such coastal groups are encountered on the shores of the Baltic (the Maglemosian culture) and in Great Britain, Portugal, and Brittany, and similar groups also existed along the great rivers of Russia and Ukraine. Certain groups even domesticated wolves, which subsequently became domesticated dogs, not as a food source but in a reciprocal arrangement between humans and canids.

The Neolithic revolution

This picture is not unique to Europe. All over the globe we encounter hunter-gatherer cultures which in every case adapted to local resources. But soon, in several separate regions, human groups would begin to domesticate certain species of animals and plants: millet, rice, and buffalo in eastern Asia and pumpkin, maize, beans, llamas, and guinea pigs in America, for example.[6]

In the Near East, around 9000 BCE, within a region that extends from Syria to the Negev, bordered to the east by the Zagros Hills which form the frontier between Iran and Iraq, a hunter-gatherer culture known as the Natufians settled down and progressively domesticated sheep, goats, cattle, and pigs, as well as wheat and barley.[7] This new economy of agriculturalists and livestock rearers, also known as the "Neolithic," meant better control over food resources which, along with sedentarism, led to rapid population growth evidenced in an increase in the size and numbers of villages. These Neolithic farmers would soon spill out of their original zone to occupy the entire Fertile Crescent and Turkey.

Around 6500 BCE, in this continuous process of expansion, they reached southeastern Europe, specifically the Balkan Peninsula (Greece, Bulgaria, Albania, ex-Yugoslavia) and from here, still accompanied by their domesticated animals and plants, most of which were not indigenous to Europe, they spread westward over the entire continent. Some groups moved along the coastline of the Mediterranean but most, once they had occupied all of the Balkan Peninsula, made their way toward Central Europe up through the Danube Basin.[8] On reaching the Middle Danube region, they left their Mediterranean-type environment behind for the first time; they and their domesticated species now had to adapt to a temperate continental climate. A new culture emerged on this frontier, namely the Linear Ceramic culture, also known as the Danubian, the *Rubanée* (in French), and the *Bandkeramik* (in German). We have already seen[9] how this culture had been identified by German researchers at the beginning of

[6] Demoule, 2007a, 2010.
[7] Lichardus et al., 1985; Cauvin, 1994; Aurenche and Kozłowski, 1999.
[8] Lichardus et al., 1985; Fowler et al., 2015; see Appendix 9.
[9] See Chapter 7, p. 147.

the twentieth century and how Gordon Childe recognized its importance in the neolithization of the continent.

These two currents of colonization met up once more on the western extremity of Europe, and in particular in what is now France. This peninsula, on the edge of Eurasia, was neolithized last via the "Mediterranean" current from about 5800 BCE and then via the "Danubian" current from about 5000 BCE. By around 4500 BCE, all of the regions of Europe most favorable for agriculture were occupied by Neolithic farmers. This large-scale migration can be traced in great detail, almost on a site-to-site basis, by comparing pottery forms, house types, and stone and bone tools. Funerary and ritual practices also underwent gradual transformations over both time and space. The migrations can also be modeled from a demographic point of view. Thus, after the arrival of modern humans in Eurasia, the Neolithic represents the second archaeological period that could possibly correspond to a historical incarnation of the presumed original Indo-European people—a hypothesis that was particularly promoted in the media by English archaeologist Colin Renfrew.[10]

Sedentary hunter-gatherers

In the face of this large-scale colonization, the small bands of indigenous Mesolithic hunter-gatherers clearly had little chance of resisting and were quickly absorbed (a fact confirmed by DNA analysis), with territories most favorable for primitive agriculture—alluvial valleys and regions with light soils such as loess—being the first to be settled. It was only in marginal regions, less suited to agriculture or, inversely, where the environment offered hunter-gatherers particularly favorable settlement conditions, that such groups managed to survive longer and even maintained contact and carried out exchanges with farming communities.

One such region was the Baltic and North Sea coast line. Here Maglemosian populations hunted a variety of animals (elk and reindeer) and also exploited marine resources (fish, shell fish, marine mammals, etc.). Their settlements are characterized by large shell middens which are often tens of meters high and several hundreds of meters in length (these middens are known as *kjøkkenmødding* in Danish). In the first half of the fifth millennium BCE, these groups came into contact with pioneering groups of Danubian Neolithic farmers who had ventured into neighboring areas; these farmers belonged to the region's Rössen culture, which is attested to over a large part of present-day Germany. Through this contact a novel culture emerged, known as the Ertebølle (or Ellerbeck in Northern Germany), in which hunter-gatherers produced coarse pottery and

---

[10] See Chapter 13.

244 THIRD MOVEMENT (1945–THIRD MILLENNIUM)

gradually began to domesticate pigs and cattle. Certain forms of wheat and barley cultivation may even have been practiced. But this particular economy would soon be absorbed by the extension of the Neolithic into all areas of Northern Europe with the spread of what is known as the Funnel Beaker culture. As we have seen,[11] this culture, characterized by megalithic tombs and pottery vessels featuring outward-flaring necks, had already been identified in Kossinna's time, but Kossinna himself believed that it derived from the Ertebølle culture. In reality, its distribution, dates, and the number of sites make such an origin impossible; instead, most of the characteristics of its material culture resemble those of the Neolithic of Danubian tradition from which it evolved.

At the same time, at the other end of Europe, other hunter-gatherer populations had established camps on the northern coasts of the Black Sea and the Caspian Sea and along the banks of the great rivers that flowed into them—the Prut, Bug, Dniester, Dnieper, Donets, Don, Volga, and all of their tributaries.[12] This region, which spans present-day southern Ukraine and Russia, also forms part of the steppic band, some 1,000 kilometers wide and stretching over 7,000 kilometers from the Danube delta and the eastern slopes of the Carpathians to Xinjiang (formerly Sinkiang, and also referred to as "Chinese Turkestan" or "East Turkestan"). The true steppe lies furthest south, and, to the north, the forest steppe forms a transition zone with the great Russian forest. In these areas, the hunting of wild boar, aurochs, red deer, roe deer, and even European bison and wild horse was supplemented by fishing and intensive gathering of shellfish. The abundance of aquatic resources allowed certain forms of sedentism to develop; the same was happening elsewhere at this time, on the banks of the Middle Danube (the Lepenski Vir culture) for example, or in northeastern Eurasia and even as far away as Japan. When Neolithic farmers arrived in the Lower Danube and penetrated the Carpathian Basin, they initially did not seek to move further east into regions that were firmly held by hunter-gatherers and where the steppic soils were less favorable for agriculture; instead they concentrated their efforts on the colonization of Central and then Western Europe.

Nonetheless, during the second half of the sixth millennium BCE, it is clear that hunter-gatherers living on the banks of the Bug and the Dniester, the zone closest to the Balkan Neolithic frontier, began to produce a relatively coarse type of pottery whose incised decoration was partly inspired by the pottery of neighboring contemporary Neolithic cultures, namely the Cris and Linear Ceramic cultures: this is known as the Bug-Dniester culture. Over time, groups belonging to this culture began to domesticate pigs and cattle (species that existed locally in their wild forms), and, subsequently, domesticated species from outside the

---

[11] See Chapter 6, pp. 146–147 and Chapter 7, p. 163.
[12] Wechler, 2002; Ošibkina, 1996; Parzinger, 2009.

WHAT ARCHAEOLOGY TELLS US TODAY   245

region, namely sheep and goats, were introduced. Cereal cultivation was also introduced from outside but appears to have been very limited. Little by little, ceramics and then animal husbandry spread throughout the Pontic Steppe, while, at the same time, other influences probably also came from the Caucasus and ultimately the Near East. Hunting, however, continued to provide the bulk of meat in the diet.

These steppic societies therefore attest to an original form of neolithization through progressive acculturation rather than colonization. In addition to the Bug-Dniester culture, several other cultural groups can be distinguished in the period corresponding to the end of the sixth and beginning of the fifth millennium.[13] In the lower basins of the Dnieper and the Donets, we encounter the Sursk-Dnieper culture, which was succeeded by the Dnieper-Donets culture.[14] Finally, to the east of the Caspian Sea and the Ural River (which more or less artificially marks the boundary between Europe and Asia), the Kelteminar culture, which spread over a large part of western Kazakhstan, combined a hunter-gatherer economy with ceramic vessels featuring pointed bases and incised ornament, and can thus be considered a transitional culture. Comparable but older phenomena are evident in Siberia and Russia as far as the Pacific coast.[15]

At the same time, in other marginal regions of Europe less favorable for agriculture, particularly at several locations on the Atlantic coast, from Portugal to Holland, sedentary hunter-gatherer communities have been identified but they are much more limited in scale; temporary and limited interactions with the agricultural colonization frontier are also evident (see Appendix 9).

The rise of chiefdoms

By the middle of the fifth millennium BCE, almost the entire continent of Europe, apart from the northern fringes and the most mountainous regions, was occupied by farmers and stock rearers. There was no more virgin territory available for colonization, and demographic growth was continuing. Over the course of the following six millennia, right up to the period when Europeans began to colonize overseas territories, the same space and the same environmental resources had to suffice to support an ever-growing population. It is for this reason that several novel innovations, both technical and social, appeared at this date. In terms of technology, we see that the invention of the ard, while animal traction and the wheel allowed better yields and permitted heavier, less favorable soils

[13] Lichardus et al., 1985, pp. 318–323; Danilenko, 1969; Dolukhanov, 1979; Markevič, 1974; Wechler, 2002; Mallory, 1989; Artemenko, 1985; Telegin and Potekhina, 1987.
[14] Wechler, 2002.
[15] Jordan and Zvelebil, 2011; Brunet, 2011; Ošibkina, 1996.

246 THIRD MOVEMENT (1945–THIRD MILLENNIUM)

to be exploited. We also observe intensification in the production and exchange of utilitarian objects—flint and green stone axes, flint blades, salt, etc.—which implies a much more specialized organization.

As regards social innovations, we witness the emergence throughout Europe, but with different regional forms, of the first signs of inequality and social hierarchy. Up until then, Neolithic villages and burials reveal no obvious differences between individuals in terms of wealth, although there is evidence for gender and age differentiation. From this time onward, this would no longer be the case. In Bulgaria, for example, within the Gumelniţa-Karanovo VI culture, certain individuals were buried with gold personal ornaments, scepters, bracelets, beads, and costume details. On the Atlantic façade of Europe, the first megalithic tombs were constructed with their burial chambers built of massive blocks of granite, often weighing tens of tons, and covered by huge mounds of earth and stones. Such tombs were reserved for a handful of individuals who were buried with personal ornaments made of semi-precious stones and long axes of green stone imported from the Alps.

This new period, which spans between 4500 and 2200 BCE, is often referred to as the "Chalcolithic" or "Copper Age" (*âge-de-la-pierre-et-du-cuivre* in French, *Kupferzeit* in German) because this was when the first metallurgy, based on the working of copper and also of gold and silver, appeared (iron metallurgy would not appear in Europe until the first millennium BCE).[16] However, until it was alloyed with tin around 1500 BCE, copper remained a relatively soft material. Therefore, metal essentially acted as a sign of social prestige; its technical usefulness would come later. The chalcolithic was, first and foremost, a social revolution which saw the emergence in Europe of the first inegalitarian societies, often referred to as "chiefdom societies"—the first states, comparable to those that developed in Egypt and Mesopotamia from 3000 BCE onward, appeared with the first Cretan and Mycenaean palaces and, especially, with the emergence of the city states of Greece and Italy, in the first millennium BCE. These inequalities can be observed in tombs displaying varying degrees of wealth and particularly in "rich" child burials which indicate that this inequality was becoming perennial; such differences in status are also evident in domestic architecture.

This social revolution was of course accompanied by intense ideological upheavals revolving around the justification of the new social order. In the Neolithic, religious activities, the evidence for which includes small, mostly female figurines, appear to have been practiced exclusively at a domestic level. In the Chalcolithic, however, collective sanctuaries, such as large ceremonial enclosures defined by monumental ditches and palisades, were erected in an area stretching from Central Europe to Scandinavia and Great Britain. Similarly,

---

[16] Lichardus et al., 1985; Lichardus-Itten and Demoule, 1997; Guilaine, 2007.

WHAT ARCHAEOLOGY TELLS US TODAY 247

the dead, who up to now were permanently buried in individual pits, were now buried in collective tombs in which the deceased were interred successively and where the human remains frequently show evidence that they were manipulated, reduced, moved, or even dispersed.

In the archaeological literature of the English-speaking world, these decisive socioeconomic mutations are often reduced to a "secondary products revolution," such as that envisaged by British archaeologist Andrew Sherratt.[17] In order to cope with their continuous population growth within a finite territory, European Neolithic societies would have developed their means of production and particularly the exploitation of milk, wool, and animal traction—in other words "secondary animal products"—as well as associated techniques. This vision of the Chalcolithic is very simplistic and, moreover, inaccurate. In fact, as regards milk products, we now know that they were produced from the earliest phases of the European Neolithic.[18] The castration of animals has been identified in the earliest Neolithic of the Balkans, at Kovačevo in Bulgaria, from the end of the seventh millennium BCE[19]; castration, and in particular of bullocks, results in larger, more docile animals that are particularly suited for draft purposes.

The Chalcolithic also witnessed the emergence of a new phenomenon: warfare. While individual violence is attested in all periods of human history, in the Chalcolithic we observe collective organized violence. A number of villages were established on sites that were naturally defensive, situated either on a height or surrounded by water. This is the period of the famous lake villages of the Alps and Jura, which do not attest to an idyllic way of life but rather to tensions that incited certain groups to settle in areas that were less attractive but easier to defend. Larger settlements were fortified using wooden palisades, dry-stone ramparts, earthen banks, and ditches. Traces of injuries, and even evidence for massacres, become increasingly common, as does evidence for the deliberate burning of entire villages. Specific types of weapons, such as stone "battle axes," also developed.

While demographic and territorial factors undoubtedly played a role in establishing this new social order, they were insufficient on their own. A global, historical explanation needs to take account of a complex combination of economic, social, and ideological causes.[20] In fact, throughout the world, not all egalitarian agricultural societies gave rise to chiefdoms. Furthermore, in the millennia that followed, periods of marked social inequality (like the first European Chalcolithic, with its precious metallurgy and megalithic tombs) were followed by periods of less pronounced differences. In reality, there is a regular

[17] Sherratt, 1981.
[18] Vigne, 2008; Vigne and Helmer, 2007.
[19] Identified by Norbert Benecke, Deutsches archäologisches Institut, Berlin.
[20] Lichardus-Itten and Demoule, 1997; Coudart, et al., 1999; Lichardus, 1991.

248   THIRD MOVEMENT (1945–THIRD MILLENNIUM)

balancing between tendencies toward the concentration of power and tendencies toward resistance to power, a phenomenon that is not exclusive to Europe.[21]

What happened on the steppes?

In the context of this "Chalcolithization" of Europe, certain regions merit particular attention with regard to the Indo-European question: foremost among these regions are the Pontic Steppes. In fact, during the fifth millennium BCE, the Neolithization front that emanated from the Balkans and, as we have seen, had stabilized immediately to the east of the Carpathians and in the vicinity of the Bug River, began to shift eastward once more to the Plains of Moldova and Ukraine and as far as the Dnieper; this is what is referred to as the *Cucuteni-Trypillia culture*. Hundreds of villages consisting of quadrangular longhouses of earth and timber have been identified, and some may have counted several thousands of inhabitants. Among the domesticated animals we find the first horses, which existed in the wild state on the Pontic Steppes. This culture produced magnificent ceramics decorated with painted motifs in several colors and also practiced the first copper and gold metallurgy in the region; in short, it gradually became "chalcolithized." It maintained close ties with other prominent Balkan Chalcolithic cultures, the most famous being the aforementioned Gumelnița-Karanovo VI culture whose cemeteries, such as Varna in Bulgaria, contain gold prestige objects (see Appendix 12).

The Cucuteni-Trypillia culture also had a profound influence on the Mesolithic populations mentioned above who were undergoing a transition toward neolithization and who occupied the territory immediately to the east, in the remaining part of modern-day Ukraine and neighboring regions. Some of these groups were specialized in hunting the herds of wild horses that had found refuge in the region at the end of the last glaciation. This specialized hunting gradually led to the domestication of the horse, one of the oldest attested instances of horse domestication in the world but probably not the only one in Europe. The exact timing of the shift from hunting to domestication is still a matter of debate because at this early stage it is difficult to distinguish between wild and domesticated forms of horse. It is only after several centuries of systematic selection by these horse breeders that clear differences between wild and domesticated animals become apparent. Settlement forms, ceramics, and stone and bone tools all follow older technical and stylistic traditions. However, we observe the appearance of limited copper metallurgy and the deposition of various prestige objects within the richest graves. These rich burials were sometimes covered

---

[21] Demoule, 1993; Miller et al., 1995; Flannery and Marcus, 2012; Graeber and Wengrow, 2021.

WHAT ARCHAEOLOGY TELLS US TODAY   249

by a mound of earth and stones. Various names have been given to the steppic populations that were going through this process of chalcolithization. The archaeologist Dmitri Telegin grouped them together within a single cultural group known as the Sredny Stog II (named after a particular site); in contrast, his compatriot, Yuri Rassamakin, tends to distinguish between different regional facies, each with a particular history.[22]

In any case, a certain process of stylistic unification took place over time, and, in the following phase (known as the "Middle Chalcolithic" or "Early Bronze Age" depending on regional terminology; see Appendices 1 and 13), from the end of the fourth millennium BCE, the entire Pontic Steppes region is generally considered to have been occupied by a single culture known as the Pit Grave culture because its dead were buried in circular, well-like pits. Sometimes the deceased were accompanied by solid-wheeled wooden carts, a recent invention, and sometimes horse bones (and indeed other animal bones) are present. This was also a period of increasing climatic aridity during which forests disappeared or retreated to humid valleys. This aridity gave rise to a semi-nomadic economy in which the horse played an important role even though the forms of its domestication remain a matter of debate.

But before the emergence of this Pit Grave horizon, we observe the gradual disappearance of the rich Neolithic cultures of the Balkans, such as the Cucuteni-Trypillia in Ukraine and Moldova or the Gumelnița-Karanovo in Bulgaria and southern Romania. At the same time, certain objects considered to be typical of steppic cultures appear in these Balkan regions; these include a type of stone club in the form of a horse's head, which are interpreted as scepters.[23] There has therefore been a strong temptation to attribute this decline of the Balkan cultures to a violent intrusion of nomadic herders, along with their domesticated horses, from the steppes. It must be remembered that, since Schrader, the issue of steppic Indo-European invasions was very much present in the minds of archaeologists working in these regions. In a later chapter,[24] we will attempt to show that the archaeological facts are more complex and can be interpreted differently.

From the Copper Age to the Bronze Age

From about 3500 BCE, at the time when the Pit Grave culture was spreading its influence over the Pontic Steppes, we witness the emergence in Central Europe, the

[22] Telegin, 1973; Telegin et al., 2001; Rassamakin, 1999, 2002, 2004; Lichardus et al., 1985, pp. 355–366; Lichardus and Lichardus-Itten, 1998; Parzinger, 2009; Govedarica, 2004.

[23] Lichardus et al., 1985, pp. 391–393; Dodd-Opritescu, 1978; Morintz and Roman, 1968; Lichardus and Lichardus-Itten, 1998; Mallory, 1989; Parzinger, 2009; Govedarica, 2004.

[24] See Chapter 14, pp. 301–314.

250   THIRD MOVEMENT (1945–THIRD MILLENNIUM)

Balkan Peninsula, and northwest Turkey, of a vast complex of cultures grouped together under the term "Baden culture"; this culture encompasses numerous regional variants and is characterized by dark-colored, groove-decorated ceramics. Throughout Northern Europe, the Funnel Beaker culture continued to evolve. Finally, various cultures characterize Western Europe (in the Paris Basin, we refer to the "Seine-Oise-Marne culture"). These cultures often buried their dead not under monumental dolmens reserved for the select few, but within collective chambers known as *allées couvertes* built of thin slabs of stone. The deceased, who often numbered in their hundreds, represent the entire community, or at least a family line, and were buried one after the other as they died.

Following this chronological horizon of the Middle Chalcolithic (already termed the "Bronze Age" in the Balkans, including Greece), the Chalcolithic culminated in what is termed the "Late" Chalcolithic, between about 2800 and 2200 BCE (see Appendices 1 and 14). In Central and Western Europe, this phase is characterized by two main cultural phenomena: the Corded Ware culture and the Bell Beaker Culture. The former group, who decorated their pottery with impressed cord motifs, occupied the entire northern half of Europe; their dead were buried beneath earthen tumuli and were accompanied by ostentatious "battle axes." We have already seen how, in the period before the Second World War,[25] this culture, known as the "Battle Axe culture" (*Streitaxtkultur* in German), played an important role in the Indo-European question. One of the debates focused on the origins and diffusion of the culture, with certain researchers, including Kossinna, advocating a Scandinavian origin and others a steppic origin. Today, while the first hypothesis has been abandoned by archaeologists, opinion remains divided over whether the culture emerged in the steppes or whether it developed in situ from the Funnel Beaker culture—with intermediate variants. In any case, the Corded Ware culture appears to have been a relatively recent historical phenomenon, one that cannot be identified with an original migration but, at best, with a secondary late migration.

The second western phenomenon is the Bell Beaker culture (*culture des Gobelets Campaniformes* in French, *Glockenbecherkultur* in German) whose most characteristic pottery takes the shape of an inverted bell decorated with horizontal bands of incised motifs. Such pottery is encountered in an area stretching from the Iberian Peninsula to Holland, and from Great Britain to Hungary. However, this occupation was not monolithic, but rather consisted of a patchwork of discontinuous entities, with bell beaker pottery often accompanying local ceramics that vary from region to region. The origin and direction of diffusion of this ceramic tradition are still problematic, with Holland and the Iberian Peninsula being most often cited as points of origin despite being a considerable

[25] See Chapter 6, pp. 120 and Chapter 7, p. 147.

WHAT ARCHAEOLOGY TELLS US TODAY   251

distance apart. Certain researchers even argue that this particular type of pottery was simply an item of exchange that circulated throughout Europe without being linked to one particular cultural group.

In southeastern Europe, the term "Bronze Age" is applied to the period immediately following the Middle Chalcolithic horizon, in other words from about 3500 BCE, even though copper and bronze (an alloy consisting of 90% copper and 10% tin) metallurgy play a decidedly modest role, particularly in the initial phases. In Greece, this is the period of the Early Helladic civilization, which lasts up until the end of the third millennium BCE, at which point the Middle Helladic begins on the mainland and the Middle Minoan in Crete; the latter is marked by the emergence of the first Cretan palaces and thus the first state-like urban phenomena in Europe. While this emergence takes the form of a smooth transition in Crete, on the mainland we observe a series of ruptures toward the end of the Early Helladic which certain researchers attribute to "Indo-European invasions," referred to more precisely as "the coming of the Greeks" in English-language publications.[26] The Mycenaean civilization, with its imposing fortresses at Mycenae and Tiryns and its gold funerary masks, began around 1500 BCE with the Late Helladic and extended as far as Crete (Late Minoan). Its script, known as Linear B, was used to write an archaic form of Greek that, along with Hittite and the language of the Indian Vedic hymns, constitutes one of the three oldest known Indo-European languages.

Further north, the Pit Grave culture (also classified as the Early Bronze Age by Russian researchers) is followed without a major break, around 2400 BCE, by the Catacomb culture, named for its important burials that were accessed by subterranean corridors. Episodes of climatic aridity endured, which favored a semi-nomadic lifestyle although fortified villages also appeared; these differed significantly in size, indicating that a hierarchy existed among settlements. Certain groups in northern Ukraine decorated their pottery with impressed cord motifs that are sometimes likened to the Corded Ware of Northern Europe. Thus, throughout the Eastern European and Central Asian steppes in the third and second millennia BCE we encounter various interacting cultures that either emerged in the Pontic zones or developed from local substrata, as in the case of the Botaj culture; many of these are grouped together under the term "Andronovo culture."[27]

From about 2200 BCE, the Bronze Age begins in most parts of Europe—even though, as we have seen, this term is applied in Eastern Europe and the Balkans to cultures that are elsewhere classified as Middle and Late Chalcolithic (i.e., more than 2,000 years earlier). The Bronze Age was once seen as a major rupture.

[26] See Chapter 15, pp. 320–327.
[27] See Chapter 15.

252 THIRD MOVEMENT (1945–THIRD MILLENNIUM)

In fact, it does not constitute an essential historic break since the invention of bronze was only a marginal technical advance: the true break in tradition—the emergence of inegalitarian chiefdom societies—dates back to the Chalcolithic. In reality, apart from in Greece, Bronze Age societies maintained the same level of social and economic organization even though extensive exchange networks for prestige goods associated with an aristocratic culture developed throughout Europe and beyond.[28]

New power networks

Copper working, the oldest form of metallurgy in the world, is attested to from at least the beginning of the fifth millennium BCE, most notably in the Balkans (it should be noted that the hammer-working of native copper existed in the Near East in at least the ninth millennium).

In any case, at the moment, the earliest known true reduction of mined copper ore in bloom furnaces, as distinct from simple melting of native copper in crucibles, occurred in the fifth millennium, in the Levant, whence it spread gradually in various directions.[29] This first metallurgy was not a radical technological revolution: in fact, copper is too soft to produce efficient tools and thus stone and bone continued to be used for this purpose for a considerable time. However, personal ornaments and other prestige objects of copper (and of gold, which began to be worked at the same time) are strong indicators of emerging powers. Such objects are found in the richest burials and also in particular domestic contexts. The Croatian site of Vučedol, situated on the banks of the Danube near Vukovar, is an emblematic example dating to the third millennium[30]: situated on a hilltop dominating the rest of the village and enclosed by a bank and ditches are two large buildings accompanied by evidence for metalworking and the tombs of an adult couple and a number of children.

In fact, copper is not equally distributed in nature; entire regions, such as Scandinavia and Mesopotamia, lack this metal. The emergence of elites whose prestige was essentially built on the possession of copper objects meant that they had to develop extensive long-distance exchange networks in order to procure it. At the end of the third millennium, no doubt due to the observation that copper with natural impurities such as tin or arsenic tended to be more resistant, the notion of deliberately adding tin to the copper in a ratio of about 1:9 arose, allowing a new much harder alloy, bronze, to be produced. This alloy lent itself

---

[28] See this Chapter, pp. 245–247; Appendices 1 and 15; Kristiansen and Larsson, 2005; Fokkens and Harding, 2013.

[29] Pigott, V., 1999; Amzallag, 2009.

[30] Schmidt, R., 1945.

to the manufacture of new forms of objects, not simple copies of stone and bone objects, that were as spectacular as they were efficient. Thus we observe the development of long swords, which allowed the wielder to kill from a distance; helmets; greaves; body armor; lances; and, of course, a wide variety of personal ornaments. Tin, however, is even rarer than copper, and the two minerals are generally not found in the same regions. At the time, important deposits of tin existed in the southern British Isles (which the Greeks called the "Cassiterides," from the Greek word for tin, which itself may derive from the ancient Kassite people), Portugal, Spain, Brittany, the Ore Mountains (Erzgebirge) on the border between Germany and the Czech Republic, and also in South East Asia, especially in the Chinese province of Yunnan and in Malaysia, areas that are still important producers of tin today.[31] Near Eastern texts such as those found at Alalakh, Ebla, Mari, and Ugarit attest to the importance of these tin exchanges throughout western Asia as far as the Indus Valley, on the one hand, and with Iberia, on the other.

As the use of bronze became more widespread during the second millennium BCE, vast networks for the exchange of copper and tin in ingot form, as well as of finished bronze objects, were established throughout Eurasia within the framework of a true "Bronze Age."[32] The individual needs of Near Eastern kingdoms and empires, of the Minoan and Mycenaean civilizations, and of the powerful chiefdoms of Northern Europe led to the generalization of these exchanges, along with that of other prestige goods—such as Baltic amber, salt, animal products, and slaves—that traveled with the copper or circulated in the opposite direction. Bronze metallurgy spread as far as Shang Dynasty China, which had the benefit of important tin resources and which witnessed the establishment of the first centralized kingdoms under the successive Erlitou and Erligang cultures and the birth of writing.[33] Thus a continuous chain of exchanges and interactions spread throughout Eurasia, linking neighboring groups all the way from the shores of the Atlantic to the shores of the Pacific.

In the first half of the second millennium BCE, a new prestigious and warlike invention, the spoke-wheeled chariot, made its first appearance, probably initially in central Asia. The horse had been domesticated on the Ukrainian steppes during the fifth or fourth millennium, at first for its meat and later for draft purposes, and the bit was developed to facilitate riding.[34] Over time the animals increased in stature, and it appears that they, too, formed part of exchanges of prestige goods. The wheel is well-attested in Europe and the East from the

[31] Muhly, 1985; Amzallag, 2009.
[32] Kristiansen and Larsson, 2005; Kohl, 2007; Fokkens and Harding, 2013; see Appendices 1 and 15.
[33] Bagley, 1999; Mei, 2000.
[34] See Chapter 14, pp. 303–308.

254   THIRD MOVEMENT (1945–THIRD MILLENNIUM)

fourth millennium onward but initially in a heavy solid-wheeled form. The invention of the spoked wheel allowed the development of rapid and more maneuverable vehicles which were used in ranged battles by the great eastern empires (the indecisive battle of Kadesh between the Egyptian army of Ramses II and the Hittites is one of the best known examples), and these are also found in the burials of European elites. The chariot, spear, and sword led to the development of new fighting techniques but also contributed greatly to the prestige of those who possessed them.

The manufacture and handling of this new equipment necessitated the acquisition of new and very specialized know-how and skills. Ancient mythologies, as well as ethnological research in various parts of the world, provide ample evidence for the special status enjoyed by metallurgists, often considered to be magicians and holders of secret knowledge, and also, of course, by warriors. In fact, archaeology shows us that deep-rooted ideological transformations were taking place throughout Eurasia at this date. Representations of females, typical of the art of the Paleolithic and Mesolithic, disappeared to be replaced by representations of armed warriors, chariots, weapons, wheels, ships, and astral bodies.[35] The recently discovered bronze and gold disc from Nebra in northern Germany, which was found along with a number of swords in what was probably the site of a sanctuary, is typical of the latter. Such representations are common in European rock art from the Alps to Scandinavia in the same period. A style of decoration, qualified as "aristocratic," composed of curvilinear motifs and interlocking spirals, is found on many prestige items, including bone whip handles, in an area stretching from the Carpathians to the Mycenaean world and Turkey.[36]

From proto-history to history

Similarly, the first phases of the Iron Age, which began around 750 BCE, were not accompanied by major social upheaval. It was only with the definitive emergence of the city states of Greece and Italy that decisive transformations took place. In Europe, we see the emergence of writing and, with this, the description and naming of a certain number of European "peoples" and, for some of them, the appearance of a written corpus in their own language.

From the fifth century BCE onward, the ethnographic and linguistic descriptions provided to us by the Greeks and later the Romans, despite their many shortcomings and biases, are invaluable. They allow us to assign a specific

[35]   Briard, 1991; Brun, 1996; Kaul, F., 1998; Demoule, 2007b.
[36]   Kristiansen, 2009; Brun and Ruby, 2008.

WHAT ARCHAEOLOGY TELLS US TODAY   255

geographical and temporal position to a certain number of populations. In broad terms, the peoples known as "Celts" and "Gauls" essentially inhabited the present-day territories of France, Great Britain, southern Germany, Austria, and Switzerland. Further north we encounter the Germanic tribes. The Iberian, Italian, and Greek peninsulas each had its own unique cultures. The Thracians occupied present-day Bulgaria, the Illyrians former Yugoslavia, the Getae and Dacians present-day Romania, and the Scythians present-day Ukraine; while the language of the Scythians is known to have belonged to the Indo-Iranian group of Indo-European languages, the languages of the four other "peoples" mentioned are barely known. The situation is even more obscure for distant parts of Central and northeastern Europe.

Nonetheless, if we compare this ethnic panorama covering the last centuries BCE (i.e. the Bronze Age and the Iron Age) with the archaeological reality for the last two millennia BCE, we observe a certain level of coincidence. Several "cultural complexes" that can be identified from about 2000 BCE (in other words, in the period when the Corded and Bell Beaker phenomena came to an end) are still to be found, with their boundaries more or less unchanged, in the historic period.[37] Thus we tend to identify the "North-Alpine complex" where, in the Iron Age, the archaeologically attested Hallstatt culture is followed by the La Tène culture, with the so-called Celtic peoples who spoke languages of the same name, and the "Nordic culture" with the so-called Germanic peoples. But, during the Bronze Age and a significant portion of the Iron Age, we also distinguish an "Atlantic complex" which encompasses southwestern England, western France, and the northwest of the Iberian Peninsula; this complex is not, however, identifiable with a historically attested "people." Furthermore, it is by no means certain that the term "people," defined as a historically homogenous entity, is applicable when describing protohistoric realities. Finally, the accounts of ancient historians have to be taken with a degree of caution.

The search for the Indo-Europeans

If, however, we retain the canonical hypothesis of an original Indo-European People, it is clear that, at the period when archaeology and ancient texts converge (i.e., in the final centuries BCE), we are looking at a situation in which the Indo-European languages are already significantly distant from each other. And if we accept that a proportion of these Indo-European languages are spoken by members of cultures that appear to have occupied the same areas since the beginning of the Bronze Age, then it is reasonable to assign the break-up of the original

---

[37] Brun, 1987; Kristiansen and Larson, 2005.

256 THIRD MOVEMENT (1945–THIRD MILLENNIUM)

people to an earlier period (see Appendices 2 and 8). In the following chapters, therefore, we will review the different hypotheses that are currently proposed, resuming in each case the supporting arguments and associated problems. At the same time, we will see how each is rooted in a long historiographical tradition and how, regardless of the wealth of archaeological data that has emanated from excavations over recent decades—upon which the historical panorama we just presented is based—the current theories in fact represent a perpetuation of earlier hypotheses.

In every case, the hypotheses ought to respond to two conditions:

1. Does there exist, in any part of Eurasia, an archaeological culture whose characteristics correspond to the notion of the original People as inferred from linguistic paleontology, comparative mythology, and all other linguistic or textual data?
2. Once such a culture is singled out, can we identify, on the basis of its original Cradle, successive migratory movements the culmination of which ultimately coincides with the geographical locations of peoples described by ancient historians?

The first question is by no means trivial because we have seen the difficulties posed by the representations that we might have of the original People as gleaned from textual data. The second presupposes that we can identify migrations archaeologically and is dependent on a strong assumption: namely, the permanence of ethnic entities over time.

12

Archaeology

What if the Indo-Europeans had always been there?

The most economical hypothesis regarding the original People is undoubtedly that of an autochthonous origin. In this scenario, the Paleolithic populations of Europe and their Mesolithic descendants would already have been speaking Indo-European languages and the question of a recent migration would not arise. This hypothesis is not new. In his day, Paul Broca defended it vigorously: it was languages, and not people, that diffused throughout Europe.[1] Already the stakes were clear: it was vital to defend the indigeneity of the two French "races" in the face of German assertions that the original People were a tall, blond race who emanated from an original Asian Cradle. This transparent claim was not confined to France. Today, certain Indian archaeologists locate the original Homeland in India, just as, for more recent periods, certain Polish archaeologists have identified Poland as the birthplace of the Slavs, while in Albania and the Basque Country others claim that they can observe a continuity in population from the Paleolithic right down to today.

A nebulous autochthony

Faced with Broca's French claims, Kossinna would soon shift the indigenous homeland to the other side of the Rhine. The "original race" was tall, blond, and now originated in Northern Germany and Scandinavia; the Proto-Indo-Europeans were descendants of Magdalenian hunters who, having moved northward at the end of the last glaciation, founded the Ertebølle-Ellerbeck culture in the region, whence they ventured forth in fourteen successive waves to conquer all of Europe. Paradoxically, Kossinna was the first Indo-Europeanist to forward an archaeological demonstration for the identification of the original Homeland, an approach that Déchelette praised for its "real competence" and that Childe lauded for its "elegance." Prior to the First World War and during the interwar years, Kossinna's model was without doubt among the most favored by

[1] See Chapter 4, pp. 77–78.

258   THIRD MOVEMENT (1945–THIRD MILLENNIUM)

archaeologists with an interest in the Indo-European question. In Germany, the theory was endorsed by numerous leading academics including Walther Schulz, Alfred Götze, Herbert Kühn, Martin Jahn, and Hans Seger.[2] Thus the position held by Kühn, a student of Kossinna, was not, as termed by Colin Renfrew,[3] simply an "interesting suggestion" but was in fact firmly rooted in the intellectual context of the time. It is worth remembering that Kühn was forced to give up his chair in Cologne University in 1935 because his wife, Rita Gersmann, was Jewish; it was not until 1946 that he managed to reintegrate academic life, this time in Mainz.

Kossinna's hypothesis, in its canonical form, collapsed in 1945. Directly linked to National Socialist ideology, it was shunned for three decades. At the same time, the progress of archaeological research rendered it irrelevant. In effect, it assumed a linear development from the Mesolithic Maglemosian culture, through the partly neolithized Ertebølle-Ellerbeck culture, culminating in the fully Neolithic, or even Chalcolithic, Funnel Beaker culture. However, all evidence indicates that the neolithization of the Ertebølle culture was not an internal process but rather that it was the result of contact with farming colonists belonging to the Rössen culture. As regards the emergence of the Funnel Beaker culture, it is difficult to attribute it to Mesolithic hunter-gatherers even if they were partially neolithized. In fact, its territory is much larger than that of the Ertebølle, extending as far as Poland, Bohemia, Northern Germany, and Holland; furthermore, it shares certain common elements with other cultures of Central European origin, such as megalithic tombs (dolmens) and large ceremonial enclosures defined by ditches, palisades, and banks. The small groups of surviving hunter-gatherers were subsequently absorbed by the Funnel Beaker culture, leaving little or no trace. In the end, there is no archaeological evidence for migrations from Scandinavia; if such migrations took place we would expect, for example, to find objects invented in Scandinavia spreading gradually southward. In reality, this marginal northern region, which was poorly suited to agriculture, was colonized relatively late by humans and its population remained sparse for a long time.

Despite the lack of support from archaeologists, the Kossinnian hypothesis reared its head once more in the 1970s in the "scientific" literature of the extreme right.[4] Archaeologically untenable, it re-emerged after three decades of silence, making no excuses for its origins. Kossinna was no longer consigned to the past.

---

[2] In particular, Kühn, 1932. See Chapter 7, p. 159.
[3] Renfrew, 1987, p. 36.
[4] See Chapter 9, p. 203 and 215–216.

WHAT IF . . .   259

Paleolithic continuity?

Today, there are nonetheless archaeologists and linguists who, independently of Kossinna and extreme right-wing ideologies, believe that the first *Homo sapiens* of the Upper Paleolithic were already speaking Indo-European languages. Among linguists, we can cite the Italian Mario Alinei and his Paleolithic Continuity Paradigm.[5] In his principal work, which is encyclopedic and expansive (among other feats, he claims in passing to be able to decipher Etruscan using Hungarian), he draws on linguistics, archaeology, genetics, geography, geology, ethnology, toponymy, paleoanthropology, cognitive sciences, and more to support the claim that the various families of Indo-European languages have been distinct from each other for a very long time, with a degree of permanency stretching back to the Paleolithic. This theory involves abandoning many of the central principles, laws, and evolutionary rhythms of traditional comparative grammar. In fact, Alinei's reasoning is essentially based on lexical comparisons with little consideration given to grammatical structures. Likewise, he focuses heavily on dialects which he believes to be more conservative than standardized official languages. In terms of continuity, the Celts had thus inhabited the British Isles and western France since the Mesolithic, and the widely accepted Celtic invasions from Central Europe never took place. One of the proofs offered is the frequency of borrowed Celtic words in Germanic languages and the absence of inverse borrowings; of particular note are supposedly Celtic terms referring to fishing found in other Indo-European languages. Furthermore, the phonetic mechanism known as "lenition," the shift from "hard" consonants to "soft" consonants (the shift from *t* to *d*, for example, with the Latin *vita* becoming *vida* in Spanish), would have been a characteristic of this original Celtic zone; this was also the region where megaliths were constructed, hence providing proof of its antiquity.

Thus, in dealing with isolated facts, Alinei combines linguistics and archaeology. Noting the presence of the word for "death" (**mer*) in the shared vocabulary, but the absence of a common term for "grave" or "cemetery," he comes to the conclusion that the various Indo-European peoples split up before the invention of graves—thus in the Paleolithic. In this particular instance, he is mistaken: the earliest graves are, in fact, attested among the Neanderthals, at least 100,000 years ago. The reliability of the archaeological references used by Mario Alinei varies. Thus he argues for permanency in linguistic boundaries over millennia, mirroring the permanency of archaeological boundaries; but the example he uses— namely, the (recent) frontier between speakers of Romance

---

[5] Alinei, 1996–2000, 2000, 2004; Ballester, 2009. See also http://www.continuitas.org/

260 THIRD MOVEMENT (1945–THIRD MILLENNIUM)

languages and speakers of Germanic languages—does not correspond, despite what he might claim, to any cultural frontier in the Neolithic period.

In so far as the "Paleolithic Continuity Paradigm" has been little discussed by other linguists,[6] one could be forgiven for thinking that it is a marginal scientific phenomenon, like those that exist in other disciplines. However, the theory has been endorsed by at least two prominent archaeologists: Paleolithic specialist Marcel Otte in Belgium[7] and Neolithic specialist Alexander Häusler in Germany.[8] More accurately, each considers that, from an archaeological point of view, there have been no significant population upheavals in Europe since the arrival of *H. sapiens* some 40,000 years ago, and thus the original Indo-European linguistic community must date back to the Paleolithic. This hypothesis has also been defended by American archaeologist Homer Thomas, who postulates continuity from the Gravettian culture (25,000 years ago) right up to the Neolithic, and more recently by Greek archaeologist Theodoros Giannopoulos[9] in the context of the "arrival of the Greeks in Greece."

This confidence relies on the interpretation of the Neolithic phenomenon in Europe. A number of researchers, outside of all linguistic concerns and in the anti-diffusionist tradition of the English-speaking world, have a tendency to minimize the demographic input of farming populations from the Near East. For the most part they prefer to interpret neolithization as a phenomenon of technological transfer. This position is difficult to endorse for many reasons.[10] When looked at in detail, the propagation of resemblances between styles of objects, techniques, ways of life, and economies can be traced over a period of two millennia from the shores of the Bosporus to the Atlantic coastline. Furthermore, all of the European domesticated animal species are genetically linked to Near-Eastern stock and none was domesticated indigenously. The only notable exception in which indigenous hunter-gatherer populations appear to have adopted agriculture and animal husbandry occurred on the steppes of Eastern Europe where the Bug-Dniester culture, through contact with the Balkan Neolithic, gradually took on the new way of life—a process known as *acculturation*. But this is the only region where, through this process of cultural borrowing (which remains debatable), hunter-gatherers remained in the majority—a fact that still needs to be confirmed, notably through DNA analysis.

Just like Colin Renfrew's hypothesis of a Near Eastern Neolithic Indo-Europeanness, the idea of linguistic continuity since the Paleolithic and the arrival of *H. sapiens* in Europe runs headlong into the problem of the ancient

---

[6] Favorable account in Le Dû, 2003; critical account in Adiego, 2002; Renzi, 1997.
[7] Otte, 1995, 2012.
[8] Häusler, 1998, 2002a, 2002b.
[9] Thomas (H. L.), 1991, 1992; Giannopoulos, 2012.
[10] See Chapter 11, pp. 242–243.

existence of non–Indo-European languages in Europe.[11] The question of the duration of the evolution of Indo-European languages, which would then have been much longer than proposed by the steppic or Anatolian models, also arises— even though there is always the risk of circular reasoning in attempts to calculate this duration because there is no independent external chronology available. Finally, DNA analyses of ancient European populations indicate that the contribution of indigenous Mesolithic populations is very low.

It is for these reasons that the Paleolithic thesis, setting aside the ideological dimension linked to the extreme right, remains anecdotal.

Having put to one side the hypothesis of an indigenous presence dating back to the Paleolithic of Indo-European languages in Europe, we will now turn our attention to the two other principal hypotheses, both migrationist and both with a long history (although regularly updated): on the one hand, a Near Eastern origin linked to the arrival of Neolithic colonists, and, on the other, an origin in the steppes to the north of the Black Sea. We will see that the difficulties which they pose ought to prompt us to question the overly simplistic model on which they are both founded.

[11] See Chapter 13, p. 2.

13

Did the Indo-Europeans really come from Turkey?

Given the weaknesses of the Paleolithic or autochthonous hypothesis, which we looked at in the preceding chapter, the second most economical hypothesis is to make the Indo-Europeanization of the continent coincide with Neolithic colonization. Again, this is not a new hypothesis. It is, in fact, one of the oldest theories and deserves a short historical recap. No sooner were the original Indo-Europeans invented at the beginning of the nineteenth century than they were located in Asia, whence they migrated and brought all of the benefits of civilization to Europe. As stated a little later by Alexandre Bertrand, who based his conclusions on the available archaeological data of the time, the Asian origin of the "Aryan civilization" is an "unassailable axiom" that is accepted "by all academic bodies in Europe" and endorsed by numerous authors.[1] According to this hypothesis, it was the Indo-Europeans who brought agriculture, animal husbandry, and metallurgy to Europe, and, in doing so, they pushed the indigenous populations to the margins of the continent where their only surviving legacy are the dolmens. This "unassailable axiom" was questioned at the end of the nineteenth century by Salomon Reinach who, like Alexandre Bertrand, was a conservator at the Musée des Antiquités Nationales and who became the principal critic of the *ex oriente lux* ("out of the East came the light") credo. This was the period when the original Homeland was being repatriated back toward Europe. Therefore, the appearance of agriculture and animal husbandry, the eastern origins of which were rarely contested, gradually became dissociated from the Indo-European migration. In addition, under the influence of Schrader, the primordial People lost their ideal, bucolic qualities so dear to Pictet and assumed the more classic characteristics of a warlike, conquering people. Moreover, the shared vocabulary seemed to support the hypothesis that agriculture played a relatively minor role in their way of life.

---

[1] Bertrand, 1864. See also, in the same volume of the *Bulletins de la Société d'anthropologie de Paris*, pp. 316–317; Schmidt (J.), 1890; Link, 1821; Brunnhofer, 1885; Hehn, 1870; Delitzsch, 1873; Hommel, 1879.

TURKEY 263

Ex oriente lux

As archaeological knowledge gradually improved, the earliest European Neolithic, namely the Painted Ceramic cultures of the Balkans and Linear Ceramic cultures (also known as *Rubanée* and Danubian) of Central Europe, seemed to correspond less and less to the warrior model postulated by Schrader. Childe drew the obvious conclusion: the "feminine conservatism" and "peasant mentality" of the Danubian farmers of the Linear Ceramic precluded them from being the original People.[2] The German prehistorian Max Ebert was of the opposite opinion. Contrary to the view of Kossinna, whom he succeeded as professor of prehistory in Berlin, Ebert proposed that the Neolithic cultures of Europe—including the Cucuteni-Trypillia of the Balkans, the Linear Ceramic of Central Europe, and the Nordic Neolithic with its dolmens (i.e., the Funnel Beaker culture)—all belonged to a single cultural entity: the *Alteuropäisch* (Old Europe), which can be identified with the Indo-Europeans.[3]

This hypothesis remained very marginal and was eventually forgotten after Ebert's death in 1929. Without reference to Ebert and in a different context, the same term *Alteuropäisch* was reused by the linguist Krahe to explain the affinities between a certain number of European hydronyms (river names); these he believed to be evidence for a disappeared common language, that spoken by the Indo-Europeans when they arrived in the continent, before it split up into the known languages.[4] The same term, translated into English as "Old Europe," was then used by archaeologist Marija Gimbutas, again without reference, to designate the same thing as did Ebert: namely, the ensemble of European Neolithic cultures which, according to her, were destined to be invaded by Indo-Europeans from the steppes.[5]

Ebert's thesis implicitly assumed that the Indo-European languages had an Asian origin because this was where the European Neolithic clearly had its origins. Childe would subsequently develop this last point in his numerous publications. And this is why, in 1927, Adalbert Sayce situated the primitive Homeland in Anatolia.[6] Three decades later, it was more or less this same Ebert-Sayce hypothesis that was taken up, with the benefit of improved archaeological data, by Catalan archaeologist Pedro Bosch Gimpera (who became a Mexican citizen after the Spanish Civil War) in a book published in 1960, which was swiftly translated into French.[7] For Bosch Gimpera, the cradle of the Indo-European

---

[2] Childe, 1926, pp. 140–143. See Chapter 7.
[3] Ebert, 1921. See Chapter 7.
[4] Krahe, 1954, 1957.
[5] See Chapter 14, pp. 294–296.
[6] Sayce, 1927. See chapter 7.
[7] Bosch Gimpera, 1960; for a somewhat imprecise French translation by Raymond Lantier, see the 1961 edition.

264 THIRD MOVEMENT (1945–THIRD MILLENNIUM)

peoples was the Central European Linear Ceramic culture, which included a significant indigenous hunter-gatherer component that would soon be infiltrated by the diffusion of the Near Eastern Neolithic. He nonetheless stressed the eminently unstable character of pre- and protohistoric cultural entities and rejected the family tree model. He constantly reminds us of the instability and "fluidity" of ethnic entities that emerge, evolve, and eventually disappear through the processes of "agglomeration," "crystallization," "contact," and "infiltration." The archaeological data used by Bosch Gimpera are now largely obsolete, and the most recent DNA analyses, in particular, have revealed the very small indigenous component among the bearers of Linear Ceramic culture. However, the methodological originality of this work remains intact. From a historiographical point of view, the theory is also an important milestone in the persistence of the hypothesis which links Europe's neolithization and Indo-Europeanization.

In parallel with these archaeological approaches, several Soviet linguists in the 1980s proposed a Near-Eastern birthplace for the Indo-Europeans. They based their hypotheses on the supposed resemblances, interpreted as evidence of ancient contacts, between the Indo-European group of languages, Semitic languages, and southern Caucasian languages (including Georgian). Since the Near East was the only geographical point of contact between these three language groups, certain scholars, among them Tamaz Gamkrelidze and Vjačeslav Ivanov, proposed a Caucasian homeland while another, Aaron Dolgopolsky, favored an Anatolian origin.[8]

A new hypothesis?

Thus, when it appeared in 1987,[9] Colin Renfrew's book, *Archaeology and Language: The Puzzle of Indo-European Origins*, did not simply appear out of nowhere, despite what the extensive media coverage wanted us to believe. On the contrary, it was part of a continuous scientific tradition that can be traced back to the very origins of the Indo-European question. In reality, it simply revived a traditional hypothesis that had been relegated to the wings by Marija Gimbutas's recent proposals regarding the steppic invasions[10]—proposals that themselves had loudly reanimated the debate on the original Homeland that, apart from a few notable exceptions (including the work of Bosch Gimpera), had languished in oblivion since 1945. Renfrew's thesis is simple and its development barely occupies 10% of the 300 pages of the 1987 publication. The bulk of the book

---

[8] Gamkrelidze and Ivanov, 1984 (see Appendix 4); Dolgopolsky, 1988.
[9] Renfrew, 1987.
[10] See Chapter 14.

focuses on providing a very didactic exposé of all of the historiographical and methodological problems posed by the "Indo-European puzzle": the Neolithic farmers from the Near East who colonized Europe from the end of the seventh millennium BCE were Indo-Europeans whose original Homeland can thus be located in Turkey (see Appendices 9 and 10).

The reaffirmation of this old hypothesis was, however, a paradox in the context of Colin Renfrew's intellectual journey. British archaeologists of the postwar era tended to define themselves in opposition to the diffusionist tradition of German archaeology. From the 1960s onward, and due in large part to the development of radiocarbon dating, they tended to stress the autonomy of European development. In his intellectual testament, Childe recalls with a degree of irony that a large part of his works had been placed under "the unifying theme of the irradiation of European barbarity by Eastern civilization."[11] For instance, dolmens and menhirs had traditionally been considered to be distantly related to the Egyptian pyramids. Radiocarbon dating has since revealed that these megalithic monuments in reality predate the famous pyramids by about 3,000 years, a fact that provided Renfrew with the title for another of his books: *Before Civilization, the Radiocarbon Revolution and Prehistoric Europe*,[12] which parallels Childe's "Neolithic revolution" from the Near East.

Renfrew also argued that metallurgy developed independently in Europe, without influence from the Near East, at the same time that other English-speaking archaeologists were claiming that the European Neolithic was invented in Europe, again without any input from the Near East. More generally, archaeology in the English-speaking world in the 1960s and '70s was characterized by a particular focus on the study of prehistoric environments and the processes of in-situ adaptation of ancient societies, favoring evolution over diffusion; it also emphasized the necessity for thoroughness in the reasoning and proof mechanisms applied. Renfrew himself coordinated the publication of several collective works on archaeological methodologies and theory which emphasized the need to develop much more complex explanatory models in archaeology.

In view of this, it might seem very surprising that a leading light of this school of archaeology suddenly showed a deep interest in one of the most traditional, even well-worn, problems of archaeology within the German tradition and, what is more, which was at the very center of all diffusions and migrationist debates. However, because Colin Renfrew was a respected archaeologist, his book was an immediate success and was translated into numerous languages, including Japanese (in the year of its publication, this was

[11] Childe, 1958, p. 70; see Chapter 7, pp. 151–152.
[12] Renfrew, 1973.

266   THIRD MOVEMENT (1945–THIRD MILLENNIUM)

the biggest selling Japanese translation of an English-language book in Japan). It provoked considerable media interest, and detailed debates regarding its theses appeared in several journals, such as *Antiquity* in Great Britain, *Current Anthropology* in the United States, and, on a more modest level, the University of Lyon II's *Topoï* journal.[13] In no time, the notion of a Near Eastern origin for the Indo-Europeans was presented as being patently evident and an accepted fact in popular English-language publications.[14] Shortly afterward, Colin Renfrew was made a Lord by Elizabeth II (with the title Baron of Kaimsthorn), a distinction which only one other archaeologist before him had received: John Lubbock, inventor of the terms "Neolithic" and "Paleolithic" and an ardent opponent of diffusionism.

At this point, we should remind ourselves that any original Homeland should fulfill two conditions: (a) it must be possible to prove its Indo-Europeanness, and (b) it must be the epicenter of a migratory phenomenon. Renfrew elegantly deals with both requirements by selecting the only large-scale migration that is virtually unanimously accepted by European prehistorians and by ignoring the first condition. In our case, the issue therefore is not to discuss the reality of the migration of Neolithic farmers,[15] but rather to ask ourselves what proof we have to link this historical fact with the Indo-Europeans. Several points are problematic, and it is worth examining each in greater detail.

a. Indo-European languages are poorly represented in the supposed original Homeland.

b. The resemblances between Indo-European languages are not organized in a gradual progression following the axis of diffusion of the Neolithic colonization of Europe, i.e., from the southeast to the northwest.

c. The wave of Neolithic (supposedly Indo-European) colonization allowed a number of non–Indo-European languages to survive in Europe.

d. The shared vocabulary lacks terms evoking the flora and fauna of the Mediterranean, the natural environment of the supposed original Homeland.

e. Finally, European Neolithic societies, which archaeology has shown to have been simple and egalitarian, possess none of the traits frequently identified by comparative studies of myths, vocabulary, and institutions, which suggest a hierarchical warrior society.

---

[13] *Antiquity*, 62, 1988; *Current Anthropology*, 29, 3, 1988; *Topoï*, vol. 2, 1992. Main criticisms in Pereltsvaig and Lewis, 2015.

[14] See Mallory and Adams, 1997, p. 307.

[15] See Chapter 11, pp. 242–243.

The language of the original Homeland

As regards the first point, it is surprising that the proposed original Homeland is a zone where few Indo-European languages have existed in the historic period. The principal languages spoken in the Near East are Semitic (Akkadian, Aramaic, Hebrew, Phoenician, Arab, etc.) or related languages (such as Egyptian). There are also a number of languages that are neither Semitic nor Indo-European: Sumerian and Elamite of Mesopotamia, and Hattic and Hurrian of Asia Minor. The only attested Indo-European languages occurred in Turkey: Hittite, Luwian, and Palaic in the second millennium BCE, and the possibly related Lycian, Lydian, and Phrygian languages of the first millennium BCE. Faced with this conundrum, Renfrew proposes to limit the original Homeland of the Indo-European languages to Turkey. But Turkey was not a primary center of origin for Neolithization. The original zone for the domestication of animals and plants essentially encompasses the present-day territories of Syria, Israel, Palestine, and western Iraq. This has recently been confirmed through genetic analyses of cereals.[16] It was in a second phase, beginning at the end of the eighth millennium, that constantly growing Neolithic populations spread out in various directions, particularly toward Turkey. Excavations in Turkey have revealed several spectacular sites, including the famous Çatal Höyük in the southeast of the country with its frescoes and bulls' skulls. However, it is highly unlikely that the Neolithic farmers who appeared and developed in a geographical area where, in historic times, only Semitic languages are attested mutated into Indo-European speakers on arriving in Turkey.

Ultimately, three possibilities exist. The first, which Renfrew does not even consider, is that the extension of the Neolithic from Syria and Iraq into Turkey involved cultural transmission rather than actual population movement. But, in reality, the entire material culture of the original zone also occurs in Turkey where previous Mesolithic settlement is evanescent.

From Indo-European to Indo-Hittite?

The second possibility, which Renfrew did not consider in the original version of his work but which he would propose later,[17] was that the Indo-European languages of Turkey (Hittite, Palaic, Louvite, etc.[18]) were the direct descendants of the "original Language." In all logic, they should be its closest descendants.

---

[16] Colledge et al., 2004.
[17] Renfrew, 1999.
[18] See Chapter 15, pp. 345–347.

268   THIRD MOVEMENT (1945-THIRD MILLENNIUM)

However, the place of Hittite in the family tree of Indo-European languages poses a problem. This language was discovered at a relatively late date, in the 1920s, when the comparative grammar had already been fully constructed. Its decipherment by Czech linguist Bedřich Hrozný belied Antoine Meillet's calm assertion, made thirty years earlier in the first edition of his *Introduction à l'étude comparative des langues indo-européennes*, that comparative grammar had reached "a point of completion that could not be surpassed" and that no new discoveries would be made.[19] The famous linguist was at first reticent to acknowledge Hrozný's discoveries[20] and then minimized their significance. Even today, the position of Hittite remains a matter of debate. For some scholars it is a language so particular that it should be classed apart; it has even been suggested, following the work of Emil Forrer and Edgar Sturtevant in the 1920s, that an umbrella term—"Indo-Hittite"—should be created to designate an even larger family of languages, a family with two branches encompassing the "classic" Indo-European languages, on the one hand, and Hittite and the other less well-known Anatolian languages, on the other. For others, Hittite had undergone a process of degradation. And for others still, Hittite was a sort of pidgin, a contact language between a strong non–Indo-European linguistic substrate (Hatti in particular) and an invasive Indo-European language with strong influences from Mesopotamian languages.[21] In short, Hittite, the oldest attested Indo-European language, poses serious classification problems which are far from being resolved. It is therefore difficult, in all cases, to see Hittite as the direct descendant of the original language spoken in the supposed original Homeland.

However, this is exactly what transpired. In 1988, and in parallel with Renfrew's work, linguist Aaron Dolgopolsky took up the Indo-Hittite hypothesis, stressing all the while the possibility of linguistic contacts between the Indo-European languages, the languages of the southern Caucasus (namely the Kartvelian group of languages of which Georgian is the best known), and the Semitic languages.[22] The proof of these contacts lay in a certain number of related words which were either borrowed from one linguistic group to another or that trace their origin back to a common ancestor: this is what is known as the "Nostratic" hypothesis, which was developed in the early twentieth century[23] and which designates a primitive language that would have given rise to the languages of Europe, western Asia, and North Africa—"Nostratic" because it is the language of "fellow

---

[19] Meillet, 1903, pp. 410–411; compare with the 1937 edition, pp. 479–480.

[20] Meillet, 1921, p. 99, note 1.

[21] Regarding this discussion, see Neu and Meid, 1979 (particularly the contributions by W. P. Schmid and W. Meid); Adrados, 1982, 1990; Justus, 1992; Schmidt (K-H.), 1992; Schmid, 1979; Oettinger, 1986; Forrer, 1921; Sturtevant, 1929, 1962; Wagner (H.), 1985; Schlerath, 1987; Voegelin and Voegelin, 1973; Finkelber, 1997; Polomé, 1980; Holm, 2008.

[22] Dolgopolsky, 1988.

[23] See Chapter 17, p. 390.

countrymen" (*nostrates* in Latin) as opposed to the language of the others. The most likely geographical setting for such contacts would be Turkey, making this also the most likely location of the original Indo-European Cradle. These possible contacts between Proto-Indo-European and Semitic had been noted since the nineteenth century, particularly the resemblances concerning the number "seven" and words for "bull," "star," "sun," "wine," "goat," "salt," etc.—in all, there are between twenty and forty comparable roots depending on the researcher. This is why, as we have seen, several linguists who have been interested in the location of the original Homeland, outside of all archaeological considerations, have regularly proposed a Near Eastern cradle because this is the supposed zone of possible contact between these two linguistic families. Hence, without going all the way back to Sayce, Hodge, in 1981, proposed an original Homeland in Egypt while at the same time Gamkrelidze and Ivanov who, like Dolgopolsky, based their reasoning on potential contacts with the languages of the Caucasus, opted for a homeland in this mountainous region.[24]

Expressed at the same time, the hypotheses of Renfrew and Dolgopolsky appeared to reach the same conclusion from different directions, a point that did not go unnoticed. However, this convergence only stands up if Renfrew's general theory (the one we are currently discussing) is proven; if the "Indo-Hittite" hypothesis, in that particular form which envisages that the Anatolian languages were the earliest to detach from the Indo-European family tree, is also validated; and, finally, if the phenomena of linguistic contact identified by Dolgopolsky can be dated to the Neolithic period. While Dolgopolsky in his 1988 article appears to favor a mechanism of borrowings, the hypothesis of a common and even earlier Proto–Indo-European language cannot be ruled out, a fact that leads us nicely on to the third possibility.

Part of the family tree of all the world's languages?

Indeed, the third possible explanation for the poor representation of Indo-European languages in the hypothetical homeland involves grouping together all of the languages of the Near East into a single linguistic family. It is this idea that Renfrew went on to develop shortly after the publication of his book. This was the time when, as we have seen, the work of American linguists and geneticists spectacularly burst on to the scene[25]; under the title of the "New Synthesis," these

---

[24] Sayce, 1927; Hodge, 1981; Gamkrelidze and Ivanov, 1984.
[25] See Chapter 10, pp. 229–230.

270   THIRD MOVEMENT (1945–THIRD MILLENNIUM)

researchers claimed to be able to reconstruct a global family tree of all the world's genes and, simultaneously, of all the world's languages.[26]

Within this model of a Great Tree, Renfrew inserted a particular hypothesis, namely that the core linguistic diffusions were linked to the diffusion of agriculture, generally through the mechanism of migration, over the course of recent millennia. More precisely, the hunter-gatherers of the Natufian culture, within which agriculture and animal husbandry gradually emerged in the Near East around 9000 BCE, spoke a particular language which lies at the origin not only of Indo-European languages, but also of other linguistic families including Semitic languages. When, as a consequence of their population growth, itself the result of their superior food production system, these proto-agriculturalists left their homeland to gradually spread out in various directions, the mother languages of the different great linguistic families developed through a process of splitting: hence, the Proto–Indo-European language would have emerged at the moment when these farmers settled in Turkey, while the ancestor of all Semitic languages undoubtedly developed in situ and the ancestor of the "Elamo-Dravidian" group would have developed in Mesopotamia, whence certain groups would have continued their travels into southern India. This would explain the handful of resemblances, noticed for more than a century, between Indo-European languages and other linguistic groups, including Semitic. But, more especially, at an even more speculative level, this would resolve the paradox of the "original Indo-European People" originating in an essentially Semitic linguistic area.

Initially, the Great Tree approach confined itself to reconciling the genetic tree and the linguistic tree by highlighting coinciding branches. These branches were not, in themselves, precisely dated in time although approximate techniques such as the "molecular clock" and, more contentiously, glottochronology were applied.[27] The branchings were not, therefore, linked to specific historical events. Renfrew's approach served to provide exactly this historical incarnation: not only in the Near East, but throughout a large part of globe, the expansion of the great linguistic families coincided with the expansion of farmers and stock rearers, to the detriment of hunter-gatherers whose populations were much less significant.[28] Nobody denies that, over the course of the last ten millennia, farmers have progressively eliminated hunter-gatherer societies from the planet, either through assimilation or straightforward annihilation. It is generally accepted that the Near Eastern epicenter was responsible for the neolithization of all western Asia, a large part of North Africa, and all of Europe. But can we relate

---

[26] Ruhlen, 1991; Cavalli-Sforza, 1997; Pellegrini, 1995; see Chapter 10, pp. 229–230, and Chapter 17, pp. 390–392; see Appendix 16.
[27] See Chapter 17, p. 395.
[28] Bellwood, 2005, 2009.

TURKEY 271

this general historical phenomenon to linguistic facts? Such a claim is founded on at least two strong assumptions:

a. that we can reconstruct a family tree of all of the linguistic families involved in this process; and
b. that we can reconstruct the migratory paths of the speakers of each of these linguistic groups by identifying over space and time a chain of archaeological cultures emanating from the Near Eastern epicenter and culminating in the societies whose languages have been identified—just as Renfrew initially proposed for the Indo-European family alone.

Concerning the difficulties of classification

The first of these assumptions is just one particular local case within the overall Great Tree. The idea that Indo-European languages are only one such particular case can be traced back, if not to the Tower of Babel, at least to Franz Bopp, the founder of comparative grammar, who attempted to push his comparisons well beyond the Indo-European group, even as far as Oceania.[29] Possible resemblances between Indo-European languages, Semitic languages, Finno-Ugric languages (Hungarian, Finnish, Estonian, Sami, Mordvinic, Mari, etc.), and even the languages of the Caucasus and the Dravidian languages of southern India were regularly suggested over the course of the nineteenth century. It was these resemblances that, in 1905, led Alfredo Trombetti to propose a family tree of the world's languages. At the same time, but without going into detail, Meillet pointed out "striking concordances" between these different language families. Urging caution, he did not rule out the possibility that a larger family tree could be constructed, but such a tree would have certain limits: "We only envisage that all the languages of peoples belonging to the 'white' race would be related to each other."[30] In the 1920s, Holger Pedersen had developed the hypothesis under the term "Nostratic"; his theory was subsequently more or less forgotten before being revived in the 1960s by Soviet linguist Vladislav Illič-Svityč, who actually compiled a dictionary of "Nostratic." After his death, the school he founded continued his work; the collapse of the Eastern Bloc and subsequent greater contacts between East and West soon gave them a much wider audience and led to the publication of numerous collective works.[31] The "Nostratic" current was soon

[29] See Chapter 2, p. 21.
[30] Meillet, 1937, pp. 38–39.
[31] Pedersen, 1931; Cuny, 1924; Illič-Svityč, 1971–1984; Dolgopolsky, 1970, 1989; Kaiser and Shevoroshkin, 1988; Shevoroshkin, 1989a, 1989b; Bomhard, 2008.

272   THIRD MOVEMENT (1945–THIRD MILLENNIUM)

joined by the universalist endeavors of Joseph Greenberg and Merritt Ruhlen and in return fed into it.[32]

In any case, as regards the question being considered here, it must be admitted that the status of these kinship relationships remains confused. In fact, in Meillet's day, researchers outlined similarities between Indo-European languages, Semitic languages, Hamitic languages (linked to the former: Ancient Egyptian, Coptic, Ethiopian languages), Caucasian languages, Finno-Ugric or Uralic languages, and Altaic languages (Turkish, Mongolian, Tungus, and related languages, which are sometimes controversially grouped together with Finno-Ugric languages within a single group known as "Uralo-Altaic"). Vladislav Illič-Svityč grouped all of these languages together within his "Nostratic." He nevertheless distinguishes between southern Caucasian languages (Kartvelian), which belong to the "Nostratic" macro-family, and northern Caucasian languages, which do not; he also includes the Dravidian group of languages within "Nostratic."

The classification devised by Greenberg and Ruhlen is quite different: they define a vast "Eurasiatic" that includes the Indo-European group, the Uralo-Altaic group (to which they add Korean, Japanese, and Ainu), Eskimo-Aleut languages, and the Siberian languages of the Chukchi and of Kamchatka. This "Eurasiatic" was in turn grouped within an even larger group, "Eurasian-American," which encompasses most of Eurasia, the Americas, and North Africa. As well as Eurasiatic, this larger group also includes Amerind (i.e., most of the Amerindian languages), the Dravidian group, the Kartvelian of the South Caucasus, and Afro-Asiatic, which more or less corresponds to the Hamito-Semitic language group. Classed apart are the languages of sub-Saharan Africa, South East Asia, and Oceania, as well as a "Dené-Caucasian" group that includes Chinese, Tibetan, Basque, Burushaski (a minor isolated language spoken in northern Pakistan), Siberian Ienissian, the northern Caucasian languages, certain North American languages, and even Sumerian—while other linguists, such as Diakonov, place the North American Na-Dené languages within "Nostratic."[33]

There is, therefore, no coincidence between the two classification systems, even if the "Eurasian-American" group, by virtue of its planetary scale, includes them both. Of course, Merit Ruhlen gives great consideration to the proponents of "Nostratic"[34]; it is true that the philological scholarship of Russian linguists is considerable and that their comparative endeavors are much more detailed than the limited, summary comparisons that they share with the wider public. At first glance, the longer history of research on "Nostratic," together with the serious scholarship of the Russian linguistic school, might appear to act as an

---

[32] See Chapter 17, pp. 390–392.
[33] For the position of Sumerian, see Bengston, 1991; Diakonoff, 1997.
[34] For example, Ruhlen, 1994, pp. 185–188.

endorsement of the Greenbergian tree. On second glance, the differences between the two systems mean that they weaken each other. Since the initial raw materials are the same, the inherent difficulties are also the same; these difficulties stem from the methods of matching, which are not based on incontrovertible and testable linguistic foundations. As in all genealogical linguistic research, but with raw materials that are far more evanescent, the first step is to seek resemblances between words and then to interpret them (Common source? Later borrowings? Chance?). It is useful to keep in mind the uncertainties of the method as well as the potential for interdisciplinary circularity with the genetic Great Tree.

The linguistic impacts of agriculture?

Above all, it is the historical explanation for this potential linguistic diffusion that poses a problem—it corresponds to the other (external) issue raised by the Nostratic hypothesis, in addition to that of its internal coherence. In Greenberg and Ruhlen's vision, humanity, in its African cradle, would have experienced an initial separation between the speakers of sub-Saharan languages, who remained in situ and gradually spread out to populate Africa, and others who were destined to populate the rest of the planet. The first to leave were the bearers of languages destined to become those of South East Asia, Oceania, and Australia. These were then followed by the Dené-Caucasian group who would go on to occupy a large part of Eurasia. But a third group, the "Eurasian-American" group, would, in turn, become detached and expand to encompass the Americas, North Africa, and, with its "Eurasiatic" subgroup, Eurasia. In this last region, they replaced the preceding group who, outside the Sino-Tibetan zone, found themselves confined in isolated enclaves (Caucasian, Basque, Burushaski, Ienissian, etc.). Ruhlen suggests that this "Eurasiatic" subgroup "probably originated in the Near East."[35] Unfortunately he has no supporting argument (such as, e.g., a shared vocabulary that might describe a Near Eastern type environment).

Renfrew, in making use of the Greenbergian language tree, adds an additional argument: the diffusion of most of the great linguistic families corresponded to the diffusion of agriculture. However, this cannot have been the case for Greenberg and Ruhlen's "Eurasian-American" macro-family since it includes the Amerind group spoken by the hunter-gatherer people who first colonized America via the Bering Strait in the Paleolithic period; agriculture would appear at a much later date in Mesoamerica and the Andes. Nor can it have been the case for the "Eurasiatic" group since it also includes well-known ancient

[35] Ibid., p. 191.

274 THIRD MOVEMENT (1945–THIRD MILLENNIUM)

hunter-gatherer societies such as the speakers of the Chukchi-Kamchatka languages, Eskimo-Aleut languages, Uralic languages, and at least some of the Altaic languages (especially if we accept the inclusion of Japanese and Ainu in this latter group). Neither the dispersion of the "Eurasian-American" macro-family nor of the "Eurasiatic" group could have coincided with the diffusion of agriculture from the Near Eastern epicenter; therefore, if these migrations occurred, they did so prior to the spread of agriculture. This would require us to envisage successive waves of migration, first of hunter-gatherers and then of farmers. But they both coexist on the various branches of the Greenberg-Ruhlen classification, just as they do within "Nostratic." In this case, everything becomes possible, which is convenient, but at the same time nothing is verifiable.

We could, of course, conserve within "Nostratic" only those languages associated with known agricultural societies in historically known periods; indeed this is more or less what Renfrew does. The Near Eastern linguistic homeland postulated by Ruhlen is also the home of agriculture recognized by archaeology; from here, the bearers of the Semitic languages (who stayed in situ or moved toward North Africa), the Dravidian group (who migrated toward India after leaving the Elamite language in Mesopotamia), the Indo-European group (who made their way toward Anatolia), and the South Caucasian group (who headed toward the mountainous region of the same name) migrated in successive waves. On the one hand, however, methodologically, this reasoning is strictly circular: since there was a diffusion of agriculture, there must have been a linguistic diffusion and thus a common source for the languages of the various agricultural civilizations of western Eurasia; since the affinities between several linguistic families allow us to postulate a common source, it follows that there must have been a general expansion of the population from an original Homeland. Moving up a notch, we re-encounter the problems posed by the equation: Indo-European expansion = Neolithic colonization of Europe.

Furthermore, several classificatory problems remain unanswered even if we accept the attested affinities. On the one hand, the expansion of the vast group of Finno-Ugric (or Uralic) and Altaic languages from this same point of origin is not demonstrated archaeologically (Renfrew, without explanation, situates it chronologically after the diffusion of agriculture[36]); however, these languages are as closely related to Indo-European languages as the Semitic languages, according to the Nostratic theory, and even more closely so according to Greenberg's theory. Moreover, Renfrew's model assumes that Proto–Indo-European separated from Proto-Semitic at the moment when Neolithic expansion reached Turkey, about 7500 BCE, and that the Proto–Indo-European of Europe then split from the Proto–Indo-European of Turkey (i.e., the ancestor

---

[36] Renfrew, 1992, pp. 457–459.

of what are termed the "Anatolian languages," like Hittite) at the moment when the Neolithic reached the Balkan Peninsula, about 6500 BCE. Following linguistic logic, we should expect to see relatively strong linguistic links between Hittite and the Semitic languages. However, this is not the case, and, for Greenberg and Ruhlen, the Semitic languages (which they include in their "Afro-Asiatic" group") are further removed from Indo-European languages than Japanese or Eskimo.

Thus, in summary, the first question raised by Renfrew's hypothesis—namely, the weak presence of Indo-European languages in the shared homeland—is not adequately answered. We might even add that the presumed, and subsequently proposed, affinities between the Indo-European languages and other language groups, including Semitic languages, pose more questions than they answer since we do not encounter the similarities that we might expect. The structure of the similarities, this time internal, is the subject of our second inquiry.

The return of Troubetzkoy

In fact, if the Indo-European languages diffused at the same time as the Neolithic colonization of Europe, it would be reasonable to expect to see a gradient in the resemblances between neighboring languages as we move from southeast to northwest.[37] Thus, Greek and Albanian (and the other little known ancient Balkan languages) should closely resemble each other and should also be close, on the one hand, to the Anatolian languages (situated in the presumed cradle) and, on the other, the Italic languages (the Neolithic spread simultaneously through Central Europe, via the Danube Basin, and along the Mediterranean coastline). The Celtic group of languages, which in the first millennium BCE were spoken in the region between Bohemia and the Paris Basin, should form a bridge between the preceding languages, located in the Mediterranean region, and the Germanic languages of Northern Europe. These two last groups should then have particular ties with the Baltic and Slavic languages situated in the northeast. The Indo-Iranian languages, located even further east, should thus have specific links with the Slavic languages, as should Tocharian, the easternmost of all the Indo-European languages. Finally, Armenian, located in the Caucasus should quite closely resemble the Anatolian languages, and particularly Hittite. Clearly, since we are dealing with a phenomenon of progressive diffusion from a single point of origin, the family tree of Indo-European languages should be organized according to this diffusion.

[37] Renfrew, 1987 [1990], pp. 192–193.

276 THIRD MOVEMENT (1945–THIRD MILLENNIUM)

However, this is not at all the case. We will see later[38] that, as things stand, there is no agreement among linguists regarding the organization of a family tree of all Indo-European languages. Even the long-held classification distinguishing between *centum* languages in the west and *satem* languages in the east[39] has been abandoned—particularly since Tocharian, far to the east, is a *centum* language. And none of the current family trees expresses the links suggested above. We will see that only one classification system, that devised by the anthropologist Alfred Kroeber, but which does not have a genealogical structure, expresses geographical affinities.[40] One could counterargue that the oldest known Indo-European languages only date back to about 1500 BCE (Hittite, Mycenaean, Sanskrit), and the others are much later, while the arrival of the Neolithic in Europe occurred about 6500 BCE. The intervening five millennia provide plenty of time during which transformations could occur, either internally in terms of the subsequent evolution of each of the languages, or externally, with the result that their known location in the historic period no longer reflects their initial location at the moment when Europe was colonized, due to probable successive migrations. Thus, it has often been assumed that the historical Greeks only arrived in Greece during the Bronze Age; the geographical location of the Slavs today dates to the beginning of the Middle Ages; the Romance languages, as we all know, resulted from the expansion of the Roman Empire; and the Celtic languages, after a vast expansion in the last centuries BCE, saw their territory drastically reduced due to the expansion of Germanic and Romance languages. However, to admit that successive migrations might have blurred the original geographical-genealogical relationships of the Indo-European languages to the point of rendering them illegible amounts to admitting that we can state nothing with certainty.

The same is true regarding the possibility of reconstructing the internal evolution of each of the Indo-European language families during these dark millennia. A number of attempts have been made, however. For Dolgopolsky,[41] once the Indo-Europeans had arrived in the Balkan Peninsula from their original Anatolian Homeland, a new linguistic fragmentation occurred when subsequent migrations radiated outward, the proof being the proportionally higher number of Indo-European languages in the Balkans compared to the rest of Europe, which would mean that this region was a springboard for Indo-European dispersion. Nevertheless, if we exclude those languages that arrived quite late in the Balkan Peninsula (southern Slavic languages, Romanian, and related Wallachian dialects) and Armenian (whose Balkan origins are controversial), most of the these ancient Balkanic languages are scarcely known (Illyrian, Thracian, Dacian,

---

[38] See Chapter 17, pp. 385–386.
[39] See Chapter 7, p. 158.
[40] See Chapter 17, pp. 396–397.
[41] Dolgopolsky, 1988.

TURKEY 277

Ancient Macedonian, and even "Pelasgian"), and our knowledge of their existence depends on the fact that literate civilizations existed on their frontiers; further north, these languages would have left no trace and so, *a contrario*, a similar prehistoric diversity could have existed in the rest of Europe.

Similarly, Colin Renfrew has attempted to revive an old hypothesis; namely, that of Hans Krahe's *Alteuropäisch*,[42] which we mentioned earlier and which should not be confused with Max Ebert's *Alteuropäisch*.[43] Using the evidence of a certain number of European place names and river names, words that are reputedly conservative, Krahe forwarded the hypothesis of an archaic linguistic layer that was Indo-European at its roots but which cannot be linked to a specific language. For example, river names such as "Alba" and "Ara" occur in an area stretching from England to Germany. He therefore considered this to be the language of the original Indo-Europeans once they had arrived in Europe. These toponymic and hydronymic studies are classics of research on lost languages, whether they are considered to be Indo-European or Pre–Indo-European, and never fail to trigger innumerable and mostly unresolvable speculations.[44] The latter were particularly developed by linguists in Balkan countries because, thanks to Greek and Latin texts that mention the names of places, peoples, and individuals in these "Barbarian" lands, a certain amount of linguistic material is available; it is also because, in these young nations, cut up and "Balkanized" by Western powers, the reconstruction at all costs of a distant past, whether imaginary or not, was a central issue and even a national cause. Even if these linguistic fossils are, in the absence of anything better, precious, it would be reckless to consider them as providing even the slightest evidence in support of Renfrew's thesis or any other thesis for that matter.

Two other British archaeologists, Andrew and Susan Sherratt,[45] in a discussion of Renfrew's hypothesis, added a contribution of their own. They suggest that the Indo-European languages dispersed from their Anatolian homeland to Europe in the form of a *koinê* (the term given to the expansion and homogenization of Greek in the Hellenistic period, following Alexander's conquests) and through extensive commercial contacts, a theory that pushes out the boundaries of the undecidable even further. It is, however, a hypothesis that Renfrew would take up some twelve years later. Subtly modifying his initial model, he suggests that such a *koinê* or *Sprachbund*, using the areal linguistic term explicitly borrowed from Troubetzkoy, may have taken form in the Balkan Peninsula thanks to

[42] Krahe, 1954, 1957; Schmid, 1968, 1987; Renfrew, 1987 [1990], pp. 194–198, 290. For a bibliography of the discussion, see Sergent, 1995, pp. 139–140.

[43] Ebert, 1921.

[44] See also Georgiev, 1961, 1973 (also cited by Renfrew) and, more generally, Sergent, 1995, pp. 96–105, 138–147.

[45] Sherratt and Sherratt, 1988.

278 THIRD MOVEMENT (1945–THIRD MILLENNIUM)

prolonged cultural contacts throughout the Neolithic and Chalcolithic.[46] So while the initial Neolithic colonization of Western Mediterranean Europe would have given rise to the Italic languages, and while the initial colonization of temperate Europe by the Linear Ceramic would have given rise to the Celtic and Germanic languages, the other Indo-European languages would have sprung from this Balkanic *Sprachbund*. Tocharian, for its part, would be the remote remnant of the initial colonization of the Pontic Steppes.

This Balkanic *Sprachbund* would account for the kinship relationships between the so-called *satem* Indo-European languages.[47] Without going into the pertinence of this ancient division, now considered obsolete, it is clear that this new hypothesis is just speculative since Renfrew's genealogical tree, which is in part inspired by that developed by the linguist Adrados,[48] is as contestable as numerous others; it does not, for example, account for the numerous affinities between Baltic languages and Germanic languages. It also takes as a given that the neolithization of the steppes occurred through colonization emanating from the Balkans (this is one of the linchpins of its critique of the steppic theory). In terms of archaeological material culture, continuity between the Chalcolithic *Sprachbund* of the Balkans and the various historically attested Indo-European languages which are supposed to have derived from it has not been demonstrated either.

In summary, no satisfactory response has been found to the second problem raised by Renfrew's model: namely, the geographical-genealogical structure that the model presumes.

A nonverifiable model

The third objection concerns the existence of non–Indo-European languages within the Eurasian space settled by the wave of Neolithic colonization from the Near East. These non–Indo-European languages have diverse statuses and histories. The late arrival of some of them is historically attested: the arrival of the Hungarians in the Carpathian Basin in the ninth century CE; the arrival of the Proto-Bulgars, speakers of an Altaic language, in Bulgaria in the seventh century CE, and the arrival of the Ottoman Turks in the Balkan Peninsula from the thirteenth century CE onwards. Others occupied the northern margins of Europe from earlier times. This is the case with the Finno-Ugric or Uralic languages: Lapp (or Sami), Finnish, Estonian, Mari, etc., and it is from this group

[46] Renfrew, 1999.
[47] See Chapter 7, p. 158.
[48] Adrados, 1987, 1990.

that the Hungarians eventually split. The present geographical locations of these languages constitute the northern limit of the extension of Indo-European languages in Europe. Likewise, the interpenetration between different linguistic groups in Asia does not pose any particular difficulties. However, not counting the numerous languages of the Caucasus; a modern language, Basque; and several ancient languages that are not considered Indo-European exist or existed in isolation surrounded by Indo-European languages. Among the ancient examples, the oldest is that written in the Linear A script of Crete in the second millennium BCE; this language, spoken in the earliest Cretan palaces, still has not been deciphered but it is generally considered to be separate from the Indo-European group. The same applies to the Etruscan language of Northern Italy in the first millennium BCE despite a number of inconclusive attempts to link it to Indo-European.[49] In the same era, the equally little-known languages of the Iberian Peninsula were transcribed using Mediterranean type alphabets at the same time that city state civilizations were emerging in the south and east of the peninsula; the latter are also considered to be non–Indo-European.[50] Finally, Pictish, known only through place names, personal names, and a few Early Medieval inscriptions, is considered to be a non–Indo-European language spoken in Scotland before the arrival of the Celts.[51]

Concerning the existence of these linguistic enclaves, Colin Renfrew suggests that either these languages predate the Neolithic colonization or that they arrived afterward—an alternative that makes a good deal of sense. The first hypothesis had been developed earlier in the global model proposed by Greenberg and Ruhlen[52] even though they did not consider the case of rare ancient languages (the language written in Linear A, Pictish, Etruscan, and Iberian). According to this model, Basque would have belonged to the vast "Dené-Caucasian" group which also included, among others, the languages of the North Caucasus, the minuscule Burushaski of Pakistan, the extensive Sino-Tibetan group, Ienissian, and the Na-Dené languages of North America. This would have constituted a first wave of expansion, emanating from the Near Eastern homeland and spreading throughout Eurasia. The next expansion, termed "Eurasian-American," would have pushed the preceding group into its present-day refuges; this scenario presents obvious difficulties when it comes to discriminating what was specifically linked to the spread of agriculture in Renfrew's version.

However, if we consider concrete archaeological evidence, this hypothesis is contradicted by the regular, methodical progression of Neolithic colonization

[49] See Sergent, 1995, pp. 149–150; Adrados, 1989.
[50] Regarding these languages in general, see Untermann, 1961, 1975, 1997; Tovar, 1961, 1987; Anderson (J.), 1980; Villar, 1990; Neumann and Untermann, 1980.
[51] Jackson, 1955.
[52] Ruhlen, 1994, p. 191.

280   THIRD MOVEMENT (1945–THIRD MILLENNIUM)

from the southeast to the northwest of the European continent. We recall[53] that three zones of early neolithization can be identified in Europe: the Balkan area, from about 6500 BCE, characterized by a very homogenous painted ceramic tradition distributed throughout the peninsula; the Mediterranean coastal zone, from about 5900 BCE, which is also characterized by a homogenous material culture that includes pottery with impressed decoration executed using sharp objects or shells; and, finally, spreading from the Balkanic zone at around 5500 BCE, the Temperate European zone, with its pottery decorated with incised motifs, known as the Linear Ceramic tradition, that eventually extended from the shores of the Black Sea to the Atlantic coast and from the Alps to the Baltic. By the early fifth millennium BCE, the entire continent, apart from the margins (the Baltic coast, the shores of the Black Sea, and the great Russian forest), had been neolithized through this continuous process.

Apart from the aforementioned margins, there is no evidence for enclaves in which neolithization was achieved through a process of adoption and borrowing of Neolithic modes of production by local hunter gatherer groups. There are no divergences evident in the North of Italy, in the Iberian Peninsula, or, despite some claims by Basque archaeologists, in southwestern France. As regards Great Britain, when agriculture and animal husbandry first appear there toward the end of the fifth millennium BCE, they are accompanied by a material and symbolic (monumental funerary architecture, large ceremonial enclosures) culture that is in every way comparable to that found on the continent at the same time. Symmetrically, in the zones where we can observe acculturation phenomena—namely, around the Baltic and to the north of the Black Sea—no non–Indo-European languages are attested. As regards the second hypothesis, there is once again a lack of archaeological evidence for the later arrival of speakers of non–Indo-European languages in the regions concerned. Clearly, there is a third possible hypothesis that has the distinction of being economical: this is the theory that all of the non–Indo-European languages, which are generally little known or undeciphered, are in fact Indo-European. The obscurity of the records lends itself to such a theory; the focus of almost exhaustive attempts at decipherment, each of these languages counts at least one linguist who has devoted him- or herself to its decryption (and many others who have refuted these efforts). Such is the case for Etruscan (even though this language is considered to be "agglutinating" in type), for the language written in the Cretan Linear A script, and even for "Tartessian," one of the Iberian languages.[54] Renfrew mentions in passing this

---

[53] See Chapter 11, pp. 242–243.
[54] For Etruscan, see Adrados, 1989; Sergent, 1995, pp. 49–50. For Linear A, see, for example, Owens, 1999. For Tartessian, Villar, 1990; Tovar, 1961; Sergent, 1995, pp. 147–148.

TURKEY 281

Indo-European theory in the case of Etruscan and Tartessian, and he himself attempted to tackle the problem of Minoan.[55]

Thus, in summary, this difficulty regarding the presence of non–Indo-European enclaves has not been meaningfully resolved: in other words, the model works except when it does not work. In short, it is not verifiable.

How can we rid ourselves of the initial brief?

The last two difficulties raised were rejected in advance by Colin Renfrew. These involve linguistic paleontological data and, more generally, the comparative study of myths, institutions, and vocabulary—none of the results of which are accepted by Renfrew. In fact, up until the present, all research on the original Homeland sought to make the observations regarding the "shared vocabulary" coincide with a particular geographical region and a particular archaeological culture. In a traditional approach, the locating of the homeland in a Mediterranean and relatively southern environment (Turkey and more generally the Near East) might also be founded on the existence of environmental data (flora, fauna, landscape, etc.) specific to this region. However, as has been noted for some time, none of the words in the shared vocabulary evokes the Mediterranean region. On the contrary, the etymology of the Greek work for "sea" (*thalassa*) is notoriously non–Indo-European, as are many Greek words referring to agriculture and plants.[56] Likewise, a significant number of plant names and terms for agricultural tools in Greek are not found in the shared vocabulary but are of Near Eastern origin, even though the Indo-Europeans are supposed to have initially passed through Greece. But since Renfrew denounced "the lure of the protolexicon"[57] from the outset, this objection does not bother him unduly.

The same applies, symmetrically, for words from the shared vocabulary pointing to a warlike, hierarchical society that had mastered the use of the horse and the chariot. Renfrew reminds us that things are not clear-cut. Supposed common terms for carts are relatively rare (Sanskrit *ratha*, "chariot," Latin *rota*, "cart," "wheel"), terms for most cart parts (apart from the yoke and axle) differ from one language to another and some of the shared technical terms referring to chariotry might only be due to the use of common metaphors to describe them.[58] Concerning the horse, the linguist Robert Coleman pointed out that several different roots existed depending on the language: moreover, nothing proves

[55] Renfrew, 1998.
[56] Haarmann, 1994, pp. 274–275.
[57] Renfrew, 1987 [1990], pp. 100–109.
[58] Renfrew, 1987, p. 86; Renfrew, 1989, p. 845; Coleman, R., 1988; Specht, 1944. See Chapter 14, pp. 309–311.

282   THIRD MOVEMENT (1945–THIRD MILLENNIUM)

that the animal designated by these terms was in fact a domesticated horse since residual wild horse populations seem to have been present in various parts of Europe and the Near East.[59] Thus, a preconceived vision of an original People as conquerors on horseback would only require a small amount of uncertain data concerning the horse and chariot in order to localize—in a circular argument— the original Cradle in the steppes, the region where this animal was supposedly first domesticated.

Similarly, in the space of ten pages, Colin Renfrew brushes aside the work of Georges Dumézil and Émile Benveniste; he points out that the structures revealed by Dumézil and Benveniste are simply general characteristics found in any hierarchical warrior society such as those whose vocabularies and mythologies they studied. In more concrete terms, while we can compare the following words meaning "king"—the Indian word *Rajah*, the Latin word *Rex*, and the Celtic word *Rix* (as in *Vercingétorix*)—nothing proves that the common root did not have a much more vague meaning originally; a root that may have undergone a subsequent evolution, but only in a few languages, to designate a royal function when such a function appeared in parallel in several European societies. Renfrew also reiterates criticisms made by anthropologist Jack Goody regarding the vocabulary of kinship which Benveniste interpreted as indicating a patrilineal society.[60]

Renfrew takes issue with Georges Dumézil on the basis that the trifunctional structure of Indo-European mythologies, with its tripartite division between king-priests, warriors, and workers, could be found in any hierarchical society, whether it be a chiefdom or a state.[61] To this effect, he cites the example of Japanese mythology, which had recently been compared by two of Dumézil's Japanese followers—Atsuhiko Yoshida and Taryô Obayashi—to Indo-European mythologies; this was a problem that I myself had already highlighted in 1980.[62] Nonetheless, Colin Renfrew has not sought to deal head on with Dumézil's findings, and, on this point, he might appear a little cavalier. He confines himself to directing the reader to two general summaries of Dumézil's work, one of which was published in the New Right's principal journal by an author sympathetic to this movement.[63] To discuss Indo-Europeanness on the basis of the structural correspondences revealed by Dumézil, as I propose to do,[64] and to deny any

---

[59] Renfrew, 1989, p. 845; Coleman (R.), 1988; Vörös, 1981; Uerpmann, 1990; Boessneck and Driesch, 1976; Levine, 2005. See Chapter 14, pp. 303–308.

[60] Goody, 1959; Renfrew, 1987, pp. 80 and 258.

[61] See Chapter 18, p. 404.

[62] Renfrew, 1987, p. 257; Yoshida, 1977, 1981; Demoule, 1980, p. 113. See Chapter 16, p. 371.

[63] Rivière, 1973; Littleton, 1973. Colin Renfrew, who certainly did not grasp the significance of it, allowed his name to feature on the list of the "scientific committee" of *Nouvelle École*.

[64] See Chapter 16, pp. 368–370.

reality to these correspondences in the name of the universality of ideologies, as Renfrew claims to do, represent two very different approaches.

However, it must be said that Colin Renfrew is not totally at ease and, in the end, admits that studies of vocabulary have some validity: "I do not doubt that a sensitive analysis and interpretation of the shared early vocabulary, insofar as it can be constructed, of very much the kind undertaken by Benveniste, can answer some of the relevant questions."[65]

An incomplete critical approach

In the end, reading Renfrew's book leaves the reader with the impression of a paradox. The author wished, in his turn, to offer a solution to a problem that has haunted Western human sciences for at least two centuries. The temptation to find a resolution was strong, but the solution was not particularly new. To do so, Renfrew, while sticking to the traditional formulation of the question (i.e., to identify the *Urheimat*, where the *Urvolk* spoke the *Ursprache*), opted to free himself from most of the constraints imposed by the usual mission statement— and in particular data gleaned from the fields of vocabulary and mythology. His hypothesis therefore, with so few constraints, becomes unverifiable—or, in epistemological terms, is not "falsifiable"; in other words we have no way of proving that it is potentially false. In the best case, we could concede "why not?" But we could just as well ask "why?" Besides, a whole body of evidence seems to contradict the Near Eastern hypothesis. It is therefore regrettable that Renfrew's critical impetus did not lead him to tackle the very heart of the model; namely, the simplistic model of a centrifugal diffusion from a single point of origin. This is precisely the direction in which his previous works, which were anti-diffusionist and respectful of the rules of validation, could have led him. This is no doubt why, symmetrically and incidentally, he feels entitled to carica- ture my own approach: "And very few indeed would agree with the French ar- chaeologist, Jean-Paul Demoule, that there really is no Indo-European language group at all, or that the similarities observed are unimportant, insignificant and fortuitous."[66]

In this regard, his most recent article, already mentioned above,[67] expresses a form of regret concerning the simplistic and diffusionist nature of his hypoth- esis. Indeed, he attempts to introduce two elements of complexity into his orig- inal theory. The first is a concession to the archaeology of the English-speaking

---

[65] Renfrew, 1987 [1990], p. 308.
[66] Renfrew, 1987, p. 42; 1990 (French translation), p. 59.
[67] Renfrew, 1999.

284 THIRD MOVEMENT (1945–THIRD MILLENNIUM)

world, which traditionally tends to be reticent toward diffusionism. In the face of all evidence to the contrary, certain archaeologists have minimized the importance of the movement of people in the diffusion of agriculture, focusing instead on simple mechanisms of contact and borrowing.[68] Observation of the material culture, however, allows us to trace this migratory movement from Anatolia all the way to northwestern Europe. Moreover, the demographical disproportion evident between the small groups of indigenous hunter-gatherers and the colonizing population could only result in the absorption of the former by the latter, even though this phenomenon was slower in marginal areas. Taking up a thesis originally forwarded by Marek Zvelebil,[69] Colin Renfrew thus concedes that hunter-gatherers on the northern fringes of Europe may have borrowed the language of the agriculturalists at the same time that they borrowed their way of life, even though, in the absence of hard evidence, he feels that this remains an intuition rather than a proven fact: "I now feel that the position as stated by Zvelebil . . . was broadly correct."[70]

The second element of complexity, already mentioned above, is the addition of an element of convergence—namely, the notion of *Sprachbund*—within a model of pure divergence. This hypothetical *Sprachbund* is an attempt to respond to one of the objections raised above: the linear model for the diffusion of Neolithic colonization does not correspond to any of the family trees (which are sometimes contradictory) proposed by linguists to account for the affinities observed between the various Indo-European languages. According to this new theory, linguistic diffusion would have occurred in two phases: the first accompanying the original diffusion of agriculture, and the second stemming from the Balkanic *Sprachbund*, which would have resulted from local interactions over the course of the two millennia of the late Neolithic and the Chalcolithic (between 5000 and 3000 BCE). Here again the question is not "Why not?," because in this area many hypotheses are admissible. But, if one intends to play by the rules of demonstrability, the question is "Why?" Furthermore, throughout his paper, Renfrew takes the precaution of using the conditional tense liberally: the word "perhaps" occurs six times in eighteen lines.[71]

Nonetheless, the considerable media attention that Renfrew's hypothesis received and his association with the proponents of the Great Family Tree of languages and genes means that this is still the dominant theory in the English-speaking media. In 1993, the *Times Atlas of World History* presented it as a given, to the point that archaeologist James Mallory, a supporter of the steppic

---

[68] For example, Dennell, 1983; Zvelebil, 1986; Zvelebil et al., 1997.
[69] Zvelebil and Zvelebil, 1990; Zvelebil, 1995.
[70] Renfrew, 1999, p. 259.
[71] Renfrew, 1999, p. 275.

hypothesis, regarded his own cause as provisionally lost, at least in terms of media coverage.[72]

In reality, among strict Indo-Europeanists, be they archaeologists or linguists, or at least among those who believe that it is possible to localize an "original Cradle" (and even though the situation differs depending on the scientific traditions of each country), the steppic theory remains predominant. We will now examine this theory in greater detail.

[72] Mallory and Adams, 1997, p. 307.

14

Did the Indo-Europeans really come from the Black Sea Steppes?

Des steppes aux océans (From the Steppes to the Oceans) is the title of the 1986 book which André Martinet, one of the principal French linguists of his generation, devoted to the Indo-European issue, with its cover graced by a dramatic photo of galloping horses. This image haunts the vision of many Indo-Europeanists to such an extent that we might think that it has always been the case. Was it not Leibniz who first hypothesized that the original People rode forth from the Black Sea steppes? However, the horses of the Indo-European chieftains have, in fact, been galloping across these steppes for less than a century! Throughout most of the nineteenth century, the original People, with their peace-loving bucolic civilization, as described by Adolphe Pictet, were believed to have hailed from distant Asia. As archaeologist Alexandre Bertrand explained to the learned fellows of the Société d'Anthropologie de Paris, the arrival of the Indo-Europeans in Europe coincided with the arrival of civilization itself (with its agriculture, animal husbandry, and metallurgy). But, toward the end of the nineteenth century, as the storm clouds of war were beginning to gather and as colonial conquests were turning ever more bloody, "noble savages" mutated into "uncouth barbarians." The ancient world was no longer the only source feeding the imagination: field ethnography and field archaeology were now providing more concrete and less idealistic raw materials. The original "cradle" slowly made its way back to Europe via the steppes of Central Europe and then those of the Ukraine; this tendency culminated with radical Germanomaniacs, including Pösche, Penka, Much, Hirt, and Kossinna, locating the Indo-Germans in Germania.

A (very) old hypothesis

German linguist Otto Schrader contributed the founding arguments of the steppic theory, a "new theory" applauded by Salomon Reinach in 1892. The entire theory rested on linguistic paleontology and a line of argument that we have already qualified as "the linguistics of absence."[1] The rarity of shared terms to designate mountains, agricultural activities, and tree species was taken to

---

[1] See Chapter 3, pp. 53–54.

THE BLACK SEA STEPPES?   287

indicate that the original People were pastoral nomads who roamed around a treeless landscape, while all other possible counterexamples (fish, the bear, salt, etc.) were disregarded under various pretexts. For the rest, Schrader, whose vast erudition and scientific honesty are unquestionable, utilized the spell-like effect of the illustrations in his *Reallexikon*, among which images relating to the archaeology of the Scythians and the ethnology of the Slavs of Russia and the Ukraine feature prominently.[2]

The methodological inconsistency of Schrader's demonstration, which as yet could not boast any archaeological proofs, and his circular reasoning would for a long time inextricably tie the Indo-Europeans to the Pontic Steppes. This was the vision held by Meillet, Benveniste, and Dumézil, when, in a roundabout way, they evoke the ancient incursions by conquering Indo-Europeans on horseback—even though Benveniste was the only one of the three to specifically refer to the Pontic Steppes.[3] It was also the vision underlying the first excavations carried out by Russian archaeologists on the Ukrainian steppes at the end of the nineteenth century. These excavations revealed earthen burial mounds (*Kurgans*), also known as ochre graves because the deceased were often sprinkled with this material. Tsarist officer Vasily Gorodtsov (who later joined the ranks of the revolution before being relieved of his functions and then rehabilitated) was the first to propose a chronology for these burials. The discoveries provided archaeological support for the steppic theory. During the interwar years, the theory, which was less popular in Germany than elsewhere, gained the support of several British scholars including John Myres, Alfred Haddon, Harold Peake, Herbert Fleure, and, with some hesitation, Gordon Childe.[4] The latter provides a pretty good overview of the state of archaeological knowledge concerning the issue at the time; in contrast, the linguistic arguments had not evolved at all since Schrader's day. The tombs were found to contain horse bones as well as copper objects and miniature chariots modeled in clay. The paucity of the funerary goods was taken to indicate a nomadic lifestyle, while their uniformity suggested common beliefs and perhaps even a common language. Despite the new archaeological data, the case remained weak, particularly because it lacked evidence for diffusion from this supposed homeland. There was, of course, the famous corded ware with its cord-impressed goblets found from Scandinavia to Poland and even in Ukraine (where they were sometimes discovered in ochre graves). But many archaeologists at the time believed that they had diffused from west to east rather than the reverse.

[2] Reinach, 1892, p. 121; Schrader, 1907; Schrader and Nehring, 1917–1929.
[3] See Chapter 5, pp. 108–110.
[4] Childe, 1926, pp. 183–200. See Chapter 7, pp. 151–155.

288 THIRD MOVEMENT (1945–THIRD MILLENNIUM)

Today, the case put forward by linguistic paleontology has not evolved greatly since Schrader. It is still founded on the horse and chariot since most of the other cultural characteristics, including copper-working, are encountered in numerous areas across Eurasia. It is this weakness in the linguistic foundations of the steppic hypothesis that allowed Colin Renfrew to brush it aside in favor of the Near Eastern hypothesis. As regards the archaeological arguments, the mass of available data has undoubtedly increased a hundredfold over the past century. The amount of information on the various cultural groups that succeeded each other from the fourth millennium onward in the Pontic Steppes is now considerable. But the demonstration of the presumed Indo-Europeanness of some of these groups is no further advanced than it was in Schrader's day (which is why Childe eventually abandoned the hypothesis). The hypothesis of widespread migrations from this region has, however, been reactivated by recent genetic research (since 2015) even though many issues remain, in particular regarding the interpretive models used.

From Vilnius to Los Angeles

When they appeared, first discretely in the 1950s and 1960s and then with great impact from 1973 onward, the successive articles on the steppic theory by American archaeologist Marija Gimbutas claimed to develop a new theory—the elaboration of which had only been made possible by the flood of new research carried out in these regions.

The daughter of two medical doctors, Marija Gimbutas was born in Lithuania in 1921 and completed the essentials of her archaeological studies in that country which, in the realm of science, was marked by a strong Germanic tradition and, more generally, by a crisis of national and cultural identity in the face of German, Russian, and Polish secular imperialism. Integrated with Poland and then occupied by Russia, Lithuania, like both other Baltic states, experienced its first taste of modern independence in 1919, following the Treaty of Versailles, although a portion of its territory was annexed by Poland. In 1940, the country was occupied by the USSR until it was invaded by Germany in June 1941. It was then placed under the protectorate of the Third Reich, which succeeded, thanks to effective local collaboration, in implementing its policy of extermination of the Jews. Even today, the official history of Lithuania, as presented in textbooks and museums, flirts with negationism.

In 1944, the Soviet Union once again entered Lithuanian territory, hot on the heels of the German army. Stalin was determined to recover the old possessions of the Russian Empire and so Lithuania became one of the Soviet Socialist Republics. Under a false identity, Marija Gimbutas and her husband

THE BLACK SEA STEPPES?   289

emigrated to Austria. In Vienna, she studied under Oswald Menghin, a proponent of Kossinna's theory, and under the latter's assistant, Christian Peschek; she also attended lectures given by Leonhard Franz in Innsbruck. But it was not long before the Red Army also entered Austria. Menghin, who had been Minister of Education, was interned in an American camp before going into exile in Argentina where he finished out his career.[5] Marija Gimbutas left for Tübingen, in Germany.[6] It was at the Institute for Prehistory in this city that she submitted a German translation of her doctoral thesis, which she had carried with her from Lithuania and which dealt with prehistoric tombs in that country. She defended it, in 1946, before Peter Goessler, a specialist in Roman archaeology who had been removed from his University position in 1934 by the Nazi regime. As she states in the preface, "the aim of the work is to provide data regarding the distribution and historical development of the Baltic tribe and their funerary cult in Lithuania."

She followed further courses at Tübingen, Munich, and Heidelberg before emigrating to the United States in 1949. Once there, she secured several temporary research and teaching positions, notably at Harvard, before securing a professorship in European archaeology in the Department of Classical Studies at the University of California, Los Angeles (UCLA) in 1963. This location was significant: from the mid-1960s, California witnessed the emergence of a well-known "cultural revolution" which was particularly marked by a feminist movement that would have direct impacts on Gimbutas's theories. Furthermore, she was based in a Department of Classics which was somewhat removed from another intellectual revolution of the time, the New Archaeology. The latter questioned traditional archaeological reasoning in favor of richer and better-argued models; this revolution was, however, confined to Departments of Anthropology—in other words, to Departments of Prehistory and Ethnology.

Because of her training, Marija Gimbutas's scientific career was shaped by the methods of reasoning and the focuses of interest that characterized German diffusionist archaeology in the first half of the twentieth century—not to mention the cultural ambiance of her native country (when I asked her once to translate the word "to bargain" in German, the language in which we used to communicate, she replied "*wie die Juden machen*"—literally, "as the Jews do"). To this was added a personal interest in history, ethnography, and the identity of Lithuania and of the Baltic peoples; during the war, between the ages of 21 and 23, she published a dozen articles on Lithuanian prehistory and the origin of the Balts,

[5] Kohl and Perez Gollan, 2002.
[6] See the interview with M. Gimbutas in *Los Angeles Times Magazine*, June 11, 1989 (cited in Poruciuc, 1995) and the CV published in her thesis (Gimbutas, 1946, pp. 233–234). I am greatly indebted to Manfred Eggert for sending me the latter document. The thesis was published under the name Marija Alseikaité-Gimbutiené, Alseika being her father's name. See also Polomé, 1987a.

290   THIRD MOVEMENT (1945–THIRD MILLENNIUM)

and, throughout her life, she maintained a deep interest in Baltic folklore. Her knowledge of Eastern European languages, particularly Russian, meant that she rapidly became an essential intermediary (especially since Childe, who formerly played this role, had died in 1957) between the abundant archaeological literature of the USSR and the English-speaking academic world. In particular, in the 1950s and 1960s, she published two syntheses, respectively dealing with the Neolithic and Chalcolithic, and then the Bronze Age, of Eastern Europe[7] as well as more popular works on the Balts and Slavs.[8]

Initial cautiousness

Her first scientific article in a Western language, published in 1952, carries the imprint of these intellectual origins. It deals with the primitive homeland of the Indo-Europeans[9] and, more precisely, that of the Indo-Europeans of Northern Europe, which include the Balts. She points out that the Balts should be distinguished from the Slavs (even though the two groups are linguistically close to each other) and that their "original territory" was once much more extensive. More generally, she wonders about the existence of a single cradle for all of the Indo-European peoples, and, in this regard, she adopts a skeptical, or even sarcastic, position: "It has become almost a tradition to look for unknown origins in the 'mysterious' steppes of South Russia."[10] While she accepted that the archaeological cultures of these steppes could have given rise to particular Indo-European groups and probably to the propagators of eastern Indo-European languages (i.e., Indo-Iranian languages), she was loath to generalize. At a time when, just before the invention of radiocarbon dating, archaeologists were still placing the beginning of the Neolithic in the third millennium BCE, she was able to assert that "The cultures in South Russia of the second millennium B.C. are not mother cultures of all later cultures which are attributed to the speakers of South, West and North 'Indo-European.'"[11]

Following in the footsteps of Max Ebert, whom she cites explicitly, and prefiguring the theses of Pedro Bosch Gimpera, Gimbutas believed that the origin of all the Indo-Europeans of Europe lay in the Linear Ceramic (or Danubian I) culture; in other words, in the earliest Neolithic of temperate Europe, which was itself, as she assumes on the basis of the work of others, of eastern origin: "The linguistic data rather coincide with the archaeological material of the 'Danubian

---

[7] Gimbutas, 1956, 1965a.
[8] Gimbutas, 1963a, 1971.
[9] Gimbutas, 1952.
[10] Ibid., p. 604.
[11] Ibid.

THE BLACK SEA STEPPES? 291

I' economy, based on the cultivation of barley, emmer wheat, beans, peas, lentils and flax."[12] She concludes,

> There is some evidence that the North "Indo-European" speakers developed from the Central European "Danubian" core, but there that the East "Indo-Europeans" also originated from Central Europe. Our ethnic group does not always impress its mark on the products of material culture. An attempt at the "reconstruction of the 'Indo-European' mother culture" by archaeological means is merely a theoretical matter; there are dialects in every stage of language and of culture and the wide "Indo-European" distribution shows that their original culture could not be restricted to a small area.[13]

Thus, in this first article, we are struck by Gimbutas's cautious methodology and her reference to Max Ebert. In fact, she has many reservations regarding the very idea of a "single unique cradle" and the possibilities offered by archaeology. Most of the time the term "Indo-European" is placed within quotation marks. She is also of the opinion that the Pontic Steppes only played a marginal role—although a little less marginal than for Ebert. She was also slow to assign a single point of origin to the Indo-Europeans, linking them instead to the entire process of neolithization in Europe. Ebert had taught archaeology in Riga after the First World War, in the early days of Latvian independence. It was also Ebert who grouped European Neolithic cultures under a single umbrella term, "Old European" (*Alteuropäisch*), which Gimbutas would subsequently adopt.

This measured and well-informed article contrasts with the author's subsequent publications. Having become familiar with developments in Soviet research carried out in the regions to the north of the Black Sea by the likes of Nikolay Merpert (whose chronological system she borrowed), Dmitri Telegin, and Valentin Danilenko, she would soon attribute a determining role to the North Pontic cultures. This was already the case in a lecture she presented to the International Congress of Ethnological Sciences held in Pennsylvania in 1956[14] and in another presented at a conference held Prague in 1959 on the subject of "Europe at the End of the Stone Age."[15] It was also the stance she took in her 1956 monograph on the Neolithic of Eastern Europe[16] and in her review of Pedro Bosch Gimpera's book on the Indo-Europeans, which was published, like her 1952 article, in *American Anthropologist*.[17]

---

[12] Ibid., pp. 606–607.
[13] Ibid., pp. 607–608.
[14] Gimbutas, 1960.
[15] Gimbutas, 1961.
[16] Gimbutas, 1956.
[17] Gimbutas, 1963b.

292   THIRD MOVEMENT (1945–THIRD MILLENNIUM)

This is why, toward the end of her life, when she revisited her 1952 article on the occasion of the publication of a collection of her Indo-Europeanist works, she did not hesitate to significantly amend the text.[18] The editors of the collection, published posthumously in 1997, noted that she was probably working on the article when she died because her notes concerning it were still incomplete.[19] Certain corrections were justified because the advent of radiocarbon dating in the meantime had pushed back the date of the European Neolithic and Chalcolithic by several millennia. But two passages are particularly revealing. In the first, that cited above, she removes the negative adverb to assert that "The cultures in South Russia of the second millennium B.C. *are* mother cultures of all later cultures which are attributed to the speakers of South, West and North 'Indo-European.'"[20] The passage regarding methodology, also cited above, in which she refers to the unlikelihood of a restricted original homeland, is now simply omitted.[21] Furthermore, on a more subtle level, the chronological corrections she makes are selective: in certain cases, she corrects the 1952 dates using absolute radiocarbon dates (the Chalcolithic now begins in the fifth millennium and no longer the second); in other instances she makes no corrections. Therefore, events that were placed in the second millennium in 1952, and which concerned the Late Neolithic and the splitting up of cultural groups belonging to the Danubian complex (according to the 1952 theory), are still placed in the second millennium in 1994 but now appear to relate to the end of the Chalcolithic and to the Bronze Age (in accordance with the 1994 theory).[22]

Thus, with a small number of corrections and a few non-corrections, Marija Gimbutas transforms an early article, which was originally hostile toward the steppic hypothesis and cautious, if not skeptical, toward the idea of an original People, into an article that is favorable to the steppic hypothesis and which even appears to lay the foundations of her subsequent work. While it is perfectly normal for a researcher's ideas to evolve and change over time as his or her knowledge develops, to intervene to this extent (and without declaring it) in one's own intellectual history is unusual and almost "Soviet" as a method.

The return of the steppes

Even in subsequent works, the system that Marija Gimbutas devised was still not established, in so far as the chronological revisions brought about by the

[18] Gimbutas, 1997, pp. 1–11.
[19] Ibid., p. xiii.
[20] Gimbutas, 1997, p. 3; emphasis added.
[21] Compare Gimbutas, 1952, pp. 607–608 and Gimbutas, 1997, p. 6.
[22] Gimbutas, 1997, pp. 5–7.

advent of radiocarbon dating in the 1950s had not yet been applied to full effect. While she now took the North Pontic cultures into account, she did not grant them a central role. It was the widespread Pit Grave culture, which she located to the east of the Lower Volga and in a large part of Central Asia, that became her "original Indo-European Homeland."[23] From its "cradle," this culture expanded, initially engulfing the entire North Pontic Steppes region and then, in a single migration, the rest of Europe; in particular, she attributed the Early Bronze Age destruction of the Early Helladic II culture in Greece and the razing of Troy II to this expansion.[24] This model was subsequently adjusted thanks in part to radiocarbon dating that extended the duration of the steppic Chalcolithic, but also more importantly thanks to the numerous excavations carried out in Ukraine, Southern Russia, and Central Asia by Soviet archaeologists during the 1950s and 1960s. Their results were gradually released into the public domain, for the most part through Russian and Ukrainian publications. At the same time, Gimbutas made several research trips to Eastern Europe. Gradually the emphasis shifted toward the North Pontic Steppes, but traces of her initial version of the steppic hypothesis would always remain: the original Homeland stays east of the Volga and north of the Caspian Sea, within the successive Samara (a tributary of the Volga) and the Khvalynsk cultures of the Chalcolithic, and the Pontic Steppes would only be "Indo-Europeanized" in a second phase. This is, therefore, a particular variation on the steppic theory, which in fact is not required by the overall model and which is not necessarily validated by the archaeological data, apart altogether from the Indo-European question.

From the 1970s onward, Marija Gimbutas's canonical model took its definitive shape (see Appendix 11). In fact, she never presented it in complete form within a general and coherent monograph but rather developed it over a dozen articles spread out over nearly four decades; these articles were in part intended for a wider audience and are somewhat repetitive, sometimes with amendments and insertions that are not always explicit. This desire to adjust her work intensified when, toward the end of her life, she undertook to group these articles together within a single volume.[25] Consequently, in the absence of a general synthesis, all we have is the result of successive sedimentations which tend to blur the details of the whole.

[23] Gimbutas, 1960, 1961, 1963b.
[24] See Chapter 15, pp. 320–327.
[25] Gimbutas, 1997.

294   THIRD MOVEMENT (1945–THIRD MILLENNIUM)

Feminism and invaders

Simple to understand, this diffusionist model differs little in its general princi-ples from that proposed by Schrader at the end of the nineteenth century and by Childe in 1926. It has simply been filled out with a considerable body of archae-ological data. But it does offer a degree of extra originality due to the Californian context mentioned above.

At the beginning of the 1970s, Indo-European studies, even in the United States, still tended to bear the stigma of their embarrassing recent past. When Marija Gimbutas participated in the founding of the *Journal of Indo-European Studies* in 1973, its editor was Roger Pearson who, in 1957, had founded an ex-treme right-wing racist movement known as the Northern League dedicated to the exaltation of the "Aryan race." Despite Pearson's involvement, which lasted a number of years, this journal remained essentially apolitical and rapidly re-ceived scientific recognition.[26] At the same time, Marija Gimbutas also accepted an invitation to be a member of the "sponsoring committee" of *Nouvelle École*, the main journal of the French Nouvelle Droite, whose favorite preoccupations include the quest for a supposed glorious Indo-European past.[27] In the intellec-tual context of Californian campuses in the 1970s, the development of theses on the origins of the Indo-Europeans was not exactly in keeping with the times. In spite of this, Marija Gimbutas took the traditional image of the conquering, warlike, primitive Indo-Europeans literally and even magnified it. But, instead of glorifying this ideology, as was the fashion up until then, she chose to con-trast it, in a rather simplistic duality, with that of the conquered societies, which were assumed to be peace-loving and feminist.[28] On the one side, she presents a sedentary farming society living in extensive settlements, with an "egalitarian, matrilineal" structure and an ideology based on the "peaceful, art-lover, woman creatress" (this is the "Old Europe"). On the other, she describes a horse-borne pastoral society, with small villages composed of rudimentary, semi-buried houses, where a "patriarchal patrilocal" system and a "warlike, man creator" ide-ology prevail.

Marija Gimbutas had a particular interest in Neolithic religions. She listed and classified the clay and stone figurines that are found in considerable numbers in the Neolithic of South Eastern Europe, and she endeavored, by identifying their recurrent features, to recreate a sort of prehistoric pantheon centered on the figure of the Mother Goddess.[29] The idea was not new. Already in the nineteenth century, the abundance of so-called Venus figurines within the art

[26] See Chapter 9, pp. 218–219.
[27] See Chapter 9, pp. 201–202.
[28] Gimbutas, 1997, table 3; 1990, tables 1 and 2; Anthony, 1996.
[29] Gimbutas, 1974, 1989 [2005, French translation].

of the Paleolithic and Neolithic had led to the hypothesis that ancient religions worshipped a great fertility goddess. It was even suggested, following the works of Swiss scholar Bachofen, that these societies lived under the political regime of the original matriarchy.[30] Mention was also made of the importance of female deities in eastern pantheons, such as Isis in Egypt and Ishtar in the Near East, as well as of certain supposedly archaic aspects of the Greek religion linked to the cult of Demeter, the Earth Mother, who was celebrated in secret rituals on the occasion of the Eleusinian Mysteries. Feminine religion and the original matriarchal society were common themes in Europe at the end of the nineteenth century and are undeniably the products of the fantasies of male scholars who described them in detail in the great evolutionary narratives that so typify the period. Childe himself refers to the "feminine conservatism" of the Neolithic Danubian farmers, which excluded them from being considered as the original Indo-European People.[31] Ever since Marx and Engels, we encounter the persistent notion that an agriculture-orientated matriarchy had been replaced by a pastoral patriarchy. This theme is often present in the works of Eastern European archaeologists eager to demonstrate their Marxist orthodoxy.[32]

Having fallen into obscurity for some time, the notion of a primitive matriarchy resurfaced in the 1960s and 1970s as part of the rise of American feminist movements that would eventually constitute one of the pillars of "political correctness." The movements' leaders would gradually sketch the outline of an ideal original society, in a time when "God was a woman" and peace and love ruled the earth.[33] Males subsequently seized power and with them came violence, inequality, and war. These political movements had their merits. Apart from the denunciation of violent or ordinary oppression of women in our contemporary societies, they also triggered, within human sciences, and particularly within ethnology and archaeology, the development of long-neglected research into the role of women in societies; thus we see the emergence of *gender archaeology* (i.e., the archaeology of the difference between the sexes).[34]

However, as regards the primitive matriarchy, in reality, this approach simply involved appropriation of a male fantasy and flipping the scale of values. The idea of a great primitive Mother Goddess, a simple inversion of male monotheism, ignores the fact that monotheism itself is a very recent concept linked to the emergence of empires with a universal vocation, one which only appeared in the final centuries BCE. All traditional societies are polytheist. Finally, the reasoning employed by Marija Gimbutas, which, as we have seen, remained untouched

[30] Bachofen, 1861; Demoule, 1994; Testart, 2010.
[31] Childe, 1926, p. 140. See Chapter 7, p. 173.
[32] For example, Neustupný, 1967.
[33] For example, Stone, 1976.
[34] Coudart and Olivier, 1995; Coudart, 1999.

296 THIRD MOVEMENT (1945–THIRD MILLENNIUM)

by the methodological revolution of the American New Archaeology, is open to criticism: circular arguments, selection of specific elements to support her theses, etc. From this point of view, it is surprising, though understandable, that, in 2005, the French publishing house Des Femmes translated and published her 1989 book, *The Language of the Goddess* (*Le Langage de la Déesse*).

As regards social organization, there is no historical, ethnological, or archaeological evidence to support the notion that matriarchal societies (i.e., societies in which political power was exclusively held by women) ever existed. Male domination, to various degrees, appears to be a universal fact. This does not preclude the possibility that a couple might reside in the wife's home (matri- or uxorilocality) or that a name, or even possessions, might be transmitted through the female line (matrilineality). As for the abundance of female depictions, often with exaggerated sexual traits, in pre- and proto-historic art, it has nothing to do with female power but simply testifies to the importance of the female principle, or even of sexuality considered from a male point of view, in these societies.[35] Societies that abundantly depict women are not necessarily those that oppress them the least—on the contrary. To be more precise, there are no indications that the earliest Neolithic societies of Europe and the Near East were ever characterized by "the peaceful creativity of women"—in fact they also yield traces of violence, as, for example, in several Linear Ceramic villages in Germany.[36] Furthermore, the Chalcolithic societies that were supposedly destroyed by Indo-European warriors were, themselves, highly stratified, with the richest burials being those of men, as can be seen, for example, at Varna in Bulgaria. Nothing in the material found in the earliest Neolithic tombs supports the notion that women had a special status. And while female representations largely predominate in this period, male depictions and phallic representations also exist.

Nevertheless, her theses earned Marija Gimbutas considerable popularity among American feminist movements, for whom she became a leading icon in the 1980s and 1990s.[37] Within this context, she took part in numerous meetings, debates, and interviews, and some of the ceremonies that took place on the occasion of her death in 1994 had a distinctly New Age flavor.

A new demonstration?

Ultimately, in the same way that her "feminism" perpetuates the evolutionist tradition of the nineteenth century, her model of the process of Indo-Europeanization

---

[35] Demoule, 2007b; Testart, 2010.
[36] Wahl and Strien, 2007; Boulestin et al., 2009.
[37] Anthony, 1996.

THE BLACK SEA STEPPES? 297

explicitly reiterates the invasion thesis. She makes reference to Antoine Meillet when she states that "the Indo-European speakers would have had to be ruled by a powerful aristocracy."[38] The "seizing of control" over two-thirds of Europe by the people of the *Kurgans* allows archaeologists to observe a "process of hybridization," with "degeneration and a gradual disappearance of local elements."[39] The shared vocabulary supposedly confirms this interpretation.

> The Kurgan elements fully correspond with the early stratum of Indo-European words concerning social structure, pattern of habitation, architecture (small rectangular timber houses), economy (predominantly stock breeding, farming on a small scale), and religion (horse sacrifice, sun symbolism, etc.). None of the cultures in the Balkans, in central and northern Europe, before the intrusion of the Kurgan peoples shows this correspondence. This is the basic argument against the assumption of the Tripolye, Danubian and Funnel-necked Beaker cultures being Indo-European.[40]

Marija Gimbutas's theses regarding the steppic origin of the Indo-Europeans have been developed further, and often in more detail, by her principal student, Irish archaeologist James Mallory.[41] They have also been taken up, sometimes in an even more simplified form, by other archaeologists including David Anthony in the United States and Kristian Kristiansen in Denmark.[42] Finally, more generally, they are in agreement with research carried out by a number of Eastern European archaeologists who, without making direct reference to the quest for an "original Indo-European People," focused on movements that appear to have caused upheavals on the Pontic Steppes during the fifth and fourth millennia BCE.[43] In any case, they could not have been unaware of this quest for the original Homeland, and it is obvious that this search has often shaped their thinking, with all the dangers of circular reasoning that this entails.

At this stage, it is pertinent to consider the case for the steppic hypothesis as a whole in terms of three questions:

1. Is the steppic theory unified, stable, and coherent?
2. What arguments, founded on texts and languages, might support the locating of the original "Indo-European Homeland" in the Pontic Steppes?

---

[38] Ibid., p. 829.
[39] Ibid., p. 827.
[40] Ibid., p. 827.
[41] Mallory, 1989; Mallory and Adams, 1997, 2006.
[42] Anthony, 1990, 1992, 2007.
[43] Telegin, 1973; Danilenko, 1974; Lichardus et al., 1985; Lichardus, 1991; Dodd-Opritescu, 1978; Morintz and Roman, 1968, 1973; Todorova, 1986.

298   THIRD MOVEMENT (1945–THIRD MILLENNIUM)

3. What archaeological evidence exists to prove that large-scale migratory movements might have gradually spread out from this supposed homeland across all of Europe and a part of Asia?

As we have seen earlier,[44] communities of hunter-gatherers living on the Pontic Steppes, between the Bug and the Volga managed to maintain their traditional way of life longer than anywhere else. Not only did these communities have access to the exceptional aquatic resources provided by the great rivers of Moldova and Ukraine, but the unfavorable nature of the steppic soils for traditional agriculture, as practiced by Balkan societies, significantly hampered the progression of the Neolithic colonization front in the region. Through gradual acculturation, these hunter-gatherers developed certain forms of animal husbandry and cultivation, but for a long time these activities remained secondary to hunting, fishing, and gathering. Horses were among the animals hunted.

Toward the middle of the fifth millennium BCE, in what is termed the Chalcolithic period, various forms of social hierarchy began to appear across most of Europe. The most spectacular examples undoubtedly occur within the context of the Balkan Neolithic on the shores of the Black Sea, where the Gumelniţa-Karanovo VI culture in Bulgaria and Romania and the Cucuteni-Trypillia culture in Romania, Moldova, and Ukraine, are associated with large fortified settlements and high-status metalworking (see Appendix 12). This inequality also develops, although in a less ostentatious fashion, within the communities descended from the hunter-gatherers of the Pontic Steppes who were in direct contact with the Trypillia culture. These contacts are attested by the circulation of objects from one region to the other. This co-existence persisted for nearly 1,000 years, during which time steppic communities, from the Dnieper to the Volga, began to bury their dead in *kurgans*. Toward the middle of the fourth millennium BCE, the exceptional Balkan civilizations gradually gave way to somewhat less flamboyant cultures such as the Baden and Ezero cultures. A new culture, still associated with *kurgans*, spread throughout the steppes. Known as the Pit Grave culture, its presence is attested in an area stretching from deep in the Urals in the western part of Central Asia to the Danube. In western Ukraine and Moldova, it occupied the former territory of the Trypillia culture (see Appendix 13).

From this overall historical picture, a number of very different conclusions can be drawn.

The interpretation proposed by Marija Gimbutas, and by her disciples and followers, is both simple and radical. In the fifth millennium BCE, in the

---

[44] See Chapter 11, pp. 248–249; Appendices 9 and 12.

steppes and forest steppes to the north of the Caspian Sea, between the Volga and the Urals, hunter-gatherer societies gradually became neolithicized and began domesticating plants and animals. To the domesticated species usually encountered in Europe and the Near East (i.e., dog, pig, cattle, sheep, and goat), they added the horse, wild herds of which roamed the steppes. This mastery of the horse allowed them to undertake seasonal movements as part of a transhumance system, and it also permitted long-distance travel. The horse was exploited for its meat but also as a draft animal (this was the time when the first wheeled vehicles appeared) and as a mount (perforated antler objects have been interpreted as elements of horse bits). A certain degree of social hierarchy appears during the second half of the fifth millennium BCE, coinciding with the emergence of a patriarchal, warlike ideology. Certain important individuals were buried under small mounds, sometimes accompanied by symbols of status, such as stone bracelets or animal figurines, especially representations of horses. Ochre was frequently sprinkled over the deceased. The largest cemeteries are those of Khvalynsk and S'eszee. Hence the terms "Samara," "Khvalynsk-S'eszee," or "Kurgan I" cultures are used to refer to these communities, which are taken to represent the "original Indo-European People" within its "original Cradle"—a region stretching more than 100,000 square kilometers, an area about the size of Kentucky.

In a second phase, around the last quarter of the fifth millennium BCE, the Khvalynsk-S'eszee culture, equipped with its mastery of the horse and its warlike ideology, would have spread from its original cradle to occupy the entire region of the Pontic Steppes as far as the Dnieper, which delineates the eastern frontier of the Cucuteni-Trypillia culture of the Balkans. This corresponds to Gimbutas's "first wave" of invasion. It would have given rise to the North Pontic Chalcolithic, often referred to under the umbrella term "Sredny Stog culture." This culture is characterized by funerary rites that are comparable to those identified in the cemeteries of Khvalynsk-S'eszee and which differ quite markedly from those of the indigenous Dnieper-Donets culture. The latest phase of the Sredny Stog is sometimes referred to as "Kurgan II." From this much larger zone, a "second wave" of invasion supposedly spread toward both the east and west around 3500 BCE. To the east, on the frontier with the Caucasus, it gave rise to the prosperous Maykop culture, whose eponymous site has yielded a spectacular princely grave. To the west, the wave led to the complete destruction of the gumelniţa-Karanovo VI culture in Bulgaria and Southern Romania and to its replacement by a group with steppic affinities, namely the Cernavoda I culture. In Moldova and western Ukraine, a mixed culture appeared, termed the Usatovo or Kurgan III culture, following the supposed taking over of the Cucuteni-Trypillia culture by the Sredny Stog warrior aristocracy.

300 THIRD MOVEMENT (1945–THIRD MILLENNIUM)

This migratory movement would have led to the formation, around 3100 BCE, of an even more extensive cultural entity which now spread from the Caucasus to the mouth of the Danube and which is known as the Pit Grave (Yamnaya) culture or Kurgan IV (see Appendix 13). Springing from this culture, Gimbutas envisaged a "third wave" of migrations that would eventually propagate the Indo-European culture throughout Europe and the Near East. In Central Europe, this would correspond to the Baden culture and in Northern Europe to the Corded Ware culture. Thus, little by little, all of Europe would find itself "kurganized," to use a term coined by Marija Gimbutas. Toward the east (i.e., toward Central Asia), the Pit Grave culture would give rise to the Afanasievo culture in the third millennium BCE, which would in turn lead to the Andronovo culture at the beginning of the second millennium BCE. The latter was supposedly the source of the Indo-Iranian migrations which carried the Indo-European languages into Pakistan and Northern India, thus causing the destruction of the Indus Civilization (this is the so-called *arrival of the Aryans*), as well as into Iran and neighboring regions.

Colin Renfrew's interpretation, which we examined in the preceding chapter, is radically opposed to that of Marija Gimbutas and her followers. According to him, there were never any migratory movements from the steppes—even though he partly revised this opinion at a recent conference.[45] The Neolithic in these regions would, instead, have been the consequence of the continuation of the wave of agricultural colonization emanating from the Balkan Peninsula and its adaptation to a different environment. The domestication of the horse for the purpose of riding was a much later phenomenon, as was the development of the war chariot. As for the presence of Indo-Iranian languages in Asia, Renfrew proposes two possible scenarios[46]: one that took place in the Early Neolithic as part of a general wave of colonization from the original Anatolian zone; or a second that took place in the Chalcolithic, consisting of a warrior migration that indeed originated from the steppes, but only after this region had already been Indo-Europeanized via the Balkan Peninsula.

Clearly there is a middle ground between these two hypotheses (i.e., those of Gimbutas and Renfrew) which would, for example, accept the possibility of migratory movements emanating from the steppes, but which would limit their impact and extent and not necessarily tie them to a hypothetical single original homeland. In this case, perhaps we could envisage models that are much more complex and elaborate than simple invasions.

---

[45] Renfrew, 2017.
[46] Renfrew, 1987, pp. 178–210, 1990, pp. 213–249.

A unified and coherent theory?

Maria Gimbutas's theory appeared in three successive forms. The first version, presented in 1952, is explicitly derived from the theses postulated by Max Ebert: the original Indo-European people has no connection with the "mysterious" Russian Steppes and must be identified with the Neolithic cultures of the Balkans and Central Europe. In the second version, dating to 1960–1963, she located the original Homeland in the steppes and more specifically the steppes in the east of the region between the Don and Volga Rivers, but at this stage she only envisaged a single migratory wave, corresponding to the Pit Grave culture. From the 1970s onward, she developed the hypothesis of three successive waves. In fact, in a less quoted 1961article, which does not feature in her collected works (1997), she appropriates the four-period chronology that had just been formulated by a young Soviet archaeologist, Nikolay Merpert (died 2012), for the Chalcolithic cultures of the steppes.[47] These correspond to the four "Kurgan" periods of her system, the last three of which each gave rise to a "wave" of expansion. In fact, Merpert's chronology was modified soon after and became much more complex as the body of available data grew; other Soviet archaeologists proposed alternative systems.

From its beginnings, the theory maintained both the idea of an original Homeland located east of the Don River and of a four-period chronology. However, she gradually became less assertive regarding the movement of the Kurgan culture toward territories west of the Don. In 1963, she claimed that the "long-lasting North Pontic culture [i.e., west of the Don] was the first victim of the invasion of the eastern steppes people."[48] But later on, this first invasion was not included as one of the three successive "waves." In 1979, Gimbutas even refers to the "horse-riding people of Khvalynsk-Sredny Stog II," thereby merging these two regions. In 1989, James Mallory, though a disciple of Gimbutas, was even more cautious: "We are still far from understanding precisely why there should have developed such a broad band of similar cultures across the Pontic-Caspian during the Early Eneolithic."[49] He simply attributes the theory of a potential anteriority of the Caspian zone over the Pontic zone to a Soviet archaeologist, Igor Vasiliev, even though it was, in fact, Marija Gimbutas's initial hypothesis.

From one article to another, the chronology and the extents of the three "waves" are plagued by the same lack of precision—admittedly, this is in part due to the inaccuracy of the chronology of the Neolithic cultures in these regions as well as that of radiocarbon dating. From this point of view, our summary of the

---

[47] Gimbutas, 1961; Merpert, 1961.
[48] Gimbutas, 1963b, p. 821. See also Gimbutas, 1965b, table 4, p. 494.
[49] Mallory, 1989, p. 210 [1997, p. 235].

302   THIRD MOVEMENT (1945–THIRD MILLENNIUM)

three-wave theory corresponds to an average view. The insertion, for example, of the postulated Cernavoda I steppic group is not always clear. But, in particular, the geographical limits of the impacts of each wave fluctuate. Sometimes, but not always, the first wave encompasses the Rössen culture in Germany, thus virtually reaching the Rhine Valley.[50] The Chalcolithic Funnel Beaker culture (*Trichterbecherkultur*, or TRBK) of Scandinavia is sometimes excluded from the zone of "kurganization" or sometimes considered as "kurganized." This is because the processes triggered by the "waves" are, as Gimbutas herself admits, very varied. They may involve mass migration but also "infiltrations" by small groups of mounted warriors or even simple "influences."

It is all of these phenomena, which are not always explicit, that are grouped together under the terms "Kurgan tradition" or "kurganization," the definition of which is broad.

> "Kurgan tradition" is defined as collective socio-economic and ideological features observable over time and space. This tradition—characterized by a pastoral economy, an agnatically-linked hierarchical social structure, seasonal settlements, small, subterranean dwellings and larger chieftain's houses, diagnostic burial rites including human and animal sacrifices and symbolic system with the sun as a dominant motif can be traced through the millennia to each geographical region the Kurgan people settled or "Kurganized" the local population.[51]

In fact, the definition is so broad that, for each of these traits, we could identify evidence significantly predating the supposed Kurgan expansion as well as counterexamples within the Kurgan space itself. James Mallory subsequently recognized this fact, admitting both that the three-wave theory was far too simple and that the definition of the "Kurgan tradition" was far too loose.[52]

Ultimately, Marija Gimbutas's three-wave theory remains, for want of an overall synthesis, incomplete and lacking in coherence, and, furthermore, apart from the general Schraderian paradigm, there is no precise agreement regarding steppic expansion. James Mallory is less detailed than Marija Gimbutas in his 1989 book and considerably more reserved, paradoxically, in the *Encyclopedia of Indo-European Culture*, which he co-edited in 1997.[53] American archaeologist David Anthony, for his part, simplifies the model and only retains the last "wave" (i.e., the wave linked to the Pit Grave culture [*Jamnaja kultura*]), which seems to be backed up by genetics for want of analyses encompassing all of the

---

[50]   Compare, for example, Gimbutas, 1997, fig. 15, p. 217 (= 1977) and table 1, p. 305 (= 1985).
[51]   Gimbutas, 1997, p. 197 (= Gimbutas, 1977).
[52]   Article on "Kurgan tradition," in Mallory and Adams, 1997, pp. 338–341.
[53]   Mallory, 1989 [1997]; Mallory and Adams, 1997.

steppic cultures.[54] As for archaeologists specialized in the Chalcolithic of Eastern Europe, they also have different points of view but these are based on concrete and accurate knowledge of archaeological data, which we will examine later on.

The horse, of course . . .

Which components of the reconstructed Indo-European proto-culture can be used as evidence of a steppic location? The shared vocabulary is littered with innumerable internal incoherencies which have been abundantly highlighted elsewhere in this book.[55] It is on these grounds that Colin Renfrew, among others, has dismissed linguistic paleontology as an effective method. However, if we decide to apply it, we are forced to recognize that most of the cultural and natural facts within the shared vocabulary can be applied to any of the Neolithic or Chalcolithic cultures of Europe, or even of part of Asia (see Appendix 5). Nevertheless, two arguments are generally singled out by the proponents of the steppic theory: the case of the horse and that of the chariot. The domesticated horse, on the one hand, and the chariot on the other, are supposedly well-attested in the shared vocabulary and are particularly valorized in the earliest Indo-European mythologies, where the sacrifice of a horse is the ultimate royal sacrifice.[56] Georges Dumézil himself stated the following with regard to the original Indo-Europeans: "For some unknown reason, thanks to the supremacy conferred on them by the war horse and the two-wheeled chariot, they spread out in all directions in successive waves, until their reserves ran out."[57]

The first archaeological evidence for the domesticated horse and for the chariot should therefore be found in the Pontic Steppes in the fifth millennium BCE. This is the linguistic foundation stone on which the steppic theory rests; other elements (such as the words for sea, mountain, salmon, certain trees, etc.) are far more general—not to mention the contradictory evidence such as the bear, the root for which, *rkPo-s, is present in seven, or perhaps eight, of the main Indo-European linguistic families, while the animal itself is conspicuously absent from the steppes. We are also dealing with the very essence of the traditional representation of Indo-Europeans as warriors surging forth from the steppes on their horses and war chariots. At the beginning of the chapter, we mentioned André Martinet's 1986 book and its cover image. With all due respect to the

---

[54] Anthony, 1986, 1990, 1992, 1994, 2007, etc.
[55] See Chapter 18, pp. 399–402.
[56] Negelein, 1903; Benveniste, 1939; Maringer, 1981; Dumézil, 1966, 1975, pp. 145–156, 177–219; Puhvel, 1970, 1987, pp. 270–276; Sergent, 1995, pp. 363–365; Polomé, 1994a, 1994b.
[57] Dumézil, 1987, p. 110.

304   THIRD MOVEMENT (1945–THIRD MILLENNIUM)

latter,[58] we could also cite the enthusiasm of Nazi raciologist Hans Günther: "In the joy for the nobly tamed horse is expressed something of the spiritual essence of the true Indo-European."[59]

The most common root for the horse is certainly found in a significant number of Indo-European languages: Latin *equus*, Sanskrit *asva*, Gaulish *epo-*, Tocharian *yakwe*, Old English *eoh*, etc., all of these words being derived from a reconstructed root **ekwo-* or **ekuo-*. This root is so well-attested, and has been for so long, that it was at the origin of Schleicher's famous fable, the first text written in reconstructed Proto-Indo-European, entitled "The sheep and the horses" (at the time Schleicher had reconstructed a root **akvas*, closer to Sanskrit), which incidentally deals with the domestication of the horse.[60] Linguists often consider this root to be recent; they sometimes compare it to an adjective meaning "fast."[61] However, the Greek *hippos* is considered to be irregular relative to the series, while the root is lacking in Armenian, Albanian, and Slavic, and its presence is debated in the case of Hittite. Its absence in Slavic is all the more surprising since the historical "cradle" of the Slavs is often said to be located in the North Pontic Steppes, or close by, precisely where the earliest domestication of the horse is reputed to have occurred.

In fact, there are four other different roots in Indo-European languages to designate the horse[62]: the root **marko-* attested in Celtic and Germanic (e.g., mare in English); the root **kurs-*, which we find in the English word horse; the root **her-*, present in Lithuanian *arklys*; and finally the word *koni*, which designates the horse in most Slavic languages. To these can be added a number of more recent innovations: the word *alogo* in Modern Greek; the Latin word *caballus* (which gives *cheval* in French and *cavallo* in Spanish), the origin of which is believed to derive either from a non–Indo-European Balkan substrate, a borrowing from Gaulish, or a Pan-European ethnonym[63]; the German *Pferd*, which derives from the Late Latin *para-veredus*, the first term being from Greek and the second borrowed from Gaulish; and the Russian *losad*, supposedly borrowed from Turkish. There are also a number of specific words in the various languages designating the mare and the foal. Finally, the root **ekwo* can also be found in the Finno-Ugric languages (where it is considered to be a borrowing from the Indo-European languages) and possibly in the Semitic and Caucasian languages; similarly, the root **marko-* has been likened to words designating the horse in Mongolian, Tungusic, Korean, Japanese, Chinese, and even Tamil.[64] In

---

[58] On Martinet and his vision of a "Jewish lobby" and a shared "Jewish cultural legacy" in linguistics, see Olender, 2009, pp. 78–79.
[59] Günther, 1934, p. 29 (cited in Römer, 1985, p. 76).
[60] Schleicher, 1868. See chapter 2, p. 27.
[61] Hamp, 1990; Meid, 1994; Zimmer, 1994; Raulwing, 2000.
[62] Coleman, R., 1988, p. 450.
[63] Ernout and Meillet, 1939, p. 124.
[64] Gamkrelidze, 1994, pp. 39, 41.

THE BLACK SEA STEPPES? 305

summary: the etymological unity and specificity of the Indo-European for horse are not as obvious as might seem.

In addition, the widespread evidence for the root *ekwo- does not imply that it designated an animal that was already domesticated. After all, the root *ulkuo- designates the wolf in most Indo-European languages and in a form that is more regular than the root for horse. It can be counterargued that while the wolf was widespread throughout Eurasia, wild horses would only have existed in the Eurasian steppes and that the oldest center of domestication would be these very Pontic Steppes. This thesis was extensively developed in the 1970 and 1980s by Hungarian archaeologist and zoologist Sándor Bökönyi[65] and Soviet zoologist Valentina Bibikova.[66] From the beginning of the Neolithic, the Pontic Steppes would have witnessed the development of autonomous forms of domestication of local species (e.g., pigs and cattle) by the Bug-Dniester and Dnieper-Donets cultures. Then, during the Chalcolithic, the Sredny Stog culture would have domesticated the horse, which existed in large wild herds that roamed the treeless landscape. The settlement of Deriivka (Dereivka) and its cemetery have yielded spectacular evidence for this activity: two-thirds of the bones found on the site belong to horses, all of which were domesticated; perforated pieces of red deer antler have been interpreted as cheek-pieces which held the bit on either side of a horse's mouth and served to attach the reins; finally, traces have been found of rituals involving horses. More generally, the animal's ideological significance manifests itself throughout the Pontic Steppes through representations on bone plaques (e.g., from the cemetery of Khvalynsk) or in the form of stone objects, resembling axes, in the shape of horses' heads and usually described as "scepters" in archaeological literature.

All the evidence seemed, therefore, to point in the same direction. However, recent research has called many of these points into question.

1. The date of domestication of the horse appears to be much later than originally believed. A re-examination of the bones from Deriivka and other comparable sites, based on their morphology and on the slaughtering age of the animals, suggests that most of the horses were still wild and therefore hunted for their meat.[67] In fact, the earliest steppic Neolithic groups, to which the early autonomous domestication of the horse and pig has traditionally been attributed, appear to have relied for the most part on hunting and fishing for their subsistence, a fact that has been revealed by recent zoological re-examinations carried out by Norbert Benecke.[68] For this reason

[65] Bökönyi, 1974, 1978, 1991.
[66] Bibikova, 1967–1970, 1986.
[67] Levine, 1990,
[68] Benecke, 1997.

306   THIRD MOVEMENT (1945–THIRD MILLENNIUM)

it comes as no surprise that, even within the Sredny Stog culture, the horse remained a game animal.

2. Following the end of the last glaciation, during which the wild horse was present throughout all ice-free parts of Europe, this animal did not confine itself to the Pontic Steppes. In reality, the presence of wild horses is attested right across Europe and even in Anatolia.[69] Its frequency simply decreases from east to west as a function of the landscape, with wild horses preferring to inhabit open spaces.

3. For this reason, the presence of other centers of autonomous domestication of the horse outside of the Pontic Steppes can be deduced from the variations in the types of domesticated horses found in Chalcolithic and Bronze Age Europe.[70] In each case, these regional domesticated forms are closer to the local wild counterparts than they are to the steppic forms. Therefore, the domestication of the horse did not necessarily occur in, and diffuse from, a single point, but, instead, several parallel domestications may have occurred in various parts of Europe at a time when Chalcolithic societies were beginning to exploit animals not only for their meat but also for draft purposes. In addition, the horses of the Corded Ware Culture are genetically not of steppic origin.[71]

4. Domestication for the specific purpose of riding is a much debated issue. The case for this relies heavily on the famous pieces of perforated red deer antler. While objects with a similar shape were used as bit components in more recent periods (e.g., during the Italian Bronze Age), detailed use-wear analyses of the perforations and extremities of the objects do not support this suggested function.[72] Furthermore, these objects are rarely found in pairs. Therefore, they could just as well be interpreted as tools, perhaps for working flint. At one time the famous perforated batons (*bâtons de commandement*) of the Upper Paleolithic, made of reindeer antler and often decorated, were interpreted as horse bits: now they are widely recognized as tools used to straighten arrow shafts. Bits of this shape would have been more suitable for driving chariots which, as we shall see, only appeared much later. Much has also been made of the skull of a stallion from Deriivka, a tooth from which displayed traces of wear caused by a bit; American archaeologist David Anthony proclaimed it to be "the oldest known mount in the world," its special status apparently reinforced by the fact that it was found in a "ritual" pit.[73] Unfortunately, a radiocarbon

---

[69] Benecke, 1994, 2002; Uerpmann, 1990, 1995; Boessneck and Van den Driesch, 1976; Becker, 1994.

[70] Benecke, 1994; Becker, 1994; Uerpmann, 1990, 1995; Müller, H. H., 1994.

[71] Librado et al., 2021.

[72] Dietz, 1992; Hüttel, 1994; Häusler, 1994; Becker, 1994; Rassamakin, 1999.

[73] Anthony and Brown, 1991; Anthony, 1994.

date for the famous skull was much more recent—by 1,500 years!—which suggests that the pit that contained it had been dug by later occupants of the site, an explanation that had already been advanced by German archaeologist Alexander Häusler.[74] The director of the Deriivka excavation, Dmitri Telegin, has since come around to this interpretation.[75] There is, therefore, no decisive proof that the horse was first ridden during the steppic Chalcolithic. Indeed, linguists have to admit that the shared vocabulary lacks words for bits, mounts, or horse riding.[76] The oldest texts confirm this, even though they are much later than the Chalcolithic: horse riding is barely mentioned in the Vedic texts of India and is almost as rarely mentioned in Homer.[77] For this reason, certain archaeologists and historians do not date the beginnings of horse riding any earlier than the last millennium BCE (i.e., during the Iron Age), some three millennia after the first evidence for domestication.[78]

5. The ideological and ritual importance of the horse must also be relativized. If we put aside the late "ritual" in Deriivka, there are several examples of horse bone deposits in the burials of the steppic Chalcolithic; however, their frequency does not exceed that of any of the other usual animals, be they wild or domesticated. Likewise, among engraved, painted, and sculpted representations associated with steppic cultures, the horse is no more commonly represented than fish, wild boar, wild birds, deer, dogs, and elk.[79] Indeed, it is worth noting that these animal representations appear, most often, to be associated with hunting, which would place the horse within the wild realm. Horse burials containing entire skeletons are not known in Eurasia before the end of the Chalcolithic or the beginning of the Bronze Age (i.e., the early second millennium BCE). As for the famous horse-head stone "scepters," these can be linked to an older and more widespread tradition of zoomorphic axes, examples of which are found among the Mesolithic hunter-gatherer societies of Eastern Europe, from Karelia in the north to Dagestan in the south, and which continue to appear in the Neolithic and Chalcolithic of the steppes; they can take the form of horses, but also elk, bears, swans, ducks, and birds of prey and are not always clearly identifiable.[80] For the Chalcolithic examples, the absence of perforations makes their function difficult to determine. In addition, none of the Chalcolithic examples that can be reasonably identified as horses'

[74] Häusler, 1994, p. 232; Rassamakin, 1999, p. 145.
[75] Telegin, 1995; Anthony and Brown, 2000.
[76] Zimmer, 1990a, 1990b, 1994; Meid, 1994.
[77] Falk, 1994; Plath, 1994.
[78] Drews, 2004.
[79] Häusler, 1994, pp. 231–244.
[80] Ibid., pp. 244–247, and fig. 14, p. 238.

308   THIRD MOVEMENT (1945–THIRD MILLENNIUM)

heads, and which belong to a relatively homogenous typological series has been found on the Pontic Steppes. Apart from one Caucasian example, they have all been found in the Balkan Peninsula, and their "steppic" origin, even though often assumed, has not been proved.[81]

6. Symmetrically, it is not certain that the horse should be attributed a special place in ancient Indo-European mythologies. Much rests on the similarity, which at first glance is enticing, identified by mythologist Georges Dumézil between the sacrifice of the October Horse to Mars in ancient Rome and the ancient Indian sacrifice of Ashvamedha; certain more disparate Celtic and Germanic elements have sometimes also been linked to this practice.[82] Although significant, these rituals do not occupy central place in their respective religious systems. Furthermore, they differ more from one another than might seem, and their resemblances do not necessarily imply a common origin.[83] Inversely, an interest in the horse is not an Indo-European specificity. It is also encountered, in potentially comparable forms, among many peoples of Eurasia, from Siberia to the Caucasus and Mongolia.[84] Earl Anderson has shown that the ritual structure of the October Horse and of the horse sacrifices that have been likened to it are found in strikingly similar forms among Mongols and Turks, who, by definition, are non–Indo-Europeans.[85] By default and by excess, it is not Indo-Europeanness per se that accounts for these mythological similarities—and this is not a unique case.

7. Finally, it is worth noting that all recent genetic studies, despite having great potential, have so far failed to shine any light on the issue of the original domestication of the horse.[86]

With such a weak case, the horse argument, which in principle is emblematic of Indo-Europeanness, greatly resembles a vicious circle. This is what German archaeologist and zoologist Norbert Benecke was suggesting when he lamented the fact that "archeozoologists and archeozoological interpretations of the data are overly influenced by the various conceptions and evolutive models of archaeologists when it comes to the domestication of the horse and the theories associated with it (for example, the 'Indo-European problem')."[87]

---

[81]   See map in Lichardus, 1988, p. 123, and Govedarica, 2004, p. 240.
[82]   Dumézil, 1966, 1975, pp. 145–156, 177–219; Puhvel, 1970, 1987, pp. 270–276; Sergent, 1995, pp. 363–365; Anderson, E., 1999.
[83]   Polomé, 1994a, 1994b.
[84]   Koppers, 1929, 1936; Uhlenbeck, 1937; Anderson, E., 1999; Brun, 2001.
[85]   Anderson, E., 1999.
[86]   Gaunitz et al., 2018; Fages et al., 2019; Librado et al., 2021.
[87]   Benecke, 1994, p. 123.

THE BLACK SEA STEPPES? 309

... And the chariot, naturally!

The nature of the chariot argument is very similar. According to a recurrent image, the first Indo-Europeans would have spread out across the known world in war chariots drawn by two horses. The reality, both linguistic and archaeological, is more complex. Here again, the argument has long been based on several shared Indo-European words designating the chariot, the wheel, and certain other parts of the chariot.[88] The principal word for cart or chariot is the root *uegh-, meaning to "move" or "to travel in a cart," which we encounter in the Latin vehiculum, Mycenaean Greek woka, German wagen, English wagon, Greek ochos, Old Church Slavonic vozu, and also in the Indo-Iranian, Celtic, and Baltic languages. But there also exists another root, namely *hem-haks-iha, attested in Greek (amaxa) and Tocharian, as well as the root *krsos, present in Celtic, which gave rise to the Latin carrus, and, in turn, the word char in French. As regards the wheel, we encounter the root *kwekwlo-, whose repeated root is perhaps onomatopoeic; it is found in the English wheel, Greek kuklos (from which comes the English word "cycle"), as well as in Tocharian (kokale), in the Indo-Iranian languages and, in a non-repeated form, in Slavic (kolo). But there also exists a second root for wheel, *rotho-, which is present in the Indo-Iranian languages (ratha, meaning "war chariot"), in Latin (rota), in Germanic (Rad in German), in Baltic and in Celtic. There are at least two other roots for wheel, *hurgi-, present in Hittite and Tocharian, which is likened to the Latin vertere, "to turn"; and *dhrogho-, attested in Greek (trochos, hence the verb trechein meaning "to run"); not counting the word a-mo, the Mycenaean Greek for a spoked wheel. There also exists a root for wheel hub (*nobh-o), which, at the same time, more broadly signifies navel; with the meaning "hub," it is encountered in the Germanic, Baltic, and Indian languages. While the designation for axel comes from the root *aks- or *heks-, present in Greek, Latin, Slavic, Baltic, Celtic, and Indo-Iranian, there are several roots for shaft (*dhur, *is, *teng-s-).

This situation prompts a number of observations. Despite the presence of common roots in several languages, sometimes geographically distant from each other, no coherent overall picture seems to emerge. Commented upon for some time,[89] this situation does not suggest that the chariot was invented in a single place at a specific moment in time. Furthermore, it does not help us to identify particular types of chariots or carts. Some of these roots have a wider meaning (e.g., navel and hub, movement and chariot, etc.) which might suggest that pre-existing words were used to designate parts of the chariot when it was invented,

---

[88] Meid, 1994; Zimmer, 1994; Gamkrelidze, 1994; Raulwing, 1998, 2000; Mallory and Adams, 1997 (pp. 625–628 and 640–641).
[89] Dressler, 1965.

310   THIRD MOVEMENT (1945–THIRD MILLENNIUM)

thus giving these words a more limited technical meaning. Colin Renfrew[90] used this as an argument to reconcile the relatively late invention of the chariot and the hypothesis of a Neolithic (i.e., much earlier) origin for the Indo-European settlement of Europe. In any case, these semantic waverings contribute to the blurring of linguistic convergences. Before the invention of the chariot per se, several rotation-based technologies are well-attested as early as the beginning of the Neolithic and even earlier. For instance, a bow was used to generate rapid rotation, in alternate directions, of a vertical shaft thus creating heat and fire through friction. The same technique was utilized for perforating objects such as beads, spindle whorls, net weights, loom weights, etc. As evidenced by ethnographic studies, these bow-driven shafts can be fitted with a disc-shaped element which acts as a flywheel. Similarly, beginning in the Early Neolithic, yarn spindles were weighted using a clay (or sometimes stone) whorl which stabilized the rotation of the implement, either in the air or on the ground in the manner of a spinning top. We should also mention the use of rolling logs to move heavy objects, in particular during the construction of megalithic monuments. All of these techniques utilize circular movement and objects which necessarily had specific designations.

As regards the first archaeological evidence for carts or chariots, it is just as problematic as the evidence for the domestication of the horse. The oldest known wheeled vehicles in the archaeological record date to the second half of the fourth millennium BCE and are found scattered across an area from Scandinavia to Mesopotamia, encompassing Switzerland, Central Europe, the steppes of Europe and Central Asia, and Syria.[91] This evidence includes representations engraved on stone and pottery, ceramic models sometimes deposited within graves,[92] and actual wheels or chariots, either found preserved on settlement sites, such as on the shores of certain Swiss lakes, or in burials, as in the Pit Grave culture of the steppes. In all cases where the type of vehicle can be identified, we are dealing with a heavy cart with two or four solid timber wheels which are usually made from three joined planks. These carts could only have been pulled by oxen as is confirmed by iconographical evidence. The horse-drawn war chariot is a much more recent development and relies on an essential technical innovation: the spoked wheel. Only such wheels are light and flexible enough to allow fast movement, be it in the context of hunting or battle, or simply for prestige. This type of wheel is not attested before the beginning of the second millennium BCE; in particular, such wheels are known from the Sintashta culture (a local variant of the

---

[90] Renfrew, 1989, p. 845, regarding an observation made by Edgar Polomé.
[91] Piggott, 1983.
[92] Bondár, 2012.

THE BLACK SEA STEPPES? 311

wider, steppic Andronovo complex) in the region to the south of the Urals where they have been found within high-ranking tombs.

There is, therefore, a significant technological hiatus, which is also geographical and chronological, between the heavy ox-drawn carts with four (or more rarely two) solid wheels and the light, horse-drawn chariots with two spoked wheels. This leads to the possibility that the wheel could have been invented independently, at least twice, and in two different forms[93]—two forms that cannot be distinguished from one another based on the different words to designate the wheel. Instead, this multiplicity of terms suggests multiple geographical origins for this invention. Ultimately, the war chariot that is so emblematic of the great battles of the second millennium BCE, from the Near East to China, and from Egypt to India (and soon afterward on the battlefields of Mycenaean Greece and Celtic and Germanic Europe) is a late invention adopted by these different civilizations, with their various languages, and should in no way be considered as a marker of "Indo-Europeanness." If there were to be a single cradle for its invention, then the case for the warlike, state-base societies of the Middle East seems to be the most solidly founded.[94]

Warrior invasions or a vicious circle?

The third version of the steppic theory concerns evidence, or otherwise, for migratory movements from the steppes. We have already seen how, from the sixth millennium BCE, the semi-sedentary hunter-gatherers in the area to the north of the Black Sea gradually adopted agriculture and stock rearing, in part through the influence of Neolithic farmers in the Balkans, but also through the influence of those of the Near East directly via the Caucasus.[95] Within these neolithicized populations, just as in Central and Western Europe, there emerged, in the fifth millennium BCE, the phenomena of social complexity that mark the Chalcolithic. Individuals who enjoyed a high status were buried with rich grave goods (the first copper objects, figurines, personal ornaments, etc.), sometimes beneath earthen mounds or *kurgans*. In the canonical steppic theory of Marija Gimbutas and James Mallory, and in the various other versions, it was these chalcolithicized populations with their hierarchical structure and warlike outlook who, having domesticated the horse, would have destroyed the rich cultures (Gumelniţa, Cucuteni-Trypillia, etc.) to the northwest and west of the Black Sea in the fifth millennium. They would have subsequently spread out, with one part

[93] Kaiser, 2011.
[94] Raulwing, 2000.
[95] See Chapter 11, pp. 248–249.

312 THIRD MOVEMENT (1945–THIRD MILLENNIUM)

of the population gradually taking control of all of Europe and imposing their Indo-European languages on the conquered peoples; another group would have chosen to migrate toward the east and south (giving rise, for example, to the Indo-Iranian, Tocharian, and Anatolian languages).

However, this apparently coherent picture could just as easily be seen as a logical vicious circle: in other words, it is because it is postulated that population movements took place from east to west that we find proof of them in the archaeological record. However, over the past two decades, a number of researchers have forwarded good archaeological arguments in support of the reverse thesis, but they have had the misfortune of publishing their results in Russian and German and so have not received the same level of media attention as their English-speaking counterparts.[96] In their contrasting version, it was the powerful Balkan and West Pontic cultures, with their innovative copper and gold metallurgy (the oldest known) and their densely populated "proto-urban" settlements (numbering several thousands of inhabitants) that influenced the evolution of the steppic cultures.

Thus, Blagoje Govedarica recently revisited the case of the oldest known tombs of "steppic" type. The bodies of the deceased were generally laid on their backs, with their legs flexed, and were sprinkled with red ochre. The graves themselves contain rare prestige goods, including copper personal ornaments and tools, long flint or bone blades, stone horse-heads (interpreted as "scepters"), stone mace heads, etc.[97] However, a fine-resolution chronological analysis, to within a century, focusing on the second half of the fifth millennium, shows that the oldest tombs, numbering about a hundred, of these first Eastern European "chieftains" are not located in the east, in a purely steppic environment but, on the contrary, are found in the west within the vast Cucuteni-Trypillia complex of Balkan origin. Furthermore, the most realistic horse-head scepters are those found in the west, while the examples found in steppic contexts appear to be rough imitations of the latter, and yet these artifacts were long regarded as "steppic" elements attesting to the arrival of warriors from the east. Similarly, perforated copper axes found in Cucuteni-Trypillia contexts are only encountered in the form of red deer antler imitations in the east. The new funerary ideology associated with the emergence of the first European elites thus seems to occur in areas where the social differences are most pronounced and subsequently spreads in a gradual manner into peripheral regions.

Yuri Rassamakin has classified the thousand or so steppic Chalcolithic graves dating from the second half of the fifth millennium and from the fourth millennium.[98] He disentangles the complex mosaic of cultures that spread out

[96] Govedarica, 2004; Rassamakin, 2004; Häusler, 2002a, 2002b.
[97] Govedarica, 2004.
[98] Rassamakin, 2004.

THE BLACK SEA STEPPES?   313

and succeeded each other during this period, from the mouth of the Danube to the Volga and the Caucasus, and identifies the exchange networks of prestige objects. The chronology shows that the bulk of cultural influences and the circulation of objects flowed from west to east (i.e., from the Balkano-Carpathian and West Pontic areas, with their powerful Gumelniţa-Karanovo VI and Cucuteni-Trypillia cultures, toward the cultures of the North and East Pontic Steppes). In particular, the steppes east of the Black Sea, occupied by the Samara and Khvalynsk-S'eszee cultures (i.e., Marija Gimbutas' "Kurgan I") only play a very peripheral role in this network of cultural exchanges, and one would be hard-pressed to consider them as the original Homeland from which all Indo-European migrations might have originated.

Nothing, therefore, indicates that these aforementioned powerful Chalcolithic cultures might have collapsed under the assault of warrior herders riding forth from the steppes. Such demises are a regular feature of proto-historic Europe and are rarely the result of violent invasions, as demonstrated by examples from other regions of the world in different eras, from Easter Island to the Maya, or from the Mycenaean world to the Mississippian culture.[99] In fact, these correspond to over-sized socioeconomic systems where the elites display a disproportionate level of ostentatious wealth (as in the Varna cemetery in Bulgaria) and where concentrations of human population, which for the first time in Europe number several thousand individuals, demand unprecedented feats of organization. As a result, these societies are very fragile and susceptible to the slightest fluctuations, be they environmental, social, economic, political, or even ideological. Indeed, toward the end of the fifth millennium BCE, throughout the Balkan and North West Pontic zone, in particular in modern-day Romania, Moldova, and western Ukraine, certain major sites were abandoned and villages shrank in size and became more scattered while elements of the material culture, such as pottery, tend to show a decline in quality.

The proponents of the steppic theory, Marija Gimbutas at the forefront, obviously use this as an argument in favor of a general collapse brought about by an invasion of warrior herders from the steppes. However, this is a hasty and biased interpretation of the facts. Detailed examination of pottery forms and decorative schemes and techniques, for example, does not reveal any evidence for stylistic discontinuity but instead shows a continuous evolution toward general simplification. Likewise, the stylistic and cultural unity characteristic of the Cucuteni-Trypillia culture during the second half of the fifth millennium, gradually gives way to regional fragmentation over the course of the fourth millennium BCE, with the emergence, for example, of the Gorodsk, Usatovo, Horodiştea, Folteşti, and Sofievka groups.[100] As in later eras (e.g., the end of the Indus civilization or

---

[99] Diamond, 2011.
[100] Lichardus et al., 1985, pp. 394–398; Lichardus and Lichardus-Itten, 1998.

314 THIRD MOVEMENT (1945–THIRD MILLENNIUM)

that of the Mycenaean world), it is not a case of the light being overwhelmed by the "Dark Ages" in a violent and generalized cataclysm, but of an oversized centralized socioeconomic system slowly collapsing in upon itself to make way for small-scale village communities that are ultimately better able to exploit their natural environment in a reasonable manner.

The fragmentation that is characteristic of the second half of the early Chalcolithic (i.e., the first half of the fourth millennium BCE) is followed, in the second half of the fourth millennium, by the re-emergence of major cultural entities within a context that can already be termed "Bronze Age" in parts of the Balkans and the Pontic Steppes but which is still considered Middle Chalcolithic in Central Europe.[101] In the Pontic Steppes, we see the spread of the Pit Grave culture, in Greece the emergence of the Early Helladic, in Hungary and neighboring regions we encounter the Baden culture (with Balkan and North West Anatolian variants), and in Northern Europe we witness the rise of the Funnel Beaker culture (see Appendix 13). These various cultures share a certain number of common features, but these are never absolute and always display considerable regional diversity. Funerary monumentalism, reserved for the most important members of society, is expressed, depending on the region, through the construction of megalithic monuments or of tumuli of earth or stone, but these lack the ostentation of the earlier megalithic tradition of Atlantic Europe or of the golden grave goods deposited in the mid-fifth millennium at the Varna cemetery in Bulgaria, for example. As regards technology, copper metallurgy continues to develop, while the wheel, the ard, and the use of draft animals, including the recently domesticated horse, become more commonplace. Settlements are increasingly protected by earthen and timber defenses and are often located on high ground. In summary, Europe carries on consolidating its "chalcolithization," particularly through the establishment of what social anthropologists term "chiefdoms."

And what of genetics?

Such was the situation in 2014, when the first French edition of this book appeared. But in June 2015, two articles on paleogenetics were published quite simply claiming that a "massive migration from the steppe was a source for Indo-European languages in Europe."[102] In October of the same year, a conference, in which I participated, was organized by the two laboratories involved in the study on the theme "Linguistics, Archaeology, and Genetics: Integrating New Evidence

---

[101] Lichardus et al., 1985; Lichardus and Lichardus-Itten, 1998. See Chapter 11, pp. 249–252.
[102] Haak et al., 2015; Allentoft et al., 2015; see Chapter 10, pp. 232–236.

for the Origin and Spread of the Indo-European Languages." While the debates were fascinating, a single consensus emerged: that there was still no consensus!

Nevertheless, a "new" narrative, which in fact only rehashed—with the addition of new arguments—the narrative that we have just examined, rapidly came to dominate a section of the scientific literature.[103] These arguments now read as follows:

1. Around 3000 BCE, a large section of the semi-nomadic herders of the so-called Yamanaya or Pit-Grave Culture (*Yamnaya kultura* in Russian, where *Yama* means *pit*) of the steppes of Southern Russia and Ukraine migrated with their oxen and newly invented heavy carts toward northwest Europe. They eventually occupied the region stretching from Poland to Denmark, forming a new culture, the Corded Ware culture, which is characterized by its tall vessels bearing impressed cord decoration. These people buried their dead beneath small mounds or tumuli. They cleared vast areas of forest to make way for their herds. Because they possessed the gene for producing lactase, they were able to digest dairy products, which gave them a significant nutritional advantage.

2. They were aided in their endeavors by a plague epidemic which decimated a large proportion of the indigenous populations but to which they themselves were immune.

3. They continued the work of the plague by massacring the remaining indigenous people, thus becoming the "most murderous people of all time."[104]

4. A portion of this group continued onward, forming a new cultural entity, the Bell Beaker people, who gained a strong foothold in Britain and Ireland and who also spread, under this form, into Central and southwestern Europe.

5. Other members of the *Yamnaya kultura* left the steppes and this time migrated toward South Asia, India, Iran, and even as far as Xinjiang in Central Asia where Indo-European languages were spoken into the Middle Ages.

6. Thus, we have a simple and definitive explanation of how, from their place of origin in the steppes of Russia and Ukraine, Indo-European languages spread throughout Europe and into a large part of Asia.

We will now consider each of these points in turn, keeping in mind that paleogenetic data continues to be generated at a steady pace.

---

[103] Kristiansen et al., 2017; Reich, 2018.
[104] Barras, 2019.

316   THIRD MOVEMENT (1945–THIRD MILLENNIUM)

The first problem is the clear difference between the material objects, especially the pottery, of the Yamnaya culture and those of the Corded Ware culture. This has forced archaeologists to demonstrate a certain virtuosity to come up with the theory that the invaders had arrived with vessels of perishable materials (e.g., of wood, leather, or textile), which therefore did not survive in the archaeological record and which local women would have imitated in clay. Furthermore, chariots and the use of animals for draft purposes were not Yamnaya inventions but had already existed in Central and Western Europe for several centuries. Likewise, forest clearances are not attested everywhere. Finally, the lactase gene still seems to be present in only a tiny minority within these populations, while at the same time various forms of dairy products were already being consumed in numerous parts of Neolithic Europe.

As regards the plague, it is not certain that its bacillus (*Yersinia pestis*) was life-threatening at the time, and evidence for a massive epidemic remains thin.

Nor is there much evidence for massacres associated with the Corded Ware culture. One example of large-scale killing was revealed at Eulau in Germany[105] and another at Koszyce in Poland.[106] But the first case concerns a clash between two Corded Ware groups and so can be regarded as a conflict between neighbors. In the second case, the victims can indeed be attributed to an indigenous culture, known as the Globular Amphora culture, which immediately preceded the Corded Ware culture and which, as initial genetic analysis indicates, is not of steppic origin; however the mass grave is not dominated by the bodies of males, as we might expect if the goal was to take possession of the womenfolk, but rather is principally composed of the remains of women and children.

As regards the relationship between the Bell Beaker culture and the Corded Ware culture, the situation is far from clear since the Bell Beaker culture is heterogeneous in terms of paleogenetics[107] but relatively homogenous in terms of material culture. In Central Europe and in Britain and Ireland, the "steppic" genetic component is indeed present, but it is virtually nonexistent in southwest Europe. We will consider the potential routes for the dispersion of the various Indo-European language families in the next chapter.

Therefore, in the present state of archaeological and genetic knowledge, the traditional invasionist model is still far from convincing in terms of providing an explanation for the kinship links observed between Indo-European languages. It seems that it would be much more reasonable to combine the phenomena of "chalcolithization" of the whole European continent mentioned above with the very progressive phenomena of genetic mixing, on the one hand, and cultural

---

[105] Haak et al., 2010.
[106] Schroeder et al., 2019.
[107] Olalde et al., 2018, 2019; see also Chapter 10, pp. 235–236.

mixing, on the other, spread out over a considerable time period and occurring in a variety of forms.

This is also the approach that has been proposed, in various forms, by archaeologists such as Martin Furholt,[108] Volker Heyd,[109] and James Mallory. In 1988, the latter, for example, stated "As a single explanatory model, the concept of an expanding Kurgan tradition as currently presented is still not robust enough to provide a convincing solution to the problem of Indo-European origins."[110]

Furthermore, Mallory, rather than arguing for military conquests, favors a peaceful and gradual linguistic diffusion:

> Appeals to the warlike character of the Kurgan tradition are also less than satisfactory and the model of Kurganized "elites" dominating Europe might be part of a solution but surely not the entire solution. The expansion of a language is a social phenomenon involving the aboriginal population adopting a new (target) language beside their own in the various social domains in which it was initially introduced. Indo-European languages would have spread from these domains to all arenas of speech to replace the local languages of a large part of Eurasia. Often, the reason for learning a new language will be the desire to associate oneself with a new ideology, social system or economic opportunity. A more nuanced reading of the steppe hypothesis would emphasize the social significance of horse-headed scepters, domestic horses, wagons, barrows, and new weapons (shaft-hole axes, daggers) associated with steppe expansions that may have reflected the new ideologies of a "steppe package." A new ideology, economy, social symbols and transportation system that could integrate larger groups of people are precisely the areas in which one might imagine the spread of a new language into previous or new social domains. The future durability of the steppe hypothesis must rely on the ability of its supporters to show how the archaeological impact of population expansions from the steppe actually effected the social and linguistic changes suggested by the dispersal of the Indo-European languages.[111]

One of the challenges for archaeological research in coming years might therefore be to test such non-invasionist models.

---

[108] Furholt, 2019a, 2019b, 2021.
[109] Harrison and Heyd, 2007; Heyd, 2021.
[110] Mallory and Adams, 1997, p. 341.
[111] Mallory, 2010, p. 35.

15

From prehistory to history

The rediscovered routes taken by the Indo-Europeans?

Diffusionist by definition, the canonical Indo-European model supposes several successive migratory phases or, more exactly, several places and moments in time which today are the focus of debates regarding potential migratory movements. In fact, the model demands that we retrace all of the migrations that, in the wake of a seminal "big bang," would have spread out from the "original Cradle" (which might be either steppic or Anatolian, depending on which of the two most popular prevailing theses we choose to accept) to the place where each of the Indo-European–speaking peoples is identified at the moment when they enter history (i.e., at the moment when they leave their first written traces). To do this, it is necessary to proceed in the opposite direction, departing each time from the region where a given people is historically attested at a precise moment in time, thanks to indisputable written sources, and then working back in time from this point. However, these moments vary significantly and are spread out over some three millennia, from the middle of the second millennium BCE with the first physical Mycenaean texts (written in Linear B) of Greece and Hittite texts of Turkey (the Indian Vedic texts are undoubtedly of a similar age but they were transcribed much later), right up to the Medieval period when a significant number of languages were written down for the first time: for example, Albanian (or rather Albanian dialects), first transcribed in the thirteenth century CE, Old Prussian (a now dead Baltic language), first transcribed in the fourteenth century, and Latvian and Lithuanian which were not written down until the sixteenth century (see Appendices 2 and 8).

How do we prove a migration?

Colin Renfrew's Anatolian theory[1] poses few migratory problems since the entire linguistic Indo-Europeanization of Europe and South West Asia is explained in terms of a single large migration, that of the first farmers and stock breeders who

---

[1] See Chapter 13.

FROM PREHISTORY TO HISTORY   319

left Turkey in the seventh millennium BCE. The only debate, in which Renfrew remains undecided, surrounds India, where he accepts that two models are possible: an agricultural colonization that emanated from the same Anatolian homeland to the west in the sixth millennium BCE or a violent invasion from the steppes to the north in the second millennium BCE.[2] We will come back to the second hypothesis later because it is shared by that other major model, namely Marija Gimbutas's steppic model.

While both models, the Anatolian and the steppic, are rooted in the Neolithic, or Chalcolithic, the ensuing migrations take place during the Bronze Age or even later. We will therefore examine in turn the main debates that surround the "arrival" of the Greeks in Greece, the Indians (or "Aryans") in India, the Tocharians in far-off Central Asia, the Italics in Italy, the Celts on the Atlantic seaboard, the Germans in North West Europe, the Slavs in Eastern Europe, and the Hittites in Turkey. Despite over a century of archaeological research, significant controversy still surrounds virtually all of these "arrivals," as has been demonstrated by James Mallory (even though he stands as a proponent of the steppic theory).[3]

Several tools are available to archaeologists to identify a migration or an invasion, and there are migratory movements which elicit a broad consensus, especially if they happen to be correlated with events mentioned in text form, such as, for instance, the expansion of the Roman Empire or the population movements of the European Early Middle Ages. For more ancient periods, in a given region, a migration or invasion event is recognized

   a. If it is observed that a number of sites are destroyed and/or abandoned over a large part of this region within the same period; or
   b. If the material culture of the new sites that succeed those destroyed/abandoned, whether they occupy the same locations or not, is significantly different and originates from a traceable geographical area outside the said region.

However, these common sense observations are not necessarily easily applicable for a number of reasons.

   a. The concept of "destruction" is sometimes based on forced interpretations and depends on the extent of excavations undertaken. If an archaeologist unearths the remains of a burned-down building in the course of a test excavation extending over just a few square meters, the evidence for burning might simply represent an accident restricted to that particular

---

[2] Renfrew, 1987 [1990], p. 244, fig. 8.4.
[3] Mallory, 1989, chapter 8.

320 THIRD MOVEMENT (1945–THIRD MILLENNIUM)

building. And even if the rest of the village was burned down, it might have been accidental since most of the structures would have been of wood, thatch, and earth. And even if one could prove that this fire was the result of some hostile action (skeletal remains exhibiting traces of wounds, scattered arrowheads, etc.), this might not constitute proof of a general invasion: it might simply represent the settling of scores between two neighboring communities at a time when centralized enforcing powers were emerging and many urban settlements were fortified.

b. One needs to prove beyond dispute that destructions of separate settlements occurred simultaneously. In fact, the archaeological dating techniques available, whether they rely on radiocarbon analyses or on ceramic typologies, are only accurate to within two or three generations at best. In which case, several fires, whether limited in extent or not, accidental or not, on several sites might give the impression of a general disaster whereas they might actually be related to events of varying importance that are spread out over time.

c. One also needs to prove that what appears to be novel really is so and that a particular new type of pottery or funerary custom is not attested, even marginally, during the preceding period.

d. And, finally, it is necessary to identify the presumed geographical origin of these innovations in order to trace the supposed migratory movement.

Genetic studies have recently contributed very significant information, sometimes even deemed "revolutionary," which needs to be cross-referenced with archaeological and even linguistic data, all the while steering clear of overly simplistic models.

The coming of the Greeks

We will first apply these methodological considerations to one of the most famous migratory puzzles linked to the Indo-European question, that of the "coming of the Greeks" to Greece. There is a degree of prestige attached to this scientific issue, which mirrors that attached to Greco-Roman culture itself. Up until recently, this culture nurtured the European intellectual elites who urged their respective nations to found the first archaeological institutes in the newly independent Greece. In addition, the language that was spoken, or at least written, during the Mycenaean period is, together with Hittite and the language of the Vedic hymns, one of the three oldest Indo-European languages known. The deciphering of the syllabic script known as Linear B by Michael Ventris in 1952[4]

---

[4] Ventris and Chadwick, 1953.

FROM PREHISTORY TO HISTORY 321

was ground-breaking and revealed that the language spoken by the aristocracy in Mycenae, Tiryns, and Pylos, and in the last palaces of Crete, was, contrary to the opinion widely held until then, already Greek. The Greeks were therefore present in Greece as early as the middle of the second millennium BCE and probably even before that since the emergence of Mycenaean civilization (referred to as the Late Bronze Age in the local terminology) seems to have occurred quite peacefully. The "coming of the Greeks" has thus become a favorite topic among Hellenists, archaeologists, historians, and philologists alike.

Yet if one goes back further in time, Neolithic communities in Greece are traditionally not regarded as Indo-European. Ancient tales from Antiquity tell of an indigenous people, the Pelasgians, who originally lived in Greece. In addition, linguists have identified certain non–Indo-European roots in Greek (words ending in –nthos, as in Corinth, or in –ssos, as in *thalassa* or Knossos, for instance—amounting to 160 words), which they attribute to a pre-existing indigenous language called a "substrate."[5] This supposed substrate is to be distinguished from the language of the first Cretan palaces, written in Linear A, which despite numerous attempts remains un-deciphered to this day.[6] Similarly, and somewhat paradoxically, the names of most of the peoples of classical Greece are believed to be etymologically non–Indo-European.

It is generally accepted that the Greek Neolithic originated from the Middle East, whether by way of mass migration or through influences or infiltrations.[7] Unless one adopts Renfrew's Anatolian theory[8] or even the theory of an autochthonous origin dating back to the Paleolithic,[9] there must have been a historical turning point either during the Neolithic period or during the succeeding Bronze Age.

The Neolithic period does not reveal any such rupture and, despite the variety of successive material cultures, it reads as a continuous evolution.[10] The Greek Bronze Age is divided into three main periods, as is often the case in archaeology on account of some inexplicable fascination with the number three. We therefore distinguish between an Early Bronze Age, a Middle Bronze Age, and finally a Late Bronze Age, the latter corresponding to the Mycenaean period. Each of these periods is itself subdivided into three sub-periods which are indicated using Roman numerals, and these are sometimes subdivided once more: so for example we end up with a Late Helladic III A2.[11] From a geographical point of

---

[5] Halley and Blegen, 1928; Van Windekens, 1952; Merlingen, 1955, 1967; Hester, 1965; Capovilla, 1964; Strunk, 2004, etc. See also Chapter 19, pp. 438–439.

[6] Duhoux, 1998.

[7] Demoule and Perlès, 1993; Perlès, 2001.

[8] Renfrew, 1987.

[9] Giannopoulos, 2012.

[10] Demoule and Perlès, 1993.

[11] Treuil et al., 2008 [1989]; Dickinson, 1994; Shelmerdine, 2008.

322   THIRD MOVEMENT (1945–THIRD MILLENNIUM)

view the mainland Bronze Age is referred to as Early-, Middle-, or Late Helladic, while it is termed Early-, Middle-, or Late Cycladic in the Cyclades, and Early-, Middle-, or Late Minoan in Crete. A distinct sequence is also applied in Northern Greece with the use of the terms "Thessalian" or even "Macedonian."

The "coming of the Greeks" can therefore only have occurred at the onset of one or other of these periods or sub-periods of the Bronze Age, each of which is distinguished by a specific material culture and, more particularly, by distinctive artifact forms and decoration (pottery, tools, weapons, figurines, etc.) as well as architecture and funerary customs. This event could, therefore, coincide with the onset of the Bronze Age (i.e., the Early Helladic I), which starts around 3200 BCE. In theory, one could also envisage the arrival of the Greeks in the Early Helladic II, starting around 2700 BCE (but there is little evidence to support this theory) or at the start of the Early Helladic III, around 2300 BCE. Other possibilities include the Middle Helladic, around 2000 BCE (but it is presently believed that the onset of this period does not coincide with any stylistic rupture) and, finally, the Late Helladic, around 1550 BCE, corresponding to the emergence of the Mycenaean civilization.[12]

However, in light of the methodological considerations stated in the introduction, we will show that none of the proposed explanations for each of the four moments of "rupture" identified is convincing, nor does any elicit even minimal consensus.

An Early Bronze Age arrival

The first proposed rupture point is therefore the start of the Early Bronze Age (i.e., the Early Helladic I).[13] One of its most recent supporters is the British archaeologist John Coleman who, in fact, simply allows Marija Gimbutas's original scenario to unfold by extending its "fourth steppic wave" as far as Greece.[14] He relies on two arguments: the first is the scarcity of archaeological sites dating to the first half of the fourth millennium BCE throughout Greece and, hence, the corollary abandonment of most Chalcolithic (Final Neolithic) sites that had been occupied up to then. The second argument consists of several typological similarities between Early Helladic pottery and that of the rest of the Balkans, and even Central Europe, which become apparent at the onset of the attested Early Bronze Age in Greece during the second half of the fourth millennium BCE (i.e., the Early Helladic I, a period that incidentally remains poorly understood).

[12] See Carruba, 1995, p. 12, reiterated by Coleman, J., 2000, p. 105.
[13] See Appendix 13.
[14] Coleman, J., 2000.

FROM PREHISTORY TO HISTORY   323

However, this argument for a fourth millennium BCE hiatus must be tempered as it depends greatly on the current state of research. In fact, several recent excavations, still largely unpublished, have revealed a number sites which belong, stratigraphically as well as from the point of view of stylistic evolution, to this interval centered around the middle of the fourth millennium BCE (e.g., Petromagoula, Mikrothivi and Palioskala in Thessaly, Dikili Tash in Macedonia, Doliana in Epirus, Rachi Panagias in Phtiotis, etc.).[15]

Exhibiting no stylistic break with the preceding period, these sites present the same pottery shapes and decorative motifs that are found during the following period, that is, during the Early Bronze Age, *stricto sensu*. These consist, for example, of bowls with inward curving rims, applied clay bands bearing finger impressions, narrow conical cups, vases with handles that extend beyond the rims, incised curvilinear motifs, vertical grooves on the collars of vessels, etc. Similar elements are found further north in the Central European cultures known as the Boleraz and Cernavoda III, but also on the northwestern coast of Turkey, for instance at Kumtepe (Layer Ib). Certain objects were physically circulated, such as terracotta lids decorated with incised spirals (referred to as "from Bratislava") or Carpathian obsidian which reached the northern edge of Greek Macedonia (at the site of Mandalo, for instance).

It remains to be explained why sites dating from this intermediate period are so scarce in Greece, a situation also observed in Bulgaria but not throughout Eastern Europe since high population densities persist in Romania and Hungary. This problem does not appear to be linked to the physico-chemical dating methods used, as is the case for other periods. There may be two, non–mutually exclusive reasons for this scarcity: either these sites are difficult to detect using current means, or else Greece was abandoned by its inhabitants at this time.

The first explanation may itself be linked to a change in lifestyle: confronted with similar cases elsewhere, archaeologists often invoke a switch toward a more nomadic and pastoral economy, implying settlements composed of lightweight structures, to explain such gaps in the record. As for the second reason, this depopulation may have had several causes: epidemics (which are difficult to prove for this period); climatic deterioration (which is not attested by climatologists); or, of course, invasion, in this case from the steppes. For this last hypothesis to be true, traces of the invaders should be found in the form of truly foreign archaeological material. However, there is no evidence for this as the handful of known Greek sites simply continue the preceding traditions and prefigure the ones that follow. Such apparent depopulations are not uncommon in archaeology. Staying in Greece, a similar case arises during the "Dark Ages" between the eleventh and ninth centuries BCE (i.e., between the collapse of the Mycenaean civilization and

---

[15] Tsirtsoni, 2010; Maran, 1998a, 1998b; Johnson, 1999; Alram, 2014.

324   THIRD MOVEMENT (1945-THIRD MILLENNIUM)

the rise of the city-states). Many hypotheses have been proposed in this case also: invasions, earthquakes, plagues, climatic deterioration, etc. Issues of archaeological legibility have also been postulated, such as burials becoming less "visible" and a shift toward building in perishable materials, although cultural continuity prevails throughout this period.[16]

In any case, from the last third of the fourth millennium BCE onward, in an area stretching from the Carpathians to Greece and northwestern Turkey, a widespread stylistic group emerges without any notable rupture in material culture. It is known under various names, the principal ones being the Baden culture in a large part of Central Europe and the Northern Balkans,[17] the Ezero-Karanovo VII in Bulgaria, Troy I in northwestern Turkey, Maliq III in Albania, Sitagroi IV-V/Dikili Tash III in Greek Macedonia, and the Early Helladic in Central and Southern Greece. Apart from the Baden culture, which forms part of the Central European Chalcolithic, all of these cultures coincide with the onset of the Early Bronze Age in the Balkans. All of the pottery associated with this group belongs to a broad common style irrespective of region: it is characterized by its dark color, ribbed decoration on the body of the vessels as well as decorative motifs incised in the clay before firing, and by small drinking vessels with one or two handles protruding above the rim.

The stylistic relationships between all of the regions within this extensive group are undeniable and have already been noted elsewhere.[18] These links do not, however, allow us to infer a specific expansion movement either from the steppes or, conversely, from Turkey (as has also been proposed), or from any other region for that matter. Regarding the steppes, this phenomenon cannot be taken as an indication that a significant population movement took place from north of the Black Sea toward the west and south, a fact that James Mallory himself concedes. He states that "many would argue that the evidence for expansions from the steppe was limited (the hard evidence seems to end with the river Tisza in Hungary) and so it is very difficult to explain IE dispersals in much of Europe, nor is the evidence for intrusions into either Greece or Anatolia particularly strong."[19] One particular detail stands out among all others: none of the sites for this period, either in Greece or in Bulgaria, has produced horse bones even though they constitute one of the most commonly invoked "markers" of the steppic theory and clearly should have accompanied any major migration.[20] In addition, funerary customs, which constitute a very strong expression of identity, vary greatly over this vast area and include cremations as well as inhumations.

---

[16] Schnapp-Gourbeillon, 2002, pp. 256-261.
[17] See Chapter 11, p. 250; Appendix 13.
[18] Nemejcova-Pavukova, 1982, 1991, 1992; Maran, 1998b.
[19] Mallory and Adams, 1997, p. 299.
[20] See Chapter 14, pp. 303-308.

However, many settlement sites were built in elevated locations and were fortified, indicating that significant tensions existed between communities.

Tiles, gray ware, and princely tombs

The second turning point proposed to coincide with the "coming of the Greeks," and the one which long remained the most popular among Hellenists, was the transition between the Early Helladic II and the Early Helladic III which occurred around 2300 BCE. This hypothesis is based on a single, albeit spectacular piece of archaeological evidence: the destruction of the "House of the Tiles" at Lerna in the Peloponnese (the place where, according to myth, the fearsome Hydra, vanquished by Heracles, dwelt). This is an impressive stone house which was roofed with clay tiles, a technique that was still rare at the time and which is indicative of high social status. The excavator, American John Caskey, drew a link between this destruction and other destructions—presumed to be contemporary—at other Greek sites and with a renewal of the material culture during the succeeding period (i.e., the Early Helladic III).[21] In fact, a complete and careful re-examination of the available archaeological documentation has exposed many of the methodological limitations that we highlighted at the start of this chapter: these destructions were not all strictly contemporary; sometimes they are only attested in test excavations of very limited extent; most of the elements regarded as novel for the Early Helladic III already existed, albeit in small numbers, during the preceding period; and, finally, none of these innovations originates from a particular location: some appear indigenous, others indeed come from north of the Balkans, while others come from Anatolia, or even from the west.[22]

Rather than a violent and sudden migration, we should envisage a situation where mid- to long-distance exchange networks would have led to stylistic innovations and where tensions between communities might have resulted in conflict and destruction but within the framework of internal political rivalry in the Peloponnese. In addition, it seems that the climate of this period was characterized by droughts, which might have exacerbated tensions. The House of the Tiles itself may have collapsed and burned down following a violent earthquake, contemporary traces of which can still be found. Indeed a funerary monument was erected on the ruins of this house, which pleads in favor of cultural and ideological continuity rather than the arrival of hostile migrants.

[21] Caskey, 1960.
[22] Forsén, 1992; Coleman, J., 2000.

326   THIRD MOVEMENT (1945–THIRD MILLENNIUM)

The third possible turning point is the emergence of the Middle Helladic, around 2000 BCE.[23] The painted ware typical of preceding periods disappears and is replaced by a fine, gray ware known as Minyan ware. Some archaeologists spent decades of the twentieth century tracking down gray-colored pottery from Greece to India via Iran as a marker for Indo-European peoples: according to their theory, a period characterized by painted pottery, typical of indigenous agricultural populations, would have been succeeded by a period when gray pottery was introduced by Indo-European invaders coming from the steppes.[24]

We should point out that the characteristic gray color arises from a physico-chemical process that occurs when ceramics are fired in a reducing atmosphere (i.e., with weak influx of oxygen from outside the kiln). Over time, proto-historical civilizations favored, in turn, bright-colored pottery obtained by oxidation firing and then dark colors. Hence, there is no question here of a global phenomenon spreading the length and breadth of Eurasia: instead we are looking at cultural choices which prevailed at a given time and which reoccurred repeatedly in various locations; at times these were no more than fashion trends. In reality, in Iran, there is no evidence that these two categories of ware (painted and gray) effectively succeeded one another. Their shapes are sometimes very similar and they are even found deposited side by side in certain tombs, as in Tepe Hissar for instance.

Consequently, the Middle Helladic is no longer considered a period of rupture, and all archaeologists now stress its stylistic continuity with the preceding period.[25] Moreover, gray ware does not appear all of a sudden, and prototypes, known as proto-Minyan ware, have been identified during the preceding period.

Finally, the last rupture proposed for the "coming of the Greeks" is the emergence of the Late Helladic and the Mycenaean civilization sometime during the sixteenth century BCE (see Appendix15). This argument relies principally on the presence of war chariots in Mycenae, an invention which was still relatively recent at the time.[26] However, we have seen the weakness of the chariot explanation: this technical innovation propagates across a great variety of cultures, with no migrations or invasions involved.[27] More generally, one can suggest long-distance cultural connections between the Mycenaean world and the steppes, in particular with the proto-urban Sintashta culture to the south of the Ural Mountains, where the more prestigious tombs contained some of the oldest known war chariots.[28] The very same culture is identified by some as the starting

---

[23] Haley and Blegen, 1928.
[24] See Chapter 7, pp. 168–169.
[25] Treuil et al., 2008, pp. 253–285.
[26] Muhly, 1979; Drews, 1988; Teufer, 2012.
[27] See Chapter 14, pp. 309–311.
[28] Lichardus and Vladar, 1996; Penner, 1998.

FROM PREHISTORY TO HISTORY 327

point for the supposed migrations of the Indo-Iranians toward Iran and India.[29] Here again, it is more likely that we are dealing with a case of exchange of high-status goods, or styles, rather than hypothetical migrations, direct evidence for which is lacking.

The same can be said for the end of the Mycenaean civilization. Formerly blamed on a Dorian invasion—as recounted by the Greek myths—the fall of Mycenae was supposedly followed by a Dark Age, between around 1150 and 800 BCE, at the end of which the "Greek Miracle" was born. First postulated at the beginning of the nineteenth century by Karl Otfried Müller, this theory of a re-generative invasion by the Dorians, who were thought to be more authentically Indo-European than the rest of the Greeks, was regarded with favor by learned Nazi Hellenists like Helmut Berve.[30] A recent re-examination of facts in the light of multiple archaeological excavations shows that, in reality, Mycenaean palace civilization collapsed by itself because it had become oversized. They also expose the so-called Dorian invasions as a Spartan founding myth and reveal that, contrary to what its name suggests, the Dark Age in fact coincided with a period of restructuring and innovation during which all of the traits of the Greek city-state civilization were gradually put in place.[31]

We are, therefore, forced to conclude that there is, to date, no convincing explanation for the "coming of the Greeks." The only certainty is that an archaic form of Greek was already spoken in the Mycenaean palaces. These various aporias have led Greek archaeologist Theodoros Giannopoulos to adopt the autochthonist Paleolithic theory, which unfortunately also raises many difficulties.[32]

Finally, it should be noted that preliminary paleogenetic analyses reveal only a very slight influence of "steppic" components in Minoan and Mycenaean Greece.[33]

The arrival of the "Aryans" in India?

India occupies a symbolic position with regard to the question of the Indo-European migrations; after all, it features in the name given to this people. Furthermore, ever since Voltaire and Schlegel, India has haunted research into Indo-European origins, to the extent that it became for a time the first original Homeland. Once it lost this status, the question arose as to how and when

[29] See Chapter 14, pp. 310–311.
[30] Müller, K. O., 1824; Will, 1956; Schnapp-Gourbeillon, 1979, 2002, pp. 344–346, note 3; see also Chapter 6, p. 139.
[31] Schnapp-Gourbeillon, 2002.
[32] Giannopoulos, 2012; see Chapter 12, p. 260.
[33] Lazaridis et al., 2017.

328   THIRD MOVEMENT (1945–THIRD MILLENNIUM)

the speakers of Indo-European languages—or more precisely those languages that belong to the so-called Indo-Aryan sub-family—arrived in India. This sub-family groups together the languages of present-day India, Pakistan, Iran, Afghanistan, and Tajikistan as well as the languages of the Kurds (who are divided up between Turkey, Iran, Iraq, and Syria), the Ossetes of the Caucasus, and also the languages once spoken by the ancient Scythians, the Alans, the population of the Near Eastern kingdom of Mittani, etc. The discovery in the 1920s of the Indus Civilization of Pakistan and Northern India by agents of the British-organized Archaeological Survey of India added a whole new archaeological dimension to these discussions. This was, in effect, a hitherto unknown urban civilization, virtually contemporary with those of Egypt and Mesopotamia, with vast cities such as Harappa and Mohenjo-daro and its own form of script, which still remains undeciphered.

British archaeologists, with Sir Mortimer Wheeler to the fore (one of the founders of the stratigraphic method of excavation), constructed a historical scenario which combined archaeological data with interpretations of the oldest known Indian texts, the Vedic hymns. According to this scenario, which still appears in numerous school textbooks in India, Indo-European invaders, the "Aryas" of the Vedic texts (from which we get the word "Aryans," synonymous with "Indo-Europeans," and which, to complicate matters, is also used to qualify the so-called Indo-Aryan language[34]), who arrived from the north in their horse-drawn war chariots, would have razed the cities of the Indus and provoked the collapse of this entire society; a collapse which, incidentally, was followed by a very poorly understood archaeological period. The scenario was embellished by the hypothesis that the bearers of the Indus civilization would have spoken Dravidian languages (a linguistic group very distant from the Indo-European languages) and that they would have retreated to the south of India where these languages are spoken today. The higher castes of India, namely the Brahmins (priests) and *kshatriyas* (warriors), would however have descended directly from the "Aryan" invaders and are often said to have lighter skin and eyes than the rest of the population. Symptomatically, this scenario suited not only the British colonizers (who, ultimately, were simply reenacting the original invasion) but also the higher castes. But this was also the scenario adopted by Marxist politicians and historians in India who simply reversed the interpretation: the domination by these higher castes is inherited from illegitimate invaders who should be put in their place—a bit like the French nobility, with their supposed Frankish origins, under the Revolution.

This vision changed with the rise of Hindu nationalism, which sometimes takes violent forms, such as the 1992 demolition of the Babri mosque in Ayodhya

---

[34] See Chapter 3, pp. 33–40.

FROM PREHISTORY TO HISTORY   329

(the ensuing riots left 2,000 people dead), not to mention regular political assassinations. Today, in a bid for autochthony, these nationalists call for the indigenization of the "Aryas." In this case, not only would the Indus civilization be Indo-European, but India itself would be the famous cradle of the original Proto–Indo-Europeans before their general dispersal, which, through an unexpected bias, is a return to the theses proposed 200 years ago by the first Indo-Europeanists. In the extreme religious version, the Hindu gods, being eternal, have always been present in India.[35] This is far from being a marginal phenomenon since the extremist Hindu party, the Bharatiya Janata Party (BJP, "the Party of the Indian people"), governs several of the states in the Indian federation and rules over the country at the national level, with the result that many educational programs have been rewritten to reflect these theories. However, support for the autochthonist thesis is not just confined to India; it is found, for example, in the work of French scholar Michel Danino and Greek scholar Nicholas Kazanas.[36] The debates surrounding this issue are heated, to the point that the *Journal of Indo-European Studies* has devoted at least two successive issues to refuting an autochthonist article by Nicholas Kazanas, which the editors of the journal nonetheless published after much hesitation.[37]

Data concerning the Indo-Europeans in India are based, as elsewhere, on linguistics, archaeology, and, secondarily, on biological anthropology with, as elsewhere, a permanent risk of interdisciplinary circular arguments, each science believing that the hypothesis is well established within the others. As is common, linguistics provide the starting point: there is general agreement that the languages mentioned above should be grouped together within what is termed the "Indo-Iranian" group, and the aim then is to find its point of origin and its modes of diffusion. The resemblances between India's most ancient texts (i.e., the Vedic hymns, including the Rig-Veda) and the oldest Iranian texts (the Avesta) suggest that a separation, if indeed there was a separation, occurred relatively recently. Since there has been a tendency in recent years to push back the date of the Iranian texts, and since the Vedic texts are traditionally dated to the second half of the second millennium BCE (although they were not actually transcribed until the last few centuries BCE when writing developed in the Indian states) this separation would have occurred at the latest in the second millennium BCE.

Such a chronology would therefore be in line with the collapse of the Indus civilization, which is firmly dated to c. 1700 BCE. The problem is that in recent decades there seems to be less and less evidence for an armed invasion that might have destroyed this civilization.[38] The great cities of the Indus were neither

---

[35] Fussman, 2003; Witzel, 2003, 2006; Trautmann, 1997.
[36] Danino, 2006, 2010; Kazanas, 2009.
[37] *Journal of Indo-European Studies*, vols. 30 and 31.
[38] Shaffer, 1984; Fussman et al., 2005; Jarrige, 1973, 1988, 1995; Danino, 2006.

330 THIRD MOVEMENT (1945–THIRD MILLENNIUM)

burned nor destroyed but simply abandoned over time. The bodies which, for past generations of British archaeologists, such as Mortimer Wheeler or Raymond and Bridget Allchin, littered the streets of the devastated cities in fact came from tombs that were perfectly normal and indeed somewhat later in date. Horses are no more common in India after the collapse of the Indus civilization than before. Thus, the general opinion among archaeologists is that this great urban civilization—contemporary with those of Egypt, Mesopotamia, and Jiroft in Iran—became oversized relative to its environmental and social resources and collapsed upon itself, a process perhaps exacerbated by climatic oscillations.[39] It was not replaced by a totally different culture, that of the supposed invader, but by traditional village communities which were less stratified and better suited to exploiting available resources.

In parallel, invasionist theorists have long turned to the Rig-Veda, the most ancient text in India, to support their idea. This collection of often obscure hymns is in part devoted to struggles between the forces of Good and Evil. On the side of the Good are the "Aryas," while their adversaries are referred to as the "Dasas." Since the latter are described as being black and "without noses," they have been identified with the supposedly Dravidian indigenous populations of the Indus civilization that would eventually be pushed southward by the "Aryan" invaders arriving from the north in their war chariots. It is believed that a vague gradient in skin color, from north to south, is observable across the Indian sub-continent, just as in Africa and Oceania, with natural selection favoring darker skin in regions more exposed to solar radiation, and vice versa. However, while the populations of Southern India do speak languages belonging to the so-called Dravidian group (e.g., Telegu, Kannada, Tamil, and Brahui), which is radi-cally different from the Indo-European family and which has been compared to Elamite of ancient Iran (not counting a third linguistic group, referred to as "Munda," found in the center of the subcontinent), it is difficult to define a "Dravidian civilization" per se. It should also be remembered that the Dasas of the Rig-Veda, in addition to their dark skin and absence of noses (or their "flat noses"), sometimes have three heads, which singularly complicates their identification with real populations! This is why physical anthropology has not contributed any meaningful results either.[40]

The Rig-Veda should not therefore be interpreted historically, just as the his-tory of Roman origins is simply the transcription of mythological tales into a historical form, as has been shown convincingly by Georges Dumézil,[41] even though such tales may naturally integrate concrete aspects of the life of past

---

[39] Francfort, 2005.
[40] Kumar, 1973.
[41] See Chapter 16, pp. 355–356.

FROM PREHISTORY TO HISTORY   331

societies. And the "Aryas" of the Rig-Veda are thus the "noble people." The word "Arya" is common to all Indo-Iranian languages and its origin remains uncertain. For linguist Oswald Szemerényi, it may even have been a borrowing from a non–Indo-European Near Eastern language such as Ugaritic and would have meant "kinsman, companion."[42] This problematic term was nonetheless chosen by many to designate, as the case may be, the Indo-European languages of India, or the Indo-European languages in general, or even the Indo-European "people" as a whole; in Nazi ideology it was used to refer to the Indo-European "race."

As well as these ancient texts, toponymy has also been used as evidence. A certain number of current place names and hydronyms of Central Asia are considered to be of Iranian or Indo-Iranian origin.[43] However, Indo-Iranian–speaking populations were also present in these regions at other moments in history. Finally, linguists have identified in Indo-Iranian languages certain borrowings from Finno-Ugric languages, which are often believed to have been the languages spoken by the hunter-gatherers of the vast Russian forests to the north of the steppes and whose descendant languages are still spoken by a number of minorities within the Russian federation (e.g., Mordvin, Mari, Komi, Syrian, Ostyak or Khanty, Vogul, Mansi, etc.). Linguists with a creative flair, such as Finnish Indianist Asko Parpola, combined archaeological evidence and supposed early contacts to come up with various imaginative but unsupported scenarios to explain these occurrences.[44]

The world of the steppes and national issues

Returning to the archaeological case file, as in Greece, we have to begin with a simple fact: the Indo-European languages of India are distant from the two other linguistic groups found on the subcontinent (i.e., Dravidian and Munda languages) and are very close to Iranian languages, which would imply a shared linguistic past at one time in history. The standard steppic theory generally identifies the undivided Indo-Iranians (i.e., the supposed ancestors of the speakers of the languages now spoken in Iran, India, and neighboring regions) with the Andronovo (Fedorovka) archaeological culture which, at the beginning of the second millennium BCE, spread across Central Asia from the Caspian and the Urals to the Yenisei River and the Altay Mountains (see Appendix 15). In fact, it is more appropriate to refer to this as an extensive cultural complex made up of numerous regional variants and chronological phases (Alakul, Fedorovo,

[42] Szemerényi, 1977, pp. 125–149.
[43] Kuz'mina, 2007.
[44] Parpola, 1999, 2012.

332 THIRD MOVEMENT (1945–THIRD MILLENNIUM)

Karasuk, Alekseyevka, Tazabagyab, Kajrak Kum, etc.) and which occupies a vast region that still remains largely unexplored in terms of archaeology. This cultural complex itself arises from a series of successive cultural phenomena starting with the eastern part of the Pit Grave culture at the end of the fourth and beginning of the third millennia BCE; this was the first steppic culture classed as belonging to the Bronze Age,[45] reaching its easternmost extent with what is termed the Afanasievo culture. Second came the Catacomb cultures in the European steppes—such as the Poltavka (which continues the Pit Grave culture) and the Abashevo and the Fatyanovo-Balanovo cultures (the latter is often regarded as the easternmost extension of the North European Corded Ware culture) in the third and early second millennia BCE. Finally, at the beginning of the second millennium, came the Sintashta-Petrovka culture, which is relatively distinct from the Andronovo. And these are just the main components of the complex. The Andronovo itself is contemporary with the Timber Grave culture in the European part of the steppes.

All of these different steppic cultures are characterized by their own styles of pottery which are exclusively hand-built using coarse clay and bear impressed or incised decoration. Funerary rites are very varied, although high-ranking individuals tended to be buried beneath *kurgans*. Prestige objects are made of bronze, in a region where mineral resources are abundant. The economy is based on crop cultivation, sometimes using irrigation, and on animal husbandry (sheep, cattle, horses, and pigs), although periods of marked climatic aridity starting at the end of the fourth millennium BCE caused forest and pastures to retreat into the valleys and imposed forms of semi-nomadic pastoralism. Nonetheless, settlements were permanent—with large timber and earth houses—and the most important were fortified. The presence of pig is an indicator of sedentarism. True horse-based nomadism, as encountered in historical periods, did not appear before the first millennium BCE.

In the canonical steppic Indo-European model, these Central Asian cultures are believed to have originated in the European steppes to the north of the Black Sea.[46] However, this is far from being a certainty. One indeed finds an eastward extension of the Pit-Grave culture from the Pontic Steppes (i.e., Indo-European according to the steppic theory) during the third millennium BCE, but the Central Asian steppes were not devoid of inhabitants before this time. Hunter-gatherer populations living there had adopted pottery making and animal husbandry; for example, the Kelteminar culture, which depended on aquatic resources, and the Botai culture, which hunted horses extensively and probably even domesticated them. The high degree of variation in the Andronovo

---

[45] See Chapter 14.
[46] See Chapter 14.

FROM PREHISTORY TO HISTORY   333

"culture" across its vast territory is due to constant multiple interactions between societies of various origins with different socioeconomic systems and whose languages and ideologies were therefore most probably distinct; as is often the case, archaeologists have conveniently grouped them together within a single "culture." Paleogenetics confirm this image of diversity.[47]

The Sintashta culture, revealed by excavations carried out over the past three decades, is quite spectacular with its circular fortified cities and its princely tombs, which contain some of the oldest known spoke-wheeled chariots. Its possible long-distance links with the Mycenaean world have already been mentioned.[48] Apart from the eponymous Sintashta site, the most mediatized site is Arkaim, discovered in 1987 and excavated by controversial archaeologist Gennady Zdanovich. No doubt in a laudable attempt to save it from being submerged by an artificial lake (he was successful in his efforts), the latter identified the site as a sort of original capital of the "Aryans." Soon baptized "Swastika City" or "Mandala City" and considered a Stonehenge-like astronomical observatory, the site has attracted the attention of a number of New Age gurus who preside over imagined pagan ceremonies every year on the occasion of the summer solstice; it has also fallen prey to certain far-right nationalist movements. Arkaim is now seen as the "City of the Aryan hierarchy and of racial purity," the place where "the Old Russian high priest Zoroaster is buried." As Russian archaeologist Viktor Shnirelman[49] has pertinently pointed out, this discovery, which coincided with the collapse of the Soviet Empire, allowed the "Slavity" of these territories (although they were only relatively recently conquered by the Tsars) to be reaffirmed through their "Aryan-ness." Naturally, Russian president Vladimir Putin has made a point of visiting these sites. Zdanovich himself has claimed: "We, the Slavs, consider ourselves as newcomers. But this is not true. The Indo-Europeans and Indo-Iranians have lived here [in the South Urals] since the Stone Age and have incorporated and unified through common ties the Kazakhs, Bashkirs and the Slavs."[50] And the circle is completed when it is claimed that the Indo-Europeans indeed came from the Far North before settling in the Urals.

We realize, therefore, that even in these faraway places, whose study requires a certain level of archaeological knowledge, issues that appear to be scientific are, in fact, anything but innocent. Thus, the identification of the Sintashta and Andronovo cultures with the original Indo-Iranians, before their southward migration, is biased from the very start. All the more so since proof of the "Indo-Iranian" character of these cultures is quite weak. The existence of hearths, even

[47] Narasimhan et al., 2018; Barros Damgaard et al., 2018a, 2018b.
[48] See Chapter 14, p. 326.
[49] Shnirelman, 1998a, 1998b, 1999, 1999–2000; Shnirelman and Komarova, 1997.
[50] Cited in Shnirelman, 1998a, p. 38.

334 THIRD MOVEMENT (1945–THIRD MILLENNIUM)

in graves, is reminiscent of the fire cult practiced by later Indo-Iranians. But, like sacrifices of horses, bulls, and sheep, it is a practice found in numerous parts of the world. Beyond the caricature of Arkaim, the affirmation of ancient cultural ties between Russia and present day Turkish-speaking Central Asia (part of the USSR until 1992) is clearly a major issue regardless of whether the archaeologists involved are aware of it or not.

But, crucially, it is proofs of a southward migration toward India and Iran that are lacking. At the start of the second millennium, a powerful and prosperous proto-urban civilization known as the "Bactria-Margiana Archaeological Complex" (BMAC; also known as the Oxus civilization) flourished in the southern oases of Central Asia. Excavations carried out over the past thirty years have revealed hundreds of sites, the most notable of which, if we ignore the older excavations at Namazga and Altyn Depe, are Gonur Depe (sometimes interpreted as a capital), Togolok, Kelleli, Taip, Djarkutan, Dashly Depe, and Sapalli Depe.[51] This is a true urban civilization, with mud-brick fortifications, temples, and palaces, founded on a prosperous agricultural economy (which involved the use of irrigation) and control over networks of neighboring villages. The graves of the elite contain high-value bronze and copper objects. Indeed, the region is rich in precious mineral resources: gold, copper, lead, silver, tin, turquoise, and lapis-lazuli. Craftsmanship was highly developed, and most of the pottery is wheel-thrown. The existence of seals attests to the degree of economic complexity, as do long-distance exchanges of luxury goods. The BMAC is therefore truly part of this urban belt of semi-arid South West Asia—stretching from Mesopotamia, through Iran (with the Elam and Jiroft cultures) to the Indus civilization in the east—which prospered during the second half of the third millennium and the early second millennium BCE. The objects exchanged also attest to contacts between the inhabitants of these cities and members of the vast Andronovo steppic culture situated immediately to the north.

Invisible migrations and *Kulturkugel*

The problematic therefore becomes obvious: Which of the two peoples are the Indo-Iranians, the Andronovo people or the BMAC people, keeping in mind that their material cultures, as well as their economic systems, were radically different? Both answers have, of course, been proposed, each with acceptable arguments, and we will not even attempt to sum up the highly technical debates—ongoing and nowhere near resolution—between the proponents of

---

[51] Sarianidi, 1999, 2005, 2007; Francfort, 1989, 2005; see Appendix 14.

FROM PREHISTORY TO HISTORY   335

the BMAC option[52] (incidentally, this is where Adolphe Pictet located the original Cradle in 1859) and proponents of the steppic option.[53] In reality, the archaeological arguments needed to certify the "Indo-Iranian-ness" of a given site are highly debatable.[54] Reference is made to the existence of a "fire cult," to the crushing of plants to obtain an inebriating drink (the *soma* of the Indians and the *haoma* of the Iranians—of which we know nothing), the exposure and defleshing of corpses, and, in contrast, their cremation, etc. However, these activities do not leave unequivocal and specific traces within the archaeological record. Cremation occurs no earlier on the steppes than in the BMAC area, and, in any case, it is not a particularly strong marker of ethnicity, regardless of the period in question.[55] The iconography found on luxury goods associated with the BMAC does not share any themes with the ancient Indo-Iranian texts. We encounter a goddess, a bird of prey hero, a dragon, and an ibex-god, which evoke both a shared Eurasian background and clear influences from Elam; only a small number of silver vessels bear scenes that, according to Henri-Paul Francfort, might potentially find comparisons in Indo-Iranian mythologies.[56]

Just as the cultures of the steppes have various historical origins and not solely Pontic, similarly, the BMAC has predecessors which are archaeologically visible in the material culture, both within its home area and further west, when the Neolithic way of life was being established. It is therefore very difficult to assign it a steppic origin. Incidentally, this is confirmed by biological anthropology, with all its limitations, which shows the permanency of physical characteristics within the BMAC and the very limited extent of mixing with steppic populations.[57]

At least one thing is sure: the collapse of both these urban civilizations (i.e., those of the BMAC and the Indus) was not caused by attacks by Andronovan barbarians from the steppes. In fact, it was the result of the slow breakdown of centralized authoritarian power, which did not leave behind a wasteland but rather gave way to more modest, village-type settlements. There are no traces of Andronovan objects south of the BMAC, and the same is true in the Hindu Kush mountain passes that lead to India. As we have seen, there are no traces either in the Indus Valley. But since the current languages spoken in Northern India indeed belong to the Indo-European group, there is only one solution left to save the invasionist model, or at least the concept of an "arrival of the Indo-Iranians": invisible migrations.

---

[52] Sarianidi, 1999; Hiebert, 1994; Hiebert and Mair, 1998. See also Sergent, 1997, with summaries in Fussman, 1998 and Elst, 1999.

[53] Kuz'mina, 2007; Mallory, 1989.

[54] Francfort, 1989, pp. 449–454; Kellens, 2005.

[55] Francfort, 2005, p. 297.

[56] Ibid., pp. 281–285 and 300–302.

[57] Ibid., pp. 302–303; Hemphill et al., 1997.

336 THIRD MOVEMENT (1945-THIRD MILLENNIUM)

To this end, James Mallory, for example, came up with the military-inspired notion of *Kulturkugel* ("culture bullets")[58]—as if, perhaps, a Germanic term might excuse, almost in a humorous manner, the use of a diffusionist model by an English-speaking author. Mallory's explanatory drawing shows a rifle cartridge (or a shell, depending) in which the bullet itself is the material culture and the charge is the language. Thus, the Indo-Aryan nomads of the steppes would have traveled across the BMAC, shedding their entire material culture on the way but not their language. Having thus become archaeologically undetectable, they would then have descended toward the Indus Plains to impose their new culture and their preserved language; this new culture would have had no known archaeological equivalent at the time.

Indianist Gérard Fussman, who is very reserved regarding the standard invasionist model, relies for his part on comparisons with historically and ethnologically attested examples of migrating populations that have left virtually no archaeological traces behind. Thus, "the Indian Lohars, itinerant blacksmiths, still travel from village to village to re-work the tools of local peasants. They can be seen camping in groups of 5 to 10 carts on the outskirts of villages and towns. There they purchase the fabric, pottery and food that they need. When they move camp, only ashes, which are quickly swept away, attest to their passage."[59] Similarly, the transhumant pastoral Pashtuns of Afghanistan live in contact with and are subservient to sedentary Uzbek- or Farsi-speaking farmers, from whom they are markedly distinct in terms of their language and customs. But when they "move camp, nothing remains but a few postholes, some refuse, ashes and bits of broken pottery and kitchen ware which were purchased at the local bazaar, in short nothing that is truly characteristic."[60] Such camps would certainly leave very few traces for future archaeologists; but, in both instances, these movements of people are not linked to linguistic diffusion phenomena.

The currently irresolvable contradictions that mar the many attempts made to reconcile the linguistic and archaeological evidence (and indeed biological anthropological evidence) for the "arrival of the Aryans in India" do not mean that the supposed "original Indo-European People" emerged in India (this would pose the same problems, but in reverse), nor do they mean that "invisible migrations" did not exist in the past. It simply means that, in the current state of knowledge, none of the hypotheses forwarded can be seriously demonstrated. Given the stakes involved, extreme caution needs to be exercised when attempting to solve this issue.

---

[58] Mallory, 1998.
[59] Fussman, 2003, p. 225.
[60] Ibid., p. 226.

FROM PREHISTORY TO HISTORY 337

While the preliminary results of paleogenetic analyses indicate the presence of a partly steppic genetic heritage in certain individuals dating to the second millennium BCE from present-day Pakistan, they are still far from easy to interpret, not least because there is a lack of analyses from India itself, where the hot climate is particularly unfavorable for the preservation of ancient DNA.[61]

The mysteries of the Tocharians

At the beginning of the twentieth century, several Western expeditions—including those led by Austro-Englishman Aurel Stein, Germans Emil Sieg, Wielhelm Siegling and Albert von Le Coq, and Frenchman Paul Pelliot—discovered in the present Chinese Province of Xinjiang manuscripts written in a hitherto unknown language using a script of Indian origin. More precisely, they were found in the Tarim Basin and in the oases located there. Dated to the seventh and eighth centuries CE and usually relating to Buddhism, these texts represented a truly remarkable and unexpected discovery since this language would subsequently be shown to belong to the Indo-European family. It was baptized "Tocharian," in reference to the *Tokharoi*, a people attested elsewhere in Central Asia by ancient Greek historians. A more recent text, written in Uyghur, mentions a people called the *Twgry* in the region. Two languages or dialects have in fact been identified; these are referred to as Tocharian A (also known as Agnean, Turfarian, and Karasahrian) and Tocharian B (also known as Kuchean)—it should be noted that the term "Tocharian," despite being the subject of debate, has passed into general use.

Linguists were struck by certain aspects of Tocharian (or versions of Tocharian). It displays fewer affinities with other geographically close Indo-European languages, such as the Indo-Iranian languages (except for certain recent borrowings) than with much more distant Indo-European languages, particularly those of Europe itself. For instance, Tocharian was, phonetically speaking, a *centum* language (i.e., belonging to the western Indo-European branch of the group which includes Latin, Greek, Germanic, etc.) and not a *satem* language (like Indo-Iranian, Baltic, and Slavic)[62]; the passive voice ends in "r" (as in Latin and Hittite); some aspects render it comparable to the Slavic languages, while others are reminiscent of Greek.[63]

Therefore, at an unknown date, the original Tocharians would have traveled at least 4,000 kilometers from Eastern Europe to Xinjiang without encountering,

---

[61] Narasimhan et al., 2018.
[62] See Chapter 7, p. 158.
[63] Pinault, 1989; Ringe, 1996.

338   THIRD MOVEMENT (1945–THIRD MILLENNIUM)

except perhaps marginally, any Indo-Iranians along the way. During the Neolithic, in the fourth millennium BCE, this region was in no way distinct from Chinese regions further east, and the Yangshao culture, with its painted pottery, and the subsequent Longshan culture, are both well-attested there. The "arrival" of the Tocharians would therefore have to have occurred in the interval between the end of the Neolithic and the middle of the first millennium CE, when the earliest known texts were produced; this is a very long interval indeed. At the time when the Tocharian texts were written, or a few centuries beforehand, the Chinese sources describe various populations in the region, but their identification with the speakers of the Tocharian languages is by no means certain since the Chinese annalists were not concerned with linguistics. In addition to the small oasis states of the Tarim Basin (Kucha, Karasahr, and Yuezhi), the sources mention, among others, the Xiongnu, the Wusun, and the Yushi, who were often at war with one another. Wall paintings also show individuals from this period, some of whom are depicted as having red hair and green eyes. Their apparently Indo-European physical characteristics caused a major stir, as did a Chinese description of the Wusun as having red hair, blue eyes, and resembling monkeys. At the end of the first millennium CE, Turkish-speaking populations from Mongolia, the Uyghurs, occupied the region and led to the disappearance of the Tocharian languages before being themselves conquered by the Manchu in the eighteenth century and integrated within the Chinese Empire in the nineteenth century with the support of the British—the word "Xinjiang" literally means "New Frontier."

The archaeology of Xinjiang, a region three times the size of France, remains largely unexplored. Nonetheless, the area became the focus of intense attention when a number of newly discovered cemeteries, such as those at Gumugou, Shanpula, Subeixi, Wupu, and Zaghunluq, yielded naturally mummified bodies which were spectacularly well-preserved because of the desert climate. Equally well-preserved were the colorful fabrics which originally enveloped the bodies. There are also a number of cemeteries where the bodies decomposed and only survive in skeletal form (e.g., Hejing, Xianbei, and Yanbulak). These tombs are spread out over time, spanning from the second millennium BCE to the first millennium CE, and are therefore, for the most part, older than the Tocharian texts. Some of the bodies are considered to be of "Europoid type" and this explains why they were naturally seen to be proof of the arrival of the Tocharians from far-away Europe.

On the basis of all this, the suggested scenario is straightforward. At the beginning of the second millennium BCE, populations belonging to the Afanasievo steppic culture (which developed from the Pit Grave culture) would have gradually expanded eastward until they reached Xinjiang, and specifically the Tarim Basin, where they settled. They were still present in the area 2,500 years later and, having converted to Buddhism in the interim, correspond to the "Tocharians" of the sixth to eighth centuries CE; they were overrun by the invading Uyghurs from Mongolia at the end of the first millennium CE. A much publicized conference organized by sinologist Victor Mair in Philadelphia in 1996 was supposed to make this solution official.

Unfortunately, the reality is much more complicated. These mummies do not represent a homogenous historical phenomenon. They are spread out over three millennia and not only is there some uncertainty regarding their dating, but, in this region where populations are constantly mixing and where the presence of "Europoids" has long been attested, the distinction between "Europoids" and "Mongoloids" is far from clear-cut. Chinese texts written about 600 CE, mention the presence along the Upper Yenisei of the Kirghiz (Turkish ethnonym) who are described as being blond or red-haired, with green eyes and white skin and who speak a Turkish language. However, modern day Kirghiz, although still Turkish-speaking, are in fact "Mongoloid."[64] For this reason German linguist Stefan Zimmer, in a well-argued warning, ridiculed the "modern necromancy" of those who would like to "make the mummies talk,"[65] once again citing Max Müller who, a century ago, had already pointed out that "Aryan blood" was as spurious as "Aryan skulls."

As regards genetics, very preliminary results obtained from a dozen individuals, dating from the last two centuries BCE, suggest that a minute part of their genetic heritage may have come from the European steppes, among many other possible sources, which is hardly surprising.[66]

We should also mention that the impression of a long, and even heroic, migration of the Tocharians from their supposed original Homeland to the Far East arises from the fact that these ancient languages are the only examples known in this region, mainly because their speakers were alone in attaining an urban, state-based, and above all literate civilization—while at the same time we know nothing of the languages spoken in the intermediary regions.

Our ancestors, the Celts

The Celts currently enjoy a position of considerable eminence in France, not only because of the famous formula that all French school children used to learn, "Our ancestors the Gauls," but also because of the current appetite for literature propounding New Age ideologies and various religious reinventions and

[64] Bazin, 1986, pp. 81–82.
[65] Mair, 1998a, 1998b; Zimmer, 1998; Francfort, 1999.
[66] Chao Ning et al., 2019, but see also Jang et al., 2021, showing that the mummies are only from a local descent.

340   THIRD MOVEMENT (1945–THIRD MILLENNIUM)

creations in which the Celts play the role of custodians of an ancient wisdom to be rediscovered. In fact, the word "Celt" covers a great many different realities.

From the point of view of ancient historians of the last centuries BCE, the word *Keltoi* was applied by the Greeks to those populations that the Romans called *Galli* (Gauls). It therefore designates, according to relatively imprecise geographical descriptions, a collection of peoples who at the time occupied temperate Europe, from Britain and Ireland to Central Europe. These peoples also made incursions southward, with the Gauls sacking Rome in 390 BCE and occupying the whole of Northern Italy (known as Cisalpine Gaul, literally "on this side of the Alps," by the Romans). They were only subjugated by Rome in the second century BCE. Other groups, namely the Scordisci, settled in the area at the confluence of the Danube and the Sava, while others still, having traveled across Greece, founded the kingdom of Galatia in Central Turkey in the third century BCE, whence they regularly waged war on Greek principalities before being eventually conquered by Rome. The only written accounts of these peoples are those partial and biased descriptions left to us by Greek and Roman historians (the most famous being Julius Caesar) who paint a less than flattering picture of the costumes, customs, and adventures of these "Barbarians."

From a linguistic point of view, the languages referred to as "Celtic" form an autonomous group within the Indo-European language family. While the surviving representatives are Breton, Welsh, Scots Gaelic, and Irish, the first usable texts only date to the Middle Ages and include Christian works and a certain number of legends from Britain and Ireland. The oldest known texts are much earlier, but they are very fragmentary: a handful of Gaulish inscriptions in France, dating to the Roman period for the most part,[67] and earlier Lepontic inscriptions, dating to between the seventh and second centuries BCE, found in the area around the Alpine lakes of Northern Italy. Therefore, it is only on the basis of medieval legends, which post-date the Christianization of Britain and Ireland by half a millennium, that mythologists such as Dumézil have been able to speculate and build a picture of what the primitive Celtic religions might have been like.

Finally, from an archaeological point of view, the historical Celts are identified with La Tène culture (named for a site on the shores of Lake Neuchatel in Switzerland) which emerged in the fifth century BCE in an area stretching from Bohemia to the Paris Basin and encompassing Switzerland, Austria, and Southern Germany; in this region, La Tène culture characterizes the "Second Iron Age." Indeed it is from this area that the Celtic migrations, attested by ancient historians, emanated in the third century BCE, the routes they took being littered with La Tène objects (iron swords, bronze bracelets, torcs and fibulae,

---

[67] Lambert, 2002.

FROM PREHISTORY TO HISTORY   341

etc.). Numerous toponyms, patronyms, and tribal names mentioned by ancient historians in this area (some of these toponyms survive, in a modified form, to this day) can be related to the Celtic language family.

There is, therefore, a relatively high degree of overlap between these various sources of information which allows us to suppose that Celtic-speaking peoples lived within this geographical area in the fifth century BCE; that, shortly afterward, a portion of these populations migrated southward before being overwhelmed or absorbed; and that a number also migrated toward Britain and Ireland at a date that remains uncertain. The Roman conquests subsequently subjugated the entire La Tène cultural zone within which the Celtic languages gradually disappeared. They only survived in Britain and Ireland, but successive invasions of Germanic Angles and Saxons and conquest by the Normans eventually confined them to Cornwall (Cornish all but died out and today is spoken only by about 1,500 enthusiasts), Wales, the Isle of Man (Manx died out in 1974, but has been revived by a few dozen enthusiasts), Scotland, and Ireland, while, in a reverse movement, Breton crossed the sea from Great Britain in the Early Middle Ages to take hold in Brittany. These Celtic languages, within the three regions or countries where they survive, suffer from the dominant position of English or French.

Therefore, in order to link the Celts to an original Indo-European Homeland, we must start from La Tène culture and work back in time from there. This culture was preceded, in almost the same geographical zone, by the Hallstatt culture (named for a cemetery site in Austria), which existed between ca. 800 and 480 BCE, and which is also known as the "First Iron Age." For a long time it was believed that La Tène culture resulted from an invasion from Central Europe which would have overpowered and assimilated the Hallstatt populations. This theory of the Celts originating in Central Asia is still frequently encountered in books relying on anterior publications. In reality, systematic regional studies have shown that in every instance there is perfect continuity, without any interruptions, between the Hallstatt and La Tène periods or, to be more exact, that the changes from one period to the next, in particular in the choice of settlement sites and the style of objects, are largely due to political and social transformations following the collapse of the network of proto-urban strongholds ("princely residences") across the Hallstatt territory.[68]

If we go back even further in time, we come to the Late Bronze Age, between 1200 and 800 BCE. For a long time, this period was referred to as the Urnfield culture in parts of Europe. In fact, while the people of the preceding periods of the Bronze Age (between 2200 and 1200 BCE; see Appendix 15)—in other words during the Middle and Early Bronze Age—generally inhumed their dead,

---

[68] Demoule, 1999a; Brun and Chaume, 1997.

342 THIRD MOVEMENT (1945–THIRD MILLENNIUM)

cremation became more widespread throughout Europe in the Late period. At the same time, a new decorative style was adopted by potters in many regions; vertical or diagonal fluting was applied to fine, dark-colored vessels. In the late nineteenth century, the term "urn field" was coined to refer to cemeteries where the ashes of the dead were buried in these fluted urns. Of course the diffusion of this stylistic and funerary fashion had to be attributed to an invasion by an "Urnfield people." This old theory is still encountered in the work of Marija Gimbutas when she lists out the succession of migrations that followed the great steppic "big bang."

However, just as for the transition from the Hallstatt to the La Tène, when archaeologists carry out a region-by-region analysis they do not find evidence for any movements of population from one location to another across the continent. The diffusion of cremation appears instead to be linked to the diffusion of a new funerary ideology, just as the new decorative style can be attributed to the diffusion of new decorative fashions.[69]

Once again, there is no evidence for discontinuity as we work our way back through the rest of the Bronze Age, nor indeed between the beginnings of the Bronze Age and the last phase of the Chalcolithic, characterized in Central and Western Europe by the Bell Beaker culture, which means that the latter could be the most likely contender for the origin of the Celts.[70] The Bell Beaker culture emerged quite rapidly around 2600 BCE; it involved the diffusion over a large part of Europe of a distinctive vessel type, shaped like an up-turned bell—hence the name given to the culture.[71] These beakers are found from the Iberian Peninsula to Denmark, and from Britain and Ireland, via the Atlantic coast of France, to Hungary, not in a continuous spread, but rather as discontinuous concentrations.[72] The territory it covers, despite its heterogeneity, encompasses the area where the historic Celts would later emerge, but also extends beyond it.

These beakers are decorated with very repetitive horizontal geometrical motifs, incised into the clay before firing, which allow the vessels to be divided into distinctive regional styles. The funerary rites are highly codified, with the bodies of the deceased being placed in a flexed position, lying on the right side for women and on the left side for men. The latter are often accompanied by flint arrowheads, copper daggers, and stone wrist guards. Certain settlements situated close to these graves yield a preponderance of Bell Beaker ceramics, while others yield various local types of pottery as well as Bell Beaker ware.

The origin of the Bell Beaker phenomenon is still a matter of ongoing debate as the number of conferences and publications dedicated to the subject

---

[69] Brun and Mordant, 1988.
[70] Brun, 2006.
[71] See Chapter 11, pp. 250–251; Appendix 14.
[72] Needham, 2005; Van der Linden, 2006; Fokkens and Nicolis, 2012.

FROM PREHISTORY TO HISTORY 343

continues to grow. Certain Spanish archaeologists argue, with some justification, that it originated in the Iberian Peninsula; for Dutch archaeologists, on the contrary, it originated in Northern Europe and is linked to a more northern element of the Corded Ware culture, the so-called "Battle Axe" culture[73]; for German archaeologists, a migration from the Iberian Peninsula would have reached Central Europe before moving back again in the opposite direction; for certain English-speaking archaeologists, the phenomenon is simply due to a network of exchanges of prestige objects between elites without any movement of population. This is the current situation. This phenomenon certainly constitutes a novel development compared to the succession of Neolithic cultures that precede it, and, rather than being reduced to a simple explanatory factor, it should be interpreted in terms of complex historical interactions. This was a period of significant reorganization that was followed by 1,500 years of relative stability of cultural boundaries, at the end of which the historic Celts emerged. A link between the Bell Beakers and the Celts is therefore plausible, but it is the origin of the former that remains to be explained; in any case it is unlikely to fit within the mold of the steppic invasionist model.

As we have seen, there is no genetic homogeneity among analyzed individuals belonging to the Bell Beaker culture.[74] As for the Celts themselves, analyses are ongoing (I myself am involved in a number of research programs), but already it is easy to envisage that, 2,500 years after the supposed steppic migrations took place, a significant degree of genetic mixing will have occurred within Celtic-speaking populations who themselves were spread out over a vast area.

Romans and Italics

Linguists believe that ancient Celtic languages are quite close to Italic languages, to the extent that they sometimes amalgamate them within a single Italo-Celtic group. Of these Italic languages, Latin, from which all present-day Romance languages are descended, is obviously the best known, but the Romans were only one of a large number of peoples who originally occupied the Italian Peninsula, and they were not necessarily the most populous group. This Italic language branch also includes more obscure languages such as Oscan, Umbrian, Samnite, Volscian, Siculian, and Venetic. Italy was only marginally impacted upon by the Bell Beaker phenomenon, which is notably present in Sicily. Prior to this, following the first wave of Neolithic colonization from the Adriatic coast of the Balkans, characterized by impressed wares, cultures succeeded one another

[73] See Chapter 11, pp. 250–251.
[74] Olalde et al., 2018, 2019; see chapter 10, p. 335.

344   THIRD MOVEMENT (1945–THIRD MILLENNIUM)

without any detectable movements of population; the southern half of the peninsula maintaining cultural links with the Aegean world, while the northern half was orientated more toward the Alpine world and its Chalcolithic Remedello culture, to which the famous Ötzi belonged. The oldest known naturally mummified individual known in Europe, Ötzi, who was found in a glacier on the Austro-Italian border, died around 3300 BCE. The Remedello culture is considered by some researchers as Indo-European because deceased high-status individuals were sometimes buried within underground chambers comparable to those of the Pit Grave culture of the steppes. However, far earlier tombs with a similar architecture have been found in Italy, as at Cuccuru S'Arriu in Sardinia,[75] where any steppic influence is highly unlikely; this proves that we are simply witnessing a convergence phenomenon since there are only so many ways of constructing funerary monuments. In addition, megalithism was current in many parts of Europe at the time and concerned various cultures but did not involve any population movements. Finally, Ötzi himself was found to have no "steppic" genetic ancestry.[76]

During the Middle and Late Bronze Age of Northern Italy, between 1650 and 1150 BCE, the Po valley was occupied by a spectacular culture known as the Terramare. The discovery of this culture in the late nineteenth century is a famous episode in the history of Italian archaeology. This was an almost proto-urban society, whose settlements are spread out, checkerboard-like, across the alluvial plain where a sophisticated networks of dykes and canals was put in place to manage water resources.[77] These settlements are hierarchized and their location within a wetland context means that their remains have been remarkably well preserved. From the outset, the sites were densely distributed, suggesting an influx of new populations, which might be confirmed by certain resemblances between the forms of ceramics and bone and metal tools (including horse bits) found in this region and examples found in Central Europe. Already in the nineteenth century, this phenomenon was linked by some scholars to the "arrival" of the Indo-Europeans and Italic languages. Linguists explained that it is because of the canals and bridges of the Terramare that *pons* has come to mean "bridge" in Latin, while the same root means "path" in Slavic (*put* in Russian), Baltic (*pinits* in Old Prussian), and Indo-Iranian (*panthah* in Sanskrit).

This remarkable society gradually collapsed over the course of the twelfth century BCE due to numerous factors including significant climatic deterioration, with colder, wetter seasons slowly getting the better of the vulnerable water management system. The population dispersed and becomes less visible

[75] Santoni, 1999.
[76] Coia et al., 2016.
[77] Bernabò Brea et al., 1997; see Appendix 15.

FROM PREHISTORY TO HISTORY   345

in the archaeological record. At the beginning of the first millennium BCE, following two centuries of archaeological vacuum, the Proto-Villanovan culture (named for a cemetery discovered near Bologna) emerged across all of Northern Italy; it was quickly followed by the Villanovan culture per se with its spectacular cemeteries and its proto-urban structure. During the same period, the Golasecca culture spread to occupy the area to the northwest (i.e., between the Po and the Alps); it is to this culture that the Celtic Lepontic inscriptions have been attributed,[78] and it is therefore reasonable to regard it, at least in part, as Celtic. It would be tempting to see the Proto-Villanovan as a continuation of the sumptuous Terramare whose population had abandoned their now inhospitable territory to seek out new lands. Both cultures share, for example, the practice of cremation burials. The only problem is that the Villanovan culture directly gave rise to the Etruscan civilization whose language is still poorly understood but is certainly not Indo-European.[79]

As things stand, therefore, there is no archaeological solution to the problem of the "arrival of the Italics" in Italy.

Hittites and Anatolians

Hittite is the oldest known Indo-European language, with its earliest texts dating back to around 1700 BCE. As is always the case, the emergence of written texts is linked to the establishment of a state-based, urban, political system, which, in other words, means that these texts were produced by and for a dominant elite but does not necessarily imply that the entire population spoke the language that has been preserved for posterity through writing.[80] In fact, in Anatolia (now part of Turkey), where the Hittite Empire flourished, several languages are known to have co-existed at the time. Apart from Hittite itself (also known as Nesite), which is the language of official texts, we find the related languages of Palaic and Luwian,[81] which can be written in cuneiform or hieroglyphics and from which descend, after the demise of the Hittite Empire, a variety of languages (some of which are barely attested in antiquity) such as Lycian, Sidetic, Lydian, Cilician, and Carian, not to mention Phrygian, which is classified separately.

But, at the same time, in the Hittite Empire people also spoke and wrote in a host of languages: Hattic and Hurrian, which are not Indo-European languages; Akkadian, which is Semitic and written in cuneiform and which was then the

[78] See this chapter, p. 340.
[79] Pallottino, 1984; Thuillier, J.-P., 2006.
[80] Bittel, 1976; Bryce, 2002.
[81] Yakubovich, 2009.

346 THIRD MOVEMENT (1945–THIRD MILLENNIUM)

language of diplomacy and international relations; Sumerian, which by then had died out but whose sacred ancient texts were still being copied; and "Mitannian," belonging to the Indo-Iranian family, of which only proper names and a few terms relating to horsemanship survive. Members of the ruling class of the Kingdom of Mitanni, who were essentially Hurrians, can bear either Hurrian or Indo-Iranian names. This linguistic proliferation is typical of a nascent empire— and we only know of those languages that have been both written down and preserved. It is also typical of traditional societies in which multilingualism is the rule and not the exception.

When it was discovered at the beginning of the twentieth century and subsequently deciphered by Czech linguist Bedřich Hrozný, the Indo-European character of Hittite was strongly disputed. The famous linguist Antoine Meillet once stated: "Its interpretation is still very hypothetical and to claim that Hittite is Indo-European would seem to be somewhat adventurous; it has been contested by most of those who have examined the documents."[82] In an attempt to redeem himself, he observed later that the language contained "innovations that were so considerable that certain linguists initially hesitated in recognizing Hittite as a completely Indo-European language."[83] In fact, Hittite displays all sorts of peculiarities, such as a reduced declension system; the absence of the feminine and dual genders; a passive voice ending in "r" as in Celtic languages and Latin; the absence of the comparative and superlative; and the absence of the aorist, subjunctive, and optative mood (the mood indicating a wish, well-known in Ancient Greek). In short, Hittite is radically different from the Sanskrit of the first Vedic hymns even though both languages are virtually contemporary with each other.

Therefore, the interpretation of Hittite in terms of historical linguistics is still hotly debated,[84] particularly between those who, like Meillet in his initial assessment, detect recent alterations within it; those who, on the contrary, consider it to represent a very early state of the language, to the extent that they propose widening the classification to create an original "Indo-Hittite" family[85]; and those for whom Hittite is a hybrid language, strongly influenced by its contacts with other languages in the region[86]—these mixed influences are equally evident in Hittite religion and institutions.

For Colin Renfrew's Anatolian theory, the geographical origin of the Hittites does not, in principle, pose any problem: they are located precisely within the original Homeland[87] (with all of the difficulties that this hypothesis entails).

[82] Meillet, 1921, p. 99, note 1.
[83] Meillet, in L'Anthropologie, 1933, p. 86.
[84] Neu and Meid, 1979; Schmidt, K.-H., 1992.
[85] Sturtevant, 1962.
[86] Wagner, H., 1985; Justus, 1992.
[87] See Chapter 13; Appendices 9 and 10.

FROM PREHISTORY TO HISTORY   347

This theory also agrees with the idea of an "Indo-Hittite," according to which Hittite would have detached first from the common trunk, while all other Indo-European languages would have become differentiated at a later stage. It also fits with certain recent statistical studies which place Hittite at the start of the general arborescence of Indo-European languages[88] except that other studies, which are just as sophisticated, support the steppic theory.[89]

In the steppic theory, the Hittites are supposed to have arrived from the steppes at a time that remains to be determined. We must keep in mind, however, that James Mallory himself admits that proofs of a migration from the steppes to Anatolia are nonexistent. This debate resembles that discussed above regarding the arrival of the Greeks in Greece, which certain researchers link to the Baden culture.[90] Admittedly, in the last quarter of the fourth millennium BCE, there is a certain stylistic "trend" within the pottery found over a large part of Central Europe and the Balkans and reaching as far as northwestern Anatolia (Troy I culture). But it is difficult to deduce from this whether a migration took place from Europe to Asia or the reverse (both theories have been proposed). There is no evidence for horses in the Balkans in this period, and the graves of the Anatolian Troy I culture do not feature the tumuli that, in principle, typify the culture of the steppic Kurgans. Here again, while nothing argues against the speakers of Hittite having arrived from the steppes at some point in time, nothing in the current archaeological record supports it either. Genetic studies of the Hittites have so far proved negative: as things stand, the "steppic" component is essentially absent from Anatolia.

Their ancestors, the *Germani*

We end this migratory inventory with a number of less controversial, or less problematic, cases. The Germanic people first make an appearance in history with the migrations of the *Cimbri* and *Tuetones* (Teutons) who were defeated by Marius in 101 BCE. But it is only later that they were identified as *Germani*, at a time when all of present day Southern Germany was part of the La Tène cultural realm, which is considered Celtic. Julius Caesar confuses things further when, against all the evidence, he identifies the Rhine as the frontier between the Gauls and *Germani*: in fact, his conquest of the Gauls was halted at this river, and he was keen for people to believe that his mission had been accomplished. The first substantial text written in a Germanic language is a

[88] Bouckaert et al., 2012.
[89] See Chapter 17, pp. 394 and 398.
[90] See this chapter, p. 324; Appendices 11 and 13.

348   THIRD MOVEMENT (1945–THIRD MILLENNIUM)

fourth-century CE translation of the Bible by the Goth bishop Wulfila (at the time the Goths occupied the shores of the Black Sea). Consequently, most of Germanic mythology has been lost because, as is often the case, the introduction of writing coincided with Christianization. The Germanic languages feature a certain number of peculiarities which set them apart as a group within the Indo-European language family and which have even prompted the idea of a pre-existing non–Indo-European indigenous substrate. Certain scholars, such as Antoine Meillet, suggested an absence of initial linguistic unity and favored the idea of an ethnic mix.

There is general agreement regarding the identification of the historical Germanic peoples with a number of archaeological cultures found in the northern half of Germany and in Scandinavia (Jastorf, Przeworsk, Wielbark, etc.), which in particular practiced cremation. All is not clear-cut, however, as the identification of these cultures with Germanic peoples or, on the contrary, with Slavic peoples obviously constitutes a major geopolitical issue. The historical Germanic peoples are often interpreted by historians as the result of highly complex ethnic mixing.[91] Most of the attested Germanic "peoples" appear in fact to correspond to opportunistic groupings, as is clear from the names of certain tribes (e.g., the Marcomanni are literally "the people of the frontier"; the Alemanni are "the people of all origins" or "all men").[92] Going back in time, there are no clear cultural breaks between these Iron Age cultures and the preceding Bronze Age culture which, in these regions, arose from the Corded Ware culture.[93] We have already mentioned the debates and the difficulties still surrounding the issue of a steppic origin for the Corded Ware culture, at least when it is conceived as a simple migratory phenomenon, as well as all the other interpretations that can be advanced.[94]

Slavs or *Germani*?

The first texts written in a Slavic language (which today is the largest linguistic family in Europe in terms of numbers of speakers) date from the end of the first millennium CE, and, as was the case with Germanic, these consist of translations of sacred Christian texts for the purposes of evangelization. At the time, scripts adapted to these languages had to be created using the Greek and Hebrew alphabets: first the Glagolitic alphabet was developed, followed by Cyrillic, while

---

[91] Ament, 1986; Pohl, 2004.
[92] Zimmer, 1990a, p. 153. See Chapter 19, pp. 427–428.
[93] See Chapter 11, pp. 249–252; Appendices 14 and 15.
[94] Furholt, 2019a, 2019b; see Chapter 14, pp. 316–317.

FROM PREHISTORY TO HISTORY   349

the Latin alphabet came to be adopted in Catholic Slavic countries. The oldest Slavic texts are written in what is known as "Old Church Slavonic," which is quite close to present-day Bulgarian. But by this time the Slavs had already been historically attested for several centuries.

The relatively close kinships between today's various Slavic languages (see Appendix 2), which is reminiscent of that which exists between the Romance languages, suggest a relatively recent separation. Their territory was once much more extensive than it is today and at its peak encompassed all of Central and Eastern Europe and the Balkans. The later arrival of the Magyars separated them geographically into Western Slavs (the Polish, Czechs, Slovaks, and Sorbs) and Southern Slavs (Slovenians, Serbs, Croats, Macedonians, Bulgarians), and ethnic cleansing in the twentieth century has reduced their presence in the Balkans.

Roman historians mention a people called the *Venedi*, situated between the *Germani* to the west and the Scythians and Sarmatians to the southeast, which are often identified with the Wends and the Slavs. These "Venedi" are not related to the Gaulish Veneti of Armorica who gave their name to the town of Vannes, nor to the Adriatic Veneti who gave their name to Veneto and who may have spoken an Italic language. It is only from the sixth century CE onward, at a time when the Byzantine Empire was under constant attack from invaders, that Byzantine historians begin to mention the "Sclaveni" and the related "Antes." Their relentless onslaught eased off for a time when, in 1014, Emperor Basil II managed to encircle and defeat the Bulgar army; he ordered the blinding of all prisoners, apart from one in every hundred who was left one-eyed, thus earning him the title *Bulgaroktonos* (Bulgar Slayer). From an archaeological point of view, the sixth century CE saw the rise of what is termed the Prague- Penkovka-Kolochin culture, which covered a wide area to the northwest of the Black Sea, between the Danube and the Volga. It is characterized by partially sunken dwellings and by relatively coarse, tall, flat-bottomed vessels with out-turned rims, known as "Prague type pottery," whose diffusion can be traced as far as the southern Balkans.

Going back in time, we find the Chernyakhov culture with its polished black pottery occupying this same region in the second quarter of the first millennium CE. However, while certain Russian and Ukrainian archaeologists see this as a Proto-Slavic culture, German archaeologists attribute it to the Goths, a Germanic people who migrated from the Baltic and who are historically attested in the region. Furthermore, the southern part of this region, corresponding to present-day Ukraine, was clearly occupied in the last half of the first millennium BCE by the famous Scythians, who spoke an Indo-Iranian language, while the western part was occupied by the Dacians. Therefore, the Chernyakhov culture might in fact constitute a complex ethnic mix, particularly since the arrival of the Huns created chaos in the area in the fourth century CE. The Huns themselves

350   THIRD MOVEMENT (1945–THIRD MILLENNIUM)

were not a homogenous ethnic entity either, and it is now known that the famous Battle of the Catalaunian Plains in 451 CE was, in reality, fought between two coalitions made up for the most part of Germanic tribes, a historical fact that should provide us with food for thought.

Earlier still, on the cusp between the last millennium BCE and the first millennium CE, we encounter the Zarubintsy culture, located immediately to the north of the Chernyakhov territory, which is also often considered to be Proto-Slavic. It is, however, geographically close to the Przeworsk culture, centered in present-day Poland and claimed as Slavic by Polish archaeologists, while German archaeologists regard it as Germanic. Likewise, if we go back even further, we find the Komarov culture in what would later become the Zarubintsy territory and the Trzciniec culture on the future Przeworsk territory (see Appendix 15); however, Baltic archaeologists vehemently claim the Trzciniec culture as one of the possible origins for the Balts. And we should also remember that, in the third millennium BCE, this very region was occupied by the vast Corded Ware culture, which could therefore be appropriated by any one of a multitude of modern nations.

And so, the further we go back in time, the more the traces of the Slavs, the Germanic peoples, and the Italic peoples become blurred and indiscernible. Consequently, in recent years a certain number of historians and archaeologists have abandoned, at least for the Early Middle Ages, the idea of culturally and linguistically homogenous ethnic groups which had been formerly envisaged as individual nation-states that remained unchanged over millennia.[95] And yet this period offers the rare advantage of allowing cross-comparisons between textual and archaeological evidence for societies that were still mainly "proto-historical" prior to becoming true states. We will come back to this debate later[96] because it is of considerable importance for representations of the Indo-European phenomenon.

The case of other Indo-European languages, such as Armenian and Albanian, not to mention more obscure languages such as Thracian, will not be dealt with here, even though there is certainly no shortage of scholarly publications on the subject. Our aim in this chapter has been to demonstrate that it is presumptuous to say the least to claim that the migratory routes traveled by the Indo-Europeans from their original Homeland have now been clearly traced.

---

[95] Pohl and Mehofer, 2010; Pohl and Zeller, 2012; Curta, 2001, 2005; Tejral, 2009.
[96] See Chapter 19, pp. 424–427.

16

Georges Dumézil, a French hero

In France, in the first quarter of the twentieth century, it was impossible to mention the Indo-Europeans without also mentioning the monumental figure of Georges Dumézil, who died in 1986 at the age of eighty-eight. Professor at the Collège de France from 1949 to 1968, member of the Académie des inscriptions et belles-lettres and of the Académie Française, Dumézil belonged to the Pantheon of the French human sciences and was among the last living representatives of the intellectual generation born in the 1890s. He spoke several dozen languages, both living and ancient, to the extent that he produced a grammar of Ubykh, a Caucasian language which at the time had only one remaining native speaker. His personality, enormous erudition, and his capacity for work fascinated all who met him. In his autumn years, he produced three books (the last of which was edited posthumously by Joël Grisward), in which, with rare intellectual generosity, he presented 100 short outlines or "sketches" of mythologies which he himself did not have time to explore fully but which he offered as works in progress to his successors.[1] At the same time, in 1984, he published *Le Moyne noir en gris dedans Varenne. Sotie nostradamique* (translated posthumously into English as The Riddle of Nostradamus: A Critical Dialogue), a Dumézilian analysis of Nostradamus, which oscillated subtly between face value and self-irony.

A sense of the epic

Dumézil was regularly interviewed in the media. The debates triggered at a late stage by his work and certain aspects of his life inspired journalist and philosopher Didier Eribon to publish a book in 1992 with the provocative title *Faut-il brûler Dumézil?* (Should we burn Dumézil?), which just missed out on winning the Médicis Essay Prize that year.[2] In the United States, with their knack for finding an apt formula, Dumézil's work was baptized "New Comparative Mythology." Even though other mythologists tackled the issue of the religions of speakers of Indo-European languages, most were, directly or indirectly, students of Dumézil whose work they endeavored to build upon. A number,

---

[1] Dumézil, 1983b, 1985a, 1994.
[2] Eribon, 1992. On Dumézil, see also Dumézil, 1987; Olender, 2009, pp. 83–94 and 138–153.

352 THIRD MOVEMENT (1945–THIRD MILLENNIUM)

following the example of Mircea Eliade, applied a form of comparatism that was even broader in scale, seeking "archetypes" of human nature: the work of others remained marginal and anecdotal. For this reason, we have decided to concentrate only on the work of Dumézil himself in our review of comparative mythology.

With the passing of time it is in fact easier to consider his work, which is by any measure considerable (17,000 pages and sixty volumes published), in total serenity and to evaluate its relevance regarding the various interpretations of the Indo-European question. His work caused tensions following its utilization by the Nouvelle Droite, an ephemeral intellectual arm of the far right in the 1970s to 1990s,[3] and the controversies that resulted therefrom. But these tensions are also linked to the man himself; he was adept at dramatizing his intellectual path, lending it a saga-like aspect and presenting it in bellicose terms as a long-lasting battle; he also claimed to relish controversy. Sometimes posturing as a victim, he (or his students in his stead) recounted that the beginnings of his academic career were difficult because, from the outset, he had a poor relationship with Antoine Meillet, who still held sway over the discipline of Indo-European studies and over the careers of those who decided to devote themselves to it.[4]

Dumézil also described his intellectual life in terms of an initiatory journey, punctuated with moments of revelation. According to his own account, his early years as a researcher, and particularly his 1924 State thesis on *Les Festins d'immortalité* (The Feasts of Immortality), were ventures into the comparatist tradition of British anthropologist James Fraser, author of the monumental twelve-volume work, *The Golden Bough* (1911–1915). At the time, in a primitivist vision of ancient societies, comparative mythologists focused on the great natural forces (sun, storm, night, etc.) which would have been vested with supernatural qualities; echoes of this vision can be found in Antoine Meillet's own work.

The three functions

But then, in 1937, Dumézil supposedly experienced an epiphany or intuition—a kind of Newton's apple or Archimedes's bathtub—which at the very least constituted an epistemological break in terms of the history of sciences: it involved making a connection between the three castes, or *varnas*, of India (namely, the priests or *brahmins*, warriors or *kshatriya*, and producers or *vaishya*) and the

---

[3] See Chapter 9.
[4] See Chapter 5.

GEORGES DUMÉZIL, A FRENCH HERO   353

three high priests or *"flamines maiores"* of Ancient Rome who respectively served Jupiter, King of the Gods; Mars, God of War; and Quirinus, who presided over the assembly of citizens. Dumézil published his intuition in a 1938 article *"La préhistoire des flamines majeurs"*[5] (The prehistory of the *flamines maiores*). Thus the original Indo-European religion was not to be sought in a sort of primitive animism but rather was already as elaborate as the known religions of the historical periods. His method of reconstruction was directly inspired by linguistics in the sense in which Antoine Meillet defined Indo-European as "a system of [linguistic] correspondences": "with all of the adaptations demanded by the differences that exist between the subjects, in the area of Indo-European studies we are attempting to obtain for religious facts, that which other comparatists have obtained for linguistic facts: namely, as exact an image as possible of a particular prehistoric system of which a certain number of historically attested systems are, for a large part, survivals."[6] Having sprung from Saussurian linguistics, structuralism, through the work of Dumézil, spread its influence to comparative mythology even though he always denied, despite the interest shown in his work by Claude Lévi-Strauss, that he was "structuralist" at a time when this movement dominated French human sciences—he would only go as far as admitting that he was, at most, "structurist." However, the 1937 discovery owed a significant debt to the structuralist intellectual climate and to Dumézil's association with Émile Benveniste, Meillet's successor, who was drawing similar conclusions at around the same time.[7]

It is generally considered that the principal achievement of Dumézil's work is the "trifunctionality" hypothesis according to which the entire ideology of Indo-European societies was organized around three poles: namely magico-religious sovereignty, warfare, and all forms of production (work, agriculture, sexuality, recreation, etc.). The idea that these three principals were originally incarnated in imposed social categories, similar to the Indian castes, was subsequently abandoned by Dumézil although he had initially envisaged it: with the exception of India, this tripartition only concerned the vision of the world or the ideology of the original society and its descendants. The fundamental comparison between the Indian castes and the three *flamines maiores* was systematically extended to other mythologies and, at the same time, was gradually refined. Thus the first function, that of magico-religious sovereignty, could often be split between a more dominating and magical sovereignty and a more serene, juridicial sovereignty, represented respectively by Varuna and Mitra in India, by Jupiter and Dius Fidius in Rome, and by Odin (Wotan) and Tyr among the Germanic

[5] Dumézil, 1938.
[6] Dumézil, 1943, p. 26.
[7] See Benveniste, 1938; Eribon, 1992, pp. 160–161.

354   THIRD MOVEMENT (1945–THIRD MILLENNIUM)

peoples. Juridicial sovereignty, for its part, could be flanked by two assistants, namely Aryaman and Bhaga in India or Baldr and Hoder among the Germanic populations. Likewise, the second function included two symmetrical aspects, brute force on the one hand and controlled force on the other, Vâyu and Indra, respectively, in India. Finally, the third function is characterized by the plurality of its manifestations, although double figures, or even twins, could often be a feature (e.g., the Vedic Aśvins and Nasatyas or the Germanic Njördr and Freyr [father and son]).

Apart from the overall trifunctional structure, narrative themes with the same structure are encountered in various parts of the Indo-European world. The cosmological clash between the gods of the two first functions and those of the third occurs in a comparable manner in India, among Germanic populations, and among the Ossetes of the Caucasus, with identical adventures and a final reconciliation. The Roman hero Horatius, who successively confronts and defeats the three Curiatii and who, on returning home, kills his sister (the lover of one of the dead Curiatii), can be compared to the Irish hero Cúchulainn, who goes through similar trials. The pairing of Odin, the one-eyed magician-god, and Tyr, who loses his hand while saving the gods by taking a false oath, evokes the two hero saviors of Rome during the war against the Etruscans: namely, the one-eyed Horatius Cocles, who confronted the entire Etruscan army, and Mucius Scaevola who discourages the enemy king from besieging Rome by taking a false oath, which he renders credible by plunging his hand into a fire. Over the course of their lives the heroes or warrior gods commit three successive "transgressions" against each of the three functions. These transgressions consist of an impiety, a murder involving treachery, and a sexual infraction, each of which is punished within the scope of the aggrieved function: this is the case of the god Indra and the hero Sisupala in India, Heracles in Greece, Sigurdr (Siegfried) and Starkadr among the Germanic peoples, and Batraz among the Ossetes of the Caucasus. In fact, there are three forms of evil against which a ruler must protect himself— deceit, enemy armies and famine—and a good ruler is revered for his virtue, the protection he provides against the enemy, and the abundance of produce that he assures.

The trifunctional structure also appears to inform various aspects of daily life, such as the three forms of medicine (by magic, by the knife, and by plants), the three forms of injury (evil spells, physical violence, theft), the three forms of expiation (ritual purification, bodily chastisement, and payment of fines), the three forms of capture (bewitchment, physical threat, and purchase), and the three forms of marriage (solemn handing over of a daughter by her father, real or simulated abduction, real or simulated purchase). In addition, three colors appear to be linked to the three functions: white for the first, red for the second, and dark blue or green for the third.

The original texts

As regards the corpus of myths both epic and legendary which allow these analyses, textual data are abundant in India and begin with the Vedic hymns, the oldest of which are traditionally dated to the second millennium BCE but they were written down much later after numerous generations of oral transmission (incidentally, the Veda has recently been added to the UNESCO List of Intangible Cultural Heritage of Humanity). In 1947, the same trifunctional structure was identified by Swedish Indianist Stig Wikander, with the endorsement of Dumézil, in the Mahabharata, an epic poem of 250,000 verse lines which is also written in Sanskrit; the oldest parts of the poem are believed to date to the last centuries BCE. The Pandava heroes, who confront the Kaurava throughout the poem, are divided into the same three functions, sometimes with duplication. In the case of the Indo-Iranian subgroup of Indo-European languages, Dumézil also carried out fruitful research on the Avesta. These sacred Iranian texts are linked to the Zoroastrian religion and are dated to the first half of the first millennium BCE. Much more recent in date, we can also cite the Narts cycle of legends, which are the work of a Caucasian Indo-Iranian-speaking people, the Ossetes, who are sometimes regarded as descendants of the ancient Scythians. Dumézil highlighted the fact that these legends are structured around the exploits of three families—namely, the Alægatæ, the Æxsærtægkatæ, and the Boratæ—whose respective characteristics appear to correspond to each of the three functions.

Staying in Asia, the religion of the Hittites, who spoke one of the three other oldest known Indo-European languages, features a few trifunctional aspects which were highlighted by Dumézil's disciples; the same disciples also proposed comparisons with other more recent mythologies in Europe.[8] But, for the most part, the Hittite religion was of the type practiced at the time in the great Near Eastern urban civilizations, which were non–Indo-European speaking.

Of course another important source of ancient texts concerns Roman religion. According to Dumézil, Roman history is largely mythological. The Romans, being a practical and concrete people, projected the trifunctional structure onto their history while their religion, which incidentally is trifunctional also, is somewhat less rich in stories than its Greek counterpart. Hence, the first four kings of Rome correspond, in order, to magico-religious sovereignty (Romulus, founder of Rome, son of Mars, and eventually deified himself), juridicial sovereignty (the wise and pious Sabine, Numa Pompilius, who was advised by the Nymph Egeria), warlike strength (the bellicose Tullus Hostilius, organizer of the army), and prosperity (Ancus Martius who is said to have founded the port of Ostia).

---

[8] For example Sergent, 1983; Masson, 1989, 1991.

356 THIRD MOVEMENT (1945–THIRD MILLENNIUM)

Rome itself was the result of the coming together of the companions of Romulus, the warriors of the Etruscan Lucumo, and the rich local Sabines of Titus Tatius.

The other great corpus of ancient texts is that of Greece. However, it is difficult to insert this corpus into the trifunctional scheme; it is not easy, for example, to divide the twelve gods of Olympus according to the three functions. Dumézil dealt with this problem by claiming that the Greek genius was exactly this ability to break free of the straitjacket of its origins. For, he claims, "I would have been horrified by what I perceive in the Indo-European world. . . . To live in a trifunctional system would give me the impression of living in a prison. Therefore, I study the three functions, I explore this prison, but I would never want to have lived there. If I was visiting cannibals, I would seek to know as much as possible about them but I would stay well away from the cauldron."[9] In contrast "Greece chose, as always, the best part: instead of the ready-made reflections, the pre-established relationships of people and things that the heritage of its northern ancestors offered it, Greece preferred the risks and opportunities offered by criticism and observation—it regarded humanity, society and the world with new eyes."[10] Of course researchers claiming to follow in Dumézil's footsteps (he himself never wanted to have any official followers) attempted to identify trifunctional organization in Greek myths and sagas (e.g., the scenes decorating the shield of Achilles as described in the Iliad), in initiation rituals, and in various local rituals.[11]

Writing, and therefore literature, is normally linked to the existence of urban, state-like societies and an associated bureaucracy. Neither the societies that spoke Celtic languages nor those that spoke Germanic languages, and *a fortiori* those that spoke Indo-European languages that are attested even later (Slavs, Balts, Armenians, Albanians and Ossetes), fall into this category until the arrival of Christianity—or the coming of Islam or Buddhism in the case of spoken and written Tocharian—in the first millennium CE. This is why comparatists must use the texts of legends or sagas that might have survived the introduction of the new religions and which are presumed to retain traces of more ancient sacred texts. Thus, the Celtic (Irish legends) and Germanic (Icelandic sagas) texts used by Dumézil and his students mostly date to the beginning of the second millennium CE (i.e., the Medieval period). From this perspective, it is not surprising that the Medieval epics, such as the *Narbonnais* Cycle studied by Joël Grisward, show similarities with Celtic texts that are, in fact, contemporary with them and that the latter can be compared to Caucasian legends that were transcribed even more recently. This example suggests that certain mythological themes may

---

[9] Dumézil, 1983a, p. 23.
[10] Dumézil, 1968, p. 633.
[11] See in particular: Yoshida, 1964; Briquel, 1982; Sergent, 1979, 1998; Vielle, 1996.

have had a considerable lifespan. In fact, Joël Grisward, one of Dumézil's most eminent disciples, demonstrated striking resemblances between the narrative schemes of certain *chansons de geste*, most notably the *Narbonnais* cycle, and the Indian epic—particularly regarding the relationships between a king and his sons—and between certain Ossetian legends and certain Celtic texts.[12] But, in the meantime, the Christian Middle Ages had adopted mythical structures that were far removed from those assumed to have been applied by the original Indo-Europeans—unless we see the three orders (clergy, nobles, and third estate) as a trifunctional resurgence as Dumézil was tempted to do. Currently, therefore, it would seem that only a small proportion of medieval narrative schemes lend themselves to such comparison.

The "Dumézil affair"

The 1980s witnessed the so-called *Dumézil affair*, which arose from supposed links between Dumézil and the far right, links that for certain commentators would have tainted his research and his vision of Indo-European societies and their ideology. These accusations and the responses provided by Dumézil and his defenders were astonishingly violent and seemingly out of proportion with the issues involved; namely very erudite studies of very ancient, disappeared religions. The controversy arose from two of Dumézil's publications.

The first of these was *Mythes et Dieux des Germains*, published in 1939, at the start of the Second World War. The following extract, taken from the last pages of the book, is often cited.

> The Third Reich did not have to create its own fundamental myths: on the contrary, perhaps it was Germanic mythology, revived in the nineteenth century, that gave its form, spirit and institutions to a Germany that unprecedented misfortunes had rendered marvelously malleable; perhaps it was because he had first suffered in the trenches haunted by the ghost of Siegfried that Adolf Hitler has been able to conceive, forge and practice a Sovereignty that no Germanic leader has known since the fabulous reign of Odin. The "Neo-pagan" propaganda of the new Germany is certainly an interesting phenomenon for historians of religions; but it is voluntary, and to some degree artificial. In any case, what is much more interesting is the spontaneous movement through which the leaders and the German masses, having eliminated foreign structures, have naturally poured their action and reactions into social and mystical molds whose conformity with the most ancient organization, the most

[12] Grisward, 1981.

358   THIRD MOVEMENT (1945–THIRD MILLENNIUM)

ancient Germanic mythologies, they are not always conscious of. . . . It is this sort of pre-established agreement between the past and the present, rather than the cases of conscious imitation of the past, that constitute the originality of the current German experience.[13]

A preceding chapter concluded as follows:

The preceding considerations perhaps explain in part certain social phenomena, among the most recent, in Germany; the development and success of paramilitary corps, the *dura virtus* and the rights of the SA Stormtroopers, the particular forms of policing that uniformed youths were sometimes tempted to perform.[14]

It is certainly true that on reading these extracts the reader might experience a sense of uneasiness, an uneasiness that is partly anachronic because Dumézil, even if he does not condemn the Nazi regime, is unaware at the time, just like many of his contemporaries, of the degree of horror that the regime will unleash. In fact, Dumézil puts himself in the detached position of a historian whose role at this stage is to describe and not to judge. Should we, however, see in these passages "a poorly disguised ideological sympathy for Nazi culture" as has been successively argued by three Italian historians, Arnaldo Momigliano, Carlo Ginzburg, and finally, in a more extensive work, Cristiano Grottanelli?[15] Dumézil himself responded vigorously and convincingly to the first two.[16]

It is true that these accusations were based on a real, but distinct, fact: Dumézil's ideological sympathy for the French extreme right, and more specifically for Action Française, in the 1920s and 1930s. His state thesis of 1924, *Les Festins d'immortalité*, is dedicated to Pierre Gaxotte, who acted as secretary to Charles Maurras and who would later become one of the movement's prominent intellectuals. In the *Entretiens* (Interviews) which he gave shortly before his death to journalist and philosopher Didier Eribon, Dumézil talks openly about his involvement, explaining that Gaxotte introduced him to Maurras, "a fascinating man—he for one was in the true sense, both instinctively and willingly, a mentor."[17] He even outlines the reasons for this attachment.

The principle, not simply monarchic but dynastic, that protects the highest post in the state from whims and ambitions seemed to me, and indeed still seems to

---

[13] Dumézil, 1939, pp. 153–157.
[14] Ibid., pp. 90–91.
[15] Momigliano, 1983; Ginzburg, 1985; Grottanelli, 1993.
[16] Dumézil, 1985a, pp. 299–318, 1985b.
[17] Dumézil, 1987, pp. 205–209.

me, to be preferable to the generalized election that we have experienced since Danton and Bonaparte.... Of course the formula is not applicable in France.... In our country, loyalism, the somewhat mystical attachment to a living, familial symbol of unity and permanency, the very pride of secular history has long disappeared. It is undoubtedly not to our benefit.[18]

In the same *Entretiens*, he states that he broke ties with Maurras, or rather that he had not seen him since 1926. However, in his fascinating and impassioned defense of Dumézil's memory, *Faut-il brûler Dumézil?*, Didier Eribon qualified this claim.[19] Between 1933 and 1936, Georges Dumézil, under the pseudonym Georges Marcenay, published numerous articles on international politics in *Le Jour*, an explicitly right-wing journal. As shown by these articles, Dumézil, in the tradition of Action Française and of Maurras, was violently anti-German and anti-Nazi, less because of the fundamental nature of the regime, but more because of the threat it posed to France's security. However, the political model he sets out as being exemplary is Mussolini's Italy and its "universalist humanism" which he admires. Without exaggeration and in a definitive reply to Momigliano (who paradoxically was a member of the Italian Fascist Party before having to flee Mussolini's anti-Semitic laws[20]) and Ginzburg, we can state that Dumézil was not a Nazi supporter in the 1930s. He was, however, a fascist in the precise meaning of the term. Perhaps his early journalistic activity was simply a means of putting food on the table, as has been argued by Didier Eribon, since Dumézil did not yet have a university position (Eribon himself was in the same position at the time of writing of his book before he too secured a university post) In fact, Dumézil abandoned this editorial activity in 1935 as soon as he was offered a job at the École pratique des hautes études. We might argue that he could have found other ways of supporting his family rather than engaging in such marked political activity. It is also true that Dumézil kept this activity concealed until Didier Eribon, who like others had heard rumors, revealed it posthumously.

Did this vision of the world, and the fact that he appears to have remained a monarchist up to his death, have an impact on his interpretation of the mythological facts that he highlighted? Eribon pertinently points out that Dumézil was part of an extremely innovative and stimulating intellectual milieu that included many Jewish scholars and within which we encounter the linguist Émile Benveniste, the communist Sinologist Marcel Granet (who undoubtedly had a great influence on him), Jules Bloch, Marcel Mauss, Sylvain Lévi, and many others.[21] In fact, a large body of correspondence provides evidence of close

[18] Ibid., p. 208.
[19] Eribon, 1992; see also García Quintela, 2001.
[20] Olender, 2009, p. 187.
[21] Eribon, 1992, pp. 145–163.

360 THIRD MOVEMENT (1945–THIRD MILLENNIUM)

intellectual bonds and of the perfect integration of Dumézil within this milieu, even though the political opinions of each individual were widely known. At the time there was perfect separation between political opinions and scientific activity—a separation that was no longer acceptable after the war, when it had become clear that ideas could kill. In the period when war was looming and Hitler's persecution of the Jews was gathering pace, none of Dumézil's Jewish colleagues or friends suspected him of anti-Semitism; likewise, none of his writings, either public or private, attests to anti-Semitic sentiments, apart perhaps from a later letter to Mircea Eliade.[22] Furthermore, in 1938, Dumézil was violently attacked, along with other colleagues, Jewish and otherwise, at the École pratique des hautes études in a sickening pamphlet entitled *L'École des cadavres*, by Louis-Ferdinand Céline. The following extract sets the tone.

No doubt you know that, under the patronage of Jewish nigger Jean Zay, the Sorbonne has been reduced to a ghetto. Everybody knows that. But there is also a sub-ghetto, a sort of concentrate of the ghetto within the Sorbonne itself, which you, taxpayers, support through your tithes and contributions, and which is called (for the subservient tadpoles) *"Ecole Pratique des hautes Etudes,"* a synagogue to the point of bursting. The pinnacle of Jewish cheek. The emblem of our unbearable stupidity, us gullible Goyim. . . . The names of some of these upstart, implausible professors: Messieurs and Mesdames Mauss, Marx, Dumézil, Elisser, Grabar, Sylvain Lévi, Stoupack (alter ego of Madame Brunschwig), Masson, Oursel, Weill, Puech, . . . etc. Jews! . . . Jews. . . . And counter-Jews.[23]

Occupation and occultism

Georges Dumézil's political opinions, which were changeable but always deeply conservative, as evidenced in his correspondence with Mircea Eliade,[24] are therefore not key to his work. As I have shown above,[25] up until 1945 the vision of the Indo-Europeans as a mounted, conquering people was not the preserve of the Right or the Left. It was shared and expressed in comparable terms by Antoine Meillet, a committed socialist; linguist Émile Benveniste, who was both Jewish and communist; and Georges Dumézil, who was so closely linked to Action Française. It was, in effect, a pluri-secular ideological construct which few at the time questioned.

[22] See this chapter, p. 367.
[23] Céline, 1938, pp. 232–233; see Eribon, 1992, pp. 176–183.
[24] Turcanu, 2013.
[25] See Chapter 5, pp. 109–110.

GEORGES DUMÉZIL, A FRENCH HERO   361

Moreover, an almost tragi-comical paradox marred Dumézil's own personal life path: he himself fell victim to the Maurrassian and Vichy far right. In the years 1935–1936 and up until the war, he was a member of Le Portique Masonic lodge, which is part of the Grande Loge de France. This affiliation appears to have gone against Dumézil's early convictions, particularly when we know that Maurras abhorred Free Masonry. Why then did he become a member? Faithful to the end to the society's traditions of secrecy and obedience, Dumézil remained very discreet on the matter in his interviews with Didier Eribon, but the latter managed to obtain a number of additional documents regarding his involvement, including the outline of a lecture given by Dumézil on "*Enseignement et liberté*" ("Teaching and liberty").[26] An important factor was no doubt his fascination for secret societies and initiation rites, one of the thematics of his work. He himself admitted to having "dreamt that this so-called 'Scottish' organization potentially had Celtic origins."[27] But, as Didier Eribon reminds us, Dumézil always had a deep fascination for occultism.[28] In the 1920s, he was introduced to radiesthesia, and Eribon, who became well acquainted with him in his final years, tells us that his work on Nostradamus, to whom he devoted one of his last books, is not to be taken simply at face value.

As crazy as it might seem, Dumézil believed in Nostradamus. Or, at least, he refused not to believe in him, he refused to reject, invoking the peculiar argument that, in the next two or three centuries, our knowledge might allow us to better understand this "second physic," to know more about this "upside-down *mundus*" and to understand how Michel de Nostre-Dame was able to access the "archives of the future." This would mean that beyond the reality that we know, and that is understood through the medium of physical and biological sciences, there exists a long thread that links the centuries together allowing the phenomenon of thought transmission: exceptional individuals would be capable of tapping into future events, of connecting their neural equations to the experiences and thoughts of an individual in the future, and it was in this way that Nostradamus captured the thoughts of Louis XVI.[29]

Of course, as Eribon also reminds us, these strange beliefs in no way influenced Dumézil's rigorous comparative method. We will, however, at a later stage question his ultimate interpretations regarding continuity and inheritance.

In any case, his membership in the Free Masons would lead to his suspension from the public education system in November 1941, under the laws against Jews

---

[26] Eribon, 1992, pp. 164–175.
[27] Dumézil, 1987, p. 74, 1985a, p. 210.
[28] Eribon, 1992, pp. 170–172.
[29] Ibid., p. 171.

362 THIRD MOVEMENT (1945–THIRD MILLENNIUM)

and Free Masons instigated by the Vichy regime (following in the vein of Action Française)—which caused Dumézil to bitterly regret having attempted the experience. In the meantime, he had converted to Catholicism, which he practiced with all the fervor of a neophyte, periodically going on retreat to a Dominican priory.[30] However, this fervor was short-lived, and, toward the end of the war, he had renounced Catholicism and henceforth confined himself definitively to atheism. This episode clearly indicates the changing or even whimsical character of part of Dumézil's world vision, or at least "that he possesses several levels of consciousness."[31] His suspension from the education system only lasted a year, and he was reintegrated in December 1942, in accordance with provisions which permitted such reinstatement, including for Jewish intellectuals, in the case of outstanding services; furthermore, the new government under Laval was hostile to these dismissals. Marcel Mauss, who himself was under threat and who resigned from the Collège de France even before the implementation of the anti-Semitic laws,[32] later wrote a note in support of Dumézil. Symmetrically, Dumézil had to appear before a purge committee (which he did successfully) since his reintegration under the Vichy government was deemed suspicious by some.[33]

Nazi intellectual Karl Epting, who was appointed head of the German University Office in France before the war, and who, under the Occupation, became director of the German Institute under the authority of the ambassador Otto Abetz, was mandated to attract French intellectuals toward the new order. His correspondence with Céline, whom he admired, was published, as was Epting's own book *Réflexions d'un vaincu*, in 1953. After the war he produced a list of thirty intellectuals with whom he had particularly close associations. Side by side with known collaborators, including writer Maurice Bardèche and biologist Alexis Carrel, we find the name Georges Dumézil. However, since the list also contains the name of historian Paul Hazard, who took part in the Resistance, it appears that Epting's associations were eclectic, just as Dumézil's ideological fascinations were; in fact, as pointed out by Philippe Burrin, who relates this fact in his book *La France à l'heure allemande (1940–1944)*, "this era was not black and white."[34]

At worst, we could cite the 1941 article, published in the *Nouvelle Revue Française*, then under the direction of fascist writer Pierre Drieu La Rochelle (who committed suicide in 1945), which we mentioned earlier.[35] In it, Dumézil reflects on "the most important event in the recent temporal history of humanity,"

---

[30] Ibid., p. 216.
[31] Ibid., 1992, p. 170.
[32] Olender, 2009, p. 203.
[33] Eribon, 1992, pp. 244–257.
[34] Burrin, 1997, p. 361, and note 85, p. 530.
[35] See Chapter 5, pp. 109–110.

namely the era of the Indo-European conquests, whose causes remain unknown: "Innate imperialism, a confused call of destiny, the blossoming into maturity of a privileged human group?" And he concludes: "Today, beyond fratricidal wars that may constitute the difficult birth of a stable order, there is only one corner of the earth where an *appelant* of this triumph might emerge. But in all likelihood he would arrive too late" This text was also used in the preface to *Jupiter, Mars, Quirinus*,[36] which appeared the same year. Curiously, this strange phrase has never been cited in charges against Dumézil even though it could quite easily be interpreted as a call to, or at least a resignation in the face of, collaboration. Furthermore, the terms "innate," "destiny," "privileged" are surely out of place in a purely scientific observation.

Drieu La Rochelle immediately saw how he could use Dumézil's work to bolster his own collaborationist beliefs.

> In France, Georges Dumézil has done much in recent years to allow us to have a much broader and more precise understanding of these ancient harmonies that connect India of the Vedas to early Rome, Gaul of the druids, Germania and Scandinavia and ancient Slavia. On such historical foundations, a solid and inspiring vision of the Europe of tomorrow might be built. . . . When we have assured ourselves of this perfect continuity of the Aryan genius throughout prehistoric, protohistoric and ancient Europe, we can look afresh at the mix of Celts and Germanic peoples in these three great countries [Germany, France, and England].[37]

Brief consideration must also be given to another more recent controversy which in fact surrounds one of Dumézil's earliest works, published in 1927, in the *Turkish Review of Anthropology* while he held a chair in the history of religions at Istanbul University. Entitled "*De quelques faux massacres*" (Regarding a number of false massacres), the article examines massacres that in certain Greek and Indian mythologies were used to justify ritual practices. He had already explored this theme in 1924, in his supplementary thesis, *Le Crime des Lemniennes*. In 1990, American mythologist Bruce Lincoln republished this forgotten article and suggested that Dumézil, while in receipt of a salary from the Turkish government, came to the rescue of the state in its denial of the Armenian genocide by citing ancient examples of "false massacres." To the overhasty reader, this might indeed seem like a worrying coincidence but Dumézil in fact concludes the article with the following: "The world has seen enough authentic killings to allow us to leave slumbering, within the peaceful treasure house of human fictions,

---

[36] Dumézil, 1941a, 1941b.
[37] Drieu La Rochelle, 1943; cited in Olender, 2009, pp. 106–107.

364   THIRD MOVEMENT (1945–THIRD MILLENNIUM)

massacres that can only be understood as myths."[38] Paradoxically, Bruce Lincoln was one of the American disciples of Romanian-born Mircea Eliade, a prolific writer on mythology and esotericism, who was a close friend of Dumézil, but whose sympathies with the Romanian fascist regime and whose youthful anti-Semitism are well established.[39]

One College, two Academies, and a New Right

The postwar years were undoubtedly Dumézil's glory years. He was elected to the Collège de France in 1949 (by a margin of eighty-five votes to fifteen) at the age of just fifty, despite opposition from more conservative ancient historians and medievalists such as André Mazon, André Piganiol, and Edmond Faral; the latter, an administrator of the Collège, was personally supportive of the candidature of Jesuit Pièrre Teilhard de Chardin to the chair of prehistory, which had been left vacant by the retirement of Abbé Breuil two years earlier.[40] Two decades later, Dumézil was elected to the Académie des inscriptions et belles-lettres in 1970, and then to the Académie Française in 1978, and thus passed from the status of groundbreaker, or even outsider, in the field of human sciences to being a scholar of considerable influence. We might ask ourselves how such a turnaround was possible. In fact, these two Academies are not known for their willingness to embrace modernist tendencies, be it in the sciences, literature, or thought. Indeed it would be easy to make a list of eminent French historians of the second half of the twentieth century who never found a place within those hallowed institutions, or, more accurately, who were never solicited to join their ranks. And the same is true of the Académie des sciences morales et politiques in the fields of modern and contemporary history, philosophy, sociology, and law. A stout conservatism has always prevailed, and this is not solely due to the advanced ages of the members.

As regards the Académie Française,[41] we recall the ironic verses penned by Edmond Rostand (who nevertheless entered the Académie a few years later!): "*Porchères, Colomby, Bourzeys, Bourdon, Arbaud . . . / Tous ces noms dont pas un ne mourra, que c'est beau!*" ("Porchères, Colomby, Bourzeys, Bourdon, Arbaud . . . / All of these names of which none will die, how wonderful!) In recent decades, the following have actually refused to become members: Marcel Aimé, Georges Bernanos, Daniel Pennac, Jean Echenoz, Simon Leys, Le Clézio, Patrick Modiano, Milan Kundera, Pascal Quignard, and Tonino Benacquista.[42]

---

[38] Dumézil, 1927; Lincoln, 1990; Eribon, 1992, pp. 48–50.
[39] Dubuisson, 2005. See this chapter, p. 377.
[40] Eribon, 1992, p. 263.
[41] Garcia, 2014.
[42] According to the entry for "*Académie Française*" in French Wikipedia.

GEORGES DUMÉZIL, A FRENCH HERO 365

This is the same Académie that, in the prewar years, counted among its members Philippe Pétain, Charles Maurras, Vichy minister Abel Bonnard, and collaborationist writer Abel Hermant. Following the Liberation, it felt obliged to expel them but, in the case of the first two, their seats remained unfilled until their deaths. Also, before the war, it awarded a prize to René Martial for his eugenist and anti-Semitic work *La Race Française*; Martial also played an active part in formulating the anti-Semitic policies of the Vichy regime.[43] When Dumézil was elected in 1978, the Permanent Secretary of the Academy was the now long-forgotten Jean Mistler, originally a prominent radical-socialist writer, deputy, and minister who subsequently became a collaborator and member of the "Conseil national," the pseudo-parliamentary body of the Vichy regime. It should be remembered that there was considerable prestige attached to the position of Permanent Secretary of the Académie at the time; in fact the Permanent Secretary was ranked tenth in the protocol of the French Republic, above the Chief of Staff of the Armed Forces. Mistler was also a friend of Dumézil from his student days, and it was he who presented Dumézil with his ceremonial sword during his installation ceremony. In 1975, three years before Dumézil, the Académie inducted writer Félicien Marceau (pseudonym Louis Carette), who was convicted in Belgium of collaboration and anti-Semitism; this induction led to the resignation of poet and Resistance member Pierre Emmanuel, and, in an ultimate irony, it was on Marceau's seat that essayist Alain Finkelkraut was elected to the Académie in 2014.

If we are to believe Alain de Benoist's interview account, Jean Mistler requested him to send all members of the Académie a copy of a special issue of the *Nouvelle École* journal devoted to Dumézil which he had just published; the subsequent election of Dumézil was "largely the fruit" of this campaign.[44] In fact, at the same time the Académie Française awarded its essay prize to Alain de Benoist's *Vu de droite*.[45] Already in 1974, in his role as Permanent Secretary, Jean Mistler had addressed a letter of support to *Nouvelle École*, which was founded and directed by Alain de Benoist.[46] In 1989, this same Académie would award a prize to a highly controversial book on Africa by far-right historian Bernard Lugan, a lecturer at the University of Lyon-III.

Inevitably these associations also raise the familiar question of Dumézil's relationship with the Nouvelle Droite.[47] Alain de Benoist had suggested to Dumézil that a special edition of *Nouvelle École* be consecrated to him; this edition was largely produced by Dumézil and his disciples and friends, but the preface was

---

[43] See Chapter 8, p. 195.
[44] Benoist, 1997. See Chapter 9, p. 207.
[45] See Chapter 9, p. 207.
[46] *Nouvelle École*, no. 25–26, winter 1974–1975.
[47] See Chapter 9.

366 THIRD MOVEMENT (1945–THIRD MILLENNIUM)

prepared by de Benoist who was editor of the journal at the time. In particular, this preface claimed

> The Indo-European heritage that we discover and cultivate within ourselves, we thus doubly project into history, both as a representation of the past and as an "imagination" of the future. . . . And so, when we speak of Indo-European traditions, or when we bring into the light forgotten traces of the myth, religion, ideology and history of the peoples in which we recognize our ancestors, we are not simply looking back. On the contrary, like Janus, we are envisaging the future.[48]

At the same time, Dumézil entered the patronage committee of *Nouvelle École*, thereby lending it his scientific backing. There are diverging interpretations of this episode. According to Didier Eribon, Georges Dumézil, by then disheartened by his failure to make a name for himself, accepted this offer from a journal whose orientation he was completely unaware of. The late mythologist and linguist Georges Charachidzé, one of Dumézil's closest collaborators, gave different but not incompatible versions. In an account sent to Maurice Olender, he wrote that Dumézil admitted to him in retrospect: "My poor friend, what kind of a wasps' nest have I dropped you into, inadvertently, I assure you!"[49] In 1981, Georges Charachidzé told me himself that Dumézil invited him to collaborate on the special edition, pointing out, "with a chuckle," that it was "for *Nouvelle École*."[50] In any case what is certain is that Dumézil removed himself from said patronage committee shortly afterward. We could therefore assume that Dumézil initially thought he understood the general orientation of the journal but that, on reading the introduction text of the issue dedicated to him, he found that it was a bit extreme.

In any case, this is what he confided directly to Maurice Olender.[51] In another interview with Olender (that cited above in which he stated that he kept "far away from the cauldron") he also affirms: "I take responsibility only for what I do or what I approve of publicly. There are studies that claim to follow the same direction as my work and that make my hair stand on end. I don't have to say it. I don't want to have to deal with the fantasies of others. I don't approve them and I don't cite them. There, that's all I have to say!"[52]

Nonetheless, several members of the Nouvelle Droite, including Alain de Benoist and Jean-Claude Rivière, would claim to have had friendly relations,

---

[48] *Nouvelle École*, no. 20–21, 1972, pp. 10–12.
[49] Olender, 1991, pp. 200–201, 2009, pp. 332–333.
[50] Interview between Georges Charachidzé and the author in February 1981.
[51] Olender, 1991, p. 200.
[52] Dumézil, 1983a. See Olender, 2009, p. 150.

GEORGES DUMÉZIL, A FRENCH HERO   367

if not intellectual common ground, with Dumézil.[53] Likewise, linguist Jean Haudry, another influential figure in this movement and who was equally skilled at appropriating endorsements, wrote in the introduction to his book on *Les Indo-Européens* for the *"Que sais-je?"* series[54]: "I thank M. Georges Dumézil for having agreed to read the manuscript of this book; it goes without saying that I alone am responsible for the content."[55] In a paper in the *Nouvel Observateur* published a few days before his death, Dumézil, commenting on Haudry's other *"Que sais-je"* volume, this time a purely linguistic work on *L'Indo-Européen*, stated: "Since 1979 a very good introductory work has been available: Jean Haudry's *L'Indo-Européen*, published in the '*Que sais-je?*' collection."[56]

We could conclude this aspect of George Dumézil's work with the balanced statement made by Pierre Vidal-Naquet on the death of the scholar: "He was used by the '*Nouvelle Droite*' and delayed a little in extricating himself."[57]

However, the recent publication of the correspondence between Georges Dumézil and Romanian-born mythologist Mircea Eliade provides additional detail concerning his personal opinions. In a letter dated April 1, 1982, four years before his death, he shows his true feelings regarding the linguist Haudry and his group. But his remarks regarding "a group of Jews, some young and some not so young" throw a dark shadow over his opinions (without naming him, he particularly targets archaeologist Alain Schnapp who, in a volume dedicated to Léon Poliakov,[58] evoked Dumézil's infamous passage from the *Dieux des Germains*).

> Senseless controversies (racist, or so-called racist, versus antiracist) into which they wanted to drag me and in which they unscrupulously used me, have been blighting my life since December. Indeed, under the direction of linguist Jean Haudry a "Centre *d'études indo-européennes*" (Centre for Indo-European Studies), which is both mediocre and compromising, has been founded at the *Université de Lyon-III*. Jean Varenne lords over it. Furthermore, a group of Jews, some young and some not so young, are busy composing sadly authentic *Protocoles* . . . Look at the journal—4 issues per year—*Le Genre humain* and the *Léon Poliakov* publication that appeared in Brussels (with Olender as editor!). How miserable![59]

[53] Rivière, 1979, p. 15.
[54] See Chapter 9, pp. 213–216.
[55] Haudry, 1981, p. 3.
[56] Dumézil, 1986; Olender, 2009, p. 335, note 33.
[57] Vidal-Naquet, 1986, p. 67. See also Duranton-Crabol, 1988, pp. 167–168.
[58] Olender, 1981; Schnapp, 1981.
[59] Turcanu, 2013, p. 132.

368   THIRD MOVEMENT (1945–THIRD MILLENNIUM)

Trifunctionality and Indo-Europeanness

We now shift our attention from the man to his considerable output. In general, we find that his work poses at least five main problems:

a. Are the comparisons developed by Dumézil well-founded?

b. Does the trifunctionality scheme function without fail in all of the mythologies concerned?

c. Is trifunctionality specific to the Indo-Europeans, or is it a general, even banal, organization found in all human societies? Does it not occur in societies that speak, or spoke, non–Indo-European languages?

d. How does Dumézil represent and explain the mode of transmission of this ideological heritage over millennia?

e. Can an alternative explanation be offered for the undeniable mythological and narrative correspondences identified by Dumézil?

As regards the first point, it is difficult to find fault with Dumézil's colossal scholarship. Criticisms made concerning his methodology are rarely based on concrete arguments but rather on general considerations or even judgments of intentions. Hence the violent tirade delivered in 1949 by Slavic scholar André Mazon, a student of Antoine Meillet and member of the Académie des inscriptions et belles-lettres, against Dumézil's candidature to the Collège de France—a candidature that was vigorously supported, ultimately successfully, by another of Meillet's protegés, Émile Benveniste: "Does a community of language necessarily imply a community of civilization? And several millennia after the fact, is it possible, using a small number of etymologies and texts whose interpretation is uncertain, to reconstruct an actual Indo-European civilization with all its customs, its beliefs, its social structure, its institutions and the entire complex that constitutes a civilization? Today, such a view strikes us as anachronic and, let's not mince words, fanciful." André Mazon also lashed out: "the risks inherent to these domains: contempt for time and space, cavalier use of critical judgement, facile and flimsy constructs, hypotheses that have no future unless their author, as happens all too often, insists on vindicating them and, having become their prisoner, is doomed to defend them in endless controversies."[60]

When we read Mazon's words we realize how, in the space of a few decades, Dumézil had gone from being a marginal researcher to being a giant of French human sciences. However, there is still room for debate on certain aspects of his work. Historians and archaeologists specializing in ancient Rome have

---

[60] *Proposition soumise à l'assemblée par M. Émile Benveniste sur les titres de M. Georges Dumézil*, Collège de France, February 13, 1949; cited in Eribon, 1992, p. 272, as well as for what follows.

often pointed out that, although organized in a trifunctional mythic system, the origins of Rome are also based on concrete historical facts such as the presence of Sabines and subsequently Etruscans on the site of the city. Furthermore, Horatius Cocles, who is supposed to have formed the one-eyed half of a pair with one-handed Mucius Scaevola, like the Odin-Tyr pair of Germanic myth, is not always described as one-eyed in the stories: according to Plutarch, for instance, he had a terrifying appearance because "the upper part of his nose was so flattened, so sunken, that there was no separation between his eyes and his eyebrows merged into one."

The second problem is the capacity of the trifunctional structure to accommodate all mythological, epic, and ritual phenomena. Indeed, since the first two functions can overlap and the third is by nature multiform due to the fact that it simultaneously encompasses work, pleasure, wealth, reproduction, etc., is there a risk that every god, and even every action, could be fitted into the model? Archaeologist and historian André Piganiol described the third function as a "catch-all," a suggestion that Dumézil rejected.[61] A certain porosity, which of course can be explained, exists between the three functions. The third function, as we have seen, frequently involves twins. But one of the divine twins who founded Rome is Romulus, the first king and thus an incarnation of the magico-religious function. In general, the kings oscillate between the first and second functions and sometimes even combine all three or borrow elements of each; Dumézil himself recognized this problem and referred to it as the "king problem." Among the Germanic peoples, the warrior function appears to take prominence, a fact which could be attributed to the bellicose nature of these societies—while the hammer-wielding god, Thor, is also a fertility god. In Greece the Dioscures belong to the third function but are also warriors. More generally, the theologies of the first function are more complex than those of the second and even more so than those of the third, which is explained by the fact that priests belong to the first function, a function that is nonetheless multiform as it encompasses all of the intellectual activities of a society. Finally, while a large number of ternary structures exist, structures with four, five, or even more divisions are also encountered in the mythologies concerned.[62] In short, detractors frequently speak of an "elasticity" that is so great that everything becomes possible[63] although we must also take into account the evolution of Dumézil's thought over time and the numerous modifications that he regularly made to the model.[64]

Without going into the details of the scholarly debates here (which the interested reader might wish to follow up), it is worth mentioning, as an example,

---

[61] Dumézil, interview in Bonnet, 1981, pp. 37–38.
[62] Dubuisson, 1985. On the porosity between the functions, see also Polomé, 1996.
[63] Belier, 1991; Schlerath, 1995–1996.
[64] Vielle, 1992, p. 165, note 2.

370 THIRD MOVEMENT (1945–THIRD MILLENNIUM)

the specific philological criticisms made by German Indianist and Iranianist Bernfried Schlerath regarding Dumézil's treatment of the Vedic hymns.[65] According to Schlerath, the Vedic gods never appear in the form of a trifunctional triad, and it is only through a series of approximations that Dumézil managed to fit them into his desired scheme. He voices the same criticism of Dumézil's claim that the trifunctional structure also exists in the Nart legends of the Ossetes, among Romanian tribes, and in the Germanic religion. Similarly, Indian marriages, which are compared to Romanian marriages, are difficult to fit within the structure.[66]

In response to his critics who claimed that the three functions are constants of all human societies (government, combat, and work) and even of human nature in general, Dumézil always replied that the Indo-Europeans were the only group in the world to use them to create an articulate vision of the world, unlike other mythologies from Mesopotamia to China and from the Arab world to the Americas. Nevertheless, it may seem that this universal aspect serves to reinforce a tripartition that is sometimes somewhat loose and changeable. It is worth noting that one of Dumézil's students and once most ardent defender, Bernard Sergent, later sought to be much less affirmative: "In the end nobody ever claimed that trifunctionality was an Indo-European monopoly."[67]

By excess and by default

This brings us to the third issue; namely the coincidence, or otherwise, between Indo-European–speaking societies and societies with a trifunctional ideology. Dumézil himself admitted that tripartition did not operate in the religion of ancient Greece even though occasional examples do occur, the Judgement of Paris being one of the best-known. He provides reasons for this: "Greece—no doubt as a consequence of the 'Greek miracle,' and also because the oldest civilizations of the Aegean had overly influenced the invaders from the North—contributes little to comparative study."[68] In other words, the model works, except when it does not. Similarly, the Hittite religion is much closer to the religions of other Near Eastern peoples with whom they had constant political and economic interaction.

Symmetrically, the trifunctional ideology occurs, to an excessive degree, among peoples who do not speak Indo-European languages. As early as 1980, I drew attention to the case of Japan, which Dumézil himself had validated

---

[65] Schlerath, 1995–1996.
[66] Malamoud, 2005.
[67] Sergent, 1995, pp. 340–341.
[68] Dumézil, 1958, p. 91. See also this chapter, p. 356.

GEORGES DUMÉZIL, A FRENCH HERO   371

shortly before, where two of his students, Yoshida and Obayashi, had noted such a structure in the Japanese and Korean pantheons and also in the three sacred objects required for the coronation of the Japanese emperor (a mirror, a sword, and a jewel.)[69] Similarly, Dumézil had accepted the tripartition of the Mesopotamian pantheon into sovereign gods, savior gods, and earthly gods, as well as the three castes of Egypt in the second millennium BCE. For the last two cases, he proposed a direct influence from the Indo-Europeans; for the Japanese case he envisaged a process of borrowing from one steppic region to another. As regards the Caucasus, Dumézil argued that while the cycle of Nart legends existed among the Ossetes' non–Indo-European neighbors (Abkhazians, Circassians, Chechens, Ingush, etc.) it did so in a degraded form; the trifunctionality of the original Indo-European version had been misunderstood and had disappeared.[70] However, Georges Charachidzé, Dumézil's closest collaborator in the area of the Caucasus (they both recorded the last speaker of Ubykh) demonstrated the opposite: "the Indo-European memory of the Caucasus," including its complete structure, was perfectly preserved among these famous neighbors.[71] Prior to this, he had also shown that the Georgians, who were non–Indo-European speakers, shared myths with Indo-European–speaking peoples, including the myth of Prometheus who is said to have been chained in the Caucasus.[72]

Naturally Dumézil refuted certain extra–Indo-European examples of trifunctionality which were cited in opposition to his theory. He thus responded sharply to English academic John Brough who claimed to have discovered a number of trifunctional structures in the Bible—it is even said he learned Hebrew specifically to do this.[73] Likewise, one of the reasons for which he learned Quechua and spent six months in Peru was to verify possible affinities between this language and culture and those of the Indo-Europeans; in the end, he concluded that none existed but he did propose lexical comparisons between Quechua and Turkish which he attributed to a possible common origin. Nevertheless, undeniable trifunctional traits are encountered here and there throughout the world, notably in Africa.[74]

In reality, only a tiny portion of Indo-European mythologies are known. Successive Roman conquests followed by the spread of Christianity, Islam, and Buddhism wiped out almost all written traces of the original religions of the Thracians, Dacians, Phrygians, Illyrians, Slavs, Celts (to a large extent), Tocharians, Armenians, and Albanians. Symmetrically, our sources are equally

---

[69] Yoshida, 1977; Obayashi, 1977; Dumézil, 1978, p. 13. See Demoule, 1980.
[70] Dumézil, 1968, p. 570, 1978.
[71] Charachidzé, 1987.
[72] Charachidzé, 1968 (with a preface by Georges Dumézil), 1986.
[73] Dumézil, 1973, pp. 338–361.
[74] Grottanelli, 1993.

372 THIRD MOVEMENT (1945–THIRD MILLENNIUM)

mute or indecipherable for the mythologies of resolutely non–Indo-European peoples of protohistoric Europe; for example, the Minoans (whose writings in Linear A remain undeciphered), the Iberians, the Picts, the Paleo-Basques, the Etruscans (even though Dumézil devoted a small appendix to them[75]), and probably many others.

Finally, certain traits of Indo-European mythologies are shared with non–Indo-European mythologies; for example, shamanism, which is characteristic of Finno-Ugric-speaking populations of Siberia (and which also occurs, depending on the definition used, among the Amerindians, including the Aztecs and Incas, and in China and Japan) and which is also encountered among the Celts and Germanic tribes[76]—even in the Middle Ages of Europe.

Therefore, how can we distinguish between "genetic" heritage and borrowing if everything becomes possible? The following table, which cross-references mythologies and languages, indicates that, in terms of logical validation, the model is not testable or, in other words, is not "falsifiable": it cannot be proved that is either true or false.

	"Classic" Indo-European mythologies	Mythologies that are in part non–Indo-European	Mythologies that are somewhat or not at all Indo-European	Little-known or unknown original mythologies
Indo-European languages	Indo-Iranians, Romans, Germanic peoples	Germanic peoples, Scythians	Greeks, Hittites	Slavs, Dacians, Thracians, Balts, Phrygians, Armenians, Tocharians, etc.
Non–Indo-European languages	Japanese, Koreans (for the general structure)	Mesopotamians, Egyptian castes, Caucasians	Finns, Lapps, Turks, Siberians, etc.	Basques, Minoans, Hungarians, Etruscans, Iberians, etc.

---

[75] Dumézil, 1966, pp. 611–680.
[76] Eliade, 1968, pp. 296–334; Sergent, 1995, p. 381.

GEORGES DUMÉZIL, A FRENCH HERO   373

This certainly does not mean that the undeniable mythological correspondences identified by Dumézil do not exist. On the contrary; but their explanation in terms of a conquering prehistoric people is not the only possibility. Before tackling what the archaeological data can tell us, we should at least mention the counterexample of the "Balkan laboratory." Within this cauldron, for 500 years a province of the Ottoman Empire which abolished all political frontiers and thus all obstacles to the movement of people and ideas, a uniform folklore developed in a context of cultural and linguistic diversity that included Turks, Albanians, Romani, Greeks, Slavs, Sefardi Jews, Romanians and Romanian-speaking minorities, Tatars, Pomaks, and Gagauzes. The impact of these centripetal phenomena extended as far as linguistic structures.[77]

Heritages and heredities

This brings us to the issue of the mode of transmission of this mental heritage of supposed Indo-European origin. This issue was examined, for example, by the Indianist Charles Malamoud[78] who took his cue from a controversial paragraph in Dumézil's *L'Héritage indo-européen à Rome* (1949) that speaks again of the tripartition of Nazism, adding the examples of Medieval France and the Soviet Union into the mix (this paragraph reappeared in its entirety as the conclusion to Dumézil's 1985 work *L'Oubli de l'homme et l'Honneur des dieux*).

That the tripartite ideology conforms to the nature of things is probable, and the undoubted temporal success of the Indo-Europeans is perhaps due to the fact that they, more than any other society, including many societies that were just as gifted, were aware of this natural division in the functions of community life. It cannot be fortuitous that some of the greatest successes and demonstrations of power, right up to the modern history of Europe, are based on clear and simple revivals of this ancient archetype, as has been elegantly stated by Mr. Mircea Eliade: the three orders that existed under the French monarchy (clergy, nobility and third estate), the three essential linchpins of the Soviet State (the Party with its police, the Red Army and the workers and farmers) and the three cornerstones of the Nazi State (the *Partei* with its police, the *Wehrmacht* and the *Arbeitsfront*) constituted, or still constitute, machines of incontestable efficiency.[79]

[77] See Chapter 19, pp. 442–445.
[78] Malamoud, 1991.
[79] Dumézil, 1949, p. 241, 1985, p. 323.

374   THIRD MOVEMENT (1945–THIRD MILLENNIUM)

However, as contended by Charles Malamoud, we can ask legitimate questions regarding the philosophy of history that underlies these considerations, according to which the Indo-European societies that experienced such "temporal success" could only be Western, post-Renaissance Christian societies since, at an earlier date, other societies such as China enjoyed just as much "success." And in this case, did European nations, between the three-order society of the Middle Ages and the totalitarian regimes of the twentieth century, simply live in some sort of unreality outside of this "nature of things"? And why then, to consider the case of Soviet society, were these "clear and simple revivals of this ancient archetype" not recognized as such by those concerned? Malamoud points out that, in official speak, "other distinctions were formulated: the Party and the people; the working class and the other social classes; and, before the USSR became the 'State of the whole people,' it defined itself as the State of the workers and peasants; it was also said that the Revolution resulted from the actions of councils (soviets) of workers, peasants and soldiers." And he concludes: "Exactly what sort of lifeform are archetypes, given that they are habits of thought specific to a particular culture and not universal constructions? In short, how can we understand the idea of a tradition when we cannot imagine the means that allowed it to silently traverse the centuries?"[80]

We have mentioned Dumézil's complex relationship with occultism and transmission across centuries. While these beliefs did not impact on the thoroughness of the comparative method, such might not be the case when it comes to the ultimate interpretation of the identified correspondences in terms of what he describes elsewhere as a "heritage" or a "hereditary path." In fact, like many Indo-Europeanists (such as Meillet[81]), Dumézil oscillates between a purely methodological attitude, in which a mythological Indo-Europeanness, as in the case of languages, is nothing but a purely "logical system of correspondences," and a spontaneous representation of conquering barbarians made of actual flesh and bone. Hence, in the case of Greece, we encounter the idea of "invaders from the North."[82] On several occasions he also states that some of the differences between the mythologies of Vedic India and of Rome were due to the fact that the latter was a society of sedentary farmers while the former was a society of nomads—a claim that is not in any way supported by the material culture.[83]

---

[80] Malamoud, 1991, pp. 120–121, 2005, pp. 268–271.
[81] See Chapter 5, pp. 103–106.
[82] Dumézil, 1958, p. 91. See this chapter, p. 370.
[83] Dumézil, 1941a, pp. 385–387 (see also this chapter, p. 370); 1987, pp. 110–114.

The unavoidable detour into archaeology

We will now make an inevitable detour into the realm of archaeology. In 1967, when as a young student I outlined my career plans during my one and only short conversation with Dumézil, he commented soberly: "My greatest enemies have been archaeologists." Nevertheless, in the last page of his *Entretiens* with Didier Eribon, he compares himself to an archaeologist who constantly revises his interpretations from one excavation to another and who "corrects himself from report to report."[84]

We have already seen why the two main archaeological diffusionist theories—the steppic and the Near Eastern (not to mention the doomed Scandinavian theory)—fall short of providing a convincing explanation in light of existing data. Moreover, Colin Renfrew's Near Eastern or Anatolian theory is incompatible with the findings of comparative mythology since the relatively peaceful and egalitarian agricultural societies that were established in Europe from the seventh millennium onward have little in common with the hierarchical and belligerent world view of the mythologies. This is why Renfrew deftly dismissed Dumézil's findings as universal truths of human societies, or at least of warrior societies.[85] However, it is difficult to bypass the mass of comparative data that reveals undeniable and specific resemblances between various parts of Eurasia in terms of a warlike and hierarchical world view.

However, neither is it necessary, when seeking to historically incarnate the mythological correspondences highlighted by Dumézil, to return to the arborescent model of dispersion used by comparative linguists to explain linguistic correspondences. While this model came naturally to the spirit of scholars in the nineteenth and twentieth centuries, it is not the only possible model, particularly since it corresponds to warrior societies that are already highly hierarchized. In fact, such societies did not really emerge in Europe until the Bronze Age in the second millennium BCE,[86] just as the social and political structures of Vedic India developed after the collapse of the cities of the Indus. During the Bronze Age we have noted the permanent long-distance circulation between elites of several prestige objects (chariots, swords, lances, personal ornaments, composite bows, horses, etc.) and of sought-after raw materials (tin, copper, amber), but also of the knowledge and know-how that necessarily accompanied these exchanges of objects and techniques. This implies the existence of an aristocratic, ideological community, which is, incidentally, reflected in representations brought to light by archaeology from one end of the continent to the other. The differences that

---

[84] Dumézil, 1987, p. 220.
[85] See Chapter 13, pp. 282–283.
[86] See Chapter 11, pp. 249–254; Appendix 15.

376 THIRD MOVEMENT (1945–THIRD MILLENNIUM)

we observe in each literary tradition could be just as easily interpreted as the de-formation of the mythologies as they diffused across space rather than as traces of a distant common heritage. Also, by definition, the texts bear testimony to the religious ideologies of the elites rather than the religions of the common people, which probably varied much more from region to region. The same hypothesis can be forwarded for certain poetic formulae that occur in Greece and India, or for certain metaphors, such as the comparison of the sun to a chariot wheel, which is precisely one of the prestige objects that characterizes the Bronze Age.[87]

A mythological model based on a network, rather than on a tree, would ex-plain not only the existence of non–Indo-European elements (like shamanism, for example) in the mythologies of peoples who speak Indo-European languages, but also, inversely, the existence of trifunctional elements in the mythologies of peoples who do not speak Indo-European languages, such as those that we have already mentioned in the Caucasus[88] or, at the other extremity of Eurasia, in Korea and Japan.[89] It is worth remembering that bronze metallurgy and chariots appear to have diffused from the West toward China, which was, incidentally, a region that produced tin.

Without calling into question Dumézil's comparative analyses, we can pro-pose models that are richer and more subtle than that of the centrifugal and diffusionist family tree—and we should also keep in mind that Dumézil, even though he always had this model in mind,[90] always refused to go further in terms of the implied historical incarnation.

Other mythologists?

Of course, Indo-European comparative mythology extended beyond the work of Georges Dumézil. But his work dominated the field to such an extent in the second half of the twentieth century that it is difficult to find other avenues of research that diverged significantly from it. In 1996, ten years after his death, a collective work was published with the programmatic and revealing title *Indo-European Religion After Dumézil*.[91] The ten contributors seemed to believe that this "after" would not be very different to what went before and contented them-selves with developing certain points in greater detail; the same is true of the two subsequent conferences organized on the twentieth and thirtieth anniversaries of Dumézil's death.[92] For the most part, studies in mythology were limited to

[87] See Chapter 11, p. 254, and Chapter 18, pp. 408–409.
[88] Charachidzé, 1987.
[89] Obayashi, 1977; Yoshida, 1977.
[90] For example, Dumézil, 1941a, pp. 385–387, 1987, pp. 110–114.
[91] Polomé, 1996.
[92] Delpech and Garcia Quintela, 2009; Émion, forthcoming

GEORGES DUMÉZIL, A FRENCH HERO   377

furthering Dumézil's hypotheses by systemizing the comparisons, particularly in the area of Greece which seemed to resist being pigeon-holed within the overall model, just as Dumézil himself admitted.[93]

Regardless of the interesting results of these other comparative studies and the validity of the comparisons between myths and stories that are geographically and temporally distant from each other, they change nothing concerning the fundamental question raised earlier: Do these resemblances necessarily imply a single origin 6,000 or 7,000 years ago (at least) or are other models, most notably involving millennia of centripetal mixing, also conceivable?

We should perhaps consider separately the prolific work of Mircea Eliade. The historian of religions of Romanian origin, already mentioned above, who finished his academic career under a shower of honors in the United States, was a close friend of Dumézil—they died just a few months apart during the same year. In 1945, Dumézil invited Eliade to lecture at the École pratique des hautes études following his arrival in Paris after the fall of the Romanian dictatorship, and he also provided a preface for Eliade's 1949 work *Traité d'histoire des religions*, the translation of which he supervised[94]; likewise, Eliade invited Dumézil to the University of Chicago in 1972. A fluent French-speaker, Eliade would always maintain close ties with France and was part of the patronage committee of the far-right journal Nouvelle École[95] from its inception, even though he was perfectly aware of its political orientation.[96] Long considered "the greatest historian of religions in the twentieth century," his work underwent serious re-evaluation from the 1990s onward. It has been demonstrated that his intellectual and political past, which was explicitly fascist, had been carefully masked through blatant lies on his part and also that his ideology, which was steeped in anti-Semitism and esotericism (with reference to René Guénon, Julius Evola, and Ananda Coomaraswany), had a direct influence on his conceptions of religion and on his work.[97] In fact, seen from a distance, all of his themes revolving around the "sacred," "hierophanies," and great mythical universals appear to spring more from esoteric ideologies, if not downright intellectual "imposture" (Daniel Dubuisson), than from a scientific approach.

When he tackles the Indo-Europeans, his later works are based on those of Dumézil, but he claims to go beyond the latter's interpretation in favor of a universal cosmogony.[98] The most enduring aspects of Eliade's work are undoubtedly the documentary comparisons, facilitated by his vast scholarship, between

[93] For example, Vielle, 1996; Sergent, 1983; see also Delpech and Garcia Quintela, 2009.
[94] Eliade,1949.
[95] See Chapter 9, p. 219.
[96] Maurice Olender, personal communication.
[97] Dubuisson, 2005; Laignel-Lavastine, 2002. See also Turcanu, 2013; Idel, 2014; Junginger, 2008; Olender, 2009, pp. 161–174, and note 8, p. 344.
[98] Eliade, 1979, pp. 199–227.

378 THIRD MOVEMENT (1945–THIRD MILLENNIUM)

mythical themes that are often very distant from each other—but many of these comparisons had, in fact, already been made by James Fraser. Among Eliade's disciples we encounter American mythologist Bruce Lincoln, who was also one of those who criticized Dumézil regarding "false massacres," an attitude that contrasts starkly with his great leniency toward his mentor. Nonetheless, in their method and results, his studies depart little from those of Dumézil.[99]

In another perspective, Italian historian Carlo Ginzburg, who was also one of Dumézil's accusers and a proponent of "micro-history," conducted a detailed study of the inquisitory judgments against witches from the fourteenth to seventeenth centuries. He hypothesized that behind the responses suggested by the judges to the accused under torture there were references to particular cults which may be evidence of ecstatic shamanic practices, with or without the use of hallucinogenic substances (mushrooms, rye ergot), traces of which he identifies, with great scholarship, in various regions of Eurasia as well as in folklore and tales. He perceives the existence of a prehistoric foundation for such practices and thus contends that beliefs and rites traversed both time and space.[100] Ginzburg's work in this particular instance is exemplary of a comparative approach in the area of religion which identifies homologies over a considerable and discontinuous space without it being necessary to interpret them in terms of a strict family tree.

Finally, we should mention the most recent work which attempts to reconstruct a family tree of all the world's myths from a single point of origin, the mythology of the first *Homo sapiens* who emerged some 100,000 years ago in Africa.[101] In fact, certain mythological resemblances might be explained not only by contacts but also by common origins in the distant past. This possibility was proposed a short time ago by Hellenist Pierre Lévêque, who built on a resemblance first noted in the early twentieth century between the Greek myth of Demeter, who abandoned humanity after the kidnapping of her daughter Persephone and thus caused crops to fail, and the Japanese myth of the sun goddess Amaterasu, who hid away in a cave after the sacrilege of her brother Susanoo. In both cases, these goddesses, who were essential to human life, are derided by the intervention of a woman who dances while exposing her sex: namely the second-ranking goddess Baubo in Greece and the young goddess Ame-no-Uzume in Japan. Similar forms of this myth are even found in North America.[102]

[99] Lincoln, 1981, 1986, 2000.
[100] Ginzburg, 1992.
[101] Berezkin, 2007, 2013; D'Huy, 2018; Le Quellec, 2021. Also Witzel, 2013; Thuillard et al., 2018.
[102] Lévêque 1988; see also Lévi-Strauss, 1967, p. 326.

GEORGES DUMÉZIL, A FRENCH HERO   379

Dumézil and the myths

In 1979, during his reception speech to the Académie Française in which, according to the established tradition, he paid homage to his seat's former occupant, historian and diplomat Jacques Chastenet, Georges Dumézil pronounced these strange words:

> Deep down, anyone who today dedicates himself to the traditional works of the spirit lives in a messianic perspective: in the manner of Cardinal Bessarion, we know that our Constantinople will soon fall and, in the still free islands of our Aegean, we are feverishly having copied the manuscripts which, in a rebirth in which we also insist on believing, will bring back to life, somewhere in the world, our Greece and our Byzantium; I am speaking of the letters and sciences of Europe.[103]

Thus, in a world in distress, like Constantinople besieged by the Turks, does the historian of religions become the "messianic" savior of fragments of prehistoric mythologies, destined to be recopied from copyist to copyist until the dawn of this hypothetical and distant "renaissance"? We could consider this view pessimistic or optimistic, reactionary or relativist. But, in this, Dumézil arrives at a conclusion similar to that of Charles Malamoud, published in an issue of the *Revue d'histoire des religions* dedicated to the Indo-European problem and which we quoted earlier as an epigraph to this book.

> In truth, when we become aware of the extraordinary fruitfulness of the comparative approach in the area of Indo-European studies . . .; and when we recognize the elusive nature of the realities to which the substantives which qualify the adjective "Indo-European" refer, we tell ourselves that the researcher, when he attempts to explore the relationships between the human spirit and the cultures, fabricates myths himself. In this instance, Freud perhaps offers us a foothold and the inestimable gift of lucidity: speaking of the theory of drives, a theory that he invented and that forms the basis of his scientific work, he remarks on several occasions that it is "in a manner of speaking, our mythology."[104]

[103] Dumézil, 1979, p. 36.
[104] Malamoud, 1991, p. 121.

380 THIRD MOVEMENT (1945–THIRD MILLENNIUM)

Dumézil had provided a response to this in advance.

> Assuming that I am completely wrong, my Indo-Europeans would be like the geometries of Riemann and Lobatchevski: constructions outside of reality. It is already not that bad. I will just have to switch shelves in the library. I will move to the "fiction" section.[105]

---

[105] Dumézil, 1987, p. 220.

17

Linguistic reconstructions and models in the twenty-first century

After the Second World War, comparative grammar continued its scholarly pursuits, deciphering and editing new texts, debating reconstructions, and proposing hypotheses—but without eliciting strong consensus except for a general unanimity regarding a kinship relationship between these languages—generally outside the field of the most innovative linguistic research (ethno-linguistics, sociolinguistics, etc.). "Revolutionary" hypotheses, such as the "Glottalic theory" developed in Russia, were frequently proposed. Nonetheless, the basic underlying assumption remained that of a family tree. This was still the case when computer techniques for the creation of tree models were introduced with great fanfare. However, a small number of linguists have attempted to develop more complex models.

Discovering original sounds?

The reconstruction of phonemes (sounds) relies on establishing "rules (or laws) of correspondences." In plain language, for a given word, this involves comparing the attested forms in each of the languages that are presumed to be related. Thus, to take a concrete example, the word for "mother" is *mater* in Latin and also in Greek, *mathir* in Old Irish, *mothar* in Gothic, and *matar* in the Indo-Iranian languages. Or, staying with the Romance languages, in the same way that we can compare *huit* (eight) in French, *otto* in Italian, and *ocho* in Spanish, we have *nuit* (night) in French, *notte* in Italian, and *noche* in Spanish; thus the sound *-uit* in French systematically corresponds to *-ott* in Italian and *-och* in Spanish. We know that in the specific case of these three languages these correspondences are explained by a common ancestor, namely Latin, in which "eight" is expressed as *octo* and "night" as *noctem* (in the direct object or accusative). There are therefore two successive steps in this approach: first, the establishment of systematic rules of correspondences and, second, the interpretation of these correspondences through the existence of a "common ancestor."

The example of the Romance languages is particularly relevant. The family tree of these languages, which is founded on twenty-five centuries of

382 THIRD MOVEMENT (1945–THIRD MILLENNIUM)

documentation, is by far the best understood. It represents, including in the historical circumstances of its diffusion, the implicit or explicit model for the entire Indo-European hypothesis, with all of the potential risks of circular reasoning that this entails. Latin allows us to study these correspondences over time; in other words, from a diachronic point of view. For example, *c* in Latin (which is pronounced [k]) transformed into *ch* in French when it was placed before an *a*—*caballus* thus became *cheval* (horse) and *cantare* became *chanter* (to sing); but it transformed into a soft *c* (pronounced [s]) before *i* or *e*—*civitas* thus became *cité* and *cervus* became *cerf.* Exceptions to the general laws are explained by specific laws: *vincam* in Latin gives *que je vainque* in French (and not *que je vainche*) through analogy with the indicative tense; *canine, cantique,* and *cavalier* in French are erudite forms, created directly from the Latin relatively recently. Generally speaking, and like the laws of physics which act as explicit or implicit models for Indo-Europeanists, "phonetic laws do not tolerate exceptions": if they did then anything would become possible. Dozens of such laws exist, each named for its discoverer[1]; indeed, for an Indo-Europeanist to give his or her name to a law is one of the highest forms of professional recognition. This corpus of laws is simultaneously the foundation, the result, and the justification of the comparative method.

One of the additional achievements of the comparative method is that, just like any other science, it is capable of predicting a result. The classic example is the Laryngeal Theory, which refers to the sounds produced by a kind of clearing of the throat, similar to the Spanish *j* in *jota*, for example. In one of his earliest works, Ferdinand de Saussure suggested the existence of these sounds in the primordial language, even though they are rare in historically attested languages. The deciphering of Hittite several decades later revealed the existence of laryngeals in the oldest known Indo-European language. The story is as perfect as that of astronomer Le Verrier who, in 1846, predicted the existence and position of the planet Neptune on the basis of anomalies in the orbit of Uranus (it is also true that, using similar calculations, he erroneously suggested the existence of another planet situated between the Sun and Mercury—in this case the anomalies were due to the laws of General Relativity). However, the story of de Saussure's prediction is only perfect if Hittite is in fact an Indo-European language with an early structure, which is but one possible hypothesis. If, however, Hittite underwent relatively late degradations, to the point of even being considered a pidgin,[2] then it follows that the existence of these specific sounds no longer attests to a primitive Indo-European state.

---

[1] For a catalog, see Collinge, 1985.
[2] See Chapter 13, pp. 267–269 and Chapter 15, pp. 345–347

LINGUISTIC RECONSTRUCTIONS   383

The honest man or woman in the street hoping to learn something of the current state of the phonology of reconstructed "Indo-European" has numerous handbooks to turn to for answers. Certain disappointment awaits however. Since Schleicher's first attempt, such handbooks have appeared on a regular basis, but, as time goes on, they increasingly contradict each other, often quite markedly.[3] One recent illustration of this is the Glottalic Theory, which suggests that the primordial language included consonants that were produced by a kind of clicking of the glottis, a sound that is normally unknown in the languages of Europe but which is well-attested among non–Indo-European languages of the Caucasus, and in particular occurs in Georgian. This theory was developed from 1973 onward by linguist Tamas Gamkrelidze, who incidentally was Georgian, and a Russian colleague, Vjačeslav Ivanov, who was a leading figure of Soviet dissidence.[4] An American linguist, Paul Hopper,[5] independently came to similar conclusions the same year. The existence of glottals, if accepted, would require an overhaul of the entire system of consonants postulated for the primordial language.

This is not the place to explore this theory in detail. However, it highlights the fact that, in terms of the history of science, and despite so many studies and "laws," it is possible to completely remodel at any time a system that is apparently well-founded. It is also significant that this theory is taken very seriously, definitively accepted by some and hotly contested by others,[6] and agreement has still to be reached. Objections have been raised regarding a number of aspects of the new theory: it relies on the supposed inexistence of the *b* sound in the primordial language even though this sound appears to be well-attested, particularly in the middle of words, in numerous shared Indo-European roots. It also relies on the phonetics of Germanic and Armenian, which are generally considered to be much more evolved relative to the primordial language than other languages. Furthermore, the theory does not explain how the supposed glottals were phonetically replaced by the historically attested sounds. Indeed, the presence of glottals in Armenian could just as easily indicate contamination from neighboring non–Indo-European languages of the Caucasus.[7]

At an international conference held in Paris in 1985 on the problem of the Glottalic Theory (and, in passing, laryngeals), the organizer concluded that

---

[3] Among the most recent: Bader, 1994; Beekes, 1995; Clackson, 2004; Fortson, 2009; Klein et al., 2017–2018; Lehmann, 1996; Meier-Brügger, 2010; Szemerényi, 1996; Tremblay, 2005, Klein et al, 2017–2018.

[4] Gamkrelidze and Ivanov, 1973, 1984; a brief article was published in 1972.

[5] Hopper, 1973.

[6] Among the opponents, see, for example, Back, 1979; Dunkel, 1981; Szemerényi, 1985; Haider, 1985; Djahukian, 1986; Pisowicz, 1989; Winter, 1992; partial response and debate in Gamkrelidze, 1992.

[7] Winter, 1992.

384   THIRD MOVEMENT (1945–THIRD MILLENNIUM)

nothing was resolved and that a manual of Indo-European phonetics, equivalent to that produced by Fritz Bechtel in 1892,[8] was still a long way off.

Indeed, the situation is no clearer in other areas of reconstructed phonetics. Laryngeals, for example, the model's great success, which classically numbered three, became ten in the 1950s (this was the opinion of the great French linguist André Martinet) but then shrank in numbers to just one in (as postulated by the Hungaro-German linguist Oswald Szemerényi, one of the most prominent Indo-Europeanists of the second half of the twentieth century[9]): in short, there is little agreement among researchers regarding how many laryngeals actually existed.

The same is true of the vowels of the primordial language. In the nineteenth century, general agreement was reached that there were three primordial vowels: *a, e, o*. Then, in the 1930s, there was a tendency to reduce these to a single vowel, *the* primitive vowel from which all of the others developed. In the face of such reductionist impulses, it is difficult not to think of India where Brahmanical teaching sometimes considers the sacred onomatopoeia, *Om*, as the resonance of the creator Verb, which alone sums up not only all of the liturgical texts of the Veda, but even the cosmos itself. This primordial vowel takes us back to the beginnings of comparative grammar, when the history of languages was also the history of the human Spirit. The single vowel has another advantage: it simplifies the problems of phonetic correspondences. It is the ideal point of origin from which any other vowel can be freely deduced.

However, the notion of a single primordial vowel did elicit objections; the most logical, raised by structuralist linguist Roman Jakobson, is that no known human language possesses just a single vowel.[10] In the 1960s, Jakobson's objection itself provoked heated discussions centered on the Caucasian languages.[11] These languages are, in fact, renowned for their phonetic complexity. Ubykh, for example (the language whose grammar was established by Georges Dumézil and Georges Charachidzé with the help of its last living speaker, Tevfik Esenç, who died in 1992), contains eighty-three consonants for just two vowels. But, in the end, it was accepted that none of the Caucasian languages has just a single vowel. And since the tendency was to reduce the number of laryngeals, symmetrically, because these sounds have a phonetic function that is close to that of vowels, there was a tendency to once again increase the number of "primordial vowels."

---

[8] Vennemann, 1989, p. 269.
[9] Szemerényi, 1985, 1996. See also Polomé, 1987b.
[10] Jakobson, 1958.
[11] Discussions resumed in Szemerényi, 1985, § VI.6.8.

What exactly are we reconstructing?

These cyclical or erratic uncertainties go beyond simple anecdote. The phonetic correspondences between languages are less to blame than their interpretation in terms of the reconstruction—or construction—of the primordial language. Within the terms of the phonetic system of a single and coherent primordial language, attempting to explain not only the correspondences but also all of the phonetic systems of the various languages presumed to have evolved from the primordial language has presented problems that, to date, have proved insoluble.

It must be acknowledged that a large number of Indo-Europeanists do not aspire to "reconstructing" the entire primordial language but, rather, hope to establish a series of "laws" or abstract facts. As linguist Ernst Pulgram once stated, "No reputable linguist pretends that Proto-Indo-European reconstructions represent a reality, and the unpronounceability of the asterisked formulae is not a legitimate argument against reconstruction"[12] (as we have seen elsewhere, phonemes or roots that are considered to be "reconstructed" but not necessarily attested in a known language are conventionally preceded by an asterisk). Furthermore, as once pointed out by Holger Pedersen,[13] the various "primordial" words that make up August Schleicher's famous Indo-European fable, and even the phonemes of a single word, were undoubtedly never all contemporaneous but instead represent linguistic phenomena that were spread out over a relatively long time period.

For Guy Jucquois and Christophe Vielle, who were more radical in their opinions, comparative grammar and comparative mythology are only "meta-systems, oh so useful and revelatory of meanings, but just meta-systems, which . . . neither prove nor depend on the hypothesis of an original linguistic or ethnic unity."[14] Wolfgang Schmid for his part speaks of "an abstract inventory of selected correspondences between a given number of compared languages," of "a more or less fragmentary theory about the common properties of individual Indo-European languages," which does "not lead to a specific point of origin, but rather purely and simply to glottogonic speculation"; to the extent that "the accusation that one is pursuing a phantasm would, under such circumstances, be made on good grounds."[15]

In fact, it is patently clear that the differences between the dozen versions of Schleicher's fable of "The Sheep and the Horses," including the ten most recent versions, are striking. This does not rule out the possibility of an *Ursprache*, but it does show that consensus is still a long way off, if indeed it is ever reached.[16]

---

[12] Pulgram, 1959, p. 423. See also Pulgram, 1953.
[13] Cited in Mounin, 1967, p. 198.
[14] Jucquois and Vielle, 1997, p. 179.
[15] Schmid, 1987, pp. 325 and 328.
[16] See Chapter 2, p. 27; and https://en.wikipedia.org/wiki/Schleicher%27s_fable.

386   THIRD MOVEMENT (1945–THIRD MILLENNIUM)

Disagreement, or even contradiction, can occur within the work of a single author. We have already seen how one of the icons of Indo-European linguistics, Antoine Meillet, could in turn write that the comparative grammar only provided "a defined system of correspondences between the historically attested languages" while asserting elsewhere that an "Indo-European nation" once existed.[17]

Ultimately, every more specific hypothesis concerning, for example, the original Homeland and the supposed migrations of the original People must depend on the particular position of each linguist regarding the status of the reconstruction. This quarrel between the proponents of incarnate reality and those of rigorous abstraction, between realists and nominalists, is not confined to Indo-European studies. It can be observed in all human sciences as soon as elaborate models begin to be developed. But after two centuries of reconstruction, is everything still just a question of belief?

In reality, there is no definitive agreement on the methods of reconstruction. As André-Georges Haudricourt pointed out regarding Oceanic languages, "the mechanical application of the principal of regular correspondence leads to the multiplication of reconstructed phonemes and, consequently, the multiplication of purely accidental similarities."[18] In other words, in order to explain the phonetic correspondences in terms of a single original language, we have to consciously adjust our vision. Scholars have been aware of the problem for more than a century, ever since Antoine Meillet's 1908 book *Les Dialectes indo-européens*,[19] in which he notes that it is impossible to trace all the way back to a single language but that we should instead think in terms of initial contemporaneous "dialects" that would eventually give rise to the various Indo-European language families. He represented the whole as a kind of pie, with a central point and radii separating six parts, namely Greek, Italic, Celtic, Germanic, Baltic and Slav together and finally Iranian which itself encompasses three subgroups (Albanian, Armenian, and Sanskrit). It is surprising to find him using the term "dialect" because he was generally very reticent regarding the subject of dialectology.[20] The term has been reused and debated[21] ever since, as has the manner in which the various Indo-European language families should be organized geographically.[22] For our purposes, the important point to take away from Meillet is that, from the very beginning, there was no single original language.

[17]   Meillet, 1937, pp. 47 and 418. See Chapter 5, pp. 167–171.
[18]   Haudricourt, 1972, p. 358.
[19]   Meillet, 1908.
[20]   Meillet, 1928c, p. 16. See Chapter 19, pp. 432–434.
[21]   Pedersen, 1925; Bonfante, 1931; Tovar, 1980; Porzig, 1954; Levin, 1988, among others.
[22]   See this chapter, p. 389.

LINGUISTIC RECONSTRUCTIONS 387

Certain French linguists who are very attached to the arborescent model in its strictest interpretation have not taken kindly to my reminders of its uncertainties. In good faith or otherwise, they have imagined that I am questioning the very existence of historical linguistics, which of course is not the case.[23]

Of roots and words

Indo-Europeanists have a very complicated relationship with Indo-European words. For Antoine Meillet, for example, "The facts of vocabulary depend on influences exerted on the civilization and are, for a large part, independent of the structure of the language."[24] In other words, it is the structure of languages, along with their syntax and morphology, that are relevant when assessing linguistic relationships, whereas any given individual word could, in fact, have been borrowed. This is why linguistic paleontology was virtually abandoned in the interwar period. We will return to this issue a little later[25] as our mission here is to discuss words and their roots rather than their meaning.

It is worth remembering that the number of words common to the entire group of Indo-European languages is quite limited. If we consider the list of Indo-European roots established by Norman Bird on the basis of Julius Pokorny's[26] etymological dictionary of Indo-European, only about 2,000 known roots are common to some or all of the fourteen Indo-European language families (Indian, Iranian, Celtic, Slav, Germanic, etc.). However, the number of roots common to all fourteen families amounts to just one: namely the root *te-u- which signifies "to swell." If we reduce the number of families to thirteen, then we encounter eight common roots: *au- (to spray), *bher- (to carry), *dhe- (to put), *in (in), *es- (to be), *me (me), *sker- (to cut), and *trei (three). Some of these roots are important, others less so. Moving down to twelve families, we still only find twenty-eight common roots including *bhrater (brother), *mater (mother), *tu (you), and the numbers five, six, seven, eight, and nine. Thirty-six roots are common to eleven families, seventy-six to ten families, eighty-five to nine families, and one hundred and twelve to eight families. The root *duo (two) is only present in eleven families and *kuetuer (four) in ten.

James Mallory and Douglas Adams have established an even more restrictive list based on 1,464 reconstructed roots: they only identify fourteen or fifteen roots common to twelve language families (i.e., 1% of the total number of identified roots)[27]; twenty-three roots common to eleven families (i.e., 2% of the

---

[23] Pellard et al. 2018; response in Bergounioux and Demoule, 2020.
[24] Meillet, 1938, p. 105. See also 1937, p. 32.
[25] See Chapter 18, pp. 399–402.
[26] Bird, 1982; Pokorny, 1959–1969.
[27] Mallory and Adams, 2006, p. 108.

388   THIRD MOVEMENT (1945–THIRD MILLENNIUM)

total); and fifty-two roots common to ten families (i.e., 4% of the total). In reality, three-quarters of reconstructed Indo-European roots are attested in six or less language families, and a quarter are only attested in two or three families. Of course, this excludes hazard (which incidentally no one defends), but considerably relativizes the notion of a well-established "original language" with a homogenous, compact vocabulary (*Ursprache*) and instead suggests a network of very open linguistic relationships. We can understand why certain Indo-Europeanists have preferred to down-play the importance of the vocabulary in their definitions of "Indo-European."

Italian linguist Angela Marcantonio[28] has completed an even more radical study, published in a collective volume which she coordinated and which was published by the same editor as the *Journal of Indo-European Studies,* not generally known for a reserved approach to the original People. Taking the 2001 dictionary of Indo-European verbal roots[29] (which number 683) as a reference, she notes that one-third of these reconstructed roots only exist in a single language (or family of languages). At the very least this allows their Indo-Europeanness to be questioned since they could be unique to the language in question or could even be of non–Indo-European origin. A second third of such roots are only attested in two languages or language families; we should remember that Antoine Meillet himself required that a fact be attested to in at least three languages to be deemed relevant. If we increase this requirement to at least six languages, then only fourteen verbal roots are common. To this we must add the ambiguity introduced by the use of laryngeals—these controversial reconstructed sounds—and also the fact that each root may have several variants and that most of the time there are more variants than actual attested languages. In reality, only one-tenth of roots possess fewer variants than the number of languages in which they are attested, and barely half of these are attested in three languages or more.

These observations have allowed Angela Marcantonio to conclude that much of the reasoning behind the reconstructions provided by comparative grammar is, in fact, circular since it proceeds as follows:

a. We assume that a given group of words are of Indo-European origin;
b. We reconstruct the origin and history of the words in question;
c. We observe that the words conform to the reconstruction;
d. We conclude that the words that we compare are of Indo-European origin because they conform to the reconstruction.

---

[28] Marcantonio, 2009.
[29] Rix and Kümmel, 2001.

LINGUISTIC RECONSTRUCTIONS 389

Therefore, we can justifiably ask ourselves if this approach does not in fact amount to "construction" rather than reconstruction.

Thinking in trees

Behind individual reconstructions lies the general model of the tree or *Stammbaum*. Arborescent thinking evokes both the memory of ancestors organized in terms of a genealogical tree and the representation of social hierarchy, such as the feudal model imposed by medieval society and which the French Revolution sought to abolish. Following Court de Gébelin's "*Arbre généalogique des langues mortes et vivantes*" (Genealogical Tree of Living and Dead Languages) developed in the late eighteenth century, which even at this early stage allowed for language mixing,[30] Schleicher's *Stammbaum* made explicit references to Darwin, literally comparing languages to "natural organisms."[31] This proclaimed marriage thus began a scientific tradition that has endured right up until today; thanks to the appeal of the sophisticated statistical techniques used (skeptics speak of "magimathics" or "mathemagics"), it has garnered considerable media favor while presenting what is in effect the application of a 250-year-old paradigm as a series of ground-breaking discoveries. This current fascination with trees runs counter to the linguistic opinion prevailing at the time when the formal and much more complex models developed by Chomsky and structural linguists were at the fore. As we have seen, this was the era when Georges Mounin was in a position to state with confidence in 1967 that Schleicher's *Stammbaum* "has not withstood criticisms" and "appeared unacceptable with respect to the well-attested facts."[32] Simply typing the words "*Stammbaum*" (or "tree model") and "Indo-European" (*indo-européen, indo-germanisch*, etc.) on the internet reveals a large number of these representations, all pretty similar despite a few attempts at innovation, including the prudent "pie" variant (without branches) as published in the *American Heritage Dictionary of the English Language* in 2000.

Nevertheless, the tree model has regularly been the subject of methodological criticism due to its singularly simplistic character, particularly in the field of linguistics; quite simply, it is unable to accommodate the phenomena of borrowings and convergences.[33] Very serious attempts have been made to test other forms of kinship relationships in the wake of Troubetzkoy and chaos theory, most notably in the case of Semitic languages.[34]

---

[30] See Chapter 1, p. 12.
[31] See Chapter 2, p. 26; Appendix 3.
[32] See Chapter 2, pp. 28–29.
[33] Bateman et al., 1990; Robb, 1991, 1993; Drinka, 2009.
[34] Edzard, 1998.

390   THIRD MOVEMENT (1945–THIRD MILLENNIUM)

The tree of all the world's languages

Far from confining themselves to individual identified and defined language families, certain trees claim to organize all of the world's languages. This is not something completely new. In 1905, barely forty years after Schleicher, Alfredo Trombetti claimed in *L'unità d'origine del linguaggio* to have reconstructed, in a series colored maps, the journey of all the "races" and languages of the world from a single point of origin.[35] For Trombetti, this origin lay in the Himalayas, in line with the early nineteenth-century scholarly tradition locating the cradle of the Indo-Europeans in the same region. Trombetti was writing when raciology was in its heyday and the arborescent model was applied equally to the "races" as defined by craniology and to languages. But this was also the era, in the fields of both history and anthropology, that witnessed the demise of the great origin epics so typical of the last quarter of the nineteenth century with the works of Tylor, Lecky, Lubbock, James Atkinson, and Westermarck. The decades that followed were characterized by a much more precise and prudent outlook, already marked by functionalist, structuralist, and synchronic approaches, whether in the fields of ethnology with Malinowski and Radcliffe-Brown, sociology with Durkheim, or linguistics with Saussure and Meillet. There was no longer any place for wide-ranging speculation within the human sciences.

Things began to change at the end of the 1980s, and, strangely enough, this was in part linked to the collapse of the Soviet Union. In fact, in this country, there continued a largely silent, underfunded and minority encyclopedic linguistic tradition exemplified by the work of researchers such as Vladislav Illič-Svityč (who died at the age of thirty-two in 1966), Igor Diakonoff (died 1999), Sergej Starostin (died 2005), Aaron Dolgopolsky (died 2012), and Vitaly Shevoroshkin. Following in the footsteps of Illič-Svityč, these researchers took up and developed the hypotheses of language "macro-families"—including Pedersen's "Nostratic"[36]—and the monogenesis of all the world's languages, which Shevoroshkin termed the "Proto-World." In the years following 1990, the circulation of researchers and ideas became freer, leading to an upsurge in conferences and publications on the hypothesis of a universal mother language, a notion that was all the more convincing since, in the United States, Joseph Greenberg and his disciple Merritt Ruhlen were independently reaching similar conclusions by grouping all of the world's languages within a single family tree.[37] Since the 1950s, Greenberg had proposed to classify all African languages within four macro-families, an approach that he subsequently extended to Oceania

---

[35] Trombetti, 1905.
[36] See Chapter 13, pp. 268 and 271.
[37] Ruhlen, 1996; see Appendix 16.

and then America; by the 1980s, almost all of the Amerindian languages (usually spread over almost 200 families) had been grouped together within a single macro-family which he termed "Amerind."

Moving from group to group, Greenberg and then Ruhlen gradually assembled a single family tree of the world's 6,000 known languages according to their affinities. It is important to note that their work focused primarily on the lexicon rather than on morphological or syntactical structures. Ultimately, Ruhlen succeeded in isolating some thirty words which he claimed belonged to the "original mother tongue" and which would have survived over the tens of thousands of years of linguistic evolution since the first *Homo sapiens* emerged in the original African cradle: *(m)ama* for "mother," *(p)apa* for "father," *maliq'a* for "breast" or "to suckle," *puti* for "vulva," *tik* for "finger" or the number "1," *aq'wa* for "water," *kuan* for "dog," *tika* for "earth," etc.

This hypothesis of the monogenesis of all human languages, which would soon become known as the Greenberg-Ruhlen theory, enjoyed a very high profile in the 1990s. In fact, Ruhlen was gifted in the field of popularization and his principal work, *The Origin of Language: Tracing the Evolution of the Mother Tongue*, originally published in 1994, gives readers the impression that they themselves are discovering the kinships between languages, culminating in the discovery of the thirty words of the "original mother tongue." He also handles controversy with great skill. Detractors who express their skepticism regarding his methodology and who contrast his linguistic approximations with the rigor of the comparative grammar of the Indo-European languages are accused of being racist on the basis that they deny to the other peoples of the world that which they only accept for the languages of White Europeans—an argument that carries considerable weight in the land of "political correctness."

Nevertheless, numerous linguists have effectively criticized the Greenberg-Ruhlen method. In fact, the method accepts many equivalences between the various phonemes of the different languages. Thus, depending on the languages, the primordial root for water, *aq'wa*, can occur in many forms—*kwe, uuku, agu-d, hoko, gugu, k'oy, waho, ku,* etc.—which creates a certain degree of latitude. Of course we can counterargue, for example, that the French word *fils* corresponds exactly, and this is scientifically proved, to the Spanish word *hijo* and that both derive from the Latin *filius* even though, at first glance, they seem to have little in common, which thus permits a certain degree of flexibility in the comparisons (another classic example is the equivalence between the number *deux* [two] in French and its analog *erku* in Armenian, which, as demonstrated by Meillet, both derive from an original root **dw-*); however, in the case of *filius*, the derivation from Latin is completely demonstrable, which is not the case for the similarities identified by Greenberg and Ruhlen. Furthermore, Greenberg and Ruhlen's theory accepts numerous

392 THIRD MOVEMENT (1945–THIRD MILLENNIUM)

possible meanings for a single root depending on the languages. Thus *bu(n) jka* can mean "knee," but also "bend," "meander," "hook," etc., and *aq'wa* can mean "to drink," "to rain," "cloud," "river," "to suck," "thirst," "out of the water," "to wash," etc. Under these conditions, with a just small number of vowels and consonants (even though we can identify about 200 vowels and 700 consonants within all the world's languages), several linguists and statisticians have calculated that we have a 100% chance of finding similarities between any given language from any given family and any other language.[38]

We have seen in the case of Colin Renfrew's Neolithic hypothesis[39] how this linguistic tree presents numerous difficulties and even contradictions with regard to Indo-European languages and potentially related languages and also with regard to equivalence between the diffusion of these languages and the diffusion of agriculture. And this despite the fact that this equivalence was supposed to anchor the linguistic diffusion within a historical reality, namely the Neolithic. Nevertheless, this world tree received considerable support from what was presented as a totally new scientific discovery: the reconstruction of a tree of all the world's genes by the American-Italian team led by Luigi Luca Cavalli-Sforza.[40] The asserted coincidence, with the same pattern of branchings between the two trees, is taken as an indication that the trees validate each other, but it can also be seen as an interdisciplinary vicious circle.[41]

French research on this central question has been more reserved. In 1981, in what was still a very marginal manner, Éric de Grolier, specialist in the history of communication and documentation sciences, organized a conference on "Glossogenetics" in Paris under the aegis of UNESCO ("despite its clear interest," a paper which I presented on "The Indo-European Question and the Tree Model" was not included in the resulting publication due to lack of space).[42] However, it was only in the 2000s that the French National Centre for Scientific Research (CNRS), in an explicit reference to the work of Greenberg, Ruhlen, and also Cavalli-Sforza, decided to fund a program of research on "the origins of man, languages and language," which would subsequently lead to several publications and conferences.[43]

---

[38] Boë et al., 2008. See also Victorri, 2000; Fracchiolla, 2006; Campbell, 2008; Campbell and Poser, 2008; Auroux, 2010; Métoz et al., 2003; Métoz, 2005; etc.

[39] See Chapter 13, pp. 273–275.

[40] See Chapter 10, pp. 229–230.

[41] Sims-Williams, 1998.

[42] Grolier, 1983.

[43] Hombert, 2005; Laks et al., 2008.

An apple, a hat, and a car

In light of the shortcomings of the Great Tree, let us turn our focus once more to the trees of the Indo-European languages, the first of which was planted by Schleicher. The growing interest in the Indo-European question from the 1970s onward and the mediatization of the works of Colin Renfrew and the "New Synthesis" in the 1990s triggered an international race, typical of the academic system in the English-speaking world, to produce increasingly novel and sophisticated trees of Indo-European languages; some, such as those produced by linguists Russell Gray and Quentin Atkinson,[44] enjoyed, and indeed still enjoy, widespread approval.

These phylogenetic trees, borrowed from biology and applied to linguistics, pose two problems. The first is that it is always possible to impose a tree structure on any objects that we might wish to compare. Such a tree will always express relationships of distance as a function of the descriptive framework chosen at the outset and to which each language being compared is reduced (in concrete terms, using a type list of words or perhaps of morphological or grammatical traits). But it is something entirely different to decide that this tree is genealogical—in other words, that it expresses kinship relationships between the chosen languages. Depending on the pre-established descriptive framework, I could, for example, compare an apple with a hat and a car: it is probable that the tree I would obtain, using an automatic classification (sophisticated or otherwise), would feature an initial branching separating the car, on the one hand, from the apple and the hat, on the other, and that the latter two would then split from each other to form separate branches. However, nothing in the model allows me deduce that at a specific moment in time a proto-object became separated into two families—that of the car, on the one hand, and that of the proto-apple-hat, on the other—which will in turn split into apple, on the one hand, and hat, on the other. The same is true for languages. A phylogenetic tree measures distances between languages according to the criteria selected; nothing indicates that it strictly expresses a general genetic evolution. Perhaps the solution is an alternative model.

The second problem involves validation. The various trees that have been produced in ever growing numbers over the past thirty years are all pretty similar in terms of their main branching pattern when viewed from a distance. We could even go as far as to say that they differ little from the Schleicher's founding tree, produced more than 150 years ago. We encounter the same nine principal linguistic groups (see Appendices 3 and 4), with the same kinship relationships: Baltic with Slavic, which are themselves close to Germanic; Celtic with Italic; Iranian with Indo-Aryan; Greek on its own; and Albanian

---

[44] Gray and Atkinson, 2003; Bouckaert et al., 2012.

394   THIRD MOVEMENT (1945–THIRD MILLENNIUM)

also floating on its own (Armenian was not included). Since Schleicher's time, Tocharian and Hittite have been discovered, and these two languages are set apart as early as the first two branchings in current trees. However, if we examine the detail of these trees, a number of unsolvable issues immediately become apparent.

Hence, in a 2005 article devoted to the construction of *perfect phylogenetic networks* (PPN), three eminent linguists and computer scientists proposed a series of trees of the Indo-European languages in which we encounter more or less the same principal kinships as presented in Schleicher's tree.[45] But, looking at the detail, they discovered a closeness between Proto-Tocharian and Proto-Slavic, while, according to the classic theory,[46] the Tocharians are believed to have developed from a steppic migration towards Xinjiang (where they have been identified in the first millennium CE) dating back to at least the second millennium BCE, very far from the postulated cradle of the Slavs in Eastern Europe. The only solution is to assume "a long migration eastward in a relatively short period of time,"[47] which, from the point of view of logic, greatly resembles a vicious circle. Similarly, a degree of proximity is suggested between the Celtic group and the Balto-Slavic group even though the populations who spoke these languages were very far apart from each other in the periods in which they are historically known. In this case, it is postulated that "the linguistic geography of eastern Europe could have been very different in, say, the third millennium BC."[48] Finally, the same is true of closeness between Proto-Italic and Proto-Greco-Armenian, the speakers of which were also separated by considerable distances; here again, the result is "surprising but cannot be excluded (given how little we know about the prehistoric linguistic geography of eastern Europe)."[49] Furthermore, the statistic basis for this closeness remains relatively weak.

Here again, the issue is not whether the propositions that arise from these models are true or false—they are above all interesting and stimulating. The issue is that said propositions are unverifiable (or unfalsifiable), or, in other words, that a possible explanation will always be found. Thus, we have not moved on much from Otto Schrader and his century-old circular reasoning.[50]

---

[45]   Nakhleh et al., 2005.
[46]   See Chapter 15, pp. 337–339.
[47]   Nakhleh et al., 2005, p. 402.
[48]   Ibid., p. 403.
[49]   Ibid.
[50]   See Chapter 3, pp. 47–54.

Measuring the speed of language evolution

An additional problem posed by these trees concerns the dating of their branchings and, in particular, the speed at which linguistic changes evolve. Long believed to be variable or even random, this speed of evolution, or this rate of linguistic renewal, was subsequently deemed to be constant and reconstructable following the work of American linguist Morris Swadesh in the years after the Second World War. Swadesh, founder of glottochronology and specialist in Amerindian languages, was a victim of McCarthyism, which forced him into a life in exile. Following in the footsteps of eighteenth-century Swedish scholar Philipp Johann Tabbert von Strahlenberg,[51] Swadesh established a list of the principal 100 (or 200) words of the basic vocabulary of all languages (pronouns, parts of the body, kinship terms, colors, natural phenomena such as rain and the stars, simple action verbs such as "to see" and "to give"), words that are assumed to be much less likely to be the subject of borrowings. Then he compared each human language with each of the others, estimating that when 70% or more words are shared, two languages could be considered to be related (i.e., they have a common origin). Then, on the basis of known languages (specifically Indo-European languages), he estimated that the rate of transformation or loss over time of this fundamental vocabulary was in the order of 14% per 1,000 years; in other words, over an interval of 1,000 years, 14% of the original words are replaced by others. This method is termed "lexicostatistics" or "glottochronology."[52]

From the outset we can see the interest in and limits of this method, one that provoked and indeed still provokes numerous debates, the details of which are beyond the scope of the current work. In short, broadly speaking it works, but clearly not in the details, and it cannot be validated if we do not have a second method of dating at our disposal. Often compared to radiocarbon dating, it suffers from the same limitations: if we did not have dendrochronology (tree-ring dating), at least for recent millennia, then we would not be able to "calibrate" or correct the Carbon 14 method because the phenomenon that it measures is not constant. Yet it is the principles of glottochronology, which are relatively complex in their implementation, that are applied in mathematical models that aim to reconstruct language trees and their dating.

---

[51] See Chapter 1, pp. 7–8.
[52] Swadesh, 1972; Hymes, 1960; Bergsland and Vogt, 1962; Embleton, 1986; McMahon and McMahon, 2006.

396   THIRD MOVEMENT (1945–THIRD MILLENNIUM)

From the tree to the network

Clearly there are other alternatives to the arborescent structure for charting relationships. Schleicher's tree, and those of a number of other researchers that followed him, did not result from sophisticated quantitative techniques but rather from an intuitive knowledge of languages. From the end of the nineteenth century, statistical techniques began to be developed, such as those devised by Francis Galton in a eugenist approach to psychology. Polish ethnologist and anthropologist Jan Czekanowski was undoubtedly a pioneer when, in 1928, he proposed a quantitative classification of Indo-European languages based on nine of the principal languages and twenty-two linguistic characters.[53] This work was continued in1937 by anthropologist Alfred Kroeber and linguist Douglas Chrétien,[54] this time with sixty-four characters taken from Antoine Meillet's *Les Dialectes indo-européens* (The Indo-European Dialects); Kroeber, was one of the most influential anthropologists of the twentieth century and, in the 1930s, was also one of the first to apply statistical analysis to archaeological material. Their pioneering article made little impact, but its content was republished by Kroeber himself in 1960, the year of his death, in a new article in which he added two graphic representations of the similarities calculated some twenty years earlier. He was already working on these representations in 1937, but, in the end, omitted them from the original article because, as he explained, "I was unable to make my partner see its significance, other than for its obvious geographical sense."

Returning to the issue, Kroeber constructs, for the first time, a non-arborescent graphic representation of the relationships between the nine principal Indo-European language families (see Appendix 19). The polygon obtained expresses, in a coherent way, both linguistic and geographical proximities. The Celtic languages and Indo-Iranian languages are at opposing angles of the polygon, and the same is true of the other languages. Furthermore, the polygon is three-dimensional because Armenian actually projects from the strictly two-dimensional plane in a bid to express its relationships with the other languages. Hittite cannot be fitted within the model, a fact which clearly sets it apart. This graphic is far from trivial. It clearly indicates that the resemblances between two languages are all the stronger if the languages are geographically close together. It does not really fit with the notion of a "big bang" emanating from a single point.

It is for this reason that Kroeber insists on the necessity to go beyond explaining these resemblances simply in genealogical terms.

[53] Czekanowski, 1928.
[54] Kroeber and Chrétien, 1937.

It is increasingly becoming evident that the difference is far from complete, that alien and kindred contacts measurably influence language also, and that the belief in the seeming prevalence of automatic, orderly, slow genetic differentiation as the sole or even dominant process in the history of linguistic change must be questioned and perhaps abandoned. . . . But they may be considerably modified by the recognition of other processes which comparativists have mostly ignored; and the hitherto accepted results will at any rate have to be viewed as forming only part of a larger web of causes and effects.[55]

He also reminds us that his master, Franz Boas, was already convinced that "genetic reconstructions would be increasingly interfered with and sullied by diffusions and influences between originally distinct genetic units."[56]

It must be admitted that, half-a-century later, Kroeber's modest yet devastating remarks have not produced much in the line of reaction or vocations. Taxonomical studies of the phenomena of mixing, contacts, and borrowings remain somewhat marginal, although their publication is often surrounded by considerable hype. Nevertheless, certain recent studies of these phenomena have attempted relatively elaborate approaches, even using non-arborescent models.[57]

We can thus conclude as follows:

a. A century-and-a-half after the first tree was published by botanist August Schleicher, quantitative linguistics continues, at what seems to be a growing pace (thanks, in part, to the competitive academic system of the English-speaking world), to produce genealogical trees of the Indo-European languages; in terms of their principal branchings these trees do not differ greatly from that proposed by Schleicher, and they display numerous contradictions with each other.

b. Thus, at present, there is no consensus regarding a detailed tree of Indo-European languages, and each tree producer has good arguments against his or her colleagues, particularly since, without going into the arcane details of statistical techniques, "cleaning" processes applied to both the initial data and to the resulting graphs allow a certain degree of latitude. Likewise, there is no consensus regarding the eventual insertion of Indo-European languages within the Great Tree of all the world's languages postulated by Greenberg and Ruhlen, or within its Nostratic version, or within any other version for that matter.

---

[55] Ibid., pp. 17 and 18, note 2.

[56] Ibid., 1960, p. 19.

[57] Edzard, 1998; Dragiev et al., 2012; Layeghifard et al., 2013; Heggarty, 2000 and 2006; Heggarty et al., 2010; Drinka, 2009; François, A., 2014. See Appendix 18.

398   THIRD MOVEMENT (1945–THIRD MILLENNIUM)

c. Some of these trees support the Anatolian hypothesis (Gray and Atkinson), while others support the steppic hypothesis (Hans Holm, Tandy Warnow).

d. Nor is there any agreement regarding the calculation of the time taken for languages to evolve since this measurement must be based on either the regular rate of linguistic change proposed by glottochronology (but which is the subject of well-founded criticism) or on correspondences with archaeological events (migrations, invasions, etc.), which again currently elicit no general consensus.

e. Besides these standard arborescent models, very few attempts have been made to propose alternative logical models that integrate the phenomena of contacts, borrowings, mixing, etc. Nevertheless, we will return to this subject a little later.[58]

---

[58] See Chapter 19.

18

Words and things of the Indo-Europeans

While archaeology is meant to reveal the ultimate material incarnation of the original Indo-Europeans, it could not begin to do so until the last quarter of the nineteenth century. It had to wait until excavation campaigns were organized to far off lands and until excavations began to multiply in Europe itself. Up until then, attempts to grasp primitive realities had to rely on the study of words and, in particular, on Adolphe Pictet's linguistic paleontology. These avenues of research were nevertheless pursued in parallel, and Schrader's monumental encyclopedia was still largely founded on such an approach.[1] However, over the course of the twentieth century, a certain mistrust crept in when it became apparent that vocabulary was not the most pertinent raw material for defining the primitive language.[2] Hence Antoine Meillet considered that "the vocabulary facts depend on influences exerted on the civilization and are largely independent of the structure of the language."[3] Furthermore, linguistic paleontology fell out of favor during this period, and it was not until the re-emergence of the Indo-Europeans on the scientific scene in the1970s that it regained popularity, while its numerous defects and risks remained intact. In what follows, we will examine the current state of linguistic paleontology and, more generally, the state of what we might call "cultural paleontology"; in other words, the study of ancient societies through their texts but with a focus on an *Urvolk* or original founding People.

The dead-ends of linguistic paleontology

We have already seen[4] that, contrary to the generally accepted view, the shared proto–Indo-European vocabulary is anything but extensive. Of the 1,500 estimated roots, only one (the word for "to swell") is common to all fourteen identified Indo-European linguistic families, and three-quarters are only found in six language families or less. This is sufficient to allow us to talk about a

---

[1] See Chapter 3, pp. 42–43.
[2] See Chapter 5, and Chapter 17, pp. 387–389.
[3] Meillet, 1938, p. 105. See also 1937, p. 32.
[4] See Chapter 17, pp. 387–389.

400   THIRD MOVEMENT (1945–THIRD MILLENNIUM)

"family" of Indo-European languages but is somewhat insufficient when it comes to describing an entire civilization. It is with this critical eye that the recent textbook by Douglas Adams and James Mallory[5] should be approached; using vocabulary as the basis, this work devotes seventeen chapters and 325 pages to listing the various aspects of the primitive Indo-European "reality" (fauna, flora, anatomy, family, society, food, emotions, activities, etc.). One Indo-European term is always present in at least one language to describe one of these realities, just as in any other language family on the planet—in the same way that it is reasonable to expect that any language in the world would possess a word for mother, food, colors, parts of the body, and house. This in no way supports the existence of a primordial society and culture (the *Urvolk* in its *Urheimat*), especially given the extreme compactness of the reconstructed common vocabulary. In fact it betrays a persistent and no doubt unconscious confusion between "Indo-European," "European," and "human."

The blind alleys of linguistic paleontology have long been highlighted and continue to be so.[6] In 1950, for example, archaeologist Stuart Piggott commenting on words present in or absent from the common vocabulary quotes Indianist Arthur Berriedale Keith (not to be confused with raciologist Sir Arthur Keith): "by taking the linguistic evidence too literally one could conclude that the original Indo-European speakers knew butter, but not milk; snow and feet but not rain or hands!"[7] In the same era, Ernst Pulgram, in an *argumentum ad absurdum* based on shared words in the Romance languages, proposed a reconstruction of a "proto-Roman" or "Latin" culture dominated by kings, priests, and bishops, where people smoked tobacco, drank beer and coffee, and waged war ("*guerre*," a word inherited from the Frankish) on horseback ("*chevaux*," from the late-Latin "*caballus*" which replaced the classic "*equus*").[8] In reality, we know that all of these words and the items which they designate appeared in the Romance languages after the Roman era. But this knowledge is only possible if written evidence is available.

We could argue that we know that coffee originated in the Arab world and that the word (which is non Indo-European) arrived with the item. But the words for "potato" (which are sometimes Indo-European in origin), clearly an imported item also, differ from country to country depending on the manner in which the tuber spread within European peasant society (unlike coffee, which only circulated among the upper echelons of European society). Thus, to designate the potato (which originally came from the Americas), the pre-existing word *tartuffo* (truffle) was used when it arrived in Italy (*trufa* or *tartiffle* in Provençal,

---

[5]   Mallory and Adams, 2006, pp. 120–422.
[6]   Renfrew, 1987; Tremblay, 2005, pp. 121–147.
[7]   Piggott, 1950, p. 246; A. B. Keith, 1938.
[8]   Pulgram, 1958.

WORDS AND THINGS 401

truffe in Berrichon), which in turn became *Kartoffel* in German (perhaps also through confusion or fusion with *Erdapfel*, literally "earth apple" or *pomme de terre* in French), then *kartofel* in Russian, *kartopili* in Georgian, etc. The Arawak Amerindian word *batata* gave us the Spanish *patata*, the English *potato*, and the French *patate* (via French Canada), which is also found in Demotic Greek, Turkish, Arabic (*batata*), Albanian, and the Scandinavian languages. Since the potato is believed to have arrived in Bohemia through Brandenburg, it is designated *brambor* in Czech. Similarly it is known as *burgonya* in Hungary because it was believed to have come from Burgundy. Finally, equivalents of the French *pomme de terre* also exist: *aardappel* in Dutch, *geomelon* in "purified" Greek, *sibzamini* in Iranian, *ziemniak* in Polish, *lursagar* in Basque, *qednakhntzor* in Armenian, and *tapu 'akh adama* in modern Hebrew. But the term *Grundbirne* ("ground pear") also existed in German, essentially in the Austro-Hungarian Empire, which became *krumpir* in Serbo-Croat, *krompir* in Walloon, and *Gromper* in the dialect of Luxemburg. If we did not have the benefit of all of the historical information one can only imagine the difficulty we would have in reconstructing these connections after millennia; thus, all things being equal, we get some idea of the difficulty involved in attempting to understand the similarities and differences that can be envisaged for a large part of the vocabulary of Indo-European languages.

Even when we can rely on concrete facts, numerous contradictions exist. Why is the root **kuwon* for dog, the earliest domesticated animal in both Europe and the Near East (tenth millennium BCE), absent in the Slavic languages, Hittite, and Albanian? And while the root **gwou* for ox/bull/cow is present in most Indo-European languages, the animal is also designated by the word *gu* in Sumerian, *ngu* or *gu* in Chinese, *kuos* in Yakut, *g'w* in ancient Egyptian, and even *ko* in the Sudan and *ngome* in the Bantu languages. In the same way, the root **marko* exists for horse (see *mare* in English) alongside the classic root **ekwos*, but this animal is also called *ma* in Chinese, which is comparable to words used for horse in Korean, Japanese, Tungusic, Mongolian, and even Tamil. These similarities are sometimes attributed to borrowings and sometimes to a potential common origin; in all cases, these facts, and others, complicate the model. We have already seen the problems posed by the horse, the wheel, and the chariot.[9]

The following table attempts to summarize the many difficulties posed by the shared vocabulary and linguistic paleontology by illustrating them for comparative purposes using current realities and the words that designate these realities.

---

[9] See Chapter 14, pp. 303–311.

402   THIRD MOVEMENT (1945–THIRD MILLENNIUM)

	Common ancient realities	Common current realities
A common Indo-European root	copper, king, beaver, squirrel, beech, salmon, father, butter, snow, foot, birch, etc.	beer, telephone, cherry, bishop, chess, taxi, tennis, etc.
Several Indo-European roots	dog, gold, milk, iron, wheel, rain, hand, horse, liver, etc.	corn, potato, turkey, computer, rocket, orange, car, crayon, etc.
A common non– (or not exclusively) Indo-European root	ox/cow/bull, axe, field, wine, etc.	coffee, tobacco, tea, banana, admiral, tattoo, taboo, algorithm, alcohol, etc.

Demonstration by absence

But linguistic paleontology, by definition, has an answer for everything. We remember for instance the following arguments from Schrader's time: if there are no bears on the steppe, but if they occur in the common vocabulary, then they must have existed there in the past. If the common root *sal for salt is not attested among the Indo-Europeans of Asia, it is due to dietary preferences. For Meillet, if there are several words for goat (which is also one of the earliest domesticated animals), it is due to the "popular nature of the denomination"[10]—which brings us back to the potato. The notion of "Taboo" is used as a foolproof argument which has the advantage of being irrefutable in the true sense of the term. Already Schrader had proposed a dietary taboo to explain the absence of words for fish (apart from salmon, *laks) even though the rivers of Ukraine were teeming with them. The absence of the root *tauros (bull) among the Indo-Iranians was also explained by a taboo. The absence of shared names for the gods, which is paradoxical if we accept the concept of an all-encompassing "trifunctional" ideological structure, is also attributed to taboo, as is the absence of common terms for wild animals.

This "linguistics of absence" has always played an important role since Justi, who deduced that the absence of words for illnesses meant that the Indo-Europeans were perfectly healthy, or Schrader, who noted the absence of restroom facilities in the original Homeland. The supposed pastoral nomadism of

---

[10] Sergent, 1995, p. 173.

WORDS AND THINGS 403

the *Urvolk* is essentially based on the fact that the shared vocabulary contains more words referring to animals and stock rearing than to crop growing. According to Meillet, "the imprecision in the meaning and the small number of names for plants contrasts with the specific value and abundance of terms designating animals; we are tempted to conclude that the 'flesh' of wild and domesticated animals . . ., along with milk (the names for which, undoubtedly used mainly by women, have different forms), formed the greater part of the diet of the Indo-European aristocracy."[11] Indeed, why not? But then again, why? We pass unconsciously from lexical inventory to pure invention, which is certainly plausible but in no way verifiable. The mental representations suggested by researchers, namely an *Urvolk* conceived on the model of the Great Invasions of the Middle Ages, are paramount, and linguistic realities have to fall into line, no matter what. In addition, there is the major problem that extensive nomadic pastoralism, as we know it, did not emerge until around the first millennium BCE.

As regards a coincidence between the supposed Indo-European expansion and the "secondary products revolution" hypothesized by British archaeologist Andrew Sherratt, we have seen how the latter is nothing more than a partial aspect of a global historical phenomenon—namely the Chalcolithic—and is based, among other things, on data now known to be inexact concerning dairy products and the castration of animals.[12] The fact that the root for castration is found in Greek (*ethris*) and also in Sanskrit (*vadhris*)[13] is not, therefore, an argument since castration is attested from the earliest phases of the European Neolithic, as are dairy products. Through circular reasoning, the predominance of stock rearing over crop cultivation—despite the abundance of roots for agricultural plants—is reinforced if needs be using unproved claims: "All of these terms refer back, not to the shared Indo-European past, but rather to borrowings made by the Indo-European conquerors in Europe of the plants and their names from the pre-existing Neolithic culture of 'Old Europe.'"[14] Archeology, however, shows us that the steppic societies of the fifth millennium BCE, the putative "conquerors," had an excellent mastery of agriculture[15] even if agriculture and animal husbandry were introduced to these regions through acculturation from the Balkans over the course of the sixth millennium BCE.

[11] Meillet, 1937, pp. 398–399.
[12] See Chapter 11, p. 247.
[13] Sergent, 1995, pp. 175–176; Sherratt, 1981.
[14] Sergent, 1995, p. 177.
[15] Pashkevich, 2003.

404   THIRD MOVEMENT (1945–THIRD MILLENNIUM)

From words to meaning

This blatant failure of linguistic paleontology, which in no way discouraged its practitioners, would nonetheless be compensated by research in the realm of meaning rather than in the realm of straightforward vocabulary. Until he suffered a stroke in 1969, Émile Benveniste was France's pre-eminent linguist, alongside André Martinet. He both followed and developed the tradition of structural linguistics but applied it to semantics, the meaning of words which cannot be understood in isolation but rather must be comprehended within a system of opposition: "Since they are signs, it is in the nature of linguistic facts to become realities in opposition and to signify only in this way."[16] It is no longer the etymology of individual words that is important but rather the underlying conceptual structures; the emphasis thus shifts from "designation" to "meaning" thanks to the rigorous rules of semantic reconstruction.[17] Benveniste puts this approach into practice in the two volumes of his *Vocabulaire des institutions indo-européennes*[18] (Vocabulary of Indo-European Institutions), a collection of detailed studies developed from lectures he gave at the Collège de France.

Benveniste shows, for example, that the common vocabulary does not really contain terms for commercial exchange but rather notions that deal with systems of gift-giving, reciprocity, and *potlatch*, like those encountered in traditional societies. The kinship system appears to be patriarchal and patrilocal, with a significant number of kinship terms to refer to a wife's family-in-law, but it also contains traces of a matrilinear system, with a particularly important role for the maternal uncle (it should be noted, however, that this claim has been disputed by English anthropologist Jack Goody[19]). Slavery and the clear distinction between free men and slaves appear to be constants in the societies studied. Among the Greeks, Italics, and Indo-Iranians, at least, we encounter a division of society into three or four categories: priests, warriors, farmers, artisans (which Dumézil, who was intellectually close to Benveniste, formalized as the "three functions"). The king also seems to have had an important religious role, the root of this word (*rex, rix, rajah*, although this last comparison is sometimes challenged) being related to words connected to rectitude and the law (*rectus* in Latin, *recht* in German).

The sacred is generally broken down into two notions: that which is charged with divine power and that which is taboo. We must also avoid imagining these societies as having a "primitive" level of reasoning in which every abstract idea initially arose from a concrete fact. Thus, it is not the herd (**peku, pecus* in Latin) that would eventually have given rise to certain words with the meaning of

[16] Benveniste, 1950.
[17] Benveniste, 1954.
[18] Benveniste, 1969; Malamoud, 1971.
[19] Goody, 1959; Renfrew, 1987, pp. 80 and 258.

material wealth (*pecunia* in Latin), but rather the inverse: the abstract notion of wealth would have been particularly incarnated in the herd. This process has, however, been questioned by certain linguists for whom the abstract notion must derive from the concrete.[20] "Fidelity" (*Treue* in Germany) would have inspired the name for oak (*drus* in Greek). Finally, it was the general notion of "crossing" (**ponthos*) which would have given rise to concepts as diverse as bridge (*pons* in Latin), sea or inlet (*pontos* in Greek), and path (*put* in Russian).

Regarding Indo-Europeanness

These studies are fascinating and stimulating, but what exactly do they tell us about the supposed original Indo-European society (the *Urvolk*)? Benveniste is explicit in this regard:

> We have in no way sought to come up with a new inventory of Indo-European realities as they are defined by major lexical correspondences. On the contrary, most of the data that we are dealing with does not belong to the shared vocabulary. As terms of institutions, they are specific, but only in particular languages and it is their genesis and the Indo-European connection that we analyze.[21]

Steering clear of all extrapolation, he only considers historically situated societies that post-date the supposed original society by several millennia and which, in any case, are not contemporary with each other. Hittite and Mycenaean texts are barely exploitable, and we cannot reasonably study Greek society before Homer in the eighth or seventh centuries BCE and Roman society before the comedies of Plautus in the second century BCE. While the Vedic hymns undoubtedly date back to the second half of the second millennium BCE, the Slavic and Germanic realities can only be gleaned from the translations of Christian texts which date to the end of the first millennium CE at the earliest, and Baltic and Albanian texts are even later. In all cases, societies only turned to writing after they had attained a certain degree of complexity, generally with the emergence of cities and states. In fact, two-thirds of the vocabulary studied by Benveniste comes from Greek, Latin, and Indo-Iranian languages; these are the languages of urban societies, city states, kingdoms, and empires and are therefore far removed from the protohistoric societies that spoke the Indo-European languages of the Neolithic period.

[20] Lamberterie, 1978, p. 276.
[21] Benveniste, 1969, I, p. 9.

406   THIRD MOVEMENT (1945–THIRD MILLENNIUM)

The only facts of a less urban or non-urban nature might be those concerning Germanic societies. Indeed, the practice of raiding by bands of youths united by their fidelity to their chief appears to oppose that of the armed populaces of the city-states of Greece and Italy. Likewise, small-scale trafficking (*kaufen* in German, *kupiti* in the Slavic languages—words derived from the Latin *caupo*), which would have been practiced among Barbarians on the frontiers of the Roman Empire (*limes*), is to be opposed to the commerce organized by specialists within the Greek and Italic cities all around the Mediterranean and defined as *neg-otium* (in Latin), an activity in its own right. But this Germanic and Slavic petty trading nevertheless supposes the existence of the Roman Empire. And it is because he has access to historical knowledge concerning these different ancient societies that Benveniste can give meaning to these studies of vocabulary.

The absence of common roots for particular notions may be due to very different causes. It could be that a concept is so general and evident that it simply was not named, such as religion in societies in which atheism has no meaning. Or that some ideas only appeared at a late stage as a function of the degree of complexity of social organization, such as commerce. Or, perhaps for similar reasons, some notions were named in each language according to terms and modes that differed in each society; as, for instance, the vocabulary pertaining to the sacred, to rites, and to sacrifice. Or, again, to the names of gods, which apart from rare exceptions (such as Uranus and the Indian god Varuna) are all different, even though we might have thought that these were fundamental notions in the original shared ideology.

In addition there is the problem of knowing whether the facts of civilization highlighted by Émile Benveniste are specifically Indo-European or, on the contrary, whether they are more generally "European"—we will come back to this issue later. In order to solve this we must be able to compare these facts with those of other contemporary European societies possessing the same social organization but non–Indo-European-speaking. However, this evidence does not exist. The ancient non–Indo-European languages of Europe are as yet undeciphered (Etruscan, Iberian, Pictish, and Minoan). Ancient Near Eastern languages (Sumerian, Elamite, Akkadian, etc.) already correspond to societies that are urbanized, state-based, or even imperial—it is telling that what we know of the Hittite religion does not allow it to be easily distinguished from other eastern religions of the period.

We have seen that Benveniste "believed" in the Indo-Europeans, at least he did so in the period before the Second World War because, in 1939, he published, like Dumézil and Meillet did at the time, the startling text on their "conquering instinct" and their "taste for open spaces"[22] just as, in 1936, he contributed to a

[22] See Chapter 5, pp. 108–110.

WORDS AND THINGS   407

tribute volume to Herman Hirt edited by Nazi Ideologue Helmuth Arntz.[23] In any case, nowhere in *Le Vocabulaire des institutions indo-européennes* does he risk proposing more concrete historical hypotheses, no more so than Dumézil, even though the idea of an original People remained firmly in the back of his mind. This should not, however, prevent us from benefiting from his semantic studies.

A primordial poetry?

Another domain of Indo-European words, one that Benveniste did not venture into but which Meillet highlighted as early as 1923, and which has been the subject of numerous studies since, is the realm of poetry.[24] There supposedly exists a certain number of concordances between the poetic forms, especially meter (rhyming schemes, regulated alternation of syllable length, divisions, etc.), and between certain formulae and metaphors found in Indo-European poetic texts. From the outset, Meillet and many of his successors attributed these concordances or resemblances to a common origin: "If Indo-European was widely propagated in Europe and Asia, it is because the nation that used this language, or at least the aristocracy of this nation, had a sense of social organization and dominance that went hand-in-hand with an intellectual culture."[25]

In reality, the concordances concern only a small number of Indo-European languages, and the texts involved vary greatly in age. Comparisons tend to be confined to Indian and Greek texts, even though some similarities can be observed with much more recent Slavic and Baltic folklore and certain Celtic texts. The defense is the usual one: over time, the other languages changed their poetic rules as they evolved. Meillet finds similarities between the relatively monotonous Vedic texts and only one form of Greek poetry—namely the song— even though a great variety of poetic genres exist in this language. It is striking that the Homeric songs, the oldest poetic texts in Greek and among the oldest attested in an Indo-European language, do not fit within the comparison. But Meillet has another classic defense up his sleeve, that of the "substrate." If the "Homeric era has no exact counterpart in the Indo-European world," it is simply due to the influence of the pre–Indo-European Aegean cultural substrate, which predated the arrival of the Greeks. Using this assumption, the great linguist invented a little historical narrative: "This does not preclude the possibility that,

[23] See Chapter 6, p. 109.
[24] Meillet, 1923; Swiggers, 1991; Bader, 1989; Campanile, 1977; Nagy, 1974; Schmitt, 1967; Toporov, 1981; Watkins, 1995; West, 1999, 2008; Pinault and Petit, 2006; criticism: Tremblay, 2005, pp. 151–159.
[25] Meillet, 1923, p. 3.

408   THIRD MOVEMENT (1945–THIRD MILLENNIUM)

in the beginning, when the Hellenes were still 'Barbarians,' the poets who plied their art at aristocratic gatherings might have received lessons from the epic poets who took part in the feasts of Aegean princes."[26] An ingenious explanation that has just one problem: when Meillet was writing, no one was yet aware that the "Aegean princes" of Mycenae or of the second palaces of Knossos, where the Pre-Hellenic *aoidoi* would have first sung before transmitting their art to the Greeks, were already speaking and singing in Greek!

Meillet, with characteristic lucidity, did not underestimate the limits of a theory based on the comparison of only two poetic systems.

> There are drawbacks with founding a theory on the comparison of just two sources of evidence. The reconstruction of a common point of departure only emerges, in fact, when at least three sources are compared: in the case where there is a divergence between two compared sources, the choice is arbitrary. Here we attempt to get over this difficulty in as far as it is possible to do so, but it needs to be signaled from the outset and we must never forget the resulting uncertainty.[27]

Since then, other languages have been added, but to a much lesser degree, while a number of poetic formulae found in texts written in different languages have been collated. The most famous, again associating Sanskrit and Greek, is that of the "immortal glory": *kleos aphthiton* in Greek, *sravas aksitam* in Sanskrit, which seem to overlap perfectly. Its relevance is sometimes questioned but it is one of several that have been identified. However, as pointed out by linguist Xavier Tremblay, such shared formulae are not very numerous.

> The number, length and geographical distribution of non-trivial formulae, stereotyped and associating words that are used in the same way from language to language, are limited: about ten formulae never exceeding two words (noun and adjective, verb and noun) are found in two, sometimes three, language families (never more). This is a poor return compared to the hundreds of formula comparisons that can be made between India and Iran or between Akkadian, Hebrew and Arabic.[28]

Among the metaphors that are encountered, one is particularly striking: namely, the comparison of the sun to the wheel of a war chariot, which is found in several languages.[29] Indeed we re-encounter the image of the solar chariot in religions

---

[26] Ibid., p. 63.
[27] Ibid., p. 18.
[28] Tremblay, 2005, p. 151.
[29] West, 1999; Bader, 1989.

WORDS AND THINGS   409

of the historic periods. We can also cite the famous bronze and gold statue of a sun chariot from Trundholm in Denmark: a bronze horse pulls a chariot of the same metal with spoked wheels, on which rests a vertical bronze disc covered in gold leaf—clearly a representation of the sun. The problem is that, as we have already seen,[30] the spoke-wheeled war chariot was developed no earlier than the beginning of the second millennium BCE; the Trundholm statue itself dates to the middle of the same millennium.

This confirms what we have already observed regarding the interpretation of a portion of the Dumézilian mythology: it is much more coherent historically to place the latter in parallel with the emergence in parts of Europe of an aristocratic, warlike, and heroic culture at the time of the development of exchange networks for prestige goods that accompanied the development of the European Bronze Age in the second millennium BCE.[31] The idea of interpreting these poetic correspondences as a steppic tradition that predated the Vedic and Greek texts by three or four millennia is a much more tenuous and far less likely explanation.

We know that rhythms, sounds, and narratives can travel and that part of the Bible has antecedents in Mesopotamia, as do certain myths which are considered to be Indo-European. Hence Martin West highlights Babylonian influences on Greece, such as the myth of the complaint made by Gaea/Gaia (the Earth) to Zeus as a prelude to the Trojan War, which can be compared to the complaint made by Prithivi to Brahma in the Mahabharata, a preliminary to the great battle at the heart of the epic, and one that is encountered again, at an earlier date, in a Babylonian poem.[32] These studies of the poetry of these ancient texts are certainly fascinating and convincing. Far less so is their ultimate interpretation in the impoverishing terms of an original *Urvolk*.

From words to things and creating
the "impression of reality"

The first "Indo-European Encyclopedia," that compiled by Schrader, drew on an inextricable mix of different sources.[33] This is why it can be justifiably described as a work of Indo-European linguistic paleontology buried within an archaeological, historical, and cultural dictionary of Ancient Europe in general and of its neighboring regions, which in itself is in no way specifically Indo-European unless we accept that everything European is Indo-European. Indeed the book is appropriately subtitled *Grundzüge einer Kultur- und Völkergeschichte Alteuropas*

---

[30] See Chapter 14, pp. 253–254.
[31] Kristiansen, 2009. See Chapter 11, pp. 249–254.
[32] West, 1999, 2008.
[33] See Chapter 3, pp. 47–54.

410 THIRD MOVEMENT (1945–THIRD MILLENNIUM)

(Elements of a Cultural History of the Peoples of Ancient Europe). The use of more than 200 illustrative plates and figures creates a strong "impression of reality." Because this encyclopedia was overflowing with images and concrete objects, it was difficult not to believe that the Indo-Europeans had actually existed. The sheer scale of Schrader's work discouraged others from undertaking a similar endeavor for several decades. However, toward the end of the twentieth century, new publications began to appear. These varied in their degree of elaboration, from the asserted encyclopedia to synthetic works aimed at a more general readership, and it is striking that the same demonstrative processes used by Schrader continued to be employed. Five recurrent characteristics of these works are particularly worthy of note.

a. Confusion between "European" and "Indo-European" and even "universal";
b. The large-scale return of linguistic paleontology from the 1980s onward;
c. The creation of an impression of reality through the use of images (depending on the publication);
d. Circular reasoning;
e. Preconceived ideas regarding the nature of the proposed original Indo-European society.

It is beyond the scope of the present work to examine in detail all of these recent publications that claim to provide a synthesis of current knowledge on the Indo-Europeans and which tend to be all the more repetitive since they feed into this new "market" they have contributed to create. However, among those that explicitly claim to revisit Schrader and Nehring's encyclopedia, we must mention the *Encylopedia of Indo-European Culture* by Douglas Adams and James Mallory, and *Les Indo-Européens* by Bernard Sergent; among those volumes that are more synthetic, and excluding those that are strictly linguistic in their scope, we should mention those by David Anthony, André Martinet, James Mallory, Iaroslav Lebedynsky, Georges Sokoloff, Jean Haudry (a single-volume edition of the original two "*Que sais-je?*" publications), and Colin Renfrew.[34] Apart from the last two, which support the Scandinavian (even North Pole) and Anatolian hypotheses respectively, the others favor the steppic theory, a fact that is made immediately obvious by the cover illustrations, with (wild?) horses on the steppe (Anthony), horses galloping across the steppe (Martinet, Mallory), or the steppe minus the horses but with yurts (Sokoloff); in the case of Lebedynsky, the cover bears a map with the superimposed drawing of a statue menhir. Adams and Mallory break the mold with an image of one of the silver Thracian horse-harness

---

[34] Mallory and Adams, 1997; Sergent, 1995; Mallory, 1989 [1997]; Martinet, 1986; Anthony, 2007; Haudry, 2010; Lebedynsky, 2006; Sokoloff, 2011.

WORDS AND THINGS   411

ornaments found at Letnica in Bulgaria, depicting what may be a hero slaying a triple monster. Sergent reproduces one of the two magnificent bronze horned helmets found in Viksø bog in Denmark and dating to the beginning of the first millennium BCE. On the cover of the re-edition of Haudry's book we encounter a proud blond-haired warrior, his back to the sea, bareheaded, blowing a horn, with an axe in hand and a sword at his waist.

Within the covers of these publications, those that have opted for the Pontic Steppes are abundantly illustrated with images of Neolithic and Chalcolithic archaeological material (Anthony, Lebedynsky, and Mallory). In one of them, we can even gaze on the faces of "original Indo-Europeans" thanks to facial reconstruction methods originally developed by Soviet archaeologists.[35]

Indo-European or universal?

As regards the techniques of persuasion, one of the most important is the permanent ambiguity—one might even say confusion—between characteristics of civilization that might be specifically Indo-European and others that we encounter throughout Europe and even beyond. The works of Adams, Mallory, and Sergent are extremely scholarly and make useful and fruitful reading, but at times we might ask ourselves what exactly is specifically Indo-European about the phenomena that are so carefully described and listed on the basis of texts that are disparate and scattered through time and space and which are compared to those of other eras and other parts of the world.[36] Such phenomena include the following: initiation rites (which "have parallels in numerous regions of the world"); the myth of the found child; the education of children (which is "like in many societies, the preserve of women"); marriage by abduction of women (which "has numerous parallels in the Amerindian world, among others"); the institution of marriage, which is supported by recent general ethnographical observations in Europe; the segregation of menstruating women ("as among most peoples"); trial by ordeal (judgment by God); funerary rituals such as keening ("more or less universal"), the funerary feast, a specific mourning color, the making of noise to frighten away demons; the importance of music; kings who are rich and powerful and linked to the sacred; warlike practices revolving around massacres, the abduction of women, and pillaging ("as among the Amazonian Amerindians," "this pillaging activity defined warriors" as "in the Indian societies of North America"); warriors who grimaced to terrorize

---

[35] Lebedynsky, 2006, p. 119.
[36] For example, Sergent, 1995, pp. 216, 219, 225, 231, 233, 237, 272, 285, 294, 297, 298, 306, 313, 319, 351, 356, 437.

412 THIRD MOVEMENT (1945–THIRD MILLENNIUM)

their adversaries ("like the soldiers of traditional China") and who also wished to be invisible and invulnerable; the practice of collective feasting, assemblies, vendetta, exchanges, and gifts to maintain social cohesion; the banishment of murderers; myths concerning a flood (also known among "a large number of peoples in Asia and the Americas") and Judgment after death; the importance of the number three; the color white as a symbol of purity (as was also the case "among the ancient Egyptians, the Hebrews, the Aztecs, Turkish peoples"); etc.

On the one hand, all sorts of cultural practices are in no way specifically Indo-European and are found far beyond the areas occupied by societies that speak/spoke Indo-European languages; on the other, a certain number of other practices attest to an absence of unity within said societies. Most of the authors acknowledge that there is no common doctrine or vocabulary for individual or collective eschatology (in other words, regarding the ultimate destiny of mortals), nor for the cosmogonic myths regarding the creation of the world, nor for the names of the gods or the denomination of priests. Reincarnation is only attested in India and in certain Greek beliefs. A degree of elasticity is required in order to find the list, in descending order of importance, of sacrificial beings in India (human, horse, cattle, sheep, goat) juxtaposable with that of ancient Rome (horse, cattle, sheep, pig). In fact, rituals vary greatly over the territory identified as Indo-European, and there is also no common vocabulary for sacrifices ("a religious practice that is practically universal"), which, incidentally, are very rarely organized in a "trifunctional" manner.[37]

Another procedure used for persuasion is circular reasoning borrowed from linguistic paleontology. If a given institution is not attested everywhere in the same form, then it must have been transformed since the time when it originated. In other words, what we might call the reasoning of "cultural paleontology" works, even when it does not. If the various musical instruments and games, which are nonetheless found in various similar forms throughout a large part of Eurasia, lack common designations, "it is completely normal: games, just like technical objects, are the subject of frequent improvement and renewal." While "pedagogical homosexuality" is attested in some parts of the Indo-European territory, and, incidentally, in other regions of the world such as New Guinea, its absence in Rome and among the Indo-Iranians "is probably due to repression at an early stage."[38] Likewise, if the study of European Neolithic skeletons (within the context of traditional physical anthropology) reveals no traces of migrations from the steppes, it is because these people from the steppes "became swamped within the indigenous population which was always relatively more dense," thus

[37] Ibid., pp. 355, 358, 361, 374.
[38] Ibid., pp. 254, 285.

WORDS AND THINGS   413

implicitly confirming their status as a conquering military elite—which brings us back to the linguistics of absence.

Inversely, if a given supposed Indo-European phenomenon occurs outside this linguistic zone, it is due to Indo-European influence. The trifunctional structures of Japanese religion can be explained in this way,[39] as can the practice of "circumambulation" (a circular procession intended to sanctify an area), which is also attested among the Semites, Turks, and Mongolians.[40]

How to always be right

In the end, we re-encounter the original hypotheses regarding what the original People should be—namely, mounted warriors—based on the model of the "Barbarian Invasions" of the Middle Ages (or rather, on the long-held image that we have had of them) and directly descended from the claims of Meillet, Benveniste, and Dumézil in the 1930s: "Aryan tribes from the Kuban (or Maykop) culture, driven by a desire for conquest and having dragged along with them the speakers of the Macro-Baltic languages"; "each Indo-Europeanized culture, adopting the value system of their conquerors, tended in turn to become expansionist"; "the Indo-Europeans, a rough people, were no strangers to human sacrifice."[41] Likewise, we are informed in a single phrase within an otherwise scholarly and stimulating philological study that "for Nomads like the Indo-Europeans, wandering could be fatal," without any evidence being offered in support of this assumed nomadism.[42]

Finally, we sometimes encounter a certain failure to consider the level of complexity of protohistoric societies in favor of a sort of Indo-European "spirit" or *Volksgeist*. From this springs the notion that there was a "taboo" on writing and a "primacy of orality" among the Indo-Europeans—an idea that was already present in the work of Antoine Meillet.[43] This is to forget the fact that all of the societies of Eurasia, whether they spoke Indo-European languages or not, developed writing as soon as they became urbanized and acquired a state structure; writing became an essential tool in the management and control of large human populations. The manipulation of abstract symbols had existed since the Paleolithic, but their combination in the form of writing only occurred with the emergence of cities and states. Chiefdom-type communities limited to a few hundred or thousand individuals can get by without writing, depending instead on

[39] See Chapter 16, pp. 370–371; Dumézil, 1978, p. 13.
[40] Sergent, 1995, p. 366.
[41] Ibid., p. 423, 431.
[42] Bader, 1989, p. 215.
[43] Meillet, 1923, p. 5. On writing in India, see Malamoud, 2002.

414   THIRD MOVEMENT (1945–THIRD MILLENNIUM)

the oral transmission of religious hymns, epics, and genealogical lists from generation to generation. Writing disappeared with the collapse of the Mycenaean urban world and the Indus civilization and reappeared a little later as cities rose once more. The use of Germanic runes, borrowed from the Latin alphabet, was limited to the realm of magic in these pre-urban societies at the beginning of the Common Era—and, symmetrically, the fact that runes play an important part in the Germanic myths proves that these stories are relatively late in date. The Gaulish societies described by Caesar, which were in the process of becoming urbanized, were exactly at the tipping point where writing (borrowed from the Greek or Latin alphabets) was beginning to be used for economic necessities while religious teachings continued to be transmitted orally.[44]

Similarly, if the ritual sites of protohistoric type societies are rarely imposing, this is not the result of a cultural choice but of the technical capacities of these simple societies, which have limited available manpower. Likewise, a formal, professional priesthood is only attested in societies that are urbanized or in the process of becoming so (e.g., the Celts), just as in the non Indo-European empires of the East. Finally, steppic societies were not inherently warlike. There is occasional evidence for massacres in the Neolithic societies of Western Europe (and elsewhere) in the sixth millennium BCE, which are assumed to be non–Indo-European, while evidence of warfare on the steppes is almost as underwhelming for the same period. It is only with the onset of the Chalcolithic, which is associated with demographic pressure and the occupation of the entire European continent by farmers, that a considerable increase in the evidence for massacres, fortified settlements, and violent injuries is widely observed.[45] This is a general historical phenomenon and is in no way linked to the "Indo-European spirit." Furthermore the reasoning of the various proponents of the steppic theory often gives the impression of being founded on three stages, none of which is validated but each of which supports the others:

1. The original Indo-Europeans were conquerors, since they imposed their original language on the whole of Europe and part of Asia.
2. The peoples who built the *kurgans* were conquerors since they possessed weapons, the domesticated horse, and the chariot and spread throughout Europe.
3. Therefore, the original Indo-Europeans were the *Kurgan*-builders, which proves that they were conquerors, etc.

---

[44] Caesar, *De Bello Gallico*, VI, 14, 3–4.
[45] Patou-Mathis, 2013; Guilaine and Zammit, 2001.

It is clear that the many erudite studies on the civilizations of ancient Europe and of some regions of Asia, based on surviving texts (a source whose potential is still not fully exploited), have yielded a wealth of fascinating insights into the history and culture of these societies. They show the extent to which these societies evolved through constant interaction with each other. To account for this in terms of an original minor steppic people who, through their own genius and superior weapons, would have imposed their language and culture on all of the populations of these vast areas would undoubtedly be the easiest explanation to understand. But, despite its long ideological history, is it not also the poorest and most reductive explanation?

V

FINALE AND SECOND OVERTURE

19

Models, countermodels, ideologies, and errors of logic

Are there any alternatives?

Coming toward the end of our journey and its many dead ends, it is now time to return to the heart of the canonical Indo-European model itself. This model, whether it be Anatolian, steppic, or otherwise, rests on four major assumptions, which we could conveniently term "Kossinnian," in reference to the German archaeologist who, at the beginning of the twentieth century, located the original People on the shores of the Baltic from where they spread out in fourteen successive invasions.[1] Regardless of the geographical locations proposed, the standard model postulates that:

1. language changes are due to movements of people, in particular via the mechanism of conquest;
2. "archaeological" cultures correspond to homogenous ethnic groups, with fixed boundaries, conceived on the model of nineteenth- and twentieth-century nation states but also on the model of biological entities that reproduce through a process of parthenogenesis;
3. there is a requisite coincidence between language and material culture;
4. ultimately, languages are also autonomous, homogenous, well-defined biological entities that also reproduce themselves through parthenogenesis or splitting.

However, none of these assumptions can be taken as a given and all lack validation, particularly archaeological validation; in reality, there is no shortage of counterexamples.

---

[1] See Chapter 6, pp. 121–123.

420   FINALE AND SECOND OVERTURE

How languages change

Usually, linguistic change is attributed to one or more of four processes, which may operate in combination: (a) the normal internal evolution of a given language; (b) the diffusion of a language in space but without movements of population; (c) the large-scale replacement of one population by another, either through absorption or destruction; (d) military conquest followed by political domination by a politico-military elite.

We will return to the first case a little later on. The second, diffusion without population movements, was the process proposed by Paul Broca, who explained the kinship relationships between Indo-European languages as follows: "What spread throughout Europe was not a race but a civilization which, in a manner of speaking, was transmitted from population to population, since good is as contagious as bad."[2] For Broca and other French anthropologists of the nineteenth century, the issue was the indigeneity of the dark-haired, brachycephalic French "race" in the face of German invasionist ambitions. But it must be acknowledged that ethnographic or historical examples for this mode of linguistic diffusion are few and far between. A notable exception was the widespread use of French in the eighteenth and nineteenth centuries, but this diffusion was ultimately ephemeral and limited to the cultivated elites of Europe. Another example, this time contemporary, is that of English, but up until now its diffusion has been limited to certain situations and contexts (e.g., diplomacy, commerce, academia, entertainment, etc.).

The third process is that which underpins much of Renfrew's Anatolian model.[3] The migratory movement in question, namely the neolithization of Europe from the Middle East, is perfectly validated in archaeological terms. It is possible to follow, and even to model, the gradual diffusion as far as the Atlantic coast of a complete homogenous material culture, which evolves at the same time, accompanied by continuous demographic expansion—the only question which remains controversial is the demographic contribution of the absorbed, indigenous, Mesolithic populations. However, it is actually the Indo-European character of this movement that is problematic and unsubstantiated.

The fourth process, namely military conquest, is that most frequently invoked to explain the diffusion of Indo-European languages according to the steppic theory and the now virtually defunct Scandinavian theory. This is the very mechanism by which Latin imposed itself over a large part of Europe, giving rise to the Romance languages; by which Arabic is spoken throughout much of the Middle East and North Africa; through which Turkish is spoken in Central Asia,

---

[2] Broca, 1864, pp. 313–315. See Chapter 4, pp. 77–78.
[3] See Chapter 13.

MODELS, COUNTERMODELS, IDEOLOGIES, ERRORS   421

Anatolia, and right up to the edges of Europe; Russian in Siberia; and French in West Africa. It is also the reason why Spanish and Portuguese spread throughout South America and why English came to dominate North America (along with a little Spanish and French), Australia, New Zealand, and part of East and South Africa—to the extent that some maps delight in showing how, over the course of the past few centuries, Indo-European languages have spread out to occupy huge swathes of the globe, with the exception of Arabic- and Chinese-speaking zones.

Invisible conquerors and secular empires

The problem is validation. There is no doubt that in a few centuries into the future, even if written documents did not exist, field archaeology would be able to trace the extension of European colonization. Similarly, it is impossible to ignore the reality of Roman colonization, which has left so many physical traces in the landscape, from London to Damas and from Budapest to the oases of Egypt, and which is often cited as a model to explain the diffusion of Indo-European languages from a restricted original Homeland (in this case Latium). But this wealth of archaeological evidence for Roman expansion, and indeed that for the Neolithic colonization of Europe, has no equivalent for the steppic model and is similarly lacking for any supposed later migrations.[4] There is in fact no evidence for the gradual progression of an entire material culture from the shores of the Black Sea to those of the Atlantic or the Ganges—unless, of course, we drastically force the data.

This is why scholars often resort to the idea of an invisible migration of "courageous small groups" (Benveniste) of "determined horsemen" (Dumézil) who appear to have been "absorbed within the mass of often more civilized peoples whom they conquered," to the point that "a long period of silence followed their conquest" (Benveniste),; their centrifugal outpouring over a couple of centuries allowed them "to overrun all of Northern, Western, Southern and South-Eastern Europe" (Dumézil).[5] As an alternative to the "Roman model," another Indo-European model was therefore proposed, namely the "Conquistador model." This is based on the fact that, within the space of a few months, a few hundred determined and well-armed men succeeded in subjugating the powerful Aztec and Inca empires. However, most historical examples contradict this hypothesis. Foreign military elites are generally absorbed within conquered populations and lose their language and culture within the space of a few generations. This was what happened in the case of the Franks within the Gallo Roman population;

---

[4] See Chapters 14 and 15.
[5] See Chapter 5, pp. 108–110.

422 FINALE AND SECOND OVERTURE

the former have left us little apart from the name of the country and a handful of words (e.g., *guerre, épieu, éperon, garçon, haine, trêve,* etc., and the names of colors), and they even adopted the religion of their subjects. We could also cite the example of the Vikings who settled in Normandy, Ukraine, and Sicily; or the Visigoths in Spain and the Langobards in Italy; or the Turco-Mongol Proto-Bulgars who, having arrived in the area of present-day Bulgaria under the command of Khan Asparuh in 681, subsequently disappeared within the conquered Slav population, leaving behind just a few words of their language.

In all other cases, the "Roman model" prevails. In Latin America, it took five centuries of Spanish or Portuguese state domination, with the support of the administration, the army, and the church, to impose these two Romance languages in South America. And even so, indigenous Amerindian languages have still not been completely eliminated: Guarani, for example, is an official language of Paraguay, just as Quechua is still spoken by millions of people and is an official language of Peru, Bolivia, Ecuador, Chile, Argentina, and Colombia. More generally, many such indigenous languages, such as Nahuatl, Mapuche, and Aymara, have survived and are still spoken by more than a million people. The Romance languages, which are derived from Latin, benefitted from 500 years of Roman domination but nevertheless many local languages (e.g., Greek, the ancestor of Albanian, Basque, Celtic, Berber, and Germanic languages) survived, while later migrations introduced foreign languages to what were once Roman territories (Slavic, Germanic, Arabic, Magyar, Turkish, Romani, Judeo-Spanish, etc.). Likewise, Arabic was imposed by the authorities of the various states that emerged from the conquest but, again, this did not prevent the survival of Berber languages, particularly in Algeria and Morocco. The Turkish example, cited by Mallory as a possible historical reference for Indo-European linguistic expansion,[6] is actually closer to the Roman model. The expansion of the Turkish model from its original Central Asian territory was dependent on a strong and long-lasting state structure which nonetheless failed to eliminate pre-existing local languages (Balkan languages, Caucasian languages, Armenian, Arabic, Kurdish, etc.).

An example closer to home is the case of English. Despite the Norman Conquest, French is not spoken in England or, as a consequence, in the rest of the former British Empire, including India and the United States. However, English is, to a certain degree, a mixed language, featuring a significant proportion of words of French origin. As such it has an intermediate status and thus represents an interesting model, one which we will return to later. This is also the case for Romanian, which, with a Romance base inherited from Latin, also includes a significant proportion of Slavic words, as does Albanian.

---

[6] Mallory, 1989, p. 147.

When confronted with the historical and archaeological data, the standard migrationist models fail to explain the diffusion of Indo-European languages. In other words, if such phenomena did in fact occur, there are no verifiable traces in the archaeological record as it stands today, and current paleogenetic data, as we have seen, also falls short of identifying a large-scale migration movement from a single point of origin.

Cultures and ethnic groups

The Indo-European model can be termed "Kossinnian" not only because of its focus on migration, but also because of the notions of "culture" and "ethnicity" that it propounds. The concept of archaeological culture first appeared and prospered in the nineteenth century, when it constituted one of the principal tools for interpreting the archaeological record. It is underpinned by several paradigms. The first is borrowed from geology. The history of the Earth has produced successive geological layers, which allow us to define "eras," "ages," and "periods," each characterized by certain types of fossils, rocks, etc. Prehistory would thus follow suit since it was geology that revealed the antiquity of mankind when, for instance, Boucher de Perthes discovered Paleolithic flint bifaces mixed with the remains of extinct animals in the layers making up the alluvial terraces of the River Somme.[7] Thus, in a spatial metaphor, archaeologists referred to "Lower," "Middle," and "Upper" Paleolithics, which were then subdivided according to the discovery sites into "Abbevillian," "Chellean," "Acheulean," "Mousterian," "Levallois," "Magdalenian," etc. The use of these names spread beyond the borders of France, and they were eventually adopted across much of the Old World. Each of these "cultures" or "civilizations" is like a box containing a range of "indicator fossils" (*Leitfossil* in German), such as carinated scrapers for the Aurignacian or barbed bone harpoons for the Magdalenian.

These types are themselves defined according to a naturalist model, this time borrowed from biology, as indicated by the use of the term "fossil." Swedish archaeologist Oscar Montelius provides an explicit description of this approach in his *Die typologische Methode* (The Typological Method) published in 1903: archaeologists, he argued, must be able to define their types of axes and pots "just as" zoologists and botanists are able to classify animal and plant species.[8] This demand for rigor is not anodyne. It implicitly presupposes that the axes and pots encountered by archaeologists enjoyed lives of their own and

[7] Boucher de Perthes, 1847.
[8] Montelius, 1903.

424   FINALE AND SECOND OVERTURE

reproduced among themselves. This is also the explicit assumption underlying the tree (*Stammbaum*) of Indo-European languages.

Furthermore, the invention of prehistory also coincided with the construction of nation states in the nineteenth century, a concept that emerged with the French Revolution and the Romantic Movement. A nation exists eternally within a defined territory. It possesses its own "spirit" (*Volksgeist* in German) and may even be embodied in a "race" (or, where necessary, two "races," as claimed by Broca and other French anthropologists). Thus, in the same vein, General de Gaulle proclaimed that "*La France vient du fond des âges* (France comes from the depths of time)." Kossinna makes the connection between the "cultural box" and the "nation" in his famous phrase: "Cultural provinces that are clearly delimited from an archaeological perspective coincide, in all eras, with specific peoples or tribes."[9] There is a clear overlap (*sich decken*, in Kossinna's words) between people or nation, on the one hand, and archaeological culture, on the other, with the latter underpinned by the same naturalist model. In this phrase, Kossinna uses the term *Völkerstämme*, which is usually translated as "tribes"; the botanic term *Stamm* also occurs in the word *Stammbaum* (family tree), where it refers to the tree trunk and, by extension, to the tribe, the "race," the lineage, but also to the grammatical root. It thus encapsulates all of these shifts and assimilations.

Almost all archaeologists at the time, Childe included,[10] shared Kossinna's vision even though criticisms on methodological grounds began to be voiced in Germany in the 1930s by, for example, Eggers and Wahle.[11] As we have seen, this Kossinnian model escaped direct criticism in the postwar years. Kossinna's work, considered an aberrant ideological subversion of true science, was simply erased from the official history of archaeology. His equation, however, has continued to underpin much of archaeological reasoning. Of course a certain number of articles and books on the subject of methodology continue to discuss the notion of archaeological culture from a variety of points of view, ranging from implicit (or unconscious) references to Kossinna to a relativist vision which sees "cultures" and "types" as no more than a construction on the part of the archaeological observer.[12]

Archaeological culture as Nation State?

The reality is clearly somewhere in between and much more subtle. Most of the time we encounter, at a given moment in time and within a delimited region, a

---

[9] See Chapter 6, p. 121.
[10] Veit, 1984.
[11] See Chapter 6, p. 128.
[12] Trigger, 1989; Klejn, 1971.

MODELS, COUNTERMODELS, IDEOLOGIES, ERRORS   425

kind of community of forms and decoration in material objects for which the term "culture" allows an initial descriptive and classificatory approach to the material. But this approach becomes "Kossinnian" when, on the one hand, these "cultures" are seen to correspond to homogenous peoples or ethnic groups with their own language and unified system of beliefs, all within a strictly delimited territory (on the model of the nation state), and, on the other, when these cultures are believed to give birth to each other in an unbroken line, thereby maintaining, beyond normal evolutions, a form of linguistic, political, and ideological permanence. This is exactly the model at work in Indo-Europeanist research on various supposed "arrivals" (i.e., those of the Greeks, Slavs, Tocharians, Indians, etc.).

Such a model presupposes that ethnic identities (and therefore archaeological cultures) perpetuate themselves unchanged, or virtually so, over centuries. Archaeology, however, demonstrates the complete opposite. For the periods that interest us here, several centuries of research have meant that the cards are continually being reshuffled. As we have seen,[13] the earliest Neolithic of temperate Europe coincides with the Linear Ceramic culture (5500 to 4900 BCE), which stretches from the Black Sea to the Atlantic and from the Alps to the Baltic. Originating in the Balkans and initially very uniform, this culture gradually became regionalized as it spread, before eventually dissolving in the first quarter of the fifth millennium. In France, for example, we subsequently encounter the Michelsberg culture occupying the northwestern quadrant of the Paris Basin (it also extends into part of Southern Germany), while the rest of the present-day territory of France is occupied by variants of what is termed the Chasséen culture, which is also attested in similar forms in Switzerland and Northern Italy and which partly springs from the Mediterranean stream of Neolithic colonization. Despite having different origins, the Michelsberg and Chasséen nonetheless share a number of common cultural traits, such as the construction of large earth and timber enclosures and a marked decline in the production of clay female figurines. Subsequently, in the south, toward the middle of the fourth millennium BCE, the Chasséen makes way for a host of local groups while in the northern half of France, totally different styles collectively known as the Seine-Oise-Marne culture emerge, variations of which also occur in Switzerland, and so on and so forth. And this pattern is repeated throughout Europe.[14]

In summary, from an archaeological point of view, the Neolithic "cultures" succeed each other without strict continuity and without overlapping between given cultural zones at a particular moment in time and those of the following period. Cultural elements are constantly rearranged, and we are unable to trace any given delimited entity that might have evolved imperceptibly and regularly over the

[13] See Chapter 11, pp. 242–243.
[14] Lichardus et al., 1985. See Buchvaldek et al., 2007 ; Fowler et al., 2015.

426 FINALE AND SECOND OVERTURE

course of the millennia in question. Certain Indo-Europeanists are aware of this problem when they admit: "The further we trace back the antiquity of a people in the archaeological record, the less it is certain that the cultures evoked belong only to this people."[15] In concrete terms, this means that the purported "synthesis" between the steppic conquerors, the supposed original Indo-Europeans, and the conquered peoples is simply not visible: "These syntheses are subtle and complex, so that it is sometimes difficult to make the connection between the movements of the Kurgan people and the historical Indo-European peoples who, precisely, almost all appear after—2000."[16] But, in this case, it is futile to attempt to work progressively back in time, even when one's goal is to meet up with the ancestors of the ancestors of the Indo-Europeans: "We observe that at the end of the Paleolithic, more than 10,000 years ago, the Indo-Europeans, who were as yet undifferentiated, were a small people living close to the Semito-Hamites of the Near East."[17] As another author has rightly pointed out in this regard, "It is as spurious to speak of Indo-Europeans, even 'as yet undifferentiated' ones, in the Paleolithic as it is to speak of 'French people (as yet undifferentiated) in the Roman period.'"[18]

Modeling "archaeological culture" on the notion of the nation state is outdated, all the more so in the light of criticisms of the classic concept of the "Nation" as an eternal entity, along the lines of the *Volksgeist*, published by Benedict Anderson, Eric Hobsbawm, and others in the 1980s and 1990s[19]; it is worth mentioning that it took fifteen years for Anderson's seminal work on nations as "imagined" or "imaginary communities" to appear in French. Working alongside or in the wake of these authors, a number of French historians also conducted critical studies on the construction of national narratives and the invention of traditions.[20] In parallel, certain ethnologists, particularly in France, reflected on the notion of ethnicity which, also long seen in terms of the traditional nation state model, has been revealed as a much more fluctuating and constantly changing reality.[21] This should not, however, lead to the total relativism once applied by English-speaking scholars engaged in so-called postmodern anthropology since ethnic groups do exist and perceive themselves as such. But these are not intangible realities "from the depths of time" that might be traced down through the generations. In fact, there is often no overlap between material

[15] Sergent, 1995, p. 416.
[16] Ibid., p. 408.
[17] Ibid., p. 434.
[18] Lebedynsky, 2006, p. 141.
[19] Anderson, B., 1983; Hobsbawm, 1990; Hobsbawm and Ranger, 1990; Gellner, 1983; Detienne, 2010.
[20] Citron, 1987; Thiesse, 1999; Fabre, 1996.
[21] Amselle and M'Bokolo, 1985; Chrétien and Prunier, 1989; Poutignat and Streiff-Fenart, 1995; Gossiaux, 1997.

MODELS, COUNTERMODELS, IDEOLOGIES, ERRORS   427

culture and ethnic sentiment, and even less so between material culture and linguistic unity, and the processes of ethnic recomposition are unending. English-speaking archaeologists working on the intersection between ethnic groups and their material culture have, in their turn, shown that the coincidence between the two is often far from perfect.[22]

Lessons from the barbarians

This fact can be confirmed by considering another period of history, namely the Early Middle Ages, the era of "great migrations" which in France is known as the period of "Barbarian invasions." In fact this is one of the few periods for which it is possible to cross-reference written sources and archaeological data regarding populations that are still "proto-historic" in character, just before the formation of true states. While this period has long been thought of in "Kossinnian" terms, with ethnically and linguistically homogenous peoples, based, as always, on the nation state, archaeological and historical research carried out in the past two or three decades by the likes of Walter Pohl in Austria, Florin Curta in the United States, and Bruno Dumézil in France has greatly altered our perception.[23]

In fact, these "Barbarians" are impossible to characterize within a delimited area on the basis of either their clothing or the objects found in the excavations of their tombs. An iconic example, rediscovered in 1653, is the tomb of the Frankish king Childeric, the father of Clovis, who died in 481 and was buried at Tournai in Belgium. The tomb contained an impressive number of typically Frankish weapons (a throwing axe or francisca, a scramasax, a lance, a long sword) but some bear decoration of Byzantine or Danubian inspiration. The grave goods also included a gold fibula, which would have been used as a cloak fastener in the Roman fashion; a gold ring bearing an image of the king in a Roman cloak (*paludamentum*), but with a "Barbarian" long hairstyle and inscribed *Childerici Regis* in Latin; 300 decorative gold bees with garnet insets, in a style borrowed from the Hun-dominated Thuringii; gold bracelets of Germanic style, etc. In accordance with "Barbarian" custom, collective horse burials also accompanied the king's tomb. This mix of influences is encountered virtually throughout Europe at this time. Most of the barbarian peoples (*gentes* in Latin) known from textual sources are not identifiable archaeologically, and it is virtually impossible to distinguish with certainty between the tombs of the Suebi, Vandals, Burgundians, Heruli, Scirii, Goths, Ostrogoths, Alemanni, Langobards, or Bavarians—at the

---

[22] Shennan, 1989; Jones, S., 1997; Terrell, 2001.
[23] Curta, 2001, 2005, 2006; Dumézil, B., 2013; Pohl, 1997, 2004; Pohl et al., 2012; Pohl and Mehofer, 2010; Pohl and Zeller, 2012; Gillett, 2002; Tejral, 2009; Mühlmann, 1985; Bernhard and Kandler-Palsson, 1986.

428 FINALE AND SECOND OVERTURE

same time, Roman populations (or more accurately, populations that had previously been conquered by the Roman armies) adopted "Barbarian" styles of dress. Whether we are talking about dress, personal ornaments, or weapons, material objects tend not to reveal clearly defined ethnic identities.

By allowing us an opportunity to cross-compare texts and archaeological material, the example of the Early Middle Ages serves to confirm in a concrete manner that ethnic groups, peoples, or *gentes* are entities in a perpetual state of transformation. The great and indecisive battle of the Catalaunian Plains in 451 CE, which is commonly believed to have been a clash between the ferocious Asian Huns led by Attila and the civilized Roman forces led by Aetius, was in fact a battle between two coalition forces—Germanic tribes, Ostrogoths, and Gepids fought beside the Huns while Visigoths, Franks, Aluns, and Burgundians swelled the ranks of the Romans. It is impossible to trace stable ethnic entities that were able to perpetuate themselves from one century to the next, and the names used to designate "peoples" in the writings of Latin historians in the first century are not the same as those encountered in the third century CE. As regards those mentioned in the fourth and fifth centuries, most were in fact recently formed military coalitions that would only later become hereditary monarchies.

We can better understand why it is unrealistic, therefore, to wish to track stable "peoples" with clearly defined material cultures (be they "Greek," "Slavs," "Indians," or Tocharians") across centuries or even millennia from a supposed original Homeland to their final destinations. To believe that this is possible is to remain confined by the "Kossinnian" model of nineteenth-century nation states.

We have also seen that "cultures" were built on "types" that were themselves conceived as biological entities. From this point of view, the "Kossinnian" culture is both a box and a biological entity, just as the original Indo-Europeans are also sometimes a "race." This biological vision of history might appear outdated, but it has recently been rehabilitated and modernized. Still proclaiming its origins in Darwinism, it has been applied in archaeology under the form of *evolutionary archaeology*[24] and in cultural history generally by, for example, Cavalli-Sforza, one of the proponents of the "New Synthesis" and the great tree of languages and genes.[25] This "biologizing" vision has been particularly criticized by social anthropologist Alain Testart.[26]

[24] For example, Shennan, 2003.
[25] Cavalli-Sforza, 2005.
[26] Testart, 2011.

MODELS, COUNTERMODELS, IDEOLOGIES, ERRORS   429

Languages and material cultures

The third Kossinnian assumption is that there is a coincidence between language and material culture; in other words, that a given group with a defined and delimited material culture will speak the same language in a homogenous way. This assumption might appear self-evident but for the fact that, even without considering the increasingly globalized and standardized world in which we live, there is an abundance of contemporary counterexamples. The inhabitants of Switzerland, for example, speak three official languages and five in reality (not counting dialects). The Bosnians, who all speak Serbo-Croat, were at war with each other in the 1990s in the name of three different religions, resulting in 200,000 deaths—to the point that some tried desperately to make people believe that there were three different languages. Conversely, English, French, and Spanish are spoken in various regions of the world with very different material cultures. Returning to more traditional societies that are closer to those of the era of the supposed Indo-European migrations, ethnologists and in particular ethno-archaeologists have described a number of counterexamples. Ethno-archaeology involves fieldwork among living societies but is carried out by archaeologists. In fact ethnologists (or social anthropologists) are especially interested in the immaterial and more "noble" aspects of traditional societies: myths, kinship systems, initiation ceremonies, funerary rites, etc. On the other hand, archaeologists necessarily apply very developed techniques to systematically describe, classify and compare material objects. Thus, among the Angas of New Zealand—an ethnic group that shares a common language—it has been found that architecture, which is emblematic of identity, differs considerably between the northwest and southeast of the region; the same is true among another ethnic group, the Simbaris.[27] Conversely, the Tewas of Arizona and the Hopi, with whom they live in symbiosis, are indistinguishable in terms of their material cultures. However, their languages are quite separate and coexist without mixing; in fact, the Hopis do not understand the Tewa language.[28] Large-scale studies carried out by Belgian ethno-archaeologist Olivier Gosselain in Cameroon, Niger, and Benin have clearly demonstrated the lack of coincidence between pottery shapes and decoration, on the one hand, and the distribution of languages, on the other.[29]

Coming back to historical examples, some of the Greek-speaking peoples of Ancient Greece were not regarded as Greek by the Athenians, examples being the Epirotes and Aetolians who occupied northwestern Greece but who did not

[27] Personal communication from Anick Coudart, CNRS. See also Roberts et al., 1995.
[28] Dozier, 1954; Zimmer, 1990a.
[29] Gosselain, 2011, 2012.

430   FINALE AND SECOND OVERTURE

have city states, did not fight like the Athenian hoplites, were difficult to understand, had kings instead of democratic regimes or oligarchies, and who were even accused of eating raw meat.[30] More recently, the material culture of the Turkish-dominated Magyars and of their Ottoman rulers were indistinguishable while, yet again, their languages were quite separate.[31]

Languages without frontiers

The fourth premise of the canonical Indo-European model is that languages themselves are homogenous biological entities that reproduce through parthenogenesis. More specifically, languages

a. will have clear boundaries, just like biological organisms (e.g., skin);
b. will be internally homogenous and coherent;
c. will not intermingle with other languages, nor will they able to combine with others to give rise to something new, apart perhaps, in a very marginal and anecdotal way.

As regards the first two points, the notion of standard, homogenous languages, which is reinforced by modern media, is a recent idea essentially dating, once again, to the nineteenth century although a number of nations with a longer history of centralized power experimented with the idea at an earlier date. In France, for example, the 1539 royal Ordinance of Villers-Cotterêts decreed that the *langage maternel francoys* was to be used for legal and administrative acts. A century later, the creation of the Académie Française and the publication of the *Grammaire de Port-Royal* codified the language while writers standardized it. But this official French was only one of the many dialects originally spoken in the northern half of France, and it only managed to supersede all of the others because it was spoken where political power was based. It still had to fight for supremacy over several dozen regional languages which did not really begin to die out until the second half of the twentieth century. The canonical Indo-European model is therefore built on an anachronistic notion of language.

Study of linguistic functioning in traditional societies, whether through the lens of ethnolinguistics[32] or dialectology,[33] offers a completely different picture. Language changed from village to village in traditional France and intercomprehension diminished progressively with distance. Just as there

---

[30] Tremblay, 2005, p. 143.
[31] Róna-Tas, 1988; Zimmer, 1990a.
[32] Palmer, 1996; Bouquiaux, 2004.
[33] Pop, 1950; Weinreich (U.), 1954; Chambers and Trudgill, 1980; Trudgill, 1986.

MODELS, COUNTERMODELS, IDEOLOGIES, ERRORS   431

was no linguistic homogeneity within a given territory, likewise there were no clearly defined linguistic boundaries. Hugo Schuchardt, the first linguist to have studied creoles and who was also a specialist in Romance languages, noted that one could travel from Rome to Paris, going from village to village, without ever encountering a clearly delimited linguistic frontier, even though French and Italian are two distinct languages.[34] In fact, one passed from Roman dialects to those of Central Italy, to Lombardic, to Piedmontise (already markedly different from standard Italian) before encountering the speakers of Franco-Provençal (in the Aosta Valley; while French and Italian are the official languages, in reality, the inhabitants communicate in Franco-Provençal) in the Alpine Valleys, in the western foothills of the Alps as far as the Jura; then, having passed this intermediary zone, one encounters the transitional dialects of the Charolais and Mâconnais regions, then those of the rest of Burgundy, which are now clearly *langues d'oïl* (French languages), before finally meeting the dialects of Île-de-France.

The very notion of Franco-Provençal, created by Italian linguist Graziado Ascoli in 1873, and to which a large body of literature has been devoted,[35] is enlightening: classically the *"Langue d'oïl"* of the northern half of France is contrasted with the *"Langue d'oc"* of the southern half (Occitan, Provençal, Niçard, Gascon, Auvergnat, etc.), but there is, in fact, no clear linguistic frontier between these two major zones and there has never been a political boundary in this area either. It was therefore necessary to create the concept of a "Franco-Provençal," a buffer zone stretching from Central France to Switzerland (Swiss "Romandy" was in fact a rural Swiss "Franco-Provençal," where only the urban elites spoke standard French) and the northern part of Alpine Italy. This Franco-Provençal has, itself, no clear frontier either to the north or south, and many linguists refuse to recognize it as an autonomous dialect but rather see it as a "broad transition zone."[36] But, in this case, what is the status of this crescent-shaped transition zone spanning what was once known as the County of Marche and the historical Limousin region?[37]

Occitan dialects, because of the lack of a unified central state, vary greatly. There is in effect no standard Occitan, and even today there is lively debate between the proponents of the revamped spelling devised by Joseph Roumanille and Frédéric Mistral in the nineteenth century and those who favor the conventions practiced by Occitan speakers of Béziers and Toulouse. Similarly, there is ongoing debate as to whether Gascon is a variety of Occitan or a completely separate language, and the same debate also surrounds Catalan(s), which

[34] Schuchardt, 1922, p. 145.
[35] For example, Jochnowitz, 1973; Tuaillon, 1972.
[36] Hall, 1949.
[37] Brun-Trigaud, 1990.

432 FINALE AND SECOND OVERTURE

is (are) very close to Languedocian. In fact the distinction, which in principle is hierarchical, between language, dialect, and patois is purely conventional and subject to variations.

Taking just one ancient example, it is striking that there was no "single" Greek language in the Archaic and Classical periods; instead, within this small territory composed of a network of independent city states, there existed numerous dialects whose history and interrelationships with each other are still a matter of debate among specialist linguists. The idea of an original Proto-Greek which would subsequently have become differentiated is but one hypothesis for which a number of strong counterarguments can be forwarded; likewise it is probable that instances of linguistic unification through convergence occurred, initially in the Mycenaean world and subsequently with the *koinê* of the Hellenistic world from the third century BCE.[38] It is clear, therefore, that as soon as we have sufficient information at our disposal, the complexity of true linguistic functioning becomes apparent.

The inadequacy of trees

This is why, since the nineteenth century, linguists have searched for alternative models to the tree in order to represent dialectal profusion. How, in fact, can the relationships within this profusion be represented in time and space when there is neither a center nor boundaries? Antoine Meillet, yet again, made a striking admission in this regard in 1928. Agreeing (uncharacteristically) with Hugo Schuchardt, but without explicitly saying so, he writes,

> There exists a serious ambiguity, which the nature of the facts prevents us from ignoring: here a single language name designates two distinct things: on the one hand, a common language of relationships, such as French, English or Italian, and on the other, a collection of local dialects [*parlers* in French], which can differ greatly from each other, just as French local dialects differ for example, but which are the result of more or less autonomous parallel developments of the same original language, in this case Latin. This second notion is relatively vague. We know what we mean when we speak of French or Italian as fixed, literary languages; in contrast, we pass from local dialects of French type to local dialects of Italian type, for example, by way of a series of imperceptible transitions, and we are unable to draw a precise geographical boundary between the two types.[39]

---

[38] Schnapp-Gourbeillon, 2002, pp. 157–160; Bartoněk, 1991; Duhoux, 1983.
[39] Meillet, 1928c, p. 16.

MODELS, COUNTERMODELS, IDEOLOGIES, ERRORS 433

To sum up, there is a kind of "noble linguistics," that of "fixed, literary languages," and then there are "local dialects [*parlers*]," which are a source of "serious ambiguity" and "a relatively vague notion." This, alas, is "the nature of the facts."

The Indo-European languages that Meillet studied and that have come down to us through literary or religious texts belong to the first kind of linguistics. But the "nature of the [linguistic] facts" in actual stateless, protohistoric societies has nothing to do with noble linguistics but rather is the stuff of dialectology, an empirical discipline linked to the description of spatial variations but which has difficulty theorizing them or does not see the need to. In addition, dialectology studies popular linguistic variations—which are partly threatened with extinction in the face of official, standardized language—often within the framework of contemporary state-based societies. Ethnolinguists, for their part, study the linguistic situation in traditional societies on other continents. Such studies show that most of these societies are in fact multilingual. Given the relatively limited size of ethnic groups and the circulation of individuals within the framework of matrimonial and trade networks, it is normal and commonplace to speak several languages. This was also the case in many parts of Europe, particularly in Central and Eastern Europe, before the two world wars and associated ethnic cleansing imposed a degree of order. Our monolingualism, which seems so natural, is in fact a historical and undoubtedly temporary exception; while the use of English continues to spread, the situation in the southwestern US, for example, is one of increasing English-Spanish bilingualism. The oldest written evidence for Indo-European languages confirms this pattern: as we have seen, in Anatolia (present-day Turkey[40]) in the second millennium BCE, at least ten written languages were in use, side by side and in combination, and it is probable that an even greater number of purely oral popular languages also existed.

Even in modern Europe, no state is linguistically homogenous.[41] All contain linguistic minorities of various sizes (not to mention recent immigrant populations), and all have groups of speakers of their official language living outside their political boundaries and who are generally officially recognized as such: France has a number of "regional languages," but there are also officially recognized French-speaking minorities in Switzerland, Belgium, Italy, and Quebec; Germany, which is home to a Slavic Sorbian minority, among others, and whose language and its dialects are also spoken in Belgium, France, Switzerland, Austria, Italy, Romania, etc.; Italy, which includes French-, German-, Ladin-, Greek-, and Sard-speaking linguistic minorities and whose language is also spoken in the Swiss Ticino; Greece, with its Turkish, Albanian, Pomak, Slav, and Wallachian minorities, while Greek is also spoken in Albania; Finland with its

---

[40] See Chapter 15, pp. 345–347.
[41] Fodor and Hagège, 1983; Giordan, 1992; Plasseraud and Marin, 2005.

434 FINALE AND SECOND OVERTURE

Sami and Swedish minorities while Finnish is also spoken by minorities within the Russian Federation; and Estonia, with its significant Russian minority, etc. In Switzerland, apart from the official languages (German, Italian, French, and, to a certain extent, Romansh), all of which are also spoken outside of the country, a large portion of the population in reality speaks a fifth, unofficial, language: Swiss German (*Schwizerdütsch*), which includes numerous local variants and whose intercomprehension with standard German (*Hochdeutsch*) is relatively limited. A similar situation prevails in Luxemburg. It is therefore impossible to identify a single European country which could be considered linguistically homogenous and whose language does not spill over into neighboring countries, and this after centuries of state domination. We can thus imagine what the situation might have been in pre-state societies.

"No language is totally pure"

This intermingling of traditional languages, which themselves are subject to significant internal spatial variations, results in their being in constant contact, whether at the level of "dialects" of the same language, creating these permanent transition zones, or between different languages. Just as racial mixing was an impossibility for Broca (otherwise the notion of "race" would disappear), so, too, was the notion of language mixing for Meillet and his contemporaries.[42] However, examples of contacts, and hence of mixing, between languages are so numerous that they can be considered the rule rather than the exception. The notion of "languages in contact" is not new and was at the core of Johannes Schmidt's "wave theory" (*Wellentheorie*)[43]; it was also central to Hugo Schuchardt's work prompting him to state that "No language is totally pure."[44]

While Schuchardt's work would long remain marginal and dissenting, the study of creoles and pidgins, and more generally of contacts and interferences between languages, has become an important branch of linguistics since the 1950s, particularly through the pioneering work carried out by Uriel Weinreich.[45] Since then, the number of conferences, specialized journals, and field work campaigns devoted to the subject have continued to multiply.

There exists an entire scale of linguistic contacts and mixing. The most muted form is the borrowing of words. These borrowings might be from an earlier substrate, such as Gaulish or Frankish words in present-day French, or Pre-Greek

---

[42] See Chapter 5, pp. 112–114.
[43] See Chapter 2, pp. 30–31.
[44] Schmidt, J., 1872; Schuchardt, 1884, p. 5. See Chapter 2, pp. 31–32.
[45] Weinreich (U.), 1953; Thomason and Kaufman, 1988; Thomason, 2001; Matras and Bakker, 2003; Nicolaï, 2001.

words in Ancient Greek. They might also arise from cultural influences, such as Arab and Hebrew words found in French, French words found in numerous European languages (dating from the past prestige attached to this language in the eighteenth and nineteenth centuries), or, symmetrically, English words found in most contemporary languages. This voyaging of words means that the most rigorous of Indo-Europeanists do not consider vocabulary when comparing two languages, but rather focus on their morphology or, more generally, their grammar.

The phenomena of frontiers, such as those already mentioned in the case of neighboring Romance languages, and fusion, in the strictest sense, are more complex. Hence in India, at the frontier between Hindi-type Indo-European languages and Dravidian languages, which are very different, forms of intermediary languages of communication have developed that borrow from both linguistic families.[46] Likewise, there is a zone of transition between standard "High German" and "Low German."

Mixes and interferences

These influences from one language to another can be substantial: Romanian, for example, a language that in principle is Romance and arose from Roman colonization, contains about 30% Slavic words which led certain Romanian linguists of the Stalinist era to claim that it was in fact a Slavic language that had been influenced by Latin. It is considered that only about 10% of Albanian is made up of strictly Albanian words, the rest resulting from "contamination" from Italian, Slavic languages, Greek, etc. Similarly, the proportion of Finno-Ugric words is very high in the Indo-European Baltic languages (Latvian and Lithuanian) due to their long co-existence with neighboring peoples to the north (Estonian, Finnish, etc.). Vietnamese is officially a Mon-Khmer language (like the Mon spoken in Myanmar and the Khmer spoken in Cambodia), but, after a thousand years of Chinese domination, it has become a tonal language, like Chinese (which belongs to the very distant family known as Sino-Tibetan), from which it has borrowed at least half of its vocabulary, to the point that it is sometimes considered to be a mixed language; it is also considered to be a useful window for understanding archaic Chinese due to the fact that many of these borrowings took place in the ancient past. Maltese, which, along with English, is one of the official languages of the island of Malta and thus an official language of the European Union, is in fact an Arabic dialect dating back to the brief occupation of the island in the eleventh and twelfth centuries; despite a long history of domination by the Order of Malta,

---

[46] Gumperz and Wilson, 1971.

436 FINALE AND SECOND OVERTURE

the language has survived. However, it contains a large number of English and Italian words, expressions and phonemes that render it virtually incomprehensible to Arab-speakers of North Africa.[47] In the Americas, Spanish and English have had a considerable influence on Amerindian languages; however, Spanish words designating new realities are borrowed directly and introduced into the indigenous languages, while, in the case of contacts with English, equivalents are often found to translate these realities in the local languages.[48]

Once a certain degree of interpenetration has occurred, we can truly speak of a "mixed language" (*Mischsprache* in German). Yiddish is a well-known example.[49] It developed around 1000 CE with a grammatical foundation derived from Rhenish and Bavarian German dialects and a lexicon of Hebrew words; it subsequently integrated a large number of Slavic words as it spread eastward with Jewish populations fleeing various persecutions. The genocide of the Jews during the Second World War virtually wiped it out.[50] Comparable linguistic creations occurred among other Jewish communities, such as the Judeo-Spanish or Ladino of Thessaloniki, which developed from the Castilian spoken by Jews expelled from Spain in 1492; or the Judeo-Piedmontese mentioned by Primo Levi; or the Judeo-Provençal, which disappeared in the 1960s.[51] The example of Yiddish was actually what incited a certain number of linguists, including Uriel Weinreich, George Jochnowitz, John Gumperz, and Claude Hagège, to study the phenomena of contact and mixing.

A striking and familiar example, highlighted by Saussure for example, is the case of English. We know that the Norman Conquest of 1066 imposed French as the language of the military elite and therefore of the aristocracy; it survives in certain official expressions (e.g., the motto "*honi soit qui mal y pense*," which appears on the Royal coat of arms; "*oyez*," the call for attention still used in court rooms, etc.). Walter Scott's famous novel *Ivanhoe* opens with a linguistic debate between Gurth the swineherd and Wamba the jester: the ox, the calf, and the pig are Saxon when they are alive but become French once they have been slaughtered and served up on the lord's table (beef, veal, pork). In the paradoxical words of New Zealand-born linguist Robert Coleman, "In spite of the elite dominance of the French-speaking Normans after 1066, English has remained as Germanic in its lexicon as it is in its phonology and grammar"[52]; however, half of the words in the English language are of Roman (or Greek) origin and entered English via French, and this is even before we consider syntax. This is particularly true for a

[47] Comrie et al., 2009; Vanhove, 1993.
[48] Brown et al., 1994.
[49] Katz, 1987; King, 1992; Weinreich, M., 1980.
[50] Ertel, 2003.
[51] Banitt, 1963.
[52] Coleman, R., 1988.

MODELS, COUNTERMODELS, IDEOLOGIES, ERRORS   437

large number of abstract words in English. The order of words and the disappearance of declensions are part of the same trend. Meillet states: "English represents the extreme culmination of a development: it represents a linguistic type that is different from the Indo-European type and has retained virtually nothing of the Indo-European morphology."[53] There is, therefore, a debate among linguists as to whether English might actually be a pidgin, a mixture of Saxon and French.[54] Its success is not simply due to political, economic, and therefore cultural domination, but also to the simplicity of its grammar, a fact that facilitates its acquisition; this is a characteristic common to most pidgins. The debate is far from won as there are also good linguistic counterarguments. However, the fact that the debate exists at all illustrates the complexity of the issue of contact between languages.

Another example worthy of mention is Mbugu, which is spoken by a few thousand Tanzanian pastoralists known by the same name. Its grammar is borrowed from Asu, one of the country's Bantu languages, but its vocabulary is derived from a Cushitic language of Ethiopia, the region from which this people is assumed to have originated.[55] Songhai, spoken by about six million people in Mali and neighboring regions, is another example and has been studied in detail by French linguist Robert Nicolaï, a specialist in the study of languages in contact.[56] Swahili is better known as it is spoken by around forty million people and is an official language of Tanzania, Kenya, Uganda, and the Democratic Republic of the Congo.[57] Swahili, which is composed of numerous local dialects, appears to owe its structure to Bantu, but its vocabulary is 40% Arabic, not counting words that have come from Iran, India, and, more recently, from the languages of European colonizers. However, it is essentially a language of communication and is the mother tongue of only a few million speakers. Afrikaans began as a Dutch dialect spoken by the first European colonists in South Africa. Over time, it evolved toward significant grammatical simplification, phonetic transformations, and foreign lexical inputs, to the extent that speakers of standard modern Dutch often find it difficult to understand. The language of Afrikaner political power, but in competition with English which has largely won out, it is nonetheless one of the eleven official languages of the country. A number of linguists consider it to be a pidgin.[58]

---

[53] Meillet, 1917.

[54] Domingue, 1977; Bailey and Maroldt, 1977; Whinnom, 1980; *contra*, see Thomason and Kaufman, 1988; Polomé, 1980; Dalton-Puffer, 1995.

[55] Goodman, 1971; Tucker and Bryan, 1974; Mous, 2003.

[56] Nicolaï, 1990, 2003

[57] Nurse and Hinnebusch, 1993; Polomé, 1967.

[58] Raidt, 1983; Markey, 1982; Zimmer, 1991.

438 FINALE AND SECOND OVERTURE

Substrates, adstrates, and superstrates

A classic theme of debates on interferences between languages, and particularly Indo-European languages, is the notion of "substrates." This is where a language replaces another through conquest but retains some elements of the original language because the conquered natives simply have difficulty speaking the imposed language correctly. Thus the Gauls might have learned Latin, but not very well and not without phonetic modifications (the development of the *u* consonant; nasal vowels such as *on*, *an*, and *in*; the reduction of vowels at the ends of words; etc.) and the addition of several hundreds of indigenous words still present in the language (e.g., *alouette*, *ambassadeur*, etc.). This is why French is not simply Latin; like other Romance languages, from Portugal to Romania, it has its own particularities. Symmetrically, there exist "superstrates," in other words linguistic layers that are superimposed on the principal language. This is precisely the case with Romanian, 30% of whose vocabulary is made up of Slavic words that were added to the Latin layer at the beginning of the Early Middle Ages. Likewise, but more discretely, the Frankish language has bequeathed a few words to French. The term "adstrate" designates a simple influence of one language on another.

These problematics have quite a long history and for the most part pre-date recent debates on linguistic interferences and mixing and on creoles and pidgins. The prevailing idea up until recently was that languages essentially perpetuated themselves as they were, although they did evolve over time. These substrate impacts were therefore to be minimized. As stated by Antoine Meillet,

> Each of the Indo-European languages has its own type: in each, pronunciation and morphology have special characteristics; and we do not perceive any condition that might determine these differences, which are profound, apart from the particularities of the language of the pre-existing populations which was replaced by Indo-European. This influence of languages that were replaced by Indo-European is what we call "substrate action." Unfortunately, these substrates are almost universally unknown so we have to resort to indemonstrable hypotheses.[59]

In other words, the differences between Indo-European languages do not allow us to deduce a simple arborescent evolution and cannot be explained directly. The "substrate" is therefore an easy explanation, all the more so since it is unverifiable: nevertheless, as we have seen,[60] it is regularly called upon in the event of difficulty.

---

[59] Meillet, 1937, p. 25.
[60] See Chapter 15, pp. 321 and 348, and Chapter 17, p. 407.

MODELS, COUNTERMODELS, IDEOLOGIES, ERRORS   439

This is why the "substrate" has proved to be a popular notion in various situations. In fact, most "substrates" remain hypothetical, and there are very few full-scale contemporary observations of the substrate phenomenon. One of the classic examples is what is termed the "pre-Hellenic" or "Pelasgic" substrate, which is said to have preceded the arrival of the Indo-European Greeks[61] and which has prompted numerous but somewhat inconclusive publications[62] and also some severe criticism.[63] Similarly, the distinctive character of Germanic languages has led some to propose the existence of a particular substrate, a hypothesis that has also attracted its fair share of criticism.[64] Various pre–Indo-European languages have been hypothesized for Europe, particularly focusing on Basque and place name evidence. In fact, the question of "substrates" should be seen, above all, as a symptom of the difficulties involved in constructing a coherent *Stammbaum* of the Indo-European languages.

Pidgins and creoles

A particularly interesting case of mixed language formation is, therefore, that of pidgins and creoles. These languages, made from bits of other languages for the purposes of communication, are generally based on a dominant language, usually that of the colonizers. The difference between "pidgin" and "creole" is somewhat vague. In principle, the term "pidgin" designates the first state in such a process and is associated with a very simplified grammar. This then goes through a process of "creolization" toward a fully formed language with a much richer vocabulary (linguists refer to "relexicalization") and becomes maternal; however, the national common language of Papua New Guinea, originally developed from an English-based pidgin is called *Tok Pisin,* a term that derives from the phrase "Talk Pidgin," with the word "pidgin" itself said to derive from the English word "business." Pidgin, creole, and "noble language" are therefore three steps in a continuum. Almost 200 of these pidgins and creoles, some of which have now disappeared, have been recorded throughout the world, often in coastal areas that are particularly subject to exchange phenomena.[65] The two best known historical conditions for their development are, on the one hand, commercial relationships between trading partners with different languages and, on the other, colonization phenomena.

[61] See Chapter 15, p. 321.
[62] For example Van Windekens, 1952; Merlingen, 1955; Hester, 1965; Capovilla, 1964; Strunk, 2004; etc.
[63] Francis, 1992.
[64] Neumann, 1971.
[65] Hancock, 1971; Kouwenberg and Singler, 2008; Mufwene, 2005; Thomason and Kaufman, 1988; McWhorter, 2005; Chaudenson, 2003.

440   FINALE AND SECOND OVERTURE

One of the principal examples, typical of the first case, is the *lingua franca* which was spoken throughout the Mediterranean coastal region from the Middle Ages right up until the nineteenth century and which had already been highlighted by Schuchardt.[66] It served as a bridge language between sailors and between merchants and was also known as Sabir from the word *saber* meaning "knowledge" in many Romance languages. In fact it was based on Romance languages (especially Provencal, but also Italian, Spanish, French, etc.), with numerous influences from Turkish, Arabic, Maltese, etc. Similarly, Chinook developed along the western coast of North America to facilitate trade through a convergence of local Amerindian languages (Chinook, Salish, Nootka or Nuu-chah-nulth, etc.) to which were added English and French words; it is even hypothesized that this language existed before the arrival of the Europeans.[67] In fact, there are many traces of purely indigenous precolonial communication pidgins (e.g., in Africa and in the lower Mississippi Valley).[68] Michif (or Métchif, the old French prononciation of "*métis*") was developed in Canada by Amerindian-French Métis communities and combines verbs from the indigenous Cree language with French nouns and various other local borrowings.[69] Russenorsk, combining Russian and Scandinavian, was used up until the early decades of the twentieth century by Russian, Scandinavian, and Sami fishermen and sailors in the Arctic region.[70] A *lingua franca* also existed during the Viking Age in the Baltic region and along the great rivers of Russia and Ukraine but unfortunately is poorly documented; the Hanseatic League established a language of communication based on Low German in the Baltic region in the twelfth to seventeenth centuries.[71] Likewise, Portuguese trading and conquests in the coastal regions of Asia led to the emergence Portuguese, Indo-Portuguese, and Malayo-Portuguese creoles, some of which were also studied by Schuchardt.[72]

Most of the recorded and spoken pidgins and creoles are associated with European colonization, although there are also a few African pidgins linked to Arab colonization on the east coast—Swahili being one form. The above-mentioned Tok Pisin of Papua New Guinea, which is based on English, allows the speakers of the island's 800 languages to communicate with each other and has become the national language. It is similar to the Bislama of Vanuatu, where it is one of three official languages along with French and English. The development of creoles in zones of direct colonization involving mass population movements was, however, much more brutal; in the West Indies, for example,

---

[66] Schuchardt, 1909; Dakhlia, 2008.
[67] Regarding Chinook, see Phillips, 1913.
[68] Bender, M., 1987; Drechsel, 1987.
[69] Bakker, 1997.
[70] Broch, 1927.
[71] Ureland, 1994, 2010.
[72] Schuchardt, 1889, 1890; Valkhoff, 1972.

MODELS, COUNTERMODELS, IDEOLOGIES, ERRORS 441

where hundreds of thousands of slaves uprooted from several regions of Africa (in total it is estimated that thirteen million were transported in the context of the Atlantic slave trade) and speaking a huge variety of languages were suddenly thrown together and expected to obey the language of their masters—be it French, English, Spanish, Portuguese, or Dutch—and to communicate among themselves. Thus were born the creoles of the Americas and the Indian Ocean which went on to become the mother tongues of the descendants of the first slaves. These creoles remain very much alive and have given rise to a written literature, even though the standardized languages of the former colonizers remain dominant. In particular, such creoles developed in insular or geographically limited regions with plantation economies. None, for example, developed in the United States, Mexico, or Peru.

Long disparaged by linguists who, like Meillet,[73] viewed them as anecdotal curiosities, the study of pidgins and creoles has really only taken off in the past fifty years. In 1959, only thirteen linguists attended the first Congrès International de Créolistique (First International Conference on Creolistics) organized by Robert Le Page at Mona University, Jamaica; by 1968, the numbers had swelled to fifty and included leading linguists such as Dell Hymes, Derek Bickerton, William Labov, and Charles Ferguson[74]; by 1980, the conference attracted no fewer than a thousand! Even by 1975, John Reinecke was able to count 8,000 books and articles devoted to the subject. Since then, conferences and journals on the subject have multiplied.[75] Apart from their individual historical interest, the theoretical issues attached to the study of creoles and pidgins center, first and foremost, on the question of the origin of language in general. While American linguist Derek Bickerton has no doubt been at the forefront in advancing these studies,[76] we also draw attention to more recent work carried out by French- and English-speaking linguist Salikoko Mufwene.[77]

Second, by offering much more complex models, these languages raise questions regarding the arborescent evolution of "normal" languages. This is why several Indo-Europeanists have wondered if convergence models might not solve the difficulty, or indeed impossibility, of reconstructing a single and homogenous family tree for the Indo-European languages. Stefan Zimmer, for example, has suggested that the original People were not homogenous but were composed of a conglomerate of protohistoric tribes, a situation exactly like that illustrated by the migrations of the Middle Ages, with their temporary aggregations, which

[73] See Chapter 5, pp. 112–114.
[74] Hymes, 1971.
[75] Arends et al., 1995; Valdman, 1977; Valdman and Highfield, 1980; Le Page and Tabouret-Keller, 1985.
[76] Bickerton, 1981, 1984, 2009.
[77] Mufwene, 2001, 2005, 2008.

442 FINALE AND SECOND OVERTURE

the ancient historians somewhat disparagingly referred to as *colluvies gentium* (which translates as something like "an agglomerated chaos of peoples," *colluvies* often being used to designate dirty water); moreover, Zimmer took the case of Afrikaans as an example of the process of creolization.[78] Likewise, Franco Crevatin was explicitly inspired by Swahili when he suggested that original Indo-European could have been a language of communication created by the interaction of several languages and peoples, and the *Stammbaum* might therefore be an inadequate model.[79] In fact, this was the hypothesis forwarded by archaeologists Susan and Andrew Sherratt[80] (although they did not elaborate it further) and the same one that Colin Renfrew had adapted when he hypothesized that the initial Neolithic Indo-European colonization might have been followed in the Balkans by *Sprachbund* type linguistic mixing in the Chalcolithic period.[81] As early as the 1930s, Dutch linguist Uhlenbeck had suggested that the original Indo-European language emerged through the convergence of two linguistic complexes, one Caucasian and the other Uralo-Altaic.[82]

Sprachbund and the Balkan laboratory

Up until now we have only talked about how interferences between two or more languages can give rise to a new language. But, within a given geographical area, these convergence phenomena can also involve several languages that interact among themselves without ceasing to exist individually; this is the focus of what is known as *areal linguistics*. The first to define this notion was Russian linguist Nikolai Troubetzkoy, who, in "Proposition 16" presented at the first International Congress of Linguistics in the Hague in 1928,[83] introduced it using the term "language union" or *Sprachbund*.[84] Within a given region, several languages of different origins can converge over time, not only in terms of their vocabulary but also their morphology, syntax, and phonology.[85]

The best known example, and the one presented by Troubetzkoy in this "Proposition 16," is that of the Balkan languages. In this region, there are four Indo-European languages belonging to four distinct groups: Modern Greek (which constitutes a group on its own), Albanian with its two principal dialects

---

[78] Zimmer, 1990c, pp. 24–33, 1991.
[79] Crevatin, 1979, after Lincoln, 2000, p. 213.
[80] Sherratt and Sherratt, 1988.
[81] See Chapter 13, pp. 275–278.
[82] Uhlenbeck, 1937.
[83] See Chapter 5, pp. 115–116.
[84] Troubetzkoy, 1930, p. 18, 1939, p. 215.
[85] Aikhenvald and Dixon, 2001; Muysken, 2008.

MODELS, COUNTERMODELS, IDEOLOGIES, ERRORS 443

(also constituting a group of its own), Bulgarian and Macedonian (which belong to the group of southern Slavic languages—the southern Serbian dialects being less concerned), and, finally, Romanian and related languages spoken by Romanian-speaking populations, namely Wallachian, Meglenitic, Aromanian, etc. (the Romanian language group). These four groups do not include the Ladino or Judeo-Spanish spoken by Sefardi Jews of Thessaloniki and Kastoría, the Judeo-Greek or Yevanic spoken by other Jewish communities, Romani dialects, and, of course, Turkish. For five centuries this region was part of the Ottoman Empire, which imposed Turkish as the administrative language while also erasing all internal political boundaries. A certain religious freedom prevailed, although a number of populations converted to Islam while retaining their language (e.g., the Pomaks of the Bulgaro-Greek Rhodope Mountains, the Albanians, the Romanian-speaking Meglenites of Macedonia, and the urban elites of Bosnia). Multilingualism was, in fact, widespread.

These 500 years of border-free mixing—which, by the way, followed a millennium-and-a-half of Roman and then Byzantine rule—means that the ethnographic and linguistic maps produced in the nineteenth century provide a very complex picture. (This was before the political "Balkanization" of the beginning of the twentieth century, which led to the creation of a host of small nation states, a painful process of fragmentation that is still unfolding before our eyes. Nineteenth century revolutionaries called for a great Balkan federation; but because it would have been Orthodox and linked to nearby Russia, Western powers delayed the independence of these countries for as long as possible . . . thus the word and the concept of "balkanization" were invented. Although not strictly comparable to protohistoric societies, the societies of the Balkans, in general rural, multilingual, and lacking internal political borders, can nonetheless offer us a useful analogy.)

While these ethnographic maps tend to locate Greeks in the south, Bulgarians in the northeast, Romanians further to the northeast but also involved in permanent transhumance, and Albanians in the west, there also exist a dense Albanian settlement in the Peloponnese (most of the leaders of the Greek liberation movement were Albanian); largely Greek cities on the Bulgarian and Romanian coasts of the Black Sea; Romanian-speaking semi-nomadic pastoralists more or less throughout the region; and Roma, not to mention Armenian, Sefardi, and of course Turkish communities. Nobel Prize winner for literature, Elias Canetti, for example, recounts in his memoirs how seven or eight languages were spoken in his native town of Ruse (Rustchuk) in Ottoman-ruled Bulgaria. (Canetti, who was born in 1905, was a Sefardi Jew whose family was of Turkish origin. He spoke Ladino at home but wrote in German; he died a British citizen in Switzerland.) This Balkan intermingling had a significant impact on the languages of all these

444 FINALE AND SECOND OVERTURE

peoples, and, as early as the 1920s, the results of these linguistic interactions were being studied in detail by Danish linguist Kristian Sandfeld.[86]

There are numerous examples of borrowings from one language to another, particularly from Greek and Turkish, but also from French in the nineteenth century and from English more recently. At the end of the nineteenth century these Balkan languages underwent a process of standardization and became national languages, and attempts were made, in so far as was possible, to eliminate Turkish words. The most pathetic case was that of so-called purified Greek (*Katharevousa*), which was reinvented on the model of a simplified Ancient Greek but which never managed to supplant the normal, "popular" language (*Dimotiki*) despite its use being obligatory for a long time in the University of Athens. During the Regime of the Colonels between 1967 and 1974, the powers that be attempted to generalize its use but they themselves were unable to speak it correctly. In the end, Turkish words remain an important element in local dialects of the various national languages.

The most interesting "Balkanisms" concern grammar rather than vocabulary. Thus, in all of these languages, the declensions, which are so typical of ancient Indo-European languages such as Greek, Latin, and Sanskrit, and which are still very much present in German and the Slavic languages, were greatly reduced to the extent that they have virtually disappeared in, for example, Bulgarian (a Slavic language); where they survive, the genitive and dative tend to fuse. Likewise, the infinitive has disappeared, often to be replaced by the subjunctive. Also worth noting is the formation of the future tense using the verb "to want" and the perfect tense using the verb "to have," as in Latin. The definite article is attached to the end of the word in Bulgarian, Albanian, and Romanian. Vowel harmony is well-attested, whereas o tends toward u and the same particular vowel (denoted as /ə/ in the international phonetic alphabet) exists in Romanian (ă), Albanian (ë), and Bulgarian (ъ, transcribed as ă). The Slavic diminutive -*ica* is also encountered in Greek and Romanian. These languages can distinguish between two verbal forms depending on whether the action occurs once or is continuous. Turkish itself, at least the version of it spoken in Bulgaria, has been influenced grammatically by the Balkan languages. We also encounter numerous linguistic *calques* (loan translations): in other words, expressions that occur in each language and are organized in the same way, such as expressions of welcome and their associated responses.

Much research has focused on trying to explain these "Balkanisms." Sandfeld, who was the first to study them, believed that the primary influence came from Greek via the Byzantine Empire, thus making Greek the most "noble" and venerable of these languages. Linguists no longer believe that this is the case and

---

[86] Sandfeld, 1930; Lindstedt, 2000; Joseph, 1983.

MODELS, COUNTERMODELS, IDEOLOGIES, ERRORS   445

instead tend to agree that there was no single source language. We are in fact looking at a highly complex phenomenon of interference between multiple languages. Unfortunately we will never know what the result might have been of several more centuries of such convergences or if they might have created false impressions of genealogical kinships.

"Areal" linguistics

Even though it is well-known simply because it is European, the Balkan example is not the only example. Another classic example is the region around the Sepi River in Papua New Guinea, an island famous for its large number of languages. In particular, three languages—Yimas, Alamblak, and Enga—belonging to three distinct families share a certain number of convergent grammatical traits.[87] Likewise, on the northwestern coast of North America, three language families— Salish, Wakashan, and Chimakuan—which together represent some thirty languages, display numerous convergences, phonetic as well as morphological.[88] The high plateaus of Ethiopia have witnessed the formation of a *Sprachbund* between Cushitic and Semitic languages.[89] And, of course, there is also the case of Central America.[90]

A final notable example is India, where three very distinct linguistic families converge: Indo-Iranian (Indo-European) languages, Dravidian languages (independent), and Munda languages (attached to the Austroasiatic family). Linguist Colin Masica has highlighted thirty characteristics of the Indian zone, some of which also occur in other Asian languages (e.g., Japanese, Burmese, Turkish, Chinese, Tibetan) but not in all (Thai is very far removed). However, only a third of these traits are found in the Indo-European languages of Western Europe (e.g., German, Spanish, and English).[91]

It is easy to see why the *Sprachbund* areal model and its concrete examples have attracted the attention of a number of linguists as a credible alternative to the genealogical *Stammbaum* model. Along with Troubetzkoy, this was also the hypothesis forwarded by Vittore Pisani in the 1960s.[92] We could also mention the reasonable suggestion made by Guy Jucquois and Christophe Vielle: "The prehistory of the Indo-European linguistic zone can, in fact, be considered as

[87] Foley, 1986.
[88] Thomason, 2001.
[89] Ferguson, 1976.
[90] Campbell et al., 1986.
[91] Masica, 1976; see Appendix 17.
[92] Pisani, 1966.

446 FINALE AND SECOND OVERTURE

centuries of interactions between a series of connected peoples occupying a geographical and dialectal continuum over a relatively wide area."[93]

This model is undoubtedly no easier to validate than the genealogical tree, but perhaps no more difficult either. It is undoubtedly also true that those linguists who are most specialized in Indo-European comparative grammar and who are most erudite have nothing to gain from sawing off the branch on which they are seated.

The tools of sociolinguistics

In any case, the underlying model of language as an autonomous biological entity appears to be inadequate. Essentially, language is a material object, just like any other tool used and manipulated by human beings. In its most material form, setting aside the written word, it is made up of sounds emitted by each person's vocal apparatus. These sounds vibrate in the air in the form of waves that are received by the human ear—just as a piece of flint struck by a knapper using a hammer stone produces a flake. The sounds may have no particular meaning, just as it is possible, in theory, for a person to perform actions that produce no end product. But, for the most part, the sounds produced by the human voice have, as we know, a communication function. These sounds are thus organized in a language, a coded system that also exists in various forms among animals (these forms include dialects, as has been observed among certain birds, for example); our primate cousins use several dozen meaningful sounds. We know that the vocal apparatus of the Neanderthals, who developed from *Homo erectus* in Europe some 300,000 years ago, is virtually identical to our own and even features the same hyoid bone. Language complexity has, therefore, evolved continuously over about 8,000,000 years, from the common ancestors of primates and humans, right down to ourselves.

As a material object, language obeys the same social rules as the other material objects produced and manipulated by a given society. For example, the decoration applied to pottery in a traditional society has a double function, which is not always immediately apparent: it serves to signal one's belonging to the group (the potter draws on the group's repertoire of motifs), and, at the same time, and to various degrees, it signals the potter's individuality through the use of specific ornamental motifs. Ethnographic research has thus shown that, among a group of potters, each is capable of identifying the work of another. Thus, over and beyond the purely material function of a given object, elements of its form and decoration play a role in affirming collective and individual identity. Some types of

---

[93] Jucquois and Vielle, 1997, pp. 178–179, note 11.

MODELS, COUNTERMODELS, IDEOLOGIES, ERRORS   447

objects, for example stone axes, which are reduced to their practical function, lend themselves less to this than others. Furthermore, some societies are more constraining than others and significantly control the element of personal inventiveness. These observations are true of all of the material objects that make up the "material culture" of a given society, be they tools, weapons, pottery, architecture, funerary practices, and, of course, language.

At the beginning of the twentieth century, Ferdinand de Saussure[94] was one of the first to apply this evidence to languages: "This awareness [of the differences between languages] gives rise to the notion among primitives that language is a habit, a custom that is comparable to that of costume or weapons. The term 'idiom' precisely designates language as reflecting the characteristic traits of a community (the Greek word *idioma* had the meaning 'special custom')."[95] Indeed, for the linguist, the evolution of a language is the result, "just like any other habit" of "two forces continually acting simultaneously and in opposite directions: on the one hand, the particularist spirit, the parochial spirit, and, on the other, the spirit of 'intercourse' that creates communication between human beings."[96] This is exactly the way that material objects function in general.

However, in the nineteenth century, archaeologists put forward a "biologizing" vision of material objects; Oscar Montelius, for example, believed that axes and pottery should be classified within defined "types," as in botany and zoology. Implicit is the idea that axes and pottery would reproduce themselves autonomously. The structuralist paradigm marks a rupture with this naturalist paradigm; in the last lines of his *Cours*, Saussure is perfectly clear when he radically rejects the organic vision in all its forms.[97]

As general linguistics has gradually moved away from the comparative grammar of Indo-European languages and gained its own independence, it has developed new methods and theories, while comparative grammar has imperturbably labored on using the same tools and the same hypotheses. Hence the paths sketched out by Saussure, with his interplay between "intercourse" and "parochialism," gave rise to a new field of research—that of sociolinguistics—in the 1960s. For this very diverse, even heterogeneous, discipline, language is inseparable from society or, more precisely, from the various social groups that manipulate it, each for its own ends. It is in this way that linguistic evolutions, in particular, occur. By definition, the fascinating research carried out by sociolinguists focuses on living, and thus directly observable, populations, while Indo-Europeanists spend most of their time looking at languages that are scholarly, preserved in texts, and/or dead.

[94] See Chapter 5, pp. 99–102.
[95] Saussure et al., 1972, p. 261.
[96] Ibid., p. 281.
[97] See Chapter 5, p. 102.

448   FINALE AND SECOND OVERTURE

The various linguistic phenomena of mixing, interaction, convergence, etc. thus offer us models that are infinitely more complex than that of the "pure" genealogical tree, with its regularly separating branches. It is not that kinships between languages are nonexistent, quite the contrary in fact; but the relationships follow pathways that are much less simplistic than those of the famous *Stammbaum*. We are aware of the amount of abusive simplification and arbitrary pruning that real cultural, historical, and linguistic evolutions have to be subjected to in order to obtain a purified *Stammbaum*, one which ultimately finds no general agreement among linguists. The point of origin is shown to be nothing but a fantasy. We are no closer to building the family tree of all languages than we are to building trees of all the axes of the world, all the pottery of the world, or all the houses of the world.

To sum up, if we return to the four assumptions of the canonical model which we outlined at the beginning of the chapter, we can confidently counterargue that

1. Linguistic changes can be due to numerous factors, often working in combination, of which migrations and military conquests are only two possible causes which never operate alone and which are not the most common.
2. Archaeological cultures, just like ethnic groups, are unstable, permeable, temporary entities, which are in a constant state of recomposition and, therefore, do not have a timeless essence that can be traced over centuries, let alone millennia.
3. There is not necessarily a coincidence between language and material culture, or between language and ethnic group.
4. Languages are not homogenous, autonomous, well-defined biological entities that reproduce through parthenogenesis or splitting; on the contrary, they are material and social objects, created by human groups for the purpose of communication, subject to considerable internal variation, and constantly evolving.

However, it is a mundane reality that simple, or even simplistic, interpretations are always easier to understand than complex interpretations!

Epilogue

The canonical, arborescent, centrifugal, and invasionist Indo-European model is without doubt the poorest, least interesting, and least convincing model that can be proposed to explain the undeniable similarities between the languages, myths, and perhaps even the genes of a large part of Eurasia. It is fraught with contradictions and does not permit any satisfactory archaeological solution. The time has come to approach this old and fascinating problem from a fresh perspective; born in the eighteenth century out of the quest for an alternative origin myth to the Bible of the Jews, the Indo-European myth gathered momentum in the context of European colonization of the world in the nineteenth century and was led astray in various ways during the turmoils of the twentieth century. The vast wealth of linguistic, literary, cultural, archaeological, and anthropological information that ancient societies have bequeathed us deserves far better.

But in this case, having come to the end of our journey, and even if we accept all of the reservations expressed and all of the dead ends encountered along the way, what is *the* solution? Especially since all previous solutions, be they Scandinavian, Anatolian, or steppic, have always been simple and easy to understand. On what grounds should we refute, or even condemn, three centuries of scholarly and methodic research and the tens of thousands of books and articles which appear to have provided irrefutable evidence for the existence, the beliefs, and the destinies of the Indo-Europeans? Surely to invoke archaeology and its tangible material realities is to exercise the narrow positivism and effrontery of these "historical illiterates" (as German Nobel Prize-winning historian Theodor Mommsen once described archaeologists)? In the end, can we shy away from answering the question that we have chosen to consider?

The answer is that (as of today) there is no definitive answer.

We can easily imagine the consternation of the believer suddenly confronted by an empty heaven. Human beings cannot live without social adherences or affiliations. But at a time when questions of origins and identities are posed with such singular acuity, scientists have a duty and a responsibility to warn against false origins and false identities.

In fact, the construction of the Indo-European myth amounts to the construction of both an origin myth and an identity myth. From the end of the eighteenth century, it has accompanied the emergence of European nation states and their national identities, but it has done so on the scale of Europe as a whole. It became inextricably linked to their destinies, and soon their pathologies, including the

450   EPILOGUE

most monstrous. There is, therefore, no pure science, just as there is no pure language, as pointed out more than a century ago by Hugo Schuchardt. Every construct has a history, and we cannot address the Indo-European problem without exploring and explaining this history.

From its beginnings, the Indo-European question has stood at the cross-roads of four disciplinary fields which themselves have never ceased to develop and be transformed: linguistics, archaeology, mythology, and biological anthropology— not to mention straightforward history. This question has accompanied the evolutions, metamorphoses, and successes of these four disciplines. Thus, for each of them, it constitutes one of their illustrations, one of their stumbling blocks, one of their symptoms, and one of their follies.

Comparative grammar, which represented an innovative branch of classical philology in the nineteenth century, gave rise in the early twentieth century to general linguistics. The latter, initially structural and then generative, continued to diversify and become enriched, intersecting with ethnology (ethnolinguistics) and sociology (sociolinguistics), investigating the origins of languages and of language itself, exploring mixed or developing languages (creoles, pidgins, etc.) using the sophisticated tools of computer technology and statistics but also falling into the trap of simplistic mediatization.

Archaeology, which was virtually nonexistent at the beginning of the nineteenth century, has since never ceased exploring the soils of Eurasia and further afield, accompanying the large-scale infrastructural developments that dramatically erode our finite and ever-shrinking historical heritage, accumulating and classifying discoveries, developing increasingly complex interpretive models, and applying techniques and methods borrowed from other sciences.

Comparative mythology, and more generally the study of ancient texts, is committed to uncovering and deciphering traces of long-disappeared beliefs and stories, organizing this evidence, and reconstructing the ideologies of the distant past.

After its dead-ends, its mistakes, and even its crimes, biological anthropology has finally embarked on new avenues, some of which hold great potential, exploring the very archaeology of our genes. It has much more to offer provided that geneticists do not become trapped by the allure of simplistic models and instead collaborate as part of a truly multidisciplinary approach.

Up until now, these four disciplines have continually tied themselves up in interdisciplinary vicious circles. This is because the Indo-European origin myth is a genealogical myth which only conceives history (of languages as well of society) through the prism of a genealogical tree. Regardless of the fact that we have at our disposal an ever-growing body of new archaeological, linguistic, mythological, and anthropological information, this corpus can only ever serve to support the established Adamic and Babelian genealogical model.

EPILOGUE   451

This book is not intended as a condemnation but rather as a call to move beyond the genealogical myth, and my criticism seeks, above all, to be dynamic and positive. For example, the convergence between textual evidence and archaeology certainly seems to suggest the emergence of a Bronze Age aristocratic, heroic ideology in part of Eurasia in the second millennium BCE; this would explain the similarities that we observe in myths, poetry, and also in ornamentation and iconography and does away with the need to invoke a single, shared origin many thousands of years earlier. Likewise, we should no longer see the prehistory and protohistory of Europe as a genealogical succession of societies, ethnic groups, or "cultures" but rather as a multipolar world that was constantly in a state of reconfiguration, and such a model should be just as valid for languages.

Research should now turn its focus to testing network models, multipolar models, and "chaotic" models utilizing this enormous corpus of new and existing data.

In conclusion, we can now propose twelve "antitheses" to the twelve canonical theses outlined at the beginning of this book; these antitheses represent avenues for future investigation, and some are already being pursued, albeit only marginally. The overall model, which remains to be constructed but which will be one day, will undoubtedly be very complex: it will involve the intertwining of diffusion, mixing, acculturation, and convergence phenomena and, yes, even conquests, over a long time scale.

An alternative vision: The twelve Indo-European antitheses

Antithesis 1. The Indo-European languages, spoken 3,000 years ago in a large part of western Eurasia, and today over a large part of the globe, form a coherent family of languages made up of twelve principal subfamilies (see Appendix 2, p. 676). The various arborescent models, which for certain linguists explain this family, are not the only possible logical models capable of describing the relationships between these languages.

Antithesis 2. The 300-year-long quest for a kinship link between these languages and for their presumed area of origin has effectively resulted in the construction of an origin myth with a view to offering European peoples an identity that differs from that provided by their official origin myth, the Bible; the latter renders them indebted to the Jews, whom they have constantly persecuted for centuries, thus creating a schizophrenic situation.

Antithesis 3. Despite two centuries of linguistic research and the support of the most up-to-date methods of quantitative linguistics, the reconstructions of the original language (*Ursprache*) and the family tree of Indo-European

452 EPILOGUE

languages (*Stammbaum*) still lack overall consensus among leading linguists.

Antithesis 4. Nor is there a consensus regarding the status of the reconstructed language (*Ursprache*), seen as a simple abstraction and a "system of correspondences" by some and as a true language that was actually spoken by an original People (*Urvolk*) by others; this double-speak is often maintained in Indo-Europeanist publications.

Antithesis 5. The idea of a single, localized, original Homeland (*Urheimat*) which was the cradle of the original People is just one of the possible hypotheses that might account for the similarities between the Indo-European languages.

Antithesis 6. The use of linguistic paleontology gives rise to numerous contradictions, aporias, and instances of circular reasoning.

Antithesis 7. The model of diffusion of "archaeological cultures," each corresponding to a given "people," is both naturalist and directly inspired by the nation states of the nineteenth century; it does not correspond to numerous situations provided, for example, by the ethnology of other continents or by the history and archaeology of protohistoric peoples of Early Medieval Europe.

Antithesis 8. Without reiterating the subversions and errors committed by European physical anthropology, even as recently as the 1980s, the potential of bone chemistry and paleogenetic analyses to throw light on prehistoric migrations is extremely promising but provides an image that is becoming increasingly complex as publications multiply, which, on the one hand, requires us to avoid confusing culture and biology and, on the other, demands complex multidisciplinary models.

Antithesis 9. While undeniable resemblances and correspondences exist between a certain number of Eurasian mythologies, it is overly simplistic to attribute these to an original, homogenous, Indo-European mythology; there are no one-to-one correspondences between languages and mythologies, and this applies equally to the analysis of other ancient texts that have survived down to today.

Antithesis 10. There is no consensus regarding the supposed original Homeland of the original People; currently, two opposing hypotheses dominate in the media, namely the steppes to the north of the Black Sea, on the one hand, and Anatolia, on the other. Each of these principal theses provides convincing arguments against the other. Likewise, there is no consensus but, rather, numerous contradictory hypotheses regarding the paths that each of the Indo-European peoples would have taken to end up in their historical locations (see Appendix 8, p. 683).

EPILOGUE 453

Antithesis 11. The past and present exploitation by nationalist and extremist movements of the canonical Indo-European model of an original People who emerged from an original Homeland is a magnified reflection of the ideological representations that are underpinned by this model.

Antithesis 12. While no one would dream of questioning the resemblances between the various so-called Indo-European languages, the centrifugal arborescent model in its current forms cannot be considered as validated due to the numerous contradictions that it contains. Furthermore, abuses, both past and present, of this model should incite us to the utmost rigor. We must therefore turn toward much more complex and multidisciplinary models concerning historical phenomena that span millennia if we are to meaningfully explore the multiplicity of problems that make up the "Indo-European question."

Appendices

Appendix 1. Simplified chronological table of the main archaeological cultures and civilizations in Eurasia (from 300,000 BCE to the present)

Countries Western European Chronology	Dates BC	Northwestern Europe (Scandinavia, Benelux, Nortccccchern France, Southwestern Germany)	Southwestern Europe (Spain, Italy Southern France)	Central Europe (Eastern Germany, Switzerland, Austria, Poland, Czech Rep., Slovakia, Hungary)	Northeastern Europe (Russia, Baltic countries)	Southeastern Europe (Balkan Peninsula)	Pontic Steppes (Ukraine, South Russia)	Near and Middle East (Turkey, Levant, Mesopotamia, Egypt)	Iran and India (Iran, India, Pakistan, Afghanistan)	Central Asia (Central Asia, Xinjiang, Mongolia)	Far East (China, Korea, Japan—without South-Eastern Asia)
Middle Paleolithic	− 300,000 − 35,000	Middle Paleolithic. (Neanderthal)	Middle Paleolithic. (Neanderthal)	Middle Paleolithic. (Neanderthal)	Middle Paleolithic. (Neanderthal)	Middle Paleolithic. (Neanderthal)	Middle Paleolithic. (Neanderthal)	Middle Paleolithic. (Neanderthal)	Middle Paleolithic.	Middle Paleolithic. (Neanderthal and Denisovans)	Peking Man, Denisovans
Upper Paleolithic	− 35,000 − 10,000	Aurignacian/ Gravettian/ Solutrean/ Magdalenian	Aurignacian/ Gravettian/ Solutrean/ Magdalenian	Aurignacian/ Gravettian/ Swiderian, Hamburgian	Aurignacian/ Gravettian/ Epigravettian/ Swiderian	Aurignacian/ Gravettian/ Epigravettian	Aurignacian/ Gravettian/ Epigravettian	Upper Paleolithic, Kebaran	Upper Paleolithic	Upper Paleolithic	Sedentary hunter-gatherers, first ceramics
Mesolithic	− 10,000 − 6,500	Azilian/ Beuronian, Maglemosian,/ Tardenoisian	Valorguian/ Montadian/ Castelnovian	Ahrensburgian/ Beuronian/	Kunda	Mesolithic, Lepenski Vir	Mesolithic	Natufian, Jarmo, Pre-Pottery Neolithic	Mesolithic	Mesolithic	Hunter-gatherers, Jomon,
Neolithic	− 6,500 − 4,500	Ertebølle-Ellerbeck (acculturated Mesolithic), Linear Ceramic	Cardial/ Epicardial/Early Chasséen	Final Mesolithic/ Linear Ceramic, Rössen	Sedentary hunter-gatherers with pottery	Neolithic: Karanovo, Criş-Körös, Dimini, Vinča, Boian, etc	Bug-Dniester, Dnieper-Donets	Samarra/Halaf/ Obeid	Neolithic: Sialk, Mergahr	Kelteminar,	Agriculture in China, Jomon in Japan
Early Chalcolithic	− 4,500 − 3,500	Funnel Beakers (TRBK), Michelsberg	Chasséen, Lagozza, Sepulcros de Fosa	Tiszapolgár, Lengyel Boleraz	Narva, Pit-Comb Ware culture	Rachmani, Gumelniţa, Cucuteni	Cucuteni-Trypillia, SrednyStog, Cernavoda	Obeid/Uruk, Nagada	Neolithic	Kelteminar, Djeitun, Namazga,	Yangshao in China, Jomon in Japan
Middle Chalcolithic	− 3,500 − 2,700	Funnel Beakers, Seine-Oise-Marne	Ferrières, Fontbouisse, Gaudo, Remedello, Los Millares, Veraza	Baden, Salzmünde Globular Amphora culture, Złota	Pit-Grave culture (*Jamnaja kultura*)	"Early Bronze Age", Early Helladic, Cycladic, Ezero	Gorodsk-Usatovo, Pit-Grave culture (*Jamnaja kultura*), Maykop, Kouban	First Egyptian and Mesopotamian states, Troy	Chalcolithic, Susa	Afanasievo, Botaj,	Yangshao/ Longshan in China, Jomon in Japan
Late Chalcolithic	− 2,700 − 2,200	Corded Ware/ Bell Beakers	Bell Beakers	Corded Ware/ Bell Beakers	Fatyanovo,	Minoan (Crete), Early and Middle Helladic	Catacomb culture	Old Egyptian Kingdom, Sumer, Akkad, Ur,	Jiroft, Indus civilization, Elam	Andronovo, *Bactria–Margiana Archaeological Complex* (BMAC)	Longshan in China, Jomon in Japan

Period	Dates										
Bronze Age	− 2,200 − 800	Nordic, Atlantic and North-Alpine Bronze Age	El Argar, Polada/ Terramare/ Protovillanova/ Villanova	"Tumulus"/ "Urnfield culture", Trzciniec, Lusatian culture	Abashevo/ Trzciniec-Komarov-Sosnica/Lusatian culture	Middle and Late Minoan (palaces), **Mycenaean**/ "Dark Ages"	Timber-grave culture (*Srubnaja kultura*)	Egyptian empire, **Hittites**, Assyrians, Mitanni, Hebrews, Phoenicians,	Indus civilization, Iron Age (**Vedas**), Yaz,	Andronovo-Fedorovka, Sintashta, Karakol,	Jomon in Japan, Erlitou/Erligang in China: Xia, Shang, Zhou dynasties
Early Iron Age	− 800 − 480	Hallstatt, Jastorf (emergence of Celts and Germanic peoples)	Italic cities (**Rome**, Etruscans, Magna Graecia) and Iberians, **Osques, Ombriens**	Lusatian culture, Hallstatt	Lusatian culture	Growth of the **Greek** cities	"prescythian" cultures/ Cimmerians, Sauromates, **Scythians**	Assyrians, Egyptian empire, **Persian** empire, Hebrews, Phoenicians, **Phrygians**,	Middle and Late Vedic period, Medes, **Persians**,	Saka,	Zhou dynasty in Chinea Jomon in Japan
Late Iron Age	− 480 − 20	Jastorf, La Tène, **Celts** and Germanic peoples	Growth of Rome, Celtic migrations, Celtiberians, Carthaginians	Przeworsk, Celts (La Tène culture),	Zarubinec	**Thracians, Illyrians**, classical Greece/Hellenistic World/Rome	Zarubinec/ Chernyakhov, Scythians, Germanic peoples	Persian empire/ Hellenistic World, **Lycians**, **Lydians**	Maurya empire, Achaemenids	Xiongnu, Ordos,	Warring States/ Qin dynasty in China, yayoi in Japan
Roman Empire	− 20 + 500	Roman Empire, "Free" **Germania**	Roman Empire	Wielbark, Roman Empire,	Slavs, Balts	Roman Empire, Dacians	Prag-Penkov-Kolochina, Slavs	Roman Empire	Parthians, Sassanians	Huns	Hans China, Yayoi in Japan
Early Middle Ages (Great Migrations)	+ 500 + 1000	Merovingians, Carolingians, Vikings, christianization	« Barbarian» Kingdoms, Lombards, etc	« Barbarian » Kingdoms », Slavs, Magyars, etc	Slavs, Balts, Varangians	Byzantine empire, Slavs, first **Slavic** writings	Slavs	Byzantine empire, first **Armenian** writings	Middle Age Umayyads	Turks, Uyghurs, **Tocharians** (in the Xinjiang)	Chinese empire, Japanese and Korean states
Classic Middle Ages	+ 1000 + 1500	Feudal Monarchies	Feudal Monarchies	First cities, christianization,	First cities, christianization, first **Baltic** writings	Byzantine empire, Slav kingdoms, first **albanian** writings	Russian empire	Byzantine empire, Ottoman empire	Mongols	Mongols, Russian and Chinese empires	Chinese empire, Japanese and Korean states
Modern times	+ 1500 + 2000	Absolute Monarchies/ Republics	Absolute Monarchies/ Republics	Absolute Monarchies/ Republics	Russian empire	Ottoman empire/ balkanization	Russian empire	Colonizations/ Independences	Colonizations/ Independences	Russian empire, Chinese empire	Chinese empire, Korea, Japan

The slash (/) separates successive cultures; the comma (,) separates more or less contemporaneous cultures. In **bold**, the first historic appearance of every Indo-European language or linguistic family.

Source: Author.

Appendix 2. Dates of emergence of the major Indo-European languages

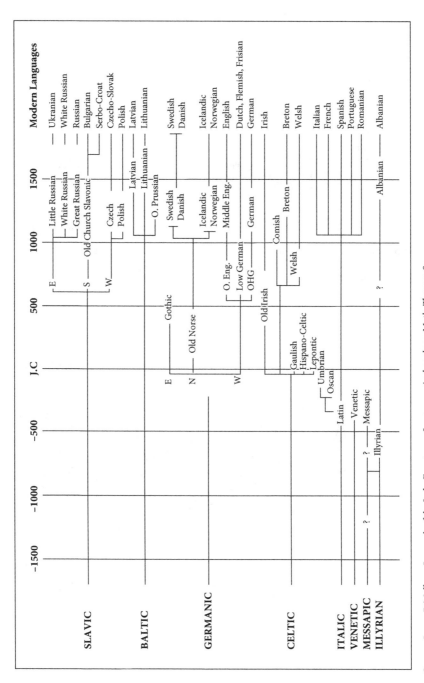

Source: James P. Mallory, *In search of the Indo-Europeans. Language, Archaeology, Myth*, Thames & Hudson, 1989, p. 15.

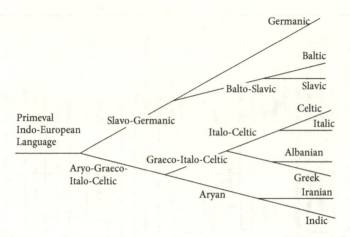

Appendix 3. August Schleicher's tree of the Indo-European languages

Source: James P. Mallory, *In search of the Indo-Europeans. Language, Archaeology, Myth*, Thames & Hudson, 1989, p. 18.

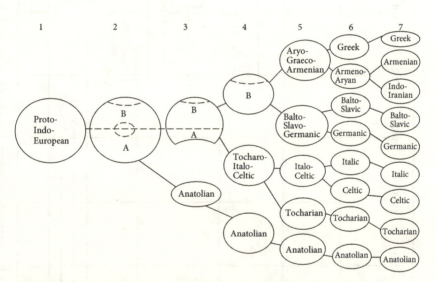

Appendix 4. The development of the Indo-European languages according to Gamkrelidze and Ivanov (1985)

Source: James P. Mallory, *In search of the Indo-Europeans. Language, Archaeology, Myth*, Thames & Hudson, 1989, p. 21.

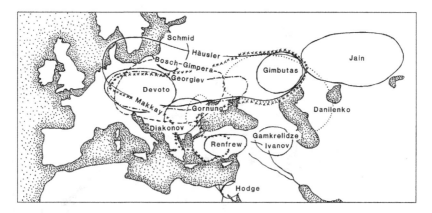

Appendix 5. A map of some of the solutions of the Indo-European homeland problem *proposed since 1960*
Source: James P. Mallory, *In search of the Indo-Europeans. Language, Archaeology, Myth*, Thames & Hudson, 1989, p. 144.

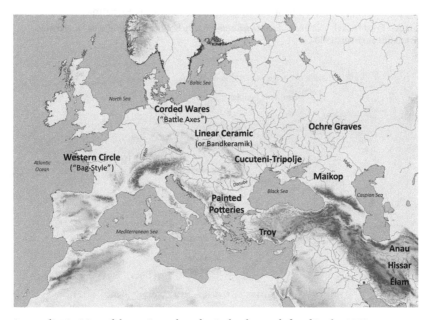

Appendix 6. Map of the main archaeological cultures defined in the 1930s
Source: Author.

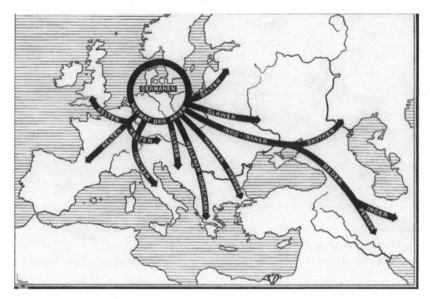

Appendix 7. The Indo-European migrations, after Gustav Kossinna
Source: Ernst Nickel, *Volk und Führer. Geschichte for Mittelschulen*. Verlag Moritz Diesterweg, Frankfurt am Main, 1940.

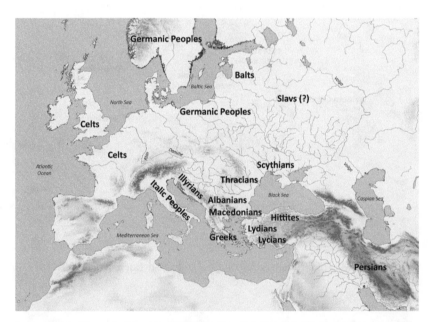

Appendix 8. The early historical distribution of the main Indo-European–speaking peoples
Source: Jean-Paul Demoule, "Les Indo-Européens ont ils existé?", *L'Histoire*, 28, 1980, p. 108.

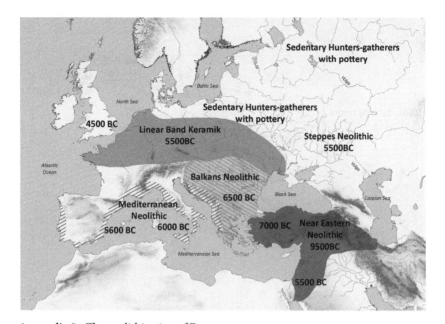

Appendix 9. The neolithization of Europe
Source: Jean-Paul Demoule, *L'Europe, un continent redécouvert par l'archéologie*, Gallimard, 2009, p. 50.

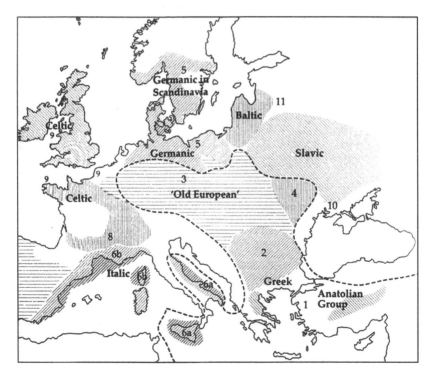

Appendix 10. The spread of Indo-European languages, after Colin Renfrew
Source: Colin Renfrew, Marek Zvelebil, *Les Dossiers de l'Archéologie*, no. 338, March-April 2010, p. 45.

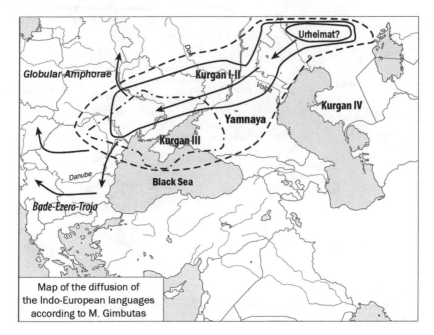

Appendix 11. The spread of Indo-European people, after Marija Gimbutas's theories

Source: "Kurgan Hypothesis", Wikipedia, after Marija Gimbutas.

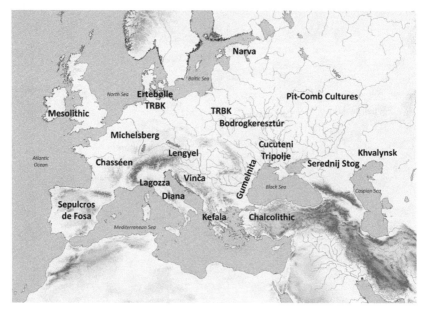

Appendix 12. Map of the Chalcolithic cultures in the fifth millennium BCE
Source: Author.

Appendix 13. Map of the Chalcolithic cultures in the fourth millennium BCE
Source: Author.

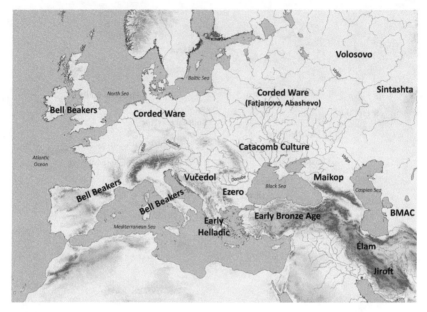

Appendix 14. Map of the Chalcolithic cultures in the third millennium BCE
Source: Author.

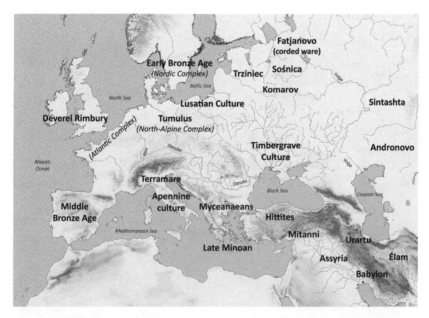

Appendix 15. Map of the Chalcolithic cultures in the second millennium BCE
Source: Author.

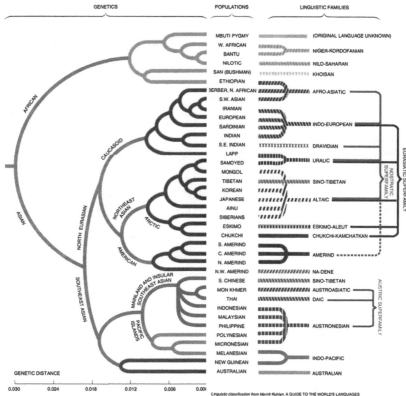

Appendix 16. Comparative trees of human genes and language families
Source: Luca Cavalli-Sforza, *Genes, Peoples, and Languages,* Penguin, 2001.

Trait No.	1	2	3	4	5	6	7	8	9	10	11	12	13	14	15	16	17	18	19	20	21	22	23	24	25	26	27	28	29	30	SCORE
Hindi	+	+	+	+	+	+	+	+	+	+	+	+	+	+	+	+	+	+	+	+	+	+	+	+	+	+	+	+	+	+	30
Telugu	+	+	+	+	+	+	+	+	+	+	+	+	+	+	+	+	+	+	+	+	+	+	+	+	+	+	+	+	+	+	30
Bengali	+	+	+	+	+	+	+	+	+	+	+	+	+	+	+	+	+	+	+	+	+	−	+	+	+	+	+	+	+	+	29
Sinhalese	+	−	+	+	+	+	+	+	+	+	+	+	+	+	+	+	+	+	+	+	+	−	+	+	+	+	+	+	+	+	28
Japanese	+	+	+	+	+	+	+	+	+	+	+	+	+	+	+	+	+	+	+	+	+	+	+	+	+	+	+	−	−	−	27
Burmese	+	+	+	+	+	+	+	+	+	−	+	+	+	+	+	+	+	+	+	+	−	−	+	+	+	+	+	−	−	+	25
Amharic	+	+	−	+	+	+	−	+	+	+	+	+	+	+	+	+	+	+	−	+	+	+	+	+	+	+	−	−	+	+	25
Turkish	+	+	+	+	−	+	+	+	+	+	+	+	+	−	+	+	+	+	+	+	+	+	+	+	+	−	−	−	−	+	24
Tibetan	+	+	+	+	+	+	+	+	+	−	−	+	+	−	−	+	+	+	−	−	−	−	+	+	−	−	−	−	−	+	18
Chinese	+	−	−	−	−	+	−	+	−	+	+	+	+	+	+	+	−	−	−	−	−	−	−	−	+	−	−	−	−	−	13
Persian	+	+	−	+	−	−	−	+	−	−	−	+	+	+	+	+	−	+	+	−	−	+	−	+	−	−	−	−	−	−	12
Russian	−	−	−	−	−	−	−	−	−	+	+	−	−	+	+	+	+	−	−	+	+	−	+	−	−	−	−	+	−	+	11
German	−	−	−	+	−	+	−	−	+	−	+	+	−	+	+	+	−	+	−	−	+	−	−	+	−	−	−	+	−	−	11
Spanish	−	−	+	−	−	−	−	−	−	−	−	+	+	+	+	+	−	+	−	−	+	−	−	−	+	−	−	+	−	−	9
English	−	−	−	−	−	−	−	−	+	+	−	+	+	+	+	−	+	−	−	−	+	−	−	−	−	−	−	−	−	−	8
Swahili	−	−	+	−	−	−	−	−	−	−	−	−	−	−	−	−	−	+	+	+	+	−	−	−	−	−	−	−	−	−	5
Arabic	−	−	−	−	−	−	−	−	−	−	−	−	+	−	−	−	−	−	−	+	+	−	−	−	−	−	−	+	−	−	4
Thai	−	−	−	−	−	−	−	−	−	−	−	−	−	−	−	−	−	−	−	−	−	−	−	+	−	−	−	−	−	−	1

Appendix 17. The Indian linguistic area, after Colin Masica

Source: Colin P. Masica, *Defining a Linguistic Area*, The University of Chicago Press, 1976.

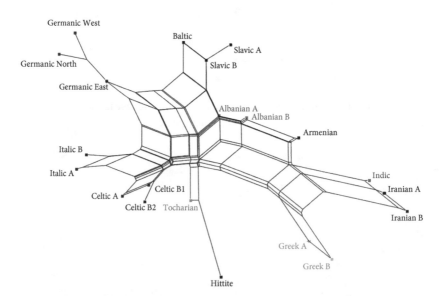

Appendix 18. Relationships between the Indo-European languages, after Paul Heggarty

Source: Paul Heggarty, Warren Maguire, and April McMahon, "Splits or waves? Trees or webs? How divergence measures and network analysis can unravel language histories", *Philosophical Transactions of the Royal Society*, B (2010) 365, fig. 3, p. 3833.

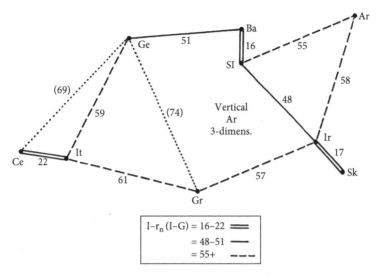

Appendix 19. Relationships between the Indo-European languages, after Alfred Kroeber
Source: Alfred Kroeber, "Statistics, Indo-European, and Taxonomy", *Language*, 36, 1, 1960, p. 4.

Bibliography

Aberg, Nils. 1918. *Das Nordische Kulturgebiet in Mitteleuropa während der Jüngeren Steinzeit*, Uppsala, Almqvist and Wiksells.

Adam, Jean-Pierre. 1988. *Le Passé recomposé, chroniques d'archéologie fantasque*, Paris, Seuil.

Adams, Mark B. (ed.). 1990. *The Wellborn Science: Eugenics in Germany, France, Brazil, and Russia*, New York, Oxford University Press.

Adiego Lajara, Ignasi-Xavier. 2002. "Indoeuropeïtzació al paleolític? Algunes reflexions sobre la 'teoria della continuità' de Mario Alinei," *Estudis romànics*, 24: 7–30.

Adrados, Francisco Rodríguez. 1982. "The Archaic Structure of Hittite: The Crux of the Problem," *Journal of Indo-European Studies*, 1-2, 10: 1–35.

Adrados, Francisco Rodríguez. 1987. "Ideas on the Typology of Proto-Indo-European," *Journal of Indo-European Studies*, 1-2, 15: 97–119.

Adrados, Francisco Rodríguez. 1989. "Etruscan as an IE Anatolian (but not Hittite) Language," *Journal of Indo-European Studies*, 17: 363–383.

Adrados, Francisco Rodríguez. 1990. "The New Image of Indoeuropean, the History of a Revolution," *Indogermanische Forschungen*, 97: 5–28.

Aikhenvald, Alexandra Yurevna, and Dixon, Robert Malcolm Ward (eds.). 2001. *Areal Diffusion and Genetic Inheritance Problems in Comparative Linguistics*, Oxford, Oxford University Press.

Algazy, Joseph. 1989. *L'Extrême Droite en France de 1965 à 1984*, Paris, L'Harmattan.

Alinei, Mario. 1996–2000. *Origini delle lingue d'Europa. La teoria della continuità*, Bologne, Mulino, 2 vols.

Alinei, Mario. 2000. "An Alternative Model for the Origins of European Peoples and Languages: The Continuity Theory," *Quaderni di Semantica*, 21: 21–50.

Alinei, Mario. 2004. "Colloquium 7.3: Intrusive Farmers or Indigenous Foragers: The New Debate about the Ethnolinguistic Origins of Europe," *in Proceedings of the XIVth UISPP Congress, September 2001, The Mesolithic*, Oxford, BAR International Series, 1302: 77–114.

Allentoft, Morten et al. 2015. "Bronze Age Population Genomics of Eurasia," *Nature*, 522: 167–172.

Alram, Eva. 2014. "Times of Change: Greece and the Aegean During the 4th Millennium BC," *in* Barbara Horeis and Mathias Mehofer (eds.), *Western Anatolia Before Troy Proto-Urbanisation in the 4th Millennium BC?*: 305–328.

Ament, Hermann. 1986. "Die Ethnogenese der Germanen aus der Sicht der Vor- und Frühgeschichte," *in* Wolfram Bernhard and Anneliese Kandler-Pálsson (eds.), *Ethnogenese Europäischer Völker*, Stuttgart-New York, Urban-Fischer bei Elsev: 247–256.

Amselle, Jean-Loup, and M'Bokolo, Elikia (eds.). 1985. *Au cœur de l'ethnie. Ethnies, tribalisme et État en Afrique*, Paris, La Découverte.

Amzallag, Nissim. 2009. "From Metallurgy to Bronze Age Civilizations: The Synthetic Theory," *American Journal of Archaeology*, 113, 4: 497–519.

472 BIBLIOGRAPHY

Anderson, Benedict R. 1983. *Imagined Communities: Reflections on the Origin and Spread of Nationalism*, London, Verso (French translation: *L'Imaginaire national. Réflexions sur l'origine et l'essor du nationalisme*, Paris, La Découverte, 1996).

Anderson, Earl R. 1999. "Horse-Sacrifice and Kingship in the Secret History of the Mongols and Indo-European Cultures," *Journal of Indo-European Studies*, 27, 3-4: 379–393.

Anderson, James M. 1980. "Languages of Ancient Spain and Portugal," *in* Herbert J. Izzo (ed.), *Italic and Romance, Linguistic Studies in Honor of Ernst Pulgram*, Amsterdam, Benjamins: 247–256.

Andree, Christian. 1976. *Rudolf Virchow als Prähistoriker*, Cologne-Vienna, Böhlau.

Anthony, David W. 1986. "The Kurgan Culture, Indo-European Origins, and the Domestication of the Horse: A Reconsideration," *Current Anthropology*, 27, 4: 291–313.

Anthony, David W. 1990. "Migration in Archaeology: The Baby and the Bathwater," *American Anthropologist*, 92: 895–914.

Anthony, David W. 1992. "The Archaeology of Indo-European Origins," *Journal of Indo-European Studies*, 19, 3-4: 193–222.

Anthony, David W. 1994. "The Earliest Horseback Riders and Indo-European Origins: New Evidence from the Steppes," *in* Bernhardt Hänsel and Stefan Zimmer (eds.), *Die Indogermanen und das Pferd, Festschrift B. Schlerath*, Budapest, Archaeolingua: 185–196.

Anthony, David W. 1996. "Nazi and Eco-Feminist Prehistories: Ideology and Empiricism in Indo-European Archaeology," *in* Philip L. Kohl and Clare Fawcett (eds.), *Nationalism, Politics, and the Practice of Archaeology*, Cambridge University Press, Cambridge: 82–98.

Anthony, David W. 2007. *The Horse, the Wheel, and Language: How Bronze-Age Riders from the Eurasian Steppes Shaped the Modern World*, Princeton, NJ, Princeton University Press.

Anthony, David W., and Brown, Dorcas R. 1991. "The Origins of Horseback Riding," *Antiquity*, 65: 22–38.

Anthony, David W., and Brown, Dorcas R. 2000. "Eneolithic Horse Exploitation in the Eurasian Steppes: Diet, Ritual and Riding," *Antiquity*, 74: 75–86.

Arends, Jacques, Muysken, Pieter, and Smith, Norval. 1995. *Pidgins and Creoles: An Introduction*, Amsterdam, John Benjamins.

Arendt, Hannah. 1951. *The Origins of Totalitarianism*, New York, Harcourt Brace & Co., 3 vols. (French translation: *Les Origines du totalitarisme*, Paris, Le Seuil, 2005–2006).

Arens, Hans. 1969. *Sprachwissenschaft: Der Gang ihrer Entwicklung von der Antike bis zur Gegenwart*, Fribourg-en-Brisgau/Munich, Orbis Academicus, 2nd ed.

Arne, Ture Algot Johnsson. 1945. *Excavations at Shah Tepé, Iran*, Stockholm-Göteborg, Reports from the scientific expedition to the north western provinces of China, 27.

Arntz, Helmuth (ed.). 1936. *Germanen und Indo-Germanen, Volkstum, Sprache, Heimat, Kultur. Festschrift für Hermann Hirt*, Heidelberg, Carl Winter, 2 vols.

Arntz, Helmuth. 1937. "Rasse, Sprache, Kultur und ihre Beziehungen zum Volkstum," *Zeitschrift für deutsche Bildung*, 13: 265–274.

Artemenko, I. I. (ed.). 1985. *Arkheologiya Ukrainskoy SSR*, Kiev, Naukova dumka, vol. 1.

Art Press. April 1997. Dossier: "L'extrême droite attaque l'art contemporain," 223: 52–65.

Arvidsson, Stefan. 2006. *Aryan Idols: Indo-European Mythology as Ideology and Science*, University of Chicago Press.

BIBLIOGRAPHY   473

Aurenche, Olivier, and Kozłowski, Stefan Karol. 1999. *La Naissance du néolithique au Proche-Orient, ou le Paradis perdu*, Paris, Errance.

Auroux, Sylvain. 1982. *Linguistique et Anthropologie en France (1600–1900)*, Paris, Département de recherches linguistiques, Université Paris-VII.

Auroux, Sylvain (ed.). 1988. *Antoine Meillet et la linguistique de son temps*, numéro de *Histoire, Épistémologie, Langage*, 10, II.

Auroux, Sylvain. 1989. "La question de l'origine des langues: ordres et raisons du rejet institutionnel," *in* Joachim Gessinger and Wolfert von Rahden (ed.), *Theorien vom Ursprung der Sprache*, Berlin, de Gruyter: 122–150.

Auroux, Sylvain (ed.). 1992. *Histoire des idées linguistiques*, t. II: *Le Développement de la grammaire occidentale*, Liège, Mardaga.

Auroux, Sylvain (ed.). 2000. *Histoire des idées linguistiques*, t. III: *L'Hégémonie du comparatisme*, Liège, Mardaga.

Auroux, Sylvain. 2010. "Les limites des reconstructions linguistiques," *in* Jean-Paul Demoule (ed.), *La Révolution néolithique dans le monde*, Paris, CNRS Éditions: 331–341.

Auroux, Sylvain, and Horde, Tristan. 1992. "Les grandes compilations et les modèle de mobilité," *in* Sylvain Auroux (ed.), *Histoire des idées linguistiques*, t. II: *Le Développement de la grammaire occidentale*, Liège: Mardaga: 538–579.

Äyräpää, Aarne. 1936. "Über die Streitaxtkultur in Russland," *Eurasia Septentrionalis Antiqua*, 8n: 1–159.

Bachofen, Johann Jakob. 1861. *Das Mutterrecht, eine Untersuchung über die Gynaikokratie der alten Welt nach ihrer religiösen und rechtlichen Natur*, Stuttgart, Verlag von Krais and Hoffmann (French translation: *Le Droit maternel, recherche sur la gynécocratie de l'Antiquité dans sa nature religieuse et juridique*, Paris, L'Âge d'Homme, 1996).

Back, Michael. 1979. "Die Rekonstruktion des indogermanischen Verschlusslautsystems im Lichte der einzelsprachlichen Veränderungen," *Zeitschrift für vergleichende Sprachforschung*, 93: 179–195.

Bader, Françoise. 1989. *La Langue des dieux, ou l'Hermétisme des poètes indo-européens*, Pisa, Giardini.

Bader, Françoise (ed.). 1994. *Langues indo-européennes*, Paris, CNRS Éditions.

Baggioni, Daniel. 1988. "Le débat Schuchardt / Meillet sur la parenté des langues (1906–1928)," *in* Sylvain Auroux (ed.), *Antoine Meillet et la linguistique de son temps, numéro de Histoire, Épistémologie, Langage*: 10, II.

Bagley, Robert. 1999. "Shang Archaeology," *in* Michael Loewe and Edward L. Shaughnessy (eds.), *The Cambridge History of Ancient China, from the Origins of Civilization to 221 BC*, Cambridge, Cambridge University Press: 125–231.

Bailey, Charles J., and Maroldt, Karl. 1977. "The French Lineage of English," *in* Jürgen Meisel (ed.), *Langues en contact—Pidgins—Creoles—Languages in Contact*, Tübingen, Gunter Narr: 21–53.

Bailey, Geoff, and Spikins, Penny (eds.). 2008. *Mesolithic Europe*, Cambridge, Cambridge University Press.

Bakker, Peter. 1997. *A Language of Our Own: The Genesis of Michif, the Mixed Cree-French Language of the Canadian Métis*, Oxford, Oxford University Press.

Ballester, Xaverio. 2009. *Lingüística Indo-Europeia Tradicional e Paradigma da Continuidade Paleolítica Cara a Cara*, Lisbon, Aprenas Libros.

Banitt, Menahem. 1963. "Une langue fantôme: le judéo-français," *Revue de linguistique romane*, 27: 245–294.

474 BIBLIOGRAPHY

Barkan, Elazar. 1992. *The Retreat of Scientific Racism: Changing Concepts of Race in Britain and the United States between the World Wars*, Cambridge, Cambridge University Press.

Barney, David. June-July 1982. "Le stade pipi-caca de la pensée," *Éléments*, 42: 5–14.

Barras, Colin. March 27, 2019. "Story of Most Murderous People of All Time Revealed in Ancient DNA," *New Scientist*. https://www.newscientist.com/article/mg24132230-200-story-of-most-murderous-people-of-all-time-revealed-in-ancient-dna/.

Barros Damgaard, Peter de et al. 2018a. "137 Ancient Human Genomes from across the Eurasian Steppes," *Nature*, 557 (7705): 369–374.

Barros Damgaard, Peter de et al. 2018b. "The First Horse Herders and the Impact of Early Bronze Age Steppe Expansions into Asia," *Science*, 360 (6396): 74–168.

Barsanti, Giulio et al. 1986. *Misura d'uomo. Strumenti, teorie e pratiche dell' antropometria e della psicologia sperimentale fra Ottocento e Novecento*, Florence, Giunti.

Bartoněk, Antonín. 1991. "L'evoluzione dei dialetti greci nella dimensione geografica delle età oscure," *in* Dominico Musti (ed.), *La transizione dal Miceneo all'alto arcaismo. Dal palazzo alla città*, Rome, Istituto per gli Studi Micenei ed Egeo-Anatolici: 241–250.

Bateman, R. I. Goddard et al. 1990. "Speaking of Forked Tongues: The Feasibility of Reconciling Human Phylogeny and the History of Language," *Current Anthropology*, 31, 1: 1–24.

Bazin, Louis. 1986. "Les peuples turcophones d'Eurasie: un cas majeur d'expansion linguistique," *Hérodote (Géopolitique des langues)*, 46: 75–109.

Becker, Cornelia. 1994. "Zur Problematik früher Pferdenachweise im östlichen Mittelmeergebiet," *in* Bernhardt Hänsel and Stefan Zimmer (ed.), *Die Indogermanen und das Pferd, Festschrift B. Schlerath*, Budapest, Archaeolingua: 145–178.

Beekes, Robert Stephen Paul. 1995. *Comparative Indo-European Linguistics: an Introduction*, Amsterdam, John Benjamins.

Beger, Bruno. April 1944. "Das Rassenbild des Tibeters in seiner Stellung zum mongoliden und europiden Rassenkreis," *Asienberichte. Vierteljahresschrift für asiatische Geschichte und Kultur*, 21: 29–53.

Belaval, Yvon. 1947. "Leibniz et la langue allemande," *Études germaniques*, 2: 121–132.

Belier, Wouter W. 1991. *Decayed Gods: Origin and Development of Georges Dumézil's "idéologie tripartie,"* Leyde, Brill.

Bellwood, Peter S. 2005. *First Farmers: The Origins of Agricultural Societies*, Malden (MA), Wiley-Blackwell.

Bellwood, Peter S. 2009. "La diffusion des populations d'agriculteurs dans le monde," *in* Jean-Paul Demoule (ed.), *La Révolution néolithique dans le monde*, Paris, CNRS Éditions: 239–262.

Bender, Harold Herman. 1922. *The Home of the Indo-Europeans*, Princeton, Princeton University Press.

Bender, Marvin Lionel. 1987. "Some Possible African Creoles: A Pilot Study," *in* Glenn G. Gilbert (ed.), *Pidgin and Creoles Languages: Essays in Memory of John E. Reinecke*, Honolulu, University of Hawaiii Press: 30–67.

Benecke, Norbert. 1994. "Zur Domestikation des Pferdes in Mittel und Osteuropa," *in* Bernhardt Hänsel and Stefan Zimmer (ed.), *Die Indogermanen und das Pferd, Festschrift B. Schlerath*, Budapest, Archaeolingua: 123–144.

Benecke, Norbert. 1997. "Archaeological Studies on the Transition from the Mesolithic to the Neolithic in the North Pontic Region," *Anthropozoologica*, 25–26: 631–641.

BIBLIOGRAPHY 475

Benecke, Norbert. 2002. "Zu den Anfängen der Pferdehaltung in Eurasien. Aktuelle archäozoologische Beiträge aus drei Regionen," *Ethnographisch-Archäologische Zeitschrift*, 43: 187–226.

Benfey, Theodor. 1868. "Vorwort," *in* August Fick (ed.), *Wörterbuch der indogermanischen Grundsprache in ihrem Bestande vor der Völkertrennung. Ein sprachgeschichtlicher Versuch. Mit einem Vorwort von Theod. Benfey*, Göttingen, Vandenhoeck: 3–19.

Benfey, Theodor. 1869. *Geschichte der Sprachwissenschaft und orientalischen Philologie in Deutschland seit dem Anfange des 19. Jahrhunderts: mit einem Rückblick auf die früheren Zeiten*, Munich, Cotta.

Bengston, John D. 1991. "Notes on Sino-Caucasian," *in* Vitaly Victorovich Shevoroshkin (ed.), *Dene-Sino-Causasian Languages*, Bochum, Brockmeyer: 67–129.

Benoist, Alain de. 1978. *Vu de droite. Anthologie critique des idées contemporaines*, Paris, Copernic.

Benoist, Alain de. 1981. *Comment peut-on être païen?*, Paris, Albin Michel.

Benoist, Alain de. 1997. "Penser le paganisme. Entretien avec Alain de Benoist. Entretien recueilli par Christopher Gérard," *Antaios* (December 1996–May 1997): 10–23.

Bentley, R. Alexander, Price, T. Douglas, Luning, Jens, Gronenborn, Detlef, Wahl, Joachim, and Fullagar, D. 2002. "Prehistoric Migration in Europe, Strontium Isotope Analysis of Early Neolithic Skeletons," *Current Anthropology*, 43, 5: 799–804.

Benveniste, Émile. 1938. "Traditions indo-iraniennes sur les classes sociales," *Journal asiatique*, 230: 528–549.

Benveniste, Émile. 1939. "Les Indo-Européens et le peuplement de l'Europe," *Revue de synthèse*, 17: 16–18.

Benveniste, Émile. 1950. "Actif et moyen dans le verbe," *Journal de psychologie*, 43: 121–129.

Benveniste, Émile. 1954. "Problèmes sémantiques de la reconstruction," *Word*, 10, 2–3: 298–301.

Benveniste, Émile. 1969. *Le Vocabulaire des institutions indo-européennes*, Paris, Les Éditions de Minuit, 2 vols.

Berezkin, Yuri E. 2007. *Mify Zaseliaut Ameriku. Arealnoe Raspredelenie Folkornyh Motivov I Rannie Migratsü v Novy Svet,* Moscow, O.G.I.

Berezkin, Yuri E. 2013. *Afrika, Migracii, Mifologija. Arealyrasprostranenija fol'klornyx motivov v istoriceskoj perspektive*, Saint Petersburg, Nauka.

Bergounioux, Gabriel. 1984. "La science du langage en France de 1870 à 1885: du marché civil au marché étatique," *Langue française*, 63, 1: 7–41.

Bergounioux, Gabriel, March 2002. "La sélection des langues: darwinisme et linguistique," *Langages*, 145: 7–18.

Bergounioux, Gabriel, and Demoule, Jean-Paul. 2020. "L'indo-européen entre épistémologie et mythologie,": https://hal.archives-ouvertes.fr/halshs-02924306/

Bergounioux, Gabriel, and Lamberterie, Charles de (ed.). 2006. *Meillet aujourd'hui. Actes du colloque de Noirlac, 21 octobre 2000*, Leuven-Paris, Peeters, Société de linguistique de Paris, vol. 89.

Bergsland, Knut, and Vogt, Hans. 1962. "On the Validity of Glottochronology," *Current Anthropology*, 3: 115–153.

Bernabò Brea, Maria, Cardarelli, Andrea, and Cremaschi, Mauro (ed.). 1997. *Le terramare: la più antica civiltà padana*, Milan, Electa.

Bernard, Jean, and Ruffié, Jacques. 1966. *Hématologie géographique. Caractères héréditaires du sang*, Paris, Masson, vol. 1.

476 BIBLIOGRAPHY

Bernhard, Wolfram, and Kandler-Pálsson, Anneliese. 1986. *Ethnogenese europäischer Völker: aus der Sicht der Anthropologie und Vor- und Frühgeschichte*, Stuttgart, Fischer.

Bernier, François. 1684. "Nouvelle division de la Terre, par les différentes Espèces ou Races d'Hommes qui l'habitent," *Journal des savants* (24 April 1684): 85–89.

Bertrand, Alexandre. 1864. "Sur les origines indo-européennes," *Bulletins de la Société d'anthropologie de Paris*, 5, 1: 367–383.

Berve, Helmut. 1937. *Sparta*, Leipzig, Meyers.

Berve, Helmut (ed.). 1942. *Das neue Bild der Antike*, Leipzig, Koehler & Amelang.

Berve, Helmut. 1986. "A Study of the Earliest Domestic Horse of Eastern Europe (Appendix 2). On the History of Horse Domestication in South-East Europe (Appendix 3)," *in* Dmitri Telegin (ed.), *Dereivka. A Settlement and Cemetery of Copper Age Horse Keepers on the Middle Dniepr*, Oxford, British Archaeological Reports, International Series, 287: 135–180.

Bibikova, Valentina Ivanovna. 1967–1970. "Kizučeniju drevnejsikh domsnikh lošadej Vostocnoj Evropy," *Bjulleten'Moskoskogo Obščestva Ispytatelej Prirody, Otdel Biologii*, 72–73: 106–118; 75: 118–125.

Bickerton, Derek. 1981. *Roots of Language*, Ann Arbor, Karoma.

Bickerton, Derek. 1984. "The Language Bioprogram Hypothesis," *Behavioral and Brain Sciences*, 7, 2: 173–221.

Bickerton, Derek. 2009. *Adam's Tongue: How Humans Made Language, How Language Made Humans*, New York, Hill and Wang.

Bierhahn, Erich. 1964. "Blondheit und Blondheitskult in der deutschen litteratur," *Archiv für Kulturgeschichte*, 46: 309–333.

Billig, Michael. 1981. *L'Internationale raciste. De la psychologie à la "science" des races*, Paris, François Maspero.

Bird, Norman. 1982. *The Distribution of Indo-European Root Morphemes: a Checklist for Philologists*, Wiesbaden, Harrassowitz.

Biscarat, Pierre-Jérôme. 2000. *De quelques usages politiques de l'idée indo-européenne en France de 1968 à nos jours*, Diplôme d'études approfondies, École des hautes études en sciences sociales, Paris.

Bittel, Kurt. 1976. *Die Hethiter: die Kunst Anatoliens vom Ende des 3. bis zum Anfang des 1. Jahrtausends vor Christus*, Munich, Beck (French translation: *Les Hittites*, Paris, Gallimard, "L'univers des formes," 1976).

Bjerrum, Marie. 1980. "Rasmus Kristian Rask," *Historiographica Linguistica*, 7, 3: 403–408.

Black, Edwin. 2012. *War Against the Weak: Eugenics and America's Campaign to Create a Master Race*, New York, Thunder's Mouth Press, new edition.

Blanckaert, Claude. 1981. *Monogénisme et Polygénisme en France de Buffon à P. Broca (1749-1880)*, Thèse de l'université de Paris-I, miméographié, 4 vols.

Blanckaert, Claude. 1982. "L'anthropologie au féminin: Clémence Royer (1830–1902)," *Revue de synthèse*, 105: 23–38.

Blanckaert, Claude. 1987. " 'Les vicissitudes de l'angle facial' et les débuts de la craniométrie (1765-1875)," *Revue de synthèse*, 4, 3–4: 417–453.

Blanckaert, Claude. 1988. "On the Origin of French Ethnology. William Edwards and the Doctrine of Race," *in* George W. Jr. Stocking (ed.), *Bones, Bodies, Behavior. Essays on Biological Anthropology*, Madison, University of Wisconsin Press: 18–55.

Blanckaert, Claude. 1989a. "L'anthropologie en France. Le mot et l'histoire (xvie-xixe siècle)," *Bulletins et Mémoires de la Société d'anthropologie de Paris*, 1, 3–4: 13–44.

BIBLIOGRAPHY 477

Blanckaert, Claude.1989b. "L'indice céphalique et l'ethnogénie européenne: A. Retzius: Broca, F. Pruner-Bey," *Bulletins et Mémoires de la Société d'anthropologie de Paris*, 1, 3–4: 165–202.

Blanckaert, Claude. 1989c. "'L'anthropologie personnifiée,' Paul Broca et la biologie du genre humain. Préface," *in* Paul Broca, *Mémoires d'anthropologie*, Paris, Jean-Michel Place, "Les Cahiers de Gradhiva," 12: 3–27, partial reprinting of the Paris edition, Reinwald et Cie, 1871.

Blanckaert, Claude. 1993. "La science de l'homme entre humanité et inhumanité," *in Des sciences contre l'homme*, vol. 1: *Classer, hiérarchiser, exclure*, Paris, Autrement, "Sciences et sociétés," no. 8: 14–46.

Bloch, Maurice. 1985. *Marxism and Anthropology: The History of a Relationship*, Oxford, Oxford University Press.

Boas, Franz. 1902. "Rudolph Virchow's Anthropological Work," *Science*, 16: 441–445.

Boas, Franz. 1911. "Changes in the Bodily form of Descendants of Immigrants," in *Senate Document*, 208: 60–75 (republished in *Race, Language and Culture*, New York, MacMillan, 1940).

Bocquet-Appel, Jean-Pierre. 1989. "L'anthropologie physique en France et ses origines institutionnelles," *Gradhiva*, 6: 23–34.

Bocquet-Appel, Jean-Pierre. 1996. "Note sur l'origine de deux interviews: Henri-Victor Vallois et Gustave Malécot," *Gradhiva*, 8: 115–124.

Bocquet-Appel, Jean-Pierre. 2008. *La Paléodémographie: 99,99% de l'histoire démographique des hommes*, Paris, Errance.

Boë, Louis-Jean, Bessière, P., Ladjili, N., and Audibert, N. 2008. "Simple Combinatorial Considerations Challenge Ruhlen's Mother Tongue Theory," *in* B. L. Davis and K. Zajdo (eds.), *The Syllable in Speech Production: Perspectives on the Frame Content Theory*, New York, Laurence Erlbaum Associates: 63–92.

Boessneck, Joachim, and Driesch, Angela von den. 1976. "Pferde im 4./3. Jahrtausend v. Chr. in Ostanatolien," *Säugetierkundliche Mitteilungen*, 24, 2: 81–87.

Boettcher, Carl-Heinz. 1996. "Pouvoir centralisé ou pouvoir partagé. L'Orient et l'Occident au cuprolithique," *Études indo-européennes*, 14th year: 103–147.

Böhme, Klaus. 1976. "Kriegdienst mit der Feder. Der erste Weltkrieg im politischen Urteil deutscher Professoren," *Quaderni di Storia*, 3: 49–67.

Bökönyi, Sándor. 1974. *History of Domestic Mammals in Central and Eastern Europe*, Budapest, Akadémiai Kiadó.

Bökönyi, Sándor. 1978. "The earliest waves of domestic horses in East Europe," *Journal of Indo-European Studies*, 6, 1–2: 17–76.

Bökönyi, Sándor. 1991. "Pferde—und Schafdomestikation bzw.—haltung in der frühen Kupferzeit Eurasiens," *in* Jan Lichardus (ed.), *Die Kupferzeit als historische Epoche*, Bonn, Habelt, Saarbrücker Beiträge zur Altertumskunde: 549–556.

Bollmus, Reinhard. 1970. *Das Amt Rosenberg und seine Gegner; Studien zum Machtkampf im nationalsozialistischen Herrschaftssystem*, Stuttgart, Deutsche Verlags-Anstalt.

Bomhard, Allan R. 2008. *Reconstructing Proto-Nostratic: Comparative Phonology, Morphology, and Vocabulary*, Leiden-Boston, Brill, 2 vols.

Bondár, Mária. 2012. *Prehistoric Wagon Models in the Carpathian Basin (3500–1500 BC)*, Budapest, Archaeolingua.

Bonfante, Giuliano. 1931. "I dialetti indoeuropei," *Annali*, 4: 69–185.

Bonfante, Giuliano. 1953–1954. "Ideas on the Kinship of the European languages from 1200 to 1800," *Cahiers d'histoire mondiale*, 1: 679–699.

478 BIBLIOGRAPHY

Bonnafé, Lucien, and Tort, Patrick. 1996. *L'Homme, cet inconnu? Alexis Carrel, Jean-Marie Le Pen et les chambres à gaz*, Paris, Syllepse.

Bonnefoy, Yves. 2013. "Jean-Pierre Vernant et la poésie," *in* Maurice Olender and François Vitrani (eds.), *Jean-Pierre Vernant dedans dehors, Le Genre humain*, Paris, Seuil: 99–110.

Bonnet, Jacques (ed.). 1981. *Georges Dumézil, Cahier pour un temps*, 3, Paris, Éditions du Centre Georges-Pompidou.

Bopp, Franz. 1816. *Über das Conjugationssystem der Sanskritsprache in Vergleichung mit jenem der griechischen, lateinischen, persischen und germanischen Sprache*, Frankfurt.

Bopp, Franz. 1820. "Analytical Comparison of the Sanskrit, Greek, Latin, and Teutonic Languages, Shewing the Original Identity of Their Grammatical Structure," *Annals of Oriental Literature*, I: 1–64.

Bopp, Franz. 1833–1852. *Vergleichende Grammatik des Sanskrit, Zend, Griechischen, Lateinischen, Litauischen, Altslawischen, Gotischen und Deutschen*, Berlin, Dummler, 6 vols.; 2nd ed. 1856 (French translation de M. Bréal, *Grammaire comparée des langues indo-européennes comprenant le sanscrit, le zend, l'arménien, le grec, le latin, le lithuanien, l'ancien slave, le gothique et l'allemand*, Paris, Hachette, 5 vols., 1866–1874).

Borst, Arno. 1957–1963. *Der Turmbau von Babel, Geschichte der Meinungen über Ursprung und Vielfalt der Sprachen und Völker*, Stuttgart, Deutscher Taschenbuch, 6 vols.

Bosch Gimpera, Pedro. 1960. *El problema indoeuropeo*, Mexico, Université autonome de Mexico (French translation by Raymond Lantier, *Les Indo-Européens, problèmes archéologiques*, Paris, Payot, 1961).

Boucher de Perthes, Jacques. 1847. *Antiquités celtiques et antédiluviennes. Mémoire sur l'industrie primitive et les arts à leur origine*, Paris, Jung-Treuttel.

Bouckaert, Remco, Lemey, Philippe, Dunn, Michael, Greenhill, Simon J., Alekseyenko, Alexander V., Drummond, Alexei J., Gray, Russell D., Suchard, Marc A., and Atkinson, Quentin D. 2012. "Mapping the Origins and Expansion of the Indo-European Language Family," *Science*, 337, 6097: 957–960.

Boule, Marcellin. 1921. *Les Hommes fossiles: éléments de paléontologie humaine*, Paris, Masson.

Boulestin, Bruno, Zeeb-Lanz, Andrea, Jeunesse, Christian, Haack, Fabian, Arbogast, Rose-Marie, and Denaire, Anthony. 2009. "Mass Cannibalism in the Linear Pottery Culture at Herxheim (Palatinate, Germany)," *Antiquity*, 83: 968–982.

Bouquiaux, Luc. 2004. *Linguistique et Ethnolinguistique. Anthologie d'articles parus entre 1961 et 2003*, Louvain, Peeters.

Brandt, Guido et al. 2013. "Ancient DNA Reveals Key Stages in the Formation of Central European Mitochondrial Genetic Diversity," *Science*, 342, 6155 (October 11, 2013): 257–261.

Bréal, Michel. 1866. "Introduction," *in* F. Bopp (ed.), *Introduction de la grammaire comparée des langues indo-européennes*, translation by Michel Bréal, Paris, Imprimerie impériale: 4–72.

Bréal, Michel. 1891. "Le langage et les nationalités," *Revue des Deux Mondes*, 61e année, t. 108: 615–639.

Briard, Jacques. 1991. *Mythes et Symboles de l'Europe préceltique. Les religions de l'âge du bronze (2500-800 av. J.-C.)*, Paris, Errance.

Briquel, Dominique. 1982. "Initiations grecques et idéologie indo-européenne," *Annales, Économies, Société, Civilisation*, 37: 454–464.

BIBLIOGRAPHY 479

Broberg, Gunnar, and Roll-Hansen, Nils (ed.). 2005. *Eugenics and the Welfare State: Sterilization Policy in Denmark, Sweden, Norway, and Finland*, East Lansing, Michigan State University Press.

Broca, Paul. 1860. "Recherches sur l'ethnologie de la France," *Bulletins de la Société d'anthropologie de Paris*, t.1: 6–15.

Broca, Paul. 1862. "La linguistique et l'anthropologie," *Bulletins de la Société d'anthropologie de Paris*, 3: 264–319 (republished in Broca. 1871. t. I: 232–276).

Broca, Paul. 1864. "Discussion sur les origines indo-européennes," *Bulletins de la Société d'anthropologie de Paris*, 5: 194–196.

Broca, Paul. 1866. "Anthropologie," *in Dictionnaire encyclopédique des sciences médicales*, Paris, t.5: 276 *sq.* (republished in Paul Broca. 1989. *Mémoires d'anthropologie*, Paris, Jean-Michel Place, I: 1–41).

Broca, Paul. 1871. *Mémoires d'anthropologie*, Paris, Reinwald & Cie.

Broch, Olaf. 1927. "Russenorsk," *Archiv für Slawische Philologie*, 41: 209–262.

Brown, Cecil H., Callaghan, Catherine A., Casson, Ronald W., Etxebarria, Jose Maria, Hill, Jane H., Lehman, F. K., Oswalt, Robert L., and Proulx, Paul. 1994. "Lexical Acculturation in Native American Languages," *Current Anthropology*, 35, 2: 95–117.

Brugmann, Karl, and Delbrück, Berthold. 1897–1916. *Grundriss der vergleichenden Grammatik der indogermanischen Sprachen*, Strasbourg, Trübner.

Brun, Patrice. 1987. *Princes et Princesses de la Celtique*, Paris, Errance.

Brun, Patrice. 1996. "Représentations symboliques, lieux de culte et dépôts votifs dans l'est de la France au Bronze final et au 1er âge du fer," *in* Matrin Almagro-Gorbea (ed.), *Archäologische Forschungen zum Kultgeschehen in der jüngeren Bronzezeit und frühen Eisenzeit Alteuropas*, Bonn, Habelt: 183–201.

Brun, Patrice. 2001. *Le Cheval, symbole de pouvoirs dans l'Europe préhistorique: exposition du 31 mars au 12 novembre 2001*, Nemours, Musée de préhistoire d'Île-de-France.

Brun, Patrice. 2006. "L'origine des Celtes. Communautés linguistiques et réseaux sociaux," *in* Daniele Vitali (ed.), *Celtes et Gaulois. L'archéologie face à l'histoire. La préhistoire des Celtes*, Glux-en-Glenne, Bibracte: 29–44.

Brun, Patrice, and Chaume, Bruno (eds.). 1997. *Vix et les éphémères résidences princières*, Paris, Errance.

Brun, Patrice, and Mordant, Claude (eds.). 1988. *Le Groupe Rhin-Suisse-France orientale et la Notion de civilisation des Champs d'Urnes*, Nemours, APRAIF, "Mémoires du Musée de préhistoire d'Île-de-France."

Brun, Patrice, and Ruby, Pascal. 2008. *L'Âge du fer en France. Premières villes, premiers États celtiques*, Paris, La Découverte-Inrap.

Brun-Trigaud, Guylaine. 1990. *Le Croissant: le concept et le mot. Contribution à l'histoire de la dialectologie française au xixe siècle*, Université Lyon-III, "Centre d'études linguistiques Jacques Goudet."

Brunel, Samantha et al. 2020. "Ancient Genomes from Present-Day France Unveil 7,000 Years of Its Demographic History," *Proceedings National Academy of Sciences*, 117(23): 12791–12798.

Brunet, Frédérique. 2011. "Comment penser la néolithisation en Asie centrale (xe-ive millénaire)? L'émergence de nouveaux modèles de sociétés entre sédentaires et nomades," *in* Éric Coqueugniot and Olivier Aurenche (eds.), *Néolithisation: nouvelles données, nouvelles interprétations. À propos du modèle théorique de Jacques Cauvin*, Paris, CNRS Éditions, Paléorient, 37/1: 187–204.

480   BIBLIOGRAPHY

Brunn, Julien. 1979. *La Nouvelle Droite. Le dossier du "procès,"* Paris, Nouvelles Éditions Oswald.

Brunnhofer, Hermann. 1885. *Über den Ursitz der Indogermanen: Vortrag,* Bâle, Benno Schwabe.

Bryce, Trevor. 2002. *Life and Society in the Hittite World,* Oxford, Oxford University Press.

Buchsenschutz, Olivier, and Schnapp, Alain. 1993. "Alésia," *in* Pierre Nora (ed.), *Les Lieux de mémoire,* Paris, Gallimard, vol. 3, 3: 272–315.

Buchvaldek, Miroslav, Lippert, Andreas, Košnar, Lubomír, Popelka, Miroslav, Krenn-Leeb, Alexandra, and Klír, Tomáš. 2007. *Archeologický atlas pravěké Evropy = Atlas zur Prähistorischen Archäologie Europas,* Prague, Univerzita Karlova v Praze, Nakladatelství Karolinum.

Bueltzingsloewen, Isabelle von. 2007. *L'Hécatombe des fous. La famine dans les hôpitaux psychiatriques français sous l'Occupation,* Paris, Aubier.

Bulkin, V. A., Klejn, Leo S., and Lebedev, G. S. 1982. "Attainments and Problems of Soviet Archaeology," *World Archaeology,* 13, 3: 272–295.

Burkhardt, Richard W. Jr. 1993. "Konrad Lorenz et le pas de l'oie," *in Des sciences contre l'homme,* vol. 2: *Au nom du bien,* Paris, Autrement, "Sciences et sociétés" no. 9: 46–57.

Burkhardt, Richard W. Jr. 2005. *Patterns of Behavior: Konrad Lorenz, Niko Tinbergen, and the Founding of Ethology,* Chicago, University of Chicago Press.

Burrin, Philippe. 1997. *La France à l'heure allemande: 1940–1944,* Paris, Seuil.

Buttler, Werner. 1938. *Der donauländische und der westische Kulturkreis der jüngeren Steinzeit,* Berlin-Leipzig, De Gruyter, Handbuch der Urgeschichte Deutschlands.

Campanile, Enrico. 1977. *Ricerche di cultura poetica indoeuropea,* Pisa, Giardini.

Campbell, Lyle. 2008. "What Can We Learn About the Earliest Human Language by Comparing Languages Known Today?," *in* Bernard Lacks, Serge Cleuziou, Pierre Encrevé, and Jean-Paul Demoule (eds.), *The Origin and Evolution of Languages: Approaches, Models, Paradigm,* London, Equinox Editions: 79–111.

Campbell, Lyle, Kaufman, Terrence, and Smith-Stark, Thomas C. 1986. "Meso-America as a Linguistic Area," *Language,* 62, 3: 530–539.

Campbell, Lyle, and Poser, William John. 2008. *Language Classification: History and Method,* Cambridge, Cambridge University Press.

Camper, Peter. 1791. *Dissertation sur les variétés naturelles qui caractérisent la physionomie des hommes des divers climats et des différens ages,* Paris, Jansen.

Camus, Jean-Yves. 2006. "La Nouvelle Droite: bilan provisoire d'une école de pensée," *La Pensée,* 345: 23–33.

Camus, Jean-Yves, and Monzat, René. 1992. *Les Droites nationales et radicales en France. Répertoire critique,* Lyon, Presses universitaires de Lyon.

Cannon, Garland. 1987. "Sir William Jones and Applied Linguistics," *in* Hans Aarsleff, Louis Gérard Kelly, and Hans-Josef Niederehe (eds.), *Papers in the History of Linguistics. Proceedings of the Third International Conference on the History of the Language Sciences (ICHoLS III),* Amsterdam, Benjamins, Amsterdam Studies in the Theory and History of Linguistic Science: 379–390.

Capovilla, Giovanni. 1964. *Praehomerica et praeitalica: Ricerche mitiche, protostoriche e linguistiche,* Rome, L'Erma di Bretschneider.

Carnoy, Albert Joseph. 1921. *Les Indo-Européens. Préhistoire des langues, des mœurs et des croyances de l'Europe,* Brussels-Paris, Vromant.

Carol, Anne. 1995. *Histoire de l'eugénisme en France. Les médecins et la procréation: xixe-xxe siècle,* Paris, Seuil.

BIBLIOGRAPHY 481

Carruba, Onofrio. 1995. "L'arrivo dei Greci, le migrazioni indoeuropee e il "ritorno" degli Eraclidi," *Athenaeum*, 83, 2: 5–44.

Caskey, John L. 1960. "The Early Helladic Period in the Argolid," *Hesperia* 29, 3: 285–303.

Caussat, Pierre. 1988. "Langue et nation," *in* Sylvain Auroux (ed.), *Antoine Meillet et la linguistique de son temps*, numéro de *Histoire, Épistémologie, Langage*, 10, II: 195–204.

Cauvin, Jacques. 1994. *Naissance des divinités, naissance de l'agriculture*, Paris, CNRS Éditions.

Cavalli-Sforza, Luigi Luca. 1997. *Qui sommes-nous? Une histoire de la diversité humaine*, Paris, Flammarion.

Cavalli-Sforza, Luigi Luca. 2005. *Évolution biologique, évolution culturelle*, Paris, Odile Jacob.

Cavalli-Sforza, Luigi Luca, Kidd, J. R., Kidd, K. K., Bucci, C., Bowcock A. M., and Helett, B. S. 1986. "DNA Markers and Genetic Variation in the Human Species," *Cold Spring Harbor Symposia on Quantitative Biology*, 51: 411–417.

Cavalli-Sforza, Luigi Luca, Luca, Luigi, Menozzi, Paolo, and Piazza, Alberto. 1994. *The History and Geography of Human Genes*, Princeton, Princeton University Press.

Cavalli-Sforza, Luigi Luca, Piazza, Alberto, Menozzi, Paolo, and Mountain, Joanna. 1988. "Reconstruction of Human Evolution: Bringing Together Genetic, Archaelogical and Linguistic Data," *Proceedings of National Academy of Sciences*, 85 (16): 6002–6006.

Céline, Louis-Ferdinand. 1938. *L'École des cadavres*, Paris, Denoël.

Chambers, Jack K., and Trudgill, Peter. 1980. *Dialectology*. Cambridge, Cambridge University Press.

Chao Ning et al. 2019. "Ancient Genomes Reveal Yamnaya-Related Ancestry and a Potential Source of Indo-European Speakers in Iron Age Tianshan," *Current Biology* 29: 1–7.

Chapoutot, Johann. 2008. *Le National-Socialisme et l'Antiquité*, Paris, PUF.

Chapoutot, Johann. 2012. *Le Nazisme et l'Antiquité*, Paris, PUF.

Charachidzé, Georges. 1968. *Système religieux de la Géorgie païenne. Analyse structurale d'une civilisation*, Paris, Maspero.

Charachidzé, Georges. 1986. *Prométhée ou le Caucase. Essai de mythologie contrastive* (préface de Georges Dumézil), Paris, Flammarion.

Charachidzé, Georges. 1987. *La Mémoire indo-européenne du Caucase*, Paris, Hachette.

Charpentier, Jarl. 1926. "The Original Home of the Indoeuropeans," *Bulletin of the School of Oriental Studies*, 4, 1: 147–170.

Chase, Allan. 1977. *The Legacy of Malthus: The Social Costs of the New Scientific Racism*, New York, Knopf-Random House.

Chaudenson, Robert. 2003. *La Créolisation: théorie, applications, implications*, Paris, L'Harmattan.

Chavée, Honoré. 1862a. *Les Langues et les Races*, Paris, Chamerot.

Chavée, Honoré. 1862b. "Sur le parallèle des langues sémitiques et des langues indo-européennes," *Bulletin de la Société d'anthropologie de Paris*, 3: 198–205.

Childe, Vere Gordon. 1925. *The Dawn of European Civilization*, London/New York, Routledge-Kegan Paul (6th ed. augmented 1957) (French translation: *L'Aube de la civilisation européenne*, Paris, Payot, 1949).

Childe, Vere Gordon. 1926. *The Aryans. A Study of Indo-European Origins*, New York, Alfred A. Knopf.

Childe, Vere Gordon. 1936. "The Antiquity of Nordic Culture," *in* Wilhelm Koppers (ed.), *Die Indogermanen- und Germanenfrage. Neue Wege zu ihrer Lösung*, Salzbourg-Leipzig: 517–530.

482 BIBLIOGRAPHY

Childe, Vere Gordon. 1958. "Retrospect," *Antiquity*, 32: 69–74.

Chrétien, Jean-Pierre, and Prunier, Gérard (ed.). 1989. *Les ethnies ont une histoire*, Paris, Karthala.

Citron, Suzanne. 1987. *Le Mythe national: l'histoire de France revisitée*, Paris, Éditions ouvrières (re-edited 2008, Paris, L'Atelier).

Clackson, James. 2004. *Indo-European Linguistics: An Introduction*, Cambridge, Cambridge University Press.

Clauss, Ludwig Ferdinand. 1934. *Die nordische Seele: eine Einführung in die Rassenseelenkunde*, Munich, J. F. Lehmanns Verlag, 2nd ed.

Cleuziou, Serge. 1986. "Tureng Tepe and Burnished Grey Ware: A Question of "Frontier"?," *Oriens Antiquus, Roma*, 25, 3–4: 221–256.

Cleuziou, Serge, Coudart, Anick, Demoule, Jean-Paul, and Schnapp, Alain. 1991. "The Use of Theory in French Archaeology," *in* Ian Hodder (ed.), *Archaeological Theory in Europe (The Last Three Decades)*, London, Routledge: 91–128.

Cluet, Marc, and Repussard, Catherine (ed.). 2013. *"Lebensreform": die soziale Dynamik der politischen Ohnmacht*, Tübingen, Francke Verlag.

Cœurdoux, Gaston-Laurent. 1808. "Question posée à Monsieur l'abbé Barthélémy et aux autres membres de l'Académie des belles-lettres et inscriptions. D'où vient que dans la langue sanscroutane il se trouve un grand nombre de mots qui lui sont communs avec le latin et le grec, et surtout avec le latin," in *Mémoires de l'Académie des inscriptions et belles-lettres*, 49: 647–697.

Coia, V. et al. 2016. "Whole mitochondrial DNA sequencing in Alpine populations and the genetic history of the Neolithic Tyrolean Iceman," *Nature, Scientific Reports*, 6: 18932.

Coleman, John E. 2000. "An Archaeological Scenario for the 'Coming of the Greeks', ca. 3200 BC," *Journal of Indo-European Studies*, 28, 1–2: 101–154.

Coleman, Robert. 1988. "Book Review: Archaelogy and Language. The Puzzle of Indo-European Origins, by Colin Renfrew," *Current Anthropology*, 3, 29: 449–453.

Colledge, Sue, Conolly, James, and Shennan, Stephen. 2004. "Archaeobotanical Evidence for the Spread of Farming in the Eastern Mediterranean," *Current Anthropology*, 45, Suppl.: 35–58.

Collinge, N. E. 1985. *The Laws of Indo-European*, Amsterdam, Benjamins.

Comrie, Bernard, Fabri, Ray, Hume, Elizabeth, Mifsud, Manwel, Stolz, Thomas, and Vanhove, Martine (eds.). 2009. *Introducing Maltese Linguistics Selected Papers from the 1st International Conference on Maltese Linguistics*, Amsterdam, John Benjamins, Studies in Language Companion Series, 113.

Conte, Édouard, and Essner, Cornelia. 1995. *La Quête de la race. Une anthropologie du nazisme*, Paris, Hachette.

Coon, Carleton Stevens. 1939. *The Races of Europe*, New York, Macmillan Company.

Coon, Carleton Stevens. 1962. *The Origin of Races*, New York, Knopf.

Coudart, Anick. 1999. "Is Post-Processualism Bound To Happen Everywhere? The French Case," *Antiquity*, 73, 279: 161–166.

Coudart, Anick, Manolakakis, Laurence, and Demoule, Jean-Paul. 1999. "Égalité/inégalité sociale et division du travail en Europe durant le néolithique," *in* Philippe Descola, Jacques Hamel, and Pierre Lemonnier (eds.), *La Production du social. Autour de Maurice Godelier (Colloque de Cerisy)*, Paris, Fayard: 267–288.

Coudart, Anick, and Olivier, Laurent. 1995. "French Tradition and the Central Place of History in Human Sciences," *in* Peter J. Ucko (ed.), *Theory in Archaeology: A World Perspective*, London/New York, Routledge: 363–381.

BIBLIOGRAPHY 483

Court de Gébelin, Antoine. 1773–1784. *Le Monde primitif analysé et comparé avec le monde moderne considéré dans son génie allégorique et dans les allégories auxquelles conduisit ce génie*, 9 vols. (new edition 1786), Paris, Valleyre l'aîné.

Coye, Noël. 1997. *La Préhistoire en parole et en acte. Méthodes et enjeux de la pratique archéologique (1830–1950)*, Paris, L'Harmattan.

Crawfurd, John. 1820. *History of the Indian Archipelago. Containing an Account of the Manners, Arts, Languages, Religions, Institutions, and Commerce of its Inhabitants*, Edinburgh, A. Constable and Co.

Crevatin, Franco. 1979. *Ricerche sull'antichità indoeuropea*, Trieste, Edizioni LINT.

Cuisenier, Jean. 1990. *Ethnologie de l'Europe*, Paris, PUF, "Que-sais-je?"

Cuny, Albert Louis Marie. 1924. *Études prégrammaticales: sur le domaine des langues indo-européennes et chamito-sémitiques*, Champion, Paris.

Curta, Florin. 2001. *The Making of the Slavs History and Archaeology of the Lower Danube Region, Ca. 500–700*, Cambridge, Cambridge University.

Curta, Florin (ed.). 2005. *Borders, Barriers, and Ethnogenesis: Frontiers in Late Antiquity and the Middle Ages*, Turnhout, Brepols.

Curta, Florin. 2006. *Southeastern Europe in the Middle Ages, 500–1250*, Cambridge, Cambridge University Press.

Czekanowski, Jan. 1928. *Na marginesie recenzji P.K. Moszyńskiego o książce "Wstęp do historji Słowian,"* re-edited, Lvov, Towarzystwo Ludoznawcze, series II, vol. 7.

Daim, Wilfried. 1958. *Der Mann, der Hitler die Ideen gab: von den religiösen Verirrungen eines Sektierers zum Rassenwahn des Diktators*, Munich, Isar Verlag.

Dakhlia, Jocelyne. 2008. *Lingua franca*, Arles, Actes Sud.

Dalton-Puffer, Christiane. 1995. "Middle English Is a Creole and Its Opposite: On the Value of Plausible Spéculation," *in* Jacek Fisiak (ed.), *Linguistic Change Under Contact Conditions*, Berlin, Mouton de Gruyter: 35–50.

Daniel, Glyn Edmund. 1950. *A Hundred Years of Archaeology*, London, Duckworth.

Danilenko, Valentin Nikolaevich. 1969. *Ukrainy: Glavy drevnej istorii Jugo-Vostočnoj Evropy*, Kiev.

Danilenko, Valentin Nikolaevich. 1974. *Eneolit Ukrainy: Etnoistoričeskoe Isledovanie*, Kiev, Akademia Nauk.

Danino, Michel. 2006. *L'Inde et l'Invasion de nulle part. Le dernier repaire du mythe aryen*, Paris, Les Belles Lettres.

Danino, Michel. 2010. *The Lost River: On the Trail of the Sarasvatī*, New Delhi, Penguin Books India.

Daube, Anna. 1940. *Der Aufstieg der Muttersprache im deutschen Denken des 15. und 16. Jahrhunderts*, Frankfurt-sur-le-Main, M. Diesterweg.

Davis, Richard S. 1983. "Theoretical Issues in Contemporary Soviet Paleolithic Archaeology," *Annual Review of Anthropology*, 12, 1: 403–428.

Day, John V. 2001. *Indo-European Origins: The Anthropological Evidence*, Washington, DC, Institute for the Study of Man.

Day, John V. 2002. "In Quest of Our Linguistic Ancestors. The Elusive Origins of the Indo-European," *The Occidental Quaterly*, 2, 3: 5–20.

Déchelette, Joseph. 1914. *Manuel d'archéologie préhistorique celtique et gallo-romaine*. Paris, Picard (2nd ed. 1927), 3 vols.

Delitzsch, Friedrich. 1873. *Studien über indogermanisch-semitische Wurzelverwandtschaft*, Leipzig, G. Kreysing.

484 BIBLIOGRAPHY

Delpech, François, and Garcia Quintela, Marco V. (eds.). 2009. *Vingt ans après Georges Dumézil (1898–1986). Mythologie comparée indo-européenne et idéologie trifonctionnelle; bilans, perspectives et nouveaux domaines*, Budapest, Archaeolingua.

de Mauro, Tullio. 1972. "Notes biographiques et critiques sur F. de Saussure," *in Cours de linguistique générale*, published by Charles Bally and Albert Séchehaye, in collaboration with Albert Riedlinger, critical edition prepared by Tullio de Mauro, Paris, Payot: 319–389 (2nd ed. 1985).

de Mauro, and Formigari, Lia. 1990. *Leibniz, Humboldt, and the Origins of Comparativism*, Amsterdam, Benjamins.

Demoule, Jean-Paul. 1980. "Les Indo-Européens ont-ils existé?," *L'Histoire*, 28: 108–120.

Demoule, Jean-Paul. 1991. "Réalité des Indo-Européens: les diverses apories du modèle arborescent," *Revue de l'histoire des religions*, 208, 2: 169–202.

Demoule, Jean-Paul. 1993. "L'archéologie du pouvoir: oscillations et résistances dans l'Europe protohistorique," *in* Alain Daubigney (ed.), *Fonctionnement social de l'âge du fer. Opérateurs et hypothèses pour la France*, Université de Besançon: 259–274.

Demoule, Jean-Paul. 1994. "L'amour passé," *Nouvelle Revue de psychanalyse*, 49: 103–117.

Demoule, Jean-Paul. 1998. "Les Indo-Européens, un mythe sur mesure," *La Recherche*, 29, 308: 40–47.

Demoule, Jean-Paul. 1999a. *Chronologie et Société des nécropoles celtiques de la culture Aisne-Marne. Supplément à la Revue archéologique de Picardie*, Amiens.

Demoule, Jean-Paul. 1999b. "Ethnicity, Culture and Identity: French Archaeologists and Historians," *Antiquity*, 73, 279: 190–198.

Demoule, Jean-Paul (ed.). 2007a. *La Révolution néolithique en France*, Paris, La Découverte-Inrap.

Demoule, Jean-Paul. 2007b. *Naissance de la figure. L'Art du paléolithique à l'âge du fer*, Paris, Hazan.

Demoule, Jean-Paul (ed.). 2009. *L'Europe, un continent redécouvert par l'archéologie*, Paris, Gallimard-Inrap.

Demoule, Jean-Paul (ed.). 2010. *La Révolution néolithique dans le monde*, Paris, CNRS Éditions.

Demoule, Jean-Paul. 2012a. *On a retrouvé l'histoire de France. Comment l'archéologie raconte notre passé*, Paris, Robert Laffont.

Demoule, Jean-Paul. 2012b. "Rescue Archaeology: A European View," *Annual Review of Anthropology*, 41: 611–626.

Demoule, Jean-Paul, and Perlès, Catherine. 1993. "The Greek Neolithic: a New Review," *Journal of World Prehistory*, 7: 355–416.

Deniker, Joseph. 1900. *Les Races et les peuples de la terre*, Paris, Masson (2nd ed., 1926).

Dennell, Robin. 1983. *European Economic Prehistory: A New Approach*, London/New York, Academic Press.

Desbuissons, Ghislaine. 1984. *La Nouvelle Droite (1968–1984). Contribution à l'étude des idées de droite en France*, Doctorat en sciences politiques, Institut d'études politiques, Université des sciences sociales de Grenoble.

Detienne, Marcel. 2010. *L'Identité nationale, une énigme*, Paris, Gallimard.

Devoto, Giacomo. 1962. *Origini indoeuropee*, Florence, Sansoni, Istituto Italiano di Preistoria e Protoistoria Italiana.

D'Huy, Julien. 2018. *Cosmogonies, la préhistoire des mythes*, Paris, La Découverte.

BIBLIOGRAPHY 485

Diakonoff, Igor Mikhailovich. 1997. "External Connections of the Sumerian Language," *Mother Tongue—Journal of the Association for the Study of Language in Prehistory*, 3: 54–62.

Diamond, Jared M. 2011. *Collapse: How Societies Choose to Fail or Succeed*, New York, Penguin Books (review edition) (French translation: *Comment les sociétés décident de leur disparition ou de leur survie*, Paris, Gallimard, 2006).

Dias, Nélia. 1989. "Séries de crânes et armées de squelettes: les collections anthropologiques en France dans la seconde moitié du xixe siècle," *in* Claude Blanckaert, Albert Ducros, and Jean-Jacques Hublin (eds.), *Histoire de l'anthropologie. Hommes, idées, moments*, numéro spécial de *Bulletins et Mémoires de la Société d'anthropologie de Paris*, 1, 3–4: 203–230.

Dias, Nélia. 1993. "Langues inférieures, langues supérieures," *in* Claude Blanckaert (ed.), *Des sciences contre l'homme*, vol. 1: *Classer, hiérarchiser, exclure*, Paris, Autrement: 95–110.

Dickinson, Oliver. 1994. *The Aegean Bronze Age*, Cambridge, Cambridge University Press.

Diederischen, Paul. 1974. "The Foundation of Comparative Linguistics: Revolution or Continuation?," *in* Dell H. Hymes (ed.), *Studies in the History of Linguistics. Traditions and Paradigms*, Bloomington-London, Indiana University Press: 277–306.

Dietz, Ute Luise. 1992. "Zur Frage vorbronzezeitlicher Trensenbelege in Europa," *Germania*, 70, 1: 17–36.

Djahukian, Gevorg B. 1986. "O tak nazyvaemoj 'glottal'noj teorii' v indoevropeistike," *Vestnik Drevnej Istorii*, 3: 160–165.

Dodd-Opritescu, Ann. 1978. "Les éléments steppiques dans l'énéolithique de Transylvanie," *Dacia, N.S.*, 22: 87–97.

Dolgopolsky, Aaron. 1970. "A Long-Range Comparison of Some Languages of Northern Eurasia," *in* Sergej P. Tolstov (ed.), *VII International Congress of Anthropological and Ethnographical Sciences*, Moscow, vol. 5: 620–634.

Dolgopolsky, Aaron. 1988. "The Indo-European Homeland and Lexical Contacts of Proto-Indo-European with other Languages," *Mediterranean Language Review*, 3: 7–31.

Dolgopolsky, Aaron. 1989. "Problems of Nostratic Comparative Phonology," *in* Vitaly Viktorovich Shevoroshkin (ed.), *Reconstructing Languages and Cultures*, Bochum, Brockmeyer: 90–98.

Dolukhanov, Paul. 1979. *Ecology and Economy in Neolithic Eastern Europe*, London, Duckworth.

Domingue, Nicole Z. 1977. "Middle English: Another Creole?," *Journal of Creole Studies*, 1, 1: 89–100.

Dotan, Aron. 1987. "From the Beginning of Medieval Hebrew-Arabic Lexicography," *in* Hans Aarsleff, Louis Gérard Kelly, and Hans-Josef Niederehe (eds.), *Papers in the History of Linguistics. Proceedings of the Third International Conference on the History of the Language Sciences (ICHoLS III)*, Amsterdam, Benjamins: 77–84.

Dozier, Edward P. 1954. *Hano, a Tewa Indian Community in Arizona*, Berkeley, University of California.

Dragiev, Plamen, Nadon, Robert, and Makarenkov, Vladimir. 2012. "Two Effective Methods for Correcting Experimental High-Throughput Screening Data," *Bioinformatics*, 28, 13: 1775–1782.

Drechsel, E. 1987. "Metacommunicative Fonctions of Mobilian Jargon, an American Indian Pidgin of the Lower Mississippi River Region," *in* Glenn G. Gilbert (ed.), *Pidgin*

486 BIBLIOGRAPHY

and Creole Languages: Essays in Memory of John E. Reinecke, Honolulu, University of Hawaii Press: 433–444.

Dressler, Wolfgang U. 1965. "Methodische Vorfragen bei der Bestimmung der 'Urheimat,'" *Die Sprache*, 11: 25–60.

Drews, Robert. 1988. *The Coming of the Greeks: Indo-European Conquests in the Aegean and the Near East*, Princeton, Princeton University Press.

Drews, Robert. 2004. *Early Riders: The Beginnings of Mounted Warfare in Asia and Europe*, New York, Routledge.

Drieu La Rochelle, Pierre. 1943. "France, Angleterre, Allemagne," *Deutschland-Frankreich*: 28–42.

Drinka, Bridget. 2009. "Stratified Reconstruction and a New View of the Family Tree Model," *in* Angela Marcantonio (ed.), *The Indo-European Language Family: Questions about its Status*, Washington, DC, Institute for the Study of Man: 7: 1–39.

Drobin, Ulf. 1980. "Indogermanische Religion und Kultur? Eine Analyse des Begriffes Indogermanisch," *Temenos*, 16, Helsinki; republished in *Skrifter utgivna av Religionshistoriska institutionen vid Stokholms universitet*, 2, 16: 26–38.

Droit, Roger-Pol. July 13, 1993. "La confusion des idées. Quarante intellectuels appellent à une Europe de la vigilance face à la banalisation de la pensée d'extrême droite," *Le Monde*. https://www.lemonde.fr/archives/article/1993/07/13/la-confusion-des-idees-quarante-intellectuels-appellent-a-une-europe-de-la-vigilance-face-a-la-banalisat ion-de-la-pensee-d-extreme-droite_3949845_1819218.html.

Droixhe, Daniel. 1978. *La Linguistique et l'Appel de l'histoire (1600–1800). Rationalisme et révolutions positivistes*, Geneva/Paris, Droz.

Droixhe, Daniel (ed.). 1984. "Genèse du comparatisme indo-européen," *Histoire, Épistémologie, Langage*, 6: 2.

Drosdowski, Günther. 1966. "Die Erforschung des indo-germanischen Altertums (1816–1966)," *Die Wissenschaftliche Redaktion*, 20: 51–69.

Dubuisson, Daniel. 1985. "Matériaux pour une typologie des structures trifonctionnelles," *L'Homme*, 25/1: 105–121.

Dubuisson, Daniel. 2005. *Impostures et Pseudo-science. L'œuvre de Mircea Eliade*, Villeneuve-d'Ascq, Presses universitaires du Septentrion.

Duhoux, Yves. 1983. *Introduction aux dialectes grecs anciens. Problèmes et méthodes, recueil de textes traduits*, Louvain, Cabay.

Duhoux, Yves. 1998. "Pre-Hellenic Language(s) of Crete," *Journal of Indo-European Language*, 26, 1–2: 1–40.

Dumézil, Bruno. 2013. *Des Gaulois aux Carolingiens*, Paris, PUF.

Dumézil, Georges. 1927. "De quelques faux massacres," *Revue turque d'anthropologie*, 3, 4 March: 39–46.

Dumézil, Georges. 1938. "La préhistoire des flamines majeurs," *Revue de l'histoire des religions*, 118: 188–200.

Dumézil, Georges. 1939. *Mythes et Dieux des Germains, essai d'interprétation comparative*, Paris, Librairie Ernest Leroux-PUF.

Dumézil, Georges, 1941a. "L'étude comparée des religions indo-européennes," *Nouvelle Revue Française*, 29: 385–399.

Dumézil, Georges. 1941b. *Jupiter, Mars, Quirinus. Essai sur la conception indo-européenne de la société et sur les origines de Rome*, Paris, Gallimard.

Dumézil, Georges. 1943. *Servius et la fortune. Essai sur la fonction sociale de louange et de blâme et sur les éléments indo-européens du cens romain*, Paris, Gallimard.

BIBLIOGRAPHY 487

Dumézil, Georges. 1949. *L'Héritage indo-européen à Rome*, Paris, Gallimard.

Dumézil, Georges. 1958. *L'Idéologie tripartite des Indo-Européens*, Brussels, Latomus.

Dumézil, Georges. 1966. *La Religion romaine archaïque*, Paris, Payot.

Dumézil, Georges. 1968. *Mythe et Épopée*, I: *L'Idéologie des trois fonctions dans les épopées des peuples indo-européens*, Paris, Gallimard.

Dumézil, Georges. 1973. *Mythe et Épopée*, III: *Histoires romaines*, Paris, Gallimard.

Dumézil, Georges. 1975. *Fêtes romaines d'été et d'automne*, Paris, Gallimard.

Dumézil, Georges. 1978. *Romans de Scythie et d'alentour*, Paris, Payot.

Dumézil, Georges. 1979. *Discours de réception à l'Académie française et réponse de M. Claude Lévi-Strauss*, Paris, Gallimard.

Dumézil, Georges. 1983a. "Les festins secrets de G. Dumézil. Entretien avec Maurice Olender," *Le Nouvel Observateur*, 949, 14–20 January (republished in Maurice Olender, *Race sans histoire*, Paris, Seuil, 2009: 138–160).

Dumézil, Georges. 1983b. *La Courtisane et les Seigneurs colorés et autres essais: vingt-cinq esquisses de mythologie*, Paris, Gallimard.

Dumézil, Georges. 1985a. *L'Oubli de l'homme et l'Honneur des dieux*, Paris, Gallimard.

Dumézil, Georges.1985b. "Science et politique. Réponse à Carlo Ginzburg," *Annales. Économies, Sociétés, Civilisations*, 40, 5: 985–989.

Dumézil, Georges. 1986. "Parlez-vous l'indo-européen," *Le Nouvel Observateur*, 1142: 104.

Dumézil, Georges. 1987. *Entretiens avec Didier Eribon*, Paris, Gallimard.

Dumézil, Georges. 1994. *Le Roman des jumeaux. Esquisses de mythologie*, posthumous edition by Joël Grisward, Paris, Gallimard.

Dunkel, Georges. 1981. "Typology versus Reconstruction," *in* Y. L. Arbeitman and Alan Bomhard (eds.), *Bono Homini Donum: Essays in Historical Linguistics, in Memory of J. Alexander Kerns*, Amsterdam, Benjamins, 2 vols.: 559–569.

Duranton-Crabol, Anne-Marie. 1988. *Visages de la Nouvelle Droite. Le G.R.E.C.E. et son histoire*, Paris, Presses de la Fondation nationale des sciences politiques.

Duranton-Crabol, Anne-Marie. 1991. *L'Europe de l'extrême droite de 1945 à nos jours*, Brussels, Complexe.

Dutour, Olivier, Hublin, Jean-Jacques, and Vandermeersch, Bernard (eds.). 2005a. *Objets et Méthodes en paléoanthropologie. Comité des travaux historiques et scientifiques*, Paris, Comité des travaux historiques et scientifiques.

Dutour, Olivier. 2005b. *Origine et Évolution des populations humaines*, Paris, Comité des travaux historiques et scientifiques.

Dutta, Pratap C. 1972. "The Bronze-Age Harappans: A Re-Examination of the Skulls in the Context of the Population Concept," *American Journal of Physical Anthropology*, 36, 3: 391–396.

Ebert, Max. 1921. *Südrussland im Altertum*, Bonn-Leipzig, Kurt Schroeder.

Edwards, William Frédéric. 1829. *Des caractères physiologiques des races humaines considérés dans leurs rapports avec l'histoire; Lettre à M. Amédée Thierry*, Paris, Compère jeune.

Edzard, Lutz. 1998. *Polygenesis, Convergence, and Entropy: an Alternative Model of Linguistic Evolution Applied to Semitic Linguistics*, Wiesbaden, Harrassowitz.

Eggers, Hans Jürgen. 1939. "Natürliche Erkenntnisgrenzen bei vorgeschichtlichen und volkskundlichen Fundkarten," *in* Karl Kaizer (ed.), *Beiträge zur Volkskunde Pommerns*, Greifswald, L. Bamberg: 166–173.

Eggers, Hans Jürgen. 1950. "Das Problem der ethnischen Deutung in der Frühgeschichte," *in* Horst Kirchner (ed.), *Ur- und Frühgeschichte als Historische Wissenschaft: Wahle Festschrift*, Heidelberg, Carl Winter: 49–59.

488 BIBLIOGRAPHY

Eggers, Hans Jürgen. 1959. *Einführung in die Vorgeschichte*, Munich, Sammlung Piper.

Ehrenreich, Eric. 2007. *The Nazi Ancestral Proof: Genealogy, Racial Science, and the Final Solution*, Bloomington, Indiana University Press.

Eichhoff, Frédéric Gustave. 1836. *Parallèle des langues de l'Europe et de l'Inde, ou Étude des principales langues romanes germaniques, slavonnes et celtiques comparées entre elles et à la langue sanscrite, avec un essai de transcription générale*, Paris, Imprimerie royale.

Eickstedt, Freiherr Egon von. 1934. *Rassenkunde und Rassengeschichte der Menschheit*, Stuttgart, F. Enke.

Eickstedt, Freiherr Egon von. 1936. *Grundlagen der Rassenpsychologie*, Stuttgart, F. Enke.

Eliade, Mircea. 1949. *Traité d'histoire des religions*, préface de Georges Dumézil (republished in 1964, 1974, 1977, 1983, 1989), Paris, Payot.

Eickstedt, Freiherr Egon von. 1968. *Le Chamanisme et les Techniques archaïques de l'extase*, Paris, Payot, 2nd ed.

Eickstedt, Freiherr Egon von. 1979. *Histoire des croyances et des idées religieuses*, I: *De l'âge de la pierre aux mystères d'Éleusis*, Paris, Payot.

Elst, Koenraad. 1999. *Update on the Aryan Invasion Debate*, New Delhi, Aditya Prakashan.

Embleton, Sheila M. 1986. *Statistics in Historical Linguistics*. Bochum, Brockmeyer.

Émion, François, forthcoming, *Mythologies. Colloque en hommage à Georges Dumézil* (working title), Paris, Garnier.

Engelhardt, Isrun. 2008. "Nazis of Tibet: A Twentieth Century Myth," *in* Monica Esposito (ed.), *Images of Tibet in the 19th and 20th Centuries*, Paris, École française d'Extrême-Orient, vol. 1: 63–96.

Eribon, Didier. 1992. *Faut-il brûler Dumézil? Mythologie, science et politique*, Paris, Flammarion.

Ernout, Alfred, and Meillet, Antoine. 1939. *Dictionnaire étymologique de la langue latine*, Paris, Klincksieck, 2nd ed. (4th ed. 1967).

Ertel, Rachel. 2003. *Brasier de mots*, Paris, Liana Levi.

Eugène, Éric. 1998. *Wagner et Gobineau: existe-t-il un racisme wagnérien?*, Paris, Le Cherche Midi.

Eysenck, Hans Jürgen. 1973. *The Inequality of Man*, Farnham, Ashgate Publishing Limited.

Fabre, Daniel (ed.). 1996. *L'Europe entre cultures et nations. Actes du colloque organisé par la Mission du Patrimoine ethnologique*, Paris, Éditions de la Maison des sciences de l'homme.

Fages, Antoine et al. 2019. "Tracking Five Millennia of Horse Management with Extensive Ancient Genome Time Series," *Cell*, 177: 1419–1435.

Falk, Harry. 1994. "Der Reitpferd im Vedischen Indien," *in* Bernhardt Hänsel and Stefan Zimmer (eds.), *Die Indogermanen und das Pferd, Festschrift B. Schlerath*, Budapest, Archaeolingua: 91–102.

Fassin, Éric. 1997. "Discours sur l'inégalité des races. *The Bell Curve*: polémique savante, rhétorique raciale et politique publique," *Hérodote*, 85: 61–88.

Faye, Guillaume. 1983. *Sexe et Idéologie*, Paris, Le Labyrinthe.

Faye, Jean-Pierre, *Langages totalitaires*. 1972. Paris, Hermann (republished and expanded, Paris, Hermann, 2004).

Feist, Sigmund. 1913. *Kultur, Ausbreitung und Herkunft der Indogermanen*, Berlin, Weidmann Buchhandlung.

Feist, Sigmund. 1914. *Indogermanen und Germanen: Ein Beitrag zur europäischen Urgeschichtsforschung*, Halle, Niemeyer.

Feist, Sigmund. 1916. "Archäologie und Indogermanenproblem," *Correspondenzblatt der deutschen Gesellschaft für Anthropologie, Ethnologie und Urgeschichte*, 47: 61–68.

BIBLIOGRAPHY 489

Feist, Sigmund. 1926. "Germanen," in Max Ebert (ed.), *Reallexikon der Vorgeschichte*, Berlin, De Gruyter, 4: 273–289.

Feist, Sigmund. 1927. "Indogermanen," in Max Ebert (ed.), *Reallexikon der Vorgeschichte*, Berlin, De Gruyter, vol. 6: 54–67.

Feist, Sigmund. 1932. "The Origin of the Germanic Languages and the Indo-Europeanising of North Europe," *Language*, 8: 245–254.

Feist-Hirsch, Elisabeth. 1970. "Mein Vater Sigmund Feist," *in* Herbert Arthur Strauss and Kurt Richard Grossmann (eds.), *Gegenwart und Rückblick. Festgabe für die jüdische Gemeinde in Berlin 25 Jahre nach Neubeginn*, Heidelberg, L. Stiehm.

Fellman, Jack. 1975. "The First Comparative Indo-Europeanist," *Linguistics*, 145: 83–86.

Ferembach, Denise. 1980. "Rapport moral," *Bulletins et Mémoires de la Société d'anthropologie de Paris*, vol. 7–4: 351–353.

Ferembach, Denise. 1981. "Rapport moral," *Bulletins et Mémoires de la Société d'anthropologie de Paris*, vol. 8–4: 473–477.

Ferguson, Charles Albert. 1976. "The Ethiopian Language Area," *in* Marvin Lionel Bender, J. Donald Bowen, Robert L. Cooper, and Charles Albert Ferguson (eds.), *Language in Ethiopia*, Oxford, Oxford University Press: 63–76.

Ferraresi, Franco (ed.). 1984. *La destra radicale*, Milan, Feltrinelli.

Fetten, Frank. 2000. "Archaeology and Anthropology in Germany Before 1945," *in* Heinrich G. H. Härke (ed.), *Archaeology, Ideology and Society. The German Experience*, Frankfurt, Peter Lang: 140–179.

Fichte, Johann Gottlieb. 1978. *Reden an die deutsche Nation hilosophische Bibliothek*, vol. 204, Hamburg, Meiner (5th edition, 1st edition. 1808) (French translation: *Discours à la nation allemande*, Paris, Imprimerie nationale, 1992).

Field, Geoffrey. 1977. "Nordic Racism," *Journal of the History of Ideas*, 38: 523–540.

Field, Geoffrey. 1981. *Evangelist of Race: The Germanic Vision of Houston Stewart Chamberlain*, New York, Columbia University Press.

Finkelberg, Margalit. 1997. "Anatolian Languages and Indo-European Migrations to Greece," *Classical World*, 91: 3–20.

Finzsch, Norbert. 1999. "Wissenschaflicher Rassismus in den Vereinigten Staaten—1850 bis 1930," *in* Heidrun Kaupen-Haas and Christian Saller (eds.), *Wissenschaftlicher Rassismus. Analysen einer Kontinuität in den Human- und Naturwissenschaften*, Frankfurt-sur-le-Main/New York, Campus Verlag: 84–110.

Fischer, Claude S., Hout, Michael, Jankowski, Martin S., Lucas, Samuel Roundfield, and Voss, Kim (eds.). 1996. *Inequality by Design: Cracking the Bell Curve Myth*, Princeton, Princeton University Press.

Fischer, Eugen. 1913. *Die Rehobother Bastards und das Bastardierungsproblem beim Menschen: anthropologische und ethnographiesche Studien am Rehobother Bastardvolk in Deutsch-Südwest-Afrika*, Jena, G. Fischer.

Flannery, Ken, and Joyce, Marcus. 2012. *The Creation of Inequality: How Our Prehistoric Ancestors Set the Stage for Monarchy, Slavery, and Empire*, Cambridge, Harvard University Press.

Fodor, István, and Hagège, Claude (eds.). 1983. *Language Reform: History and Future = La réforme des langues: histoire et avenir = Sprachreform: Geschichte und Zukunft*, Hamburg, John Benjamins.

Fokkens, Harry, and Harding, Anthony (eds.). 2013. *The Oxford Handbook of the European Bronze Age*, Oxford, Oxford University Press.

490 BIBLIOGRAPHY

Fokkens, Harry, and Nicolis, Franco (eds.). 2012. *Background to Beakers: Inquiries into the Regional Cultural Background to the Bell Beaker Complex*, Leyde, Sidestone Press.

Foley, William A. 1986. *The Papuan Languages of New Guinea*, Cambridge, Cambridge University Press.

Forrer, Emil. 1921. "Ausbeute aus den Boghazköi-Inschriften," *Mitteilungen der deutschen Orient-Gesellschaft zu Berlin*, 61: 20–39.

Forsén, Jeannette. 1992. *The Twilight of the Early Helladics: A Study of the Disturbances in East-central and southern Greece towards the end of the Early Bronze Age*, Jonsered, Paul Astroms Forlag, SIMAPB, 116.

Fortson, Benjamin W. 2009. *Indo-European Language and Culture: An Introduction*, Malden (MA), Blackwell.

Fowler, Chris et al. (ed.). 2015. *The Oxford Handbook of Neolithic Europe*, Oxford, Oxford University Press.

Fracchiolla, Béatrice (ed.). May 2006. "L'origine du langage et des langues," *Marges linguistiques—Revue électronique en sciences du langage*, http://www.revue-texto.net/Parutions/Marges/00_ml112006.pdf.

Fraisse, Geneviève. 1983. "Clémence Royer (1830–1902), lecture de Darwin et regard féministe," *Raison présente*, 67: 87–101.

Frankfurt, Henri-Paul. 1989. *Fouilles de Shortugaï. Recherches sur l'Asie centrale protohistorique*, Paris, De Boccard, 2 vols.

Frankfurt, Henri-Paul. 1999. "Compte-rendu de: V. H. Mair (dir.): The Bronze Age and Early Iron Age Peoples of Eastern Central Asia," *Bulletin de l'École française d'Extrême-Orient*, 86: 449–458.

Frankfurt, Henri-Paul. 2005. "La civilisation de l'Oxus et les Indo-Iraniens et Indo-Aryens en Asie centrale," *in* Henri-Paul Frankfurt, Gérard Fussman, Jean Kellens, and Xavier Tremblay (eds.), *Aryens et Iraniens en Asie centrale*, Paris, Collège de France, Publications de l'Institut de civilisation indienne, fasc. 72: 253–328.

Francis, E. D. 1992. "The Impact of Non-Indo-European Languages on Greek and Mycenian," *in* Edgar C. Polomé and Werner Winter (eds.), *Reconstructing Languages and Cultures*, Berlin, Mouton de Gruyter: 469–506.

François, Alexandre. 2014. "Trees, Waves and Linkages: Models of Language Diversification," *in* Cl. Bowern and B. Evans (eds.), *The Routledge Handbook of Historical Linguistics*, Routledge: 161–189.

François, Stéphane. 2006. *La Musique europaïenne. Ethnographie politique d'une subculture de droite*, Paris, L'Harmattan.

François, Stéphane. 2007. *Le Néo-Paganisme: une vision du monde en plein essor*, Apremont, MCOR-Table d'émeraude.

François, Stéphane. 2008. *Les Néo-Paganismes et la Nouvelle Droite*, Milan/Paris, Archè.

Freu, Jacques. 1989. "L'arrivée des Indo-Européens en Europe," *Bulletin de l'Association Guillaume Budé*, 1: 3–41.

Friedrich, Paul. 1970. "Proto-Indo-European Trees," *in* George Cardona, Henry M. Hoenigswald, and Alfred Senn (eds.), *Indo-European and Indo-Europeans*, Philadelphia, University of Pennsylvania Press: 11–34.

Frieman, Catherine J., and Hofmann, Daniela. 2019. "Present Pasts in the Archaeology of Genetics, Identity and Migration in Europe: A Critical Essay," *World Archaeology*, 51, 4: 528–545.

Furholt, Martin. 2003. *Die absolutchronologische Datierung der Schnurkeramik in Mitteleuropa und Südskandinavien*, Bonn, Rudolf Habelt.

BIBLIOGRAPHY 491

Furholt, Martin. 2019a. "Re-integrating Archaeology: A Contribution to aDNA Studies and the Migration Discourse on the 3rd Millenium BC in Europe," *Proceedings of the Prehistoric Society*, 85: 1–15.

Furholt, Martin. 2019b. "De-contaminating the aDNA: Archaeology Dialogue on Mobility and Migration Discussing the Culture-Historical Legacy," *Current Swedish Archaeology*, 27: 53–68.

Furholt, Martin. 2021. "Mobility and Social Change: Understanding the European Neolithic Period After the Archaeogenetic Revolution" *Journal of Archaeological Research*, 29: 481–535.

Fussman, Gérard. 1998. "Compte-rendu de: Bernard Sergent, Genèse de l'Inde. 1997." *Bulletin de l'École française d'Extrême-Orient*, 85: 476–485.

Fussman, Gérard. 2003. "Entre fantasmes, science et politique: l'entrée des Āryas en Inde," *Annales, Histoire, Sciences sociales*, 58e année, 4: 781–813 (reprinted in Fussman et al., 2005: 197–232).

Fussman, Gérard, Kellens, Jean, Frankfurt, Henri-Paul, and Tremblay, Xavier. 2005. *Āryas, Aryens et Iraniens en Asie centrale*, Paris, Collège de France.

Galton, S. Francis. 1865. "Hereditary Talent and Character," *Macmillan's Magazine*, 12, 68: 157–165, 345–349.

Galton, S. Francis. 1869. *Hereditary Genius*, London, MacMillan (new edition 1892).

Galton, S. Francis. 1883. *Inquiries into Human Faculty and Its Development*, London, MacMillan.

Galton, S. Francis. 1907. *Inquiries into Human Faculty and Its Development*, London, Dent (new edition).

Gamkrelidze, Tamaz V. 1992. "Comparative Reconstruction and Typological Verification: The Case of Indo-European," *in* Edgar C. Polomé and Werner Winter (eds.), *Reconstructing Languages and Cultures*, Berlin/New York, Mouton de Gruytertp. 63–71.

Gamkrelidze, Tamaz V. 1994. "PIE "Horse" and "Cart" in the Light of the Hypothesis of Asiatic homeland of the Indo-Europeans: Indo-European—Caucasian aspects," *in* Bernhardt Hänsel and Stefan Zimmer (eds.), *Die Indogermanen und das Pferd, Festschrift B. Schlerath*, Budapest, Archaeolingua: 37–42.

Gamkrelidze, Tamaz V, and Ivanov, Vjačeslav Vsevolodovič. 1973. "Sprachtypologie und die Rekonstruktion der gemeinindogermanischen Verschlüsse. Vorläufiger Bericht," *Phonetica*, 27: 150–156.

Gamkrelidze, Tamaz V, and Ivanov, Vjačeslav Vsevolodovič. 1984. *Indoevropejskij jazik i Indoevropejcy. Rekonstrukcija i istoriko-tipologičeskij analiz prajazyka i protokul'tury*, Tbilissi, State University Editions, 2 vols.

Garcia, Daniel. 2014. *Coupole et Dépendances. Enquête sur l'Académie française*, Paris, Éditions du Moment.

García Quintela, Marco V. 2001. *Dumézil. Une introduction suivie de l'affaire Dumézil*, Crozon, Éditions Armeline.

Gasman, Daniel. 1971. *The Scientific Origins of National Socialism*, London, MacDonald.

Gasparov, Boris. 1987. "The Ideological Principles of Prague School Phonology," *in* Elzbieta Chodakowska, Hugh Mclean, Brent Vine, and Krystyna Pomorska (eds.), *Language, Poetry and Poetics. The Generation of the 1890s: Jakobson, Trubetzkoy, Majakovskij. Proceedings of the First Roman Jakobson Colloquium*, Berlin, Mouton de Gruyter: 49–78.

492 BIBLIOGRAPHY

Gaunitz, Charleen et al. 2018. "Ancient Genomes Revisit the Ancestry of Domestic and Przewalski's Horses," *Science*, 360 (6384), 111–114.

Geiger, Lazarus. 1871. "Über die Ursitze der Indogermanen," *in Zur Entwicklungsgeschichte der Menschheit*, Stuttgart, Cotta (2nd ed. 1878).

Gellner, Ernest (ed.). 1980. *Soviet and Western Anthropology*, London, Duckworth.

Gellner, Ernest. 1983. *Nations and Nationalism*, Ithaca, Blackwell (French translation: *Nations et Nationalismes*, Paris, Payot, 1994).

Gentile, Emilio. 2013. *Pour ou contre César? Les religions chrétiennes face aux totalitarismes*, Paris, Aubier (original Italian edition: *Contro Cesare. Cristianesimo e totalitarismo nell'epoca dei fascismi*, Milan, Feltrinelli, 2010).

Georgiev, Vladimir Ivanov. 1961. *La Toponymie ancienne de la péninsule Balkanique et la Thèse méditerranéenne*, Sofia, Bulgarian Academy of Sciences.

Georgiev, Vladimir Ivanov. 1973. "Raetisch oder Nordetruskisch," *Orbis*, 22: 232–247.

Gérard, René. 1963. *L'Orient et la Pensée romantique allemande*, Nancy, Imprimerie G. Thomas.

Germinario, Francesco. 2002. *La destra degli dei: Alain de Benoist e la cultura politica della Nouvelle Droite*, Turin, Bollati Boringhieri.

Gessinger, Joachim. 1992. "Les traditions nationales, Allemagne," *in* Sylvain Auroux (ed.), *Histoire des idées linguistiques*, t. II: *Le Développement de la grammaire occidentale*, Sylvain Auroux (ed.), Liège, Mardaga: 387–405.

Ghesquière, Emmanuel, and Marchand, Gregor. 2010. *Le Mésolithique en France*, Paris, La Découverte.

Giannopoulos, Theodoros G. 2012. *"Pothen kai pote oi Ellines"* ["The Greeks: Whence and When?" The Mainstream Scientific Responses and the Present State of Research on the First Beginning of the Greek Civilization], Heraklion, Crete University Press.

Giles, Peter. 1922. "The Aryans," *in* Edward James Rapson (ed.), *Cambridge History of India*, vol. 1, New York, MacMillan: 58–68.

Gillett, Andrew (ed.). 2002. *On Barbarian Identity: Critical Approaches to Ethnicity in the Early Middle Ages*, Turnhout, Brepols.

Gimbutas, Marija. 1946. *Die Bestattung in Litauen in der vorgeschichtlichen Zeit*, Inaugural-Dissertation zur Erlangung des Doktorgrades einer Hohen Philosophischen Fakultät der Eberhard-Karls, Universität zu Tübingen, Tübingen.

Gimbutas, Marija. 1952. "On the Origin of the North-Indo-Europeans," *American Anthropologist*, 54: 601–602.

Gimbutas, Marija. 1956. *The Prehistory of Eastern Europe*, t. I: *Mesolithic, Neolithic and Copper Age Cultures in Russia and the Baltic Area*, Harvard, Peabody Museum, American School of Prehistoric Research, no. 20.

Gimbutas, Marija. 1960. "Culture Change in Europe at the Start of the Second Millenium BC, A Contribution to the Indo-European Problem," *in Men and Cultures. Selected Papers of the Fifth International Congress of Anthropological and Ethnological Sciences, Philadelphia*, Philadelphia, University of Pennsylvania Press: 540–552.

Gimbutas, Marija. 1961. "Notes on the Chronology and Expansion of the Pit-Grave Culture," *in* Jaroslav Böhm and Sigfried De Laet (eds.), *L'Europe à la fin de l'âge de la pierre. Actes du Symposium consacré aux problèmes du néolithique européen*, Prague, Éditions de l'Académie techécoslovaque des sciences: 193–200.

Gimbutas, Marija. 1963a. *The Balts*, New York/London, Thames & Hudson.

Gimbutas, Marija. 1963b. "The Indo-European: Archaeological Problems," *American Anthropologist*, 65: 815–836.

BIBLIOGRAPHY   493

Gimbutas, Marija.1965a. *Bronze Age Cultures in Central and Eastern Europe*, La Haye/ London, Walter De Gruyter.
Gimbutas, Marija. 1965b. "The Relative Chronology of Neolithic and Chalcolithic Cultures in Eastern Eeurope North of the Balkan Peninsula and the Black Sea," *in* Robert W. Ehrich (ed.), *Chronologies in Old World Archaeology*, Chicago, Chicago University Press, 2nd ed.: 459–502.
Gimbutas, Marija. 1970. "Proto-Indo-European Culture, The Kurgan Culture During the Fifth, Fourth, and Third Millennia BC," *in* George Cardona, Henry M. Hoenigswald, and Alfred Senn (eds.), *Indo-European and Indo-Europeans*, Philadelphia, University of Pennsylvania Press: 155–197.
Gimbutas, Marija 1971. *The Slavs*, London, Thames & Hudson.
Gimbutas, Marija. 1973. "Old Europe C. 7000–3500 BC: The Earliest European Civilization Before the Infiltration of the Indo-European Peoples," *Journal of Indo-European Studies*, 1, 1: 1–20.
Gimbutas, Marija. 1974. *The Gods and Goddesses of Old Europe: 7000–3500 BC: Myths, Legends and Cult Images*, Berkeley, University of California Press.
Gimbutas, Marija. 1977. "The First Wave of European Steppe Pastoralists into Copper Age Europe," *Journal of Indo-European Studies*, 5: 277–338.
Gimbutas, Marija. 1985. "Primary and Secondary Homeland of the IE: Comments on Gamkrelidze-Ivanov Articles," *Journal of Indo-European Studies*, 13, 1–2: 185–202.
Gimbutas, Marija. 1989. *The Language of the Goddess*, San Francisco, HarperCollins (French translation: *Le Langage de la déesse*, Paris, Des femmes Antoinette Fouque, 2005).
Gimbutas, Marija. 1990. "The Collision of Two Ideologies," *in* Thomas Markey and John A. C. Greppin (eds.), *When Words Collide: The Indo-Europeans and the Pre-Indo-Europeans*, Ann Arbor, Karoma Publishers: 171–178.
Gimbutas, Marija. 1997. *The Kurgan Culture and the Indo-Europeanization of Europe: Selected Articles Form 1952 to 1993, Journal of Indo-European Studies*, Monograph Series, 18, Washington, DC, Institute for the Study of Man (available at www.jies.org).
Ginzburg, Carlo. 1985. "Mythologie germanique et nazisme. Sur un livre ancien de Georges Dumézil," *Annales. Économies, Sociétés, Civilisations*, 40, 4: 695–715.
Ginzburg, Carlo. 1992. *Le Sabbat des sorcières*, Paris, Gallimard.
Giordan, Henri (ed.). 1992. *Les Minorités en Europe. Droits linguistiques et droits de l'homme*, Paris, Éditions Kimé.
Gobineau, Arthur de. 1853. *Essai sur l'inégalité des races humaines*, Paris, Firmin-Didot.
Goldberg, Amy et al. 2017. "Ancient X chromosomes reveal contrasting sex bias in Neolithic and Bronze Age Eurasian migrations." *Proceedings of the National Academy of Sciences USA*, 114: 2657–2662.
Goodman, Mooris. 1971. "The Strange Case of Mbugu," *in* Dell H. Hymes (ed.), *Pidginization and Creolization of Languages*, Cambridge, Cambridge University Press: 243–254.
Goodrick-Clarke, Nicholas. 1989. *Les Racines occultistes du nazisme. Les Aryosophistes en Autriche et en Allemagne, 1890–1935*, Puiseaux, Pardès (*The Occult Roots of Nazism: Secret Aryan Cults and Their Influence on Nazi Ideology: The Ariosophists of Austria and Germany, 1890–1935*, London, Aquarian Press, 1985).
Goody, Jack. 1959. "Indo-European Society," *Past and Present*, 16: 88–92.

494 BIBLIOGRAPHY

Gosselain, Olivier Pierre. 2011. "Pourquoi le décorer? Quelques observations sur le décor céramique en Afrique," *Azania: Archaeological Research in Africa*, 46, 1: 3–19.

Gosselain, Olivier Pierre. 2012. "D'une histoire à l'autre. Retour sur une théorie des liens entre langues et techniques en Afrique," *in* Nathan Schlanger and Anne-Christine Taylor (eds.), *La Préhistoire des autres. Perspectives archéologiques et anthropologiques*, Paris, La Découverte: 83–98.

Gossett, Thomas F. 1963. *Race: The History of an Idea in America*, Dallas, Southern Methodist University Press.

Gossiaux, Jean-François. 1997. "Ethnie, ethnologie, ethnicité," *Ethnologie française*, 27, 3: 329–333.

Gould, Stephen Jay. 1981. *The Mismeasure of Man*, Harmondsworth, Penguin Books (French translation: *La Mal-Mesure de l'homme*, Paris, Ramsay, 1983).

Goury, Georges. 1931–1933. *L'Homme des cités lacustres*, Paris, Picard, 2 vols.

Govedarica, Blagoje. 2004. *Zepterträger—Herrscher der Steppen: die frühen Ockergräber des älteren Äneolithikums im karpatenbalkanischen Gebiet und im Steppenraum Südost- und Osteuropas*, Mayence, Von Zabern.

Graeber, David, and Wengrow, David. 2021. *The Dawn of Everything: A New History of Humanity*, New York, Farrar, Straus and Giroux.

Graebner, Fritz Robert. 1911. *Methode der Ethnologie*, Heidelberg, C. Winter, Kulturgeschichtliche Bibliothek.

Gran-Aymerich, Ève. 1998. *Naissance de l'archéologie moderne, 1798–1945*, Paris, CNRS Éditions.

Gray, Russell D., and Atkinson, Quentin D. 2003. "Language-Tree Divergence Times Support the Anatolian Theory of Indo-European Origin," *Nature*, 426 (27 November): 435–439.

Green, Sally. 1981. *Prehistorian: A Biography of V. Gordon Childe*, Bradford-on-Avon, Moonraker Press.

Greenberg, Joseph. 1987. *Language in the Americas*, Stanford, Stanford University Press.

Greenberger, Allen Jay. 1969. *The British Image of India: A Study in the Literature of Imperialism, 1880–1960*, London, Oxford University Press.

Greene, John C. 1961. *The Death of Adam: Evolution and Its Impact on Western Thought*, New York, Mentor (2nd edition Iowa State Press, 1996).

Grimm, Jacob. 1848. *Geschichte der deutschen Sprache*, Leipzig, Weidmann.

Grisward, Joël H. 1981. *Archéologie de l'épopée médiévale. Structures trifonctionnelles et mythes indo-européens dans le cycle des Narbonnais*, Paris, Payot.

Groenen, Marc. 1994. *Pour une histoire de la préhistoire. Le paléolithique*, Grenoble, Jérôme Milloon.

Grolier, Éric de (ed.). 1983. *Glossogenetics: The Origin and Evolution of Language: Proceedings of the I st International Transdisciplinary Symposium on Glossogenetics*, London, Harwood Academic Publishers.

Grottanelli, Cristiano. 1993. *Ideologia miti massacri. Indoeuropei di Georges Dumézil*, Palermo, Sellerio Editore.

Grünert, Heinz. 2002. *Gustaf Kossinna (1858–1931). Vom Germanisten zum Prähistoriker. Ein Wissenschaftler im Kaiserreich und in der Weimarer Republik*, Rahden/Westf., Marie Leidorf, Vorgeschichtliche Forschungen, vol. 22.

Guibert de, Michel, and Souchon, Georges. 1974. *"Morituri": ceux qui doivent mourir: la délivrance par la mort, l'humanisme biologique et le "racisme scientifique,"*

BIBLIOGRAPHY 495

La Celle-Saint-Cloud, Éditions du Groupe d'action et de recherche pour l'avenir de l'homme (GARAH).

Guignes, Joseph de. 1777. "Réflexions sur un libre indien appelé *Bagavadam*, un des dix-huit *Pouranas* ou livres sacrés des Indiens," *Mémoires de littérature tirés des registres de l'Académie royale des inscriptions et belles-lettres*, 38: 312–336.

Guilaine, Jean (ed.). 2007. *Le Chalcolithique et la Construction des inégalités*, t. I, *Le Continent européen*, Arles, Errance.

Guilaine, Jean, and Jean Zammit. 2001. *Le Sentier de la guerre. Visages de la violence préhistorique*, Paris, Seuil.

Guiral Pierre, and Temime, Émile (ed.). 1977. *L'Idée de race dans la pensée politique française contemporaine*, Paris, CNRS Éditions.

Gumperz, John J., and Wilson, Robert. 1971. "Convergence and Creolization. A Case from the Indo-Aryan/Dravidian Border in India," *in* Dell H. Hymes (ed.), *Pidginization and Creolization of Languages*, Cambridge, Cambridge University Press: 151–167.

Güntert, Hermann. 1934. *Der Ursprung der Germanen*, Heidelberg, Kultur und Sprache IX.

Günther, Hans Friedrich Karl. 1933. *Rassenkunde des deutschen Volkes*, Munich, J. F. Lehmann (16th edition).

Günther, Hans Friedrich Karl. 1934. *Die nordische Rasse bei den Indogermanen Asiens. Zugleich ein Beitrag zur Frage nach der Urheimat und Rassenherkunft des Indogermanen*, Munich, J. F. Lehmann.

Haak, Wolfgang et al. 2010. "Die schnurkeramischen Familiengräber von Eulau: ein außergewöhnlicher Fund und seine interdisziplinäre Bewertung," *Tagungen des Landesmuseums für Vorgeschichte Halle*, 4: 80–89.

Haak, Wolfgang et al. 2015. "Massive Migration from the Steppe Is a Source for Indo-European Languages in Europe," *Nature*, 522: 207–211.

Haarmann, Harald. 1994. "Contact Linguistics, Archaeology and Ethnogenetics: An Interdisciplinary Approach to the Indo-European Homeland Problem," *Journal of Indo-European Studies*, 22, 3–4: 265–288.

Hachmann, Rolf. 1970. *Die Goten und Skandinavien*, Berlin, De Gruyter.

Haddon, Alfred C. 1925. *The Races of Man and Their Distribution*, New York, MacMillan & Co (1st ed. London, Milner & Company, 1909; French translation: A. Van Gennep, *Les Races humaines et leur répartition géographique*, Paris, Félix Alcan, 1930).

Haider, Hubert. 1985. "The Fallacy of Typology, Remarks on the Proto-Indo-European Stop System," *Lingua* 65: 1–27.

Hale, Christopher. 2005. *Himmler's Crusade: The Nazi Expedition to Find the Origins of the Aryan Race*, Hoboken (NJ), John Wiley & Sons.

Haley, Joseph Boyd, and Blegen, Carl William. 1928. "The Coming of the Greeks," *American Journal of Archaeology*, 32: 141–154.

Hall, Robert Anderson. 1949. "The Linguistic Position of Franco-Provençal," *Language* 25: 1–14.

Halle, Uta. 2002. *"Die Externsteine sind bis auf weiteres germanisch!" Prähistorische Archäologie im Dritten Reich*, Bielefeld, Verlag für Regionalgeschichte.

Hamp, Eric P. 1990. "The Indo-European Horse," *in* Thomas Markey and John A. C. Greppin (eds.), *When Words Collide: The Indo-Europeans and the Pre-Indo-Europeans*, Ann Arbor, Karoma Publishers: 211–225.

496 BIBLIOGRAPHY

Hancock, Ian. 1971. "A Survey of the Pidgins and Creoles of the World," *in* Dell H. Hymes (ed.), *Pidginization and Creolization of Languages*, Cambridge, Cambridge University Press: 509–523.

Hänsel, Bernhardt, and Zimmer, Stefan (eds.). 1994. *Die Indogermanen und das Pferd, Festschrift B. Schlerath*, Budapest, Archaeolingua.

Hansen, Sven. "Once Again: Farewell to the Indo-Europeans," *in* S. Hansen, V. I. Molodin, and L. N. Mylnikova (eds.), *Mobility and Migration: Concepts, Methods, Results*, Novosibirsk, IAET SB RAS Publishing: 44–60.

Harrison, Richard, and Heyd, Volker. 2007. "The Transformation of Europe in the Third Millennium BC: the example of 'Le Petit-Chasseur I + III' (Sion, Valais, Switzerland)," *Prähistorische Zeitschrift*, 82: 129–2014.

Harvey, Joy. 1983. *Races Specified, Evolution Transformed: The Social Context of Scientific Debates Originating in the Société d'anthropologie de Paris, 1859–1902*, PhD dissertation, Harvard University, Cambridge Press.

Harvey, Joy. 1984. "L'évolution transformée: positivistes et matérialistes dans la Société d'anthropologie de Paris du Second Empire à la IIIe République," *in* Britta Rupp-Eisenreich (ed.), *Histoires de l'anthropologie (XVIe-XIXe siècle)*, Paris, Klincksieck: 387–410.

Hassmann, Henning. 2000. "Archaeology in the "Third Reich," *in* Heinrich Härke (ed.), *Archaeology, Ideology and Society. The German Experience*, Frankfurt, Peter Lang: 65–139.

Haudricourt, André-Georges. 1972. *Problèmes de phonologie diachronique*, Paris, SELAF.

Haudry, Jean. 1979. *L'Indo-Européen*, Paris, PUF, coll. "Que sais-je?."

Haudry, Jean. 1981. *Les Indo-Européens*, Paris, PUF, coll. "Que sais-je?."

Haudry, Jean. 1987. *La Religion cosmique des Indo-Européens*, Milan/Paris, Archè-Les Belles Lettres.

Haudry, Jean. 1997. "L'habitat originel des Indo-Européens au regard de la linguistique; les Indo-Européens et le Grand Nord; Chronologie de la tradition indo-européenne; Indo-européen et 'mentalité indo-européenne'," *Nouvelle École*, 49: 109–142.

Haudry, Jean. 2010. *Les Indo-Européens*, Forcalquier, Éditions de la Forêt (augmented re-edition of the 1981 work).

Häusler, Alexander. 1994. "Archäologische Zeugnisse für Pferd und Wagen in Ost- und Mitteleuropa," *in* Bernhardt Hänsel and Stefan Zimmer (eds.), *Die Indogermanen und das Pferd, Festschrift B. Schlerath*, Budapest, Archaeolingua: 217–258.

Häusler, Alexander. 1998. "Zum Ursprung der Indogermanen. Archäologische, anthropologische und sprachwissenschaftliche Gesichtspunkte," *Ethnographisch-Archäologische Zeitschrift*, 39: 1–46.

Häusler, Alexander. 2002a. "Ursprung und Ausbreitung der Indogermanen. Alternative Erklärungsmodelle," *Indogermanische Forschungen*, 107: 47–75.

Häusler, Alexander. 2002b. *Nomaden, Indogermanen, Invasionen. Zur Entstehung eines Mythos*, Halle-Wittenberg, Orientwissenschaftliches Zentrum der Martin-Luther-Universität, Orientwissenschaftliche Hefte, 5.

Hearnshaw, Leslie Spenser. 1979. *Cyril Burt, Psychologist*, London, Hodder & Stoughton.

Heggarty, Paul. 2000. "Quantifying Change over Time in Phonetics," *in* Colin Renfrew, April McMahon, and Larry R. Trask (eds.), *Time-Depth in Historical Linguistics*, Cambridge, McDonald Institute for Archaeological Research: 531–562.

BIBLIOGRAPHY 497

Heggarty, Paul. 2006. "Interdiscipline Indiscipline," *in* Peter Forster and Colin Renfrew (eds.), *Phylogenetic Methods and the Prehistory of Languages*, Cambridge, McDonald Institute for Archaeological Research (McDonald Institute Monographs): 183–194.

Heggarty, Paul, Maguire, Warren, and McMahon, April. 2010. "Splits or Waves? Trees or Webs? How Divergence Measures and Network Analysis Can Unravel Language Histories," *Philosophical Transactions of the Royal Society (Biological Sciences)*, 365, 1559: 3829–3843.

Hehn, Victor. 1870. *Kulturpflanzen und Haustiere in ihrem Übergang aus Asien nach Griechenland und Italien sowie in das übrige Europa: historisch-linguistische Skizzen*, Berlin, Borntraeger.

Hehn, Victor. 1873. *Das Salz: Eine kulturhistorische Studie*, Berlin, Borntraeger.

Hemmerdinger, Bertrand. 1971. "La théorie irano-germanique de Juste Lipse (1598)," *Indogermanische Forschungen*, 76: 20–21.

Hemphill, B. E., Christensen, A. F., and Mustafakulov, S. I. 1997. "Trade or Travel: An Assessment of Interpopulational Dynamics Among Bronze Age Indo-Iranian Populations," *in* Bridget Allchin and Raymond Allchin (eds.), *South Asian Archaeology 1995*, New Delhi, Oxford-IBH Publishing, vol. 2: 855–871.

Henry, Clarissa, and Hillel, Marc. 1975. *Children of the SS*, London, Hutchinson.

Hermann, Joachim. 1981. "Heinrich Schliemann and Rudolf Virchow," *in* Glyn Edmund Daniel (ed.), *Towards a History of Archaeology*, London, Thames & Hudson: 127–132.

Herrnstein, Richard J., and Murray, Charles A. 1994. *The Bell Curve: Intelligence and Class Structure in American Life*, New York, Free Press.

Hester, David A. 1965. " 'Pelasgian': A New Indo-European Language?," *Lingua*, 13: 335–384.

Heyd, Volker. 2021. "Yamnaya, Corded Wares, and Bell Beakers on the Move," *in* V. Heyd, G. Kulcsár, and B. Preda-Bălănică (eds.), *Yamnaya Interactions*, Budapest, Archaeolingua: 383–414.

Heyer, Évelyne. 2020. *L'Odyssée des gènes*, Flammarion, Paris.

Hiebert, Fredrik Talmage. 1994. *Origins of the Bronze Age Civilization in Central Asia*, Cambridge, Peabody Museum, American School of Prehistoric Research, 42.

Hiebert, Fredrik Talmage, and Mair, Victor H. 1998. "Central Asia and the Iranian Plateau: A Model for Indo-European Expansionism," *in* Victor Mair (ed.), *The Bronze Age and Early Iron Age Peoples of Eastern Asia*, Washington, DC, Institute for the Study of Man: 148–161.

Hirt, Hermann. 1892. "Die Urheimat der Indogermanen," *Indogermanische Forschungen*, I: 464–485 (republished in Anton Scherer [ed.], *Die Urheimat der Indogermanen*, Darmstadt, Wissenschaftliche Buchgesellschaft, 1968: 1–24).

Hirt, Hermann. 1905–1907. *Die Indogermanen; ihre Verbreitung, ihre Urheimat und ihre Kultur*, Strasbourg, K. J. Trübner, 2 vols.

Hitler, Adolf. 1925–1926. *Mein Kampf*, Munich, Franz Eher Nachfolger, 2 vols. (re-edition Zentralverlag der NSDAP, Munich, Franz Verlag Nachfolger, 1940).

Hjelmslev, Louis. 1951. *Commentaires sur la vie et l'œuvre de Rasmus Rask*, Paris, Institut de linguistique de l'université de Paris-X, vol. 10: 143–157 (reproduced in *Essais linguistiques*, Copenhagen, Nordisk Sprogog Kulturforlag, 1973, II: 3–16).

Hobsbawm, Eric. 1990. *Nations and Nationalism since 1780: Programme, Myth, Reality*, Cambridge, Cambridge University Press (French translation: *Nations et Nationalismes depuis 1780. Programme, mythe et réalité*, Paris, Gallimard, 1992).

498 BIBLIOGRAPHY

Hobsbawm, Eric, and Ranger, Terence (eds.). 1983. *The Invention of Tradition*, Cambridge, Cambridge University Press (French translation: *L'Invention de la tradition*, Paris, Éditions Amsterdam, 2006).

Hodge, Carleton Taylor. 1981. "Indo-Europeans in the Near East," *Anthropological Linguistics*, 23: 227–244.

Hofmann, Daniela, 2019. "Commentary. Archaeology, Archaeogenetics and Theory Challenges and Convergences," *Current Swedish Archaeology*, 27: 133–140.

Hoernes, Moritz, and Menghin, Oswald. 1925. *Urgeschichte der bildenden Kunst in Europa von den Anfängen bis um 500 vor Christi*, Vienna, A. Schroll & Co., 3rd ed.

Holm, Hans J. 2008. "The Distribution of Data in Word Lists and its Impact on the Subgrouping of Languages," *in* Christine Preisach, Hans Burkhardt, Lars Schmidt-Thieme, and Reinhold Decker (eds.), *Data Analysis, Machine Learning, and Applications*, Heidelberg-Berlin, Springer-Verlag: 629–636.

Hombert, Jean-Marie (ed.). 2005. *Aux origines des langues et du langage*, Fayard, Paris.

Hommel, Fritz. 1879. *Die Namen der Säugethiere bei den südsemitischen Völkern als Beiträge zur arabischen und äthiopischen Lexicographie, zur semitischen Kulturforschung und Sprachvergleichung und zur Geschichte der Mittelmeerfauna*, Leipzig, J. C. Hinrichs.

Hopper, Paul J. 1973. "Glottalized and Murmured Occlusives in Indo-European," *Glossa*, 7: 141–166.

Hovelacque, Abel. 1873. *Langues, Races, Nationalités*, Paris, Ernest Leroux.

Hovelacque, Abel. 1878. "L'œuvre linguistique de Chavée," *Bulletin de linguistique et de philologie comparée*, 11, 2: 105–118.

Humboldt, Wilhelm von. 1974. *Introduction à l'œuvre sur le kavi et autres essais*, translated by Pierre Caussat, Paris, Seuil (*Über die Verschiedenheit des menschlichen Sprachbaus und seinen Einfluss auf die geistige Entwicklung des Menschengeschlechts*, Berlin, Königliche Akademie des Wissenschaften, in Commission bei Dämmler, 1836).

Humboldt, Wilhelm von. 2000. *Sur le caractère national des langues*, Paris, Seuil.

Hurel, Arnaud. 2007. *La France préhistorienne de 1789 à 1941*, Paris, CNRS Éditions.

Hurel, Arnaud, and Coye, Noël. 2011. *Dans l'épaisseur du temps: Archéologues et géologues inventent la préhistoire*, Paris, Muséum national d'histoire naturelle.

Hüttel, Hans-Georg. 1994. "Zur archäologischen Evidenz der Pferdenutzung in der Kupfer- und Bronzezeit," *in* Bernhardt Hänsel and Stefan Zimmer (eds.), *Die Indogermanen und das Pferd, Festschrift B. Schlerath*, Budapest, Archaeolingua: 197–216.

Huxley, Julian, Haddon, Alfred C., and Carr-Saunders, A. M. 1935. *We Europeans: A Survey of "Racial" Problems*, London, Jonathan Cape.

Hymes, Dell H. 1960. "Lexicostatistics So Far," *Current Anthropology*, 1, 1: 3–44.

Hymes, Dell H. (ed.). 1971. *Pidginization and Creolization of Languages*, Cambridge, Cambridge University Press.

Idel, Moshe. 2014. *Mircea Eliade from Magic to Myth*, New York, Peter Lang.

Illič-Svityč, Vladislav Markovich. 1971–1984. *Opyt sravnenija nostraticeskih jazykov (semitoxamitskij, kartvel'skij, indoevropejskij, ural'skij, dravidijskij, altajskij). Sravnitel'nyj slovar'*, Moscow, Nauka, 3 vols.

Jackson, Kenneth Hurlstone. 1955. "The Pictish Language," *in* Frederick Threlfall Wainwright (ed.), *The Problem of the Picts*, Edinburgh, Nelson: 129–166.

Jahn, Martin. 1941. "Die deutsche Vorgeschichtsforschung in einer Sackgasse?" *Nachrichtenblatt für deutsche Vorzeit*, 17, 3–4: 73–82.

Jakobson, Roman. 1938. "Sur la théorie des affinités phonologiques entre les langues," *in* *Actes du quatrième Congrès international de linguistes tenu à Copenhague du 27 août*

BIBLIOGRAPHY   499

au 1er septembre 1936: 48–58, Copenhagen, Einar Munksgaard (republished with modifications in Nikolaï Troubetzkoy, *Principes de phonologie*, Paris, Klincksieck, 1949: 351–365).

Jakobson, Roman. 1952. *Studies in Comparative Slavic Metrics*, Oxford, Oxford Slavonic Papers, 3.

Jakobson, Roman. 1958. "Typological Studies and Their Contribution to Historical Comparative Linguistics," *in* Eva Sivertsen (ed.), *Proceedings of the Eighth International Congress of Linguists*, Oslo, Oslo University Press: 17–35.

Jang Fan et al. 2021. "The Genomic Origins of the Bronze Age Tarim Basin Mummies," *Nature*, 599 (7884): 256–261.

Jardin, André. 1977. "Alexis de Tocqueville, Gustave de Beaumont et le problème de l'inégalité des races," *in* Pierre Guiral and Émile Temime (eds.), *L'Idée de race dans la pensée politique française contemporaine*, Paris, CNRS Éditions: 200–219.

Jarrige, Jean-François. 1973. "La fin de la civilisation harappéenne," *Paléorient*, 1, 2: 263–287.

Jarrige, Jean-François. 1988. *Les Cités oubliées de l'Indus: archéologie du Pakistan: [exposition]*, Musée national des arts asiatiques-Guimet, November 1988–January 1989, Paris, Association française d'action artistique.

Jarrige, Jean-François. 1995. "Du néolithique à la civilisation de l'Inde ancienne: contribution des recherches archéologiques dans le nord-ouest du sous-continent indo-pakistanais," *Arts asiatiques*, 50, 1: 5–30.

Joachimsen, Paul Fritz. 1951. *Die Reformation als Epoche der deutschen Geschichte*, Munich, R. Oldenburg.

Jochnowitz, George. 1973. *Dialect Boundaries and the Question of Franco-Provençal*, La Haye, Mouton.

Johnson, Mats. 1999. "Chronology of Greece and South-East Europe in the Final Neolithic and Early Bronze Age," *Proceedings of the Prehistoric Society*, 65: 319–336.

Jones, Siân. 1997. *The Archaeology of Ethnicity: Constructing Identities in the Past and Present*, London, Routledge.

Jones, Sir William. 1799. *The Works of Sir William Jones in Six Volumes*, London, Robinson and Evans, vol. 1.

Jones, Sir William. 1807a. "The Third Anniversary Discourse: On the Hindus," *in* Lord Teignmouth (ed.), *The Works of Sir William Jones, with the Life of the Author*, London, John Stockdale, vol. 13.

Jones, Sir William. 1807b. "The Ninth Anniversary Discourse: On the Origin and Families of Nations," *in* Lord Teignmouth (ed.), *The Works of Sir William Jones, with the Life of the Author*, London, John Stockdale, vol. 3: 185–204.

Jordan, Peter, and Zvelebil, Marek. 2011. *Ceramics Before Farming: The Dispersal of Pottery among Prehistoric Eurasian Hunter-Gatherers*, Walnut Creek, Left Coast Press Inc.

Joseph, Brian D. 1983. *The Synchrony and Diachrony of the Balkan Infinitive: A Study in Areal, General, and Historical Linguistics*, Cambridge, Cambridge University Press.

Jouanna, Arlette. 1976. *L'Idée de race en France au xvie siècle et au début du xviie siècle (1498–1614)*, Lille, Atelier de reproduction des thèses (diffusion Champion), 3 vols.

Jouty, Sylvain. 1991. "À la recherche du paradis terrestre," *L'Histoire*, 149: 90–97.

Jucquois, Guy, and Vielle, Christophe. 1997. "Illusion, limites et perspectives du comparatisme indo-européen. Pour en finir avec le mythe scientifique des proto-langues/-peuples," *in Festschrift for Eric P. Hamp*, vol. 1, Washington, DC, *Journal of Indo-European Studies*, Monograph, 23: 162–184.

500 BIBLIOGRAPHY

Junginger, Horst (ed.). 2008. *The Study of Religion under the Impact of Fascism*, Leyde, Brill.

Justi, Ferdinand. 1862. "Über die Urzeit der Indogermanen," *in* Friedrich von Raumer (ed.), *Historisches Taschenbuch*, Leipzig, F. A. Brockhaus: 301–342.

Justus, Carol F. 1992. "The Impact of non-Indo-European Languages on Anatolian," *in Reconstructing Languages and Cultures*, Edgar C. Polomé and Werner Winter (eds.), Berlin/New York, Mouton de Gruyter: 443–467.

Kaiser, Elke. 2011. "Wurde das Rad zweimal erfunden? Zu den frühen Wagen in der eurasischen Steppe," *Prähistorische Zeitschrift*, 85, 2: 137–157.

Kaiser, Mark, and Shevoroshkin, Vitaly Victorovich. 1988. "Nostratic," *Annual Review of Anthropology*, 17, 1: 309–329.

Kater, Michael H. 1974. *Das "Ahnenerbe" der SS 1935–1945: ein Beitrag zur Kulturpolitik des Dritten Reiches*, Stuttgart, DVA.

Katz, Dovid (ed.). 1987. *Origins of the Yiddish Language: Papers from the First Annual Oxford Winter Symposium in Yiddish Language and Literature*, Oxford, Pergamon Press.

Kaul, Flemming. 1998. *Ships on Bronzes: A Study in Bronze Age Religion and Iconography*, Copenhagen, Publications from the National Museum Studies in Archaeology and History, vol. 3, 1–2.

Kaul, Friedrich Karl. 1968. "Das 'Ahnenerbe' und die 'jüdische Schädelsammlung' an der ehemaligen 'Reichsuniversität Strassburg,'" *Zeitschrift für Geschichtswissenschaft*, 11: 1460–1474.

Kaupen-Haas, Heidrun, and Saller, Christian (ed.). 1999. *Wissenschaftlicher Rassismus: Analysen einer Kontinuität in den Human- und Naturwissenschaften*, Frankfurt-sur-le-Main/New York, Campus Verlag.

Kazanas, Nicholas. 2009. "Indo-European Linguistics and Indo-Aryan Indigenism," *in* Angela Marcantonio (ed.), *The Indo-European Language Family: Questions about Its Status*, Washington, DC, Institute for the Study of Man, 9: 1–60.

Keith, Arthur Berriedale. 1938. "The Relation of Hittite, Tocharian and Indo-European," *Indian Historical Quaterly*, 14: 201–233.

Kellens, Jean. 2005. "Les Airiia- ne sont plus des Aryas: ce sont déjà des Iraniens," *in* Jean Kellens, Henri-Paul Frankfurt, Gérard Fussman, and Xavier Tremblay (eds.), *Aryens et Iraniens en Asie centrale*, Paris, Collège de France, Publications de l'Institut de civilisation indienne, 72: 233–252.

Keyser, C., Bouakaze, C., Crubézy, E., Nikolaev, V. G., Montagnon, D., Reis, T., and Ludes, B. 2009. "Ancient DNA Provides New Insights into the History of South Siberian Kurgan People," *Human Genetics*, 126 (3): 395–410.

Khomyakov, Aleksěj Stepanovič, and Hilferding, Alexander Fedorovič. 1873. *Zapiski o vsemirnoj istorii*, Moscow, Tipografija Lebedeva, t. II.

King, Robert D. 1992. "Migration and Linguistics as Illustrated by Yiddish," *in* Edgar C. Polomé and Werner Winter (eds.), *Reconstructing Languages and Cultures*, Berlin, Mouton de Gruyter: 419–438.

Kivikoski, Ella. 1954. "A. M. Tallgren," *Eurasia Septentrionalis Antiqua*, Supplementary volume: 77–121.

Klaproth, Julius von. 1830. "Réponse à quelques passages de la préface du roman chinois intitulé "Hao khieou tchouan," *Journal asiatique*, 4, 99–122.

Klee, Ernst. 2005. *Das Personenlexikon zum Dritten Reich: wer war was vor und nach 1945?*, Frankfurt-sur-le-Main, Fischer-Taschenbuch-Verlag.

Klein, Jared, Joseph, Brian, and Fritz, Matthias (eds.). 2017–2018. *Handbook of Comparative and Historical Indo-European Linguistics*, Berlin/Boston, De Gruyter Mouton, 3 vols.

BIBLIOGRAPHY 501

Klejn, Lev S. 1971. "Was ist eine archäologische Kultur?," *Ethnographisch-Archäologische Zeitschrift*, 12: 321–345.

Klejn, Lev S. 1974. "Kossinna im Abstand von vierzig Jahren," *Jahresschrift Mitteldeutschen Vorgeschichte*, 58: 7–55.

Klejn, Lev S. 1999. "Gustaf Kossinna, 1858–1931," *in* Tim Murray (ed.), *Encyclopedia of Archaeology: The Great Archaeologists*, Santa Barbara, ABC-CLIO, vol. 1: 233–246.

Kline, Wendy. 2001. *Building a Better Race Gender, Sexuality, and Eugenics from the Turn of the Century to the Baby Boom*, Berkeley, University of California Press.

Koerner, Ernst Frideryk Konrad. 1973. *Ferdinand de Saussure: Origin and Development of his Linguistic Thought in Western Studies of Language: A Contribution to the History and Theory of Linguistics*, Braunschweig, Vieweg.

Koerner, Ernst Frideryk Konrad. 1982. "Observations on the Sources, Transmission, and Meaning of "Indo-European" and Related Terms in the Development of Linguistics," *in* J. P. Maher, A. R. Bomhard, and E. F. K. Koerner (eds.), *Papers from the 3rd International of Historical Linguistics*, Amsterdam, Benjamins: 153–180.

Koerner, Ernst Frideryk Konrad. 1987. "The Importance of Saussure's "Mémoire" in the Development of Historical Linguistic," *in* George Cardona and Norman H. Zide (eds.), *Festschrift for Henry Hoenigswald: On the Occasion of his Seventieth Birthday*, Tübingen, Günter Narr: 201–217.

Kohl, Philip. 2007. *The Making of Bronze Age Eurasia*, Cambridge, Cambridge University Press.

Kohl, Philip, and Perez Gollan, Jose Antonio. 2002. "Religion, Politics, and Prehistory, Reassessing the Lingering Legacy of Oswald Menghin," *Current Anthropology*, 43, 5: 61–586.

Kollmann, Julius. 1882. "Menschenrassen Europas und die Frage nach der Herkunft der Arier," *Correspondenzblatt für Anthropologie, Ethnologie und Urgeschichte*, 23: 102–106.

Kollmann, Julius. 1892. "Les races humaines de l'Europe et la question arienne," *in Congrès international d'archéologie préhistorique et d'anthropologie*, Moscow, 11th session, 1: 249–262.

Koppers, Wilhelm. 1929. "Die Religion der Indogermanen in ihren kulturhistorischen Beziehungen," *Anthropos*, 24: 1073–1089.

Koppers, Wilhelm. 1935. "Die Indogermanenfrage im Lichte der historischen Völkerkunde," *Anthropos*, 30: 1–31.

Koppers, Wilhelm. 1936. *Die Indogermanen- und Germanenfrage. Neue Wege zu ihrer Lösung*, Salzbourg-Leipzig, Anton Pustet, Wiener Beiträge zur Kulturgeschichte und Linguistik, Jahrgang IV.

Kossinna, Gustaf. 1896. "Die vorgeschichtliche Ausbreitung der Germanen in Deutschland," *Zeitschrift des Vereins für Volkskunde*, 6: 1–14.

Kossinna, Gustaf. 1902. "Die indogermanische Frage archäologisch beantwortet," in *Zeitschrift für Ethnologie*, 34: 161–222 (republished in Anton Scherer ed., *Die Urheimat der Indogermanen*, Darmstadt, Wissenschaftliche Buchgesellschaft, 1968: 25–109).

Kossinna, Gustaf. 1911. *Die Herkunft der Germanen: zur Methode der Siedlungsarchäologie*, Leipzig, Kabitzsch.

Kossinna, Gustaf. 1912. *Die deutsche Vorgeschichte, eine hervorragend nationale Wissenschaft*, Würzburg, Mannus Bibliothek 9.

Kossinna, Gustaf. 1921. *Die Indogermanen: Ein Abriss*, t. I: *Das indogermanische Urvolk*, Leipzig, Kabitsch.

502 BIBLIOGRAPHY

Kossinna, Gustaf. 1926. *Ursprung und Verbreitung der Germanen in vor- und frühgeschichtlicher Zeit*, Würzburg, Mannus-Bibliothek 6.

Kouwenberg, Silvia, and Singler, John (eds.). 2008. *The Handbook of Creole Linguistics*, Oxford, Basil Blackwell.

Kozłowski, Leon. 1924. *Młodsza epoka kamienna w Polsce*, Lvov, Towarzystwa Naukowego II, 2.

Krabbe, Wolgang R. 1974. *Gesellschaftsveranderung durch Lebensreform: Strukturmerkmale einer sozialreformerischen Bewegung im Deutschland der Industrialisierungsperiode*, Göttingen, Vandenhoeck und Ruprecht.

Krahe, Hans. 1954. *Sprache und Vorzeit: europäische Vorgeschichte nach dem Zeugnis der Sprache*, Heidelberg, Quelle & Mayer.

Krahe, Hans. 1957. "Indogermanisch und Alteuropäisch," *Saeculum*, 8, no 1: 1–16.

Krall, Katharina. 2005. *Prähistorie im Nationalsozialismus: ein Vergleich der Schriften von Herbert Jankuhn und Hans Reinerth zwischen 1933 und 1939*, Mémoire de master, Université de Constance, département d'histoire et sociologie.

Kriševskij, Yevgeni. 1933. "Indogermanskij vopros arkheologičeski razrasonnyi," *in* S. N. Bykovski et al. (eds.), *Iz istorii dokapitalističeskih formacii*, Leningrad-Moscow, Izvestija Gos, Akademija Istorii Materialnoj Kultury, 100: 158–202.

Kristiansen, Kristian. 2009. "Premières aristocraties—Pouvoir et métal à l'âge du bronze," *in* Jean-Paul Demoule (ed.), *L'Europe, un continent redécouvert par l'archéologie*, Paris, Gallimard: 73–84.

Kristiansen, Kristian et al. 2017. "Re-Theorizing Mobility and the Formation of Culture and Language Among the Corded Ware Cultures in Europe," *Antiquity*, 91, 356: 334–347.

Kristiansen, Kristian, and Larsson, Thomas B. 2005. *The Rise of Bronze Age Society: Travels, Transmissions and Transformations*, Cambridge, Cambridge University Press.

Kroeber, Alfred Louis. 1960. "Statistics, Indo-European, and Taxonomy," *Language*, 36, 1: 1–21.

Kroeber, Alfred Louis, and Chrétien, Douglas. 1937. "Quantitative Classification of Indo-European Languages," *Language*, 13, 2: 83–103.

Kühl, Stefan. 1994. *The Nazi Connection: Eugenics, American Racism, and German National Socialism*, New York, Oxford University Press.

Kuhn, Adalbert. 1845. *Zur ältesten Geschichte der indogermanischen Völker*, Berlin, Nauck.

Kühn, Herbert. 1932. "Herkunft und Heimat der Indogermanen," *in Proceedings of the 1st International Congress of Prehistoric and Protohistoric Sciences (London)*, London, Oxford University Press: 237–242 (republished in Anton Scherer [ed.], *Die Urheimat der Indogermanen*, Darmstadt, Wissenschaftliche Buchgesellschaft, 1968: 110–116).

Kumar, G. D. 1973. "The Ethnic Components of the Builders of the Indus Valley Civilization and the Advent of the Aryans," *Journal of Indo-European Studies*, 1, 1: 66–80.

Kümmel, Werner. 1968. "Rudolf Virchow und der Antisemitismus," *Medizin-Historisches Journal*, 3: 165–179.

Kuz'mina, Elena E. 2007. *The Origin of the Indo-Iranians*, Leyde, Brill.

Lafont, Max. 1993. *L'Extermination douce. La mort de 40 000 malades mentaux dans les hôpitaux psychiatriques en France, sous le régime de Vichy*, Ligné, Éditions de l'AREFPPI.

Laignel-Lavastine, Alexandra. 2002. *Cioran, Eliade, Ionesco. L'oubli du fascisme: trois intellectuels roumains dans la tourmente du siècle*, Paris, PUF.

BIBLIOGRAPHY 503

Laks, Bernard, Demoule, Jean-Paul, Encrevé, Pierre, and Cleuziou, Serge (eds.). 2008. *The Origin and Evolution of Languages: Approaches, Models, Paradigm*, London, Equinox.

Lambert, Pierre-Yves. 2002. *La Langue gauloise. Description linguistique, commentaire d'inscriptions choisies*, Paris, Errance.

Lamberterie, Charles de. 1978. "Armeniaca I-VIII: études lexicales," *Bulletin de la Société de linguistique de Paris*, 73, 1: 243–285.

Laming-Emperaire, Annette. 1964. *Origines de l'archéologie préhistorique en France. Des superstitions médiévales à la découverte de l'homme fossile*, Paris, Picard.

Lang, Hans-Joachim. 2004. *Die Namen der Nummern*, Hoffmann.

Lanz-Liebenfels, Jörg. 1905. *Theozoologie oder die Kunde von den Sodoms-Äfflingen und dem Götter-Elektron: eine Einführung in die älteste und neueste Weltanschauung und eine Rechtfertigung des Fürstentums und des Adels*, Vienna, Moderner Verlag.

Lanz-Liebenfels, Jörg. 1918. *Die Blonden als Schöpfer der Sprachen, ein Abriß der Ursprachenforschung (Protolinguistik)*, Vienna, Mödling, Ostara, Bücherei der Blonden 52.

Larbiou, Benoît. 2005. "René Martial, 1873–1955. De l'hygiénisme à la raciologie, une trajectoire possible," *Genèses*, 60, 3: 98–120.

Laruelle, Marlène. 1999. *L'Idéologie eurasiste russe, ou Comment penser l'Empire*, Paris, L'Harmattan.

Laruelle, Marlène. 2010. "Le berceau aryen: mythologie et idéologie au service de la colonisation du Turkestan," *Cahiers d'Asie centrale*, 17–18: 107–131.

Laruelle, Marlène, and Taguieff, Pierre-André. 2005. *Mythe aryen et Rêve impérial dans la Russie du XIXe siècle*, Paris, CNRS Éditions.

Lassen, Christian. 1847. *Indische Altertumskunde*, Bonn, König, 4 vols. (2nd ed. 1867–1874).

Latham, Robert Gordon. 1862. *Elements of Comparative Philology*, London, Walton and Maberly.

Layeghifard, Medhi, R. Peres-Neto, Pedro, and Makarenkov, Vladimir. 2013. "Inferring Explicit Weighted Consensus Networks to Represent Alternative Evolutionary Histories," *BMC Evolutionary Biology*, 13: 274.

Lazaridis, Iosif et al. 2017. "Genetic Origins of the Minoans and Mycenaeans," *Nature*, 548: 214–220.

Lebedynsky, Iaroslav. 2006. *Les Indo-Européens. Faits, débats, solutions*, Paris, Errance.

Le Bras, Hervé. 1997. "Compte-rendu de: Benoist de (Alain), Famille et Société," *Origines, Histoire, Actualité, Population*, 52, 1: 245–249.

Leclainche, Emmanuel. 1937. "Séance publique annuelle du lundi 20 décembre 1937," *Comptes-rendus de l'Académie des sciences*, 205, 25: 1269–1282.

Le Dû, Jean. 2003. "Compte-rendu de: Mario Alinei, Origini delle lingue d'Europa," *Études celtiques*, 35: 351–358.

Lehmann, Winfred Philipp. 1996. *Theoretical Bases of Indo-European Linguistics*, London, Routledge.

Lehmann, Winfred Philipp, and Zgusta, Ladislav. 1979. "Schleicher's Tale After a Century," in Bela Brogyanyi (ed.), *Studies in Diachronic, Synchronic, and Typological Linguistics, Festschrift for Oswald Szemerényi on the Occasion of His 65th Birthday*, Amsterdam, Benjamins: 455–466.

Leibniz, Gottfried Wilhelm. 1838 [1679]. "Unvorgreifliche Gedanken betreffend die Ausübung und Verbesserung der Teutschen Sprache," in Gottschalk Eduard Guhrauer (ed.), *Deutsche Schriften*, Berlin, vol. 1: 440–486.

504 BIBLIOGRAPHY

Leibniz, Gottfried Wilhelm. 1993. *Nouveaux Essais sur l'entendement humain*, Flammarion, Paris (1st ed. 1765).

Leopold, Jean. 1970. "The Aryan Theory of Race in India, 1870–1920, Nationalist and Internationalist Visions," *Indian Economic and Social Review*, 2: 271–297.

Le Page, Robert Broch, and Tabouret-Keller, Andrée. 1985. *Acts of Identity: Creole-Based Approaches to Language and Ethnicity*, Cambridge, Cambridge University Press.

Le Quellec, Jean-Loïc. 2021. *Avant nous, le Déluge—L'humanité et ses mythes*, Paris, Éditions du Détour. Leroy, Maurice. 1963. *Les Grands Courants de la linguistique moderne*, Paris, PUF (2nd ed. 1971).

Lester, Paul, and Millot, Jacques. 1939. *Les Races humaines*, Paris, Armand Colin (2nd ed.).

Lévêque, Pierre. 1988. *Colère, sexe, rire: le Japon des mythes anciens*, Paris, Les Belles Lettres.

Lévi-Strauss, Claude. 1967. *Mythologiques*, ii: *Du miel aux cendres*, Paris, Plon.

Levin, Saul. 1988. "The Misnomer Indo-European Dialects," *General Linguistics*, 28, 3: 159–162.

Levine, Marsha A. 1990. "Dereivka and the Problem of Horse Domestication," *Antiquity*, 64: 727–740.

Levine, Marsha A. 2005. "Domestication and Early History of the Horse," *in* Daniel Mills and Sue McDonnell (eds.), *The Domestic Horse: The Evolution, Development and Management of its Behaviour*, Cambridge, Cambridge University Press: 5–22.

Ley, Willy. 1947. "Pseudoscience in Naziland," *Astounding Science Fiction*, 39: 90–98.

L'Hermitte, René (ed.). 1969. "La linguistique en URSS; choix, présentation et traduction de textes," *Langage*, 15: 1–133.

Liauzu, Claude. 1992. *Race et Civilisation. L'autre dans la culture occidentale: anthologie historique*, Paris, Syros.

Liauzu, Claude. 1999. "L'obsession des origines, démographie et histoire des migrations," *Mots*, 60, 1: 155–165.

Liberman, Anatoly. 1980. "Review of R. Jakobson (ed.), N. S. Trubetzkoy's Letters and Notes," *Linguistics*, 18: 543–546.

Librado, Pablo et al. 2021. "The Origins and Spread of Domestic Horses from the Western Eurasian Steppes," *Nature*, 598: 634–652.

Lichardus, Jan (ed.). 1988. "Der Westpontische Raum und die Anfänge der kupferzeitlichen Zivilisation," *in* Alexander Fol and Jan Lichardus (eds.), *Macht, Herrschaft und Gold*, Sarrebruck, Moderne Galerie des Saarland-Museums: 79–130.

Lichardus, Jan. 1991. *Die Kupferzeit als historische Epoche*, Bonn, Habelt, Saarbrücker Beiträge zur Altertumskunde, 2 vols.

Lichardus, Jan, and Lichardus-Itten, Marion. 1998. "Nordpontische Gruppen und ihre westlichen Nachbarn, Ein Beitrag zur Entstehung der frühen Kupferzeit Alteuropas," *in* Bernhardt Hänsel and Jan Machnik (eds.), *Das Karpatenbecken und die osteuropäische Steppe*, Munich-Rahden, Verlag Marie Leidorf: 99–122.

Lichardus, Jan, Lichardus-Itten, Marion, Bailloud, Gérard, and Cauvin, Jacques. 1985. *Protohistoire de l'Europe. Le néolithique et le Chalcolithique*, Paris, PUF.

Lichardus, Jan, and Vladàr, J. 1996. "Karpatenbecken—Sintašta—Mykene. Ein Beitrag zur Definition der Bronzezeit als historischer Epoche," *Slovenská Archeológia*, 44–1: 25–93.

Lichardus-Itten, Marion, and Demoule, Jean-Paul. 1997. "Cerny et le chalcolithique européen," *in* Claude Constantin, Daniel Mordant, and Daniel Simonin (eds.), *La Culture de Cerny, nouvelle économie, nouvelle société au néolithique*, Nemours, Mémoires du Musée de préhistoire d'Île-de-France: 689–700.

BIBLIOGRAPHY   505

Lilienthal, Georg. 2003. *Der "Lebensborn e.V": ein Instrument nationalsozialistischer Rassenpolitik*, Stuttgart, Fischer.

Lincoln, Bruce. 1981. *Priests, Warriors, and Cattle: A Study in the Ecology of Religions*, Berkeley, University of California Press.

Lincoln, Bruce. 1986. *Myth, Cosmos, and Society: Indo-European Themes of Creation and Destruction*, Cambridge, Harvard University Press.

Lincoln, Bruce. 1990. "Mito e storia nello studio del mito: un testo oscuro di Georges Dumézil," *Quaderni di storia*, 16, 32: 5–30.

Lincoln, Bruce. 2000. *Theorizing Myth: Narrative, Ideology and Scholarship*, Chicago, University of Chicago Press.

Lindenschmit, Ludwig. 1880. "Einleitung," in *Handbuch der deutschen Alterthumerskunde*, vol. 1, Braunschweig, F. Vieweg und Sohn.

Lindstedt, Jouko. 2000. "Linguistic Balkanization, Contact-Induced Change by Mutual Reinforcement," *in* D. G. Gilbers et al. (eds.), *Languages in Contact*, Amsterdam/ Atlanta, Rodopi: 231–246.

Link, Heinrich Friedrich. 1821. *Die Urwelt und das Alterthum erläutert durch die Naturkunde*, Berlin, F. Dümmler.

Linné, Carl von. 1758. *Caroli Linnaei Systema naturae per regna tria naturae, secundum classes, ordines, genera, species, cum characteribus, differentiis, synonymis, locis*, Holmiae, Laurentii Salvii (10th edition).

Linse, Ulrich. 1983. *Barfussige Propheten: Erloser der zwanziger Jahre*, Berlin, Siedler Verlag.

Lipphardt, Veronika. 2008. "Das "schwarze Schaf" der Biowissenschaften. Marginalisierungen und Rehabilitierungen der Rassenbiologie im 20. Jahrhundert," *in* Dirk Rupnow, Jens Thiel, Christina Wessely, and Veronika Lipphardt (eds.), *Pseudowissenschaft. Konzeptionen von Nichtwissenschaftlichkeit in der Wissenschaftsgeschichte*, Frankfurt-sur-le-Main, Suhrkamp: 223–250.

List, Guido von. 1908. *Die Armanenschaft der Ario-Germanen*, Leipzig, Steinhacker.

List, Guido von. 1914. *Die Ursprache der Ario-Germanen und ihre Mysteriensprache*, Leipzig, Lechner.

Littleton, C. Scott. 1973. *The New Comparative Mythology: An Anthropological Assessment of the Theories of Georges Dumézil*, Berkeley, University of California Press.

Lombard, L. 1889. "Description ethnographique sommaire de l'Europe. Question aryenne," *Bulletins de la Société d'anthropologie de Paris*, t. 12, 3rd series: 472–497.

Lorenz, Konrad. 1940. "Durch Domestikation verursachte Störungen arteigegenen Verachtens," *Zeitschrift für angewandte Psychologie und Characterkunde*, 59: 2–80.

Lorenz, Konrad. 1943. "Die angeborenen Formen möglicher Erfahrung," *Zeitschrift für Tierpsychologie*, 5, 2: 235–409.

Losemann, Volker. 1977. *Nationalsozialismus und Antike: Studien zur Entwicklung des Faches Alte Geschichte 1933–1945*, Hambourg, Hoffmann & Campe.

Luschan, Felix von. 1922. *Völker, Rassen, Sprachen anthropologische Betrachtungen*, Berlin, Welt-Verlag.

Lutzhöft, Hans-Jürgen. 1971. *Der Nordische Gedanke in Deutschland 1920–1940*, Stuttgart, Ernst Klett, Kieler historische Studien, Bd. 14.

Maas, Utz. 2010. *Verfolgung und Auswanderung deutschsprachiger Sprachforscher 1933–1945*, Tübingen, Stauffenburg, 2 vols.

Madsen, Torsten. 1997. "Ideology and Social Structure in the Earlier Neolithic of South Scandinavia. A View from the Sources," *Analecta Praehistorica Leidensia*, 29: 75–81.

506 BIBLIOGRAPHY

Mair, Victor H. (ed.), 1998a. *The Bronze Age and Early Iron Age Peoples of Eastern Central Asia*, Washington, DC, Institute for the Study of Man, University of Pennsylvania Museum.

Mair, Victor H. 1998b. "Comments on Stefan Zimmer, "Modern Necromancy, or How to Make Mummies Speak," *Journal of Indo-European Studies*, 26, 1-2: 181-190.

Malamoud, Charles. 1971. "L'Œuvre d'Émile Benveniste: une analyse linguistique des institutions indo-européennes (note critique)," *Annales ESC*, 26, 3: 653-663.

Malamoud, Charles. 1991. "Histoire des religions et comparatisme, la question indo-européenne. Présentation," *Revue de l'histoire des religions*, 208, 2: 115-121.

Malamoud, Charles. 2002. "Noirceur de l'écriture," *in* Charles Malamoud (ed.), *Le Jumeau solaire*, Paris, Seuil: 127-149.

Malamoud, Charles. 2005. "Les Indo-Européens, les femmes et les chemins de la liberté," *in* Charles Malamoud (ed.), *Féminité de la parole. Études sur l'Inde ancienne*, Paris, Albin Michel: 261-271.

Malina, Jaroslav, and Vašíček, Zdeněk. 1990. *Archaeology Yesterday and Today: The Development of Archaeology in the Sciences and Humanities*, Cambridge, Cambridge University Press.

Mallory, James P. 1973. "A Short History of Indo-European Problem," *Journal of Indo-European Studies*, 1: 21-65.

Mallory, James P. 1989. *In Search of the Indo-Europeans: Language, Archaeology and Myth*, London, Thames and Hudson (French translation: *À la recherche des Indo-Européens*, Paris, Seuil, 1997).

Mallory, James P. 1998. "A European Perspective on Indo-European in Asia," *in* Victor H. Mair (ed.), *The Bronze Age and Early Iron Age Peoples of Eastern and Central Asia*, Washington, DC, The Institute for the Study of Man: 175-201.

Mallory, James P. 2010. "L'hypothèse des steppes," *Dossiers d'archéologie*, 338: 28-35.

Mallory, James P., and Adams, Douglas Q. (eds.). 1997. *Encyclopedia of Indo-European Culture*, London/Chicago, Fitzroy Dearborn.

Mallory, James P., and Adams, Douglas Q. 2006. *The Oxford Introduction to Proto Indo European and the Proto Indo European World*, Oxford, Oxford University Press.

Malmberg, Bertil. 1991. *Histoire de la linguistique. De Sumer à Saussure*, Paris, PUF.

Maran, Joseph. 1998a. *Kulturwandel auf dem griechischen Festland und den Kykladen im späten 3. Jahrtausend v. Chr.: Studien zu den kulturellen Verhältnissen in Südosteuropa und dem zentralen sowie östlichen Mittelmeerraum in der späten Kupfer- und frühen Bronzezeit*, Bonn, Habelt.

Maran, Joseph. 1998b. "Die Badener Kultur und der ägäisch-anatolische Bereich, eine Neubewertung eines alten Forschungsproblems," *Germania*, 76, 2: 497-525.

Marcantonio, Angela. 2009. "Evidence that most Indo-European Lexical Reconstructions Are Artefacts of the Linguistic Method of Analysis," *in* Angela Marcantonio (ed.), *The Indo-European Language Family: Questions about Its Status*, Washington, DC, Institute for the Study of Man: 10: 1-46.

Maringer, Johannes. 1981. "The Horse in Art and Ideology of Indo-European Peoples," *Journal of Indo-European Studies*, 9: 177-204.

Markevič, V. I. 1974. *Bugo-dnestrovskaja kul'tura na territorii Moldavii*, Kišinev, Academia.

Markey, Thomas L. 1982. "Afrikaans, Creole or Non-Creole?," *Zeitschrift für Dialektologie und Linguistik*, 49, 2: 169-207.

Maroger, Katherine. 2008. *Les Racines du silence*, Paris, Éditions Anne Carrière.

BIBLIOGRAPHY 507

Marr, Nikolaï Jakovlevitch. 1923. *Der Japhetitische Kaukasus und das dritte ethnische Element im Bildungsprozess der mittelländischen Kultur*, Berlin, W. Kohlhammer, Japhetitische Studien, II.

Martial, René. 1942. *Les Métis. Nouvelle étude sur les migrations, le mélange des races, le métissage, la retrempe de la race française et la révision du code de la famille*, Paris, Flammarion.

Martial, René.1955. *Les Races humaines*, Paris, Hachette.

Martinet, André. 1986. *Des steppes aux océans. L'indo-européen et les "Indo-Européens,"* Paris, Payot.

Masica, Colin P. 1976. *Defining a Linguistic Area: South Asia*, Chicago, University of Chicago Press.

Massin, Benoît. 1993. "Anthropologie raciale et national-socialisme, heurs et malheurs du paradigme de la "race," *in* Josiane Olff-Nathan (ed.), *La Science sous le Troisième Reich. Victime ou alliée du nazisme?*, Paris, Seuil: 197–262.

Massin, Benoît. 1996. "From Virchow to Fischer: Physical Anthropology and 'Modern Race Theories' in Wilhelmine Germany," *in* George W. Stocking Jr. (ed.), *Volksgeist as Method and Ethic Essays on Boasian Ethnography and the German Anthropological Tradition*, Madison, Wisconsin University Press: 79–154.

Massin, Benoît. 1998. "Préface aux deux volumes," *in* Paul Weindling (ed.), *L'Hygiène de la race*, t. I: *Hygiène raciale et Eugénisme médical en Allemagne, 1870–1933* (abridges French translation), Paris, La Découverte: 5–66.

Massin, Benoît. 1999. "Anthropologie und Humangenetik im Nationalsozialismus oder: wie schreiben deutsche Wissenschaftler ihre eigene Wissenschaftgeschichte," *in* Heidrun Kaupen-Haas and Christian Saller (eds.), *Wissenschaftlicher Rassismus. Analysen einer Kontinuität in den Human- und Naturwissenschaften*, Frankfurt-sur-le-Main/New York, Campus Verlag: 12–64.

Masson, Émilia. 1989. *Les Douze Dieux de l'immortalité. Croyances indo-européennes à Yazilikaya*, Paris, Les Belles Lettres.

Masson, Émilia. 1991. *Le Combat pour l'immortalité. Héritage indo-européen dans la mythologie anatolienne*, Paris, PUF.

Matras, Yaron, and Bakker, Peter (ed.). 2003. *The Mixed Language Debate Theoretical and Empirical Advances*, Berlin, Mouton de Gruyter.

McMahon, April M. S., and McMahon, Robert. 2006. *Language Classification by Numbers*, Oxford, Oxford University Press.

McNairn, Barbara. 1980. *The Method and Theory of V. Gordon Childe: Economic, Social, and Cultural Interpretations of Prehistory*, Edinburgh, Edinburgh University Press.

McWhorter, John H. 2005. *Defining Creole*, New York, Oxford University Press.

Mees, Bernard. 2008. *The Science of the Swastika*, Budapest, Central European University Press.

Mei, Jianjun. 2000. *Copper and Bronze Metallurgy in Late Prehistoric Xinjiang: Its Cultural Context and Relationship with Neighbouring Regions*, Oxford, Archaeopress, British Archaeological Reports (BAR) International.

Meid, Wolfgang. 1994. "Die Terminologie von Pferd und Wagen im Indogermanischen," *in* Bernhardt Hänsel and Stefan Zimmer (eds.), *Die Indogermanen und das Pferd, Festschrift B. Schlerath*, Budapest, Archaeolingua: 53–66.

Meier-Brügger, Michael. 2010. *Indogermanische Sprachwissenschaft*, Berlin/New York, Walter de Gruyter, 9th edition.

Meillet, Antoine. 1908. *Les Dialectes indo-européens*, Paris, Champion.

508 BIBLIOGRAPHY

Meillet, Antoine. 1917. *Caractères généraux des langues germaniques*, Paris, Hachette.
Meillet, Antoine. 1921. *Linguistique historique et Linguistique générale*, I, Paris, Klincksiek.
Meillet, Antoine. 1923. *Les Origines indo-européennes des mètres grecs*, Paris, PUF.
Meillet, Antoine. 1928a. "Caractères généraux de la langue grecque," in *Actes du premier Congrès international de linguistes à La Haye, du 10 au 15 avril*, Leyde, Sijthoff: 164–165.
Meillet, Antoine. 1928b. *Esquisse d'une histoire de la langue latine*, Paris, Klincksieck.
Meillet, Antoine. 1928c. *Les Lanues dans l'Europe nouvelle (avec un appendice de Lucien Tesnière sur la statistique des langues de l'Europe)*, Paris, Payot, 2nd ed.
Meillet, Antoine. 1937. *Introduction à l'étude comparative des langues indo-européennes*, Paris, Hachette, 8th dition (1st ed. 1903); re-edition Alabama, University of Alabama Press, 1964.
Meillet, Antoine. 1938. *Linguistique historique et Linguistique générale*, II, Paris, Klincksiek.
Menghin, Oswald. 1934. *Geist und Blut; Grundsätzliches um Rasse, Sprache, Kultur und Volkstum*. Vienna, A. Schroll & Co.
Menghin, Oswald.1935. Die Ergebnisse der urgeschichtlichen Kulturkreislehre, Berlin, *Neue Jahrbücher für Wissenschaft und Jugenbildung*, 11: 71–81.
Menk, Roland. 1980. "A Synopsis of the Physical Anthropology of the Corded Ware Complex on the Background of the Expansion of the Kurgan Culture," *Journal of Indo-European Studies*, 8, 3–4: 361–392.
Menk, Roland. 1981. *Anthropologie du néolithique européen: analyse multivariée et essai de synthèse*, thèse de l'université de Geneva.
Menozzi, Paolo, Alberto Piazza, and Luigi Luca Cavalli-Sforza. 1978. "Synthetic Map of Human Gene Frequencies in Europe," *Science*, 201: 786–792.
Merkenschlager, Friedrich, and Saller, Karl. 1934. *Ofnet, Wanderungen zu den Mälern am Weg der deutschen Rasse*, Berlin, Kurt Wolff.
Merlingen, Weriand. 1955. *Das "Vorgriechische" und die sprachwissenschaftlich-vorhistorischen Grundlagen*, Vienna, Gerold.
Merlingen, Weriand. 1967. "Fair Play for 'Pelasgian,'" *Lingua*, 18: 144–167.
Merpert, Nikolay Ya. 1961. "L'Énéolithique de la zone steppique de la partie européenne de l'URSS," *in L'Europe à la fin de l'âge de la pierre. Actes du Symposium consacré aux problèmes du néolithique*, Prague, Éditions de l'Académie techécoslovaque des sciences: 176–192.
Meščaninov, Ivan Ivanovič. 1949. *Die neue Sprachtheorie auf ihrer heutigen Entwicklungsstufe*, Berlin-Leipzig, Volk-Wissen.
Metcalf, George Joseph. 1974. "The Indo-European Hypothesis in the Sixteenth and Seventeenth Centuries," *in* Dell H. Hymes (ed.), *Studies in the History of Linguistics. Traditions and Paradigms*, Bloomington, Indiana University Press: 233–257.
Métoz, Laurent. 2005. *De la glottochronologie à la "Nouvelle Synthèse." Histoire de la linguistique comparative américaine de 1950 à nos jours: concepts et méthodes*, thesis presented at l'École normale supérieure lettres et sciences humaines de Lyon, 2 vols.
Métoz, Laurent, Vallée, Nathalie, and Rousset, Isabelle, 2003 "Ruhlen's 'Mother Tongue Theory' Subjected to the Test of Probabilities," http://www-uilots.let.uu.nl/latest_n ews/Mededelingen-archief/2003/2003-06-25.html#item2a.
Michell, John. 1982. *Megalithomania: Artists, Antiquarians, and Archaeologists at the Old Stone Monuments*, London, Thames & Hudson.
Midgley, Magdalena S. 1992. *TRB Culture: The First Farmers of the North European Plain*, Edinburgh, Edinburgh University Press.

BIBLIOGRAPHY   509

Mierau, Peter. 2006. *Nationalsozialistische Expeditionspolitik. Deutsche Asien-Expeditionen 1933–1945*, Munich, Herbert Utz.

Miller, Dan, Rowlands, Michael, and Tilley, Christopher (eds.). 1995. *Domination and Resistance*, London, Routledge.

Miller, Mykhaïlo Oleksandrovych. 1956. *Archaeology in the U.S.S.R.*, London, Atlantic Press.

Milza, Pierre. 2002. *L'Europe en chemise noire. Les extrêmes droites européennes de 1945 à aujourd'hui*, Paris, Fayard.

Momigliano, Arnaldo. 1983. "Permesse per una discussione di Georges Dumézil," *OPVS. Rivista internazionale per la storia economica e sociale dell'antichità*, 2, 2: 329–341.

Montelius, Oscar. 1903. *Die typologische Methode*, Stockholm, Selbstverlag des verfassers.

Monzat, René. 1992. *Enquêtes sur la droite extrême*, Paris, Le Monde Éditions.

Monzat, René. 1997. "La culture graphique de la nouvelle droite," *Art Press*, 223: 55–61.

Morgan, Jacques Jean Marie de. 1925–1927. *La Préhistoire orientale*, posthumous work published by Louis Germain, Paris, Paul Geuthner, 3 vols.

Morintz, Sebastian, and Roman, Petre. 1968. "Aspekte des Ausgangs des Äneolithikums und der Übergangsstufe zur Bronzezeit im Raum der Niederdonau," *Dacia*, special number, 12: 45–128.

Morintz, Sebastian, and Roman, Petre. 1973. "Über die Übergangsperiode vom Äneolithikum zur Bronzezeit in Rumänien," *in* Bohuslav Chropovsky (ed.), *Symposium über die Entstehung und Chronologie der Badener Kultur*, Bratislava, Archäologisches Institut der Slowakischen Akademie der Wissenschaften: 81–136.

Mortillet, Gabriel de. 1879. "Sur l'origine des animaux domestiques," *Bulletins de la Société d'anthropologie de Paris*, 3rd series, 2, 1: 232–240.

Mosse, George. 1964. *The Crisis of German Ideology*, New York, Grosset & Dunlap.

Mosse, George. 1975. *The Nationalization of the Masses*, New York, H. Fertig.

Mounin, Georges. 1967. *Histoire de la linguistique*, Paris, PUF (corrected 4th ed.1985).

Mounin, Georges. 1972. *La Linguistique du xxe siècle*, Paris, PUF.

Mous, Maarten. 2003. *The Making of a Mixed Language the Case of Maʾa/Mbugu*, Amsterdam, John Benjamins.

Moussa, Sarga (ed.). 2003. *L'Idée de "race" dans les sciences humaines et la littérature (xviiie-xixe siècle)*, Paris, L'Harmattan.

Much, Matthäus. 1902. *Die Heimat der Indogermanen im Lichte der urgeschichtlichen Forschung*, Berlin, H. Costenoble.

Much, Rudolf, Jankuhn, Herbert, and Lange, Wolfgang (eds.). 1967. *Die Germania des Tacitus erläutert*, Heidelberg, Carl Winter (augmented re-edition of the 1937 work).

Mufwene, Salikoko S. 2001. *The Ecology of Language Evolution*, Cambridge, Cambridge University Press.

Mufwene, Salikoko S.2005. *Créoles, écologie sociale, évolution linguistique*, Paris, L'Harmattan.

Mufwene, Salikoko S.2008. *Language Evolution: Contact, Competition and Change*, London/New York, Continuum International Publishing.

Mühlmann, Wilhelm Emil. 1985. *Studien zur Ethnogenese*, Opladen, Westdeutscher Verlag.

Muhly, James D. 1979. "On the Shaft Graves at Mycenae," *in* Marvin A. Powell and Ronald Herbert Sack (eds.), *Studies in Honor of Tom B. Jones*, Neukirchen-Vluyn, Neukirchener Verlag: 311–323.

510 BIBLIOGRAPHY

Muhly, James D. 1985. "Sources of Tin and the Beginnings of Bronze Metallurgy," *American Journal of Archaeology*, 89, 2: 275–291.

Müller, Friedrich Max. 1872. *Lectures on the Science of Language*, New York, Scribner, vol. 1.

Müller, Friedrich Max. 1876. *Einleitung in die Sprachwissenschaft*, Vienna, Grundriss der Sprachwissenschaft.

Müller, Friedrich Max. 1888. *Biographies of Words and the Home of the Aryas*, London, Logmans, Green & Co.

Müller, Friedrich Max. 1889. *Three Lectures on the Science of Language and Its Place in General Education: Delivered at the Oxford University Extension Meeting 1889, with a Supplement "My Predecessors," an Essay on the Genesis of the Idea of the Identity of Thought and Language in the History of Philosophy*, Chicago, Open Court Pub. Co.

Müller, Hans-Hermann. 1994. "Das domestizierte Pferd in Mitteleuropa," *in* Bernhardt Hänsel and Stefan Zimmer (eds.), *Die Indogermanen und das Pferd, Festschrift B. Schlerath*, Budapest, Archaeolingua: 179–184.

Müller, Karl Otfried. 1824. *Die Dorier*, Breslau, Max (2nd ed. 1844).

Müller-Hill, Benno. 1984. *Tödliche Wissenschaft: Die Aussonderung von Juden, Zigeunern und Geisteskranken, 1933–1945*, Hambourg, Rowohlt (English translation: *Murderous Science: Elimination by Scientific Selection of Jews, Gypsies and Others, Germany, 1933–1945*, Oxford University Press, 1988).

Mund, Rudolf J. 1982. *Der Rasputin Himmlers: die Wiligut-Saga*, Vienna, Volkstum-Verlag.

Murra, John V., Hankin, Robert M., and Holling, Fred. 1951. *The Soviet Linguistic Controversy*, New York, Columbia University Press.

Muysken, Pieter (ed.). 2008. *From Linguistic Areas to Areal Linguistics*, Amsterdam, John Benjamins.

Myres, John Linton. 1911. *The Dawn of History*, London, Williams & Norgate.

Nagel, Günter. 1975. *Georges Vacher de Lapouge (1854–1936): ein Beitrag zur Geschichte des Sozialdarwinismus in Frankreich*, Fribourg-en-Brisgau, Schulz.

Nagy, Gregory. 1974. *Comparative Studies in Greek and Indic Meter*, Cambridge, Harvard University Press.

Nakhleh, Luay, Ringe, Donald, and Warnow, Tandy. 2005. "Perfect Phylogenetic Networks: A New Methodology for Reconstructing the Evolutionary History of Natural Languages," *Language (Journal of the Linguistic Society of America)*, 81, 2: 382–420.

Narasimhan, Vagheesh M. et al. 2018. "The Genomic Formation of South and Central Asia," *BioRxiv*.

Narasimhan, Vagheesh M. et al. 2019. "The Genomic Formation of South and Central Asia," *Science*, 365 (6457).

Needham, Stuart. 2005. "Transforming Beaker Culture in North-West Europe: Processes of Fusion and Fission," *Proceedings of the Prehistoric Society*, 71: 171–217.

Negelein, Julius von. 1903. *Das Pferd im arischen Altertum*, Königsberg, Teutonia von Uhl.

Nemejkova-Pavukova, Viera. 1982. "Periodisierung der Badener Kultur und ihre chronologischen Beziehungen zu Südosteuropa," *Thracia Praehistorica* (Supplementum Pulpudeva 3): 150–176.

Nemejkova-Pavukova, Viera.1991. "Typologische Fragen der relativen und absoluten Chronologie der Badener Kultur," *Slovenská Archeológia* 39, 1–2: 59–90.

Nemejkova-Pavukova, Viera.1992. "Kulturhistorische Verhältnisse in Südosteuropa zu Beginn des Horizontes Ezero-Baden und die möglichen Wege von Kontakten mit dem ägäisch-anatolischen Gebiet," *Studia Praehistorica*, 11–12: 362–384.

BIBLIOGRAPHY 511

Neu, Erich, and Meid, Wolfgang. 1979. *Hethitisch und Indogermanisch: Vergleichende Studien zur historischen Grammatik und zur dialektgeographischen Stellung der indogermanischen Sprachgruppe Altkleinasiens*, Innsbruck, Innsbrucker Beiträge zur Sprachwissenschaft.

Neumann, Günter. 1971. "Substrate im Germanischen?," *Nachrichten der Akademie der Wissenschaften, Philol.-Histor. Klasse*, 4: 75–99.

Neumann, Günter, and Untermann, Jürgen. 1980. *Die Sprachen im römischen Reich der Kaiserzeit*, Cologne-Bonn, Rheinland-Verlag.

Neustupný, Evžen. 1967. *K počátkům patriarchátu ve střední Evropě*, Prague, Akademie Věd.

Neuville, Henri. 1933. *L'Espèce, la race et le métissage en anthropologie. Introduction à l'anthropologie générale*, Paris, Masson, Archives de l'Institut de paléontologie humaine, 11.

Nicolaï, Robert. 1990. *Parentés linguistiques (à propos du songhay)*, Paris, CNRS Éditions.

Nicolaï, Robert. 2001. "Contacts et dynamique(s) du contact: à propos des alliances de langue, des koiné et des processus de leur actualisation," *in Les Langues de communication: Quelles propriétés structurales préalables ou acquises?*, Paris, Mémoire de la Société de linguistique de Paris, t. 11: 95–119.

Nicolaï, Robert. 2003. *La Force des choses ou l'Épreuve "nilo-saharienne": questions sur les reconstructions archéologiques et l'évolution des langues*, Cologne, Rüdiger Köppe, SUGIA 13.

Nurse, Derek, and Hinnebusch, Thomas J. 1993. *Swahili and Sabaki: A Linguistic History*, Berkeley, University of California Press.

Obayashi, Taryô. 1977. "La structure du panthéon nippon et le concept de péché dans le Japon ancien," *Diogène*, 98: 125–142.

Oettinger, Norbert. 1986. *"Indo-Hittite" -Hypothese und Wortbildung*, Innsbruck, Innsbrucker Beiträge zur Sprachbildung.

Olalde, Iñigo et al. 2018. "The Beaker Phenomenon and the Genomic Transformation of Northwest Europe." *Nature*, 555 (7695): 190–196.

Olalde, Iñigo et al. 2019. "The Genomic History of the Iberian Peninsula over the Past 8000 Years," *Science*, 363: 1230–1234.

Olalde, Iñigo, and Posth, Cosimo. 2020. "Latest Trends in Archaeogenetic Research of West Eurasians," *Current Opinion in Genetics & Development*, 62: 36–43.

Olender, Maurice (ed.). 1981. *Le Racisme. Mythes et sciences. Pour Léon Poliakov*, Brussels, Éditions Complexe.

Olender, Maurice. 1983. "Au sujet des Indo-Européens," *Archives de sciences sociales des religions*, 55, 2: 163–167. Extended version in Olender, 2009.

Olender, Maurice. 1989. *Les Langues du paradis. Aryens et Sémites, un couple providentiel*, Gallimard-Seuil, Paris.

Olender, Maurice. 1991. "Georges Dumézil et les usages "politiques" de la préhistoire indo-européenne," *in* Roger-Pol Droit (ed.), *Les Grecs, les Romains et nous. L'Antiquité est-elle moderne?*, Paris, Le Monde Éditions: 191–228. Extended version in Olender, 2009.

Olender, Maurice, 2008. The *Languages of Paradise? Race, Religion and Philology in the Nineteenth Century*, Harvard University Press, translated by Arthur Goldhammer, paperback edition. Translated from the French, *Les Langues du paradis. . .* (1989). Originally published in English in 1992.

Olender, Maurice. 2009. *Race sans histoire*, Paris, Seuil (Republished in slightly abridged form in English in 2009 as *Race and Erudition;* all references are to the French edition).

512 BIBLIOGRAPHY

Olff-Nathan, Josiane (ed.). 1993. *La Science sous le Troisième Reich. Victime ou alliée du nazisme?*, Seuil, Paris.

Olivier, Georges. 1965. *Morphologie et types humains*, Lyon, Vigot frères.

Olivier, Laurent. 2012. *Nos ancêtres les Germains. Les archéologues français et allemands au service du nazisme*, Paris, Tallandier.

Omalius d'Halloy, Jean-Baptiste Julien. 1848. "Observation sur la distribution ancienne des peuples," *Bulletin de l'Académie de Belgique*, 15: 549.

Omalius d'Halloy, Jean-Baptiste Julien. 1864. "Sur les origines indo-européennes," *Bulletins de la Société d'anthropologie de Paris*, 5, 1: 187–190.

Omalius d'Halloy, Jean-Baptiste Julien. 1865. "Sur la prétendue origine asiatique des Européens," *Bulletins de la Société d'anthropologie de Paris*, 6, 1: 237–248.

Orlando, Ludovic. 2021. *L'ADN fossile, une machine à remonter le temps: Les tests ADN en archéologie*, Paris, Odile Jacob.

Ošibkina, Svetlana Viktorovna (ed.). 1996. *Neolit Severnoj Evrazii*, Moscow, Nauka.

Otte, Marcel. 1995. "Diffusion of Modern Languages in Prehistoric Eurasia," *Comptes-rendus de l'Académie des sciences*, series 2, fasc. A 321, 12: 1219–1220.

Otte, Marcel. 2012. "Les Indo-Européens sont arrivés en Europe avec Cro-Magnon," *in* Daniel Le Bris (ed.), *Aires linguistiques, aires culturelles. Études de Concordances en Europe occidentale: Zones Manche et Atlantique*, Brest, Centre de recherche bretonne et celtique-Université de Bretagne occidentale: 19–51.

Owens, Gareth. 1999. "The Structure of the Minoan Language," *Journal of Indo-European Studies*, 27, 1–2: 15–55.

Pallottino, Massimo. 1984. *Etruscologia*, Milan, Hoepli.

Palmer, Gary B. 1996. *Toward a Theory of Cultural Linguistics*, Austin, University of Texas Press.

Parpola, Asko. 1999. "The Formation of the Aryan Branch of Indo-European," *in* R. Blench and M. Spriggs (eds.), *Archaeology and Language: Artefacts, Languages and Texts*, London, Routledge: 180–207.

Parpola, Asko. 2012. "Formation of the Indo-European and Uralic (Finno-Ugric) Language Families in the Light of Archaeology. Revised and Integrated 'Total' Correlations," *in* Riho Grünthal and Petri Kallio (eds.), *Linguistic Map of Prehistoric North Europe*, Suomalais-Ugrilaisen Seuran Toimituksia = Mémoires de la Société Finno-Ougrienne, 266, Helsinki, Société finno-ougrienne: 119–184.

Parry, Benita. 1972. *Delusions and Discoveries. Studies on India in the British Imagination, 1880–1930*, Berkeley, Berkeley University Press.

Parzinger, Hermann. 2009. "Le monde des steppes. Cinq millénaires du Danube à l'Oural," *in* Jean-Paul Demoule (ed.), *L'Europe, un continent redécouvert par l'archéologie*, Paris, Gallimard-Inrap: 61–72.

Pashkevich, Galina. 2003. "Palaeoethnobotanical Evidence of Agriculture in the Steppe and the Forest-Steppe of East Europe in the Late Neolithic and Bronze Age," *in* Marsha A. Levine, Colin Renfrew, and Katherine V. Boyle (eds.), *Prehistoric Steppe Adaptation and the Horse*, Cambridge, McDonald Institute for Archaeological Research: 287–298.

Passler-Mayrhofer, Edeltraut. 1948. "Das Buchenargument," *in* Wilhelm von Brandenstein (ed.), *Frühgeschichte und Sprachwissenschaft*, Vienna, Institut für allgemeine und vergleichende Sprachwissenschaft: 155–161.

Patou-Mathis, Marylène. 2013. *Préhistoire de la violence et de la guerre*, Paris, Odile Jacob.

Patte, Étienne. 1938a. "Le problème de la race. Le cas de l'Europe passé et présent," *Cahiers de la Démocratie*, 52.

BIBLIOGRAPHY 513

Patte, Étienne. 1938b. *Race, races, races pures*, Paris, Hermann.

Pauwels, Louis, and Bergier, Jacques. 1960. *Le Matin des magiciens. Introduction au réalisme fantastique*, Paris, Gallimard.

Paxton, Robert Owen, and Hoffman, Stanley. 1999. *La France de Vichy, 1940–1944*, Paris, Seuil.

Peake, Harold John Edward. 1922. *The Bronze Age and the Celtic World*, London, Benn.

Peake, Harold John Edward, and Fleure, Herbert John. 1928. *The Corridors of Time*, Oxford, Clarendon Press.

Pearson, Karl. 1905. *National Life from the Standpoint of Science*, Cambridge, Cambridge University Press.

Pedersen, Holger. 1925. *Le Groupement des dialectes indo-européens*, Det Kgl. Danske Videnskabernes Selskab, Historisk-filologiske Meddelelser XI, 3, Copenhagen, A. F. Høst & Søon.

Pedersen, Holger. 1931. *Linguistic Science in the Nineteenth Century: Methods and Results*, Cambridge, Harvard University Press (English translation of the original Danish edition of 1924, re-edition 1959, Bloomington, Indiana University Press).

Pellard, Thomas et al. 2018. "L'indo-européen n'est pas un mythe," *Bulletin de la société de linguistique de Paris*, 113 (1): 79–102.

Pellegrini, Béatrice. 1995. *L'Ève imaginaire. Les origines de l'homme, de la biologie à la paléontologie*, Paris, Payot.

Penka, Karl. 1883. *Origines ariacae. Linguistisch-ethnologische Untersuchungen zur ältesten Geschichte der arischen Völker und Sprachen*, Vienna, K. Prochaska.

Penner, Silvia. 1998. *Schliemanns Schachtgräberrund und der europäische Nordosten: Studien zur Herkunft der frühmykenischen Streitwagenausstattung*, Bonn, Habelt.

Pereltsvaig Asya, and Lewis, Martin W. 2015. *The Indo-European Controversy. Facts and Fallacies in Historical Linguistics*, Cambridge, Cambridge University Press.

Perlès, Catherine. 2001. *The Early Neolithic in Greece, the First Farming Communities in Europe*, Cambridge, Cambridge University Press.

Perrot, Jean. 1988. "Antoine Meillet et les langues de l'Europe: l'affaire hongroise," in Sylvain Auroux (ed.), *Antoine Meillet et la linguistique de son temps, Histoire, Épistémologie, Langage*, 10, II: 195–204.

Phelps, Reginald H. 1963. " 'Before Hitler Came': Thule Society and Germanen Orden," *Journal of Modern History*, 25: 245–261.

Phillips, Walter Shelley. 1913. *The Chinook Book: A Descriptive Analysis of the Chinook Jargon in Plain Words*, Seattle, R. L. Davis Printing Company (reprinted 2012).

Pichot, André. 2000. *La Société pure: De Darwin à Hitler*, Paris, Flammarion.

Pictet, Adolphe. 1837. *De l'affinité des langues celtiques avec le sanscrit*, Paris, Duprat.

Pictet, Adolphe. 1859–1863. *Les Origines indo-européennes, ou les Aryas primitifs, essai de paléontologie linguistique*, Paris, J. Cherbuliez.

Piétrement, Charles-Alexandre. 1879. "Les Aryas et leur première patrie," *Revue de linguistique et de philologie comparée*: 99–158, separate reprint, Paris, Maisonneuve.

Piggott, Stuart. 1937. "Prehistory and the Romantic Movement," *Antiquity*, 11: 31–38.

Piggott, Stuart. 1950. *Prehistoric India to 1000 B.C.*, Harmondsworth, Penguin.

Piggott, Stuart. 1983. *The Earliest Wheeled Transport: From the Atlantic Coast to the Caspian Sea*, Ithaca, Cornell University Press.

Pigott, Vincent C. (ed.). 1999. *The Archaeometallurgy of the Asian Old World*, Philadelphia, University of Pennsylvania Press.

514   BIBLIOGRAPHY

Pinault, Georges-Jean. 1989. "Introduction au tokharien," *Lalies*, 7, Paris, Presses de l'École normale supérieure: 5–224.

Pinault, Georges-Jean, and Petit, Daniel (ed.). *La langue poétique indo-européenne*, Leuwen Paris, Peeters.

Pisani, Vittore. 1966. "Entstehung von Einzelsprachen aus Sprachbünden," *Kratylos*, 11: 125–141.

Pisowicz, Andrzej. 1989. "Objections d'un arménologue contre la théorie glottale," *Folia Orientalia*, 25: 213–225.

Plasseraud, Yves, and Marin, Cécile (eds.). 2005. *Atlas des minorités en Europe: de l'Atlantique à l'Oural, diversité culturelle*, Paris, Autrement.

Plath, Robert. 1994. "Pferd und Wagen im Mykenischen und bei Homer," *in* Bernhardt Hänsel and Stefan Zimmer (eds.), *Die Indogermanen und das Pferd, Festschrift B. Schlerath*, Budapest, Archaeolingua: 103–114.

Poewe, Karla, and Hexham, Irving. 2005. "Jakob Wilhelm Hauer's New Religion and National Socialism," *Journal of Contemporary Religion*, 20, 2: 195–215.

Pohl, Walter (ed.). 1997. *Kingdoms of the Empire: The Integration of Barbarians in Late Antiquity*, Leyde, Brill.

Pohl, Walter, 2004. *Die Germanen. Enzyklopädie deutscher Geschichte*, 57, Munich, R. Oldenbourg.

Pohl, Walter, Gantner, Clemens, and Payne, Richard (eds.). 2012. *Visions of Community in the Post-Roman World the West, Byzantium and the Islamic World, 300–1100*, Farnham, Ashgate.

Pohl, Walter, and Mehofer, Mathias (eds.). 2010. *Archaeology of Identity = Archäologie der Identität*, Vienna, Verlag der Österreichischen Akademie der Wissenschaften.

Pohl, Walter, and Zeller, Bernhard (eds.). 2012. *Sprache und Identität im frühen Mittelalter*, Denkschriften, Bd. 426, Vienna, Verlag der Österreichischen Akademie der Wissenschaften.

Poisson, Georges. 1928–1929. "Les civilisations néolithiques et énéolithiques de la France," *L'Anthropologie*: 239–256 and 368–379; 1929: 45–62.

Poisson, Georges. 1934. *Les Aryens*, Paris, Payot.

Poisson, Georges. 1939. *Le Peuplement de l'Europe. État actuel, origines et évolution*, Paris, Payot.

Pokorny, Julius. 1959–1969. *Indogermanisches etymologisches Wörterbuch*, Bern, Franke, 2 vols.

Poliakov, Léon. 1968. *Histoire de l'anti-sémitisme*, t. III: *De Voltaire à Wagner*, Paris, Calmann-Lévy.

Poliakov, Léon. 1971. *Le Mythe aryen. Essai sur les sources du racisme et des nationalismes*, Paris, Calmann-Lévy, Paris; extended re-edition, Brussels, Éditions Complexe, 1987.

Poliakov, Léon, and Wulf, Josef (eds.). 1983. *Das Dritte Reich und seine Denker*, Berlin, Ullstein (1st ed. 1959).

Polomé, Edgar C. 1967. *Swahili Language Handbook*, Washington, DC, Center for Applied Linguistics.

Polomé, Edgar C. 1980. "Creolization Processes and Diachronic Linguistics," *in* Albert Valdman and Arnold R. Highfield (eds.), *Theoretical Orientations in Creole Studies*, New York, Academic Press: 185–202.

Polomé, Edgar C. 1987a. "Marija Gimbutas, a Biographical Sketch," *in* Susan Nacev Skomal and Edgar C. Polomé (eds.), *Proto-Indo-European: The Archaeology of a*

BIBLIOGRAPHY   515

Linguistic Problem: Studies in Honor of Marija Gimbutas, Washington, DC, Institute for the Study of Man: 375–378.

Polomé, Edgar C. 1987b. "Recent Developments in the Laryngal Theory," *Journal of Indo-European Studies*, 15, 1–2: 159–167.

Polomé, Edgar C. 1994a. "Das Pferd in der Religion der eurasischen Völker," *in* Bernhardt Hänsel and Stefan Zimmer (eds.), *Die Indogermanen und das Pferd, Festschrift B. Schlerath*, Budapest, Archaeolingua: 43–52.

Polomé, Edgar C. 1994b. "L'Asvamedha est-il un rituel de date indo-européenne?," *in* Chantal Kirchner-Durand (ed.), *Nomina Rerum. Hommage à Jacqueline Manessy-Guitton*, Nice, Université, LAMA, 13: 349–361.

Polomé, Edgar C. (ed.). 1996. *Indo-European Religion After Dumézil*, Washington, DC, Institute for the Study of Man.

Pomian, Krzysztof. 1992. "Francs et Gaulois," *in* Pierre Nora (ed.), *Les Lieux de mémoire*, Paris, Gallimard, vol. 3: 40–105.

Poniatowski, Michel. 1978. *L'avenir n'est écrit nulle part*, Paris, Albin Michel.

Pop, Sever. 1950. *La Dialectologie, aperçu historique et méthodes d'enquêtes linguistiques*, Louvain, J. Duculot, 2 vols.

Poruciuc, Adrian. 1995. "Marija Gimbutas, 1921–1994," *Arheologia Moldovei*, 18: 361–364.

Porzig, Walter. 1954. *Die Gliederung des indogermanischen Sprachgebiets*, Heidelberg, Carl Winter.

Pott, August Friedrich. 1833–1836. *Etymologische Forschungen auf dem Gebiete der Indo-Germanischen Sprachen: mit besonderem Bezug auf die Lautumwandlung im Sanskrit, Griechischen, Lateinischen, Littauischen und Gothischen*, Lemgo, Meyersche Hof-Buchhandlung, 2 vols. (2nd ed. 1859–1876, 6 vols.).

Pott, August Friedrich. 1856. *Die Ungleichheit menschlicher Rassen, hauptsächlich vom sprachwissenschaftlichem Standpunkte, unter besonderen Berücksichtigung von des Grafen von Gobineau gleichnamigem Werke. Mit einem Überblicke über die Sprachverhältnisse der Völker. Ein ethnologischer Versuch*, Lemgo & Detmold, Meyer.

Pouchain, Delphine. 1999. *Alain de Benoist. Une appropriation tactique de l'écologie*, Mémoire de DEA, Université de Lille-II.

Poutignat, Philippe, and Streiff-Fenart, Jocelyne. 1995. *Théories de l'ethnicité, suivi de "Les groupes ethniques et leurs frontières" de Frederick Barth*, Paris, PUF.

Price, T. Douglas, and Borić, Dušan. 2013. "Strontium Isotopes Document Greater Human Mobility at the Start of the Balkan Neolithic," *Proceedings of the National Academy of Sciences of the United States of America*, 110, 9: 3298–3303.

Prichard, James Cowles. 1813. *Researches into the Physical History of Man*, re-edited by University of Chicago Press.

Pringle, Heather Anne. 2006. *The Master Plan: Himmler's Scholars and the Holocaust*, New York, Hyperion.

Pruner-Bey, Franz. 1864. "Questions relatives à l'anthropologie générale," *Bulletins de la Société d'anthropologie de Paris*, 5: 64–135.

Puhvel, Jaan. 1970. "Aspects of Equine Functionality," *in* Jaan Puhvel (ed.), *Myth and Law among the Indo-Europeans: Studies in Indo-European Comparative Mythology*, Berkeley, University of California Press: 159–172.

Puhvel, Jaan. 1987. *Comparative Mythology*, Baltimore/London, John Hopkins University Press.

Pulgram, Ernst. 1953. "Family-Tree, Wave-Theory and Dialectology," *Orbis*, 2: 67–72.

516 BIBLIOGRAPHY

Pulgram, Ernst. 1958. *The Tongues of Italy: Prehistory and History*, Cambridge, Harvard University Press.

Pulgram, Ernst. 1959. "Proto-indo-european Reality and Reconstruction," *Language*, 35, 3: 421–426.

Pulzer, Peter G. J. 1964. *The Rise of Political Anti-Semitism in Germany and Austria*, New York, Wiley.

Pumpelly, Raphael (ed.). 1908. *Explorations in Turkestan, Expedition of 1904: Prehistoric Civilizations of Anau, Origins, Growth, and Influence of Environment*, Washington, DC, Carnegie Institute of Washington, 2 vols.

Quatrefages de Bréau, Armand de. 1871. "Histoire naturelle de l'homme. La race prussienne," *Revue des Deux Mondes*, 91: 647–669; separate re-edition, Paris, Hachette.

Quatrefages de Bréau, Armand de. 1887. *Histoire générale des races humaines. Introduction à l'étude des races humaines. Questions générales*, Paris, Hennuyer.

Quattordio Moreschini, Adriana (ed.). 1987. *L'Opera Scientifica di Antoine Meillet. Atti del Convegno della Società Italiana di Glottologia*, Pisa, Giardini.

Raidt, Edith H. 1983. *Einführung in Geschichte und Struktur des Afrikaans*, Darmstadt, Wissenschaftliche Buchgesellschaft.

Rapp, Adolf. 1920. *Die deutsche Gedanke, seine Entwicklung im politischer und geistigen Leben seit dem 18. Jahrhundert*, Bonn, K. Schroeder.

Rask, Rasmus Kristian. 1818. *Undersögelse om det gamle nordiske eller islandske sprogs oprindelse*, Copenhagen, Gyldenlal.

Rask, Rasmus Kristian. 1932–1937. *Ausgewählte Abhandlungen*, Louis Hjelmslev (ed.), Copenhagen, Levin and Munksgaard, 3 vols.

Rask, Rasmus Kristian. 1993. *Investigation of the Origin of the Old Norse or Icelandic Language*, English translation by Niels Ege, Copenhagen, Travaux du Cercle linguistique de Copenhague, XXIV (re-edited Amsterdam, Benjamins, 2013).

Rassamakin, Yuri. 1999. "The Eneolithic of the Black Sea Steppe: Dynamics of Cultural and Economic Development 4500–2300 BC," *in* Marsha A. Levine, Yuri Rassamakin, Aleksandr Kislenko, and Nataliya Tatarintseva (eds.), *Late Prehistoric Exploitation of the Eurasian Steppe*, Cambridge, McDonald Institute Monographs: 59–182.

Rassamakin, Yuri. 2002. "Aspects of Pontic Steppe Development (4500–3000 BC) in the Light of the New Cultural-Chronological Model," *in* Katherine V.Boyle, Colin Renfrew, and Marsha A. Levine (eds.), *Ancient Interactions: East and West in Eurasia*, Cambridge, McDonalds Institute Monographs: 49–75.

Rassamakin, Yuri. 2004. *Die nordpontische Steppe in der Kupferzeit: Gräber aus der Mitte des 5. Jts. bis Ende des 4. Jts. v. Chr.*, Mayence, Von Zabern, 2 vols.

Raulwing, Peter. 1998. "Pferd, Wagen und Indogermanen: Grundlagen, Probleme und Methoden der Steitwagenforschung," *in* Wolfgang Meid (ed.), *Sprache und Kulture der Indogermanen. Akten der X. Fachtagung der Indogermanischen Gesellschaft*, Innsbruck, Innsbrucker Beiträge zur Sprachwissenschaft, Bd. 93: 523–546.

Raulwing, Peter. 2000. *Horses, Chariots, and Indo-Europeans: Foundations and Methods of Chariotry Research from the Viewpoint of Comparative Indo-European Linguistics*, Budapest, Archaeolingua.

Ravdonikas, Vladislav Iosifovič. 1932. "Peščernye goroda Kryma i gotskaja problema v svjazi so stadial'nym razvitijem severnovo pričernomor'ja," *Gotskij Sbornik*, 12, 1–2: 5–106.

Reich, David. 2018. *Who We Are and How We Got Here*, Oxford, Oxford University Press.

BIBLIOGRAPHY 517

Reinach, Salomon. 1892. *L'Origine des Aryens. Histoire d'une controverse*, Paris, Ernest Leroux.

Reinach, Salomon. 1898. "Esquisse d'une histoire de l'archéologie gauloise," *La Revue celtique*, 19: 101–117 and 292–307.

Renfrew, Colin. 1973. *Before Civilization: The Radiocarbon Revolution and Prehistoric Europe*, London, Pimlico (French translation: *Les Origines de l'Europe: la révolution du radiocarbone*, Paris, Flammarion, 1983).

Renfrew, Colin. 1987. *Archaeology and Language: The Puzzle of Indo-European Origins*, London, Jonathan Cape (French translation: *L'Énigme indo-européenne. Archéologie et langage*, Paris, Flammarion, 1990).

Renfrew, Colin. 1989. "They Ride Horses, Don't They? Mallory on the Indo-Europeans?" *Antiquity*, 63, 241: 843–847.

Renfrew, Colin. 1992. "Archaeology, Genetics and Linguistic Diversity," *Man (N.S.)*, 27: 445–478.

Renfrew, Colin. 1998. "Word of Minos: The Minoan contribution to Mycenaean Greek and the Linguistic Geography of the Bronze Age Aegean," *Cambridge Archaeological Journal*, 8: 239–264.

Renfrew, Colin. 1999. "Time Depth, Convergence Theory, and Innovation in Proto-Indo-European, "Old Europe" as a PIE Linguistic Area," *Journal of Indo-European Studies*, 27, 3–4: 257–293.

Renfrew, Colin. 2017. "Marija Rediviva: DNA and Indo-European Origins," Lecture at the Oriental Institute Lecture Series: Marija Gimbutas Memorial Lecture, Chicago, November 8, 2017 [online].

Renzi, Lorenzo. 1997. "Alinei, ovvero il latino prima di Roma," *Rivista italiana di dialettologia*, 21: 191–202.

Retzius, Anders. 1846. "Mémoire sur les formes du crâne des habitants du Nord," *Annales des sciences naturelles*, 3rd series, "Zoologie," t. VI: 133–171.

Retzius, Anders. 1864. *Ethnologische Schriften: Nach dem Tode des Verfassers gesammelt*, Stockholm: A. Norstedt & Söner.

Reynaud Paligot, Carole. 2006. *La République raciale: paradigme racial et idéologie républicaine, 1860–1930*, Paris, PUF.

Reynaud Paligot, Carole. 2007. *Races, racisme et antiracisme dans les années 1930*, Paris, PUF.

Rhode, Johann Gottlieb. 1820. *Die heilige Sage und das gesammte Religionssystem der alten Baktrer, Meder und Perser oder des Zendvolkes*, Frankfurt-sur-le-Main, Hermann.

Ridé, Jacques. 1966. "La fortune singulière du mythe germanique en Allemagne," *Études germaniques*, 21, 4: 489–505.

Ridé, Jacques. 1976. *L'Image du Germain dans la pensée et la littérature allemandes de la redécouverte de Tacite à la fin du XVIe siècle: contribution à l'étude de la genèse d'un mythe*, thèse de doctorat d'État, Université de Paris-Sorbonne.

Ringe, Donald A. 1996. *On the Chronology of Sound Changes in Tocharian*, vol. 1: *From Proto-Indo-European to Proto-Tocharian*, New Haven, American Oriental Society.

Ripley, William Zebina. 1899. *The Races of Europe. A Sociological Study*, New York, D. Appleton (republished, Johnson Reprint Corp., 1965).

Riquet, Raymond. 1951. "Essai de synthèse sur l'ethnogénie des néo-énéolithiques en France," *Bulletins et Mémoires de la Société d'anthropologie de Paris*, 2, 4: 201–233.

Rivière, Jean-Claude. 1973. "Pour une lecture de Dumézil," *Nouvelle École*, 21–22: 14–79.

Rivière, Jean-Claude. 1979. "Actualité de Georges Dumézil," *Éléments*, 32: 15–17.

518   BIBLIOGRAPHY

Rix, Helmut, and Kümmel, Martin. 2001. *LIV, Lexikon der indogermanischen Verben: die Wurzeln und ihre Primärstammbildungen*, Wiesbaden, Reichert, 2nd ed.

Robb, John E. 1991. "Random Causes with Directed Effects: The Indo-European Language Spread and the Stochastic Loss of Lineages," *Antiquity*, 65: 287–291.

Robb, John E. 1993 "A Social Prehistory of European Languages," *Antiquity*, 67: 747–760.

Roberts, John M., Moore, Carmella C., and Romney, Antone Kimball. 1995. "Predicting Similarity in Material Culture Among New Guinea Villages from Propinquity and Language: A Log-Linear Approach," *Current Anthropology*, 36, 5: 769–788.

Robins, Robert H. 1967. *A Short History of Linguistics*, London, Routledge (French translation: *Brève histoire de la linguistique*, Paris, Seuil, 1976).

Rochet, Charles. 1871. "Sur le type prussien," *Bulletins de la Société d'anthropologie de Paris*, 2nd series, 6, 1: 189–196.

Römer, Ruth. 1981. "Sigmund Feist: Deutscher—Germanist—Jude," *Muttersprache*, 91: 249–308.

Römer, Ruth. 1985. *Sprachwissenschaft und Rassenideologie in Deutschland*, Munich, Wilhelm Fink.

Róna-Tas, András. 1988. "Ethnogenese und Staaatsgründung. Die turkische Komponente in der Ethnogenese des Ungartums," in *Studien zur Ethnogenese*, Opladen, Westdeutscher Verlag, vol. 2: 107–142.

Rosenberg, Alfred. 1930. *Der Mythus des 20. Jahrhunderts. Eine Wertung der seelisch-geistigen Gestaltenkämpfe unserer Zeit*, Munich, Hoheneichen Verlag (7th edition 1942).

Rosser, Zoë H., Zerjal, Tatiana, Hurles, Matthew E., Adojaan, Maarja, Alavantic, Dragan, Amorim, António, Amos, William et al. 2000. "Y-Chromosomal Diversity in Europe Is Clinal and Influenced Primarily by Geography, Rather Than by Language," *American Journal of Human Genetics*, 67: 1526–1543.

Rostovtzeff, Mihail Ivanovich. 1922. *Iranians and Greeks in South Russia*, Oxford, Clarendon Press.

Rousseau, Jean. 1981. "R. Rask (1787–1832) et la transcription des langues amérindiennes—Une lettre inédite à J. Pickering," *Histoire Épistémologie Langage*, 3, 2: 69–83.

Rousso, Henry. 1990. *Le Syndrome de Vichy: de 1944 à nos jours*, Paris, Seuil, 2nd ed.

Rousso, Henry. 2004. *Le Dossier Lyon III: le rapport sur le racisme et le négationnisme à l'université Jean-Moulin*, Paris, Fayard.

Royer, Clémence. 1862. "Préface," in Charles Darwin (ed.), *De l'origine des espèces ou des lois du progrès chez les êtres organisés*, Paris, Guillaumin et Cie-Victor Massin et Fils, 1862.

Royer, Clémence. 1870. *Origine de l'homme et des sociétés*, Paris, Guillaumin et Cie (re-edited J.-M. Place, Cahiers de Gradhiva, Paris, 1990).

Ruhlen, Merritt. 1991. *A Guide to the World's Languages*, vol. 1: *Classification*, Stanford, Stanford University Press.

Ruhlen, Merritt. 1996. *The Origin of Language: Tracing the Evolution of the Mother Tongue*, New York, John Wiley & Sons (French translation: *L'Origine des langues. Sur les traces de la langue mère*, Paris, Belin, 1997).

Saller, Karl. 1961. *Die Rassenlehre des Nationalsozialismus in Wissenschaft und Propaganda*, Darmstadt, Progress-Verlag.

Sandfeld, Kristian. 1930. *Linguistique balkanique: problèmes et résultats*, Paris, Champion.

BIBLIOGRAPHY 519

Santoni, Vincenzo. 1999. "Le néolithique moyen-supérieur de Cuccuru S'Arriu (Cabras-Oristano, Sardaigne)," *in* Jean Vaquer (ed.), *Actes du colloque international sur le néolithique nord-ouest méditarranéen*, Paris, Congrès préhistorique de France, Société préhistorique française: 77–87.

Sarianidi, Viktor. 1999. "Near Eastern Aryans in Central Asia," *Journal of Indo-European Studies*, 27, 3–4: 295–326.

Sarianidi, Viktor. 2005. *Gonurdepe: City of Kings and Gods*, Aşgabat, Miras.

Sarianidi, Viktor. 2007. *Necropolis of Gonur*, Athènes, Kapon Éditions.

Saussure, Ferdinand de, Bally, Charles, Sechehaye, Albert, Riedlinger, Albert, and de Mauro, Tullio. 1972. *Cours de linguistique générale*, published by Charles Bally and Albert Séchehayein in collaboration with Albert Riedlinger, critical edition prepared by Tullio de Mauro, Paris, Payot (2nd edition. 1985).

Sayce, Archibald Henry. 1884. *Principes de philologie comparée*, Paris, C. Delagrave.

Sayce, Archibald Henry.1927. "The Aryan Problem. Fifty Years Later," *Antiquity*, 1: 204–214.

Schemann, Ludwig. 1913–1916. *Gobineau. Eine Biographie*, Strasbourg, K. J. Trübner.

Scherer, Anton. 1968. *Die Urheimat der Indogermanen*, Darmstadt, Wissenschaftliche Buchgesellschaft.

Schiller, Francis. 1979. *Paul Broca, Founder of French Anthropology, Explorer of the Brain*, Berkeley, University of California Press.

Schleicher, August. 1861. *Compendium der vergleichenden Grammatik der indogermanischen Sprachen. Kurzer Abriss einer Laut- und Formenlehre der indogermanischen Ursprache, des altindischen, alteranischen, altgriechischen, altitalischen, altkeltischen, altslavischen, litauischen und altdeutschen*, Weimar, Böhlau.

Schleicher, August. 1863a. "Der wirtschaftliche Kulturstand des indogermanischen Urvolkes," *Jahrbücher für Nationaloekonomie*: 401–411.

Schleicher, August. 1863b. *Die Darwinsche Theorie und die Sprachwissenschaft. Offenes Sendschreiben an Herrn Dr. Ernst Häckel*, Weimar, Böhlau.

Schleicher, August. 1868. "La théorie et la science du langage," *in Recueil de travaux originaux ou traduits relatifs à l'histoire littéraire*, vol. 1, trad. de *Die darwinsche Theorie und die Sprachwissenschaft*, Paris, A. Franck.

Schlerath, Bernfried. 1987. "On the Reality and Status of a Reconstructed Language," *Journal of Indo-European Studies*, 1–2, 15: 41–46.

Schlerath, Bernfried. 1995–1996. "G. Dumézil und die Rekonstruktion indogermanischer Kultur," *Kratylos*, 40: 1–48; 41: 1–67.

Schliemann, Heinrich. 1992. *Une vie d'archéologue*, Paris, Jean-Cyrille Godefroy.

Schliz, Alfred. 1906. "Die Schnurkeramische Kulturkreis und seine Stellung zu den anderen neolitischen Kulturformen in Südwestdeutschland," *Zeitschrift für Ethnologie*, 38: 312–345.

Schmid, Wolfgang Paul. 1968. *Alteuropäisch und Indogermanisch*, Mayence, Steiner, Akademie der Wissenschaften und Literatur.

Schmid, Wolfgang Paul. 1979. "Das Hethitische in einem neuen Verwandtschaftsmodell," *in* Erich Neu and Wolfgang Meid (eds.), *Hethitisch und Indogermanisch. Vergleichende Studien zur historischen Grammatik und zur dialektgeographischen Stellung der indogermanischen Sprachgruppe Altkleinasiens*, Innsbruck, Innsbrucker Beiträge zur Sprachwissenschaft, I: 231–236.

Schmid, Wolfgang Paul. 1987. ""Indo-European"—"Old European" (On the Reexamination of Two Linguistic Terms)," *in* Susan Nacev Skomal and Edgar C. Polomé

520 BIBLIOGRAPHY

(eds.), *Proto-Indo-European: The Archaeology of a Linguistic Problem: Studies in Honor of Marija Gimbutas*, Washington, DC, Institute for the Study of Man: 322–338.

Schmidt, Erich Friedrich. 1933. "Tepe Hissar Excavations 1931," *Museum Journal of Philadelphia*, 23, 4: 322–485.

Schmidt, Erich Friedrich. 1937. *Explorations at Tepe Hissar, Damghan*, Philadelphia, University of Pennsylvania Press.

Schmidt, Johannes. 1872. *Die Verwandtschaftsverhältnisse der indogermanischen Sprachen*, Weimar, Hermann Böhlau.

Schmidt, Johannes. 1890. *Die Urheimath der Indogermanen und das Europäische Zahlsystem*, Berlin, Verlag der Königl, Akademie der Wissenschaften, in Commission bei G. Reimer.

Schmidt, Karl-Horst. 1992. "Contributions from New Data to the Reconstruction of the Proto-Language," *in* Edgar C. Polomé and Werner Winter (eds.), *Reconstructing Languages and Cultures*, Berlin/New York, Mouton de Gruyter: 35–62.

Schmidt, Robert Rudolf. 1945. *Die Burg Vučedol*, Zagreb, Arheološki Muzeum.

Schmidt, Wilhelm. 1926. *Die Sprachfamilien und Sprachkreise der Erde*, Heidelberg, Carl Winter, 2 vols.

Schmitt, Rüdiger. 1967. *Dichtung und Dichtersprache in indogermanischer Zeit*, Wiesbaden, Otto Harrassowitz.

Schmuhl, Hans-Walter. 2005. *Grenzüberschreitungen. Das Kaiser-Wilhelm-Institut für Anthropologie, menschliche Erblehre und Eugenik 1927–1945, in Geschichte der Kaiser-Wilhelm-Gesellschaft im Nationalsozialismus*, 9, Göttingen, Wallstein.

Schmuhl, Hans-Walter. 2008. *The Kaiser Wilhelm Institute for Anthropology, Human Heredity, and Eugenics, 1927–1945 Crossing Boundaries*, New York, Springer, Boston Studies in the Philosophy of Science, vol. 259.

Schnapp, Alain. 1977. "Archéologie et nazisme," *Quaderni di storia*, 5: 1–26.

Schnapp, Alain. 1980. "Archéologie et nazisme (II)," *Quaderni di storia*, 11: 19–33.

Schnapp, Alain. 1981. "Archéologie, archéologues et nazisme," *in* Maurice Olender (ed.), *Le Racisme: mythes et sciences. Pour Léon Poliakov*, Brussels, Éditions Complexe: 289–315.

Schnapp, Alain. 1993. *La Conquête du passé. Aux origines de l'archéologie*, Paris, Éditions Carré; English translation: *The Discovery of the Past: The Origins of Archaeology*, London, British Museum, 1996.

Schnapp, Alain, and Svenbro, Jesper. 1980. "Du nazisme à "Nouvelle École": repères sur la prétendue Nouvelle Droite," *Quaderni di storia*, 11: 107–119.

Schnapp-Gourbeillon, Annie. 1979. "Le mythe dorien," *Annali del Seminario di Studi del Mondo Classico, Sezzione di Archeologia e Storia Antica*, I: 1–11.

Schnapp-Gourbeillon, Annie. 2002. *Aux origines de la Grèce, xiiie-viiie siècle avant notre ère. La genèse du politique*, Paris, Les Belles Lettres.

Schneider, William H. 1990. *Quality and Quantity: The Quest for Biological Regeneration in Twentieth-Century France*, Cambridge, Cambridge University Press.

Schneider, William H. 1994. "Hérédité, sang, et opposition à l'immigration dans la France des années trente," *Ethnologie française*, 24, 1: 104–117.

Schneider, William H. 1995. "Blood Group Research in Great Britain, France, and the United States Between the World Wars," *Yearbook of Physical Anthropology*, 38, 21: 87–114.

Schrader, Otto. 1907. *Sprachvergleichung und Urgeschichte: linguistisch-historische Beiträge zur Erforschung des indogermanischen Altertums*, Iéna, Hermann Costenoble (1st ed. 1883; augmented 2nd ed. 1890).

BIBLIOGRAPHY   521

Schrader, Otto, and Nehring, Alfons (eds.). 1917–1929. *Reallexikon der indogermanischen Altertumskunde: Grundzüge einer Kultur- und Völkergeschichte Alteuropas*, Berlin-Leipzig, de Gruyter, 2 vols. (1st ed. 1901).

Schroeder, Hannes et al. 2019. "Unraveling Ancestry, Kinship, and Violence in a Late Neolithic Mass Grave," *Proceedings of the National Academy of Sciences*, 116 (22): 10705–10710.

Schuchardt, Hugo Ernst Mario. 1884. *Slawo-deutsches und slawo-italienisches*, Graz, Leuschner & Lubensky.

Schuchardt, Hugo Ernst Mario. 1885. *Über die Lautgesetze: gegen die Junggrammatiker*, Berlin, Oppenheim.

Schuchardt, Hugo Ernst Mario. 1889. "Allgemeineres über das Indoportugiesisch (Asioportugiesische)," *Zeitschrift für romanische Philologie*, 13: 476–516.

Schuchardt, Hugo Ernst Mario. 1890. "Über das Malaioportugiesische von Batavia und Tugu," *Sitzungberichte der phil.-histor. Classe der kaiserlichen Akademie der Wissenschaften in Wien*, 122: 1–256.

Schuchardt, Hugo Ernst Mario. 1909. "Die Lingua franca," *Philologie*, 33, 4: 441–461.

Schuchardt, Hugo Ernst Mario. 1922. *Hugo Schuchardt-Brevier: ein Vademecum der allgemeinen Sprachwissenschaft, als Festgabe zum 80. Geburtstag des Meisters zusammengestellt und eingeleitet von Leo Spitzer*, Halle, Niemeyer (2nd ed. 1928).

Schuchardt, Hugo Ernst Mario. 2011. *Textes théoriques et de réflexion, 1885–1925*, Limoges, Éditions Lambert-Lucas (bilingues en sciences humaines).

Schuchardt, Karl. 1919. *Alteuropa: Kulturen—Rassen—Völker*, Berlin-Strasbourg, de Guyter.

Schulenburg, Sigrid von der. 1973. *Leibniz als Sprachforscher*, Frankfurt-sur-le-Main, Veröff. des Leibniz-Archivs, 4.

Schultz, Bruno Kurt. 1934. *Erbkunde, Rassenkunde, Rassenpflege; ein Leitfaden zum Selbststudium und für den Unterricht*, Munich, J. F. Lehmann.

Schulz, Heinrich. 1826. *Zur Urgeschichte des deutschen Volksstamms*, Hamm, Schulzische Buchhandlung.

Schulz, Walther. 1935. "Die indogermanische Frage in der Vorgeschichtsforschung. Völkerbewegungen während der Jüngeren Steinzeit (3. Jahrtausend v. Chr.)," *Zeitschrift für Vergleichende Sprachforschung*, 62: 184–198 (republished in Anton Scherer [ed.], *Die Urheimat der Indogermanen*, Darmstadt, Wissenschaftliche Buchgesellschaft, 1968: 141–157).

Schulz, Walther. 1938. *Indogermanen und Germanen*, Leipzig-Berlin, Teubner.

Schwab, Raymond. 1950. *La Renaissance orientale*, Payot, Paris.

Schwidetzky, Ilse. 1954. *Das Problem des Völkertodes. Eine Studie zur historischen Bevölkerungsbiologie*, Stuttgart, Ferdinand Enke.

Schwidetzky, Ilse. 1980. "The Influence of the Steppe People Based on the Physical Anthropological Data in Special Consideration to the Corded-Battle Axe Culture," *Journal of Indo-European Studies*, 8, 3–4: 345–360.

Searle, Geoffrey Russel. 1976. *Eugenics and Politics in Britain: 1900–1914*, Leyde, Noordhoff.

Seger, Hans. 1936. "Vorgeschichtsforschung und Indogermanenproblem," *in* Helmuth Arntz (ed.), *Germanen und Indo-Germanen, Volkstum, Sprache, Heimat, Kultur. Festschrift für Hermann Hirt*, Heidelberg, Carl Winter, vol. 1: 1–14.

Seidel, Gillian. 1981. "Le fascisme dans les textes de la Nouvelle Droite," *Mots, les langages du politique*, 3: 47–62.

522 BIBLIOGRAPHY

Sergent, Bernard. 1979. "Les trois fonctions des Indo-Européens dans la Grèce ancienne: bilan critique," *Annales, Économies, sociétés, civilisations*, 34, 6: 1155–1186.

Sergent, Bernard. 1982. "Penser—et mal penser—les Indo-Européens (note critique)," *Annales. Économies, sociétés, civilisations*, 37, 4: 669–681.

Sergent, Bernard. 1983. "Panthéons hittites trifonctionnels," *Revue de l'histoire des religions*, 200, 2: 131–153.

Sergent, Bernard. 1990. "La religion cosmique des Indo-Européens (note critique)," *Annales. Économies, sociétés, civilisations*, 45, 4: 941–949.

Sergent, Bernard. 1995. *Les Indo-Européens, histoire, langues, mythes*, Paris, Payot.

Sergent, Bernard. 1997. *Genèse de l'Inde*, Paris, Payot.

Sergent, Bernard. 1998. *Les Trois Fonctions indo-européennes en Grèce ancienne*, vol. 1: *De Mycènes aux Tragiques*, Paris, Economica.

Sergi, Giuseppe. 1903. *Gli Arii in Europa e in Asia*, Turin, Fratelli Bocca.

Sériot, Patrick. 1999. *Structure et totalité. Les origines intellectuelles du structuralisme en Europe centrale et orientale*, Paris, PUF.

Sériot, Patrick. 2005. "Si Vico avait lu Engels, il s'appellerait Nicolas Marr," *Cahiers de l'ILSL*, n° 20: 227–254.

Shaffer, Jim G. 1984. "The Indo-Aryan Invasions, Cultural Myth and Archaeological Reality," *in* John R. Lukacs (ed.), *The People of South Asia: The Biological Anthropology of India, Pakistan and Nepal*, New York, Plenum Press: 77–89.

Shapiro, Fred R. 1981. "On the Origin of the Term "Indo-Germanique," *Historiographia Linguistica*, 8, 1: 165–170.

Shelmerdine, Cynthia W. (ed.). 2008. *The Cambridge Companion to the Aegean Bronze Age*, Cambridge, Cambridge University Press.

Shennan, Stephen J. (ed.). 1989. *Archaeological Approaches to Cultural Identity*, London-Boston, Unwin Hyman (re-edited London/New York, Routledge, 2003).

Shennan, Stephen J. 2003. *Genes, Memes and Human History: Darwinian Archaeology and Cultural Evolution*, London, Thames & Hudson.

Sherratt, Andrew. 1981. "Plough and Pastoralism: Aspects of the Secondary Products Revolution," *in* Ian Hodder, Glynn Isaac, and Norman Hammond (eds.), *Pattern of the Past: Studies in Honour of David Clarke*, Cambridge, Cambridge University Press: 261–305.

Sherratt, Andrew, and Sherratt, Susan. 1988. "Agricultural Transition and Indo-European Dispersals," *Antiquity*, 62: 584–595.

Shevoroshkin, Vitaly Victorovich. 1989a. *Reconstructing Languages and Cultures. Abstracts and Materials from the First International Interdisciplinary Symposium on Language and Prehistory*, Bochum, Brockmeyer.

Shevoroshkin, Vitaly Victorovich (ed.). 1989b. *Explorations in Languages Macro-Families*, Bochum, Brockmeyer.

Shnirelman, Victor A. 1995. "From Internationalism to Nationalism: Forgotten Pages of Soviet Archaeology in the 1930s and 1940s," *in* Philip L. Kohl and Clare Fawcett (eds.), *Nationalism, Politics, and the Practice of Archaeology*, Cambridge, Cambridge University Press: 120–138.

Shnirelman, Victor A. 1998a. "Archaeology and Ethnic Politics: The Discovery of Arkaim," *Museum International (Unesco, Paris)*, 50, 2: 32–39.

Shnirelman, Victor A. 1998b. *Russian Neo-Pagan Myths and Antisemitism*, Jerusalem, Hebrew University of Jerusalem, Series: Analysis of Current Trends in Antisemitism, 13.

BIBLIOGRAPHY   523

Shnirelman, Victor A. 1999. "Passions About Arkai: Russian Nationalism, the Arians, and the Politics of Archaeology," *Inner Asia*, 1: 267–282.

Shnirelman, Victor A. 1999–2000. "Perun, Svarog and Others: Russian Neo-Paganism in Search of Itself," *Cambridge Anthropology*, 21, 3: 18–36.

Shnirelman, Victor A., and Komarova, Galina. 1997. "Majority as a Minority: The Russian Ethno-Nationalism and Its Ideology in the 1970s–1990s," *in* Hans-Rudolf Wicker (ed.), *Rethinking Nationalism and Ethnicity: The Struggle for Meaning and Order in Europe*, Oxford, Berg: 211–224.

Siegert, Hans. 1941–1942. "Zur Geschichte der Begriffe 'Arier' und 'Arisch'," *Wörter und Sachen, Zeitschrift für indogermanische Sprachwissenschaft, Volksforschung und Kulturgeschichte*, Neue Folge, 4: 73–99.

Sims-Williams, Patrick. 1998. "Genetics, Linguistics and Prehistory: Thinking Big and Thinking Straight," *Antiquity*, 72, 277: 505–527.

Sklenář, Karel. 1983. *Archaeology in Central Europe: The First 500 Years*, Leicester, Leicester University Press.

Smolla, Günter. 1979–1980. "Das Kossinna-Syndrom," *Fundberichte aus Hessen*, 19/20: 1–9.

Smolla, Günter. 1984–1985. "Gustaf Kossinna nach 50 Jahren. Kein Nachruf," *Acta Praehistorica et Archaeologica*, 16/17: 9–14.

Sokoloff, Georges. 2011. *Nos ancêtres les nomades. L'épopée indo-européenne*, Paris, Fayard.

Spearman, Charles. 1927. *The Abilities of Man: Their Nature and Their Measurements*, London, Macmillan.

Specht, Franz. 1944. *Der Ursprung der indogermanischen Deklination*, Göttingen, Vandenhoek & Ruprecht.

Speer, Albert. 1976. *Inside the Third Reich*, New York, Avon (original German edition: *Erinnerungen*, Frankfurt/Main, Ullstein, 1969).

Spiegel-Rösing, Ina, and Schwidetzky, Ilse. 1982. *Maus und Schlange. Untersuchungen zur Lage der deutschen Anthropologie*, Munich, Oldenburg.

Stalin, Joseph V. 1950. *Le Marxisme et les Problèmes de linguistique*, Moscow, Éditions en langues étrangères (Marxism and Problems of Linguistics, by J. V. Stalin, Moscow, Foreign Languages Publishing House, 1950).

Stanton, William. 1960. *The Leopard's Spots: Scientific Attitudes towards Race in America, 1815–1859*, Chicago, Chicago University Press.

Steegmann, Robert. 2005. *Struthof, le KL-Natzweiler et ses Kommandos. Une nébuleuse concentrationnaire des deux côtés du Rhin, 1941–1945*, Strasbourg, La Nuée Bleue.

Sterling, Eleonore. 1969. *Judenhass. Die Anfänge des politischen Antisemitismus in Deutschland (1815–1850)*, Frankfurt-sur-le-Main, Europäische Verlagsanstalt.

Stern, Alexandra. 2005. *Eugenic Nation Faults: and Frontiers of Better Breeding in Modern America*, Berkeley, University of California Press.

Stern, Fritz Richard. 1961. *The Politics of Cultural Despair: A Study in the Rise of the Germanic Ideology*, Berkeley, University of California Press.

Sternhell, Zeev. 1978. *La Droite révolutionnaire. 1885–1914. Les origines françaises du fascisme*, Paris, Seuil.

Sternhell, Zeev. 1983. *L'Idéologie fasciste en France*, Paris, Seuil.

Steuer, Heiko. 1997. "Gedenkrede für Herbert Jankuhn am 21. November 1991 in Göttingen," in H. Beck, H. Steuer (ed.), *Haus und Hof in ur- und frühgeschichtlicher Zeit*, Abh. Akad. Wiss. Göttingen, Phil. Hist. Klasse, Dritte Folge Nr. 218, Festschrift Jankuhn, Göttingen: 547–568.

524 BIBLIOGRAPHY

Stoczkowski, Wiktor. 1994. *Anthropologie naïve, anthropologie savante de l'origine de l'homme, de l'imagination et des idées reçues*, Paris, CNRS Éditions.

Stoczkowski, Wiktor. 1999. *Des hommes, des dieux et des extra-terrestres. Ethnologie d'une croyance moderne*, Paris, Flammarion.

Stone, Merlin. 1976. *When God Was a Woman*, New York, Barnes & Noble (French translation: *Quand Dieu était une femme*, Québec, SCE, 1978).

Strahlenberg, Philipp Johann Tabbert von. 1730. *Das nord- und ostliche Theil von Europa und Asia*, Stockholm, *in* Verlegung des Autoris (fac-similé *Studia uralo-altaïca*, 8, Szeged, 1975).

Streitberg, Wihlelm. 1915. "Zur Geschichte der Sprachwissenschaft," *Indogermanische Forschungen*, 35: 182–197.

Strunk, Klaus. 2004. "Vorgriechisch/"Pelasgisch": Neue Erwägungen zu einer älteren Substrathypothese," *in* Joachim Bammesberger and Theo Vennemann (eds.), *Languages in Prehistoric Europe*, Heildelberg, Winter: 85–98.

Sturtevant, Edgar Howard. 1929. "The Relationship of Hittite to Indo-European," *Transactions and Proceedings of the American Philology Association*, 60: 25–37.

Sturtevant, Edgar Howard. 1962. "The Indo-Hittite Hypothesis," *Language*, 38: 105–110.

Sulimirski, Tadeusz. 1933. "Die Schnurkeramischen Kulturen und das indoeuropäische Problem," *in La Pologne au VIIe Congrès international des sciences historiques*, Varsovie, vol. 1: 287–308 (republished in Anton Scherer [ed.], *Die Urheimat der Indogermanen*, Darmstadt, Wissenschaftliche Buchgesellschaft, 1968: 117–140).

Sünner, Rüdiger. 1999. *Schwarze Sonne. Entfesselung und Missbrauch der Mythen in Nationalsozialismus und rechter Esoterik*, Fribourg-en-Brisgau, Herder Spektrum.

Swadesh, Morris. 1972. *The Origin and Diversification of Language*, London, Taylor & Francis.

Swiggers, Pierre. 1991. "The Indo-European Origin of the Greek Meters: Antoine Meillet's Views and Their Reception by Émile Benveniste and Nikilai Trubetzkoy," *in* Karl Pearson (ed.), *Perspectives on Indo-European Language, Culture and Religion: Studies in Honor of Edgar C. Polomé*, Washington, DC, Institute of the Study of Man, JIES Monograph, 7, vol. 1: 199–215.

Szemerényi, Oswald John Louis. 1977. *Studies in the Kinship Terminology of the Indo-European Languages: With Special Reference to Indian, Iranian, Greek, and Latin*, Acta Iranica 16, Téhéran-Liège, Éditions Bibliothèque Pahlavi.

Szemerényi, Oswald John Louis. 1985. "Recent Developments in Indo-European Linguistics," *Transactions of the Philological Society*, 83, 1: 1–71.

Szemerényi, Oswald John Louis. 1996. *Introduction to Indo-European Linguistics*, Oxford, Oxford University Press.

Taguieff, Pierre-André. 1981. "L'héritage nazi. Des nouvelles droites européennes à la littérature niant le génocide," *Les Nouveaux Cahiers*, 64: 3–22.

Taguieff, Pierre-André. 1984. "La stratégie culturelle de la 'Nouvelle Droite' en France (1968–1983)," *in* Antoine Spire (ed.), *Vous avez dit fascismes?*, Paris, Montalba-Artaud: 13–52.

Taguieff, Pierre-André. 1994. *Sur la Nouvelle Droite. Jalons d'une analyse critique*, Paris, Descartes-Galilée.

Taguieff, Pierre-André et al. 1999. *L'Antisémitisme de plume, 1940–1944, études et documents*, Berg International.

Tallgren, Aarne Michaël. 1926. "La Pontide préscythique après l'introduction des métaux," *Eurasia Septentrionalis Antiqua*, 2.

BIBLIOGRAPHY 525

Tallgren, Aarne Michaël. 1936a. "Sur la méthode de l'archéologie préhistorique," *Eurasia Septentrionalis Antiqua*, 10: 16–24.

Tallgren, Aarne Michaël. 1936b. "Archaeological Studies in Soviet Russia," *Eurasia Septentrionalis Antiqua*, 10: 129–170.

Tallgren, Aarne Michaël. 1939. *Etnogenesis eli ajatuksia kansakuntain synnystä* [L'ethnogénèse, ou réflexions sur la naissance des nations], Helsinki.

Taylor, Isaac. 1890. *The Origin of the Aryans: An Account of the Prehistoric Ethnology and Civilisation of Europe*, London, W. Scott.

Tejral, Jaroslav. 2009. "Les grandes migrations, depuis les Germains jusqu'à l'an mille," *in* Jean-Paul Demoule (ed.), *L'Europe, un continent redécouvert par l'archéologie*, Paris, Gallimard: 125–136.

Telegin, Dmitri. 1973. *Seredno-Stogivska kul'tura epokhy midi*, Kiev, Naukova Dumka.

Telegin, Dmitri, Nečitaljlo, A. L., Potekhina, I. D., and Pančenko, V. Ju. 2001. *Srednestogovskaja i novodanilovskaja kul'tury ėneolita Azovo-Černomorskogo regiona*, Lougansk, Shlyahh.

Telegin, Dmitri, and Potekhina, I. D. 1987. *Neolithic Cemeteries and Populations in the Dnieper Basin*, Oxford, British Archaeological Reports, International series, S383.

Terrell, John E. 2001. *Archaeology, Language, and History: Essays on Culture and Ethnicity*, Westport (CT), Bergin & Garvey.

Testart, Alain. 2010. *La Déesse et le Grain. Trois essais sur les religions néolithiques*, Paris, Errance.

Testart, Alain. 2011. "Les modèles biologiques sont-ils utiles pour penser l'évolution des sociétés?," *Préhistoires méditerranéennes*, 2: 105–122.

Teufer, Mike. 2012. "Der Streitwagen: iene 'indo-iranische' Erfindung? Zum Problem der Verbindung von Sprachwissenschaft und Archäologie," *Archäologische Mitteilungen aus Iran und Turan*, 44: 271–312.

Thiesse, Anne-Marie, *La Création des identités nationales: Europe xviiie-xxe siècle*, Paris, Seuil, 1999.

Thiolay, Boris. 2012. *Lebensborn, la fabrique des enfants parfaits. Ces Français qui sont nés dans une maternité SS*, Paris, Flammarion.

Thomas, Homer L. 1991. "Indo-European: From the Paleolithic to the Neolithic," *in* Roger Pearson (ed.), *Perspectives on Indo-European Language, Culture and Religion: Studies in Honor of E.C. Polomé*, Washington, DC, Institute for the Study of Man, vol. I: 12–37.

Thomas, Homer L. 1992. "Archaeology and Indo-European Comparative Linguistics," *in* Edgar C. Polomé and Werner Winter (eds.), *Reconstructing Languages and Cultures*, Berlin/New York, Mouton de Gruyter: 281–315.

Thomason, Sarah Grey. 2001. *Language Contact: An Introduction*, Edinburgh, Edinburgh University Press.

Thomason, Sarah Grey, and Kaufman, Terrence. 1988. *Language Contact, Creolization, and Genetic Linguistics*, Berkeley, University of California Press.

Thuillard, Marc et al. 2018. "A Large-Scale Study of World Myths," *Trames*, 22 (4): 407–424.

Thuillier, Guy. 1977. "Un anarchiste positiviste, G. Vacher de Lapouge," *in* Pierre Guiral and Émile Temime (eds.), *L'Idée de race dans la pensée politique française contemporaine*, Paris, CNRS Éditions: 48–65.

Thuillier, Jean-Paul. 2006. *Les Étrusques*, Paris, Éditions du Chêne.

Thuillier, Pierre. 1981. *Les biologistes vont-ils prendre le pouvoir? La sociobiologie en question*, t. I: *Le Contexte et l'Enjeu*, Brussels, Éditions Complexe.

526 BIBLIOGRAPHY

Tilak, Bâl Gangâdhar. 1903. *The Arctic Home in the Vedas*, Poona, Tilak Bros (French translation: *L'Origine polaire de la tradition védique*, Milan, Archè, 1979).

Todorova, Henrieta. 1986. *Kamenno-mednata Epoha v Bǎlgarija (peto hiljadoleti predi novata era)*, Sofia, Izdatelstvo Nauka i Iskustvo.

Toman, Jindrich. 1987. "Trubetzkoy Before Trubetzkoy," *in* Hans Aarsleff, Louis Gérard Kelly, and Hans-Josef Niederehe (eds.), *Papers in the History of Linguistics*, Amsterdam, Benjamins: 627–638.

Topinard, Paul. 1891. *L'Homme dans la nature*, Paris, Bibliothèque scientifique internationale.

Toporov, Vladimir Nikolaevic. 1981. "Die Ursprünge der indoeuropäischen Poetik," *Poetica*, 13: 189–251.

Tournier, Maurice. 1992. "Des mots en politique. 'Race,' un mot qui a perdu la raison," *Mots*, 32: 105–107.

Tovar, Antonio. 1961. *The Ancient Languages of Spain and Portugal*, New York, Vanni.

Tovar, Antonio. 1980. "Die Bildung der indogermanischen Dialekte," *in* Joachim Göschel, Pavle Ivić, and Kurt Kehr (eds.), *Dialekt und Dialektologie*, Beihefte NF 26, Wiesbaden, Franz Steiner: 143–153.

Tovar, Antonio. 1987. "Lenguas y pueblos de la antigua Hispania," in Joaquin Gorrochategui, José L. Melena, and Juan Santos (eds.), *Actas del IV Coloquio sobre las lenguas y culturas paleohispanicas*, Vitoria, Victoriaco vasconum: 15–34.

Trautmann, Thomas R. 1997. *Aryans and British India*, Berkeley, University of California Press.

Trautmann-Waller Céline (ed.). 2004. *Quand Berlin pensait les peuples. Anthropologie, ethnologie, psychologie, 1850–1890*, Paris, CNRS Éditions.

Tremblay, Xavier. 2005. "Grammaire comparée et grammaire historique: quelle réalité est reconstruite par la grammaire comparée?," *in* Henri-Paul Frankfurt, Gérard Fussman, Jean Kellens, and Xavier Tremblay (eds.), *Aryens et Iraniens en Asie centrale*, Paris, Collège de France, Publications de l'Institut de civilisation indienne, fasc. 72: 21–196.

Treuil, René, Darcque, Pascal, Poursat, Jean-Claude, and Touchais, Gilles (eds.). 2008. *Les Civilisations égéennes du néolithique et de l'âge du bronze*, Paris, PUF (1st ed. 1989).

Trigger, Bruce G. 1980. *Gordon Childe, Revolutions in Archaeology*, New York, Columbia University Press.

Trigger, Bruce G. 1989. *A History of Archaeological Thought*, Cambridge-New York, Cambridge University Press.

Trombetti, Alfredo. 1905. *L'unità d'origine del linguaggio*, Bologne, Luigi Beltrami.

Troubetzkoy, Nikolaï Serguevitch. 1930. "Proposition 16," in *Actes du premier Congrès international de linguistes à La Haye, du 10 au 15 avril 1928*, Leyde, A. W. Sijthoff, vol. 1: 17–18.

Troubetzkoy, Nikolaï Serguevitch. 1939. "Gedanken über das Indogermanenproblem," *Acta Linguistica*, 1: 81–89.

Troubetzkoy, Nikolaï Serguevitch. 1949. *Principes de phonologie*, Paris, Klincksieck,

Troubetzkoy, Nikolaï Serguevitch. 1975. *N. S. Trubetzkoy's Letters and Notes*, Roman Jakobson (ed.), La Haye, Mouton.

Troubetzkoy, Nikolaï Serguevitch. 1996. "Réflexions sur le problème indoeuropéen," *in* Patrick Seriot (ed.), *N. S. Troubetzkoy. L'Europe et l'Humanité. Écrits linguistiques et paralinguistiques*, Liège, Mardaga: 211–230.

Troubetzkoy, Nikolaï Serguevitch. 2006. *Correspondance avec Roman Jakobson et autres écrits*, edition established by Patrick Seriot, Lausanne, Payot.

BIBLIOGRAPHY   527

Trudgill, Peter. 1986. *Dialects in Contact*, Oxford, Blackwell.
Tsirtsoni, Zoï. 2010. "To telos tis neolithikis epochis stin Ellada kai ta Balkania," *in* Zoï Tsirtsoni and Nikos Papadimitriou (eds.), *La Grèce dans le contexte culturel des Balkans du Ve et IVe millénaire av. J.-C.*: 93–103, Athens, Fondation N. P. Goulandris-Musée d'art cycladique.
Tuaillon, Gaston. 1972. "Le franco-provençal: progrès d'une définition," *Travaux de linguistique et de littérature*, 10: 293–339.
Tucker, A. N., and Bryan, M. A. 1974. "The 'Mbugu'Anomaly," *Bulletin of the School of Oriental and African Studies*, 37, 1: 188–207.
Ţurcanu, Florin. 2003. *Mircea Eliade. Le prisonnier de l'histoire*, Paris, La Découverte.
Ţurcanu, Florin. 2013. "Mircea Eliade et Georges Dumézil, "une amitié dans la liberté"?," *Historia Religionum*, 5: 109–134.
Uerpmann, Hans-Peter. 1990. "Die Domestikation des Pferdes im Chalkolithikum West- und Mitteleuropas," *Madrider Mitteilungen*, 31: 109–153.
Uerpmann, Hans-Peter. 1995. "Domestication of the Horse: When, Where, and Why?," *in* Liliane Bodson (ed.), *Le Cheval et les Autres Équidés. Aspects de l'histoire de leur insertion dans les activités humaines*, Liege, Université de Liège: 15–29.
Uhlenbeck, Christianus Cornelius. 1935. "Oer-Indogermaansch en Oer-Indogermanen," *Medeleelingen der Koninklijke Akademie van Wetenschappen, Afdeeling Letterkunde*, 77, series A, 4.
Uhlenbeck, Christianus Cornelius. 1937. "The Indogermanic Mother Language and Mother Tribes Complex," *American Anthropologist*, 39, 3: 385–393.
Ujfalvy, Charles Eugène de. 1884. *Le Berceau des Aryas d'après des ouvrages récents*, Paris, A. Hennuyer.
Ujfalvy, Charles Eugène de. 1887a. "Quelques observations sur les Tadjiks des montagnes, appelés aussi Galtchas," *Bulletins de la Société d'anthropologie de Paris*, 10, 1: 15–43.
Ujfalvy, Charles Eugène de. 1887b. "L'influence du milieu sur les peuples de l'Asie centrale," *Bulletins de la Société d'anthropologie de Paris*, 10, 1: 436–457.
Ujfalvy, Charles Eugène de. 1896. *Les Aryens au nord et au sud de l'Hindou-Kouch*, Paris, G. Masson.
Untermann, Jürgen. 1961. *Sprachräume und Sprachbewegungen im vorrömischen Hispanien*, Wiesbaden, Harrassowitz.
Untermann, Jürgen. 1975. *Monumenta Linguarum Hispanicarum*, t. I.: *Die Münzlegenden*, Wiesbaden, Harrassowitz.
Untermann, Jürgen. 1997. *Monumenta Linguarum Hispanicarum*, t. IV: *Die tartessischen, keltiberischen und lusitanischen Inschriften*, Wiesbaden, Reichert.
Ureland, Per Sture. 1994. "Language Contact Across the Baltic," *Gothenburg Papers in Theoretical Linguistics*, 72: 199–269.
Ureland, Per Sture (ed.). 2010. *Sprachkontakt in der Hanse: Aspekte des Sprachausgleichs im Ostsee- und Nordseeraum. Akten des 7. Internationalen Symposions über Sprachkontakt*, Berlin, de Gruyter.
Vacher de Lapouge, Georges. 1899. *L'Aryen, son rôle social. Cours libre de science politique professé à l'Université de Montpellier (1889–1890)*, Paris, A. Fontemoing.
Valdman, Albert (ed.). 1977. *Pidgin and Creole Linguistics*, Bloomington, Indiana University Press.
Valdman, Albert, and Highfield, Arnold R. (eds.). 1980. *Theoretical Orientations in Creole Studies*, New York, Academic Press.

528 BIBLIOGRAPHY

Valkhoff, Marius François. 1972. *New Lights on Afrikaans and Malayo-Portuguese*, Louvain, Peeters.

Valle Rodriguez, Carlos del. 1983. "Die Anfänge der hebräischen Grammatik in Spanien," *in* C. H. M. Versteegh, Konrad Koerner, and Hans-Josef Niederehe (eds.), *The History of Linguistics in the Near East*, Amsterdam, Benjamins: 153–166.

Vallois, Henri-Victor. 1936. "Notice nécrologique de Georges Vacher de Lapouge," *L'Anthropologie*, 46: 481.

Vallois, Henri-Victor. 1938. "Les recherches sur la race au congrès pour l'étude des problèmes de la population," *L'Anthropologie*, 48: 160–161.

Vallois, Henri-Victor. 1944. *Les Races humaines*, Paris, PUF, "Que sais-je?" collection.

Van Bekkum, Wout Jan. 1983. "The Risala of Yehuda Ibn Quraysh and Its Place in Hebrew Linguistics," *in* C. H. M. Versteegh, Konrad Koerner, and Hans-Josef Niederehe (eds.), *The History of Linguistics in the Near East*, Amsterdam, Benjamins: 71–91.

Van den Gheyn, R. P. 1889. *L'Origine européenne des Aryas. Mémoire presenté au Congrès scientifique international des catholiques tenu à Paris en 1888*, Paris, Bureaux des Annales de philosophie chrétienne.

Van der Linden, Marc. 2006. *Le Phénomène campaniforme dans l'Europe du IIIe millénaire avant notre ère: synthèse et nouvelles perspectives*, Oxford, Archaeopress, BAR International Series, 1470.

Van der Linden, Marc. 2016. "Population History in Third-Millennium-BC Europe: Assessing the Contribution of Genetics," *World Archaeology*, 48, 5: 714–728.

Vanhove, Martine. 1993. *La Langue maltaise: études syntaxiques d'un dialecte arabe "périphérique,"* Wiesbaden, Harrassowitz.

Van Windekens, Albert Jan. 1952. *Le Pélasgique. Essai sur une langue indo-européenne préhellénique*, Louvain, Université de Louvain, Bibliothèque du Mouseion.

Veit, Ulrich. 1984. "Gustaf Kossinna und V. Gordon Childe: Ansätze zu einer theoretischen Grundlegung der Vorgeschichte," *Saeculum*, 35: 326–364.

Veit, Ulrich. 1989. "Ethnic Concepts in German Prehistory: A Case Study on the Relationship Between Cultural Identity and Archaeological Objectivity," Stephen J. Shennan (ed.), London, Unwin Hyman: 35–56 (re-edited Paperback Routledge, London/New York, 1994).

Veit, Ulrich. 2000. "Gustaf Kossinna and His Concept of a National Archaeology," *in* Heinrich G. H. Härke (ed.), *Archaeology, Ideology and Society: The German Experience*, Frankfurt-sur-le-Main, Peter Lang: 41–66.

Vennemann, Theo. 1989. *The New Sound of Indo-European: Essays in Phonological Reconstruction*, Amsterdam, Mouton de Gruyter.

Ventris, Michael, and Chadwick, John. 1953. "Evidence for Greek Dialect in the Mycenaean Archives," *Journal of Hellenic Studies*, 73: 84–103.

Verdu, Paul et al. 2013. "Sociocultural Behavior, Sex-Biased Admixture, and Effective Population Sizes in Central African Pygmies and Non-Pygmies," *Molecular Biology and Evolution*, 30, 4: 918–937.

Verschuer, Otmar von. 1959. *Genetik des Menschen. Lehrbuch der Humangenetik*, Munich, Urban & Schwarzenberg.

Viallaneix, Paul, and Jean Ehrard (eds.). 1982. *Nos ancêtres les Gaulois. Actes du colloque international de Clermont-Ferrand*, Clermont-Ferrand, Publications de la Faculté des lettres et sciences humaines.

Victorri, Bernard. 2000. "La langue originelle," in *Science et Avenir*, 125: 37–41.

BIBLIOGRAPHY   529

Vidal-Naquet, Pierre. 1986. "Mort d'un inventeur, Georges Dumézil," *L'Événement du jeudi*, 102 (16 to 22 October 1986).

Vidal-Naquet, Pierre. 2005. *L'Atlantide. Petite histoire d'un mythe platonicien*, Paris, Les Belles Lettres.

Viel, Michel. 1984. *La Notion de "marque" chez Trubetzkoy et Jakobson: un épisode de l'histoire de la pensée structurale*, Lille-Paris, Didier-Érudition.

Vielle, Christophe. 1992. "Idéologie, mythe et littérature. Quelles perspectives pour les acquis du comparatisme dumézilien?," *Uranie*, 2: 165–185.

Vielle, Christophe. 1994. "Sir William Jones et la comparaison génétique en mythologie," *in* Christophe Vielle, Pierre Swiggers, and Guy Jucquois (eds.), *Comparatisme, mythologies, langages, en hommage à Claude Lévi-Strauss*, Louvain-La-Neuve, Peeters, "Bibliothèque des cahiers de l'Institut de linguistique de Louvain," 73: 33–60.

Vielle, Christophe. 1996. *Le Mytho-cycle-héroïque dans l'aire indo-européenne: correspondances et transformations helléno-aryennes*, Louvain-la-Neuve, Institut orientaliste, Publications de l'institut orientaliste de Louvain, 46.

Vigne, Jean-Denis. 2008. "Zooarchaeological Aspects of the Neolithic Diet Transition in the Near East and Europe, and Their Putative Relationships with the Neolithic Demographic Transition," *in* Jean-Pierre Bocquet-Appel and Ofer Bar-Yosef (eds.), *The Neolithic Demographic Transition and Its Consequences*, New York, Springer: 179–205.

Vigne, Jean-Denis, and Daniel Helmer. 2007. "Was Milk a "Secondary Product" in the Old World Neolithisation Process?: Its Role in the Domestication of Cattle, Sheep and Goats," *Anthropozoologica*, 42, 2: 9–40.

Villar, Francisco. 1990. "Indo-Européens et pré-Indo-Européens dans la péninsule Ibérique," *in* Thomas Markey and John A. C. Greppin (eds.), *When Words Collide: The Indo-Europeans and the Pre-Indo-Europeans*, Ann Arbor, Karoma Publishers: 363–394.

Vinogradov, Viktor Vladimirovich. 1969. "Triompher du culte de la personnalité dans la linguistique soviétique," *Langage*, 15, 4: 67–84.

Virchow, Rudolf. 1872. "Über die Methode der wissenschaftlichen Anthropologie," *Zeitschrift für Ethnologie*, 4: 300–320.

Virchow, Rudolf. 1874. *Die Urbevölkerung Europa's*, Berlin, C.G. Lüderitz (French translation: "Les peuples primitifs de l'Europe," *Revue scientifique*, 4 July 1874: 1–13).

Virchow, Rudolf. 1884. "Die Rasse von La Tène," *Verhandlungen der Berliner Gesellschaft für Anthropologie, Ethnologie und Urgeschichte*: 168–181.

Virchow, Rudolf. 1886. "Gesammtbericht über die von der deutschen anthropologischen Gesellschaft veranlassten Erhebungen über die Farbe der Haut, der Haare und der Augen der Schulkinder," *Archiv für Anthropologie*, 14: 275–475.

Voegelin, C. F., and Voegelin, F. M. 1973. "Recent Classifications of Genetic Relationships," *Annual Review of Anthropology*, 2, 1: 139–151.

Von See, Klaus. 1970. *Deutsche Germanen-Ideologie vom Humanismus bis zur Gegenwart*, Frankfurt-sur-le-Main, Athenäum-Verlag.

Von See, Klaus. 1981. "Der Germane als Barbar," *Jahrbuch für internationale Germanistik*, 13: 42–72.

Vörös, I. 1981. "Wild Equids from the Early Holocene in the Carpathian Basin," *Folia Archaeologica*, 32: 37–68.

Wagner, Gottfried. 1998. *L'Héritage Wagne. Une autobiographie*, Paris, Éditions Nil.

Wagner, Heinrich. 1985. *Das Hethitische vom Standpunkte der typologischen Sprachgeographie*, Pisa, Giardini, Testi Linguistici, 7.

530 BIBLIOGRAPHY

Wahl, J., and Strien, H.-C. (eds.). 2007. *Tatort Talheim. 7000 Jahre später: Archäologen und Gerichtsmediziner ermitteln*, Heilbronn, Städtische Museen Heilbronn.

Wahle, Ernst. 1932. *Deutsche Vorzeit*, Leipzig, K. Kabitzsch (2nd ed. 1952).

Wahle, Ernst. 1940–1941. "Zur ethnischen Deutung frühgeschichtlicher Kulturprovinzen: Grenze der frühgeschichlichen Erkenntnis," *Sitzungsberichte der Heidelberger Akademie der Wissenschaft Phil.-Hist. Klasse*, I, 2.

Wahle, Ernst. 1964. *Tradition und Auftrag prähistorischer Forschung: Ausgewählte Abhandlungen*, Berlin, Duncker, Humbolt.

Walter, Henriette. 1994. *L'Aventure des langues en Occident. Leur origine, leur histoire, leur géographie* (preface by André Martinet), Paris, Robert Laffont.

Warren, William Fairfield. 1885. *Paradise Found: The Cradle of the Human Race at the North Pole: A Study of the Prehistoric World*, Boston, Houghton, Mifflin.

Watkins, Calvert. 1995. *How to Kill a Dragon: Aspects of Indo-European Poetics*, Oxford, Oxford University Press.

Wechler, Klaus-Peter. 2002. *Studien zum Neolithikum der osteuropäischen Steppe*, Mayence, Philipp von Zabern.

Weindling, Paul. 1989. *Health, Race, and German Politics Between National Unification and Nazism, 1870–1945*, Cambridge, Cambridge University Press (abridged French translation: *L'Hygiène de la race*, t. I: *Hygiène raciale et Eugénisme médical en Allemagne, 1870–1933*, Paris, La Découverte-Syros, 1998).

Weinreich, Max. 1946. *Hitler's Professors: The Part of Scholarship in Germany's Crimes Against the Jewish People*, Yale University Press (2nd edition 1999).

Weinreich, Max. 1980. *History of the Yiddish Language*, Chicago/London, University of Chicago Press.

Weinreich, Uriel. 1953. *Languages in Contact, Findings and Problems*, New York, Publications of the Linguistic Circle of New York, 1.

Weinreich, Uriel. 1954. "Is a Structural Dialectology Possible?," *Word*, 10: 388–400.

West, Martin Litchfield. 1999. *The East Face of Helicon: West Asiatic Elements in Greek Poetry and Myth*, Oxford, Oxford University Press (new edition).

West, Martin Litchfield. 2008. *Indo-European Poetry and Myth*, Oxford, Oxford University Press.

Whinnom, Keith. 1980. "Creolization in Linguistic Change," *in* Albert Valdman and Arnold R. Highfield (eds.), *Theoretical Orientations in Creole Studies*, New York, Academic Press: 203–212.

White, Charles. 1799. *Account of the Regular Gradation in Man*, London, Dilly.

Wieland, Hermann. 1925. *Atlantis, Edda und Bibel. 200 000 Jahre germanischer Weltkultur und das Geheimnis der Heiligen Schrift*, Weissenburg in Bayern, Gross-deutscher Verlag.

Wieviorka, Annette, and Laffitte, Michel. 2012. *À l'intérieur du camp de Drancy*, Paris, Perrin.

Wilke, Georg. 1918. "Archäologie und Indogermanenproblem," *Veröffentlichungen des Provinzialmuseums zu Halle*, 3, Halle: 1–18.

Will, Édouard. 1956. *Doriens et Ioniens. Essai sur la valeur du critère ethnique appliqué à l'étude de l'histoire et de la civilisation grecques*, Paris, Les Belles Lettres.

Williams, Elizabeth A. 1983. *The Science of Man: Anthropological Thought and Institutions in Nineteenth-Century France*, Bloomington, Indiana University.

Willson, Amos Leslie. 1964. *A Mythical Image: The Ideal of India in German Romanticism*, Durham, NC, Duke University Press.

BIBLIOGRAPHY 531

Wilser, Ludwig. 1899. *Herkunft und Urgeschichte der Arier*, Heidelberg, J. Hörning.

Winter, Werner. 1992. "Armenian, Tocharian, and the "Glottalic" Theory," *in* Edgar C. Polomé and Werner Winter (eds.), *Reconstructing Languages and Cultures*, Berlin/New York, Mouton & de Gruyter: 112–127.

Wirth, Hermann Felix. 1928. *Der Aufgang der Menschheit. Geschichte der Religion, Symbolik und Schrift der atlantisch-nordischen Rasse*, t. I: *Die Grundzüge*, Iéna, E. Diederichs.

Witzel, Michael. 2003. "Ein Fremdling im Rgveda," *Journal of Indo-European Studies*, 31, 1–2: 107–185.

Witzel, Michael. 2006. "Rama's Realm: Indocentric Rewritings of Early South Asian History," *in* Garrett Fagan (ed.), *Archaeolological Fantasies: How Pseudoarchaeology Misrepresents the Past and Misleads the Public*, London, Routledge.

Witzel, Michael. 2013. *The Origins of the World's Mythologies*, New York, Oxford University Press.

Wiwjorra, I. 1996. "German Archaeology and Its Relation to Nationalism and Racism," *in* Margarita Díaz-Andreu Garcia and Tim Champion (eds.), *Nationalism and Archaeology in Europe*, London, ULC Press: 164–171.

Wolff, Karl Felix. 1914. "Die Urheimat der Indogermanen," *Mannus*, 6: 309–321.

Wolfram, S. 2000. "Vorsprung durch Technik or "Kossinna Syndrome," *in* G. H. Heinrich Härke (ed.), *Archaeology, Ideology and Society: The German Experience*, Frankfurt-sur-le-Main, Peter Lang: 180–201.

Wolzogen, comte Hans von. 1882. *Die Religion des Mitleidens und die Ungleichheit der menschlichen Racen*, Bayreuth, Burger.

Wrotnowska, Denise. 1975. "Pruner-Bey, Franz Ignace," *in* Charles Coulston Gillispie (ed.), *Dictionary of Scientific Biography*, New York, Charles Scribner's Sons, t. XI: 177–179.

Wulsin, Frederick R., and Smith, Myron Bement. 1932. *Excavations at Tureng Tepe, near Asterābād, Bulletin of the American Institute for Persian Art and Archaeology*, 2, Suppl. 1 *bis*.

Xirotiris, Nikolaos I. 1980. "The Indo-European in Greece: An Anthropological Approach to the Population of the Bronze Age," *Journal of Indo-European Studies*, 8: 201–210.

Yakubovich, Ilya S. 2009. *Sociolinguistics of the Luvian Language*, Leyde, Brill.

Yoshida, Atsuhiko. 1964. "La structure de l'illustration du bouclier d'Achille," *Revue belge de philologie et d'histoire*, 42, 1: 5–15.

Yoshida, Atsuhiko. 1977. "Mythes japonais et idéologie tripartite des Indo-Européens," *Diogène*, 98: 101–124.

Yoshida, Atsuhiko. 1981. "Dumézil et les études comparatives des mythes japonais," *in* Jacques Bonnet et al. (eds.), *Pour un temps: Georges Dumézil*, Paris, Centre Georges Pompidou: 319–324.

Young, Edward J. 1968. *Gobineau und der Rassismus: eine Kritik der anthropologischen Geschichtstheorie*, Meisenheim, Hain.

Zimmer, Stefan. 1990a. "On Indo-Europeanization," *Journal of Indo-European Studies*, 18, 1–2: 141–155.

Zimmer, Stefan, 1990b. "The Investigation of Proto-Indo-European History: Methods, Problems, Limitations," *in* Thomas Markey and John A. C. Greppin (eds.), *When Words Collide: The Indo-Europeans and the Pre-Indo-Europeans*, Ann Arbor, Karoma Publishers: 311–334.

532 BIBLIOGRAPHY

Zimmer, Stefan. 1990c. *Ursprache, Urvolk und Indogermanisierung: zur Methode der indogermanischen Altertumskunde*, Innsbruck, Innsbrucker Beiträge zur Sprachwissenschaft.

Zimmer, Stefan. 1991. "On Language Genesis: The Case of Afrikaans," *in* Roger Pearson (ed.), *Perspectives on Indo-European Language, Culture and Religion: Studies in Honor of Edgar C. Polomé*, JIES Monograph, 7: 347–359.

Zimmer, Stefan. 1994. "Die Indogermanen und das Pferd—Befunde und Probleme," *in* Bernhardt Hänsel and Stefan Zimmer (eds.), *Die Indogermanen und das Pferd, Festschrift B. Schlerath*, Budapest, Archaeolingua: 29–35.

Zimmer, Stefan. 1998. "Modern Necromancy, or How to Make Mummies Speak," *Journal of Indo-European Studies*, 26: 163–180.

Zmarzlik, Hans-Günther. 1963. "Der Sozialdarwinismus in Deutschland als geschichtliches Problem," *Vierteljahreshefte für Zeitgeschichte*, 11: 245–273.

Zschaetzsche, Karl Georg. 1922. *Die Arier: Herkunft und Geschichte des arischen Stammes*, Berlin, Nicolassee (2nd ed. 1934).

Zvelebil, Marek (ed.). 1986. *Hunters in Transition: Mesolithic Societies of Temperate Eurasia and Their Transition to Farming*, Cambridge, Cambridge University Press.

Zvelebil, Marek. 1995. "At the Interface of Archaeology, Linguistics and Genetics: Indo-European Dispersals and the Agricultural Transition in Europe," *Journal of European Archaeology*, 3, no 1: 33–71.

Zvelebil, Marek, Domańska, Lucyna, and Dennell, Robin (eds.). 1997. *Harvesting the Sea, Farming the Forest: The Emergence of Neolithic Societies in the Baltic Region*, Sheffield, Sheffield Academic Press.

Zvelebil, Marek, and Zvelebil, Kamil Václav. 1990. "Agricultural Transition, "Indo-European Origins," and the Spread of Farming," *in* Thomas Markey and John A. C. Greppin (eds.), *When Words Collide: The Indo-Europeans and the Pre-Indo-Europeans*, Ann Arbor, Karoma Publishers: 237–266.

Index of personal names

For the benefit of digital users, indexed terms that span two pages (e.g., 52–53) may, on occasion, appear on only one of those pages.

Abbas Pacha, 77
Abellio, Raymond, 203–4
Åberg, Nils, 160–61
Abetz, Otto, 362
Abraham, 14
Achilles, 356–57
Adam, 10, 36–37, 63, 68
Adams, Douglas, 387–88, 399–400, 410–12
Adelung, Johann Christoph, 35
Adrados, Francisco Rodríguez, 278
Aetius, 428
Agassiz, Louis, 65
Alexander the Great, 6–7
Alinei, Mario, 259–60
Allard, Jean-Paul, 216–17
Allchin, Raymond and Bridget, 329–30
Altheim, Franz, 141, 218–19
Amenhotep IV, 153
Ammon, Otto Georg, 56–57, 93–94
Amsel, Hans Georg, 220–21
Ancus Martius, 355–56
Anderson, Benedict R., 426–27
Anderson, Earl, 308
Anquetil-Duperron, Abraham Hyacinthe, 6–7, 24–25
Anthony, David W., xvi–xvii, 297, 302–3, 306–7, 410–11
Anttila, Raimo, xvi–xvii, 218–19
Arne, Ture Algot Johnsson, 168–69
Arntz, Helmuth, 108–9, 161–62, 406–7
Aryaman, 353–54
Ascoli, Graziado, 29–30, 431
Ashkenaz, 10
Asparuh, 421–22
Aśvins, 353–54
Atkinson, James Jasper, 122, 390
Atkinson, Quentin, 393, 398
Attila, 428
Atzenbeck, Carl, 157
Augier, Marc, 206
Äyräpää, Aarne, 160–61, 172

Bachofen, Johan Jakob, 294–95
Baelz, Erwin, 87
Bailly, Jean Sylvain, 14
Baldr, 353–54
Bardèche, Maurice, 212–13, 362
Bardet, Jean-Claude, 206–7
Barney, David. *See* Benoist, Alain de
Barthel, Waldemar, 157
Barthélémy (Abbé), 6–7
Basil II, 349
Batraz, 354
Baudouin de Courtenay, Jan Niecisław Ignacy, 100
Baur, Erwin, 187
Bechtel, Fritz, 383–84
Beger, Bruno, 140–41, 188, 222
Bender, Harold Herman, 155–56
Benecke, Joachim, 142–43
Benecke, Norbert, 305–6, 308
Benoist, Alain de, 201–6, 207, 208–10, 213–14, 215–16, 217–18, 219–21, 222, 365–67
Benveniste, Émile, 4, 8–9, 19–20, 40, 103, 107–9, 110, 124, 149, 154, 161–62, 171, 282, 283, 287, 352–53, 359–60, 368, 404, 405–7, 413, 421–22
Bergier, Jacques, 200–1, 203–4, 215–16
Bernabo Brea, Luigi, 149
Bernier, François, 37, 63–64
Bersu, Gerhard, 138–39, 160
Bertillon, Adolphe, 75–76
Bertillon, Alphonse (son of the above), 75–76, 88
Bertrand, Alexandre, 35–36, 78, 262, 286
Berve, Helmut, 139, 327
Bessarion (Cardinal), 379
Bhaga, 353–54
Bibikova, Valentina Ivanova, 305
Bickerton, Derek, 441
Billig, Michael, 218
Binet, Alfred, 95
Bingen, Hildegard von, 10
Bird, Norman, 387
Bismarck, Otto von, 57, 84–85, 93–94

534 INDEX OF PERSONAL NAMES

Blavatsky, Helena Petrovna, 58–59, 60–61, 132, 133, 140–41
Bloch, Jules, 359–60
Blot, Yvan, 206–7, 209–10
Blüher, Hans, 212–13
Blume, Erich, 125–26
Blumenbach, Johann Friedrich, 66, 67–68
Boas, Franz, 87–88, 119, 184, 185, 397
Boettcher, Carl-Heinz, 215–16
Bökönyi, Sándor, 305
Bonaparte, Napoleon, 42, 69, 358–59
Bonnard, Abel, 364–65
Bonnefoy, Yves, 210
Bopp, Franz, xviii, 3–4, 19, 20–21, 22–24, 25–26, 80–81, 133, 176, 271–72
Borman, Martin, 137
Bory de Saint-Vincent, Jean-Baptiste, 65–66
Bosch Gimpera, Pedro, 149, 175–76, 263–65, 290–91
Boucher de Perthes, Jacques, 423
Bourdier, Franck, 215–16
Bourget, Paul, 93–94
Bourgine, Raymond, 201–2
Brahma, 14, 409
Brandenstein, Wilhelm von, 166
Brasillach, Robert, 212–13
Bréal, Michel, vi, 25, 80–81, 82–83, 101–2
Breker, Arno, 205–6
Breuil, Henri (Abbé), 143, 193, 364
Broca, Paul, 72–77, 78–79, 82, 83–84, 86, 87, 89, 102, 112, 180, 182, 184, 190, 191, 224–26, 257–58, 420, 424, 434
Brough, John, 371
Brugmann, Karl, 3–4, 29–30
Brunnhofer, Hermann, 38–39
Buffon, George-Louis Leclerc (Count), 13–14, 15, 64–65
Bulwer-Lytton, Edward, 58–59
Burrin, Philippe, 362
Burt, Cyril, 95, 205, 236, 405–185
Buttler, Werner, 141, 147, 148, 161

Caesar, Gaius Julius, 50, 74–75, 340, 347–48, 413–14
Caignet, Michel, 212–13
Caillois, Roger, 205
Camper, Peter, 66
Campi, Alessandro, 221
Canetti, Elias, 443–44
Carcopino, Jérôme, 193
Carnoy, Albert Joseph, 155–56
Carrel, Alexis, 191, 194–95, 205, 362
Carrel, Armand, 69

Caskey, John L., 325
Cattell, Raymond, 95, 184–85, 236
Cau, Jean, 205
Cavalli-Sforza, Luigi Luca, 229, 230–31, 392, 428, 467f
Céline, Louis-Ferdinand Destouches, 195–96, 359–60, 362
Centaurs, 48
Chamberlain, Houston Stewart, 56–57, 93–94, 131, 135, 152–53
Champollion, Jean-François, 42
Chantraine, Pierre, 103
Charachidzé, Georges, 366, 370–71
Charpentier, Jarl, 155–56
Chastenet, Jacques, 379
Chavée, Honoré, 76
Chézy, Antoine-Léonard, 20
Childe, Vere Gordon, 37–38, 121–22, 124, 127, 144–45, 148–49, 150, 151–52, 153–56, 158–59, 160, 161, 162–65, 166, 167–68, 170–72, 173–74, 175–76, 179, 241, 242–43, 257–58, 263–64, 265, 287–88, 289–90, 294–95, 424
Childeric (*Childerici*), 427–28
Chimène, 63
Chirac, Jacques, 208
Chrétien, Douglas, 396
Christ, 132, 135, 187–88
Christen, Yves, 207, 208
Class, Heinrich, 125–26
Clauss, Ludwig Ferdinand, 187–88
Clovis, 24, 427–28
Cocherel (Abbé), 42
Coeurdoux, Gaston-Laurent, 6–7, 24–25
Cohen, Marcel, 103, 111
Coleman, John E., 322
Coleman, Robert, 281–82, 436–37
Coomaraswany, Ananda, 377
Coon, Carleton Stevens, 155–56, 182, 224
Correns, Carl, 183
Court de Gébelin, Antoine, 12, 389
Crawfurd, John, 35
Creuzer, Georg Friedrich, 20
Crevatin, Franco, 441–42
Cúchulainn, 354
Curiatii, 354
Cuvier, Georges, 42–43, 65, 74
Czekanowski, Jan, 155–56, 396

Dally, Eugène, 77–78
Daniel, Glyn Edmund, 127, 149
Danielou, Alain, 212–13
Danilenko, Valentin Nikolaevich, xvi, 291
Danino, Michel, xvi, 328–29

INDEX OF PERSONAL NAMES   535

Dannehl, Alfred, 134–35
Danton, Georges Jacques, 358–59
Darwin, Charles, 3–4, 26, 27, 28, 42–43, 56–57, 59, 65, 83, 87, 93–95, 122, 183, 389
Day, John V., 219–20, 227
Déchelette, Joseph, 45, 119–20, 124, 146, 149, 158, 170, 174, 190, 224–25, 257–58
Delbrück, Berthold, 3–4, 29–30
Demangel, Robert, 143
Demeter, 294–95, 378
Deniker, Joseph, 155–56, 168
Deshayes, Jean, xvi–xvii, 169
Diakonoff, Igor Mikhailovich, 390–91
Diderot, Denis, 13–14
Dinter, Arthur, 135
Dioscuri, 369
Dius Fidius, 353–54
Dolgopolsky, Aaron, 264, 268–69, 276–77, 390–91
Doriot, Jacques, 194–95
Dörpfeld, Wilhelm, 46
Dostoevsky, Fyodor Mikhailovich, 41
Drexler, Anton, 134
Dreyfus, Alfred, 56–57, 88
Drieu la Rochelle, Pierre, 109, 212–13, 362–63
Drobin, Ulf, 28
Droit, Roger-Pol, 210
Drumont, Édouard, 91–92
Düben (Baron von), 77
Dubuisson, xvi–xvii, Daniel, 377
Dumézil, Bruno, 427
Dumézil, Georges, xvi–xvii, 4, 103, 106, 107–8, 109–10, 111, 114–15, 124, 149, 154, 182, 203, 207, 282–83, 287, 303, 308, 330–31, 340, 351–80, 384, 404, 406–7, 413, 421–22
Dupâquier, Jacques, 207–8
Durkheim, Émile, 103, 390
Dutta, Pratap C., 226

Ebert, Max, 52, 148, 156–57, 169, 171, 172–73, 263–64, 277, 290–91, 301
Eckart (Eckardt), Dietrich, 60–61, 134, 137, 201
Edwards, William Frédéric, 74–75
Eggers, Hans Jürgen, 128, 162–63, 424
Ehrhardt, Arthur, 218
Eichhoff, Frédéric Gustave, 35
Eickstedt, Freiherr Egon von, 155–56, 189, 191–92, 225–26
Eisner, Kurt, 134
Eliade, Mircea, 218–19, 351–52, 359–60, 363–64, 367, 373, 377
Elliot Smith, Sir Grafton, 155–56
Engels, Friedrich, 176–77, 178, 294–95

Epting, Karl, 362
Eribon, Didier, 351–52, 358–60, 361, 366, 375
Erzberger, Matthias, 133–34
Esenç, Tevfik, 384
Eugène, Éric, 71
Eulenburg-Hertefeld (Count von), 93–94
Evans, Sir Arthur, 151–52
Eve, 10, 36–37, 229, 239–40
Evola, Julius, 205, 206–7, 221, 377
Eysenck, Hans Jürgen, 205, 206–7, 236–37

Fabre-Luce, Alfred, 205
Faral, Edmond, 364
Faye, Guillaume, 208, 211, 220–21
Feist, Sigmund, 125–26, 156–57, 163–64
Ferembach, Denise, 223, 225–26
Ferguson, Charles Albert, 441
Fichte, Johann Gottlieb, 23, 122–23
Fischer, Eugen, 137, 155–56, 186–87, 189, 191, 192–93, 225
Fisher, Sir Ronald, 95, 184–85, 236
Fleischhacker, Hans, 188
Fleming, Alexander, 183–84
Fleure, Herbert John, 155–56, 171, 287
Forrer, Emil, 267–68
Fouillée, Alfred, 88–89
Francfort, Henri-Paul, xvi, 334–35
Frankfort, Henri, 143, 144–45
Franz, Leonhard, 288–89
Franz-JOSEF, Emperor, 56–57
Fraser, Sir James, 48, 106, 352, 377–78
Frederick Barbarossa, 140
Freud, Sigmund, vi, 111, 114–15, 205, 379
Freyr, 353–54
Frick, Wilhelm, 143–45
Fritsch, Theodor, 133–34
Frobenius, Leo, 120–21
Fussman, Gérard, 336

Gaea or Gaia, 409
Galton, Sir Francis, 93–95, 183–85, 186, 236, 396
Gamkrelidze, Tamaz, 29, 264, 268–69, 383, 460f
Gandharvas, 48
Gaulle, Charles de, 424
Gaxotte, Pierre, 358
Gayre, Robert, 218
Geiger, Abraham, 54–55
Geiger, Lazarus or Ludwig, 54–55, 79
Gérard, René, 38–39
Gersmann, Rita, 257–58
Ghirshman, Roman, 169
Giannopoulos, Theodoros G., 260, 327

536 INDEX OF PERSONAL NAMES

Giles, Peter, 155–56
Gilliéron, Jules, 111–12
Gimbutas, Marija, xvi, 8, 9, 40, 217–20, 239, 263, 288–303, 311–14, 341–42, 464*f*
Ginzburg, Carlo, 358, 359, 378
Girard De Rialle, Julien, 82–83
Giscard d'Estaing, Olivier, 207–8
Giscard d'Estaing, Valéry, 207
Glauer, Rudolf, a.k.a. Baron Rudolf von Sebottendorff, 134
Gliddon, George, 65–66
Gobineau, Joseph Arthur, a.k.a. Count of, 25–26, 70–71, 74–76, 79–80, 88–89, 92–94, 125–26, 204, 205, 219–20
God, 10, 12, 36–38, 64, 132–33, 135, 295, 411–12
Goebbels, Joseph, 182
Goessler, Peter, 288–89
Goldziher, Ignaz, 76
Gollnisch, Bruno, 216–17
Gomer, 10
Goodrick-Clarke, Nicholas, 201
Goody, Jack, 282, 404
Gorodcov, Vasily, 148, 174–75
Gosselain, Olivier Pierre, 429
Götze, Alfred, 159–60, 257–58
Goudet, Jacques, 216–17
Gould, Stephen Jay, 65
Govedarica, Blagoje, xvi, 312
Graebner, Fritz Robert, 120–21
Gramsci, Antonio, 202
Granet, Marcel, 359–60
Gray, Russell D., xvi–xvii, 393, 398
Greenberg, Joseph, 229–30, 271–72, 273–75, 279, 390–92, 397
Grimm, Jacob, 23–24, 25–26, 69, 126
Gripari, Pierre, 212–13
Grisward, Joël H., 351, 356–57
Grolier, Éric de, xvi, 392
Grottanelli, Cristiano, 358
Guénon, René, 203–4, 377
Guibert, Michel de, 208–9
Guignes, Joseph de, 24–25
Guizot, François, 69
Gumperz, John J., 436
Güntert, Hermann, 164–65
Günther, Hans Friedrich Karl, 124–25, 126, 134–35, 155–56, 161–62, 186, 187–88, 206, 213–14, 215, 218, 220–21, 303–4
Gurdjieff, Georges, 203–4

Häckel or Haeckel, Ernst, 27, 28, 56–57, 88–89, 93–94, 133

Haddon, Alfred C., 119, 155–56, 171, 185, 287
Hagège, Claude, 436
Hamlet, 66
Hammurabi, 166–67
Hamy, Ernest-Théodore, 73–74
Harder, Richard, 142–43
Harrer, Karl, 134
Haudricourt, André-Georges, 386
Haudry, Jean, 209–10, 213–17, 219, 220–21, 366–67, 410–11
Hauer, Jakob, 135
Haushofer, Karl, 201
Häusler, Alexander, 260, 306–7
Hawkes, Christopher, 143, 144–45, 149
Hazard, Paul, 362
Hector, 82–83
Hegel, Georg Wilhelm Friedrich, 23–24, 28, 122–23
Helen (of Troy), 82–83
Hellwig, Karl August, 133–34
Henry the Lion (Heinrich der Löwe), 140
Heracles, 325, 354
Herder, Johann Gottfried von, 15, 37, 55–56, 69, 122–23, 131
Hermant, Abel, 364–65
Herrnstein, Richard J., 237
Hersant, Robert, 209
Himmler, Heinrich, 126–27, 131–32, 136, 140–43, 218
Hindenburg, Paul von, 137
Hirt, August, 188
Hirt, Hermann, 61–62, 86, 108–9, 126, 157–58, 159–60, 161–63, 166, 181, 286, 406–7
His, W. 77
Hitler, Adolf, 56–57, 60–61, 62, 93–94, 118, 126–27, 130–31, 133, 134, 136–39, 144–45, 181–82, 186–87, 192–93, 200–1, 205, 357–58, 359–60
Hjelmslev, Louis, 114–15
Hobhouse, Leonard Trelawny, 122
Hobsbawm, Eric, 426–27
Hoder, 353–54
Hodge, Carleton Taylor, 268–69
Hoernes, Moritz, 126–27, 160–61, 162–63
Holbein, Hans, 66
Holm, Hans J., 398
Homer, 46–47, 50, 101, 306–7, 405, 407–8
Horatius Cocles, 354, 368–69
Hörbiger, Hans, 134–35
Hovelacque, Abel, 80–81
Hrozný, Bedřich, 267–68, 346
Huet, Pierre-Daniel (Bishop), 37
Hülle, Werner Matthias, 142–43

INDEX OF PERSONAL NAMES   537

Humboldt, Wilhelm von, 23
Hume, David, 13–14, 64–65
Huxley, Julian, 185
Hymes, Dell H., 441

Illič-Svityč, Vladislav Markovich, 271–72, 390–91
Indra, 353–54
Ishtar, 171–72, 294–95
Ivanov, Vjačeslav Vsevolodovič, 29, 264, 268–69, 383, 460*f*

Jacob, 131–32
Jacolliot, Louis, 58–59
Jäger, Andreas, 7
Jahn, Martin, 159–60, 257–58
Jakobson, Roman, 99, 114–16, 118, 384
Jankuhn, Herbert, 123, 141, 142–43, 145, 161, 206, 215
Japheth, 10, 63
Jensen, Arthur, 205, 236–37
Jochnowitz, George, 436
Jones, Sir William, xviii, 3–4, 5–8, 9, 15, 19, 26, 33–34, 35
Jucquois, Guy, 385, 445–46
Jupiter, 352–54
Justi, Ferdinand, 402–3

Kaimsthorn, Baron of. *See* Renfrew, Colin
Kant, Emmanuel, 15, 23–24
Kapp, Wolfgang, 137
Kaurava, 355
Kazanas, Nicholas, 328–29
Keith, Arthur Berriedale, 400
Keith, Sir Arthur, 155–56, 169
Khomyakov, Aleksey Stepanovich, 41
Kirchhoff, Günther, 141–42
Klaproth, Julius von, 35
Knoll, August Maria, 137
Koestler, Arthur, 203–4
Koller, Rosa, 192
Kollmann, Julius, 85–86
Koppers, Wilhelm, 120–21, 146, 162, 166
Kossinna, Gustaf, 25–26, 57–58, 62, 120, 121–29, 138–39, 141–42, 151–52, 155, 157–60, 161, 162–63, 170, 181–82, 213–16, 219–20, 243–44, 250, 257–59, 263, 286, 424, 462*f*
Kostrzewsky, Jósef, 127
Kozłowski, Leon, 160–61, 172
Krahe, Hans, 263, 277
Krause, Ernst Ludwig, 56–57
Krebs, Pierre, 220–21
Krichevsky, Yevgeni, 175–76

Kroeber, Alfred Louis, 276, 396–97, 469*f*
Kuhn, Adalbert, 27
Kühn, Herbert, 159–60, 257–58
Kühnen, Michaël, 212–13
Kumar, G. D., 226
Kurylowicz, Jerzy, 103

La Coste-Messelière, Pierre de, 143
Labov, William, 419
Laennec, René, 194–95
Lafitau, Fr. Joseph-François, 48
Lagarde, Paul de, 56–57
Langbehn, Julius, 56–57
Lange, Wolfgang, 215
Langsdorff, Alexander, 141
Lanz, Adolf Josep, a.k.a. Jorg von Liebenfels, 60–61, 132–35, 137
Laruelle, Marlène, 41
Latham, Robert Gordon, 40
Lauffer, Siegfried, 142–43
Lauterer, Ernst, a.k.a. "Tarnhari," 60–61
Laval, Pierre, 361–62
Le Bon, Gustave, 73–74, 88–89
Le Coq, Albert von, 337
Le Gallou, Jean-Yves, 206–7, 209–10
Le Page, Robert Broch, 441
Le Verrier, Urbain, 382
Lebedynsky, Iaroslav, 410–11
Leclainche, Emmanuel, 193
Leibniz, Gottfried Wilhelm, 9, 10–11, 13, 15, 19, 23–24, 40, 53–54, 131, 171, 286
Lejeune, Michel, 103
Lemerle, Paul, 143
Lenin, Vladimir Ilyich Ulyanov, 174–75
Lenz, Friedrich, 186–87
Leroi-Gourhan, André, 175–76
Lesquen du Plessis Casso, Henry de, 206–7
Levi, Primo, 436
Lévi, Sylvain, 359–60
Lévi-Strauss, Claude, 118, 196, 228, 352–53
Lévy-Bruhl, Lucien, 48, 103
Lincoln, Bruce, 363–64, 377–78
Link, Heinrich Friedrich, 38–39
Linnaeus, Carl, or von Linné, 13–14, 22, 63–64, 67–68, 89, 122
Lipse, Juste, or LIPS, Joost, 7
List, Guido von, 59–61, 131–34, 137
Littleton, C. Scott, 218–19
Lobatchevski, Nikolai Ivanovich, 380
Locchi, Giorgio, 203–4
Locke, John, 9
Lorenz, Konrad, 187, 204, 207
Louis XVI, 361

538 INDEX OF PERSONAL NAMES

Lubbock, Sir John, 45, 265–66, 390
Lucumo, 355–56
Lugan, Bernard, 216–17, 365
Lumley, Henri de, 144
Luschan, Felix von, 87
Luther, 36–37
Lutzhöft, Hans-Jürgen, 158
Lyssenko, Trofim Denisovich, 177–78

Mabire, Jean, 201–2, 209–10
Magnussen, Karin, 189
Mahieu, Jacques de, 203–4
Mair, Victor H., 338–39
Malamoud, Charles, vi, 373, 374, 379
Malinowski, Bronislaw, 119, 390
Mallory, James P., xvi, 284–85, 297, 301, 302–3,
   311–12, 317, 319, 324–25, 336, 347, 387–88,
   399–400, 410–12, 422, 458f
Malte-Brun, Conrad, 55
Marcantonio, Angela, 388
Marceau, Félicien (pseudonym Louis Carette),
   364–65
Marcenay, Georges. See Georges Dumézil
Marius (General), 347–48
Marlaud, Jacques, 216–17
Marmin, Michel, 201–2, 208
Marr, Nikolai Yakovlevich, 174, 176–78
Mars, 220–21, 308, 352–53, 355–56
Marshall, Sir John, 169
Martial, René, 191, 195–96, 364–65
Martinet, André, 103, 286, 303–4, 384, 404,
   410–11
Maruščenko, Alexander A., 168
Marx, Karl, 178, 205, 294–95, 360
Masica, Colin P., 445, 468f
Massin, Benoît, 189
Masson, Vadim, 169, 360
Matzneff, Gabriel, 212–13
Maurras, Charles, 358–59, 361, 364–65
Mauss, Marcel, 103, 359–60, 361–62
Mayakovsky, Vladimir Vladimirovich, 114–15
Mazon, André, 364, 368–69
Mcdonald, Kevin, 219–20
Mclennan, John Ferguson, 122
Médecin, Jacques, 207–8
Mégret, Bruno, 206–7, 209–10
Meillet, Antoine, 17, 19–21, 30, 31–32, 99, 102–
   9, 110, 111–14, 124, 149–50, 178, 267–68,
   271–72, 287, 296–97, 346, 347–48, 352–53,
   360, 368, 374, 386, 387, 388, 390, 391–92,
   396, 399, 402–3, 406–8, 413–14, 432–33, 434,
   436–37, 438, 441
Mendel, Gregor, 95, 183

Mengele, Josef, 189, 193, 218
Menghin, Oswald, 118, 160–61, 288–89
Menk, Roland, 226–27
Merhardt, Gero von, 138–39, 141, 161
Merkenschlager, Friedrich, 187–88
Merpert, Nikolay Ya, xvi, 291, 301
Meščaninov, Ivan Ivanovich, 177–78
Meyer, Eduard, 126–27, 137, 162–63
Michelet, Jules, 69
Miller, Alexander, 174–75
Millot, Jacques, 191, 193
Mishima, Yukio, 212–13
Mistler, Jean, 207, 364–65
Mistral, Frédéric, 431–32
Mitra, 353–54
Modrijan, Walter, 142–43
Moeller van den Bruck, Arthur, 56–57
Moltke, Helmuth von (General), 93–94
Momigliano, Arnaldo, 358, 359
Mommsen, Theodor, 449
Monboddo, Lord James Burnett, 64
Montandon, Georges, 155–56, 191, 195–96,
   203–4
Montelius, Oscar, 120, 127, 160–61, 174, 423–
   24, 447
Montfaucon, Bernard de, 42
Montherlant, Henry de, 212–13
Morgan, Jacques Jean Marie de, 166–68
Morgan, Lewis, 122, 176
Mortillet, Gabriel de, 45, 84, 87, 146, 174–75
Morton, Samuel George, 65–66
Mounin, Georges, 28, 389
Much, Matthäus, 57–58, 85–86, 124–25, 126,
   157, 215, 301
Much, Rudolf, 157, 215
Mucius Scaevola, 354, 368–69
Mufwene, Salikoko, xvi–xvii, 441–42
Müller, Friedrich Max, 31–32, 48, 112, 176, 339
Müller, Karl Otfried, 139, 327
Müller, Sophus Otto, 160–61, 163–64
Müller-Hill, Benno, 137, 189
Murray, Charles A., 237
Mussolini Benito, 212, 359
Mutti, Claudio, 221
Myres, John Linton, 151–52, 163–64, 171, 287

Napoleon III, 44–45, 70–71, 72
Naram-Sin, 166–67
Nasatyas, 353–54
Neckel, Gustav, 131–32, 157
Nehring, Alfons, 162, 166, 410–11
Neuville, Henri, 191
Nicolaï, Robert, 437

INDEX OF PERSONAL NAMES 539

Nietzsche, Friedrich, 131, 204
Njördr, 353–54
Noah, 6, 10, 38–39, 63, 84
Nostradamus, Michel de Nostre-Dame, 351, 361
Notin, Bernard, 216–17
Nott, Josiah, 65–66
Numa Pompilius, 355–56

Obayashi, Taryô, 282–83, 370–71
Odin (Wotan), 131, 133–34, 353–54, 357–58, 368–69
Olender, Maurice, xvi, 145, 210, 366, 367
Omalius d'Halloy, Jean-Baptiste Julien, 38–39, 77–78, 83
Orcival, François d', 201–2
Ormesson, Jean d', 209
Osthoff, Hermann, 29–30
Otte, Marcel, xvi, 260
Ötzi, 234, 343–44

Pandava, 355
Paris (of Troy), 82–83
Parpola, Asko, 331
Passek, Tatijana, 147–48
Pasteur, Louis, 183–84, 195
Patte, Étienne, 191
Paulsen, Peter, 142–43
Pauwels, Louis, 60–61, 200–1, 203–4, 208, 209, 215–16
Peake, Harold John Edward, 163–64, 171, 287
Pearson, Karl, 94–95, 184–85, 236
Pearson, Roger, 218–19, 294
Pedersen, Holger, 165–66, 271–72, 385, 390–91
Pelliot, Paul, 337
Penka, Karl, 55–56, 57–58, 61–62, 82–83, 87, 88–89, 126, 131–32, 152, 161–62, 286
Perrier, 75–76
Peschek, Christian, 288–89
Pétain, Philippe (Maréchal), 44, 194–95, 364–65
Petersen, Wilhelm, 205–6
Pfister, Thierry, 208–9
Pictet, Adolphe, 21, 34 --36, 39–40, 46–47, 48, 51, 53–54, 101, 110, 114, 168, 262, 286, 334–35, 399
Piétrement, Charles-Alexandre, 82–83, 167
Piganiol, André, 364, 369
Piggott, Stuart, 149, 400
Pinault, Georges, a.k.a. PENAOD, Goulven, xvi–xvii, 216–17
Pisani, Vittore, 117–18, 445–46
Pittard, Eugène, 155–56
Plantin, Jean, 216–17

Plato, 43, 58–59, 131
Plautus, 405
Ploetz, Alfred, 186
Plunkett, Patrice de, 201–2, 208, 209
Pohl, Walter, 427
Poisson, Georges, 163–64, 166
Pokorny, Julius, 387
Poliakov, Léon, 19, 69, 367
Polivanov, Yevgeny Dmitrievich, 177–78
Polomé, Edgar C., 218–19
Poniatowski, Michel, 207, 236–37
Pott, August Friedrich, 25–26, 35
Pouchet, Georges, 75–76
Prichard, Charles, 66–68
Prigent, Michel, 216
Prithivi, 409
Prometheus, 130, 370–71
Pruner-Bey, a.k.a. Bruner, Franz, 75, 77, 78–81
Pulgram, Ernst, 385, 400
Pumpelly, Raphael, 164–65, 168
Putin, Vladimir, 333
Pytheas, 134, 215–16

Quatrefages De Bréau, Armand de, 37–38, 73–74, 75, 79–80, 84–85, 87, 163–64
Quinet, Edgar, 69
Quirinus, 352–53

Radcliffe-Brown, Alfred Reginald, 119, 390
Rambousek, Anselm (Abbé), 183
Ramses II, 253–54
Ranke, Johannes, 87
Rask, Rasmus Kristian, 3–4, 19, 20–22, 23, 25–26, 35, 67–68
Rassamakin, Yuri, xvi–xvii, 248–49, 312–13
Ratzel, Friedrich, 120–21
Ravdonikas, Vladislav Iosifovič, 176–77, 178
Reagan, Ronald, 209
Rebérioux, Madeleine, 208–9
Reche, Otto, 157, 161–62, 169, 224
Reinach, Salomon, 40, 43–44, 55–56, 143, 262, 286–87
Reinecke, John, 45, 441
Reinecke, Paul, 149
Reinerth, Hans, 126–27, 138–39, 141–43, 144–45, 159–60, 161, 206
Renan, Ernest, 70–71, 75–76
Renfrew, Colin, xvi, 219–20, 239, 243, 257–58, 260–61, 264–66, 267–71, 273–75, 277–78, 279, 280–85, 288, 300, 303, 309–10, 318–19, 321, 346–47, 375, 392, 393, 410–11, 420, 441–42, 463*f*
Retzius, Anders, 22, 66–68, 77, 82

540 INDEX OF PERSONAL NAMES

Rhode, Johann Gottlieb, 33–34, 166–67, 168
Richthofen, Bolko von, 175
Rieger, Jürgen, 220–21
Riemann, Georg Friedrich Bernhard, 380
Ripley, William Zebina, 155–56, 182
Riquet, Raymond, 223–25, 227
Ritter, Carl, 120–21
Rivers, William Halse Rivers, 119
Rivet, Paul, 193
Rivière, Jean-Claude, 216–17, 366–67
Robien, Christophe-Paul, a.k.a. Président de ROBIEN, 42
Rochet, Charles, 80
Rodrigue, 63
Romulus, 355–56, 369
Roques, Henri, 216–17
Rosenberg, Alfred, 93–94, 131, 134, 136, 137, 138–39, 140–42, 159–60, 203–4, 215–16, 219
Rostand, Edmond, 364–65
Rostovtzeff, Mikhail Ivanovich, 162–63, 174–75
Roumanille, Joseph, 431–32
Royer, Clémence, 83–84, 88–89, 237
Rüdin, Ernst, 186–87
Ruffié, Jacques, 228
Ruhlen, Merritt, xvi–xvii, 229–30, 271–75, 279, 390–92, 397
Ruttke, Falk-Alfred, 186–87

Saartjie Baartman, or Sawtche, a.k.a. "The Hottentot Venus," 74
Sacy, Antoine Isaac, Baron Silvestre de, 20
Saint-Loup . See Augier, Marc
Saller, Karl, 187–88
Sandars, Nancy K., 149
Sandfeld, Kristian, 115–16, 443–45
sassetti, Francesco, 7
Saussure, Ferdinand de, 4, 20, 24–25, 32, 99–102, 103, 105, 114, 119, 382, 390, 436–37, 447
Saussure, Horace Bénédict de, 101
Sautarel, Pierre, 217–18
Sauter, Marc-Rodolphe, 226–27
Sayce, Adalbert, 165, 172–73, 263–64, 268–69
Schachermeyr, Fritz, 142–43
Schaeffer, Claude, 143
Schäfer, Ernst, 140–41
Scheidt, Walter, 224
Schemann, Ludwig, 56–57, 71, 93–94, 125–26
Schlegel, Friedrich von, 15, 20, 22–23, 28, 33–34, 35, 69, 122–23, 126, 133, 153, 176, 327–28
Schleicher, August, 3–4, 19–20, 27–29, 30–31, 39, 56–57, 101–2, 112, 114, 133, 304, 383, 385, 389, 390, 393–94, 396, 397, 460f
Schleif, Hans, 141

Schlerath, Bernfried, 369–70
Schliemann, Heinrich, 46, 84–85, 101
Schliz, Alfred, 158–60, 224
Schmid, Wolfgang Paul, 385
Schmidt, Erich Friedrich, 168–69
Schmidt, Hubert, 147–48, 151–52, 164–65
Schmidt, Johannes, 30–32, 38–39, 89–90, 117–18, 434
Schmidt, Robert Rudolf, 142–43
Schmidt, Wilhelm, 120–21, 146
Schmitt, Carl, 212
Schmitt, Rüdiger, 218–19
Schnapp, Alain, xvi, 142–43, 208–9, 367
Scholl, Hans and Sophie, 141–42
Schuchardt, Hugo Ernst Mario, 30–32, 112–14, 117–18, 430–31, 434, 440, 449–50
Schuchardt, Karl, 126–27, 139, 158–60
Schultz, Bruno Kurt, 153, 161–62
Schulz, Heinrich, 38–39
Schulz, Walther, 159–60, 257–58
Schwantes, Gustav, 160
Schwidetzky, Ilse, 189, 219–20, 225–26
Scott, Walter, 436–37
Sebaldt von Werth, Max Ferdinand, 59–60
Seger, Hans, 159–60, 257–58
Sergent, Bernard, xvi–xvii, 213–14, 370, 410–12
Sergi, Giuseppe, 82–83, 155–56, 163–64, 167
Serra Rafols, José de, 149
Shem, 63–64
Sherratt, Andrew, 247, 277–78, 403, 441–42
Sherratt, Suzan, 277–78, 441–42
Shevoroshkin, Vitaly Victorovich, 390–91
Shnirelman, Viktor A., xvi–xvii, 333
Shockley, William, 236–37
Sieg, Emil, 337
Siegfried (Sigurdr), 71, 213–14, 354, 357–58
Siegling, Wielhelm, 337
Sieyès, Emmanuel Joseph, 69
Sigurdr. See Siegfried
Sisupala, 354
Sluyterman von Langeweyde, Georg, 205–6
Sokoloff, Georges, 410–11
Solzhenitsyn, Aleksandr, 178
Sorel, Albert, 93–94
Sorel, Georges, 205, 212
Souchon, Georges, 208–9
spanuth, Jürgen, 203–4
Spearman, Charles, 95, 184–85, 236
Speer, Albert, 136
Spengler, Oswald, 206–7
Spitsyn, Alexander, 174–75
Sprockhoff, Ernst, 160
Stalin, Joseph V., 111, 175, 176, 178, 288–89

INDEX OF PERSONAL NAMES 541

Starkadr, 354
Starostin, Sergei Anatolyevich, 390–91
Stein, Aurel, 337
Steinthal, Heymann, 76
Sturtevant, Edgar Howard, 267–68
Sulimirski, Tadeusz, 163–64
Swadesh, Morris, 395
Szemerényi, Oswald John Louis, 330–31, 384

Tabbert von Strahlenberg, Philipp Johann, 7–8, 395
Tacitus, 10, 50, 59–60, 215
Tallgren, Aarne Michaël, 148, 160–61, 162–63, 170–71, 172, 174–76
Tarchi, Mario, 221
Taylor, Isaac, 86, 87, 163–64
Teilhard de Chardin, Pierre (Fr.), 364
Telegin, Dmitri, xvi, 248–49, 291, 306–7
Tesnière, Lucien, 103
Testart, Alain, 428
Teudt, Wilhelm, 141
Thatcher, Margaret, 209
Thierry, Augustin, 69
Thomas, Homer L., 260
Thomsen, Christian Jürgensen, 43, 49
Thor, 133–34, 369
Thurnam, John, 77
Tilak, Bâl Gangâdhar, 215–16
Tischler, Otto, 127
Titus TATIUS, 355–56
Tocqueville, Alexis de, 25–26, 70–71
Topinard, Paul, 87, 190, 227
Tremblay, Xavier, 408
Trombetti, Alfredo, 165–66, 223, 229–30, 271–72, 390
Troubetzkoy (Trubetzkoy), Prince Nikolai Sergeyevich, 99, 100–1, 114–18, 160–61, 177–78, 277–78, 389, 442–43, 445–46
Tschermak, Erich von, 183
Tuisto, 10
Tullus Hostilius, 355–56
Tylor, Edward Burnett, 122, 390
Týr, 353–54, 368–69

Uhlenbeck, Christianus Cornelius, 117–18, 166, 441–42
Ujfalvy, Charles Eugène de, 82–83, 167
Unverzagt, Wilhelm, 142–43
Uranus, 48, 382, 406
Uvarov, Count Aleksey Sergeyevich, 174
Uvarova, Countess Praskovya, 174

Vacano, Otto Wilhelm von, 142–43
Vacher de Lapouge, Claude, 195

Vacher de Lapouge, Georges, 55–57, 81, 88–89, 90–94, 124–25, 126, 131–32, 137, 152, 192, 195, 213–16, 219–20
Valla, Jean-Claude, 201–2, 208
Vallat, Xavier, 195–96
Vallois, Henri-Victor, 87–88, 144–45, 190, 191–93, 218, 225–26, 227
van Boxhorn, Marcus Zuerius, 12
Van der Mijl, Abraham, 7
van Gorp, Jan, a.k.a. Goropius Becanus, 9, 10
Varenne, Jean, 208, 209–10, 216–17, 367
Varuna, 48, 353–54, 406
Vasiliev, Igor, 301
Vaufrey, Raymond, 143–44
Vâyu, 353–54
Venner, Dominique, 201–2, 212–13
Ventris, Michael, 320–21
Venus, 294–95
Vercingetorix, 44, 282
Vernant, Jean-Pierre, 145
Verner, Karl Adolph, 29–30
Verschuer, Otmar von, 186–87, 189, 191, 193, 218
Vial, Pierre, 209–10, 213–14, 216–18, 220–21
Vielle, Christophe, xvi, 385, 445–46
Vincent, Louis-Claude, 206
Vines, Lucy, 210
Vinogradov, Viktor Vladimirovich, 178
Virchow, Rudolf, 46, 47–48, 84–86, 120, 126, 127, 168, 181
Virey, Jean-Joseph, 65–66
Virgil, 46–47
Vogt, Emil, 149
Voltaire, 13–14, 15, 36–37, 60–61, 327–28
Vries, Hugo De, 183
Vulcanius, Bonaventure, 7

Wagner, Gottfried, 71
Wagner, Richard, 25–26, 57, 71, 79, 93–94, 133–34, 205
Wahle, Ernst, 128, 159–60, 162–64, 170, 424
Warnow, Tandy, xvi–xvii, 398
Weigel, Karl Theodor, 141–42
Weinreich, Uriel, 434, 436
West, Martin Litchfield, 409
Westermarck, Edward, 122, 390
Wheeler, Sir Mortimer, 328, 329–30
White, Charles, 64–65
Whitney, William Dwight, 100
Wiegand, Theodor, 137, 138, 139
Wieland, Hermann, 131–32
Wikander, Stig, 355
Wilamowitz-Moellendorff, Ulrich von, 137

542 INDEX OF PERSONAL NAMES

Wilhelm II, 52, 93–94, 138–39, 232
Wiligut, Karl Maria, 136, 140, 141–42
Wilke, Georg, 159–60
Willvonseder, Kurt, 142–43
Wilser, Ludwig, 56–58, 61–62, 87, 93–94, 161–62
Wilson, Edgar, 205
Windischmann, Karl Joseph, 20
Wirth, Hermann Felix, 131–32, 137, 141–42, 203–4, 206
Wolff, Karl Felix, 125–26, 157
Woltmann, Ludwig, 56–58, 93–94
Wolzogen, Count Hans von, 57
Wotan. *See* ODIN
Wulfila (Bishop), 347–48

Wulsin, Frederick R., 168
Wüst, Walther, 131–32, 141–42

Yoshida, Atsuhiko, 282–83, 370–71

Zay, Jean, 360
Zdanovich, Gennady, 333
Zeus, 131–32, 409
Zeuss, Johann Kaspar, 21
Zimmer, Stefan, 339, 441–42
Zind, Pierre, 216–17
Zoroaster, 333
Zschaetzsch, Karl Georg, 131–32
Zvelebil, Marek, xvi–xvii, 283–84, 463*f*

Index of placenames: countries, regions, archaeological sites, toponyms, hydronyms

For the benefit of digital users, indexed terms that span two pages (e.g., 52–53) may, on occasion, appear on only one of those pages.

Achaemenid (Empire), 103–4
Adamklissi, 52
Aegean Sea, 370, 379
Afghanistan, xv, 33–34, 35, 327–28, 336, 456*f*
Africa, 13, 37–38, 48, 74, 94, 155, 227–28, 229–30, 239–40, 272, 273, 330, 365, 371, 378, 420–21, 440–41. *See also* North Africa; South Africa
Akdepe, 168
Alalakh, 252–53
Alaska, 180
Albania, 242–43, 257, 324, 433–34
Alberta (province of Canada), 184–85
Alborz Mountains, 168
Algeria, 75–76, 199, 201–2, 422
Alps, Alpine, 119–20, 148, 161, 173, 240, 246, 247, 254, 340, 343–45, 425, 430–31
Altay Mountains, 331–32
Altyn Depe (archaeological site), 334
Amazon, 411–12
America, 13, 48, 131–32, 177–78, 189, 199, 203–4, 206, 219–20, 239–40, 242, 272, 273–74, 279, 370, 378, 390–91, 400–1, 411–12, 420–21, 422, 435–36, 440–41, 445
Amu Darya (Oxus River), 33–34, 168
Anatolia, xix, 172–73, 235–36, 263–64, 274, 283–84, 306, 324–25, 345, 347, 420–21, 433, 452
Anau (archaeological site), 147–48, 164–65, 166, 168, 461*f*
Aosta Valley, 430–31
Arabia, 37, 169
Aral (Sea), 168
Argentina, 160–61, 203–4, 288–89, 422
Arizona, 429
Arkaim (archaeological site), 333–34
Armorica, 79–80, 167, 349
Ashgabat (Ashkhabad), 168
Asia, 9, 35, 37, 39–41, 43–44, 50–51, 55, 77, 82–84, 85–86, 103–4, 119, 166–67, 169, 215, 227,

239–40, 242, 245, 252–53, 262, 267, 268–69, 272, 273, 278–79, 286, 298, 300, 303, 315, 318–19, 334, 347, 355, 402, 407, 411–12, 414, 415, 440, 456*f*. *See also* Central Asia
Astarabad, 168
Atapuerca (archaeological site), 239–40
Athens, 42, 59–60, 143, 444
Atlantic (Ocean), 90, 91–92, 119–20, 146, 172–73, 232, 245, 246, 253, 260, 279–80, 319, 342, 420, 421, 425, 440–41
Auschwitz, 97, 140–41, 188–89
Austria, 30–31, 56–57, 59, 84–85, 160–61, 183, 211, 221, 238, 254–55, 288–89, 340–41, 427, 433–34, 456*f*
Austro-Hungarian (Empire), 31–32, 400–1
Ayodhya, 328–29
Azores (archipelago), 131–32

Babylon, 48–49
Bactria, 6–7, 35
Bagdad, 200–1
Balkans (Balkan Peninsula), 44–45, 84, 129, 147, 157–58, 169–70, 173, 240, 242–43, 247, 248, 249–50, 251–52, 263, 276–79, 297, 299, 300, 301, 307–8, 311–12, 314, 322, 324, 325, 343–44, 347, 349, 403, 425, 441–42, 443, 456*f*
Balkhash (lake), 82–83
Baltic Sea, xix, 17, 33, 38–39, 40, 50, 51, 53, 61, 109, 125, 146, 154, 174, 203, 207, 211, 213–14, 222, 241–42, 243–44, 279–81, 288, 349–50, 419, 425, 440, 456*f*
Basque Country, 240, 257
Bayreuth, 57, 71, 93–94
Belgium, 84–85, 221, 240, 364–65, 427–28, 433–34
Benin, 429
Berlin, 4, 52, 62, 71–72, 84–85, 87, 120, 126–27, 131–32, 137, 138, 140–41, 142–43, 153, 156–57, 159–60, 164–65, 173, 201, 218, 263

544   INDEX OF PLACENAMES

Black Sea, xviii, 8, 9, 38–39, 40, 84, 90, 91–92, 146, 154, 155–56, 174, 224–25, 230–32, 241, 244, 261, 279–81, 286, 291, 298, 311–13, 324–25, 347–48, 349, 421, 425, 443–44, 452
Bohemia, 56–57, 192–93, 258, 275, 340–41, 400–1
Bolivia, 422
Bologna, 344–45
Bornholm, 22
Borreby (site and "type"), 224
Bosporus, 260
Brandenburg, 400–1
Bratislava, 323
Breslau, 159–60
British Colombia, 184–85
British Empire, 422
British Isles, 252–53, 259
Brittany, 42, 79–80, 159–60, 205, 241–42, 252–53, 341
Brno (Brün), 183, 224
Budapest, 421
Bug (River), 244–45, 248, 298, 456*f*
Bulgaria, 142–43, 147–48, 164–65, 242–43, 246, 247, 248, 249, 254–55, 278–79, 296, 298, 299, 313, 314, 323, 324–25, 410–11, 421–22, 443–44
Burgundy, 400–1, 430–31
Byzantine Empire (Byzantium), 349, 379, 443, 444–45, 456*f*

Cairo, 65–66
Calcutta. *See* Kolkata
California, 219–20, 289, 294–71
Cambodia, 435–36
Cameroon, 429
Canada, 183–84, 400–1, 440
Cape Town, 207–8
Carpathians, 148, 173, 241, 244, 248, 254, 324
Caspian Sea, 15, 168, 241, 244, 245, 292–93, 298–99, 301, 331–32
Cassiterides (Islands), 252–53
Çatal Höyük (archaeological site), 267
Catalaunian Plains (battle site), 349–50, 428
Catalonia, 221
Caucasus, 33, 38–39, 66, 129, 148, 162–63, 166, 169–70, 176–77, 234–35, 244–45, 271–72, 275, 278–79, 299–300, 308, 311–13, 327–28, 354, 370–71, 383
Central Asia, 39–40, 41, 67–68, 82–83, 118, 155–56, 164–65, 166–69, 234–35, 253–54, 292–93, 298, 300, 310–11, 315, 319, 331–32, 333–34, 337, 341, 420–21, 456*f*
Charolais, 430–31

Chauvet (Cave), 240
Chemin des Dames (battle), 149
Chile, 422
Chinese Turkestan, 4, 241, 244
Cologne (Köln), 120–21, 159–60, 257–58
Cologne-Lindenthal (archaeological site), 147, 161
Colombia, 422
Congo, 437
Constance (Lake), 13, 145
Constantinople, 192, 379
Copenhagen, 43, 99, 114–15, 160–61, 192–93, 233
Corinth, 321
Cornwall, 341
Crete, 157–58, 251, 278–79, 320–22, 456*f*
Croatia, 142–43
Cuccuru S'Arriu, 343–44
Dagestan, 307–8
Damas, 421
Danube, 9, 123, 133, 242–43, 244, 252, 275, 298, 300, 312–13, 340, 349
Dashly Depe (archaeological site), 334
Denmark, 43, 64, 118, 150, 235–36, 315, 342, 408–9, 410–11
Deriivka (archaeological site), 305–8
Detmold, 140
Dikili Tash (archaeological site), 323, 324
Dimini (archaeological site), 147–48, 456*f*
Djarkutan (archaeological site), 334
Dmanissi (archaeological site), 239–40
Dnieper River, 172–73, 244, 245, 248, 298, 299
Doliana (archaeological site), 323
Don River, 244, 301
Donets River, 244, 245
Drancy (camp), 195–96
Düsseldorf, 42–43

Easter Island, 313
Ebla (archaeological site), 252–53
Ecuador, 422
Egypt, 5–6, 15, 42, 52, 61–62, 75–76, 77, 149–50, 164–65, 246, 268–69, 294–95, 311, 327–28, 329–30, 370–71, 421, 456*f*
Elam, 334–35, 456*f*
England, 42, 74, 77, 143, 144–45, 152–53, 184–85, 255, 277, 364, 422. *See also* Great Britain; United Kingdom
Ethiopia, 437, 445
Euphrates, 36–37
Eurasia, xv, 51, 107–8, 130, 155–56, 230–31, 237, 240, 243, 244, 253–54, 256, 272, 273, 274, 279, 288, 305, 307–8, 317, 326, 375, 376, 378, 412–14, 449, 450, 451, 456*f*
Externsteine (archaeological site), 140, 141–42

INDEX OF PLACENAMES 545

Faroe Islands, 134
Finland, 160–61, 172, 175–76, 433–34
Flanders, 205, 221
Flores Island, 239–40
France, 23–26, 44–45, 49, 56–57, 69–71, 74–75,
    79–84, 87–88, 91, 95, 102, 103, 108, 119–20, 127,
    137, 138, 143, 149, 152, 161, 166, 170–71, 175–
    76, 179, 180, 182, 190–93, 194–95, 196, 199–201,
    211, 212–13, 216, 218, 220–21, 223–24, 226,
    227–28, 238, 240, 243, 254–55, 257, 259, 280–81,
    339–40, 342, 351, 358–59, 361–62, 363, 373, 377,
    423, 424, 425, 426–27, 430–31, 433–34, 456f
Frankfurt, 138, 144–45, 188
Friesland, 58

Gaggenau, 140
Ganges, 421–22
Gaul, 9, 111, 340, 363
Geneva, 99–100, 101–2, 114, 226–27
Georgia, 239–40
Germania, 10, 54–55, 62, 119, 138–39, 286, 363,
    456f
Germany, 8–9, 15, 23–24, 25–26, 28, 45, 47–49,
    54–55, 56–57, 59, 68–69, 77, 79–80, 82–83,
    84–85, 89, 91, 93–94, 97, 99, 108–9, 120–21,
    122–23, 125–27, 129, 130, 131, 135, 144–45,
    146–47, 148, 152, 155, 156–58, 161, 164–65,
    169–70, 172, 175, 179, 180, 181, 183, 184,
    185–86, 187–88, 189, 190, 191–92, 194, 199–
    200, 205, 212, 218, 219–21, 232, 234, 238, 239,
    243–44, 252–53, 254–55, 257–58, 260, 277,
    287, 288–89, 296, 301–2, 340–41, 347–48,
    357–58, 363, 404–5, 424, 425, 433–34, 456f
Giessen, 61
Gihon (River of Eden), 36–37
Glozel, 40
Gonur Depe (archaeological site), 334
Göttingen, 25–26, 66, 215
Graz, 30–31
Great Britain, 77, 89, 91, 128, 144, 151, 175–76,
    179, 185, 186, 199–200, 218, 235–36, 241–42,
    246–47, 250–51, 254–55, 265–66, 280–81, 341
Greece, 9, 24, 25, 44, 136, 139, 142–43, 147–48,
    152, 154–55, 199, 221, 235–36, 242–43, 246,
    250, 251–52, 254, 260, 276, 281, 292–93, 311,
    314, 318, 319, 320–27, 331–32, 340, 347, 354,
    356, 369, 370, 374, 375–77, 378, 379, 406, 409,
    429–30, 433–34, 456f
Gumugou (archaeological site), 338

Hague, The, 114–16, 442
Halle (German city, also known as Saale), 159–
    60, 218

Hamburg, 141
Harvard, 65, 182, 289
Hawaii, 180
Hebron, 131–32
Hedeby (also known as Haithabu;
    archaeological site), 141–42, 161
Heidelberg, 289
Hejing (archaeological site), 338
Heligoland, 203–4
Helsinki, 160–61
Himalayas, 33, 35, 58–59, 223, 229–30, 390
Hindu Kush, 33–34, 82–83, 165–66, 168, 335
Hinkelstein (archaeological site), 224
Hohlefels (cave), 240
Hohlenstein-Stadel (cave), 240
Holland, 58, 89, 169–70, 183, 245, 250–51, 258
Houlbec-Cocherel (archaeological site), 42
Hungary, 147, 211, 234, 235–36, 250–51, 314,
    323, 324–25, 342, 400–1, 456f

Iberian Peninsula (Iberia), 235–36, 240, 250–
    51, 252–53, 255, 278–79, 280–81, 342–43
Iceland, 184–85
Île-de-France, 430–31
India, xv, 5–6, 14, 15, 17, 20–21, 24–25, 26,
    33–37, 38–39, 41, 48, 60–61, 129, 159–60,
    165–67, 168, 169, 229–30, 234–35, 257, 270,
    271–72, 274, 300, 306–7, 311, 315, 318–19,
    326–32, 334, 335, 336–37, 352–54, 355, 363,
    374, 375–76, 384, 408, 412, 422, 435, 437,
    445, 456f
Indian Ocean, 440–41
Indonesia, 199
Indus River, 169, 226, 252–53, 300, 313–14,
    327–30, 334, 335–36, 375–76, 413–14, 456f
Innsbruck, 288–89
Iran, xv, 147–48, 164–65, 166–67, 168, 169, 199,
    242, 300, 315, 326–28, 329–30, 331–32, 334,
    408, 437, 456f, See also Persia
Iraq, 242, 267, 327–28
Ireland, 44–45, 215–16, 315, 316, 340, 341, 342
Isle of Man, 341
Israel, 63, 267
Isturitz (cave), 240
Italy, 45, 104–5, 165–66, 167, 211, 221, 234, 246,
    254, 278–79, 280–81, 319, 340, 343–45, 359,
    400–1, 406, 421–22, 425, 430–31, 433–34,
    456f

Jakovica (archaeological site), 172
Jamaica, 441
Japan, 13, 184–85, 205, 226, 244, 265–66, 370–
    71, 372, 376, 378, 456f

546 INDEX OF PLACENAMES

Jiroft (archaeological site), 329–30, 334, 456*f*, 466*f*
Judea, 37
Jura, 148, 240, 247, 430–31

Kadesh (Battle of), 253–54
Kaliningrad. *See* Königsberg
Karasahr (Karashar), 337–38
Karelia, 307–8
Kashmir, 37
Kassel, 123
Kastoría, 442–43
Kazakhstan, 82–83, 245
Kelleli (archaeological site), 334
Kenya, 437
Khargush Tepe (archaeological site), 166–67
Kharkov, 142–43
Khvalynsk (archaeological site), 292–93, 298–99, 301, 305, 312–13
Kiel, 141, 160
Kiev, 142–43, 176–77
Knossos, 52, 151–52, 164–65, 321, 407–8
Kolkata (formerly Calcutta), 5
Königsberg (present day Kaliningrad), 55, 155–56, 172, 175, 187
Korea, 199, 376, 456*f*
Kovačevo (archaeological site), 247
Krasnoyarsk, 231–32
Kucha (state), 337–38
Kumtepe (archaeological site), 323

Latium, 45, 421
Latvia, 172, 291
Leipzig, 3–4, 29–30, 32, 61, 101–2, 139, 157
Lerna (archaeological site), 325
Letnica (archaeological site), 410–11
Limousin, 431
Lithuania, 288–90
London, 71–72, 95, 184–85, 236–37, 421
Los Angeles, 289
Luxembourg, 400–1, 433–34
Lvov (Lwòw, Luiv), 160–61

Mâconnais, 430–31
Mainz, 225–26, 257–58
Malaysia, 252–53
Mali, 437
Maliq (archaeological site), 324
Malta, 435–36
Mandalo (archaeological site), 323
Marburg, 138–39, 161
Marche, 431
Mari (archaeological site), 252–53

Marienburg (Castle), 140
Marseille, 134
Martinique, 112–13
Maykop, 299, 413, 456*f*
Mediterranean, 90, 138, 173, 193, 224, 226, 242–43, 266, 275, 277–78, 279–80, 281, 406, 425, 440
Mesopotamia, 38–39, 61–62, 149–50, 171–72, 246, 252–53, 267, 270, 274, 310–11, 327–28, 329–30, 334, 370, 409, 456*f*
Mikrothivi (archaeological site), 323
Mississippi, 313, 440
Mitanni, 153, 345–46
Mohenjo-daro, 169, 327–28
Moldova, 147–48, 248, 249, 298, 299, 313
Mongolia, 308, 337–39, 456*f*
Mont Blanc, 101
Morea, 65–66
Morocco, 422
Moscow, 71–72, 148
Mu (continent), 58–59, 206
Munich, 134, 141–42, 215–16, 289
Mycenae, 46, 52, 251, 320–21, 326–27, 407–8

Namazga (archaeological site), 334, 456*f*
Namibia, 187
Natzweiler (concentration camp), 188
Nazca, 200–1
Near East, 36–37, 42, 44, 53–54, 230–32, 234–35, 240, 242, 244–45, 252, 260, 264–65, 267, 269–71, 273, 278–79, 281–82, 294–95, 296, 298–99, 300, 311–12, 401, 425–26
Nebra (archaeological site), 254
Negev, 242
Neuchatel, 340–41
New Guinea, 412–13, 439, 440–41, 445
New York, 58–59, 118
New Zealand, 420–21, 429
Nice, 207–8
Niger, 429
Nile, 37
North Africa, 159–60, 268–69, 270–71, 272, 273, 274, 420–21, 435–36
North Pole, 33, 82–83, 215–16, 410–11
North Sea, 58, 89, 90, 91, 203–4, 243–44
Norway, 240
Novgorod, 176–77
Novocherkassk, 142–43
Nuremberg, 60–61, 186–87, 225

Occitanie, 205
Oceania, 239–40, 271–72, 273, 330, 390–91
Odessa, 55

INDEX OF PLACENAMES 547

Öhningen, 13
Olympia, 46, 141
Olympus, 356
Ore Mountains (*Erzgebirge*), 252–53
Ostia, 355–56
Ostmark, 125
Ottoman Empire, 13, 29–30, 44–45, 65–66, 278–79, 373, 429–30, 442–44, 456*f*
Oxford, 151–52, 163–64, 171
Oxus River. *See* Amu Darya

Pacific Ocean, 31–32, 155, 245, 253
Pakistan, xv, 33–34, 176–77, 222, 272, 279, 300, 327–28, 337, 456*f*
Palenque (archaeological site), 200–1
Palioskala (archaeological site), 323
Pamir, 33–34, 82–83, 164–65, 168
Papua New Guinea. *See* New Guinea
Paraguay, 63–64, 422
Paris, 4, 20, 23, 44–45, 71–72, 80–81, 99, 101–2, 103, 143, 147, 148, 149, 192–93, 195–96, 212–13, 249–50, 275, 340–41, 377, 383–84, 392, 425, 430–31
Peloponnese, 325, 443–44
Pennsylvania, 291
Périgord, 123, 146, 157–58, 240
Persia, 5, 39, 166–67. *See also* Iran
Peru, 183–84, 371, 422, 440–41
Petromagoula (archaeological site), 323
Philadelphia, 65, 338–39
Philippines, 180
Pisa, 78–79
Pishon (River of Eden), 36–37
Plovdiv, 147–48
Po River, 344–45
Poland, 103, 138, 142–43, 147, 160–61, 169–70, 172, 257, 258, 287, 288, 315, 316, 350, 456*f*
Poltava, 7–8
Pomerania, 84–85
Pontic Steppes, 40, 155–56, 160–61, 167–68, 171–73, 244–45, 248, 249–50, 251, 277–78, 287–88, 291, 292–93, 297–98, 299, 301, 303–4, 305, 306, 307–8, 312–13, 314, 332–33, 335, 411, 456*f*
Portugal, 199, 241–42, 245, 252–53, 438
Prague, 27, 99, 114–15, 153, 291
Pripet River and Marsh, 152
Prussia, 55, 123, 127, 172
Prut River, 244
Puerto Rico, 180
Pyatigorsk, 142–43
Pylos, 320–21
Pyrenees, 240

Quebec, 39, 433–34

Rachi Panagias, 323
Raidenstein (archaeological site), 140
Rehoboth (city in Namibia), 187
Réunion Island, 112–13
Rhine, 257–58, 301–2, 347–48
Rhodope Mountains, 442–43
Riga, 172, 291
Roman Empire, 25, 52, 219–20, 276, 319, 406, 456*f*
Romandy (Swiss), 431
Romania, 52, 147–48, 249, 254–55, 298, 299, 313, 323, 433–34, 438
Rome, 24, 25, 44, 45, 93–94, 136, 154–55, 308, 340, 352–54, 355–56, 363, 368–69, 374, 412–13, 430–31, 456*f*
Rostov, 142–43
Ruse (Roustchouk), 443–44
Russia, 8–9, 41, 47, 53, 107, 118, 119–20, 147, 169–70, 172, 232, 234, 242, 244, 245, 286–87, 288, 290, 292–93, 315, 333–34, 381, 440, 443, 456*f*

Seszee (archaeological site), 298–99
Sadowa, 56–57
Saint Petersburg, 174–75
Saint-Germain-en-Laye, 44–45, 143
Salzburg, 140
Samara, 232, 292–93
Sapalli Depe (archaeological site), 334
Sardinia, 343–44
Saxony, 140
Saxo-Thuringia, 160
Scandinavia, 45, 47–48, 54–55, 57–58, 61, 67–68, 91, 120, 127, 130, 146–47, 155–61, 162–64, 169–70, 172, 181, 192–93, 215–16, 241, 246–47, 250, 252–53, 254, 257–58, 287, 301–2, 310–11, 348, 363, 375, 410–11, 420–21, 449, 456*f*
Schleswig-Holstein, 160
Scotland, 278–79, 341
Sedan, 54–55
Senegal, 64
Serbia, 142–43
Servia (archaeological site), 147–48
Sesklo (archaeological site), 147–48
Shah Tepe (archaeological site), 168, 169
Shanpula (archaeological site), 338
Shetland Islands, 134
Siberia, 7–8, 231–32, 245, 308, 372, 420–21
Sicily, 343–44, 421–22
Sitagroi (archaeological site), 324
Slovakia, 147, 456*f*

548 INDEX OF PLACENAMES

Somme, 42–43, 419
South Africa, 74, 95, 165–66, 184–85, 187, 199, 216–17, 420–21, 437
South West Africa. *See* Namibia
Soviet Union. *See* USSR
Spain, 91, 175–76, 199, 221, 234, 239–40, 241, 252–53, 421–22, 436, 456*f*
Stonehenge (archaeological site), 203, 333
Strasbourg, 93–94, 188
Subeixi (archaeological site), 338
Sudan, 401
Susa, 147–48, 456*f*
Swabian Jura, 240
Sweden, 77, 118, 163–64, 183–85, 217–18
Switzerland, 35, 45, 77, 80–81, 84–85, 183–84, 221, 254–55, 310–11, 340–41, 425, 429, 431, 433–34, 443–44, 456*f*
Syr Darya River, 33–34, 168
Syria, 108, 199, 242, 267, 310–11, 327–28

Taip (archaeological site), 334
Tajikistan, 33–34, 327–28
Takon, 73
Tanzania, 437
Ticino, 433–34
Tigris, 36–37
Tiryns, 46, 251, 320–21
Tisza River, 324–25
Togolok (archaeological site), 334
Toulouse, 431–32
Tournai, 427–28
Transylvania, 164–65
Trobriand Islands, 119
Troy, 46, 147, 159–60, 292–93, 324, 347, 456*f*
Trundholm (archaeological site), 408–9
Tureng Tepe (archaeological site), 168
Turfan, 337–38
Turkestan, 164–65
Turkmenian steppes, 168
Turkmenistan, 147–48, 168
Tübingen, 135, 138–39, 288–89

Uganda, 437
Ukraine, 8, 47, 53, 119–20, 147–48, 169–70, 172, 241–42, 244, 248–49, 251, 254–55, 286–87, 292–93, 298, 299, 313, 315, 349–50, 402, 421–22, 440, 456*f*
United Kingdom, 41. *See also* Great Britain

United States, 24–25, 65–66, 77, 91, 92–93, 94, 107, 118, 128, 134–35, 144–45, 152, 179, 180, 183–86, 199, 218, 228, 237, 265–66, 289, 294, 297, 351–52, 377, 390–91, 422, 427, 440–41
Ural Mountains, 148, 298–99, 310–11, 326–27, 331–32, 333
Ural River, 245
USSR (Soviet Union), 118, 142–43, 170, 174–75, 176, 177–78, 202, 288–90, 333–34, 373–74, 390–91

Vanuatu, 440–41
Varna (archaeological site), 248, 296, 313, 314
Vaud (Canton), 184–85
Versailles, 54–55, 97, 125, 199, 288
Vienna (Austria), 23, 55–57, 71–72, 118, 120–21, 126–27, 132, 160–61, 162, 166, 192–93, 288–89
Vietnam, 199
Viksø (archaeological site), 410–11
Vistula River, 9
Volga River, 150, 232, 244, 292–93, 298–99, 301, 312–13, 349
Vorochilovsk, 142–43
Vučedol (archaeological site), 252
Vukovar, 252

Weimar, 133–34, 180, 205
Werfenstein (castle), 133
West Indies, 31–32, 70
Wewelsburg (castle), 140, 220–21
Wrocław. *See* Breslau
Wupu (archaeological site), 338

Xianbei, 338
Xinjiang, 244, 315, 337–39, 394, 456*f*, *See also* Chinese Turkestan

Yanbulak, 338
Yenisei River, 331–32, 339
Yugoslavia (Ex-), 242–43, 254–55
Yunnan, 252–53

Zaghunluq (archaeological site), 338
Zagros Mountains, 242
Zaraus, 73–74, 77
Zhoukoudian (archaeological site), 165–66
Zurich, 45

Index rerum: concepts, archaeological cultures, institutions, texts, etc.

For the benefit of digital users, indexed terms that span two pages (e.g., 52–53) may, on occasion, appear on only one of those pages.

"bag-shaped" (pottery). See *Beutelstil*

Abashevo (culture), 331–32, 466*f*
Abbevillian (culture), 423
abortion, 48–49, 208, 209, 212–13, 214
Académie de Médecine (France), 72, 195
Académie des Inscriptions et Belles Lettres, 6–7, 351, 364, 368
Académie des Sciences (France), 87, 193, 364
Académie Française, 195, 207, 351, 364–65, 379, 430
Academy of Sciences (Denmark), 20–21
Academy of Sciences (USSR), 174–75
Acheulean (culture), 423
Action Française, 110, 358–59, 360, 361–62
Adstrate (linguistics), 438–39
Æxsærtægkatæ, 355
Afanasievo (culture), 300, 331–32, 338–39, 456*f*
Ahnenerbe ("Heritage of the Ancestors"), 131–32, 140–42, 188, 203–4, 206, 218
Alægatæ, 355
Alakul (culture), 331–32
Alekseyevka (culture), 331–32
alphabet, xvii, 348–49, 413–14, 444
Alpine (race), 90–91, 155–56, 167, 182, 193, 224, 226
Alteuropäisch (cultural complex), 172–73, 263, 277, 291
amber, 162–63, 253, 375–76
Amt Rosenberg (Rosenberg Service), 131, 139, 140–41
Andronovo (culture), 251, 300, 310–11, 331–35, 456*f*, 466*f*
Apartheid, 94, 95, 144, 179–80, 184–85, 186, 207–8, 216–17
ape, 28, 64, 66, 74, 78, 90–91, 165–66
Arbeitsfront, 373
areal linguistics , 115–18, 277–78, 442, 445–46. See also *Sprachbund*
Ark, 38–39

Armanen Order or *Armanenschaft*, 60
Aryas, 34, 328–29, 330–31
Ashvamedha, 308
Atlantis, 58–60, 131–32, 203–4, 206, 213–14
Aurignacian, 240, 423, 456*f*
Australopithecus, 165–66
Avesta., 6–7, 33–34, 82–83, 166–67, 215–16, 329, 355, 458*f*
Azilian (culture), 241–42, 456*f*

Baas (political party), 208
Babel (Tower of), 229, 271–72
Babelian model, 6, 13, 450
Bactria-Margiana Archaeological Complex, BMAC. *See* Oxus (culture)
Baden (culture), 249–50, 298, 300, 314, 324, 347, 456*f*
Balkanism (linguistics), 444–45
Balkanization, 443, 456*f*
Bandkeramik. *See* Linear Ceramic
bathing, 50
Battle Axe culture, 147, 149–50, 157–58, 160, 162–63, 250, 342–43. *See also* Corded Ware
Baumes-Chaudes ("race"), 224
bear, 53, 61, 155–56, 286–87, 303–4, 307–8, 402
bee, 61, 162–63, 427–28
beech, 39–40, 55–56, 61, 155–56, 162–63, 402
Bell Beaker (culture), 235–36, 250–51, 255, 315, 316, 342–44, 456*f*, 466*f*
Berlin Anthropological, Ethnological and Prehistoric Society (*Berliner Gesellschaft für Anthropologie, Ethnologie und Urgeschichte*), 84–85
Beutelstil, 148, 461*f*
Bharatiya Janata Party (BJP), 328–29
Bible, biblical, xvi, 10–11, 12, 13, 15, 26, 36, 37–39, 42–43, 63–65, 70, 131–32, 180, 337, 371, 409, 449, 451
birch, 35, 39–40, 55–56, 61, 162–63, 402
bit (horse), 253–54, 298–99, 305, 306–7, 344

550 INDEX RERUM

Boleraz (culture), 323, 456*f*
Boratæ, 355
brachycephalic, brachycephaly, 66–68, 74–75, 77, 78, 82–83, 85–86, 89, 91–92, 126, 167–68, 171–72, 224, 420
Brahmins, 14, 15, 36–37, 41, 328, 352–53
Bronze Age, 43, 45, 120, 149–50, 162–63, 168–69, 172–73, 181–82, 224, 232, 233, 249–52, 253, 255–56, 276, 289–90, 292–93, 306–8, 314, 319, 320–25, 331–32, 341–42, 344, 348, 375–76, 409, 451, 456*f*
bronze, 61–62, 251–53, 254, 332, 334, 340–41, 376, 408–9, 410–11
Buddhism, Buddhist, 5–6, 140–41, 153, 337, 338–39, 356–57, 371–72
bull, 267, 268–69, 333–34, 401, 402
Bund der Germanen, 56–57

camel, 39–40, 65–66, 162–63
cart, 53–54, 61–62, 165–66, 249, 281–82, 309–11, 315, 336
caste, 41, 124, 328, 352–54, 370–71, 372
castration, 88–89, 92–93, 132–33, 247, 403
Catacomb (culture: *Katakumbnaja kultura*), 148, 251, 331–32, 456*f*, 466*f*
Catholic, Catholicism, 11, 14, 24, 68, 209, 348–49, 361–62
cattle, 242, 243–45, 298–99, 305, 332, 412
Caucasian (race), xvi, 22, 66, 67–68
Celtomania, 43–44, 59, 60–61
Centaur, 48
centum (languages), 157–58, 170, 276, 337
cephalic index, 22, 66–67, 87–88, 92–93, 184
Cernavoda (culture), 299, 301–2, 323, 456*f*
Chalcolithic, 8, 149–50, 164, 231, 246–48, 249–52, 258, 277–78, 284, 289–90, 292–93, 296, 298, 299, 300, 301–3, 305, 306–8, 311–14, 319, 322, 324, 342, 343–44, 403, 411, 414, 441–42, 456*f*, 465*f*–66*f*
chariot, 253–54, 281–82, 287–88, 300, 303–4, 306–7, 309–11, 316, 326–27, 328, 330, 333, 375–76, 401, 408–9, 414
Chasséen (culture), 148, 425, 456*f*, 465*f*
chastity, 48–49, 50
Chellean (culture), 423
Chernyakhov (culture), 349–50, 456*f*
chief, chiefdom, chieftain, 103–4, 245–48, 251–52, 253, 282–83, 286, 302, 312, 314, 406, 413–14
Christian, Christianity, Christianization, xv, 11–12, 13, 14, 15, 58, 59, 63, 83, 92–93, 131, 135, 199–200, 208–10, 211, 212, 340, 347–49, 356–57, 371–72, 374, 405, 456*f*

Church (Roman: catholic), 11, 14, 24, 135, 422. *See also* Catholic
Club de l'Horloge (The Clock Club), 206–8, 209–10
CNRS (*Centre National de la Recherche Scientifique*), 225–26, 231–32, 392
coffee, 73–74, 400–1, 402
collaboration, 44, 88–89, 179, 188, 191, 194–96, 199–200, 203–4, 218, 288, 362–63, 364–65,
Collège de France, 25, 70–71, 80–81, 102, 108, 351, 361–62, 364, 368, 404
colluvies gentium, 441–42
Commissariat général aux questions juives, 195–96
Copper Age. *See* Chalcolithic
copper, 8, 57–58, 124–25, 148, 171–72, 246, 248–49, 251, 252–53, 287–88, 311–12, 314, 334, 342, 375–76, 402
Corded Ware (culture, "race"), 119–20, 123, 147, 150, 157–58, 159–61, 162–64, 169–70, 172, 174, 224–25, 232, 233–34, 250, 251, 255, 287, 300, 306, 315, 316, 331–32, 342–43, 348, 350, 456*f*, 461*f*, 466*f*
craniometry, 22, 47–48, 65, 66–68, 73–74, 82, 87–89, 95, 140–41, 146, 150, 153, 155, 168–69, 181, 182, 187–88, 190, 192, 223, 224, 226–27, 229–30, 235–36
cremation, 324–25, 334–35, 341–42, 344–45, 348
Cris (culture), 244–45
Cro-Magnon, 82, 124, 203
cross-breed, 64–65, 74–76. *See also* mètis
crusades, 36–37
Cucuteni, Cucuteni-Trypillia (culture and site), 147–48, 248–49, 263, 298, 299, 311–14, 456*f*, 461*f*
cuneiform, 345–46
Cyrillic (alphabet), 348–49

Danubian (culture: Linear Pottery), 147–48, 149–50, 155, 164, 224, 242–44, 263, 290–91, 292, 294–95, 297, 427–28. *See also* Linear Pottery
Dark Ages, 313–14, 323–24, 327, 456*f*
Darwinism, 59, 87, 93–94, 428
declensions, 22–23, 346, 436–37, 444
Deutsches Archäologisches Institut (German Archaeological Institute), 137, 138, 143
dialect, dialectology, 10, 22, 23–24, 89–90, 105, 111–13, 117, 141–42, 259, 276–77, 291, 318, 337, 386, 396, 400–1, 429, 430–34, 435–36, 437, 442–43, 444, 445–46
Dinaric ("race"), 193, 224

DNA, xv, 219–20, 223, 227–28, 231, 234–35, 243, 260–61, 263–64, 337
Dnieper-Donets (culture), 245, 299, 305, 456*f*
dog, 111, 241–42, 298–99, 307–8, 391, 401, 402
dolichocephalic, dolichocephaly, 22, 47–48, 66–68, 74–75, 77, 78, 80–81, 82–83, 85–86, 90–92, 126, 130, 133, 157–58, 162–63, 167, 169, 171–72, 181–82, 203, 224,
dolmen , 36, 43–44, 52, 77, 119–20, 146–47, 155, 157–58, 169–70, 181–82, 249–50, 258, 262–63, 265. *See also* megalith
Dreyfus Affair, 56–57, 88
druid, 43–44, 60–61, 363

Earthly Paradise, 36–38, 84, 229–30. *See also* Eden
École Française d'Athènes, 42, 143, 147–48
École Pratique des Hautes Études, 102, 191, 359–60, 377
Edda, 131–32
Edda Society, 134–35
Eden, Garden of, 36–37, 131–32, 165–66. *See also* Earthly Paradise
eel, 55–56, 155–56, 162–63
Éléments (journal), 201–2, 205–6, 208–9, 222
elephant, 39–40
Ellerbeck (culture : Ertebølle), 124, 157–58, 181–82, 215–16, 243–44, 257–58, 456*f*. *See also* Ertebølle
Erligang (culture), 253, 456*f*
Erlitou (culture), 253, 456*f*
Ertebølle (culture), 164, 181–82, 215–16, 243–44, 257–58, 456*f*
esoteric, esotericism, 58, 59, 203–4, 206, 212, 214, 216–17, 363–64, 377. *See also* occultism
ethnic (group), ethnicity, 12, 56–57, 68, 80, 101–2, 110, 120–22, 123, 126–29, 175–76, 178, 180, 211, 212, 222, 226, 255, 256, 263–64, 291, 334–35, 347–48, 349–50, 385, 419, 423–25, 426–28, 429, 433, 448, 451
ethnic cleansing, 349
ethnolinguistics, 381, 430–31, 433, 450
Eugenics, 56–57, 59–60, 88–89, 93–95, 97, 119, 132–33, 180–81, 183–85, 186–87, 188, 191, 192–93, 208–9, 212–13, 218, 219–21, 364–65, 396
Eurasia Septentrionalis Antiqua (journal), 148, 160–61, 174–75
Ezero (culture), 298, 324, 456*f*, 464*f*, 465*f*

Family tree of languages. See *sprachbund*
Fatyanovo (culture), 119–20, 147, 331–32, 456*f*, 466*f*

Fedorovka, Fedorovo (culture), 331–32, 456*f*
Figaro Magazine, 207, 208, 209
flamines, 352–54
Flood, The, 13, 36–37, 42–43, 63, 239–40, 411–12
flower, 48–49, 53–54, 90
Folteşti (culture), 313–14
Freemason, freemasonry, 59, 361–62
French Revolution, 15, 23, 38–39, 69, 88–89, 91–92, 328, 389, 424
French School at Athens. See *École Française d'Athènes*
Front National, FN, 194–95, 199–200, 206–7, 209–10, 211, 213, 214, 216–18
Funnel Beaker (culture; also known as TRBK), 146–47, 164, 181–82, 243–44, 249–50, 258, 263, 301–2, 314, 456

gender archeology, 295
General Commission for Jewish Questions. See *Commissariat général aux questions juives*
Genesis (Book of), 36–37, 42–43, 45, 89
genetics, 38–39, 95, 119, 180, 183–84, 186, 187–88, 190, 193, 197, 223, 228, 229, 259, 302–3, 314–17, 339. *See also* DNA; eugenics
genocide, 95, 179, 180–81, 196, 205, 363–64, 436
Germanomania (Aryanomania), 57, 58, 60–61, 85–86, 87, 93–94, 130, 131–32, 134, 138–39, 140, 141–42, 157, 158, 159–60, 161–62, 206, 215, 286
Gestapo, 118, 160–61
Glagolitic (alphabet), 348–49
Globular Amphora (culture), 316, 456*f*, 464*f*, 465*f*
glottal (consonant), 383
glottalic (theory), 381, 383–84
glottochronology, 7–8, 270–71, 395, 398
gnosis, 203–4
goat, 242, 244–45, 268–69, 298–99, 402, 412
Golasecca (culture), 344–45
gold, 5, 146, 148, 246, 248, 251, 252, 254, 312, 334, 402, 408–9, 427–28
Gorodsk (culture), 313–14, 456*f*, 465*f*
Grammaire de Port-Royal, 24–25, 364
Grande Loge de France, 361
Great Migrations (period: Invasions), 427, 456*f*, *See also* Invasions
Groupement de recherche et d'études pour la civilisation européenne (GRECE), 201–2, 205–9, 212–13, 216–17, 221
Grubenhaus. See pit-dwelling

552 INDEX RERUM

Gumelnița (culture), 246, 248, 249, 298, 299, 311–13, 456*f*
Gundestrup cauldron, 52

Hallstatt (culture), 255, 341, 342, 456*f*
Hammer (movement), 133–34
Hanseatic League, 440
haoma, 334–35
Helladic (period and civilization), 251, 292–93, 314, 321–22, 324, 325–27, 456*f*, 465*f*, 466*f*
heresy, 10, 11–12
hieroglyphics, 345
Homo antecessor, 239–40
Homo erectus, 165–66, 229, 230, 239–40, 446
Homo ergaster, 239–40
Homo habilis, 239–40
Homo heidelbergensis, 239–40
Homo neanderthalensis. See Neanderthal
Homo sapiens, Homo sapiens sapiens, 229, 230, 231, 239–40, 259, 260–61, 378, 391
homosexuality, 60–61, 188, 212–13, 214, 412–13
honey, 61
Horodiștea (culture), 313–14
horse, horse riding, horsemanship, 8, 27, 53–54, 61, 82–83, 109, 124–25, 152, 154, 162–63, 164–66, 171–72, 240–41, 244, 248–49, 253–54, 281–82, 286, 287–88, 294, 297, 298–99, 300, 301, 303–8, 309, 310–12, 314, 317, 324–25, 328, 329–30, 332–34, 344, 345–46, 347, 375–76, 381–82, 385, 400, 401, 402, 408–9, 410–11, 412, 414, 421–22, 427–28
house, 49, 52, 120, 146, 147–48, 161, 243, 248, 294, 297, 302, 325, 332, 399–400

Iliad, 101, 356
Indus (civilization), 169, 226, 300, 313–14, 327–30, 334, 335, 375–76, 413–14, 456*f*
Institut d'études indo-européennes (Institute for Indo-European Studies, France), 215–17, 367
Institut de Paléontologie Humaine (Institute for Human Paleontology), 144, 191
Institut national d'études démographiques (National Institute for Demographic Studies, France), 194–95, 207–8
Institute for the Study of Man, 218–19
Invasions (Barbarian: Great Migrations), 413, 427. *See also* Great Migrations
IQ (intelligence quotient), 74, 95, 207, 236–37
Iron Age, 43, 45, 146, 155, 166–67, 224, 234, 254, 255, 306–7, 340–41, 348, 456*f*
iron, 181, 246, 340–41

Iron Curtain, 239
Ivanhoe, 436–37

Jastorf (culture), 348, 456*f*
Jiroft (culture), 329–30, 334, 456*f*, 466*f*
Jomon (culture), 226, 456*f*
Journal of Indo-European Studies, 218–19, 226, 294, 328–29, 388

Kabbalah, 59–60, 132
Kajrak Kum (culture), 331–32
Karanovo VI, VII (cultures), 246, 248, 249, 298, 299, 312–13, 324, 456*f*
Karasuk (culture), 331–32
Katakumbnaja. See Catacomb (culture)
Kelteminar (culture), 245, 332–33, 456*f*, 465*f*
Khvalynsk (culture), 59–60, 292–93, 298–99, 301, 305, 312–13, 465*f*
king, 11–12, 282–83, 352–53, 354, 355–57, 369, 400, 402, 404, 411–12, 427–28, 429–30
kinship (between languages and cultures), 7, 127–28, 139, 272, 278, 282, 316–17, 349, 381, 389, 391, 393–94, 420, 444–45, 448, 451
Kinship (system), 395, 404, 429
kiss, 50–51
kjøkkenmødding. See shell midden
koinê, 277–78, 432, 458*f*, See also *sprachbund*
Komarov (culture), 350, 456*f*
Kshatriya (warrior caste), 328, 352–53
Ku Klux Klan, 186
Kuban (culture) 413
Kugelamphorenkultur: See Globular Amphora (culture)
Kurgan (culture, graves), 8, 148, 169–70, 203, 226–27, 239, 287, 296–97, 298–300, 301–2, 311–13, 317, 332, 347, 414, 425–26, 464*f*

L'Anthropologie (journal), 143–44, 191–92
La Tène (culture), 255, 340–41, 342, 347–48, 456*f*
Lake settlements, lake villages (*palafittes*), 45, 52, 53, 119–20, 146, 148, 161, 247
laryngeals, 101–2, 382, 383–84, 388
Lebensborn, 132–33, 190
Lebensreform, 59, 212–13
Lepenski Vir, 244, 456*f*
Lepontic (inscriptions), 340, 344–45
Levallois (culture), 423
Linear A (writing), 278–79, 280–81, 321, 371–72
Linear B (writing), 251, 318, 320–21
Linear Ceramic (culture), 119–20, 147, 149, 157–58, 159–60, 161, 164, 169–70, 172, 173, 175–76, 242–43, 244–45, 263–64, 277–78, 279–80, 290–91, 296, 425, 456*f*, 461*f*, 463*f*

linguistic paleontology, xviii, 34, 35, 39–40, 49, 51, 52–53, 55–56, 101–2, 105, 146, 152, 155–58, 162–63, 171–72, 173, 256, 286–87, 288, 303, 387, 399–401, 402, 404, 409–10, 412–13, 452

Longshan (culture), 337–38, 456*f*

Louvre (museum), 25, 168

Magdalenian (culture), 157–58, 170, 240, 257–58, 423, 456*f*

Maglemose, Maglemosian (culture), 157–58, 164, 241–42, 243–44, 258, 456*f*

Mahabharata, 355, 409

Malta (Order of), 435–36

Mankind Quarterly (journal), 218, 220–21

Mannus (journal), 120, 125–26, 160

marriage, 47–48, 50–51, 68, 86, 92–93, 94, 159–60, 184–85, 186, 187, 212–13, 227, 354, 369–70, 411–12

matriarchal, matriarchy, 294–96

Maykop (culture), 162–63, 299, 413, 456*f*, 465*f*, 466*f*

medhu, 61

megalith, 42, 43–44, 45, 52, 55–56, 59–60, 85–86, 123, 146–47, 148–49, 159–60, 162–63, 164, 169–70, 172, 224, 243–44, 246, 247–48, 258, 259, 265, 309–10, 314, 343–44. *See also* dolmen

menhir, 36, 43–44, 265, 410–11. *See also* megalith

metallurgy, 8, 43–44, 57–58, 124–25, 166–67, 246, 247–49, 251, 252–53, 254, 262, 265, 286, 298, 312, 314, 376

Metapedia (internet site), 221

métis, métissage, 440. *See also* cross-breed

Michelsberg (culture), 148, 425, 456*f*, 465*f*

Middle Ages, 7–8, 12, 36–37, 63, 113–14, 271–72, 315, 319, 340, 341, 350, 356–57, 372, 374, 402–3, 413, 427, 428, 438, 440, 441–42, 456*f*

milk, milk products, 233, 247, 400, 402–3

Minoan (culture), 157–58, 251, 253, 321–22, 327, 371–72, 456*f*, 466*f*

Minyan (ware), 326

Mischsprache. See mixed language

Mississippian (culture), 313, 440

mixed language (*mischsprache*), 31–32, 112–13, 422, 435–36, 439

Monist League (*Monistenbund*), 28, 56–57, 92, 93–94, 133

monogenisis, monogenist, 14, 64, 66–67, 71–72, 75, 79–80, 390–91

monotheism, 58, 70–71, 111, 153, 295–96

Moon (sect), 218

mother language, 23–24, 26–27, 35, 230, 270, 390–91

Mousterian (culture), 423

multilingualism, 345–46, 433, 442–43

Musée de l'Homme, 74, 191, 193

Musée des Antiquités Nationales, 35–36, 40, 44–45, 143, 262

Muséum national d'histoire naturelle (Paris), 75, 191

Mycenaean (culture), 30, 235–36, 246, 251, 253, 254, 276, 309, 311, 313–14, 318, 320–22, 323–24, 326–27, 333, 405, 413–14, 432, 456*f*, 458*f*, 466*f*

Narbonnais (Cycle), 356–57

Nart legends, 355, 369–71

National Front (Great Britain), 199–200

National Institute for Demographic Studies. See *Institut national d'études démographiques*

Nationaldemokratische Partei Deutschlands (NPD), 199–200

Natufian (culture), 242, 270, 456*f*

Nazi Party (*National-Socialistische Deutsche Arbeiterpartei*), 60–61, 133, 134–35, 162, 200–1, 204, 215–16

Nazi, Nazism (National-socialism), 8–9, 44, 57–58, 59, 60–61, 62, 71, 97, 108–9, 118, 123, 124–25, 127, 128, 129–31, 133–45, 157, 158, 160–62, 169, 175, 179, 186–88, 199–201, 202–4, 205–6, 208–9, 210–11, 212–16, 218, 219–22, 225–26, 288–89, 303–4, 327, 330–31, 358, 359, 362, 373, 406–7

Neanderthal, *Homo neanderthalensis*, 42–43, 82, 84–85, 225, 230, 231, 239–40, 259–60, 446, 456*f*

negationism, 212, 216–17, 220–21, 222, 288

Neogrammarians, 27, 29–31, 32, 47, 99, 101–2

Neolithic, 8, 42, 45, 49, 77, 84, 119–20, 123, 142–43, 146–48, 149–50, 151–52, 155, 161, 164–65, 167–73, 181–82, 224, 230–31, 233–35, 239, 241–47, 248–49, 258, 259–61, 262, 263–67, 269, 274–76, 277–81, 284, 289–92, 294–95, 296, 298–99, 300, 301–2, 303, 305–6, 307–8, 309–10, 311–12, 316, 319, 321–22, 335, 337–38, 343–44, 392, 403, 405, 411, 412–13, 414, 421, 425–26, 441–42, 456*f*, 463*f*

Neo-Nazi, 212–13, 218, 220–21

New Age, 217–18, 296, 333, 339–40

New Archaeology, 122, 128, 238–39, 289, 295–96

New Synthesis, xv, 229–30, 269–70, 393, 428

Noah's ark, 38–39

554 INDEX RERUM

Nordic (race), Nordicism, 8–9, 55–56, 110, 124–25, 126, 130, 131–32, 138, 146–47, 152–53, 154–56, 157–59, 160–61, 162–65, 167, 169–70, 171–72, 174, 181–82, 186, 187–88, 193, 203, 214–15, 219–20, 224–25, 226, 255, 263, 456*f*
Nordische Ring, 161–62
Northern League for Northern European Friendship, 218, 220–21, 294
Nouvelle Droite, 187–88, 195–96, 199–222, 236–37, 294, 352, 365–67
Nouvelle École (journal), 201–3, 204, 205–6, 207, 213–14, 215–16, 218–19, 220–21, 222, 294, 365–66, 377
Nuremberg Laws, 60, 186–87

occultism, 58–61, 133, 134–35, 136, 140–41, 201, 203–4, 211–12, 214, 360–64, 374. *See also* esotericism
ochre (pigment), 148, 169–70, 298–99, 312
Ochre grave (culture), 148, 162–63, 169–70, 171–73, 174, 287
Oera-Linda Book, 58, 60–61, 131–32
Order of the New Templars, *Ordo Novi Templi*, 60–61, 133
original Homeland. See *Urheimat*
original Indo-European People. See *Urvolk*
original Language. See *Ursprache*
Ostara (journal), 133, 137
Oxus (culture), 334, 456*f*
oyster, 14, 55–56

palafittes. *See* lake settlements
palafittes. See *lake villages*
Paleolithic, 45, 53–54, 120, 123, 149, 167–68, 224, 234, 240, 254, 257, 259–61, 262, 265–66, 273–74, 294–95, 306–7, 321, 327, 413–14, 423, 425–26, 456*f*
Pan-German League (*Alldeutscher Verband*), 125–26
Pan-Germanism, 55, 56–58, 60, 79–80, 119–45, 161
Papal bull, 63–64
Paris Commune, 80, 212
patriarchy, patriarchal, 57, 60, 89–90, 294–95, 298–99, 404
pederasty. *See* homosexuality
Petrovka (culture), 331–32
Pit Grave (culture: *Jamnaja kultura,* Yamnaya), 148, 232, 234, 249–50, 251, 292–93, 298, 300, 301, 302–3, 310–11, 314, 315, 331–33, 338–39, 343–44, 456*f*
pit-dwelling (*Grubenhaus*), 49

poetry, poetic, xviii, 49, 153, 375–76, 407–9, 451
Poltavka (culture), 332
polygenism, polygenist, 64–66, 71–72, 76, 77–78, 84, 87, 180
potato, 400–1, 402
potlatch, 404
Prähistorische Zeitschrift (journal), 126–27
primitive People. See *Urvolk*
Proto-Villanovan (culture), 344–45, 456*f*
Przewalski's horse, 165–66
Przeworsk (culture), 348, 350, 456*f*

Radiocarbon dating, 149–50, 241, 265, 290, 292–93, 301–2, 306–7, 320, 395
Red Army, 202, 288–89, 373
Reformation, 11, 12, 15
Remedello (culture), 234, 343–44, 456*f*, 465*f*
Renaissance, 7, 12, 15, 57–58, 374
rest room, 48–49
Rigveda . See Vedas, Vedic hymns
Romano-Germanic Commission. See *Römisch-Germanische Komission*
Romanticism, 15, 20, 23, 37, 38–39, 43–45, 59, 69, 93–94, 116–17, 122–23, 126, 129, 153, 155, 178, 424
Römisch-Germanische Komission (Romano-Germanic Commission), 138, 144–45, 160
Rosicrucians, 59–60, 132
Rössen (culture), 243–44, 258, 301–2, 456*f*
runes, 57–58, 131–32, 134–35, 140, 141–42, 413–14

S'eszee (culture), 299, 312–13
SA (*Sturmabteilung*), 141–42, 162, 188, 358
sacrifice, 43–44, 132–33, 297, 302, 303, 308, 333–34, 406, 412, 413
sagas, 356–57
salmon, 53, 155–56, 303–4, 402
salt, 53, 61, 155–56, 245–46, 253, 268–69, 286–87, 402
Samara (culture), 232, 292–93, 298–99, 312–13
satem languages, 157–58, 170, 276, 278, 337
Sauveterrian (culture), 241–42
scepter, 246, 249, 305, 307–8, 312, 317
Schnurkeramik. See Corded Ware
Seine-Oise-Marne (culture), 148, 249–50, 425, 456*f*, 465*f*
Shang (dynasty), 253, 456*f*
sheep, 27, 51, 242, 244–45, 298–99, 304, 332, 333–34, 385, 412
shell midden (*kjøkkenmødding*), 45, 55–56, 157–58, 243–44
Sinanthropus, 165–66

INDEX RERUM 555

Single Grave (culture), 147, 160, 162–63
Sintashta (culture), 310–11, 326–27, 331–32, 333–34, 456f, 466f
slave, slavery, 14, 60, 65, 74, 77, 85–86, 124, 132–33, 180, 253, 404, 440–41
Social Darwinism, 83, 88–89, 212
Société d'anthropologie de Paris, 35–36, 119–20, 167, 189, 190, 191, 225–26, 286
Société de linguistique de Paris, 25, 102
Société préhistorique française, 81–82, 119–20
sociolinguistics, 381, 446–48, 450
Sofievka (culture), 313–14
soma, 334–35
Sorbonne (university), 217, 360
spindle whorl, 46, 309–10
Sprachbund, 115–16, 277–78, 284, 441–46. See also *koinê* and balkanization
Sredny Stog (culture), 299, 301, 305–6, 456f
Srubnaja kultura. See Timber-Grave culture
SS (*Schutzstaffel*), 60, 123, 126–27, 131–33, 136, 139, 140–43, 153, 161–62, 188, 190, 203–4, 205–6, 213, 215, 218, 220–21
Stammbaum (family tree of languages, genes), xv, 3–4, 9, 27, 28, 29, 31–32, 101–2, 117–18, 119, 122, 165–66, 239–40, 263–64, 267–68, 269–73, 275–76, 284–85, 376, 378, 381–82, 389–92, 393, 423–24, 439, 441–42, 445–46, 448, 451–52
State Academy for History and Material Culture (GAIMK, Russia), 174, 175, 176
steppes, xviii, 8, 40, 53–54, 61, 84, 146, 148, 152, 155–56, 160–61, 162–63, 164–66, 167–69, 171–73, 174, 222, 224, 226–27, 230–33, 235–36, 239, 244–45, 248–50, 251, 253–54, 260, 261, 263, 277–78, 281–82, 286–317, 318–19, 323–25, 326–27, 331–36, 339, 343–44, 347, 402, 410–11, 412–13, 414, 452, 456f, 463f
strontium isotope analysis, 236
substrate (linguistic, cultural), 121–22, 173, 203, 267–68, 304–5, 321, 347–48, 407–8, 434–35, 438–39
sun, 48, 90, 220–21, 268–69, 297, 302, 352, 375–76, 378, 408–9
Supreme Being, 11
Sursk-Dnieper (culture), 245

taboo, 53, 402, 404–5, 413–14
Tardenoisian (culture), 241–42, 456f
Tazabagyab (culture), 331–32
tell, 46, 147–48, 168
Templars, 59–61, 132, 133, 203–4, 212
Terramare (culture), 45, 52, 146, 344–45, 456f
Tetralogy (Wagner), 79

Teutonic, 78–79, 133, 136, 140
theosophy, 58–60
Third Reich, 91–92, 161–62, 187–88, 222, 223, 288, 357–58
Thule Circle (*Cercle Thulé*), 221
Thule Society (*Thule-Gessellschaft*), 60–61, 134, 200–1, 215–16, 220–21
tiger, 39–40, 61, 162–63
Timber Grave (culture; *Srubnaja kultura*), 148, 331–32, 456f, 466f
toilet. *See* rest room
tortoise, 155–56, 162–63
Trajan's Column, 52
Treaty of Versailles, 97, 199, 288
tree (linguistics). See *Stammbaum*
Trichterbecherkultur (TBRK). *See* Funnel Beaker
trifunctional, trifunctionality, 59–60, 282–83, 353–57, 368–71, 376, 402, 412, 413
Tripolye (culture), 119–20, 147–48, 172, 297, 456f, 465f
Trzciniec (culture), 350, 456f, 466f

Unesco, 185, 196, 355, 392
Union international de sciences préhistoriques et protohistoriques (UISPP: International Union for Prehistoric and Protohistoric Sciences), 144
Université de Lyon, 194–95, 215–17, 265–66, 365, 367
Urheimat (original homeland), xviii, 8, 9, 17, 29, 33–62, 82–84, 85–86, 89, 91, 103, 105, 119, 125, 131–32, 146–78, 181–82, 197, 213–14, 215, 239, 257–58, 262–85, 286–317, 327–28, 339, 350, 386, 399–400, 402–3, 421, 428, 452, 453
Urnfield (culture, period), 341–42, 456f
Ursprache (original language), xviii, 3–4, 9, 10, 12, 17, 27, 29, 33, 103, 197, 267–68, 283, 382–83, 384, 385, 386, 387–88, 414, 432, 438, 451–52
Urvolk (original people), xviii, 15, 17, 19–20, 29, 33–35, 41, 48–49, 50, 51, 62, 97, 105, 110, 116–18, 123, 150, 156–57, 158, 166, 170, 181, 197, 215–16, 222, 223, 256, 257, 262–63, 281–82, 283, 286–87, 292, 386, 388, 399–400, 402–3, 405, 406–7, 409, 413, 419, 441–42, 452–53
Usatovo (culture), 299, 313–14, 456f

Vaishya (caste), 352–53
Vase Painter (culture), 147–48, 164–65
Vedas, Vedic hymns, 48, 251, 306–7, 318, 320–21, 328, 329, 330–31, 346, 353–54, 355, 363, 369–70, 374, 375–76, 384, 405, 407–8, 409, 456f

556 INDEX RERUM

Vichy (government), 127, 191, 194–95, 207, 223, 361–62, 364–65
Villanova (culture), Villanovan, 344–45, 456f
Villers-Cotterêts (ordinance), 430
Völkisch, 56–57, 59, 60–61
Volksgeist, 28, 122–23, 126, 129, 155, 175–76, 178, 413–14, 424, 426–27

Wave theory (*Wellentheorie*), 30–31, 117, 301–3, 434
Wehrmacht, 118, 373
Weimar Republic, 133–34, 181, 205
Weiße Rose (resistance group: White rose), 141–42

Wellentheorie. See wave theory
wheel, 53, 106, 171–72, 245–46, 249, 253–54, 281–82, 298–99, 303, 309–11, 314, 333, 375–76, 401, 402, 408–9
Wicca (movement), 217–18
Wielbark (culture), 348, 456f
Wikipedia, 221, 222
Wolf, 61, 241–42, 305

Yamnaya (culture). *See* Pit Grave (culture)
Yangshao (culture), 337–38, 456f
Yayoi (culture), 226, 456f

Zarubintsy (culture), 350

Index of languages (real or supposed) and language families

For the benefit of digital users, indexed terms that span two pages (e.g., 52–53) may, on occasion, appear on only one of those pages.

Afrikaans, 437, 441–42
Afro-Asiatic, 229–30, 272, 274–75, 467f
Agglutinating, 22–23, 28, 133, 176–77, 280–81
Agnean, 337
Ainu, 193, 272, 273–74
Akkadian, 267, 345–46, 406, 408
Alamblak, 445
Albanian, 3–4, 21, 275, 304, 318, 350, 386, 393–94, 400–1, 405, 422, 433–34, 435–36, 442–43, 444, 458f
Aleut, 272, 273–74
Allemanic. *See* Swiss-German
Altaic, 22, 272, 273–75, 278–79, 441–42
Alteuropäisch, 172–73, 263, 277
Amerind, 272, 273–74, 390–91
Arabic, 7–8, 400–1, 408, 420–21, 422, 435–36, 437, 440, 468f
Aramaic, 267
Arawak, 400–1
Armenian, 3–4, 19, 21, 103, 275, 276–77, 304, 350, 383, 386, 391–92, 393–94, 396, 400–1, 422, 443–44, 458f
Aromanian, 442–43
Asu, 437
Austroasiatic, 445, 467f
Auvergnat, 431
Aymara, 422

Babylonian, 38–39, 171–72, 409
Baltic, 3–4, 50, 275, 278, 309, 318, 337, 344, 386, 393–94, 405, 407–8, 413, 435–36, 458f, 460f, 468f
Bantu, 401, 437
Basque, 15, 22, 31, 107, 176–77, 272, 273, 278–79, 400–1, 422, 439
Bavarian (dialect), 436
Berber, 230, 422
Berrichon, 400–1
Bislama, 440–41

Brahui, 330
Breton, 43–44, 107, 340, 341, 458f
Bulgarian, 349, 442–43, 444, 458f
Burmese, 445, 468f
Burushaski, 272, 273, 279

Carian, 345
Castilian, 39, 436, 458f
Catalan, 431–32
Caucasian, 21, 31, 114–15, 117–18, 165–66, 264, 272, 273, 274, 279, 304–5, 351, 356–57, 384, 422, 441–42
Celtic, 3–4, 5, 9, 12, 15, 21, 22, 31, 105, 111, 259, 275, 276, 277–78, 282, 304–5, 308, 309, 340–41, 343–45, 346, 356–57, 386, 387, 393–94, 396, 407–8, 422, 458f, 460f, 468f
Chimakuan, 445
Chinese, 12, 15, 22–23, 272, 304–5, 337–38, 339, 401, 420–21, 435–36, 445, 468f
Chinook, 440
Chukchi, 272, 273–74
Cilician, 345
Coptic, 272
Cornish, 341
Cree, 440
Creole, 31–32, 112–13, 430–31, 434, 438, 439–42, 450
Cushitic, 437, 445
Czech, 56–57, 400–1, 458f

Dené-Caucasian, 272, 273, 279
Dimotiki (Demotic or Modern Greek), 400–1, 444, 458f
Dravidian, 22, 229–30, 270, 271–72
Dutch, 400–1, 437, 440–41, 458f

Egyptian, 15, 267, 272, 401
Elamite, 267, 274, 330, 406
Enga, 445

558 INDEX OF LANGUAGES

English, 100–1, 115–16, 304–5, 309, 400–1, 420–21, 422, 429, 432, 433, 434–37, 439, 440–41, 444, 445, 458*f*, 468*f*
Eskimo, 272, 273–75, 467*f*
Esperanto, 107
Estonian, 233, 271–72, 278–79, 435–36
Ethiopian, 272
Etruscan, 259, 278–79, 280–81, 344–45, 406

Farsi, 336. *See also* Persian
Finnish, 171–72, 271–72, 278–79, 433–34, 435–36
Finno-Ugric, 7–8, 22, 107, 117–18, 141–42, 165–66, 171–72, 233, 271–72, 274–75, 278–79, 304–5, 331, 372, 435–36. *See also* Uralic
Franco-Provençal, 430–31
Frankish, 400, 434–35, 438
French, 10, 15, 23–25, 49, 63, 70–71, 89–90, 111, 112–13, 115–16, 157–58, 304–5, 309, 341, 381–82, 391–92, 400–1, 420–21, 422, 429, 430–31, 432, 433–35, 436–37, 438, 440–41, 444, 458*f*

Gascon, 431–32
Gaulish, 111, 304–5, 340, 434–35, 458*f*
Georgian, 264, 268–69, 383, 400–1
German, 7, 10–11, 17, 19, 20, 23–24, 25–26, 31–32, 35, 48–49, 55, 56–57, 63, 115–16, 153, 157–58, 289–90, 304–5, 309, 400–1, 404, 406, 433–34, 435, 436, 440, 443–44, 445, 458*f*, 468*f*
Germanic, 3–4, 9, 19, 20–21, 49, 55, 57–58, 101–2, 103, 105, 111–12, 113–14, 132, 163–64, 176–77, 259–60, 275, 276, 277–78, 304–5, 309, 336, 337, 347–49, 356–57, 383, 387, 393–94, 413–14, 422, 436–37, 439, 458*f*, 460*f*, 468*f*
Greek, 3–4, 6–7, 9, 15, 19, 21, 22–23, 24–25, 30, 42, 55, 70, 101–2, 103, 162–63, 171–72, 213–14, 235–36, 251, 252–53, 275, 277–78, 281, 304–5, 309, 320–21, 327, 337, 346, 348–49, 381, 386, 393–94, 400–1, 403, 404–5, 407–8, 413–14, 422, 429–30, 432, 433–37, 442–43, 444–45, 447, 458*f*, 460*f*, 468*f*

Hamitic, 272
Hamito-Semitic, 176–77, 272
Hattic, 267–68, 345–46
Hebrew, 7–8, 9, 12, 14, 38–39, 267, 348–49, 371, 400–1, 408, 434–35, 436
Hindi, 435, 458*f*, 468*f*
Hittite or Nesite, 4, 30, 101–2, 235–36, 251, 267–69, 275, 276, 304, 309, 318, 320–21, 337, 345–47, 382, 393–94, 396, 401, 458*f*, 468*f*
Hochdeutsch. See German

Hungarian, 107, 221, 259, 271–72
Hurrian, 267, 345–46

Iberian, 279, 280–81, 406
Ido, 107
Illyrian, 276–77, 458*f*
Indo-Iranian, 39–40, 53, 55, 103, 105, 176–77, 229–30, 235–36, 254–55, 275, 290, 300, 309, 311–12, 329, 330–32, 334–35, 337, 344, 345–46, 349–50, 355, 381, 396, 402, 405, 445,
Indo-Portuguese, 440
Iranian, 82–83, 329, 331–32, 334–35, 355, 386, 387, 393–94, 400–1, 458*f*, 460*f*, 468*f*, *See also* Indo-Iranian; Persian
Irish, 107, 340, 381, 458*f*
Isolating, 22–23, 28, 133, 176–77
Italian, 7, 31–32, 63, 89–90, 112–13, 381, 430–31, 432, 433–34, 435–36, 440, 458*f*
Italic, 275, 277–78, 343–44, 349, 386, 393–94, 458*f*, 460*f*, 468*f*

Japanese, 272, 273–75, 304–5, 401, 445, 468*f*
Japhetic, 22, 176–77
Judeo-Greek, 442–43
Judeo-Piedmontese, 436
Judeo-Provençal, 436
Judeo-Spanish, 422, 436, 442–43

Kamchatka (languages of), 272, 273–74
Kannada, 330
Karasahr, 337–38
Kartvelian, 268–69
Katharevousa (Modern Greek), 444
Khanty, 331
Khmer, 435–36
Koinê, 277–78, 432, 458*f*
Komi, 331
Korean, 272, 304–5, 401
Kuchean, 337, 458*f*
Kurdish, 55, 422, 458*f*

Ladino: see Judeo-Spanish
Languedocian, 431–32
Lapp. *See* Sami
Latin, 3–4, 5, 6–7, 9, 10, 19, 21, 23–25, 42, 49, 55, 63, 89–90, 101–2, 103, 104–5, 107, 111, 113–14, 157–58, 259, 277, 281–82, 304–5, 309, 337, 343–44, 346, 348–49, 381–82, 391–92, 400, 404–5, 406, 420–21, 422, 427–28, 432, 435–36, 438, 444, 458*f*
Latvian, 318, 435–36, 458*f*
Lingua franca, 440

INDEX OF LANGUAGES 559

Lithuanian, 19, 21, 39, 61, 101–2, 107, 304–5, 318, 435–36, 458*f*
Lombardic, 430–31
Luwian, 267, 345, 458*f*
Luxemburg dialect, 400–1
Lycian, 267, 345, 458*f*
Lydian, 267, 345, 458*f*

Macedonian (Ancient), 276–77
Macedonian (Slavic), 442–43
Magyar, 422. *See also* Hungarian
Malayo-Portuguese, 440
Maltese, 435–36, 440
Mansi, 331
Manx, 341
Mapuche, 422
Mari, 252–53, 271–72, 278–79, 331
Mbugu, 437
Meglenitic, 442–43
Michif (*Métchif*), 440
Minoan (Linear A), 278–79, 280–81, 321, 371–72, 406
Mon, 435–36
Mongolian, 272, 304–5, 401
Mon-Khmer, 435–36, 467*f*
Mordvin, 271–72, 331
Munda, 330, 331–32, 445
Mycenaean (Linear B), 30, 235–36, 251, 276, 309, 318, 320–21, 405, 458*f*

Na-Dené, 272, 279, 467*f*
Nahuatl, 422
Nesite. *See* Hittite
Niçard, 431
Nootka, 440
Nostratic, 268–69, 271–75, 390–91, 397, 467*f*
Nuu-chah-nulth. *See* Nootka

Occitan, 431–32
Oïl Languages, 430–31
Old Church Slavonic, 309, 348–49, 458*f*
Old Prussian, 318, 344
Old Slavonic, 19, 39
Oscan, 343–44, 458*f*
Ossetian, 356–57, 458*f*
Ostyak, 331

Palaic, 267–68, 345, 458*f*
Pelasgian, 15, 276–77
Persian, 3–4, 5, 7, 19, 21, 38–39, 41, 458*f*, 468*f*
Phoenician, 131–32, 267
Phrygian, 267, 345, 458*f*
Pictish, 278–79, 406

Pidgin. *See* Creole
Piedmontese, 436
Polynesian, 21, 35
Provençal, 400–1, 430–31, 436

Quebec-French, 39
Quechua, 371, 422

Rhenish (dialect), 436
Romance (languages), 24, 31, 125, 259–60, 276, 343–44, 349, 381–82, 420–21, 422, 430–31, 435–36, 438, 440
Romani, 422
Romanian, 276–77, 373, 422, 435–36, 438, 442–44, 458*f*
Romansh, 433–34
Russenorsk, 440
Russian, 35, 55, 178, 289–90, 304–5, 312, 344, 400–1, 404–5, 420–21, 440, 458*f*, 468*f*

Sabir, 440
Salish, 440
Sami, 12, 171–72, 271–72, 278–79, 433–34, 445
Samnite, 343–44
Sanskrit, 3–4, 5, 6–7, 19, 21, 22–23, 24–25, 35, 39, 40, 49, 70, 135, 157–58, 276, 281–82, 304, 344, 346, 355, 386, 403, 408, 444, 458*f*
Sard, 433–34
Saxon, 436–37
Scots Gaelic, 340
Semitic, 76, 117–18, 165–66, 176–77, 229–30, 264, 267, 268–69, 270, 271–72, 274–75, 304–5, 345–46, 389, 445
Serbian, 442–43
Serbo-Croat, 31–32, 103, 400–1, 429, 458*f*
Siculian, 343–44
Sidetic, 345
Sino-Tibetan, 273, 279, 435–36, 467*f*
Slavic, 3–4, 21, 40, 51, 103, 107, 111–12, 157–58, 275, 276–77, 304–5, 309, 337, 344, 348–50, 393–94, 401, 405, 406, 407–8, 422, 433–34, 435–36, 438, 442–43, 444, 456*f*, 458*f*, 460*f*, 468*f*
Slovenian, 31–32
Songhai, 437
Spanish, 15, 89–90, 180, 259, 304–5, 381, 382, 391–92, 400–1, 420–21, 422, 429, 433, 435–36, 440–41, 442–43, 445, 458*f*, 468*f*
Sumerian, 171–72, 267, 272, 345–46, 401, 406
Swahili, 437, 440–42, 468*f*
Swiss-German (*Schwizerdütsch*), 433–34
Syrian, 331

560 INDEX OF LANGUAGES

Tamil, 304–5, 330, 401
Tartessian, 280–81
Telugu, 330, 468*f*
Tewa, 429
Thai, 445
Thracian, 276–77, 350, 458*f*
Tibetan, 272, 273, 279, 435–36, 445, 468*f*
Tocharian, 4, 30, 161–62, 275, 276, 277–78, 304,
    309, 311–12, 337–39, 356–57, 393–94, 458*f*,
    460*f*, 468*f*
Tok Pisin, 439, 440–41
Tungusic, 272, 335, 401
Turfarian, 337
Turkish, 7–8, 12, 22–23, 41, 118, 272, 304–5,
    333–34, 337–38, 339, 371, 400–1, 420–21,
    422, 440, 442–43, 444, 445, 468*f*

Ubykh, 351, 370–71, 384
Ugaritic, 330–31

Umbrian, 343–44, 458*f*
Uralic, 272, 273–75, 278–79
Uralo-Altaic, 22, 272, 441–42

Venetic, 343–44, 458*f*
Vietnamese, 435–36
Vogul, 331
Volapük, 31
Volscian, 343–44

Wakashan, 445
Wallachian, 276–77, 442–43
Walloon, 400–1
Welsh, 340, 458*f*

Yakut, 401
Yevanic, 442–43
Yiddish, 436
Yimas, 445

Index of names of peoples

For the benefit of digital users, indexed terms that span two pages (e.g., 52–53) may, on occasion, appear on only one of those pages.

Abkhazians, 370–71
Aetolians, 429–30
Afghans, 41
Africans, 63–64, 66–67, 74, 90–91, 93–94, 95, 105, 180, 184–85, 187, 195, 229–30, 231, 233, 239–40
Afrikaners, 436–37
Ainu, 193
Alans, 327–28
Albanians, 356–57, 371–72, 373, 442–44, 462*f*
Alemanni, 348, 427–28
Alsacians, 80–81
Amerindians (American Indians), 48, 63–64, 66–67, 105, 180, 183–84, 372, 411–12
Angas, 429
Angles, 341
Antes, 349
Aquitani, 80
Arabs, 370, 400–1, 440–41
Armenians, 51, 356–57, 363–64, 371–72, 443–44
Ashkenazi Jews, 192
Assyrians, 52, 456*f*
Athenians, 139, 429–30
Atlanteans, 58–60, 132
Australians, 66–67, 193, 467*f*
Aztecs, 372, 411–12

Balts, 157–58, 288–90, 350, 356–57, 372, 456*f*, 462*f*
Bantus, 229, 467*f*
Bashkirs, 333
Basques, 67–68, 73–74, 77, 79–81, 121–22, 228, 233, 235–36, 257, 371–72
Bavarians, 80, 427–28
Berbers, 467*f*
Boers, 187
Bosnians, 429
Bulgarians, 349, 443–44
Bulgars, 278–79, 421–22
Burgundians, 80, 427–28

Bushmen, 74
Byzantines, 349, 427–28, 443, 444–45, 456*f*

Caribbeans, 66–67
Celts, 5–6, 39, 43–44, 46, 50–51, 66–68, 77, 80–81, 125–26, 157–58, 210–11, 254–55, 259, 319, 339–43, 363, 371–72, 414, 456*f*, 462*f*
Chechens, 370–71
Chinese, 5–6, 15, 73, 337–38, 435–36, 456*f*
Chukchi, 272, 273–74
Cimbri, 347–48
Circassians, 370–71
Croats, 349
Czechs, 349

Dacians, 125–26, 254–55, 349–50, 371–72, 456*f*
Dasas, 330
Dorians, 139, 327

Eburones, 131–32
Egyptians, 5–6, 15, 58–59, 246, 253–54, 370–71, 372, 411–12, 456*f*
English, 75–76, 187
Epirotes, 429–30
Ethiopians, 5–6, 229–30, 467*f*
Etruscans, 15, 344–45, 354, 356, 368–69, 371–72, 456*f*

Filipinos, 229
Finno-Ugric, 372
Finns, 51, 55–56, 66–68, 70, 79–80, 372
Franks, 24, 80, 421–22, 428
French, 69, 74–76, 86, 125, 190, 194–95, 257, 328, 339–40, 420, 425–26, 436–37

Gagauzes, 373
Galatians, 340
Gallo-Romans, 24, 421–22
Galls, 74–75, 182
Galtchas. *See* Tajiks
Gauls, 44, 80, 254–55, 339–40, 347–48, 438
Georgians, 66, 370–71

562 INDEX OF NAMES OF PEOPLES

Gepids, 428
Germanic peoples/tribes, 10, 45, 51, 57–58, 59–60, 69, 70, 74–76, 79–80, 118, 123, 124–25, 127, 130, 136, 138–39, 140, 141–42, 156–58, 164–65, 186–87, 215, 254–55, 311, 341, 347–50, 353–54, 357–58, 363, 369–70, 372, 406, 428, 456*f*, 462*f*
Germans, 10, 20, 23–24, 46, 50–51, 55, 56–57, 62, 66–68, 69, 70–71, 74, 77, 78–81, 82–83, 84–86, 93–94, 121–23, 125–26, 138–39, 143–44, 163–64, 181, 182, 184–85, 186–88, 190, 194, 215, 224, 319, 357–58
Getae, 254–55
Goths, 5–6, 39, 347–48, 349–50, 427–28
Greeks, 5–6, 46, 50–51, 55–56, 138–39, 157–58, 251, 252–53, 254–55, 260, 276, 319, 320–27, 340, 354, 372, 404, 407–8, 424–25, 439, 443–44, 456*f*, 462*f*
Greenlanders, 66–67

Hebrews, 36–37, 65–66, 411–12, 456*f*
Hereros, 187
Heruli, 427–28
Hindus (Indians), 5–6, 15, 46, 50–51, 93–94, 229, 319, 334–35, 424–25, 428
Hittites, 253–54, 319, 345–47, 355, 372, 456*f*, 462*f*
Hopi, 429
Hottentots, 13–14, 65–66, 74. *See also* Bushmen
Hungarians (Magyars), 53–54, 233, 263, 278–79, 349, 372, 429–30, 456*f*
Huns, 53–54, 146–47, 165–66, 349–50, 428, 456*f*

Iberians, 224, 371–72, 456*f*
Illyrians, 254–55, 371–72, 456*f*, 462*f*
Incas, 372, 421–22
Indians (American). *See* Amerindians
Indians (of India). *See* Hindus
Indo-Iranians, 39–40, 157–58, 326–27, 331–32, 333–35, 337–38, 372, 402, 404, 412–13, 456*f*, 462*f*
Ingush, 370–71
Iranians, 334–35
Irish, 107, 184–85
Italic peoples, 157–58, 319, 343–45, 350, 404, 406, 456*f*, 462*f*

Japanese, 5–6, 15, 205, 226, 282–83, 370–71, 372, 413, 456*f*, 467*f*
Jews, xvi, 11–12, 14, 39, 60, 69, 70, 91–92, 93–94, 130, 131–32, 135, 180, 189, 192, 193, 194, 195–96, 219–20, 288, 289–90, 359–60, 361–62, 367, 373, 436, 442–43, 449, 451

Kalmyks, 66
Khoisans. *See* Bushmen
Kimris, 74–75, 182
Kirghiz, 339
Koreans, 370–71, 456*f*, 467*f*
Kurds, 327–28

Ladins, 433–34
Langobards (Lombards), 421–22, 427–28, 456*f*
Lapps. *See* Sami
Ligurians, 80
Lombards. *See* Langobards
Lorrainians, 80–81, 224
Lycians, 456*f*, 462*f*
Lydians, 456*f*, 462*f*

Macedonians (Ancient-), 51, 462*f*
Macedonians (Slavs), 349
Magyars. *See* Hungarians
Malaysians, 66–67, 467*f*
Manchu, 337–38
Marcomanni, 348
Maya, 313
Meglenites, 442–43
Minoans, 157–58, 251, 253, 322, 327, 372, 456*f*
Mongols, 55–56, 66–67, 84, 93–94, 165–66, 308, 421–22, 456*f*, 467*f*

Normans, 100–1, 341, 422, 436–37

Ossetes, 327–28, 354, 355, 356–57, 369–71
Ostrogoths, 427–28
Ottomans. *See* Turks

Papuans, 66–67, 228
Pelasgians, 46, 321
Persians, 5–6, 50–51, 66–67, 456*f*, *See also* Iranians
Peruvians, 5–6, 15
Phoenicians (Phenicians), 5–6, 124–25, 456*f*
Phrygians, 371–72, 456*f*
Picts, 371–72
Polynesians, 35, 467*f*
Pomaks, 373, 442–43
Proto-Bulgarians. *See* Bulgars
Prussians, 56–57, 79–80, 84–85
Pygmies, 70, 467*f*

Romani, 373, 422, 442–43
Romanians, 369–70, 373, 377, 442–44
Romans, 50–51, 52, 57, 74–75, 107, 125, 136, 138–39, 219–20, 254–55, 276, 319, 330–31, 340, 341, 343–44, 349, 355–56, 371–72, 400, 405, 406, 421, 422, 427–28, 435–36, 443, 456*f*

INDEX OF NAMES OF PEOPLES 563

Russians, 4, 41, 44–45, 50, 53–54, 148, 174, 176–77, 209, 288–89, 331, 333, 433–34, 456*f*

Sabines, 355–56, 368–69
Sami (Lapps), 66–68, 372, 433–34, 440
Sards, 229, 433–34, 467*f*
Sarmatians, 349
Saxons, 341
Scirii, 427–28
Sclaveni, 349
Scordisci, 340
Scots
Scythians, 5–6, 39, 41, 51, 53–54, 235–36, 254–55, 286–87, 327–28, 349–50, 355, 372, 456*f*
Sea Peoples, 39
Sefardi (Sephardi) Jews, 373, 442–44
Semites, 38–39, 55–56, 79–80, 84, 88, 111, 145, 413
Serbs, 349
Simbaris, 429
Slavs, 41, 50–51, 53–54, 55–56, 66–68, 125–26, 157–58, 257, 276, 286–87, 289–90, 304, 319, 333, 348–50, 356–57, 371–72, 373, 394, 424–25, 428, 456*f*
Slovaks, 349
Slovenes, 349
Sorbs, 349
Spartans, 139
Suebi, 427–28
Swedes, 67–68, 433–34

Tajiks, 41, 82–83
Tatars, 53–54, 66–67, 373
Teutons (Tuetones), 133, 136, 347–48
Tewa, 429
Thracians, 51, 254–55, 371–72, 456*f*, 462*f*
Thuringii or Thuringians, 427–28
Tibetans, 140–41, 467*f*
Tocharians (Tokharoi), 319, 337–39, 372, 394, 424–25, 428, 456*f*
Turks (Ottomans), 13, 30, 44–45, 65–66, 235–36, 278–79, 308, 372–73, 379, 411–12, 413, 429–30, 442–44, 456*f*, 467*f*

Uyghurs, 337–39, 456*f*

Vandals, 427–28
Varangians, 176–77, 456*f*
Veddas, 193
Veneti, 349
Vikings, 70, 141, 161, 176–77, 203–4, 206, 421–22, 440, 456*f*
Visigoths, 421–22, 428

Wallachians, 433–34, 442–43
Wends, 349
Wusun, 337–38

Xiongnu, 337–38

Yuezhi, 337–38

Printed in the USA/Agawam, MA
April 18, 2023

808659.025